MACROTHESAURUS

for
Information Processing
in the Field of Economic
and Social Development

NEW ENGLISH EDITION

prepared by

JEAN VIET
Maison des Sciences de l'Homme, Paris

ORGANISATION FOR ECONOMIC CO-OPERATION AND DEVELOPMENT

The Organisation for Economic Co-operation and Development (OECD) was set up under a Convention signed in Paris on 14th December 1960, which provides that the OECD
shall promote policies designed:
— to achieve the highest sustainable economic growth and employment and a rising
    standard of living in Member countries, while maintaining financial stability, and
    thus to contribute to the development of the world economy;
— to contribute to sound economic expansion in Member as well as non-member
    countries in the process of economic development;
— to contribute to the expansion of world trade on a multilateral, non-discriminatory
    basis in accordance with international obligations.
The Members of OECD are Australia, Austria, Belgium, Canada, Denmark, Finland,
France, the Federal Republic of Germany, Greece, Iceland, Ireland, Italy, Japan, Luxembourg, the Netherlands, New Zealand, Norway, Portugal, Spain, Sweden, Switzerland,
Turkey, the United Kingdom and the United States.

* *

CONTENTS

I. INTRODUCTION

The purpose of this new edition of the *Macrothesaurus* is no different from that of its predecessors. It endeavours to provide a language which can process information relating to all the aspects of economic and social development and at the same time, give a common dimension to the more specific vocabularies corresponding to each of them. Its aim is therefore still to offer in several widely-spoken languages a common fund of terminology which has been duly tested in the practice of documentary analysis, in which adequate expression is given to the many approaches to development and in which the special vocabularies that translate them extensively find sufficient number of anchor points for an exchange of information among specialised agencies.

But while the purpose of the *Macrothesaurus* has not changed, this is by no means the case for its content, which has been entirely revised and considerably enlarged, to such a point that the 1973 edition, which succeeded the *Aligned List of Descriptors* published in 1969, seems now very much out of date in spite of the service its has given.

Before describing the procedure adopted for this revision and presenting its outcome, we shall say something about the use made of the *Macrothesaurus* during these last five years and the reasons why it has been completely recast. This will help to underline the continuity of an effort which has always been based on broad international co-operation.

PAST USE OF THE MACROTHESAURUS

The last edition of the *Macrothesaurus* was published by the OECD at the beginning of 1973 in four languages—English, French, German and Spanish— and ran into 6,000 copies in all. It was the product of several years' consultation between the international organisations most directly concerned with the problems of development and gave rise to a quite extraordinary demand— for a documentary language likely to interest mainly information services— so that it had to be reprinted in 1974, and no copies have been available for the last two years.

The figure given for the OECD edition is in any case lower than the real distribution. The existence of a number of parallel editions should be noted: a Spanish edition published by the Centro latin-oamericano de documentación económica y social in Santiago, Chile, in 1973; a Brazilian edition by the Instituto brasileiro de bibliografia e documentação in Rio de Janeiro in 1974; a Portuguese edition by the Missão de estudo do rendimento nacional do ultramar in Lisbon in 1973; an Arabic edition by the Industrial Development Centre for Arab States in Cairo in 1974; an Iranian adaptation in Farsi by the Iranian Planning Institute in Teheran in 1974; an Indonesian edition by the Institute for Economic and Social Research of the University of Indonesia in Djakarta in 1977; etc.

The uses of the *Macrothesaurus* appear to have taken quite a variety of forms. In the best of cases, it was adopted entirely by an organisation as *the* language for processing its information; this was the case in the OECD (Paris), the ILO (Geneva), the International Development Research Centre (IDRC, Ottawa) and in many international and national organisations concerned with the many aspects of development, such as the Nederlands Documentatiecentrum voor Ontwikkelingslanden, which publishes "Nedo Abstracts" in Amsterdam. In other circumstances, the *Macrothesaurus* provided the foundation on which an organisation built up its own vocabulary; such was the case for UNIDO (Vienna), a good half of whose thesaurus consists of descriptors from the *Macrothesaurus,* but also for UNESCO, including both its general thesaurus and sectoral thesauri (Mass Communication Thesaurus, SPINES Thesaurus, etc.), or the International Trade Centre/UNCTAD/GATT. The *Macrothesaurus* was also used in interrogating data bases, set up elsewhere with its help, by information services at the disposal of developing countries: the Development Enquiry Service, formerly attached to the OECD Development Centre, or the Development Reference Service, which currently operates in the Society for International Development. Finally, it acted as a multilingual terminology bank for many documentation centres and translation services wishing to keep to a standardized vocabulary.

It is therefore, to a large extent, thanks to the *Macrothesaurus* that a certain discipline has been maintained in the processing of information relating to development and that co-operative practices have been adopted or strengthened in the organisations responsible for such processing.

REASONS FOR A REVISION

But this discipline and these practices did not in any way mean that the language must be preserved in its original state. A thesaurus must always correspond to the information to be processed, and the more the instrument was used, the more it became evident that it had to be amended to take account of new requirements.

In fact, the situation has evolved appreciably since the 1973 edition.

In the agencies which made the *Macrothesaurus* the instrument for their information processing, needs were perceived which the language could not satisfy. Quite a large number of additions, but also modifications were made to the descriptors. These were usually notified to a network of correspondents; but in the absence of an inter-organisational system for permanent management of the documentary language, they could not be jointly examined and no generally acceptable decision was taken about them. Hence differences and incompatibilities built up over the years and soon made it necessary to begin an overhaul.

Furthermore, new thesauri more or less directly connected with economic and social development have made their appearance during the last five years. Some of them, such as the *Thesaurus of Industrial Development Terms*, whose 3rd bilingual edition (English-French) was published by UNIDO in 1976, and the *ILO Thesaurus* (2nd edition in 1978), are directly derived from the *Macrothesaurus*; others taken it more or less strict by into account, like the *Mass Communication Thesaurus*, the *Thesaurus for Information Processing in Sociology*, the *UNESCO Thesaurus*, the *UNESCO/IBE Education Thesaurus*, the *SPINES Thesaurus*, all five of which are prepared under UN-ESCO auspices, or the *EUDISED Multilingual Thesaurus for Information Processing in Education* and the *Cultural Development Thesaurus* published by the Council of Europe. In addition to these published thesauri, several are in preparation: the *Population Multilingual Thesaurus*, the *International Thesaurus of Cultural Development*, etc. The older the reference to the *Macrothesaurus*, the greater the risk of distortion. The common language must therefore learn from these new contributions and harmonize them as far as possible in order to continue to play its regulating role.

Nor can it be overlooked that development issues have changed profoundly in these last few years. The aspiration to a " new international economic order" has altered their terms. Certain descriptors relating to " development aid" are now called in question. The " developing countries" themselves have become " economically less developed countries" or, again, " countries more seriously affected" than others by the economic crisis. New international organisations have emerged; countries have changed their names.

Moreover, certain sectors which were not much in evidence in the *Macrothesaurus* have become important enough, because of the information systems now relating to them and the discussions concerning them, to warrant increasing the share allotted to their special terminologies. Science policy, environment, health, population, quality of life, habitat and cultural development not only call for a larger number of usable descriptors relating to them, but for changes in the general structure of the vocabulary in order to cater more satisfactorily for the new information needs concerning them.

Lastly, the projected International Information System for the Development Sciences (DEVSIS), following a feasibility study carried out in 1975 under the aegis of the IDRC, the ILO, the OECD, the United Nations Department of Economic and Social Affairs, the United Nations Development Programme (UNDP) and UNESCO, as well as the creation in November 1976 in the United Nations Consultative Committee on Administrative Questions of an Informal Task Force on Terminology were further inducements in complete harmony with the international co-operation established not so long ago, to review this documentary language which has proved so beneficial to every organisation.

A procedure for revising the *Macrothesaurus* was therefore worked out in Summer 1976 and became operative by the end of that year.

PROCEDURE ADOPTED

In October 1976, an agreement was first signed between the IDRC and the OECD Executive Directorate under which the former financed the revision of the documentary language, while the OECD through its Automated Documentation Unit drew up the computer programmes for the compilation and management of a multilingual thesaurus. This agreement was renewed the following year and was to permit publication of the revised edition of the *Macrothesaurus* in three languages: English, French and Spanish.

The " Maison des Sciences de l'Homme" in Paris, which had already contributed to the first edition of the *Macrothesaurus*, was once again closely associated with the work; it provided technical assistance and the guarantee of methods which it had itself evolved in preparing many documentary languages.

The work of revision comprised several phases.

It was based, to begin with, on broad consultation with those who had been the first artisans of the *Macrothesaurus* before becoming its principal users. A first meeting was held in December 1976 at the ILO in Geneva, and all the United Nations agencies with their headquarters in that city were also invited. Talks were held in April 1977 in Rome with those responsible for FAO information system. Contacts were established with the United Nations Dag Hammarskjöld Library, the World Bank, UNESCO and the International Atomic Energy Agency. Lists indicating the frequency with which *Macrothesaurus* descriptors are used were received from the ILO, the International Occupational Safety and Health Information Centre, OECD, IDRC, FAO and UNIDO. Proposals for additional descriptors as well as suggestions for possible modifications were also received from these organisations, as well as from the International Bureau of Education, the Nederlands Documentatiecentrum voor Ontwikkelingslanden, the African Studies Centre of the University of Warsaw, the Central Statistics Bureau of Hungary, etc. Similarly, institutions representing sectors which had hitherto not been well covered in the *Macrothesaurus* were also consulted: the United Nations Environment Programme, the Committee for International Co-ordination of National Research in Demography, the Secrétariat des Missions d'Urbanisme et d'Habitat, etc. All these approaches, lists and suggestions elicited a fairly clear idea of the uses which had been made of the vocabulary over the last five years and the amendments which it now needed.

In the second stage, thesauri published since 1972 and geared in any way to economic and social development were attentively examined. In each of them, two parts were distinguished, the first concerning descriptors which because of their specific nature or marginal interest were clearly not relevant to the *Macrothesaurus*, and the second containing descriptors that might be considered for insertion.

All the information concerning possible additions was then classified according to the *Macrothesaurus*, first by major topic and then in the light of its divisions and subdivisions. The work of revision was then launched in detail: deletion, modification and addition of descriptors, search for foreign-language equivalents, but also an exhaustive analysis of relations between descriptors, and sometimes a change in the distribution by subject when the great influx of new descriptors called for a different type of structuring.

At the same time, the OECD Automated Documentation Unit, under the direction of Mr. Patrice Taupin, drew up a complex set of programmes for the permanent computerised management of a multilingual thesaurus. This set of programmes, which is almost unique, had been planned at the very start of operations and was not only to control computerised data input but to authorise the modifications which these data were to undergo in the course of the work, carrying the changes considered necessary over into the different languages at all descriptor relationship levels.

Owing to the help thus provided by computer science, a first printout of the revised *Macrothesaurus* was obtained as early as Summer 1977. It was sent all over the world to the information services most interested in its preparation and was discussed at a meeting held by the OECD in Paris from 5th to 7th October 1977. Mr. Maurice Jacomet, Executive Director of the OECD, opened this meeting, which was then chaired by Mr. John Woolston, Director of the Information Sciences Division of the IDRC, and attended by many participants from these two organisations as well as representatives of other international organisations such as the United Nations, the ILO, UNESCO, FAO, the ECLA's Centro latinoamericano de documentación económica y social (CLADES), WIPO, WHO, the ITC/UNCTAD/GATT, the SMUH, the Commission of the European Communities, the European Parliament and national institutions such as the Maison des Sciences de l'Homme (Paris), the Institute for Economic and Social Research (Djakarta), the Deutsche Stiftung für internationale Entwicklung (Bonn), the Nederlands Documentatiecentrum voor Ontwikkelingslanden (Amsterdam), the Association française des instituts de recherche sur le développement (Paris), the Institute of Development Studies (Brighton) and others.

The role played by this meeting was particularly important in that it led to closer participation by the organisations represented in the joint preparation of *Macrothesaurus* and that it attracted other contributions, including those from the United Nations Environment Programme (Nairobi), the International Bureau of Education (Geneva) and the Commission of the European Communities (Brussels). After the meeting and during the following months, a great many new suggestions were received which were gradually taken into account; a preliminary critical review of the Spanish version by the CLADES was also received. This was all to such good purpose that

by May 1978 we had a second version of the revised vocabulary which was in turn subjected to a thorough scrutiny in Paris, New York, Geneva, Brussels, Ottawa and Santiago.

Lastly, the editor of the *Macrothesaurus* attended a working meeting on the revised edition with IDRC representatives during the first fortnight of July 1978. This meeting was arranged in Bogota by the CLADES and brought together representatives of the information services in most of the Latin American and Caribbean countries. The Spanish version was once again carefully screened. In order to correspond to the region's specific requirements, certain expressions were modified some descriptors were added and others deleted. The IDRC representatives having for their part put forward a good many proposals, a final revision of the three versions was then carried out. This provided a happy conclusion to what could only be a collective work, which was then continued for two days in New York in the United Nations Department of Economic and Social Affairs before a fair-copy of the manuscript was produced in the Maison des Sciences de l'Homme, followed by a last phase of data processing in the OECD by the Automated Documentation Unit.

DESCRIPTION OF THE NEW EDITION

The new edition differs from the last on five main counts: structure of the thesaurus, field covered, choice of national languages, number and form of the descriptors, printing.

1. *Structure of the thesaurus*

It is now no longer in two parts but in four, which provide as many different approaches to the relationship between descriptors.

The first part gives these and any synonyms in alphabetical order in each volume's language of publication. Each descriptor is accompanied by its equivalents in the two other basic languages of the thesaurus and a number referring to the subject or subtopic to which it is related in the second part. It is followed, where necessary, by a scope note (SN) and references to the synonymous (UF), generic (BT), specific (NT) or associated (RT) descriptors with which it is related. This alphabetical part therefore contains all the information which may be required on the significance of the descriptors themselves.

For the convenience of persons responsible for documentary analysis, we have decided to put this at the front of the thesaurus. Regrettable though this practice may be, experience in fact shows that the analyst's first reflex is to check the alphabetical part of the thesaurus to see whether the descriptors which come to his mind on reading a text do exist. It would no doubt be more useful if he were to look first for the subject suggested by this text: he would find in the subject part of the thesaurus the most useful descriptors which he was not always able to remember. But it is a fact that analysts take the opposite approach and, at the risk of reducing the usable vocabulary to what they can remember, which may not be much, they succumb to the temptation of the alphabet. We considered it pointless to fight against nature and have chosen instead to go along with it. Who knows, if analysts find things so easy, they might be prompted to consult the second part too!

The latter presents the descriptors and their synonyms by subject and sub-topic. When compiling it, we used the same principles as are defined in the previous edition. The main lines of descriptor distribution by affinity of meaning are in any case the same, in harmony with the specialisation of the institutions which have been using the *Macrothesaurus* for some years. In order to make the volume less bulky, we have avoided repeating the information given in the alphabetical part for descriptors arranged by subject; this makes for easier reference, while emphasizing that the two parts are complementary, and it is quite simple to go from one to the other, using in one case the number of the subject and the alphabetical order in the other.

The third part arranges the descriptors according to their hierarchical relationship. All the top terms are listed with all the specific descriptors subordinate to the latter themselves being placed at their different levels of specificity.

Finally, the fourth part is a permuted descriptors index which supplements the alphabetical classification given in the first part since it provides access to composite descriptors through their respective elements taken one by one.

2. *Field covered*

This is much broader and, at the request of users and in the light of the information to be processed, many sectors are developed further than in the previous edition. This is particularly true of population, health and environment, but also of cultural development, communication, education, energy conservation, etc.

This pragmatic approach to the field covered is sufficiently exemplary to merit a moment's attention. It may in fact remove one of the main obstacles to the design of certain international information systems.

One is banned to be surprised at the importance attached in the preliminary studies to theoretical discussion on the scope of the documentary language. Quite frequently, the enumeration of the subjects to be covered, the statement of the problems, the definition of sectors and the placing of surrounding barriers are given as prerequisites, and there are quite a few examples of a project encountering these stumbling-blocks.

Now while it is true that a thesaurus cannot in itself suffice to create an information system, it is also true that the design of such a system, no matter how precisely its objectives may be set down or its mechanisms described, cannot give form and content

to the documentary language itself. The latter's raison d'être first depends on the data to be processed and the data medium consisting of the documents considered useful. Of course, the criteria of this usefulness are built into the system, but there they are necessarily formulated in quite general terms which cannot really determine the vocabulary. It often happens that information regarded as valid in its reference to the system appears in relation to other information not covered by such reference; in order to be entered without giving use to distortion it must therefore be embodied in a documentary language which departs from the beaten track, sometimes in a quite unpredictable direction. Compiling such a language is a matter of actual practice and must take account of the experience gained both in analysing documents as accurately as possible and in searching for the best information to answer users' questions. To allow for appropriate broader development, it cannot be laid down initially in the system analysis.

A thesaurus cannot emerge fully equipped from a simple glance at a field of application, and this field itself cannot be exactly delimited as long as it has not been ploughed from top to bottom by the thesaurus. What counts to begin with, therefore, is a certain practice of documentation. This does not of course start at random; it finds assurance in the information needs to be met and is based on the documents required, but the actual perspective which such needs describe and the flow of information carried by the documents include a certain unpredictable element.

It is of course possible to consider that this element is now small in the *Macrothesaurus* since it has been put to the test for five years, but it would be a mistake to think that it does not exist. Who can tell exactly now what place biology, for example, will hold in the development process in ten years' time and prescribe the corresponding vocabulary?

3. *Choice of national languagues*

The three languages adopted for the revised *Macrothesaurus* are those regarded as particularly important in the DEVSIS study: "We are prepared to assert that the group of languages composed of English, French and Spanish are the most significant and widely used in the development literature and by the development community"*.

However, there is nothing against the possibility of later editions in other languages at national or regional level according to requirements and with the agreement of the OECD Executive Directorate.

The French, English and Spanish languages were given equal status at every stage in compiling the *Macrothesaurus*. It was prepared simultaneously in all three languages, each making its contribution to the common edifice. Thus, there is no source-language

* "DEVSIS Preliminary Design of an International Information System for the Development Sciences" Ottawa, IDRC, 1976, p. 51.

and no target-language. Every effort has been made throughout the operations to maintain a balance between the three language areas. In each of them account was taken of the development discourse in its effective form and only afterwards was equivalence sought between descriptors. These equivalences are sometimes a long way from translations, but this is because we have rejected any standardization, which is always arbitrary. It seemed sufficient that the terms taken in three different languages should correspond to the same concept; there was no need to pour them into the same mould. We have therefore usually taken the current expressions in each language. Any other approach to compiling a multilingual thesaurus would mean giving one language preference over the others; this introduces a bias into the documentary language which very soon becomes intolerable for users of the subordinate languages.

4. *The descriptors*

The number of descriptors has almost doubled from one edition to the next. Since we have also deleted or changed some of the old descriptors which were found irrelevant, it is easy to see the extent of the revision.

With use, a certain amount of preco-ordinations became necessary; we have adopted them when they permitted more precise documentary analysis and made it unnecessary to include too many cross-reference between descriptors in order to search for information.

Many descriptors have changed from the singular to the plural in accordance with the UNISIST recommendations and the practice adopted in most of the English-language thesauri. We have nevertheless kept in the singular descriptors which should according to the norm have been in the plural. They are the ones concerning the nature of documents: bibliography, manual, meeting report, conference paper, etc. Since they are customarily used to describe particular document being analysed, it goes without saying that they must be in the singular. In any event, this question of the use of the singular or the plural, which has long been a difficulty for information services that have elected to incorporate descriptors in the text of their abstracts, is not so important: either form, or even abbreviated descriptors, can be used for information retrieval by computer.

The number of relations between descriptors has been increased in order to overcome the disadvantages of an arrangement by subject which usually gives descriptors one place only in the thesaurus, but also in order to facilitate the compilation of microthesauri and to open new paths for users in the search for information. We have paid special attention to hierarchical relations, which give the documentary language its principal framework, although we did not consider it necessary to give special emphasis to terms governing hierarchical linkages in the alphabetical part of the thesaurus; they are sufficiently revealed in the part dealing with them.

Lastly, at the request of several information services, especially in Latin America, we have prepared new scope notes for descriptors whose meaning might give rise to ambiguity. But we have refrained from going too far in this direction and putting redundancies into the thesaurus, since we consider that the descriptors are generally given with sufficient precision through their language equivalence, their inclusion in a given subject and their network of relations.

5. *Printing*

The new version of the *Macrothesaurus* has been filmset from the magnetic tape printed by the computer. The text is entirely printed in capital letters since we wished to retain the same graphic status for the descriptors in the different parts of the thesaurus; but the words are in lighter or heavier type according to the place occupied by the descriptors and whether they refer to the descriptors themselves or to their synonyms. We hope that this will make it easier to consult the work.

DESTINATION

The *Macrothesaurus* is intended primarily for information centres or services concerned with economic and social development as a whole or with a particular aspect of it.

Experience has shown that it was particularly relevant to the requirements of institutions primarily conceived with development on an international (IDRC), regional (CLADES) or national scale (Ministries of Planning, planning institutes); or, again, institutions working in many fields (OECD) or handling information from a great variety of sources (ILO Library).

Contrary to widespread opinion, it is not necessary to have a computer in order to take advantage of the *Macrothesaurus*. It is intended for use in developing countries, notably by national documentation centres which have been set up recently and wish to control the information flows in the main social science sectors. Of course, all the possibilities of the documentary language call for an appropriate computerised infrastructure if they are to be fully exploited; but the selection of tried descriptors offered by the *Macrothesaurus* and the arrangement of these descriptors by subject are in any event very useful; by electing to base documentary work on them from the start, these centres would also increase their chances of one day belonging to an international network.

The *Macrothesaurus* is also intended for information services concerned with development from the sectoral angle. It provides them with the basic vocabulary to express their special interests and they can derive from it a microthesaurus for their specific needs. They will also find material in it to overcome their own limitations, to describe when necessary information with which they are less familiar and to consult data banks established in other sectors but likely to contain information which is nonetheless relevant to themselves.

PERMANENT MANAGEMENT

If the *Macrothesaurus* had been managed on a permanent basis since 1973 and if it had been amended daily to keep abreast of the information supplied and the requests received, it might have been possible to avoid the considerable work required over the last two years for its revision. The necessity for permanent updating was quite clear from the start, but the conditions for carrying it out were never satisfied.

This is definitely a pity, but the final outcome is not entirely without benefit. After all, if the *Macrothesaurus* has been subjected to the shock of information supply and demand, if a world-wide documentary analysis has shown the need for its adaptation and if material for improving it has been found in its actual operation, this is because it has indeed been used. There is thus no further need to furnish proof of its use. Information is a risk for any documentary language. Some take the risk, while others do not, thus keeping their hands clean but also demonstrating that they have no ground to stand on.

The experience gained with the *Macrothesaurus* shows that anyone wishing to introduce a thesaurus must ensure from the start that there are built-in mechanisms for amending it. For efficient strategy, these mechanisms should be at three levels.

One of them corresponds to data acquisition. A first possibility of altering the vocabulary should be established in the documentary analysis offices. Analysts must have a certain latitude to expand the thesaurus so that it always matches what is being said in documents. This latitude assumes, of course, that they have full mastery over the instrument and that they are familiar with its every possibility; but once this condition has been fulfilled, nothing should prevent them from borrowing from the language of documents themselves those elements which will fill any gaps in the thesaurus. Such borrowing will only be temporary, however, if the analytical unit responsible belongs to a network. At the same time as they are embodied in abstracts or appear in indexes with a special sign, the additional descriptors will at the same time be entered on worksheets; they will be subjected to a formal acceptance procedure before being reported to other units.

The second level concerns the production of other documentary languages in the field of reference. When it relates to such an extensive and varied process as economic and social development, this production cannot fail to be on a large scale, at least judging by the last five years. It is essential to take it into account, to establish relations between one thesaurus and the next and to see that the interaction of the documentary languages develops in such a way as to be of benefit to everyone.

The third level concerns the request for information. A mechanism should be set up to make the documentary language take account of the terms in which that request is made. The effect must be checked on the descriptors themselves, but still more

no doubt on the relations which the thesaurus establishes between them from the outset. It is in fact on these relations that search strategies normally rely. It is important, even though this has not hitherto received much attention, to keep track of the relations used for giving a reply so that they can be emphasized if necessary in the thesaurus or inserted if by chance they are missing.

The operation of these mechanisms comprises in its turn two requirements:

The first is for an institutional framework for the permanent management of the language. It is difficult to see how the functions described can be carried out if they are not taken over by a responsible agency.

The ups and downs of the *Macrothesaurus* are an excellent illustration of this problem. The reason why it has suddenly become necessary to revise completely a vocabulary on which so many documentary ventures are based, and at the risk of disturbing their operation, is because there has never been a place where certain essential operations could be *centralised*. Not that institutional support was really lacking: the OECD, the ILO, the IDRC and many other institutions have managed the *Macrothesaurus*, but each of them has done so on its own account. This has not only been responsible for discrepancies which were difficult to remove after the event, but important tasks have been neglected, such as the consideration of new thesauri. If these tasks are to cease being neglected and if the revised *Macrothesaurus* is to open the door for a fresh start, then it is merely necessary to appoint a caretaker institution by common agreement to initiate and supervise the management of the documentary language.

If an arrangement were concluded along these lines, it would probably have some influence on the introduction of an international information system for development as envisaged by the DEVSIS study. Being established at data processing language level, the co-operation on which such a system is based would be more than half achieved. In this respect too, a pragmatic approach may have its good points.

The second requirement for permanent management of the *Macrothesaurus* is for a computerised terminological data base. This should include, together with the revised *Macrothesaurus* in three languages, the various thesauri of most direct interest to economic and social development. A number of them are computerised and it would be relatively easy to obtain the appropriate magnetic tapes.

The data base could be consulted by means of an inverted file covering all the descriptors and would give much information. By merely retrieving a descriptor, the operator would immediately discover, the thesauri to which it belongs, its foreign language equivalents, the relations associated with it in different places, the scope notes applying to it and so on. Such information would be extremely valuable. To begin with, it would provide an excellent touchstone for the management of the *Macrothesaurus*: when considering the admission of a new descriptor, it would be possible to check immediately whether it has been accepted elsewhere, to what extent, its foreign language equivalents, etc. But, above all, it would make it possible to detect any incompatibilities between the thesauri and to prescribe some way of correcting them, with a view to achieving the integration of information systems and the convergence of services to users.

If we had had such a terminological data base, the revision of the *Macrothesaurus* would have raised far fewer problems.

*
* *

It is no doubt too soon to assess the usefulness of this revision. All we can say is that it comes at the right time. The exchange of information seems today more than ever to condition development, and the instruments for such exchanges have become so numerous that is was urgent to have a framework for their integration.

It would not have been possible to prepare that framework without the considerable help we have received. The compilation of the *Macrothesaurus* had been a collective operation and this applies even more to its revision. There is no room here to list all the 50 or so institutions, nor all the persons who took an active part in this revision. It is only right, however, to state that it would not have taken place if the IDRC, the OECD and the Maison des Sciences de l'Homme had not provided the means to start with, and, in this respect, we are particularly grateful to Mr. John Woolston, Mr. Maurice Jacomet and Mr. Clemens Heller for having taken the necessary administrative decisions. Our thanks go also to Mr. George Thompson of the ILO, Mrs. Martha Beya of the CLADES and Mrs. Elizabeth Miller of the United Nations, who provided us with useful contacts and who arranged and chaired the working meetings held in Geneva, Bogota and New York. We also wish to thank Mrs. Gisèle Morin-Labatut and her assistants at the IDRC for having shared the donkeywork of terminological revision with us. Finally, we should like to express our special gratitude to the OECD Automated Documentation Unit which, under the direction of Patrice Taupin, prepared the computerised management programmes for a multilingual thesaurus, undertook the data acquisition and processing and produced the new version of the *Macrothesaurus*.

31st October 1978   Jean VIET
Maison des Sciences de
l'Homme
54, boulevard Raspail
75270 PARIS CEDEX 06

II. ALPHABETICAL THESAURUS

ABILITY GROUPING
GROUPEMENT PAR APTITUDES / AGRUPAMIENTO POR APTITUD - 06.04.10
    UF: STREAMING
    RT: CLASSES

ABORIGINAL POPULATION
POPULATION AUTOCHTONE / POBLACION ABORIGEN - 14.03.01
SN: DENOTES PEOPLE BORN IN THE COUNTRY IN WHICH THEY ARE LIVING.
    BT: POPULATION
    NT: INDIGENOUS POPULATION

ABORTION
AVORTEMENT / ABORTO - 14.05.02
    NT: LEGAL ABORTION

ABRASIVES
ABRASIFS / ABRASIVOS - 08.12.08

ABSENTEEISM
ABSENTEISME / AUSENTISMO - 13.05.00
    RT: LEAVE OF ABSENCE

ABSORPTIVE CAPACITY
CAPACITE D'ABSORPTION / CAPACIDAD DE ABSORCION - 11.02.06
    RT: DEVELOPMENT AID
         INVESTMENTS

ABSTRACT
RESUME / RESUMEN ANALITICO - 19.02.07
    BT: SECONDARY DOCUMENTS

ABUNDANCE
ABONDANCE / ABUNDANCIA - 03.02.05
    RT: AFFLUENT SOCIETY
         WEALTH

ACADEMIC FREEDOM
LIBERTE DE L'ENSEIGNEMENT / LIBERTAD DE ENSENANZA - 04.02.02
    BT: CIVIL LIBERTIES
    RT: EDUCATIONAL SYSTEMS

ACAST
CCAST / CCACT - 01.03.02
SN: ADVISORY COMMITTEE FOR THE APPLICATION OF SCIENCE AND TECHNOLOGY TO DEVELOPMENT
    BT: ECOSOC
    RT: SCIENCE
         TECHNOLOGY

ACCELERATED COURSES
COURS ACCELERES / CURSOS ACELERADOS - 06.05.01
    UF: INTENSIVE COURSES
    BT: COURSES

ACCESS TO CULTURE
ACCES A LA CULTURE / ACCESO A LA CULTURA - 05.02.03
    RT: CULTURE
         RIGHT TO EDUCATION

ACCESS TO EDUCATION
ACCES A L'EDUCATION / ACCESO A LA EDUCACION - 06.02.02
    RT: EDUCATIONAL OPPORTUNITIES
         EDUCATIONAL SELECTION
         RIGHT TO EDUCATION

ACCESS TO INFORMATION
ACCES A L'INFORMATION / ACCESO A LA INFORMACION - 19.01.01
    RT: DATA PROTECTION
         INFORMATION
         INFORMATION DISSEMINATION
         INFORMATION EXCHANGE
         INFORMATION SOURCES
         INFORMATION USERS

ACCESS TO MARKET
ACCES AU MARCHE / ACCESO AL MERCADO - 09.03.01
    RT: BOYCOTT
         EMBARGO
         MARKET
         TRADE AGREEMENTS

ACCIDENT INSURANCE
ASSURANCE ACCIDENT / SEGURO DE ACCIDENTES - 11.02.03
    BT: INSURANCE
    RT: ACCIDENTS

ACCIDENT PREVENTION
- 13.04.00
    USE: OCCUPATIONAL SAFETY

ACCIDENTS
ACCIDENTS / ACCIDENTES - 02.04.02
    BT: SOCIAL PROBLEMS
    NT: OCCUPATIONAL ACCIDENTS
    RT: ACCIDENT INSURANCE
         CAUSES OF DEATH
         DAMAGE
         SAFETY

ACCLIMATIZATION
ACCLIMATATION / ACLIMATACION - 17.02.01
    RT: CLIMATE

ACCOUNTANTS
COMPTABLES / CONTADORES - 13.09.09
    BT: OFFICE WORKERS
    RT: ACCOUNTING

ACCOUNTING
COMPTABILITE / CONTABILIDAD - 12.09.00
    NT: COST ACCOUNTING
         NATIONAL ACCOUNTING
         PUBLIC ACCOUNTING
    RT: ACCOUNTANTS
         AUDITING

ACCT
ACCT / ACCT - 01.03.03

ACCT<CONT>
SN: AGENCY FOR CULTURAL AND TECHNICAL
COOPERATION (BETWEEN FRENCH-SPEAKING
COUNTRIES)
   BT: INTERGOVERNMENTAL ORGANIZATIONS

ACCULTURATION
ACCULTURATION / ACULTURACION - 05.02.02
   RT: CULTURAL INTEGRATION
       CULTURAL RELATIONS
       CULTURE

ACCUMULATION RATE
TAUX D'ACCUMULATION / TASA DE ACUMULACION -
03.01.02
   RT: CAPITAL FORMATION
       GROWTH RATE
       INVESTMENTS

ACDA
ACDA / ACDA - 01.03.03
SN: ASIAN CENTRE FOR DEVELOPMENT ADMINISTRATION
   BT: ASIAN ORGANIZATIONS
       NON-GOVERNMENTAL ORGANIZATIONS
   RT: ASIA
       DEVELOPMENT ADMINISTRATION

ACIDS
ACIDES / ACIDOS - 08.12.04

ACOUSTICS
ACOUSTIQUE / ACUSTICA - 08.14.08
   BT: PHYSICS

ACTIVITY ANALYSIS
ANALYSE D'ACTIVITE / ANALISIS DE ACTIVIDAD -
12.04.00
   BT: ECONOMIC ANALYSIS
   RT: ECONOMETRICS
       INPUT-OUTPUT ANALYSIS
       LINEAR PROGRAMMING

ACTUARIES
ACTUAIRES / ACTUARIOS - 13.09.09

ACUPUNCTURE
ACUPONCTURE / ACUPUNTURA - 15.04.04
   BT: MEDICINE

ACUSTIC POLLUTION
POLLUTION ACOUSTIQUE / CONTAMINACION ACUSTICA -
16.03.04
   BT: POLLUTION
   RT: NOISE

ADAPTATION
ADAPTATION / ADAPTACION - 05.03.03
   UF: ADJUSTMENT
   NT: ADAPTATION TO CHANGE
       INDUSTRIAL ADAPTATION
       SOCIAL ADAPTATION
   RT: MALADJUSTMENT

ADAPTATION TO CHANGE
ADAPTATION AU CHANGEMENT / ADAPTACION AL CAMBIO

ADAPTATION TO CHANGE<CONT>
- 05.03.04
   BT: ADAPTATION
   RT: RESISTANCE TO CHANGE
       SOCIAL CHANGE

ADC
ADC / ADC - 01.03.03
SN: ASIAN DEVELOPMENT CENTRE.
   BT: APU
       DEVELOPMENT CENTRES
   RT: ASIA

ADHESIVES
ADHESIFS / ADHESIVOS - 08.12.08

ADIPA
ADIPA / ADIPA - 01.03.03
SN: ASSOCIATION OF DEVELOPMENT RESEARCH AND
TRAINING INSTITUTES OF ASIA AND THE PACIFIC.
   BT: ASIAN ORGANIZATIONS
       NON-GOVERNMENTAL ORGANIZATIONS
   RT: ASIA
       DEVELOPMENT RESEARCH
       PACIFIC REGION
       RESEARCH CENTRES

ADJUSTMENT
- 05.03.03
   USE: ADAPTATION

ADMINISTERED PRICES
PRIX IMPOSES / PRECIOS REGULADOS - 09.02.00
SN: PRICE SET BY THE STATE.
   BT: PRICES
   RT: MARKETING BOARDS

ADMINISTRATION OF EDUCATION
- 04.03.02
   USE: EDUCATIONAL ADMINISTRATION

ADMINISTRATION OF JUSTICE
ADMINISTRATION DE LA JUSTICE / ADMINISTRACION DE
JUSTICIA - 04.03.02
   BT: PUBLIC ADMINISTRATION
   RT: CONSTITUTIONAL COURTS
       JURISPRUDENCE
       LABOUR COURTS

ADMINISTRATIVE ASPECTS
ASPECTS ADMINISTRATIFS / ASPECTOS
ADMINISTRATIVOS - 04.03.04
SN: USE IN CONNECTION WITH ADMINISTRATION ONLY,
AND DISTINGUISH FROM MANAGERIAL ASPECTS,
WHICH ARE COVERED BY THE DESCRIPTORS
'MANAGEMENT', 'PERSONNEL MANAGEMENT', ETC.
   RT: PUBLIC ADMINISTRATION

ADMINISTRATIVE LAW
DROIT ADMINISTRATIF / DERECHO ADMINISTRATIVO -
04.01.02
   BT: PUBLIC LAW
   RT: PUBLIC ADMINISTRATION

ADMINISTRATIVE REFORMS
REFORMES ADMINISTRATIVES / REFORMAS
ADMINISTRATIVAS - 04.03.04
    RT: PUBLIC ADMINISTRATION

ADMISSION REQUIREMENTS
CONDITIONS D'ADMISSION / REQUISITOS DE INGRESO -
06.04.09
SN: CONDITIONS (EXAMINATIONS, CERTIFICATES,
    PROOF OF SKILLS, ETC.) OF ENTRANCE TO AN
    EDUCATIONAL INSTITUTION.
    RT: EDUCATIONAL SELECTION

ADOLESCENCE
- 14.02.02
    USE: YOUTH

ADULT EDUCATION
EDUCATION DES ADULTES / EDUCACION DE ADULTOS -
06.03.05
    NT: EDUCATION OF WOMEN
         LIFE-LONG EDUCATION
         RECURRENT EDUCATION
    RT: ADULTS
         NIGHT SCHOOLS

ADULTS
ADULTES / ADULTOS - 14.02.02
    BT: AGE GROUPS
    RT: ADULT EDUCATION

ADVANCEMENT
- 13.02.02
    USE: PROMOTION

ADVANCEMENT OF EDUCATION
- 06.02.03
    USE: EDUCATIONAL DEVELOPMENT

ADVERTISING
PUBLICITE / PUBLICIDAD - 09.03.04
    BT: INFORMATION DISSEMINATION
    RT: PUBLIC RELATIONS

AERIAL SURVEYS
ENQUETES AERIENNES / AEREOFOTOGRAMETRIA -
18.04.00
    BT: SURVEYS
    RT: GEOLOGICAL SURVEYS
         PHOTOGRAMMETRY
         REMOTE SENSING

AEROSOLS
AEROSOLS / AEROSOLES - 16.03.04
    BT: AIR POLLUTANTS

AEROSPACE INDUSTRY
INDUSTRIE AEROSPATIALE / INDUSTRIA AEROSPACIAL -
08.14.07
    BT: INDUSTRIAL SECTOR
    RT: AIRCRAFT INDUSTRY
         OUTER SPACE

AESTHETICS
ESTHETIQUE / ESTETICA - 05.05.02
    BT: PHILOSOPHY
    RT: ART

AFFLUENT SOCIETY
SOCIETE D'ABONDANCE / SOCIEDAD OPULENTA -
03.02.05
    BT: SOCIETY
    RT: ABUNDANCE
         CONSUMPTION

AFFORESTATION
BOISEMENT / PLANTACION FORESTAL - 07.08.03
    NT: REFORESTATION

AFGHAN
AFGHAN / AFGANO - 14.03.02
    RT: AFGHANISTAN

AFGHANISTAN
AFGHANISTAN / AFGANISTAN - 01.04.06
    BT: MIDDLE EAST
    RT: AFGHAN

AFRASEC
AFRASEC / AFRASEC - 01.03.03
SN: AFRO-ASIAN ORGANIZATION FOR ECONOMIC
    COOPERATION.
    BT: NON-GOVERNMENTAL ORGANIZATIONS
    RT: AFRICA
         ASIA

AFRICA
AFRIQUE / AFRICA - 01.04.02
    NT: AFRICA SOUTH OF SAHARA
         ENGLISH SPEAKING AFRICA
         FRENCH SPEAKING AFRICA
         NORTH AFRICA
         SAHARA
    RT: AFRASEC
         AFRICAN
         AFRICAN DEVELOPMENT BANK
         AFRICAN ORGANIZATIONS
         CAFRAD
         CODESRIA
         ECA
         OAU
         OCAM

AFRICA SOUTH OF SAHARA
AFRIQUE AU SUD DU SAHARA / AFRICA AL SUR DEL
SAHARA - 01.04.02
    BT: AFRICA
    NT: CENTRAL AFRICA
         EAST AFRICA
         SOUTHERN AFRICA
         WEST AFRICA

AFRICAN
AFRICAIN / AFRICANO - 14.03.02
    RT: AFRICA

AFRICAN DEVELOPMENT BANK
BANQUE AFRICAINE DE DEVELOPPEMENT / BANCO
AFRICANO DE DESARROLLO - 01.03.03
    BT: AFRICAN ORGANIZATIONS
         DEVELOPMENT BANKS
         INTERGOVERNMENTAL ORGANIZATIONS
    RT: AFRICA

AFRICAN ORGANIZATIONS
ORGANISATIONS AFRICAINES / ORGANIZACIONES AFRICANAS - 01.03.03
> BT: REGIONAL ORGANIZATIONS
> NT: AFRICAN DEVELOPMENT BANK
>> CACEU
>> CAFRAD
>> CODESRIA
>> EAC
>> ECA
>> MPCC
>> OAU
>> OCAM
>> WARDA
> RT: AFRICA
>> REGIONAL INTEGRATION

AGE
AGE / EDAD - 14.02.02
> NT: MINIMUM AGE
> RT: AGE DISTRIBUTION
>> AGE GROUPS

AGE DISTRIBUTION
REPARTITION PAR AGE / DISTRIBUCION POR EDAD - 14.02.02
> BT: AGE-SEX DISTRIBUTION
> RT: AGE

AGE GROUPS
GROUPES D'AGE / GRUPOS DE EDAD - 14.02.02
> NT: ADULTS
>> CHILDHOOD
>> OLD AGE
>> SCHOOL AGE POPULATION
>> YOUTH
> RT: AGE
>> GENERATIONS

AGE-SEX DISTRIBUTION
REPARTITION PAR AGE ET SEXE / DISTRIBUCION POR EDAD Y SEXO - 14.02.01
> NT: AGE DISTRIBUTION
>> SEX DISTRIBUTION
> RT: POPULATION COMPOSITION

AGED
PERSONNES AGEES / ANCIANOS - 14.02.02
> UF: OLDER PEOPLE
> NT: OLDER WORKERS
> RT: AGEING
>> CARE OF THE AGED
>> OLD AGE
>> OLD AGE BENEFITS

AGEING
VIEILLISSEMENT / ENVEJECIMIENTO - 14.02.02
> RT: AGED
>> CAUSES OF DEATH
>> OLD AGE

AGGLOMERATES
AGGLOMERES / AGLOMERADOS - 08.10.02
> BT: CONSTRUCTION MATERIALS

AGGRESSION
AGRESSION / AGRESION - 01.02.07
> RT: WAR

AGRARIAN REFORMS
REFORMES AGRAIRES / REFORMAS AGRARIAS - 07.02.00
SN: REFORMS COVERING ALL ASPECTS OF AGRARIAN INSTITUTIONS INCLUDING LAND REFORMS, PRODUCTION AND SUPPORTING SERVICES STRUCTURE, PUBLIC ADMINISTRATION IN RURAL AREAS, RURAL SOCIAL WELFARE INSTITUTIONS, ETC.
> NT: LAND REFORMS

AGRARIAN STRUCTURE
STRUCTURE AGRAIRE / ESTRUCTURA AGRARIA - 07.02.00
SN: A COMPLEX OF RELATIONSHIPS WHICH EXIST AMONG TENURE, PRODUCTION AND SUPPORTING SERVICES STRUCTURE, AND OTHER RELATED RURAL INSTITUTIONS, EACH CONSTITUTING AN INTEGRAL PART OF THE WIDER WHOLE.
> UF: AGRARIAN SYSTEMS

AGRARIAN SYSTEMS
- 07.02.00
> USE: AGRARIAN STRUCTURE

AGRICULTURAL ADMINISTRATION
ADMINISTRATION AGRICOLE / ADMINISTRACION AGRICOLA - 04.03.02
SN: AT THE GOVERNMENT LEVEL. DO NOT CONFUSE WITH 'AGRICULTURAL MANAGEMENT'.
> BT: ECONOMIC ADMINISTRATION
> RT: AGRICULTURAL PLANNING
>> AGRICULTURAL POLICY

AGRICULTURAL AREAS
ZONES AGRICOLES / ZONAS AGRICOLAS - 07.05.02
SN: AREAS DEVOTED PRIMARILY TO AGRICULTURE.
> NT: FISHING GROUNDS
>> FOREST AREAS

AGRICULTURAL ASPECTS
ASPECTS AGRICOLES / ASPECTOS AGRICOLAS - 07.01.01

AGRICULTURAL BANKS
BANQUES AGRICOLES / BANCOS AGRICOLAS - 07.03.03
> BT: BANKS
> RT: AGRICULTURAL CREDIT
>> DEVELOPMENT BANKS

AGRICULTURAL CENSUSES
RECENSEMENTS AGRICOLES / CENSOS AGROPECUARIOS - 07.05.01
> BT: CENSUSES

AGRICULTURAL COMMODITIES
- 07.05.05
> USE: AGRICULTURAL PRODUCTS

AGRICULTURAL COOPERATIVES
COOPERATIVES AGRICOLES / COOPERATIVAS AGRICOLAS

AGRICULTURAL COOPERATIVES<CONT>
- 07.03.02
- BT: AGRICULTURAL ENTERPRISES
- COOPERATIVES
- RT: COOPERATIVE FARMING

AGRICULTURAL CREDIT
CREDIT AGRICOLE / CREDITO AGRICOLA - 07.03.03
- BT: CREDIT
- RT: AGRICULTURAL BANKS

AGRICULTURAL DEVELOPMENT
DEVELOPPEMENT AGRICOLE / DESARROLLO AGRICOLA -
07.01.02
- BT: ECONOMIC DEVELOPMENT
- NT: FISHERY DEVELOPMENT
- FORESTRY DEVELOPMENT
- RT: AGRICULTURAL ECONOMY
- GREEN REVOLUTION

AGRICULTURAL ECONOMICS
AGROECONOMIE / ECONOMIA AGRARIA - 07.01.01
SN: ECONOMICS AS IT RELATES TO THE AGRARIAN
SECTOR. DO NOT CONFUSE WITH 'AGRICULTURAL
ECONOMY'.
- BT: ECONOMICS
- NT: FISHERY ECONOMICS
- FORESTRY ECONOMICS
- RT: LAND ECONOMICS

AGRICULTURAL ECONOMY
ECONOMIE AGRICOLE / ECONOMIA AGRICOLA - 07.01.01
- RT: AGRICULTURAL DEVELOPMENT
- AGRICULTURAL SECTOR

AGRICULTURAL EDUCATION
ENSEIGNEMENT AGRICOLE / ENSENANZA AGRICOLA -
06.03.07
- BT: VOCATIONAL EDUCATION
- RT: AGRICULTURAL INSTITUTES
- AGRICULTURAL TRAINING
- AGRICULTURE

AGRICULTURAL ENGINEERING
GENIE AGRICOLE / INGENIERIA AGRICOLA - 07.04.00
- UF: AGRICULTURAL TECHNOLOGY
- BT: ENGINEERING
- NT: FISHERY ENGINEERING
- FOREST ENGINEERING

AGRICULTURAL ENTERPRISES
ENTREPRISES AGRICOLES / EMPRESAS AGRICOLAS -
07.03.01
- BT: ENTERPRISES
- NT: AGRICULTURAL COOPERATIVES
- FARMS
- PLANTATIONS
- RT: AGRICULTURAL WORKERS
- FARM MANAGEMENT
- FARMERS

AGRICULTURAL EQUIPMENT
EQUIPEMENT AGRICOLE / EQUIPO AGRICOLA -

AGRICULTURAL EQUIPMENT<CONT>
07.04.00
- BT: EQUIPMENT
- NT: AGRICULTURAL MACHINERY
- FISHING EQUIPMENT
- FORESTRY EQUIPMENT

AGRICULTURAL EXTENSION
VULGARISATION AGRICOLE / EXTENSION AGRICOLA -
07.01.02
- BT: EXTENSION SERVICES
- RT: AGRICULTURAL TRAINING
- AGRICULTURE

AGRICULTURAL INCOME
REVENU AGRICOLE / INGRESO AGRICOLA - 07.03.03
SN: FARMERS' INCOME. FOR THE SHARE OF
AGRICULTURE IN NATIONAL INCOME, USE
'NATIONAL INCOME' AND 'AGRICULTURE'.
- BT: INCOME

AGRICULTURAL INDUSTRY
- 07.01.01
- USE: AGROINDUSTRY

AGRICULTURAL INSTITUTES
ECOLES D'AGRICULTURE / ESCUELAS AGRICOLAS -
06.04.06
- RT: AGRICULTURAL EDUCATION
- AGRICULTURE

AGRICULTURAL INSURANCE
ASSURANCE AGRICOLE / SEGURO AGRICOLA - 07.03.03
- BT: INSURANCE

AGRICULTURAL INVESTMENTS
INVESTISSEMENTS AGRICOLES / INVERSIONES
AGRICOLAS - 07.03.03
- BT: INVESTMENTS
- RT: AGRICULTURE

AGRICULTURAL MACHINERY
MATERIEL AGRICOLE / MAQUINARIA AGRICOLA -
07.04.00
- UF: FARM MACHINERY
- BT: AGRICULTURAL EQUIPMENT
- MACHINERY
- NT: TRACTORS
- RT: AGRICULTURAL MECHANIZATION

AGRICULTURAL MANAGEMENT
GESTION AGRICOLE / GESTION AGRICOLA - 07.01.02
- BT: MANAGEMENT
- NT: FARM MANAGEMENT
- FISHERY MANAGEMENT
- FOREST MANAGEMENT

AGRICULTURAL MARKET
MARCHE AGRICOLE / MERCADO AGRICOLA - 07.01.03
- BT: MARKET

AGRICULTURAL MECHANIZATION
MECANISATION AGRICOLE / MECANIZACION AGRICOLA -

AGRICULTURAL MECHANIZATION<CONT>
07.04.00
    BT: MECHANIZATION
    RT: AGRICULTURAL MACHINERY

AGRICULTURAL PLANNING
PLANIFICATION AGRICOLE / PLANIFICACION AGRICOLA
- 07.01.02
    BT: ECONOMIC PLANNING
    NT: FISHERY PLANNING
        FORESTRY PLANNING
    RT: AGRICULTURAL ADMINISTRATION

AGRICULTURAL POLICY
POLITIQUE AGRICOLE / POLITICA AGRARIA - 07.01.02
    BT: ECONOMIC POLICY
    NT: FISHERY POLICY
        FOREST POLICY
    RT: AGRICULTURAL ADMINISTRATION

AGRICULTURAL POPULATION
POPULATION AGRICOLE / POBLACION AGRICOLA -
14.04.02
    BT: RURAL POPULATION
    NT: AGRICULTURAL WORKERS
        PEASANTS

AGRICULTURAL POTENTIAL
POTENTIEL AGRICOLE / POTENCIAL AGRICOLA -
07.01.02
    NT: LAND CAPABILITY
    RT: DEVELOPMENT POTENTIAL

AGRICULTURAL PRICES
PRIX AGRICOLES / PRECIOS AGRICOLAS - 07.01.03
    BT: COMMODITY PRICES

AGRICULTURAL PRODUCTION
PRODUCTION AGRICOLE / PRODUCCION AGRICOLA -
07.05.01
    BT: PRODUCTION
    NT: ANIMAL PRODUCTION
        FOREST PRODUCTION
        PLANT PRODUCTION
    RT: AGRICULTURAL PRODUCTS

AGRICULTURAL PRODUCTS
PRODUITS AGRICOLES / PRODUCTOS AGRICOLAS -
07.05.05
    UF: AGRICULTURAL COMMODITIES
    BT: COMMODITIES
    NT: ANIMAL PRODUCTS
        PLANT PRODUCTS
    RT: AGRICULTURAL PRODUCTION
        AGRIPRODUCT PROCESSING

AGRICULTURAL PROJECTS
PROJETS AGRICOLES / PROYECTOS AGRICOLAS -
07.01.02
    BT: DEVELOPMENT PROJECTS

AGRICULTURAL RESEARCH
RECHERCHE AGRICOLE / INVESTIGACION AGRICOLA -

AGRICULTURAL RESEARCH<CONT>
07.06.00
    BT: RESEARCH
    NT: FISHERY RESEARCH
        FORESTRY RESEARCH
    RT: AGRICULTURE
        CIAT
        CIMMYT
        EXPERIMENTAL FARMS
        ICRISAT
        IRRI

AGRICULTURAL SECTOR
SECTEUR AGRICOLE / SECTOR AGROPECUARIO -
07.01.01
SN: INCLUDES FORESTRY AND FISHERY.
    BT: PRIMARY SECTOR
    RT: AGRICULTURAL ECONOMY

AGRICULTURAL STATISTICS
STATISTIQUES AGRICOLES / ESTADISTICAS AGRICOLAS
- 07.05.01
    BT: ECONOMIC STATISTICS
    NT: FISHERY STATISTICS
        FORESTRY STATISTICS
    RT: AGRICULTURE
        PRODUCTION STATISTICS

AGRICULTURAL SURPLUSES
EXCEDENTS AGRICOLES / EXCEDENTES AGRICOLAS -
07.01.03
    BT: SURPLUSES

AGRICULTURAL TECHNOLOGY
- 07.04.00
    USE: AGRICULTURAL ENGINEERING

AGRICULTURAL TRAINING
FORMATION AGRICOLE / CAPACITACION AGRICOLA -
06.03.07
    UF: FARMER TRAINING
    BT: VOCATIONAL TRAINING
    RT: AGRICULTURAL EDUCATION
        AGRICULTURAL EXTENSION
        AGRICULTURE
        EXPERIMENTAL FARMS

AGRICULTURAL WASTES
DECHETS AGRICOLES / DESPERDICIOS AGRICOLAS -
07.05.05
    BT: WASTES

AGRICULTURAL WORKERS
TRAVAILLEURS AGRICOLES / TRABAJADORES AGRICOLAS
- 13.09.05
    BT: AGRICULTURAL POPULATION
        RURAL WORKERS
    NT: FARMERS
        FISHERMEN
    RT: AGRICULTURAL ENTERPRISES

AGRICULTURE
AGRICULTURE / AGRICULTURA - 07.01.01
SN: USE MORE SPECIFIC DESCRIPTOR, IF APPLICABLE.

AGRICULTURE<CONT>
    NT: FISHERY
         FORESTRY
    RT: AGRICULTURAL EDUCATION
         AGRICULTURAL EXTENSION
         AGRICULTURAL INSTITUTES
         AGRICULTURAL INVESTMENTS
         AGRICULTURAL RESEARCH
         AGRICULTURAL STATISTICS
         AGRICULTURAL TRAINING
         AGRIS
         AGROINDUSTRY
         CAB
         FAO

AGRIPRODUCT PROCESSING
TRAITEMENT DE PRODUITS AGRICOLES / PROCESAMIENTO DE PRODUCTO AGRICOLA - 08.06.02
    BT: PROCESSING
    NT: FOOD PROCESSING
    RT: AGRICULTURAL PRODUCTS

AGRIS
AGRIS / AGRIS - 19.01.02
SN: INTERNATIONAL INFORMATIOM SYSTEM FOR
    AGRICULTURE SCIENCES AND TECHNOLOGY.
    BT: INFORMATION SYSTEMS
    RT: AGRICULTURE
         FAO

AGROINDUSTRIAL COMPLEX
- 07.01.01
    USE: AGROINDUSTRY

AGROINDUSTRY
AGROINDUSTRIE / AGROINDUSTRIA - 07.01.01
    UF: AGRICULTURAL INDUSTRY
         AGROINDUSTRIAL COMPLEX
    RT: AGRICULTURE
         INDUSTRIAL CROPS
         INDUSTRY

AGRONOMISTS
AGRONOMES / AGRONOMOS - 13.09.09
    BT: SCIENTISTS
    RT: AGRONOMY

AGRONOMY
AGRONOMIE / AGRONOMIA - 07.06.00
    RT: AGRONOMISTS

AID BY RELIGIOUS BODIES
- 01.01.02
    USE: PRIVATE AID

AID COORDINATION
COORDINATION DE L'AIDE / COORDINACION DE LA AYUDA - 01.01.04
    RT: DEVELOPMENT AID
         OECD DAC

AID EVALUATION
EVALUATION DE L'AIDE / EVALUACION DE LA AYUDA -

AID EVALUATION<CONT>
01.01.04
    BT: EVALUATION
    RT: DEVELOPMENT AID
         PROJECT EVALUATION

AID FINANCING
FINANCEMENT DE L'AIDE / FINANCIAMIENTO DE LA AYUDA - 01.01.04
    BT: FINANCING
    RT: DEVELOPMENT AID
         DEVELOPMENT BANKS

AID IN KIND
AIDE EN NATURE / AYUDA EN ESPECIE - 01.01.03
    UF: GRANTS IN KIND
    BT: DEVELOPMENT AID

AID INSTITUTIONS
ORGANISMES D'AIDE / INSTITUCIONES DE AYUDA - 01.01.07
SN: INSTITUTION PROVIDING PRIMARILY FINANCIAL
    AID.
    NT: REGIONAL AGENCIES
    RT: DEVELOPMENT AID

AID PROGRAMMES
PROGRAMMES D'AIDE / PROGRAMAS DE AYUDA - 01.01.04
    RT: DEVELOPMENT AID
         FINANCING PROGRAMMES

AIMS OF EDUCATION
FINALITE DE L'EDUCATION / FINALIDAD DE LA EDUCACION - 06.02.01
    RT: EDUCATION

AIR
- 17.01.02
    USE: ATMOSPHERE

AIR PIRACY
PIRATERIE AERIENNE / PIRATERIA AEREA - 01.02.07
    RT: TERRORISM

AIR POLLUTANTS
POLLUANTS DE L'AIR / CONTAMINANTES ATMOSFERICOS - 16.03.04
    BT: POLLUTANTS
    NT: AEROSOLS
         NITROGEN OXIDES
         SULPHUR DIOXIDE
    RT: AIR POLLUTION
         ATMOSPHERE

AIR POLLUTION
POLLUTION DE L'AIR / CONTAMINACION ATMOSFERICA - 16.03.04
    UF: ATMOSPHERIC POLLUTION
    BT: POLLUTION
    RT: AIR POLLUTANTS
         ATMOSPHERE

AIR TRAFFIC
CIRCULATION AERIENNE / TRAFICO AEREO - 10.08.00
    BT: TRAFFIC
    RT: AIR TRANSPORT

AIR TRANSPORT
TRANSPORT AERIEN / TRANSPORTE AEREO - 10.05.00
    BT: MODES OF TRANSPORTATION
    RT: AIR TRAFFIC
        AIRCRAFT
        AIRCRAFT INDUSTRY
        AIRPORTS
        HELICOPTERS
        ICAO

AIRCRAFT
AVIONS / AVIONES - 10.04.00
    BT: MOTOR VEHICLES
    NT: HELICOPTERS
    RT: AIR TRANSPORT
        AIRCRAFT INDUSTRY
        PILOTS

AIRCRAFT INDUSTRY
INDUSTRIE AERONAUTIQUE / INDUSTRIA AERONAUTICA -
08.14.07
    BT: INDUSTRIAL SECTOR
    RT: AEROSPACE INDUSTRY
        AIR TRANSPORT
        AIRCRAFT

AIRPORTS
AEROPORTS / AEROPUERTOS - 10.03.00
    RT: AIR TRANSPORT

ALBANIA
ALBANIE / ALBANIA - 01.04.05
    BT: EASTERN EUROPE
        MEDITERRANEAN COUNTRIES
    RT: ALBANIAN

ALBANIAN
ALBANAIS / ALBANES - 14.03.02
    RT: ALBANIA

ALCOHOL
ALCOOL / ALCOHOL - 08.12.04

ALCOHOLIC BEVERAGES
BOISSONS ALCOOLISEES / BEBIDAS ALCOHOLICAS -
08.06.05
    BT: BEVERAGES
    NT: BEER
        WINE
    RT: ALCOHOLISM

ALCOHOLISM
ALCOOLISME / ALCOHOLISMO - 02.04.02
    BT: POISONING
        SOCIAL PROBLEMS
    RT: ALCOHOLIC BEVERAGES
        DRUG ADDICTION

ALECSO
ALECSO / ALECSO - 01.03.03

ALECSO<CONT>
*SN: THE ARAB LEAGUE EDUCATIONAL, CULTURAL AND
SCIENTIFIC ORGANIZATION.*
    BT: LEAGUE OF ARAB STATES
    RT: ARAB COUNTRIES
        CULTURE
        EDUCATION
        SCIENCE

ALGAE
ALGUES / ALGAS - 07.10.04
    UF: SEAWEEDS
    BT: AQUATIC PLANTS

ALGERIA
ALGERIE / ARGELIA - 01.04.02
    BT: ARAB COUNTRIES
        FRENCH SPEAKING AFRICA
        MEDITERRANEAN COUNTRIES
        NORTH AFRICA
    RT: ALGERIAN

ALGERIAN
ALGERIEN / ARGELINO - 14.03.02
    RT: ALGERIA

ALIENATION
ALIENATION / ALIENACION - 05.03.03
    RT: MARGINALITY
        PERSONALITY

ALLERGIES
- 15.04.02
    USE: IMMUNOLOGIC DISEASES

ALLIANCES
ALLIANCES / ALIANZAS - 01.02.01
    RT: INTERNATIONAL RELATIONS

ALLOYS
ALLIAGES / ALEACIONES - 08.14.02
    NT: STEEL
    RT: METALS

ALMONDS
AMANDES / ALMENDRAS - 07.07.05
    BT: FRUITS

ALTERNATIVE TECHNOLOGY
TECHNOLOGIE ALTERNATIVE / TECNOLOGIA ALTERNATIVA
- 12.06.00
    BT: TECHNOLOGY
    RT: APPROPRIATE TECHNOLOGY
        INTERMEDIATE TECHNOLOGY

ALTITUDE
ALTITUDE / ALTITUD - 18.06.00

ALUMINIUM
ALUMINIUM / ALUMINIO - 08.14.02
    BT: NON-FERROUS METALS
    RT: ALUMINIUM INDUSTRY
        BAUXITE

ALUMINIUM INDUSTRY
INDUSTRIE DE L'ALUMINIUM / INDUSTRIA DEL
ALUMINIO - 08.14.01
> *RT:* ALUMINIUM
> BAUXITE

ALUMINIUM ORE
- 08.13.00
> *USE:* BAUXITE

AMERICA
AMERIQUE / AMERICA - 01.04.03
> *NT:* CARIBBEAN
> LATIN AMERICA
> NORTH AMERICA
> SOUTH AMERICA
> *RT:* AMERICAN ORGANIZATIONS
> AMERINDIANS
> OAS
> PAHO

AMERICAN
AMERICAIN / NORTEAMERICANO - 14.03.02
SN: USE ONLY IN CONNECTION WITH NATIONALS OF THE USA.
> *RT:* USA

AMERICAN ORGANIZATIONS
ORGANISATIONS AMERICAINES / ORGANIZACIONES
AMERICANAS - 01.03.03
> *BT:* REGIONAL ORGANIZATIONS
> *NT:* CABEI
> CACM
> CARICOM
> CARIFTA
> CEMLA
> CLACSO
> ECLA
> IDB
> ILPES
> LAFTA
> OAS
> OCAS
> *RT:* AMERICA

AMERINDIANS
AMERINDIENS / AMERINDIOS - 14.03.03
> *UF:* ANDEAN INDIANS
> *RT:* AMERICA

AMINO ACIDS
ACIDES AMINES / AMINOACIDOS - 15.01.03
> *BT:* PROTEINS

AMMONIA
AMMONIAQUE / AMONIACO - 08.12.04

AMORTIZATION
AMORTISSEMENT / AMORTIZACION - 11.02.05
> *RT:* CAPITAL

ANATOMY
ANATOMIE / ANATOMIA - 15.02.01
> *BT:* NATURAL SCIENCES

ANATOMY<CONT>
> *NT:* CARDIOVASCULAR SYSTEM
> DIGESTIVE SYSTEM
> ENDOCRINE SYSTEM
> HISTOLOGY
> INTEGUMENTARY SYSTEM
> LYMPHATIC SYSTEM
> MUSCULOSKELETAL SYSTEM
> NERVOUS SYSTEM
> RESPIRATORY SYSTEM
> UROGENITAL SYSTEM

ANDEAN GROUP
GROUPE ANDIN / GRUPO ANDINO - 01.03.03
> *UF:* ANDEAN PACT
> CARTHAGENA AGREEMENT
> *BT:* LAFTA
> *RT:* LATIN AMERICA

ANDEAN INDIANS
- 14.03.03
> *USE:* AMERINDIANS

ANDEAN PACT
- 01.03.03
> *USE:* ANDEAN GROUP

ANDEAN REGION
REGION ANDINE / REGION ANDINA - 01.04.03
> *BT:* SOUTH AMERICA

ANDORRA
ANDORRE / ANDORRA - 01.04.05
> *BT:* WESTERN EUROPE

ANGOLA
ANGOLA / ANGOLA - 01.04.02
> *BT:* SOUTHERN AFRICA
> *RT:* ANGOLAN

ANGOLAN
ANGOLAIS / ANGOLENO - 14.03.02
> *RT:* ANGOLA

ANIMAL BREEDING
SELECTION ANIMALE / MEJORAMIENTO ANIMAL -
07.09.02
> *NT:* FISH BREEDING
> *RT:* ANIMALS
> ARTIFICIAL INSEMINATION
> GENETIC IMPROVEMENT
> REPRODUCTION

ANIMAL DISEASES
MALADIES ANIMALES / ENFERMEDADES ANIMALES -
15.04.01
> *BT:* DISEASES
> *RT:* ANIMALS
> PESTS OF ANIMALS
> VETERINARY MEDICINE

ANIMAL ECOLOGY
ECOLOGIE ANIMALE / ECOLOGIA ANIMAL - 16.01.01
> *BT:* ECOLOGY

ANIMAL ECOLOGY<CONT>
>RT: ANIMAL RESOURCES
>ANIMALS

ANIMAL FATS
GRAISSES ANIMALES / GRASAS ANIMALES - 08.06.06
>BT: ANIMAL PRODUCTS
>FATS

ANIMAL FEEDING
ALIMENTATION ANIMALE / ALIMENTACION ANIMAL -
07.09.03
SN: USED IN DISCUSSING PROBLEMS AND METHODS OF
>FEEDING ANIMALS. WHEN DISCUSSING WHAT THEY
>ARE TO EAT, USE 'FEED'.
>BT: FEEDING
>RT: ANIMAL NUTRITION

ANIMAL FIBRES
FIBRES ANIMALES / FIBRAS ANIMALES - 07.09.05
>BT: ANIMAL PRODUCTS
>NATURAL FIBRES
>NT: SILK
>WOOL

ANIMAL HUSBANDRY
ELEVAGE / ZOOTECNIA - 07.09.02
>NT: CATTLE PRODUCTION
>RT: ANIMAL RESOURCES
>ANIMALS
>ZOOTECHNICIANS

ANIMAL NUTRITION
NUTRITION ANIMALE / NUTRICION ANIMAL - 07.09.03
>BT: NUTRITION
>RT: ANIMAL FEEDING
>ANIMALS

ANIMAL OILS
HUILES ANIMALES / ACEITES ANIMALES - 08.06.06
>BT: ANIMAL PRODUCTS
>OILS AND FATS
>NT: FISH OILS

ANIMAL PRODUCTION
PRODUCTION ANIMALE / PRODUCCION ANIMAL -
07.09.02
>BT: AGRICULTURAL PRODUCTION
>NT: CATTLE PRODUCTION
>FISH PRODUCTION
>RT: ANIMALS

ANIMAL PRODUCTS
PRODUITS D'ORIGINE ANIMALE / PRODUCTOS ANIMALES
- 07.09.05
>BT: AGRICULTURAL PRODUCTS

ANIMAL PRODUCTS<CONT>
>NT: ANIMAL FATS
>ANIMAL FIBRES
>ANIMAL OILS
>DAIRY PRODUCTS
>EGGS
>FISHERY PRODUCTS
>HIDES AND SKINS
>HONEY
>MEAT PRODUCTS
>RT: ANIMALS

ANIMAL PROTECTION
PROTECTION DES ANIMAUX / PROTECCION DE ANIMALES
- 16.05.01
>BT: NATURE CONSERVATION
>NT: FISHERY CONSERVATION
>GAME PROTECTION
>RT: ANIMAL RESOURCES
>ANIMALS
>PROTECTED SPECIES

ANIMAL RESOURCES
RESSOURCES ANIMALES / RECURSOS ANIMALES -
16.02.02
>BT: NATURAL RESOURCES
>NT: FISHERY RESOURCES
>RT: ANIMAL ECOLOGY
>ANIMAL HUSBANDRY
>ANIMAL PROTECTION
>ANIMALS

ANIMALS
ANIMAUX / ANIMALES - 07.09.01
>NT: BIRDS
>DOMESTIC ANIMALS
>ELEPHANTS
>EQUIDAE
>FISH
>INSECTS
>LIVESTOCK
>REPTILES
>RODENTS
>RUMINANTS
>SWINE
>WILD ANIMALS
>RT: ANIMAL BREEDING
>ANIMAL DISEASES
>ANIMAL ECOLOGY
>ANIMAL HUSBANDRY
>ANIMAL NUTRITION
>ANIMAL PRODUCTION
>ANIMAL PRODUCTS
>ANIMAL PROTECTION
>ANIMAL RESOURCES
>FAUNA
>NON-MOTORIZED TRANSPORT
>ZOOLOGICAL GARDENS
>ZOOLOGY

ANIMISM
ANIMISME / ANIMISMO - 05.04.03

ANNOTATED BIBLIOGRAPHY
BIBLIOGRAPHIE ANNOTEE / BIBLIOGRAFIA ANOTADA -

ANNOTATED BIBLIOGRAPHY<CONT>
19.02.07
    BT: BIBLIOGRAPHY

ANNUAL REPORT
RAPPORT ANNUEL / INFORME ANUAL - 19.02.08

ANTARCTICA
ANTARCTIQUE / ANTARTICA - 01.04.01

ANTHROPOLOGISTS
ANTHROPOLOGUES / ANTROPOLOGOS - 13.09.09
    BT: SCIENTISTS
    RT: ETHNOLOGY

ANTHROPOLOGY
ANTHROPOLOGIE / ANTROPOLOGIA - 05.01.01
    BT: NATURAL SCIENCES
         SOCIAL SCIENCES
    RT: IUAES

ANTIBIOTICS
ANTIBIOTIQUES / ANTIBIOTICOS - 15.05.00
    BT: DRUGS

ANTIGUA
ANTIGUA / ANTIGUA - 01.04.03
    BT: WEST INDIES ASSOCIATED STATES

ANTILLES
- 01.04.03
    USE: **CARIBBEAN**

ANTITRUST LEGISLATION
LEGISLATION ANTI-TRUST / LEGISLACION ANTITRUST -
12.02.00
    BT: ECONOMIC LEGISLATION
    RT: COMPETITION
         CONSUMER PROTECTION
         RESTRICTIVE BUSINESS PRACTICES
         TRUSTS

APARTHEID
APARTHEID / APARTHEID - 04.02.04
    BT: RACIAL SEGREGATION
    RT: SOUTH AFRICA

APICULTURE
APICULTURE / APICULTURA - 07.09.02
    RT: HONEY

APO
OAP / OAP - 01.03.03
SN: ASIAN PRODUCTIVITY ORGANIZATION.
    BT: ASIAN ORGANIZATIONS
         INTERGOVERNMENTAL ORGANIZATIONS
    RT: ASIA
         PRODUCTIVITY

APPELLATION OF ORIGIN
APELLATION D'ORIGINE / DENOMINACION DE ORIGEN -
12.07.02

APPELLATION OF ORIGIN<CONT>
    RT: QUALITY STANDARDS
         SPECIFICATIONS

APPLES
POMMES / MANZANAS - 07.07.05
    BT: FRUITS

APPLIED RESEARCH
RECHERCHE APPLIQUEE / INVESTIGACION APLICADA
18.01.00
    BT: RESEARCH
    RT: RESEARCH AND DEVELOPMENT

APPRENTICES
APPRENTIS / APRENDICES - 13.09.03
    RT: APPRENTICESHIP
         VOCATIONAL TRAINING

APPRENTICESHIP
APPRENTISSAGE / APRENDIZAJE - 06.03.07
    BT: VOCATIONAL TRAINING
    RT: APPRENTICES

APPROPRIATE TECHNOLOGY
TECHNOLOGIE APPROPRIEE / TECNOLOGIA APROPIADA -
12.06.00
    BT: TECHNOLOGY
    RT: ALTERNATIVE TECHNOLOGY
         INDUSTRIAL EXTENSION
         INTERMEDIATE TECHNOLOGY
         TECHNOLOGY TRANSFER

APTITUDES
APTITUDES / APTITUDES - 06.05.04
    RT: INTELLIGENCE QUOTIENT

APU
UPA / UPA - 01.03.03
SN: ASIAN PARLIAMENTARY UNION.
    BT: ASIAN ORGANIZATIONS
         INTERGOVERNMENTAL ORGANIZATIONS
    NT: ADC
    RT: ASIA
         PARLIAMENT

AQUACULTURE
AQUICULTURE / ACUACULTURA - 07.10.03
    NT: FISH CULTURE
         OYSTER CULTURE

AQUATIC ENVIRONMENT
ENVIRONNEMENT AQUATIQUE / MEDIO AMBIENTE
ACUATICO - 16.01.02
    BT: PHYSICAL ENVIRONMENT
    NT: MARINE ENVIRONMENT

AQUATIC FAUNA
FAUNE AQUATIQUE / FAUNA ACUATICA - 07.10.04
    BT: FAUNA

AQUATIC PLANTS
PLANTES AQUATIQUES / PLANTAS ACUATICAS -

AQUATIC PLANTS<CONT>
07.07.01
>   *BT:* PLANTS
>   *NT:* ALGAE

AQUEDUCTS
AQUEDUCS / ACUEDUCTOS - 17.05.04

ARAB COUNTRIES
PAYS ARABES / PAISES ARABES - 01.04.06
>   *NT:* ALGERIA
>   EGYPT
>   IRAQ
>   JORDAN
>   LEBANON
>   LIBYA
>   MOROCCO
>   OMAN
>   PERSIAN GULF STATES
>   SAUDI ARABIA
>   SUDAN
>   SYRIA
>   TUNISIA
>   YEMEN
>   YEMEN PDR
>   *RT:* ALECSO
>   ARAB ORGANIZATIONS
>   ARABS
>   CAEU
>   IDCAS
>   MIDDLE EAST
>   NORTH AFRICA
>   OAPEC

ARAB ORGANIZATIONS
**ORGANISATIONS ARABES / ORGANIZACIONES ARABES -
01.03.03**
>   *BT:* REGIONAL ORGANIZATIONS
>   *NT:* ECWA
>   LEAGUE OF ARAB STATES
>   MPCC
>   OAPEC
>   *RT:* ARAB COUNTRIES
>   REGIONAL INTEGRATION

ARABIC
LANGUE ARABE / LENGUA ARABICA - 05.06.02
>   *BT:* LANGUAGES

ARABLE LAND
TERRE LABOURABLE / TIERRA CULTIVABLE - 07.05.02
>   *RT:* CULTIVATED LAND

ARABS
ARABES / ARABES - 14.03.02
>   *RT:* ARAB COUNTRIES

ARBITRATION
ARBITRAGE / ARBITRAJE - 05.03.06
>   *BT:* DISPUTE SETTLEMENT

ARCHAEOLOGICAL SITES
SITES ARCHEOLOGIQUES / YACIMIENTOS ARQUEOLOGICOS

ARCHAEOLOGICAL SITES<CONT>
- 05.05.01
>   *RT:* ARCHAEOLOGY

ARCHAEOLOGY
ARCHEOLOGIE / ARQUEOLOGIA - 05.05.01
>   *RT:* ARCHAEOLOGICAL SITES
>   ART
>   HISTORY

ARCHITECTS
ARCHITECTES / ARQUITECTOS - 13.09.09
>   *RT:* ARCHITECTURE

ARCHITECTURE
ARCHITECTURE / ARQUITECTURA - 05.05.03
>   *BT:* FINE ARTS
>   *RT:* ARCHITECTS

ARCHIVES
ARCHIVES / ARCHIVOS - 19.01.03
>   *BT:* INFORMATION SERVICES

AREA STUDY
- 17.03.01
>   *USE:* REGIONAL ANALYSIS

ARGENTINA
ARGENTINE / ARGENTINA - 01.04.03
>   *BT:* LATIN AMERICA
>   SOUTHERN CONE
>   *RT:* ARGENTINIAN

ARGENTINIAN
ARGENTIN / ARGENTINO - 14.03.02
>   *RT:* ARGENTINA

ARID ZONE
ZONE ARIDE / ZONA ARIDA - 17.02.03
>   *UF:* DESERT
>   *BT:* CLIMATIC ZONES
>   *RT:* DESERTIFICATION
>   DROUGHT
>   SAHARA

ARMAMENT
ARMEMENT / ARMAMENTISMO - 01.02.06
*SN: THE PROCESS OF ARMING; OTHERWISE USE
'WEAPONS'.*
>   *UF:* ARMS RACE
>   *RT:* MILITARY AID
>   MILITARY EXPENDITURES
>   WEAPON PROCUREMENT
>   WEAPONS

ARMISTICE
ARMISTICE / ARMISTICIO - 01.02.07
>   *RT:* PEACE
>   WAR

ARMS EMBARGO
EMBARGO SUR LES ARMES / EMBARGO DE ARMAS -

ARMS EMBARGO<CONT>
01.02.06
    BT: EMBARGO
    RT: WEAPONS

ARMS LIMITATION
- 01.02.06
    USE: DISARMAMENT

ARMS RACE
- 01.02.06
    USE: ARMAMENT

ARMY
ARMEE / EJERCITO - 01.02.06
    RT: MILITARY
         MILITARY SERVICE

ARRANGEMENT OF WORKING TIME
AMENAGEMENT DU TEMPS DE TRAVAIL / ORDENAMIENTO
DEL TIEMPO DE TRABAJO - 13.03.03
    NT: CONTINUOUS WORKING DAY
         HOURS OF WORK
         NIGHT WORK
         REST PERIOD
         SHIFT WORK

ART
ART / ARTE - 05.05.02
    NT: FOLK ART
    RT: AESTHETICS
         ARCHAEOLOGY
         ART EDUCATION
         ARTISTIC CREATION
         ARTS
         CREATIVITY
         CULTURE
         WORKS OF ART

ART EDUCATION
EDUCATION ARTISTIQUE / EDUCACION ARTISTICA -
06.03.07
    BT: VOCATIONAL EDUCATION
    RT: ART

ARTICLE
ARTICLE / ARTICULO - 19.02.06
    RT: PERIODICALS

ARTIFICIAL INSEMINATION
INSEMINATION ARTIFICIELLE / INSEMINACION
ARTIFICIAL - 15.02.02
    RT: ANIMAL BREEDING

ARTIFICIAL LAKES
LACS ARTIFICIELS / LAGOS ARTIFICIALES - 17.05.04
    BT: LAKES
    RT: DAMS

ARTISTIC CREATION
CREATION ARTISTIQUE / CREACION ARTISTICA -
05.05.02

ARTISTIC CREATION<CONT>
    RT: ART
         CREATIVITY

ARTISTS
ARTISTES / ARTISTAS - 13.09.09
*SN: USE FOR CREATIVE ARTISTS, OTHERWISE USE
«PERFORMERS».*

ARTS
ARTS / ARTES - 05.05.03
    NT: LITERATURE
         MUSIC
         PERFORMING ARTS
         VISUAL ARTS
    RT: ART

ASBESTOS
AMIANTE / ASBESTO - 08.10.02
    BT: REFRACTORY MATERIALS

ASEAN
ASEAN / ASEAN - 01.03.03
SN: ASSOCIATION OF SOUTH-EAST ASIAN NATIONS.
    BT: ASIAN ORGANIZATIONS
         INTERGOVERNMENTAL ORGANIZATIONS
    RT: SOUTH EAST ASIA

ASIA
ASIE / ASIA - 01.04.04
    NT: FAR EAST
         SOUTH ASIA
         SOUTH EAST ASIA
    RT: ACDA
         ADC
         ADIPA
         AFRASEC
         APO
         APU
         ASIAN
         ASIAN DEVELOPMENT BANK
         ASIAN ORGANIZATIONS
         ASPAC
         ESCAP

ASIAN
ASIATIQUE / ASIATICO - 14.03.02
    RT: ASIA

ASIAN DEVELOPMENT BANK
BANQUE ASIATIQUE DE DEVELOPPEMENT / BANCO
ASIATICO DE DESARROLLO - 01.03.03
    BT: ASIAN ORGANIZATIONS
         DEVELOPMENT BANKS
         INTERGOVERNMENTAL ORGANIZATIONS
    RT: ASIA

ASIAN ORGANIZATIONS
ORGANISATIONS ASIATIQUES / ORGANIZACIONES
ASIATICAS - 01.03.03
    BT: REGIONAL ORGANIZATIONS

ASIAN ORGANIZATIONS<CONT>
NT: ACDA
     ADIPA
     APO
     APU
     ASEAN
     ASIAN DEVELOPMENT BANK
     ASPAC
     CENTO
     COLOMBO PLAN
     ECWA
     ESCAP
     SEATO
     SPC
RT: ASIA
     REGIONAL INTEGRATION

ASPAC
ASPAC / ASPAC - 01.03.03
SN: ASIAN AND PACIFIC COUNCIL.
     BT: ASIAN ORGANIZATIONS
         INTERGOVERNMENTAL ORGANIZATIONS
     RT: ASIA
         PACIFIC REGION

ASSEMBLY LINES
CHAINES DE MONTAGE / CADENAS DE MONTAJE -
08.14.07
     RT: ASSEMBLY-LINE WORK
         INDUSTRIAL PROCESSES

ASSEMBLY-LINE WORK
TRAVAIL A LA CHAINE / LINEA DE MONTAJE -
13.03.02
     RT: ASSEMBLY LINES
         WORKING CONDITIONS

ASSOCIATIONS
ASSOCIATIONS / ASOCIACIONES - 05.03.07
     NT: EMPLOYEE ASSOCIATIONS
         EMPLOYERS ORGANIZATIONS
         OCCUPATIONAL ORGANIZATIONS
     RT: FREEDOM OF ASSOCIATION
         TRADE UNIONS

ASTHMA
ASTHME / ASMA - 15.04.02

ASTRONAUTICS
ASTRONAUTIQUE / ASTRONAUTICA - 17.07.00
     BT: SPACE SCIENCES

ASTRONOMY
ASTRONOMIE / ASTRONOMIA - 17.07.00
     BT: SPACE SCIENCES

ATHEISM
ATHEISME / ATEISMO - 05.04.02

ATLANTIC OCEAN
OCEAN ATLANTIQUE / OCEANO ATLANTICO - 17.06.00

ATLASES
ATLAS / ATLAS - 18.07.00
     RT: MAPS

ATMOSPHERE
ATMOSPHERE / ATMOSFERA - 17.01.02
     UF: AIR
     BT: PHYSICAL ENVIRONMENT
     RT: AIR POLLUTANTS
         AIR POLLUTION
         BAROMETRIC PRESSURE
         WEATHER

ATMOSPHERIC POLLUTION
- 16.03.04
     USE: AIR POLLUTION

ATMOSPHERIC SCIENCES
- 17.01.01
     USE: METEOROLOGY

ATOMIC ENERGY
- 08.11.03
     USE: NUCLEAR ENERGY

ATOMIC WEAPONS
- 01.02.06
     USE: NUCLEAR WEAPONS

ATTITUDES
ATTITUDES / ACTITUDES - 05.03.02
     NT: EMPLOYEES ATTITUDES
         MANAGEMENT ATTITUDES
     RT: BEHAVIOUR
         CONSERVATISM

AUDIENCE
PUBLIC / PUBLICO - 05.07.02
     UF: COMMUNICATION USERS

AUDIENCE RATING
EVALUATION DU PUBLIC / EVALUACION DEL PUBLICO -
05.07.02
     BT: EVALUATION

AUDIOVISUAL AIDS
MOYENS AUDIOVISUELS / MEDIOS AUDIOVISUALES -
06.05.03
SN: MATERIAL SUCH AS FILMS, TAPE RECORDINGS,
    POSTERS AND CHARTS UTILIZED FOR TEACHING AND
    RESEARCH PURPOSES.
     BT: TEACHING AIDS
     NT: EDUCATIONAL FILMS
     RT: AUDIOVISUAL MATERIALS

AUDIOVISUAL CENTRES
CENTRES AUDIOVISUELS / CENTROS AUDIOVISUALES -
19.01.03
     BT: INFORMATION SERVICES

AUDIOVISUAL MATERIALS
DOCUMENTS AUDIOVISUELS / MATERIAL AUDIOVISUAL -
19.02.01
     BT: DOCUMENTS

AUDIOVISUAL MATERIALS<CONT>
    NT: CHARTS
          DIAGRAMS
          FILMS
          GRAPHS
          MAPS
          MICROFILMS
          PHOTOGRAPHS
          SLIDES
    RT: AUDIOVISUAL AIDS
          MASS MEDIA

AUDITING
VERIFICATION COMPTABLE / AUDITORIA - 12.09.00
    RT: ACCOUNTING

AUSTERITY POLICY
POLITIQUE D'AUSTERITE / POLITICA DE AUSTERIDAD -
02.01.03
SN: RESTRICTIONS ON GOVERNMENT SPENDING; INCOME
    AND PRICE CONTROLS.
    BT: ECONOMIC POLICY
    RT: ECONOMIC RECESSION
          INFLATION

AUSTRALIA
AUSTRALIE / AUSTRALIA - 01.04.07
    BT: OCEANIA
    RT: AUSTRALIAN
          PACIFIC ISLANDS AUS

AUSTRALIAN
AUSTRALIEN / AUSTRALIANO - 14.03.02
    RT: AUSTRALIA

AUSTRIA
AUTRICHE / AUSTRIA - 01.04.05
    BT: WESTERN EUROPE
    RT: AUSTRIAN

AUSTRIAN
AUTRICHIEN / AUSTRIACO - 14.03.02
    RT: AUSTRIA

AUTHORS
AUTEURS / AUTORES - 19.02.03
    RT: COPYRIGHT

AUTOMATIC CONTROL
REGULATION AUTOMATIQUE / REGULACION AUTOMATICA -
12.07.02
SN: PRODUCTION IN WHICH ALL CONTROLS ARE
    AUTOMATICALLY CARRIED THROUGH BY MACHINERY.
    BT: PRODUCTION CONTROL
    RT: AUTOMATION

AUTOMATION
AUTOMATION / AUTOMATIZACION - 12.07.02
SN: THE USE OF AUTOMATIC DEVICES WHICH PERFORM
    PRODUCTION AND ASSEMBLY OPERATIONS AND WHICH
    PROVIDE BUILT-IN INSPECTION AND CONTROL
    FEATURES.
    NT: LIBRARY AUTOMATION

AUTOMATION<CONT>
    RT: AUTOMATIC CONTROL
          INDUSTRIALIZATION
          TECHNOLOGICAL CHANGE

AUTOMOBILE INDUSTRY
INDUSTRIE AUTOMOBILE / INDUSTRIA AUTOMOTRIZ -
08.14.07
    BT: MOTOR VEHICLE INDUSTRY
    RT: AUTOMOBILES
          ROAD TRANSPORT

AUTOMOBILE SERVICE
SERVICE AUTOMOBILE / SERVICIO AUTOMOTRIZ -
10.03.00
SN: USE IN CONNECTION WITH THE MAINTENANCE OF
    MOTOR VEHICLES.
    BT: SERVICE INDUSTRY
    RT: AUTOMOBILES
          MAINTENANCE AND REPAIR
          ROAD TRANSPORT

AUTOMOBILES
AUTOMOBILES / AUTOMOVILES - 10.04.00
    UF: MOTOR CARS
    BT: MOTOR VEHICLES
    RT: AUTOMOBILE INDUSTRY
          AUTOMOBILE SERVICE

AUXILIARY HEALTH WORKERS
- 13.09.10
    USE: **PARAMEDICAL PERSONNEL**

AUXILIARY WORKERS
TRAVAILLEURS AUXILIAIRES / TRABAJADORES
AUXILIARES - 13.09.02
    BT: WORKERS

AZORES
ACORES / AZORES - 01.04.05
    BT: WESTERN EUROPE
    RT: PORTUGAL

BACTERIA
BACTERIES / BACTERIAS - 15.01.02
    BT: MICROORGANISMS
    RT: BACTERIOLOGY

BACTERIOLOGICAL WEAPONS
ARMES BACTERIOLOGIQUES / ARMES BACTERIOLOGICAS -
01.02.06
    BT: WEAPONS
    RT: BACTERIOLOGY

BACTERIOLOGY
BACTERIOLOGIE / BACTERIOLOGIA - 15.01.01
    BT: MICROBIOLOGY
    RT: BACTERIA
         BACTERIOLOGICAL WEAPONS

BAGS
SACS / SACOS - 10.06.00
    BT: CONTAINERS
    RT: PACKAGING

BAHAMAS
BAHAMAS / BAHAMAS - 01.04.03
    BT: CARIBBEAN
    RT: BAHAMIAN
         UNITED KINGDOM

BAHAMIAN
BAHAMIEN / BAHAMES - 14.03.02
    RT: BAHAMAS

BAHRAIN
BAHREIN / BAHREIN - 01.04.06
    BT: PERSIAN GULF STATES

BAKERY PRODUCTS
PRODUITS DE BOULANGERIE / PRODUCTOS DE PANADERIA
- 08.06.04
    BT: FOOD
    NT: BREAD

BALANCE OF PAYMENTS
BALANCE DES PAIEMENTS / BALANZA DE PAGOS -
11.03.02
    NT: BALANCE OF TRADE
         CAPITAL MOVEMENTS
         EXPORTS
         IMPORTS
         INVISIBLE TRANSACTIONS
    RT: COMPENSATORY FINANCING
         DEVALUATION
         ECONOMIC STATISTICS
         EXCHANGE RATE
         EXTERNAL DEBT
         INTERNATIONAL PAYMENTS

BALANCE OF TRADE
BALANCE COMMERCIALE / BALANZA COMERCIAL -
09.05.03
    BT: BALANCE OF PAYMENTS
    RT: FOREIGN TRADE

BANANA-TREES
BANANIERS / BANANOS - 07.07.05
    BT: FRUIT TREES
    RT: BANANAS

BANANAS
BANANES / BANANAS - 07.07.05
    BT: FRUITS
    RT: BANANA-TREES

BANGLADESH
BANGLADESH / BANGLADESH - 01.04.04
    BT: SOUTH ASIA
         SOUTH EAST ASIA
    RT: BENGALI

BANK RATE
TAUX DE REESCOMPTE / TASA DE REDESCUENTO -
11.02.07
    RT: DISCOUNT
         MONETARY POLICY
         MONEY MARKET

BANKING
ACTIVITE BANCAIRE / ACTIVIDAD BANCARIA -
11.02.02
    RT: BANKING SYSTEMS
         BANKS

BANKING SYSTEMS
SYSTEMES BANCAIRES / SISTEMAS BANCARIOS -
11.02.02
    BT: SERVICE INDUSTRY
    RT: BANKING
         BANKS
         CREDIT SYSTEMS

BANKRUPTCY
FAILLITE / QUIEBRA - 12.09.00
    RT: DEFICIT
         FINANCIAL LOSS

BANKS
BANQUES / BANCOS - 11.02.02
    BT: FINANCIAL INSTITUTIONS
    NT: AGRICULTURAL BANKS
         CENTRAL BANKS
         COMMERCIAL BANKS
         DEVELOPMENT BANKS
         INDUSTRIAL BANKS
         INVESTMENT BANKS
    RT: BANKING
         BANKING SYSTEMS
         CREDIT

BARBADIAN
BARBADIEN / BARBADENSE - 14.03.02
    RT: BARBADOS

BARBADOS
BARBADE / BARBADOS - 01.04.03
    BT: CARIBBEAN
    RT: BARBADIAN

BAREFOOT DOCTORS
MEDECINS AUX-PIEDS-NUS / MEDICOS DESCALZOS -
13.09.10
SN: TYPE OF CHINESE MEDICAL AUXILIARIES.
    BT: PARAMEDICAL PERSONNEL

BARLEY
ORGE / CEBADA - 07.07.04
    BT: CEREALS

BAROMETRIC PRESSURE
PRESSION BAROMETRIQUE / PRESION BAROMETRICA -
17.01.02
    RT: ATMOSPHERE

BARTER
TROC / TRUEQUE - 09.01.01
    BT: TRADE

BASIC EDUCATION
EDUCATION DE BASE / EDUCACION BASICA - 06.03.04
*SN: INSTRUCTION IN SUBJECTS OF ELEMENTARY
    EDUCATION, SOCIAL SKILLS AND COMMUNITY
    RESPONSIBILITIES.*
    NT: CIVIC EDUCATION
        CONSUMER EDUCATION
        ENVIRONMENTAL EDUCATION
        HEALTH EDUCATION
        HOME ECONOMICS
        LITERACY
        PHYSICAL EDUCATION
        POLITICAL EDUCATION
        SAFETY EDUCATION
        SEX EDUCATION

BASIC NEEDS
BESOINS FONDAMENTAUX / NECESIDADES BASICAS -
02.01.01
    UF: CRITICAL NEEDS
    BT: DEMAND
    NT: EDUCATIONAL NEEDS
        FOOD REQUIREMENTS
        HOUSING NEEDS
        INFORMATION NEEDS
        WATER REQUIREMENTS
    RT: DEVELOPMENT POLICY
        LIVING CONDITIONS
        POVERTY
        QUALITY OF LIFE

BASIC RESEARCH
RECHERCHE FONDAMENTALE / INVESTIGACION BASICA -
18.01.00
    BT: RESEARCH

BASIC TRAINING
FORMATION DE BASE / CAPACITACION BASICA -
06.03.07
*SN: SPECIALLY ORGANIZED TRAINING, GIVEN OUTSIDE
    OF PRODUCTION ACTIVITIES OF AN UNDERTAKING,
    AND AIMED AT IMPARTING THE BASIC KNOWLEDGE
    AND SKILL REQUIRED FOR A GIVEN GROUP OF
    OCCUPATIONS.*
    BT: VOCATIONAL TRAINING

BAUXITE
BAUXITE / BAUXITA - 08.13.00
    UF: ALUMINIUM ORE
    BT: MINERALS

BAUXITE<CONT>
    RT: ALUMINIUM
        ALUMINIUM INDUSTRY

BEANS
HARICOTS / FRIJOLES - 07.07.06
    BT: LEGUMINOSAE

BEEF
VIANDE DE BOEUF / CARNE VACUNA - 07.09.05
    BT: MEAT
    RT: BOVIDAE

BEER
BIERE / CERVEZA - 08.06.05
    BT: ALCOHOLIC BEVERAGES
    RT: BREWERY

BEET SUGAR
SUCRE DE BETTERAVE / AZUCAR DE REMOLACHA -
08.06.04
    BT: SUGAR
    RT: SUGAR BEETS

BEHAVIOUR
COMPORTEMENT / COMPORTAMIENTO - 05.03.02
    NT: CONSUMER BEHAVIOUR
        ECONOMIC BEHAVIOUR
        POLITICAL BEHAVIOUR
        SEXUAL BEHAVIOUR
        SOCIAL BEHAVIOUR
        STUDENT BEHAVIOUR
    RT: ATTITUDES
        BEHAVIOURAL SCIENCES

BEHAVIOURAL SCIENCES
SCIENCES DU COMPORTEMENT / CIENCIAS DEL
COMPORTAMIENTO - 05.01.01
    NT: PSYCHOLOGY
        SOCIAL PSYCHOLOGY
    RT: BEHAVIOUR
        SOCIAL SCIENCES

BELGIAN
BELGE / BELGA - 14.03.02
    RT: BELGIUM

BELGIUM
BELGIQUE / BELGICA - 01.04.05
    BT: WESTERN EUROPE
    RT: BELGIAN

BELIEF
CROYANCE / CREENCIA - 05.03.02
    RT: IDEOLOGIES
        OPINION

BELIZE
BELIZE / BELICE - 01.04.03
    UF: BRITISH HONDURAS
    BT: CENTRAL AMERICA

BENEFIT PLANS

BENEFIT PLANS<CONT>
SYSTEMES DE PREVOYANCE / SISTEMAS DE PREVISION
SOCIAL - 02.03.02
SN: USE IN CONNECTION WITH THE VARIOUS TYPES OF
OCCUPATIONAL SCHEMES ESTABLISHED BY THE
GOVERNMENT OR BY THE EMPLOYERS TO PROVIDE
SOME DEGREE OF FINANCIAL PROTECTION FOR
EMPLOYEES AGAINST ACCIDENT, ILLNESS, OLD AGE
AND DEATH.
    RT: SOCIAL SECURITY

BENELUX
BENELUX / BENELUX - 01.03.03
SN: BENELUX ECONOMIC UNION.
    BT: CUSTOMS UNION
        EUROPEAN ORGANIZATIONS
        INTERGOVERNMENTAL ORGANIZATIONS

BENGALI
BENGALI / BENGALI - 14.03.02
    RT: BANGLADESH

BENIN
BENIN / BENIN - 01.04.02
    BT: FRENCH SPEAKING AFRICA
        WEST AFRICA
    RT: BENINESE

BENINESE
BENINOIS / BENINES - 14.03.02
    RT: BENIN

BENZENE
BENZENE / BENCINA - 08.11.06
    BT: HYDROCARBONS

BERMUDA
BERMUDES / BERMUDA - 01.04.03
    BT: NORTH AMERICA
    RT: UNITED KINGDOM

BEVERAGE INDUSTRY
INDUSTRIE DES BOISSONS / INDUSTRIA DE
ELABORACION DE BEBIDAS - 08.06.05
    BT: FOOD INDUSTRY
    NT: BREWERY

BEVERAGES
BOISSONS / BEBIDAS - 08.06.05
    NT: ALCOHOLIC BEVERAGES
        NON-ALCOHOLIC BEVERAGES

BHUTAN
BHOUTAN / BUTAN - 01.04.04
    BT: SOUTH ASIA
        SOUTH EAST ASIA
    RT: BHUTANESE

BHUTANESE
BHOUTANAIS / BUTANES - 14.03.02
    RT: BHUTAN

BIBLIOGRAPHY
BIBLIOGRAPHIE / BIBLIOGRAFIA - 19.02.07

BIBLIOGRAPHY<CONT>
    BT: REFERENCE MATERIALS
        SECONDARY DOCUMENTS
    NT: ANNOTATED BIBLIOGRAPHY
    RT: LITERATURE SURVEY

BICYCLES
BICYCLETTES / BICICLETAS - 10.04.00
    BT: NON-MOTORIZED TRANSPORT

BIG GAME
GROS GIBIER / CAZA MAYOR - 07.09.01
    BT: WILD ANIMALS
    RT: GAME PROTECTION
        HUNTING

BILATERAL AID
AIDE BILATERALE / AYUDA BILATERAL - 01.01.02
    BT: BILATERAL RELATIONS
        DEVELOPMENT AID

BILATERAL RELATIONS
RELATIONS BILATERALES / RELACIONES BILATERALES -
01.02.01
    BT: INTERNATIONAL RELATIONS
    NT: BILATERAL AID

BILHARZIASIS
- 15.04.02
    USE: SCHISTOSOMIASIS

BILINGUALISM
BILINGUISME / BILINGUISMO - 05.06.01
    BT: MULTILINGUALISM

BIOCHEMISTRY
BIOCHIMIE / BIOQUIMICA - 15.01.03
    BT: CHEMISTRY
    RT: BIODEGRADATION
        BIOLOGY

BIOCLIMATOLOGY
BIOCLIMATOLOGIE / BIOCLIMATOLOGIA - 17.01.01
    BT: CLIMATOLOGY
    RT: BIOLOGY

BIODEGRADATION
BIODEGRADATION / BIODEGRADACION - 15.01.03
    UF: BIODETERIORATION
    RT: BIOCHEMISTRY
        CORROSION
        WASTE DISPOSAL

BIODETERIORATION
- 15.01.03
    USE: BIODEGRADATION

BIOGRAPHIES
BIOGRAPHIES / BIOGRAFIAS - 19.02.02
    BT: PRIMARY DOCUMENTS

BIOLOGICAL EQUILIBRIUM
- 16.01.01
    USE: ECOLOGICAL BALANCE

BIOLOGISTS
BIOLOGISTES / BIOLOGOS - 13.09.09
    BT: SCIENTISTS
    RT: BIOLOGY

BIOLOGY
BIOLOGIE / BIOLOGIA - 15.01.01
    BT: NATURAL SCIENCES
    NT: MICROBIOLOGY
    RT: BIOCHEMISTRY
        BIOCLIMATOLOGY
        BIOLOGISTS
        MEDICAL SCIENCES

BIOMASS
BIOMASSE / BIOMASA - 16.01.02
    RT: BIOSPHERE

BIOSPHERE
BIOSPHERE / BIOSFERA - 16.01.02
    BT: PHYSICAL ENVIRONMENT
    RT: BIOMASS
        HABITAT

BIRDS
OISEAUX / AVES - 07.09.01
    BT: ANIMALS
    NT: POULTRY

BIRTH
NAISSANCE / NACIMIENTO - 14.05.01
    RT: BIRTH RATE

BIRTH CONTROL
REGULATION DES NAISSANCES / REGULACION DE LA
NATALIDAD - 14.05.02
    BT: FAMILY PLANNING
    NT: BIRTH SPACING

BIRTH RATE
TAUX DE NATALITE / TASA DE NATALIDAD - 14.05.01
    RT: BIRTH

BIRTH SPACING
ESPACEMENT DES NAISSANCES / ESPACIAMIENTO DE LOS
NACIMIENTOS - 14.05.02
    BT: BIRTH CONTROL

BITUMENS
BITUMES / ASFALTOS - 08.10.02
    BT: CONSTRUCTION MATERIALS

BLACK MARKET
MARCHE NOIR / MERCADO NEGRO - 09.01.02
    BT: MARKET

BLACKS
NOIRS / NEGROS - 14.03.03

BLINDNESS
CECITE / CEGUERA - 15.04.03
    BT: EYE DISEASES
    RT: ONCHOCERCIASIS

BLOCKADE
BLOCUS / BLOQUEO - 01.02.07

BLOOD
SANG / SANGRE - 15.02.04

BOARDING SCHOOLS
INTERNATS / INTERNADOS - 06.04.03
    BT: SCHOOLS

BOATS
- 10.04.00
    USE: SHIPS

BOILERMAKING
CHAUDRONNERIE / CALDERERIA - 08.14.01
    BT: METALWORKING INDUSTRY

BOLIVIA
BOLIVIE / BOLIVIA - 01.04.03
    BT: LATIN AMERICA
        SOUTH AMERICA
    RT: BOLIVIAN

BOLIVIAN
BOLIVIEN / BOLIVIANO - 14.03.02
    RT: BOLIVIA

BONDS
- 11.02.07
    USE: DEBENTURES

BONUSES
- 13.07.00
    USE: WAGE INCENTIVES

BOOK INDUSTRY
INDUSTRIE DU LIVRE / INDUSTRIA DEL LIBRO -
08.16.00
    BT: COMMUNICATION INDUSTRY
    NT: BOOKSELLING
        PUBLISHING

BOOK REVIEW
COMPTE RENDU DE LIVRE / RESENA BIBLIOGRAFICA -
19.02.07
    BT: SECONDARY DOCUMENTS

BOOKS
LIVRES / LIBROS - 05.07.03
    BT: MASS MEDIA
    RT: BOOKSELLING

BOOKSELLING
VENTE DE LIVRES / VENTA DE LIBROS - 08.16.00
    BT: BOOK INDUSTRY
    RT: BOOKS

BORDER INTEGRATION
INTEGRATION FRONTALIERE / INTEGRACION FRONTERIZA
- 01.02.01
SN: MECHANISM OF COMPLEMENTARITY AND COOPERATION
    BETWEEN NEIGHBOURING COUNTRIES.
    BT: ECONOMIC COOPERATION
    RT: COMPLEMENTARITY AGREEMENTS

BORDERS
- 01.02.02
    USE: BOUNDARIES

BORROWING
EMPRUNTS / EMPRESTITOS - 11.02.02
    BT: FINANCIAL TERMS
    NT: PUBLIC BORROWING
    RT: CREDIT
        DEBT
        LOANS
        MONETARY TRANSFERS

BOTANICAL GARDENS
JARDINS BOTANIQUES / JARDINES BOTANICOS -
16.05.02
    BT: PROTECTED RESOURCES
    RT: BOTANY
        PLANTS
        PROTECTED SPECIES

BOTANISTS
BOTANISTES / BOTANICOS - 13.09.09
    BT: SCIENTISTS
    RT: BOTANY

BOTANY
BOTANIQUE / BOTANICA - 07.06.00
    BT: NATURAL SCIENCES
    RT: BOTANICAL GARDENS
        BOTANISTS
        PLANTS

BOTSWANA
BOTSWANA / BOTSWANA - 01.04.02
    BT: ENGLISH SPEAKING AFRICA
        SOUTHERN AFRICA

BOUNDARIES
FRONTIERES / FRONTERAS - 01.02.02
    UF: BORDERS
        FRONTIERS
    RT: FRONTIER MIGRATIONS
        TRANSFRONTIER POLLUTION

BOURGEOISIE
BOURGEOISIE / BURGUESIA - 05.03.05
    BT: SOCIAL CLASSES

BOVIDAE
BOVIDES / BOVIDOS - 07.09.01
    BT: RUMINANTS
    NT: CALVES
        COWS
        WATER BUFFALOES
    RT: BEEF
        CATTLE

BOXES
CAISSES / CAJAS - 10.06.00
    BT: CONTAINERS
    RT: PACKAGING

BOYCOTT
BOYCOTTAGE / BOICOT - 09.05.07
    BT: TRADE BARRIERS
    RT: ACCESS TO MARKET

BRAIN
CERVEAU / CEREBRO - 15.02.04
    BT: NERVOUS SYSTEM

BRAIN DRAIN
EXODE DES COMPETENCES / EXODO INTELECTUAL -
14.07.00
    SN: USE IN CONNECTION WITH THE LOSS SUFFERED,
    FOR EXAMPLE, BY DEVELOPING COUNTRIES AS A
    RESULT OF THE MIGRATION OF HIGHLY-QUALIFIED
    SCIENTIFIC PERSONNEL TO DEVELOPED COUNTRIES.
    BT: EMIGRATION

BRAZIL
BRESIL / BRASIL - 01.04.03
    BT: LATIN AMERICA
        SOUTH AMERICA
    RT: BRAZILIAN

BRAZILIAN
BRESILIEN / BRASILENO - 14.03.02
    RT: BRAZIL

BREAD
PAIN / PAN - 08.06.04
    BT: BAKERY PRODUCTS

BREAST FEEDING
ALLAITEMENT NATUREL / LACTANCIA - 15.03.02
    BT: FEEDING
    RT: MATERNAL AND CHILD HEALTH

BREWERY
BRASSERIE / INDUSTRIA CERVECERA - 08.06.05
    BT: BEVERAGE INDUSTRY
    RT: BEER

BRICKS
BRIQUES / LADRILLOS - 08.10.03
    BT: CERAMICS

BRIDGES
PONTS / PUENTES - 10.03.00
    BT: TRANSPORT INFRASTRUCTURE

BRITISH
BRITANNIQUE / BRITANICO - 14.03.02
    RT: UNITED KINGDOM

BRITISH HONDURAS
- 01.04.03
    USE: **BELIZE**

BRITISH VIRGIN ISLANDS
ILES VIERGES BRITANNIQUES / ISLAS VIRGENES RU -
01.04.03
    BT: CARIBBEAN
    RT: UNITED KINGDOM

BROADCASTING
RADIODIFFUSION / RADIODIFUSION - 08.16.00
    BT: TELECOMMUNICATION INDUSTRY
    RT: RADIO
        TELEVISION

BRUNEI
BRUNEI / BRUNEI - 01.04.04
    BT: SOUTH EAST ASIA
    RT: UNITED KINGDOM

BUDDHISM
BOUDDHISME / BUDISMO - 05.04.03

BUDGET
BUDGET / PRESUPUESTO - 12.09.00
SN: OF AN ENTERPRISE. IN THE FRAMEWORK OF PUBLIC
   FINANCE, USE 'NATIONAL BUDGET'.
    RT: BUDGETING
        BUDGETING METHODS

BUDGETARY POLICY
POLITIQUE BUDGETAIRE / POLITICA PRESUPUESTARIA -
11.01.01
    BT: FINANCIAL POLICY
    RT: NATIONAL BUDGET

BUDGETARY RESOURCES
RESSOURCES BUDGETAIRES / RECURSOS
PRESUPUESTARIOS - 11.01.01
    BT: ECONOMIC RESOURCES
        NATIONAL BUDGET
    NT: TAX REVENUES
    RT: PUBLIC ACCOUNTING
        PUBLIC EXPENDITURES

BUDGETING
ETABLISSEMENT DU BUDGET / ELABORACION DEL
PRESUPUESTO - 12.09.00
    RT: BUDGET
        BUDGETING METHODS

BUDGETING METHODS
METHODES BUDGETAIRES / METODOS PRESUPUESTARIOS -
12.09.00
    RT: BUDGET
        BUDGETING

BUFFER STOCKS
STOCKS REGULATEURS / EXISTENCIAS REGULADORAS -
09.05.02
    BT: STOCKS
    RT: COMMODITIES
        COMMODITY AGREEMENTS
        COMMODITY PRICES
        MARKET STABILIZATION
        PRICE STABILIZATION

BUILDING INDUSTRY
- 08.10.01
    USE: CONSTRUCTION INDUSTRY

BUILDING MACHINERY
MATERIEL DE CONSTRUCTION / MAQUINARIA PARA LA
CONSTRUCCION - 08.14.06
    UF: CONSTRUCTION EQUIPMENT
    BT: MACHINERY
    NT: EARTHMOVING MACHINERY
    RT: CONSTRUCTION INDUSTRY

BUILDING MATERIALS
- 08.10.02
    USE: CONSTRUCTION MATERIALS

BUILDINGS
BATIMENTS / CONSTRUCCIONES - 08.10.01
    NT: EDUCATIONAL BUILDINGS
        FARM BUILDINGS
        INDUSTRIAL BUILDINGS
        PREFABRICATED BUILDINGS
    RT: CONSTRUCTION INDUSTRY

BULGARIA
BULGARIE / BULGARIA - 01.04.05
    BT: EASTERN EUROPE
    RT: BULGARIAN

BULGARIAN
BULGARE / BULGARO - 14.03.02
    RT: BULGARIA

BUREAUCRACY
BUREAUCRATIE / BUROCRACIA - 04.03.05
    RT: CIVIL SERVICE
        POLITICAL POWER
        PUBLIC ADMINISTRATION
        PUBLIC SECTOR

BURMA
BIRMANIE / BIRMANIA - 01.04.04
    BT: SOUTH EAST ASIA
    RT: BURMESE

BURMESE
BIRMAN / BIRMANO - 14.03.02
    RT: BURMA

BURNS
BRULURES / QUEMADURAS - 15.04.02
    BT: WOUNDS AND INJURIES

BURUNDI
BURUNDI / BURUNDI - 01.04.02
    BT: CENTRAL AFRICA
        EAST AFRICA
        FRENCH SPEAKING AFRICA

BUSES
AUTOBUS / AUTOBUSES - 10.04.00
    BT: MOTOR VEHICLES
    RT: URBAN TRANSPORT

BUSINESS CYCLE
CYCLE ECONOMIQUE / CICLO ECONOMICO - 03.02.04
SN: USE TO DENOTE AN ALTERNATE EXPANSION AND
   CONTRACTION IN OVERALL ECONOMIC ACTIVITY.
    UF: ECONOMIC FLUCTUATIONS
    NT: SEASONAL FLUCTUATIONS
    RT: ECONOMIC CONDITIONS
        ECONOMIC RECESSION
        ECONOMIC RECOVERY
        INFLATION
        TRENDS
        UNEMPLOYMENT

BUSINESS ECONOMICS
ECONOMIE DE L'ENTREPRISE / ECONOMIA DE LA
EMPRESA - 12.01.00
    BT: ECONOMICS
    RT: BUSINESS MANAGEMENT
        ENTERPRISES

BUSINESS MANAGEMENT
GESTION D'ENTREPRISES / ADMINISTRACION DE
EMPRESAS - 12.04.00
    BT: MANAGEMENT
    RT: BUSINESS ECONOMICS
        ENTERPRISES
        ENTREPRENEURS

BUSINESS ORGANIZATION
ORGANISATION DE L'ENTREPRISE / ORGANIZACION DE
LA EMPRESA - 12.04.00
*SN: THE COMPLETE STRUCTURE AND COMPOSITION OF A
BUSINESS ENTERPRISE.*
    RT: ENTERPRISES
        MANAGEMENT CONSULTANTS
        WORK RULES

BUTTER
BEURRE / MANTEQUILLA - 07.09.05
    BT: DAIRY PRODUCTS
    RT: MARGARINE

BUYING
- 09.03.02
    USE: PURCHASING

BY-PRODUCTS
SOUS-PRODUITS / SUBPRODUCTOS - 12.08.01
    BT: PRODUCTS

BYELORUSSIAN
BIELORUSSIEN / BIELORRUSO - 14.03.02
    RT: BYELORUSSIAN SSR

BYELORUSSIAN SSR
RSS BIELORUSSIE / RSS DE BIELORRUSIA - 01.04.05
    BT: EASTERN EUROPE
    RT: BYELORUSSIAN

CAB
CAB / CAB - 01.03.04
SN: COMMONWEALTH AGRICULTURAL BUREAUX.
    RT: AGRICULTURE

CABEI
BCAIE / BCIE - 01.03.03
*SN: CENTRAL AMERICAN BANK OF ECONOMIC
INTEGRATION.*
    BT: AMERICAN ORGANIZATIONS
        DEVELOPMENT BANKS
        INTERGOVERNMENTAL ORGANIZATIONS
    RT: CENTRAL AMERICA

CABLES
CABLES / CABLES - 08.14.04
    BT: METAL PRODUCTS

CACEU
UDEAC / UAEAC - 01.03.03
SN: CENTRAL AFRICAN CUSTOMS AND ECONOMIC UNION.
    BT: AFRICAN ORGANIZATIONS
        CUSTOMS UNION
        INTERGOVERNMENTAL ORGANIZATIONS
    RT: CENTRAL AFRICA

CACM
MCCA / MCCA - 01.03.03
SN: CENTRAL AMERICAN COMMON MARKET.
    BT: AMERICAN ORGANIZATIONS
        COMMON MARKET
        INTERGOVERNMENTAL ORGANIZATIONS
    NT: SIECA
    RT: CENTRAL AMERICA

CADASTRAL SURVEYS
ENQUETES CADASTRALES / CATASTROS - 18.04.00
    BT: SURVEYS

CADMIUM
CADMIUM / CADMIO - 08.14.02
    BT: NON-FERROUS METALS
        TOXIC METALS

CAEU
CAEU / CAEU - 01.03.03
SN: COUNCIL OF ARAB ECONOMIC UNITY.
    BT: LEAGUE OF ARAB STATES
    RT: ARAB COUNTRIES

CAFRAD
CAFRAD / CAFRAD - 01.03.03
*SN: AFRICAN TRAINING AND RESEARCH CENTRE IN
ADMINISTRATION FOR DEVELOPMENT.*
    BT: AFRICAN ORGANIZATIONS
        NON-GOVERNMENTAL ORGANIZATIONS
        RESEARCH CENTRES
    RT: AFRICA
        DEVELOPMENT ADMINISTRATION

CALCIUM
CALCIUM / CALCIO - 08.12.04

CALORIE DEFICIENCY
DEFICIENCE CALORIQUE / DEFICIENCIA CALORICA -

CALORIE DEFICIENCY<CONT>
15.03.02
    BT: MALNUTRITION
    RT: CALORIES

CALORIES
CALORIES / CALORIAS - 15.03.02
    RT: CALORIE DEFICIENCY
        TEMPERATURE

CALVES
VEAUX / TERNEROS - 07.09.01
    BT: BOVIDAE

CAMBODIA
- 01.04.04
    USE: KAMPUCHEA

CAMELS
CHAMEAUX / CAMELLOS - 07.09.01
    BT: LIVESTOCK
        RUMINANTS

CAMEROON
CAMEROUN / CAMERUN - 01.04.02
    BT: CENTRAL AFRICA
        FRENCH SPEAKING AFRICA
        WEST AFRICA
    RT: CAMEROONIAN

CAMEROONIAN
CAMEROUNAIS / CAMERUNES - 14.03.02
    RT: CAMEROON

CANADA
CANADA / CANADA - 01.04.03
    BT: NORTH AMERICA
    RT: CANADIAN

CANADIAN
CANADIEN / CANADIENSE - 14.03.02
    RT: CANADA

CANALS
CANAUX / CANALES - 10.03.00
    BT: INLAND WATERWAYS
        TRANSPORT INFRASTRUCTURE

CANARY ISLANDS
ILES CANARIES / ISLAS CANARIAS - 01.04.05
    BT: WESTERN EUROPE
    RT: SPAIN

CANCER
CANCER / CANCER - 15.04.02

CANE SUGAR
SUCRE DE CANNE / AZUCAR DE CANA - 08.06.04
    BT: SUGAR
    RT: SUGAR CANE

CANNED FOOD
CONSERVES ALIMENTAIRES / CONSERVAS ALIMENTICIAS

CANNED FOOD<CONT>
- 08.06.03
    BT: FOOD
    RT: CANNING INDUSTRY
        FOOD PRESERVATION

CANNING INDUSTRY
INDUSTRIE DE LA CONSERVE / INDUSTRIA CONSERVERA
- 08.06.01
    BT: FOOD INDUSTRY
    RT: CANNED FOOD
        PACKAGING

CAPE VERDE
CAP VERT / CABO VERDE - 01.04.02
    BT: WEST AFRICA
    RT: CAPE VERDEAN

CAPE VERDEAN
CAP-VERDIEN / CABOVERDIANO - 14.03.02
    RT: CAPE VERDE

CAPITAL
CAPITAL / CAPITAL - 11.02.05
    NT: FOREIGN CAPITAL
        INDUSTRIAL CAPITAL
        WORKING CAPITAL
    RT: AMORTIZATION
        CAPITAL CONCENTRATION
        CAPITAL COSTS
        CAPITAL DEPRECIATION
        CAPITAL FORMATION
        CAPITAL GAINS
        CAPITAL INTENSITY
        CAPITAL MOVEMENTS
        CAPITAL TAX
        FINANCIAL AID
        FINANCIAL NEEDS
        FINANCIAL RESOURCES
        INVESTMENTS
        MEANS OF PRODUCTION
        PRODUCTION FACTORS
        PRODUCTION GOODS

CAPITAL AID
- 01.01.03
    USE: FINANCIAL AID

CAPITAL CONCENTRATION
CONCENTRATION DU CAPITAL / CONCENTRACION DEL
CAPITAL - 11.02.05
    BT: ECONOMIC CONCENTRATION
    RT: CAPITAL

CAPITAL COSTS
COUTS DE CAPITAL / COSTOS DE CAPITAL - 12.09.00
    UF: CAPITAL EXPENDITURES
    BT: COSTS
        EXPENDITURES
    RT: CAPITAL
        FINANCIAL LOSS

CAPITAL DEPRECIATION

CAPITAL DEPRECIATION<CONT>
DEPRECIATION DU CAPITAL / DEPRECIACION DEL
CAPITAL - 11.02.05
>   RT: CAPITAL

CAPITAL EXPENDITURES
- 12.09.00
>   USE: CAPITAL COSTS

CAPITAL FLOWS
- 11.03.03
>   USE: CAPITAL MOVEMENTS

CAPITAL FORMATION
FORMATION DE CAPITAL / FORMACION DE CAPITAL -
11.02.05
>   RT: ACCUMULATION RATE
>   CAPITAL
>   INVESTMENT BANKS
>   INVESTMENTS

CAPITAL GAINS
GAINS DE CAPITAL / GANANCIAS DE CAPITAL -
12.09.00
>   BT: PROFITS
>   RT: CAPITAL

CAPITAL INTENSITY
DENSITE DE CAPITAL / INTENSIDAD DE CAPITAL -
12.06.00
SN: WITH RELATIVELY GREATER PLANT AND EQUIPMENT
>   COSTS THAN LABOUR COSTS.
>   RT: CAPITAL
>   CAPITAL-LABOUR RATIO
>   CAPITAL-OUTPUT RATIO

CAPITAL INVESTMENTS
- 11.02.06
>   USE: INVESTMENTS

CAPITAL MARKET
- 11.02.07
>   USE: FINANCIAL MARKET

CAPITAL MOVEMENTS
MOUVEMENTS DE CAPITAUX / MOVIMIENTOS DE
CAPITALES - 11.03.03
>   UF: CAPITAL FLOWS
>   BT: BALANCE OF PAYMENTS
>   NT: CAPITAL TRANSFERS
>   EXPORT OF CAPITAL
>   INTERNATIONAL INVESTMENTS
>   REPATRIATION OF CAPITAL
>   RT: CAPITAL
>   INVISIBLE TRANSACTIONS

CAPITAL NEEDS
- 11.02.05
>   USE: FINANCIAL NEEDS

CAPITAL PUNISHMENT
PEINE DE MORT / PENA DE MUERTE - 02.04.03
>   BT: PENAL SANCTIONS

CAPITAL PUNISHMENT<CONT>
>   RT: CRIMINAL LAW
>   HOMICIDE

CAPITAL RESOURCES
- 11.02.05
>   USE: FINANCIAL RESOURCES

CAPITAL TAX
IMPOT SUR LE CAPITAL / IMPUESTO AL CAPITAL -
11.01.02
>   BT: TAXES
>   RT: CAPITAL

CAPITAL TRANSFERS
TRANSFERTS DE CAPITAUX / TRANSFERENCIAS DE
CAPITALES - 11.03.03
>   BT: CAPITAL MOVEMENTS

CAPITAL-LABOUR RATIO
RAPPORT CAPITAL-TRAVAIL / RELACION
CAPITAL-TRABAJO - 12.07.03
SN: STATISTICS ON CAPITAL INVESTMENT PER WORKER.
>   BT: PRODUCTION FUNCTIONS
>   RT: CAPITAL INTENSITY
>   LABOUR INTENSITY

CAPITAL-OUTPUT RATIO
RAPPORT CAPITAL-PRODUCTION / RELACION
CAPITAL-PRODUCTO - 12.07.03
>   BT: PRODUCTION FUNCTIONS
>   RT: CAPITAL INTENSITY

CAPITALISM
CAPITALISME / CAPITALISMO - 03.03.01
>   BT: ECONOMIC SYSTEMS
>   RT: CAPITALIST
>   CAPITALIST COUNTRIES
>   CAPITALIST ENTERPRISES
>   MARKET ECONOMY
>   MODES OF PRODUCTION

CAPITALIST
CAPITALISTE / CAPITALISTA - 03.03.01
>   RT: CAPITALISM
>   CAPITALIST COUNTRIES

CAPITALIST COUNTRIES
PAYS CAPITALISTES / PAISES CAPITALISTAS -
03.03.03
>   RT: CAPITALISM
>   CAPITALIST
>   CAPITALIST ENTERPRISES

CAPITALIST ENTERPRISES
ENTREPRISES CAPITALISTES / EMPRESAS CAPITALISTAS
- 12.01.00
>   BT: ENTERPRISES
>   RT: CAPITALISM
>   CAPITALIST COUNTRIES
>   PRIVATE OWNERSHIP
>   PROFITS

CARBOHYDRATES
HYDRATES DE CARBONE / HIDRATOS DE CARBONO -

CARBOHYDRATES<CONT>
08.06.04
> *NT:* CELLULOSE
> STARCH
> SUGAR

CARD FILES
FICHIERS / FICHEROS - 19.01.04

CARDBOARD
CARTON / CARTON - 08.07.02
> *BT:* WOOD PRODUCTS
> *RT:* PULP AND PAPER INDUSTRY

CARDIOLOGY
CARDIOLOGIE / CARDIOLOGIA - 15.04.06
> *BT:* MEDICAL SCIENCES
> *RT:* HEART

CARDIOVASCULAR SYSTEM
SYSTEME CARDIOVASCULAIRE / SISTEMA
CARDIOVASCULAR - 15.02.04
> *BT:* ANATOMY
> *NT:* HEART

CARDS
FICHES / FICHAS - 19.01.04
> *NT:* PUNCHED CARDS

CARE OF THE AGED
AIDE AUX GENS AGES / ASISTENCIA A LOS ANCIANOS -
02.05.03
> *BT:* SOCIAL SERVICES
> *RT:* AGED

CARGO
CARGAISON / CARGA - 10.06.00

CARGO SHIPS
NAVIRES DE CHARGE / BUQUES DE CARGA - 10.04.00
> *BT:* SHIPS
> *RT:* MERCHANT MARINE

CARIBBEAN
CARAIBES / CARIBE - 01.04.03
> *UF:* ANTILLES
> WEST INDIES
> *BT:* AMERICA

CARIBBEAN<CONT>
> *NT:* BAHAMAS
> BARBADOS
> BRITISH VIRGIN ISLANDS
> CAYMAN ISLANDS
> CUBA
> DOMINICAN REPUBLIC
> GUADELOUPE
> HAITI
> JAMAICA
> MARTINIQUE
> MONTSERRAT
> NETHERLANDS ANTILLES
> PUERTO RICO
> TRINIDAD AND TOBAGO
> TURKS AND CAICOS ISLANDS
> UNITED STATES VIRGIN ISLANDS
> WEST INDIES ASSOCIATED STATES
> *RT:* CARICOM
> CARIFTA
> LATIN AMERICA
> WEST INDIAN

CARICOM
CARICOM / CARICOM - 01.03.03
SN: CARIBBEAN COMMUNITY
> *BT:* AMERICAN ORGANIZATIONS
> COMMON MARKET
> INTERGOVERNMENTAL ORGANIZATIONS
> *RT:* CARIBBEAN

CARIFTA
CARIFTA / CARIFTA - 01.03.03
SN: CARIBBEAN FREE TRADE ASSOCIATION; SINCE 1973
USE «CARICOM«.
> *BT:* AMERICAN ORGANIZATIONS
> INTERGOVERNMENTAL ORGANIZATIONS
> *RT:* CARIBBEAN
> FREE TRADE AREA

CARPETS
TAPIS / ALFOMBRAS - 08.08.01
> *RT:* TEXTILE INDUSTRY

CARRIERS
TRANSPORTEURS / TRANSPORTISTAS - 10.02.00
> *RT:* TRANSPORT

CARTELS
CARTELS / CARTELES - 12.02.00
> *BT:* MONOPOLIES
> RESTRICTIVE BUSINESS PRACTICES
> *RT:* PRODUCERS ASSOCIATIONS

CARTHAGENA AGREEMENT
- 01.03.03
> *USE:* ANDEAN GROUP

CARTOGRAPHY
- 18.07.00
> *USE:* MAPPING

CASE STUDIES
ETUDES DE CAS / ESTUDIOS DE CASOS - 18.04.00

CASH CROPS
- 07.07.02
    USE: INDUSTRIAL CROPS

CASH FLOW
REVENU DISPONIBLE / INGRESO EN EFECTIVO -
12.09.00
    UF: CASH INCOME
    BT: PROFITS

CASH INCOME
- 12.09.00
    USE: CASH FLOW

CASHEW NUTS
NOIX CACHOU / CASTANAS DE CAJU - 07.07.05
    BT: FRUITS

CASSAVA
MANIOC / MANDIOCA - 07.07.06
    BT: ROOT CROPS

CASTES
CASTES / CASTAS - 05.03.05
    RT: SOCIAL STRATIFICATION

CASTINGS
FONTES / COLADAS - 08.14.04
    BT: METAL PRODUCTS

CASUAL WORKERS
TRAVAILLEURS OCCASIONNELS / TRABAJADORES
OCASIONALES - 13.09.02
    BT: WORKERS
    RT: TEMPORARY EMPLOYMENT

CATALOGUE
CATALOGUE / CATALOGO - 19.02.07
    BT: SECONDARY DOCUMENTS

CATALOGUING
CATALOGAGE / CATALOGACION - 19.01.02
    BT: DOCUMENTATION

CATERING
APPROVISIONNEMENT / ABASTECIMIENTO - 09.03.02
    RT: SUPPLIERS

CATTLE
BETAIL / GANADO VACUNO - 07.09.01
    BT: LIVESTOCK
    RT: BOVIDAE
        CATTLE PRODUCTION

CATTLE PRODUCTION
PRODUCTION DE BETAIL / GANADERIA - 07.09.02
    BT: ANIMAL HUSBANDRY
        ANIMAL PRODUCTION
    RT: CATTLE

CAUSES OF DEATH
CAUSES DE DECES / CAUSAS DE MUERTE - 14.06.00

CAUSES OF DEATH<CONT>
    RT: ACCIDENTS
        AGEING
        DEATH
        DISEASES
        EUTHANASIA
        HOMICIDE
        MORTALITY

CAUSTIC SODA
SOUDE CAUSTIQUE / SODA CAUSTICA - 08.12.04
    BT: SODA

CAYMAN ISLANDS
ILES CAIMANES / ISLAS CAIMAN - 01.04.03
    BT: CARIBBEAN
    RT: UNITED KINGDOM

CCAQ
CCQA / CCCA - 01.03.02
SN: CONSULTATIVE COMMITTEE ON ADMINISTRATIVE
    QUESTIONS.
    BT: UN

CDP
CPD / CPD - 01.03.02
SN: COMMITTEE FOR DEVELOPMENT PLANNING.
    BT: ECOSOC
    RT: DEVELOPMENT PLANNING

CELIBACY
CELIBAT / CELIBATO - 14.02.05
    RT: MARITAL STATUS

CELLS
CELLULES / CELULAS - 15.02.04
    RT: CYTOLOGY

CELLULOSE
CELLULOSE / CELULOSA - 08.07.01
    BT: CARBOHYDRATES
    RT: WOOD

CEMENT
CIMENT / CEMENTO - 08.10.02
    BT: CONSTRUCTION MATERIALS
    RT: CEMENT INDUSTRY

CEMENT INDUSTRY
INDUSTRIE DU CIMENT / INDUSTRIA DEL CEMENTO -
08.10.02
    BT: INDUSTRIAL SECTOR
    RT: CEMENT
        CONCRETE

CEMLA
CEMLA / CEMLA - 01.03.04
SN: CENTRE FOR LATIN AMERICAN MONETARY STUDIES.
    BT: AMERICAN ORGANIZATIONS
        NON-GOVERNMENTAL ORGANIZATIONS
    RT: LATIN AMERICA
        MONETARY SYSTEMS

CENSORSHIP
CENSURE / CENSURA - 05.07.01
    BT: COMMUNICATION POLICY
    RT: FREEDOM OF SPEECH

CENSUSES
RECENSEMENTS / CENSOS - 18.04.00
    BT: DATA COLLECTING
    NT: AGRICULTURAL CENSUSES
        ECONOMIC CENSUSES
        HOUSING CENSUSES
        INDUSTRIAL CENSUSES
        POPULATION CENSUSES

CENTO
CENTO / CENTO - 01.03.03
SN: CENTRAL TREATY ORGANIZATION.
    BT: ASIAN ORGANIZATIONS
        INTERGOVERNMENTAL ORGANIZATIONS

CENTRAL AFRICA
AFRIQUE CENTRALE / AFRICA CENTRAL - 01.04.02
    BT: AFRICA SOUTH OF SAHARA
    NT: BURUNDI
        CAMEROON
        CENTRAL AFRICAN EMPIRE
        CHAD
        CONGO
        EQUATORIAL GUINEA
        GABON
        RWANDA
        SAHEL
        SAO TOME AND PRINCIPE
        ZAIRE
    RT: CACEU

CENTRAL AFRICAN EMPIRE
**EMPIRE CENTRAFRICAIN / IMPERIO CENTROAFRICANO -
01.04.02**
    BT: CENTRAL AFRICA
        FRENCH SPEAKING AFRICA

CENTRAL AMERICA
AMERIQUE CENTRALE / AMERICA CENTRAL - 01.04.03
    BT: LATIN AMERICA
    NT: BELIZE
        COSTA RICA
        EL SALVADOR
        GUATEMALA
        HONDURAS
        NICARAGUA
        PANAMA
        PANAMA CANAL ZONE
    RT: CABEI
        CACM
        OCAS
        SIECA

CENTRAL BANKS
BANQUES CENTRALES / BANCOS CENTRALES - 11.02.02
    BT: BANKS
    RT: MONETARY POLICY

CENTRAL GOVERNMENT
**ADMINISTRATION CENTRALE / GOBIERNO CENTRAL -
04.03.03**
    BT: GOVERNMENT
    NT: FOREIGN SERVICE

CENTRALIZATION
CENTRALISATION / CENTRALIZACION - 04.03.03
    RT: DECENTRALIZATION

CERAMICS
CERAMIQUES / CERAMICAS - 08.10.03
    BT: CONSTRUCTION MATERIALS
    NT: BRICKS
    RT: CERAMICS INDUSTRY
        REFRACTORY MATERIALS

CERAMICS INDUSTRY
**INDUSTRIE DE LA CERAMIQUE / INDUSTRIA CERAMICA -
08.10.03**
    BT: INDUSTRIAL SECTOR
    RT: CERAMICS
        CLAY
        POTTERY

CEREALS
CEREALES / CEREALES - 07.07.04
    UF: GRAINS
    BT: FOOD
        FOOD CROPS
        PLANT PRODUCTS
    NT: BARLEY
        MAIZE
        MILLET
        RICE
        RYE
        SORGHUM
        TRITICALE
        WHEAT
    RT: GREEN REVOLUTION

CERN
CERN / CERN - 01.03.03
SN: EUROPEAN ORGANIZATION FOR NUCLEAR RESEARCH.
    BT: EUROPEAN ORGANIZATIONS
        INTERGOVERNMENTAL ORGANIZATIONS
    RT: NUCLEAR ENERGY

CERTIFICATES
CERTIFICATS / CERTIFICADOS - 06.04.13
*SN: USE IN CONNECTION WITH PRIMARY EDUCATION,
    SECONDARY EDUCATION AND VOCATIONAL TRAINING;
    OTHERWISE USE «DIPLOMAS».*
    BT: QUALIFICATIONS

CEYLON
- 01.04.04
    USE: **SRI LANKA**

CHAD
TCHAD / CHAD - 01.04.02
    BT: CENTRAL AFRICA
        FRENCH SPEAKING AFRICA

CHARTING
**CARTOGRAPHIE MARINE / CARTOGRAFIA MARINA -
18.07.00**
    BT: MAPPING
    RT: CHARTS

CHARTS
CARTES MARINES / CARTAS MARINAS - 18.07.00
    BT: AUDIOVISUAL MATERIALS
    NT: GEOLOGICAL MAPS
    RT: CHARTING

CHEESE
FROMAGE / QUESO - 07.09.05
    BT: DAIRY PRODUCTS

CHEMICAL ANALYSIS
ANALYSE CHIMIQUE / ANALISIS QUIMICO - 08.12.02
    RT: CHEMISTRY

CHEMICAL CONTRACEPTIVES
CONTRACEPTIFS CHIMIQUES / ANTICONCEPTIVOS
QUIMICOS - 14.05.02
    BT: CONTRACEPTIVES

CHEMICAL ENGINEERING
TECHNOLOGIE CHIMIQUE / INGENIERIA QUIMICA -
08.12.02
    BT: ENGINEERING
    RT: FOOD TECHNOLOGY

CHEMICAL FERTILIZERS
ENGRAIS CHIMIQUES / FERTILIZANTES QUIMICOS -
08.12.05
    BT: FERTILIZERS
    RT: FERTILIZER INDUSTRY
        NITRATES
        PHOSPHATES
        POTASH

CHEMICAL INDUSTRY
INDUSTRIE CHIMIQUE / INDUSTRIA QUIMICA -
08.12.01
    BT: INDUSTRIAL SECTOR
    NT: FERTILIZER INDUSTRY
        PETROCHEMICAL INDUSTRY
        PHARMACEUTICAL INDUSTRY
        PLASTICS INDUSTRY

CHEMICAL POLLUTION
POLLUTION CHIMIQUE / CONTAMINACION QUIMICA -
16.03.04
    BT: POLLUTION
    RT: CHEMICALS

CHEMICALS
PRODUITS CHIMIQUES / PRODUCTOS QUIMICOS -
08.12.04
    NT: HYDROCARBONS
        PETROCHEMICALS
        PHARMACEUTICALS
    RT: CHEMICAL POLLUTION

CHEMISTRY
CHIMIE / QUIMICA - 08.12.02
    BT: NATURAL SCIENCES

CHEMISTRY<CONT>
    NT: BIOCHEMISTRY
        FOOD CHEMISTRY
        GEOCHEMISTRY
        ORGANIC CHEMISTRY
        PETROCHEMISTRY
        SOIL CHEMISTRY
    RT: CHEMICAL ANALYSIS
        CHEMISTS

CHEMISTS
CHIMISTES / QUIMICOS - 13.09.09
    BT: SCIENTISTS
    RT: CHEMISTRY

CHICKPEAS
POIS CHICHES / GARBANZOS - 07.07.06
    BT: LEGUMINOSAE

CHILD CARE
AIDE A L'ENFANCE / AYUDA A LA INFANCIA -
02.05.03
SN: COVERS THE VARIOUS ACTIVITIES AIMED AT
    IMPROVING THE CONDITIONS OF CHILDREN IN
    SOCIETY.
    BT: FAMILY POLICY
        SOCIAL SERVICES
    RT: CHILDREN
        PEDIATRICIANS

CHILD DEVELOPMENT
DEVELOPPEMENT DE L'ENFANT / DESARROLLO DEL NINO
- 06.05.04
    RT: CHILD REARING
        CHILDREN
        PEDIATRICIANS
        PEDIATRICS

CHILD LABOUR
TRAVAIL DES ENFANTS / TRABAJO DE MENORES -
13.09.02
    BT: LABOUR
    RT: CHILDREN

CHILD REARING
PUERICULTURE / PUERICULTURA - 15.03.02
    BT: HOME ECONOMICS
    RT: CHILD DEVELOPMENT

CHILDHOOD
ENFANCE / INFANCIA - 14.02.02
    BT: AGE GROUPS
    NT: EARLY CHILDHOOD
    RT: CHILDREN
        UNICEF

CHILDREN
ENFANTS / NINOS - 14.02.02
    NT: INFANTS
    RT: CHILD CARE
        CHILD DEVELOPMENT
        CHILD LABOUR
        CHILDHOOD
        ORPHANAGES

CHILE
CHILI / CHILE - 01.04.03
    BT: LATIN AMERICA
        SOUTHERN CONE
    RT: CHILEAN

CHILEAN
CHILIEN / CHILENO - 14.03.02
    RT: CHILE

CHINA
CHINE / CHINA - 01.04.04
    BT: FAR EAST
    RT: CHINESE

CHINESE
CHINOIS / CHINO - 14.03.02
    RT: CHINA

CHINESE LANGUAGE
LANGUE CHINOISE / LENGUA CHINA - 05.06.02
    BT: LANGUAGES

CHLORINE
CHLORE / CLORO - 08.12.04

CHOCOLATE
CHOCOLAT / CHOCOLATE - 08.06.04
    RT: COCOA

CHOICE OF PRODUCTS
CHOIX DE PRODUITS / ELECCION DE PRODUCTOS -
12.08.02
*SN: TO BE USEDDDD IN THE CONTEXT OF PRODUCTION, NOT
CONSUMPTION.*
    RT: NEW PRODUCTS
        PRODUCT DESIGN
        PRODUCT DEVELOPMENT
        PRODUCTS

CHOICE OF TECHNOLOGY
CHOIX DE TECHNOLOGIE / ELECCION DE TECNOLOGIA -
12.06.00
*SN: DECIDING ON LABOUR INTENSIVE OR CAPITAL
INTENSIVE METHODS, CHOOSING AMONG VARIOUS
PROCESSES, ETC.*
    RT: TECHNOLOGY

CHOLERA
CHOLERA / COLERA - 15.04.02
    BT: INFECTIOUS DISEASES
        TROPICAL DISEASES

CHRISTIANITY
CHRISTIANISME / CRISTIANISMO - 05.04.03
    RT: RELIGIOUS MISSIONS

CHROMIUM
CHROME / CROMO - 08.14.02
    BT: NON-FERROUS METALS

CHROMOSOMES
CHROMOSOMES / CROMOSOMA - 15.02.03

CHROMOSOMES<CONT>
    RT: GENES
        GENETICS

CHRONIC DISEASES
MALADIES CHRONIQUES / ENFERMEDADES CRONICAS -
15.04.02
    BT: DISEASES

CHRONOLOGY
CHRONOLOGIE / CRONOLOGIA - 18.10.00
    RT: TIME FACTOR

CIAT
CIAT / CIAT - 01.03.04
*SN: INTERNATIONAL CENTRE FOR TROPICAL
AGRICULTURE.*
    BT: NON-GOVERNMENTAL ORGANIZATIONS
    RT: AGRICULTURAL RESEARCH
        TROPICAL ZONE

CIMMYT
CIMMYT / CIMMYT - 01.03.04
*SN: INTERNATIONAL MAIZE AND WHEAT IMPROVEMENT
CENTRE.*
    BT: NON-GOVERNMENTAL ORGANIZATIONS
        RESEARCH CENTRES
    RT: AGRICULTURAL RESEARCH
        MAIZE
        TRITICALE
        WHEAT

CINEMA
CINEMA / CINE - 05.05.03
    BT: DRAMATIC ART
    RT: FILMS

CITIES
- 14.04.03
    USE: TOWNS

CITRUS FRUITS
AGRUMES / CITRICOS - 07.07.05
    BT: FRUITS

CIVIC EDUCATION
INSTRUCTION CIVIQUE / EDUCACION CIVICA -
06.03.04
    BT: BASIC EDUCATION
    RT: POLITICAL EDUCATION

CIVIC SERVICE
CHANTIERS NATIONAUX / SERVICIO CIVICO - 04.03.06
*SN: USE IN CONNECTION WITH THE PARTICIPATION OF
UNEMPLOYED WORKERS, VOLUNTEER WORKERS, ETC.
IN PUBLIC WORKS AND PUBLIC SERVICE.*

CIVIL ENGINEERING
GENIE CIVIL / INGENIERIA CIVIL - 12.06.00
    BT: ENGINEERING
    RT: CONSTRUCTION INDUSTRY
        PUBLIC WORKS
        TRANSPORT INFRASTRUCTURE

CIVIL LAW
DROIT CIVIL / DERECHO CIVIL - 04.01.02
    BT: LAW
    NT: FAMILY LAW

CIVIL LIBERTIES
LIBERTES CIVILES / LIBERTADES CIVILES - 04.02.02
    BT: FREEDOM
    NT: ACADEMIC FREEDOM
        FREEDOM OF ASSOCIATION
        FREEDOM OF INFORMATION
        FREEDOM OF OPINION
        FREEDOM OF SPEECH
        RELIGIOUS FREEDOM
    RT: CIVIL RIGHTS
        DEMOCRATIZATION
        OMBUDSMAN

CIVIL RIGHTS
DROITS DU CITOYEN / DERECHOS CIVILES - 04.02.01
    RT: CIVIL LIBERTIES

CIVIL SERVANTS
FONCTIONNAIRES / FUNCIONARIOS - 13.09.04
SN: USE TO DENOTE PUBLIC ADMINISTRATION
    EMPLOYEES. DO NOT CONFUSE WITH 'PUBLIC
    SERVANTS'.
    RT: CIVIL SERVICE
        PUBLIC ADMINISTRATION

CIVIL SERVICE
FONCTION PUBLIQUE / FUNCION PUBLICA - 04.03.04
    RT: BUREAUCRACY
        CIVIL SERVANTS
        PUBLIC ADMINISTRATION
        TECHNOCRACY

CIVIL WAR
GUERRE CIVILE / GUERRA CIVIL - 01.02.07
    BT: WAR
    RT: GUERRILLA
        REVOLUTION

CIVILIZATION
CIVILISATION / CIVILIZACION - 05.02.01
    RT: CULTURE

CLACSO
CLACSO / CLACSO - 01.03.03
SN: LATIN-AMERICAN COUNCIL OF SOCIAL SCIENCES.
    BT: AMERICAN ORGANIZATIONS
        NON-GOVERNMENTAL ORGANIZATIONS
    RT: LATIN AMERICA
        SOCIAL SCIENCES

CLADES
CLADES / CLADES - 01.03.02
SN: CENTRO LATINOAMERICANO DE DOCUMENTACION
    ECONOMICA Y SOCIAL.
    BT: ECLA
        INFORMATION SERVICES
    RT: DOCUMENTATION

CLAN
CLAN / CLAN - 14.02.04
    RT: KINSHIP

CLASS CONSCIOUSNESS
**CONSCIENCE DE CLASSE / CONCIENCIA DE CLASE -
05.03.05**
    RT: CLASS STRUGGLE
        SOCIAL CLASSES

CLASS STRUGGLE
LUTTE DE CLASSES / LUCHA DE CLASES - 05.03.06
    BT: INTERGROUP RELATIONS
    RT: CLASS CONSCIOUSNESS
        SOCIAL CLASSES
        SOCIAL CONFLICTS

CLASSES
CLASSES / CLASES - 06.04.10
SN: GROUPS OF STUDENTS.
    NT: EXPERIMENTAL CLASSES
    RT: ABILITY GROUPING

CLASSIFICATION
CLASSIFICATION / CLASIFICACION - 19.01.02
    NT: JOB CLASSIFICATION
        SOIL CLASSIFICATION
    RT: DOCUMENTATION

CLAY
ARGILE / ARCILLA - 08.10.03
    RT: CERAMICS INDUSTRY

CLEANING AGENTS
**PRODUITS DE NETTOYAGE / PRODUCTOS DE LIMPIEZA -
08.12.08**
    NT: DETERGENTS
        SOAP
    RT: POTASH

CLEARING AGREEMENTS
**ACCORDS DE COMPENSATION / ACUERDOS DE
COMPENSACION - 11.03.01**
    BT: MONETARY AGREEMENTS
    RT: CLEARING SYSTEMS

CLEARING SYSTEMS
**SYSTEMES DE COMPENSATION / SISTEMAS DE
COMPENSACION - 11.03.01**
    RT: CLEARING AGREEMENTS

CLERGY
CLERGE / CLERO - 05.04.04

CLERICAL WORKERS
- 13.09.07
    USE: OFFICE WORKERS

CLIMATE
CLIMAT / CLIMA - 17.02.01
    RT: ACCLIMATIZATION
        CLIMATIC INFLUENCE
        CLIMATIC ZONES
        CLIMATOLOGY
        SEASONS

CLIMATIC INFLUENCE
INFLUENCE CLIMATIQUE / INFLUENCIA CLIMATICA -

CLIMATIC INFLUENCE<CONT>
17.02.01
    RT: CLIMATE

CLIMATIC REGIONS
- 17.02.03
    USE: CLIMATIC ZONES

CLIMATIC ZONES
ZONES CLIMATIQUES / ZONAS CLIMATICAS - 17.02.03
    UF: CLIMATIC REGIONS
    NT: ARID ZONE
        COLD ZONE
        EQUATORIAL ZONE
        FRIGID ZONE
        HUMID ZONE
        SEMI-ARID ZONE
        SUBTROPICAL ZONE
        TEMPERATE ZONE
        TROPICAL ZONE
    RT: CLIMATE

CLIMATOLOGY
CLIMATOLOGIE / CLIMATOLOGIA - 17.01.01
    BT: GEOPHYSICS
        METEOROLOGY
    NT: BIOCLIMATOLOGY
    RT: CLIMATE
        SEASONS

CLOTHING INDUSTRY
INDUSTRIE DU VETEMENT / INDUSTRIA DEL VESTUARIO
- 08.08.01
    BT: TEXTILE INDUSTRY
    NT: FUR INDUSTRY

CMEA
CAEM / CAEM - 01.03.03
SN: COUNCIL FOR MUTUAL ECONOMIC ASSISTANCE.
    BT: EUROPEAN ORGANIZATIONS
        INTERGOVERNMENTAL ORGANIZATIONS
    RT: EASTERN EUROPE

COAL
CHARBON / CARBON - 08.11.05
    BT: ENERGY SOURCES
        FOSSIL FUELS
    RT: COAL MINING
        COKE
        ECSC

COAL GAS
GAZ DE HOUILLE / GAS DEL ALUMBRADO - 08.11.05
    BT: ENERGY SOURCES
        FOSSIL FUELS

COAL MINING
CHARBONNAGES / MINAS DE CARBON - 08.13.00
    BT: MINING
    RT: COAL

COASTAL AREAS
- 17.03.04
    USE: LITTORAL ZONES

COASTAL FISHING
PECHE COTIERE / PESCA COSTERA - 07.10.03
    BT: MARINE FISHING
    RT: COASTAL WATERS

COASTAL POLLUTION
POLLUTION DES COTES / CONTAMINACION DEL LITORAL
- 16.03.04
    BT: POLLUTION
    RT: COASTAL WATERS
        COASTS
        MARINE POLLUTION

COASTAL WATERS
EAUX COTIERES / AGUAS COSTERAS - 17.06.00
    RT: COASTAL FISHING
        COASTAL POLLUTION
        COASTS
        TERRITORIAL WATERS

COASTS
COTES / COSTAS - 17.03.04
    BT: LITTORAL ZONES
    RT: COASTAL POLLUTION
        COASTAL WATERS

COATING
ENROBAGE / REVESTIMIENTO - 08.12.03
    BT: INDUSTRIAL PROCESSES
    RT: PAINTS AND VARNISHES
        PLATING

COBALT
COBALT / COBALTO - 08.14.02
    BT: NON-FERROUS METALS

COCOA
CACAO / CACAO - 07.07.09
    BT: INDUSTRIAL CROPS
        NON-ALCOHOLIC BEVERAGES
    RT: CHOCOLATE

COCONUT PALMS
COCOTIERS / COCOTEROS - 07.07.05
    BT: FRUIT TREES
    RT: COCONUTS

COCONUTS
NOIX DE COCO / COCOS - 07.07.05
    BT: FRUITS
        INDUSTRIAL CROPS
    RT: COCONUT PALMS
        COIR

CODES
CODES / CODIGOS - 04.01.01
    NT: LABOUR CODE

CODESRIA
CODERESA / CODEIESA - 01.03.03
*SN: COUNCIL FOR THE DEVELOPMENT OF ECONOMIC AND
    SOCIAL RESEARCH IN AFRICA.*
    BT: AFRICAN ORGANIZATIONS
        NON-GOVERNMENTAL ORGANIZATIONS
    RT: AFRICA

COEDUCATIONAL SCHOOLS
ECOLES MIXTES / ESCUELAS MIXTAS - 06.04.03
    BT: SCHOOLS

COFFEE
CAFE / CAFE - 07.07.09
    BT: INDUSTRIAL CROPS
        NON-ALCOHOLIC BEVERAGES

COIR
FIBRE DE COCO / FIBRA DE COCO - 07.07.07
    BT: PLANT FIBRES
    RT: COCONUTS

COKE
COKE / COQUE - 08.11.05
    RT: COAL

COLD SEASON
SAISON FROIDE / ESTACION FRIA - 17.02.02
    BT: SEASONS

COLD ZONE
ZONE FROIDE / ZONA FRIA - 17.02.03
    BT: CLIMATIC ZONES
    RT: FRIGID ZONE

COLLECTIVE AGREEMENTS
CONVENTIONS COLLECTIVES / CONVENIOS COLECTIVOS -
13.06.00
*SN: AGREEMENT CONCERNING THE WORKING CONDITIONS
OF A PARTICULAR GROUP OF WORKERS CONCLUDED
BETWEEN THE WORKERS' REPRESENTATIVES AND THE
EMPLOYERS.*
    RT: COLLECTIVE BARGAINING
        WORKING CONDITIONS

COLLECTIVE BARGAINING
NEGOCIATION COLLECTIVE / NEGOCIACION COLECTIVA -
13.06.00
*SN: THE PROCESS BY WHICH REPRESENTATIVES OF
EMPLOYERS AND THOSE OF THE EMPLOYEES DISCUSS
AND NEGOTIATE THE VARIOUS PHASES OF THEIR
RELATIONSHIP WITH A VIEW TO ARRIVING AT A
MUTUALLY ACCEPTABLE LABOUR AGREEMENT.*
    RT: COLLECTIVE AGREEMENTS

COLLECTIVE ECONOMY
ECONOMIE COLLECTIVE / ECONOMIA COLECTIVA -
03.03.02
    BT: ECONOMIC SYSTEMS
    RT: COLLECTIVE FARMING
        COLLECTIVE OWNERSHIP
        COLLECTIVISM

COLLECTIVE FARMING
AGRIEXPLOITATION COLLECTIVE / EXPLOTACION
AGRICOLA COLECTIVA - 07.05.03
    BT: FARMING SYSTEMS
    RT: COLLECTIVE ECONOMY
        STATE FARMS

COLLECTIVE HOUSING
LOGEMENT COLLECTIF / VIVIENDA COLECTIVA -

COLLECTIVE HOUSING<CONT>
14.04.01
    BT: HOUSING

COLLECTIVE OWNERSHIP
PROPRIETE COLLECTIVE / PROPIEDAD COLECTIVA -
03.03.05
    BT: OWNERSHIP
    RT: COLLECTIVE ECONOMY
        PUBLIC OWNERSHIP

COLLECTIVE TRANSPORT
- 10.01.00
    USE: PUBLIC TRANSPORT

COLLECTIVISM
COLLECTIVISME / COLECTIVISMO - 03.03.01
    RT: COLLECTIVE ECONOMY
        COMMUNISM
        SOCIALISM

COLLEGE MANAGEMENT
ADMINISTRATION UNIVERSITAIRE / ADMINISTRACION
UNIVERSITARIA - 06.04.08
    BT: MANAGEMENT
    RT: HIGHER EDUCATION INSTITUTIONS

COLLEGE STUDENTS
ETUDIANTS / ESTUDIANTES - 06.06.01
    BT: STUDENTS
    NT: FOREIGN STUDENTS
        UNDERGRADUATES
    RT: STUDENT BEHAVIOUR
        STUDENT MOVEMENTS

COLLEGES OF EDUCATION
ECOLES NORMALES / ESCUELAS NORMALES - 06.04.05
    UF: TEACHER TRAINING COLLEGES
    RT: TEACHER TRAINING

COLOMBIA
COLOMBIE / COLOMBIA - 01.04.03
    BT: LATIN AMERICA
        SOUTH AMERICA
    RT: COLOMBIAN

COLOMBIAN
COLOMBIEN / COLOMBIANO - 14.03.02
    RT: COLOMBIA

COLOMBO PLAN
PLAN DE COLOMBO / PLAN COLOMBO - 01.03.03
    BT: ASIAN ORGANIZATIONS
        INTERGOVERNMENTAL ORGANIZATIONS

COLONIAL COUNTRIES
COLONIES / COLONIAS - 01.02.03
    RT: COLONIALISM
        DECOLONIZATION

COLONIALISM
COLONIALISME / COLONIALISMO - 03.03.01

COLONIALISM<CONT>
  RT: COLONIAL COUNTRIES
      DECOLONIZATION
      NATIONAL LIBERATION MOVEMENTS
      NEOCOLONIALISM

COMMENT
COMMENTAIRE / COMENTARIO - 19.02.07
  BT: SECONDARY DOCUMENTS

COMMERCIAL BANKS
BANQUES COMMERCIALES / BANCOS COMERCIALES - 09.04.03
  BT: BANKS
  RT: COMMERCIAL CREDIT
      FINANCIAL MARKET
      TRADE

COMMERCIAL CREDIT
CREDIT COMMERCIAL / CREDITO COMERCIAL - 09.04.03
  BT: CREDIT
  RT: COMMERCIAL BANKS
      TRADE

COMMERCIAL EDUCATION
ENSEIGNEMENT COMMERCIAL / ENSENANZA COMERCIAL - 06.03.07
  SN: USE IN CONNECTION WITH THE STUDY OF
      COMMERCIAL SUBJECTS.
  BT: VOCATIONAL EDUCATION
  RT: COMMERCIAL SCHOOLS

COMMERCIAL ENTERPRISES
ENTREPRISES COMMERCIALES / EMPRESAS COMERCIALES - 09.04.03
  BT: ENTERPRISES
  RT: DEALERS
      TRADE

COMMERCIAL FARMING
AGRICULTURE COMMERCIALE / AGRICULTURA COMERCIAL - 07.05.03
  BT: FARMING SYSTEMS

COMMERCIAL LAW
DROIT COMMERCIAL / DERECHO MERCANTIL - 04.01.02
  BT: LAW
  RT: TRADE

COMMERCIAL POLICY
POLITIQUE COMMERCIALE / POLITICA COMERCIAL - 09.04.02
  SN: REFERS TO DOMESTIC TRADE. DO NOT CONFUSE
      WITH «TRADE POLICY».
  BT: ECONOMIC POLICY
  RT: DOMESTIC TRADE

COMMERCIAL SCHOOLS
ECOLES COMMERCIALES / ESCUELAS DE COMERCIO - 06.04.06
  BT: SCHOOLS
  RT: COMMERCIAL EDUCATION
      VOCATIONAL SCHOOLS

COMMODITIES
PRODUITS DE BASE / PRODUCTOS BASICOS - 12.08.01
  SN: AS OPPOSED TO SEMI-MANUFACTURED OR FINISHED
      PRODUCTS; IN THEIR ORIGINAL STATE, OR
      PROCESSED ONLY ENOUGH TO BE PREPARED FOR
      MARKETING IN INTERNATIONAL TRADE.
  UF: PRIMARY PRODUCTS
  BT: PRODUCTS
  NT: AGRICULTURAL PRODUCTS
      RAW MATERIALS
  RT: BUFFER STOCKS
      COMMODITY AGREEMENTS
      COMMODITY MARKET
      COMMODITY PRICES
      MARKET STABILIZATION
      NATURAL RESOURCES

COMMODITY AGREEMENTS
ACCORDS SUR LES PRODUITS DE BASE / CONVENIOS SOBRE PRODUCTOS BASICOS - 09.05.02
  BT: TRADE AGREEMENTS
  NT: COMMON FUND
  RT: BUFFER STOCKS
      COMMODITIES
      COMMODITY MARKET
      PRODUCERS ASSOCIATIONS

COMMODITY MARKET
MARCHE DES PRODUITS DE BASE / MERCADO DE PRODUCTOS BASICOS - 09.01.02
  BT: MARKET
  RT: COMMODITIES
      COMMODITY AGREEMENTS
      COMMODITY PRICES

COMMODITY PRICES
PRIX DES PRODUITS DE BASE / PRECIOS DE PRODUCTOS BASICOS - 09.02.00
  BT: PRICES
  NT: AGRICULTURAL PRICES
  RT: BUFFER STOCKS
      COMMODITIES
      COMMODITY MARKET
      COMMON FUND
      PRODUCERS ASSOCIATIONS
      TERMS OF TRADE

COMMON FUND
FONDS COMMUN / FONDO COMUN - 09.05.02
  SN: JOINT FINANCING OF AN INTEGRATED PROGRAMME
      OF INDIVIDUAL COMMODITY BUFFER STOCKS.
  BT: COMMODITY AGREEMENTS
  RT: COMMODITY PRICES
      PRICE STABILIZATION

COMMON LAW
COMMON LAW / COMMON LAW - 04.01.02
  SN: ANGLO-AMERICAN LAW BASED MAINLY ON CUSTOM
      AND ON PREVIOUS COURT DECISIONS.
  BT: LAW
  RT: JURISPRUDENCE
      LEGISLATION

COMMON MARKET
MARCHE COMMUN / MERCADO COMUN - 01.02.01

COMMON MARKET<CONT>
SN: *USE THIS DESCRIPTOR IN ITS GENERAL MEANING.*
DO NOT RESTRICT TO THE EUROPEAN ECONOMIC
COMMUNITY.
    NT: CACM
        CARICOM
        EEC
    RT: CUSTOMS UNION
        REGIONAL INTEGRATION
        TRADE AGREEMENTS
        TRADE POLICY

COMMONWEALTH
COMMONWEALTH / COMMONWEALTH - 01.03.03
SN: *USE TO MEAN THE BRITISH COMMUNITY.*
    BT: INTERGOVERNMENTAL ORGANIZATIONS

COMMUNAL LAND
TERRES COMMUNALES / TIERRAS COMUNALES - 07.02.00
    BT: PUBLIC LAND

COMMUNICABLE DISEASES
- 15.04.02
    USE: **INFECTIOUS DISEASES**

COMMUNICATION
COMMUNICATION / COMUNICACION - 05.07.01
SN: *A PROCESS OF SHARING INFORMATION INVOLVING*
THE ENCODING, TRANSMISSION, DECODING, USE OF
AND REACTION TO THE MESSAGE.
    NT: MASS COMMUNICATION
        TELECOMMUNICATIONS
    RT: COMMUNICATION BARRIERS
        COMMUNICATION ENGINEERING
        COMMUNICATION INDUSTRY
        COMMUNICATION PLANNING
        COMMUNICATION POLICY
        COMMUNICATION RESEARCH
        COMMUNICATION SATELLITES
        COMMUNICATION SYSTEMS
        CONTENT ANALYSIS
        CYBERNETICS
        INFORMATION
        INFORMATION THEORY
        MEDIA

COMMUNICATION BARRIERS
OBSTACLES A LA COMMUNICATION / BARRERAS A LA
COMUNICACION - 05.07.01
    NT: LANGUAGE BARRIER
    RT: COMMUNICATION

COMMUNICATION ENGINEERING
TECHNOLOGIE DES COMMUNICATIONS / TECNOLOGIA DE
COMUNICACIONES - 08.16.00
    BT: ENGINEERING
    RT: COMMUNICATION
        COMMUNICATION INDUSTRY
        ELECTRONICS

COMMUNICATION INDUSTRY
INDUSTRIE DES COMMUNICATIONS / INDUSTRIA DE
COMUNICACIONES - 08.16.00

COMMUNICATION INDUSTRY<CONT>
    NT: BOOK INDUSTRY
        FILM INDUSTRY
        PRINTING INDUSTRY
        RECORD INDUSTRY
        TELECOMMUNICATION INDUSTRY
    RT: COMMUNICATION
        COMMUNICATION ENGINEERING
        INFORMATION

COMMUNICATION MEDIA
- 05.07.03
    USE: **MEDIA**

COMMUNICATION PLANNING
PLANIFICATION DE LA COMMUNICATION /
PLANIFICACION DE LA COMUNICACION - 05.07.01
SN: *DESIGN, DEVELOPMENT AND MANAGEMENT OF*
COMMUNICATION INFRASTRUCTURE.
    BT: PLANNING
    RT: COMMUNICATION

COMMUNICATION POLICY
POLITIQUE DE LA COMMUNICATION / POLITICA DE LA
COMUNICACION - 05.07.01
SN: *SETS NORMS TO GUIDE THE BEHAVIOUR OF*
COMMUNICATION INSTITUTIONS.
    BT: GOVERNMENT POLICY
    NT: CENSORSHIP
    RT: COMMUNICATION

COMMUNICATION RESEARCH
RECHERCHE SUR LA COMMUNICATION / INVESTIGACION
SOBRE LA COMUNICACION - 05.07.01
    BT: RESEARCH
    RT: COMMUNICATION

COMMUNICATION SATELLITES
SATELLITES DE COMMUNICATION / SATELITES DE
COMUNICACION - 08.16.00
    RT: COMMUNICATION
        REMOTE SENSING

COMMUNICATION SYSTEMS
SYSTEMES DE COMMUNICATION / SISTEMAS DE
COMUNICACION - 05.07.01
SN: *ALL THE ELEMENTS IMPLIED IN INFORMATION*
TRANSFER (TRANSMITTER, RECEIVER, CHANNEL,
CODE, ETC.) AND TYPES OF ORDERING.
    RT: COMMUNICATION

COMMUNICATION THEORY
- 18.08.00
    USE: **INFORMATION THEORY**

COMMUNICATION USERS
- 05.07.02
    USE: **AUDIENCE**

COMMUNISM
COMMUNISME / COMUNISMO - 03.03.01
    RT: COLLECTIVISM
        COMMUNIST
        MARXISM

COMMUNIST
COMMUNISTE / COMUNISTA - 03.03.01
    RT: COMMUNISM

COMMUNITY
COLLECTIVITE / COMUNIDAD - 14.04.01
    RT: COMMUNITY DEVELOPMENT
        COMMUNITY RELATIONS
        LOCAL GOVERNMENT
        SCHOOL-COMMUNITY RELATIONSHIPS

COMMUNITY DEVELOPMENT
DEVELOPPEMENT DES COLLECTIVITES / DESARROLLO DE
LA COMUNIDAD - 14.04.01
*SN: USE IN CONNECTION WITH THE ORGANIZATION OF
    ALL ASPECTS OF COMMUNITY LIVING, IN
    PARTICULAR WITH REGARD TO NEW SETTLEMENT
    PROJECTS AND THE IMPROVEMENT OF EXISTING
    FACILITIES IN A COMMUNITY.*
    BT: SOCIAL DEVELOPMENT
    RT: COMMUNITY
        SOCIAL PARTICIPATION

COMMUNITY RELATIONS
RELATIONS AVEC LA COLLECTIVITE / RELACION
COMUNITARIA - 14.04.01
*SN: ENTERPRISE PARTICIPATION IN COMMUNITY
    SERVICE PROGRAMMES, ENCOURAGEMENT OF
    COMMUNITY IMPROVEMENTS AND OF INDIVIDUAL
    PARTICIPATION IN COMMUNITY ACTIVITIES.*
    RT: COMMUNITY

COMMUTING
MIGRATIONS ALTERNANTES / DESPLAZAMIENTOS
RESIDENCIA-TRABAJO - 14.07.00
    BT: INTERNAL MIGRATIONS

COMORIAN
COMORIEN / COMORANO - 14.03.02
    RT: COMOROS

COMOROS
COMORES / COMORAS - 01.04.02
    BT: EAST AFRICA
        FRENCH SPEAKING AFRICA
        SOUTHERN AFRICA
    RT: COMORIAN

COMPARATIVE ADVANTAGE
AVANTAGE COMPARE / VENTAJA COMPARATIVA -
09.05.03
    RT: ECONOMIC THEORY
        INTERNATIONAL DIVISION OF LABOUR

COMPARATIVE ANALYSIS
ANALYSE COMPARATIVE / ANALISIS COMPARATIVO -
18.09.00
    UF: COMPARATIVE STUDY
    BT: RESEARCH METHODS
    NT: COMPARATIVE EDUCATION
        CROSS CULTURAL ANALYSIS
    RT: COMPARISON

COMPARATIVE EDUCATION
EDUCATION COMPAREE / EDUCACION COMPARADA -

COMPARATIVE EDUCATION\<CONT\>
06.01.00
    BT: COMPARATIVE ANALYSIS
    RT: EDUCATIONAL RESEARCH
        SCIENCES OF EDUCATION

COMPARATIVE STUDY
- 18.09.00
    USE: COMPARATIVE ANALYSIS

COMPARISON
COMPARAISON / COMPARACION - 18.09.00
    RT: COMPARATIVE ANALYSIS

COMPENSATION
- 13.07.00
    USE: WAGES

COMPENSATORY EDUCATION
EDUCATION COMPENSATOIRE / EDUCACION
COMPENSATORIA - 06.03.03
    BT: SPECIAL EDUCATION

COMPENSATORY FINANCING
FINANCEMENT COMPENSATOIRE / FINANCIAMIENTO
COMPENSATORIO - 11.02.04
*SN: COMPENSATES FOR TEMPORARY SHORTFALLS IN
    EXPORT EARNINGS.*
    BT: DEFICIT FINANCING
    RT: BALANCE OF PAYMENTS
        EXPORT EARNINGS
        IMF

COMPETITION
CONCURRENCE / COMPETENCIA - 09.01.02
    NT: UNFAIR COMPETITION
    RT: ANTITRUST LEGISLATION
        MONOPOLIES
        RESTRICTIVE BUSINESS PRACTICES

COMPETITIVE PRODUCTS
PRODUITS COMPETITIFS / PRODUCTOS COMPETITIVOS -
12.08.02
    BT: PRODUCTS

COMPLEMENTARITY AGREEMENTS
ACCORDS DE COMPLEMENTARITE / ACUERDOS DE
COMPLEMENTACION - 01.02.01
*SN: REFER TO INDUSTRIAL PRODUCTION AT THE
    SECTORIAL LEVEL BETWEEN VARIOUS COUNTRIES
    PARTICIPATING IN AN ECONOMIC INTEGRATION
    PROGRAMME.*
    BT: ECONOMIC AGREEMENTS
    RT: BORDER INTEGRATION
        INDUSTRIAL INTEGRATION

COMPREHENSIVE SCHOOLS
ECOLES GLOBALES / ESCUELAS UNITARIAS - 06.04.03
    BT: SCHOOLS

COMPULSORY EDUCATION
ENSEIGNEMENT OBLIGATOIRE / ENSENANZA OBLIGATORIA

COMPULSORY EDUCATION<CONT>
- 06.03.03
    BT: EDUCATIONAL SYSTEMS
    RT: SCHOOLING

COMPUTATION
CALCUL / COMPUTACION - 18.08.00

COMPUTER CENTRES
CENTRES DE CALCUL / CENTROS DE COMPUTACION -
18.02.00
    RT: COMPUTER PROGRAMMES
        COMPUTER SCIENCE
        COMPUTERS
        ELECTRONIC DATA PROCESSING

COMPUTER PROGRAMMES
PROGRAMMES D'ORDINATEUR / PROGRAMAS DE
COMPUTADORA - 08.15.02
    UF: SOFTWARE
    RT: COMPUTER CENTRES
        COMPUTER SCIENCE
        COMPUTERS
        ELECTRONIC EQUIPMENT
        SYSTEMS DESIGN

COMPUTER SCIENCE
INFORMATIQUE / INFORMATICA - 18.08.00
    UF: INFORMATICS
    BT: INFORMATION SCIENCES
    RT: COMPUTER CENTRES
        COMPUTER PROGRAMMES
        COMPUTERS

COMPUTERS
ORDINATEURS / COMPUTADORAS - 08.15.02
    UF: ELECTRONIC COMPUTERS
    BT: ELECTRONIC EQUIPMENT
    RT: COMPUTER CENTRES
        COMPUTER PROGRAMMES
        COMPUTER SCIENCE
        ELECTRONIC DATA PROCESSING
        LIBRARY AUTOMATION

CONCENTRATION CAMPS
CAMPS DE CONCENTRATION / CAMPOS DE CONCENTRACION
- 02.04.03
    RT: HUMAN RIGHTS
        VIOLENCE

CONCENTRATION OF POLLUTANTS
- 16.03.04
    USE: POLLUTION LEVEL

CONCILIATION
CONCILIATION / CONCILIACION - 05.03.06
    BT: DISPUTE SETTLEMENT

CONCRETE
BETON / HORMIGON - 08.10.02
    BT: CONSTRUCTION MATERIALS
    RT: CEMENT INDUSTRY
        CONCRETE CONSTRUCTION

CONCRETE CONSTRUCTION
CONSTRUCTION EN BETON / CONSTRUCCION EN HORMIGON
- 08.10.01
    BT: CONSTRUCTION TECHNIQUES
    RT: CONCRETE

CONDENSED FOOD
ALIMENTS CONCENTRES / ALIMENTOS CONCENTRADOS -
08.06.03
    BT: FOOD
    NT: FISH PROTEIN CONCENTRATE

CONDOMS
PRESERVATIFS / PRESERVATIVOS - 14.05.02
    BT: CONTRACEPTIVES

CONF
CONF / CONF - 19.04.00
SN: USE TO INDICATE THAT A PARTICULAR CONFERENCE
    HAS TAKEN PLACE.

CONFERENCE
CONFERENCE / CONFERENCIA - 19.04.00
SN: USE IN CONNECTION WITH THE ORGANIZATION,
    FINANCING, ETC., OF CONFERENCES, CONGRESSES
    AND MEETINGS. DO NOT CONFUSE WITH 'CONF'.
    RT: CONFERENCE PAPER
        CONFERENCE REPORT

CONFERENCE PAPER
DOCUMENT DE REUNION / DOCUMENTO DE REUNION -
19.02.05
    UF: MEETING PAPER
    RT: CONFERENCE
        CONFERENCE REPORT

CONFERENCE REPORT
RAPPORT DE REUNION / INFORME DE REUNION -
19.02.08
    UF: MEETING REPORT
    RT: CONFERENCE
        CONFERENCE PAPER

CONFLICT RESOLUTION
- 05.03.06
    USE: DISPUTE SETTLEMENT

CONFLICTS
CONFLITS / CONFLICTOS - 05.03.06
    NT: RACIAL CONFLICTS
        SOCIAL CONFLICTS
        WAR
    RT: DISPUTE SETTLEMENT
        VIOLENCE

CONFUCIANISM
CONFUCIANISME / CONFUCIANISMO - 05.04.03

CONGO
CONGO / CONGO - 01.04.02
    BT: CENTRAL AFRICA
        FRENCH SPEAKING AFRICA
    RT: CONGOLESE

CONGOLESE
CONGOLAIS / CONGOLENO - 14.03.02
    RT: CONGO

CONSERVATION OF CULTURAL HERITAGE
PROTECTION DU PATRIMOINE CULTUREL / PROTECCION
DEL PATRIMONIO CULTURAL - 05.02.02
    RT: CULTURAL HERITAGE
        CULTURAL INTEGRATION

CONSERVATISM
CONSERVATISME / CONSERVADURISMO - 05.03.02
    RT: ATTITUDES
        RESISTANCE TO CHANGE
        TRADITION

CONSTITUTION
CONSTITUTION / CONSTITUCION - 04.03.01
    RT: CONSTITUTIONAL COURTS
        CONSTITUTIONAL LAW

CONSTITUTIONAL COURTS
COURS CONSTITUTIONNELLES / TRIBUNALES
CONSTITUCIONALES - 04.03.01
    RT: ADMINISTRATION OF JUSTICE
        CONSTITUTION
        CONSTITUTIONAL LAW

CONSTITUTIONAL LAW
DROIT CONSTITUTIONNEL / DERECHO CONSTITUCIONAL -
04.01.02
    BT: PUBLIC LAW
    RT: CONSTITUTION
        CONSTITUTIONAL COURTS

CONSTRUCTION EQUIPMENT
- 08.14.06
    USE: BUILDING MACHINERY

CONSTRUCTION INDUSTRY
INDUSTRIE DE LA CONSTRUCTION / INDUSTRIA DE LA
CONSTRUCCION - 08.10.01
    UF: BUILDING INDUSTRY
    BT: INDUSTRIAL SECTOR
    RT: BUILDING MACHINERY
        BUILDINGS
        CIVIL ENGINEERING
        CONSTRUCTION MATERIALS
        CONSTRUCTION TECHNIQUES
        CONSTRUCTION WORKERS
        PUBLIC WORKS
        TRANSPORT INFRASTRUCTURE

CONSTRUCTION MATERIALS
MATERIAUX DE CONSTRUCTION / MATERIALES DE
CONSTRUCCION - 08.10.02
    UF: BUILDING MATERIALS

CONSTRUCTION MATERIALS<CONT>
    NT: AGGLOMERATES
        BITUMENS
        CEMENT
        CERAMICS
        CONCRETE
        LIME
        PARTICLE BOARDS
        PLYWOOD
        REFRACTORY MATERIALS
        SAND
        STONE
        TIMBER
    RT: CONSTRUCTION INDUSTRY

CONSTRUCTION TECHNIQUES
TECHNIQUES DE CONSTRUCTION / TECNICAS DE
CONSTRUCCION - 08.10.01
    NT: CONCRETE CONSTRUCTION
        STEEL CONSTRUCTION
        STONE CONSTRUCTION
        WOOD CONSTRUCTION
    RT: CONSTRUCTION INDUSTRY
        PREFABRICATED BUILDINGS

CONSTRUCTION WORKERS
OUVRIERS DU BATIMENT / OBREROS DE LA
CONSTRUCCION - 13.09.06
    BT: INDUSTRIAL WORKERS
    RT: CONSTRUCTION INDUSTRY

CONSULTANT REPORT
RAPPORT DE CONSULTANT / INFORME DE CONSULTOR -
19.02.08
SN: USE TO DENOTE A TECHNICAL ASSISTANCE STUDY
    MADE BY A CONSULTANT UNDER CONTRACT TO A
    GOVERNMENT AGENCY OR AN INTERNATIONAL
    ORGANIZATION.
    RT: CONSULTANTS

CONSULTANTS
CONSULTANTS / CONSULTORES - 01.01.07
    BT: DEVELOPMENT PERSONNEL
    RT: CONSULTANT REPORT

CONSUMER BEHAVIOUR
COMPORTEMENT DU CONSOMMATEUR / COMPORTAMIENTO
DEL CONSUMIDOR - 09.01.03
    BT: BEHAVIOUR
    RT: CONSUMER DEMAND
        CONSUMERS
        MARKET STUDIES

CONSUMER CREDIT
CREDIT A LA CONSOMMATION / CREDITO AL CONSUMIDOR
- 11.02.02
    UF: INSTALMENT CREDIT
    BT: CREDIT
    RT: CONSUMERS
        CONSUMPTION
        HIRE PURCHASE

CONSUMER DEMAND
DEMANDE DE CONSOMMATION / DEMANDA DE CONSUMO -

CONSUMER DEMAND<CONT>
09.01.03
    BT: DEMAND
    RT: CONSUMER BEHAVIOUR
         CONSUMER GOODS
         CONSUMERS

CONSUMER EDUCATION
EDUCATION DU CONSOMMATEUR / EDUCACION DEL
CONSUMIDOR - 06.03.04
    BT: BASIC EDUCATION
    RT: CONSUMER PROTECTION
         CONSUMERS

CONSUMER EXPENDITURES
DEPENSES DE CONSOMMATION / GASTOS DE CONSUMO -
09.01.03
    BT: EXPENDITURES
    RT: CONSUMERS
         FAMILY BUDGET

CONSUMER GOODS
BIENS DE CONSOMMATION / BIENES DE CONSUMO -
09.01.03
    NT: DURABLE GOODS
    RT: CONSUMER DEMAND
         CONSUMPTION

CONSUMER PRICES
PRIX A LA CONSOMMATION / PRECIOS AL CONSUMIDOR
- 09.02.00
    BT: PRICES

CONSUMER PROTECTION
PROTECTION DU CONSOMMATEUR / PROTECCION DEL
CONSUMIDOR - 09.01.03
    RT: ANTITRUST LEGISLATION
         CONSUMER EDUCATION
         CONSUMERS
         RESTRICTIVE BUSINESS PRACTICES

CONSUMERS
CONSOMMATEURS / CONSUMIDORES - 09.01.03
    RT: CONSUMER BEHAVIOUR
         CONSUMER CREDIT
         CONSUMER DEMAND
         CONSUMER EDUCATION
         CONSUMER EXPENDITURES
         CONSUMER PROTECTION
         CONSUMERS COOPERATIVES
         CONSUMPTION

CONSUMERS COOPERATIVES
COOPERATIVES DE CONSOMMATION / COOPERATIVAS DE
CONSUMO - 09.03.01
    BT: COOPERATIVES
    RT: CONSUMERS
         CONSUMPTION

CONSUMPTION
CONSOMMATION / CONSUMO - 09.01.03

CONSUMPTION<CONT>
SN: USE ONLY TO DENOTE CONSUMPTION OF A
    COMMODITY OR PRODUCT THROUGHOUT A GEOGRAPHIC
    AREA.
    NT: CONSUMPTION PER CAPITA
         DOMESTIC CONSUMPTION
         ENERGY CONSUMPTION
         FOOD CONSUMPTION
         WATER CONSUMPTION
    RT: AFFLUENT SOCIETY
         CONSUMER CREDIT
         CONSUMER GOODS
         CONSUMERS
         CONSUMERS COOPERATIVES
         CONSUMPTION FUNCTIONS
         CONSUMPTION TAX
         FAMILY BUDGET

CONSUMPTION FUNCTIONS
FONCTIONS DE CONSOMMATION / FUNCIONES DE CONSUMO
- 09.01.03
    RT: CONSUMPTION

CONSUMPTION PER CAPITA
CONSOMMATION PAR TETE / CONSUMO POR HABITANTE -
09.01.03
    BT: CONSUMPTION
    RT: STANDARD OF LIVING

CONSUMPTION TAX
IMPOT SUR LA CONSOMMATION / IMPUESTO AL CONSUMO
- 11.01.02
    UF: SALES TAX
    BT: TAXES
    NT: IMPORT TAX
         VALUE ADDED TAX
    RT: CONSUMPTION

CONTAGIOUS DISEASES
- 15.04.02
    USE: INFECTIOUS DISEASES

CONTAINERS
RECIPIENTS / RECIPIENTES - 10.06.00
    NT: BAGS
         BOXES
         TRANSPORT CONTAINERS

CONTAMINANTS
- 16.03.04
    USE: POLLUTANTS

CONTENT ANALYSIS
ANALYSE DE CONTENU / ANALISIS DE CONTENIDO -
19.01.02
    BT: INFORMATION ANALYSIS
    RT: COMMUNICATION
         DATA ANALYSIS

CONTINENTAL SHELVES
PLATEFORMES CONTINENTALES / PLATAFORMAS
CONTINENTALES - 17.03.04

CONTINENTAL SHELVES\<CONT\>
    RT: CONTINENTS
        DREDGING
        LITTORAL ZONES

CONTINENTS
CONTINENTS / CONTINENTES - 17.03.04
    RT: CONTINENTAL SHELVES

CONTINGENCY FUNDS
FONDS DE SECOURS / FONDOS PARA GASTOS
IMPREVISTOS - 02.03.02
    RT: SOCIAL SECURITY

CONTINUING EDUCATION
- 06.03.05
    USE: **LIFE-LONG EDUCATION**

CONTINUOUS WORKING DAY
JOURNEE CONTINUE / JORNADA CONTINUA - 13.03.03
    BT: ARRANGEMENT OF WORKING TIME

CONTRACEPTION
CONTRACEPTION / ANTICONCEPCION - 14.05.02
    RT: CONTRACEPTIVE METHODS
        CONTRACEPTIVES
        FAMILY PLANNING

CONTRACEPTIVE METHODS
METHODES CONTRACEPTIVES / METODOS
ANTICONCEPTIVOS - 14.05.02
    RT: CONTRACEPTION

CONTRACEPTIVES
CONTRACEPTIFS / ANTICONCEPTIVOS - 14.05.02
    NT: CHEMICAL CONTRACEPTIVES
        CONDOMS
        INTRAUTERINE DEVICES
        ORAL CONTRACEPTIVES
    RT: CONTRACEPTION
        PHARMACEUTICALS

CONTRACT LABOUR
TRAVAIL SUR CONTRAT / TRABAJO CONTRATADO -
13.02.01
SN: USE WITH REFERENCE TO LABOUR SUPPLIED BY A
    CONTRACTOR.
    RT: LABOUR CONTRACT
        WORKING CONDITIONS

CONTRACTING
CONCLUSION DE CONTRATS / CELEBRACION DE
CONTRATOS - 12.07.02
    NT: SUBCONTRACTING

CONURBATION
CONURBATION / CONURBACION - 14.04.03
    BT: URBAN CONCENTRATION

CONVENTIONAL WEAPONS
ARMES CONVENTIONNELLES / ARMAS CONVENCIONALES -
01.02.06
    BT: WEAPONS

CONVENTIONS
CONVENTIONS / CONVENIOS - 01.02.04
    RT: INTERNATIONAL AGREEMENTS

CONVERTIBILITY
CONVERTIBILITE / CONVERTIBILIDAD - 11.03.01
    RT: CURRENCIES
        GOLD STANDARD
        NON-CONVERTIBLE CURRENCIES

COOKERY
- 15.03.01
    USE: **FOOD PREPARATION**

COOLING
REFROIDISSEMENT / ENFRIAMIENTO - 08.12.03
    BT: INDUSTRIAL PROCESSES
    RT: FREEZING
        REFRIGERATION
        TEMPERATURE

COOPERATIVE FARMING
AGRIEXPLOITATION COOPERATIVE / EXPLOTACION
AGRICOLA COOPERATIVA - 07.05.03
    BT: FARMING SYSTEMS
    RT: AGRICULTURAL COOPERATIVES

COOPERATIVE MARKETING
VENTE EN COOPERATION / COMERCIALIZACION
COOPERATIVA - 09.03.01
    BT: MARKETING
    RT: MARKETING COOPERATIVES

COOPERATIVE MOVEMENTS
MOUVEMENTS COOPERATIFS / MOVIMIENTOS
COOPERATIVOS - 03.03.04
    BT: SOCIAL MOVEMENTS
    RT: COOPERATIVES

COOPERATIVES
COOPERATIVES / COOPERATIVAS - 03.03.04
    NT: AGRICULTURAL COOPERATIVES
        CONSUMERS COOPERATIVES
        CREDIT COOPERATIVES
        HOUSING COOPERATIVES
        MARKETING COOPERATIVES
        PRODUCTION COOPERATIVES
    RT: COOPERATIVE MOVEMENTS
        ECONOMIC SYSTEMS

COPPER
CUIVRE / COBRE - 08.14.02
    BT: NON-FERROUS METALS
    RT: COPPER ORE

COPPER ORE
MINERAI DE CUIVRE / MINERAL DE COBRE - 08.13.00
    BT: MINERALS
    RT: COPPER

COPYRIGHT
DROITS D'AUTEUR / DERECHOS DE AUTOR - 19.02.03
    BT: INTELLECTUAL PROPERTY
    RT: AUTHORS

CORK
LIEGE / CORCHO - 08.07.01
    BT: WOOD

CORPORATION TAX
IMPOT SUR LES SOCIETES / IMPUESTO A LAS
SOCIEDADES - 11.01.02
    BT: INCOME TAX

CORPORATISM
CORPORATISME / CORPORATISMO - 03.03.01
    BT: ECONOMIC SYSTEMS
    RT: OCCUPATIONAL ORGANIZATIONS

CORRECTIONAL EDUCATION
EDUCATION SURVEILLEE / EDUCACION CORRECCIONAL -
06.03.03
    BT: SPECIAL EDUCATION
    RT: CORRECTIONAL INSTITUTIONS

CORRECTIONAL INSTITUTIONS
CENTRES D'EDUCATION SURVEILLEE / CENTROS DE
EDUCACION CORRECCIONAL - 06.04.03
    BT: SPECIAL SCHOOLS
    RT: CORRECTIONAL EDUCATION

CORRESPONDENCE
CORRESPONDANCE / CORRESPONDENCIA - 19.02.09
    BT: PRIMARY DOCUMENTS

CORRESPONDENCE EDUCATION
ENSEIGNEMENT PAR CORRESPONDANCE / ENSENANZA POR
CORRESPONDENCIA - 06.05.03
    BT: DISTANCE STUDY

CORROSION
CORROSION / CORROSION - 08.12.03
    RT: BIODEGRADATION

CORRUPTION
CORRUPTION / CORRUPCION - 02.04.02
    BT: SOCIAL PROBLEMS
    RT: CRIMES
        PUBLIC ADMINISTRATION

COSMETICS
COSMETIQUES / COSMETICOS - 08.12.08
    BT: TOILET PREPARATIONS

COST ACCOUNTING
CALCUL DES COUTS / CONTABILIDAD DE COSTOS -
12.09.00
    BT: ACCOUNTING
    RT: COST ANALYSIS
        COSTS

COST ANALYSIS
ANALYSE DES COUTS / ANALISIS DE COSTOS -
12.09.00
    BT: ECONOMIC ANALYSIS
    RT: COST ACCOUNTING
        COST-BENEFIT ANALYSIS
        COSTS
        EFFICIENCY

COST OF EDUCATION
COUT DE L'EDUCATION / COSTO DE LA EDUCACION -
06.02.05
    UF: EDUCATIONAL EXPENDITURES
    BT: ECONOMICS OF EDUCATION
    NT: FEES
    RT: COST-BENEFIT ANALYSIS
        EDUCATIONAL OUTPUT

COST OF LIVING
COUT DE LA VIE / COSTO DE VIDA - 03.02.05
*SN: THE ACTUAL COST OF GOODS AND SERVICES
    ACCEPTED AS NECESSARY TO LIFE IN GENERAL. DO
    NOT CONFUSE WITH 'STANDARD OF LIVING'.*
    RT: LIVING CONDITIONS
        PRICE INDEX
        PURCHASING POWER

COST-BENEFIT ANALYSIS
ANALYSE COUT-AVANTAGE / ANALISIS DE COSTOS Y
BENEFICIOS - 12.09.00
    RT: COST ANALYSIS
        COST OF EDUCATION
        COSTS
        DECISION MAKING
        ECONOMIC EVALUATION
        EDUCATIONAL OUTPUT
        PROGRAMME PLANNING
        PROJECT EVALUATION

COSTA RICA
COSTA RICA / COSTA RICA - 01.04.03
    BT: CENTRAL AMERICA
    RT: COSTA RICAN

COSTA RICAN
COSTA-RICIEN / COSTARRICENSE - 14.03.02
    RT: COSTA RICA

COSTS
COUTS / COSTOS - 12.09.00
    NT: CAPITAL COSTS
        DISTRIBUTION COSTS
        EQUIPMENT COSTS
        LABOUR COSTS
        OVERHEAD COSTS
        PRODUCTION COSTS
    RT: COST ACCOUNTING
        COST ANALYSIS
        COST-BENEFIT ANALYSIS
        EXPENDITURES

COTTAGE INDUSTRY
INDUSTRIE FAMILIALE / INDUSTRIA CASERA -
08.02.02
    BT: RURAL INDUSTRY
        SMALL-SCALE INDUSTRY
    RT: HANDICRAFT PROMOTION
        WEAVING

COTTON
COTON / ALGODON - 07.07.07

COTTON<CONT>
    BT: INDUSTRIAL CROPS
          OILSEEDS
          PLANT FIBRES

COUNCIL OF EUROPE
CONSEIL DE L'EUROPE / CONSEJO DE EUROPA -
01.03.03
    BT: EUROPEAN ORGANIZATIONS
          INTERGOVERNMENTAL ORGANIZATIONS
    RT: WESTERN EUROPE

COUNTERPART
CONTREPARTIE / CONTRAPARTE - 01.01.05
    RT: COUNTERPART FUNDS
          COUNTERPART PERSONNEL

COUNTERPART FUNDS
FONDS DE CONTREPARTIE / FONDOS DE CONTRAPARTE -
01.01.05
*SN: A FUND SET UP BY A COUNTRY RECEIVING
    ECONOMIC AID, THE FUND BEING IN LOCAL
    CURRENCY AND ITS AMOUNT BEING EQUAL TO THE
    VALUE OF AID RECEIVED.*
    RT: COUNTERPART

COUNTERPART PERSONNEL
PERSONNEL HOMOLOGUE / PERSONAL DE CONTRAPARTE -
01.01.05
*SN: LOCAL PERSONNEL OF A COUNTRY RECEIVING AID,
    WHO HAVE THE SAME ROLE AS, AND COMPLEMENT
    THE WORK OF, TECHNICAL ASSISTANCE EXPERTS.*
    RT: COUNTERPART
          DEVELOPMENT PERSONNEL

COURSES
COURS / CURSOS - 06.05.01
    BT: CURRICULUM
    NT: ACCELERATED COURSES
          TRAINING COURSES
    RT: EDUCATIONAL SYSTEMS
          TEACHING

COWPEAS
NIEBES / FRIJOLES DE COSTA - 07.07.06
    BT: LEGUMINOSAE

COWS
VACHES / VACAS - 07.09.01
    BT: BOVIDAE
    RT: MILK

CRAFTSMANSHIP
DEXTERITE MANUELLE / HABILIDAD MANUAL - 13.02.01

CRAFTSMEN
ARTISANS / ARTESANOS - 13.09.06
    NT: MASTERCRAFTSMEN
    RT: HANDICRAFT

CREATIVITY
CREATIVITE / CREATIVIDAD - 05.03.02
    RT: ART
          ARTISTIC CREATION

CREDIT
CREDIT / CREDITO - 11.02.02
    NT: AGRICULTURAL CREDIT
          COMMERCIAL CREDIT
          CONSUMER CREDIT
          EXPORT CREDIT
          INDUSTRIAL CREDIT

    RT: BANKS
          BORROWING
          CREDIT COOPERATIVES
          CREDIT INSURANCE
          CREDIT POLICY
          CREDIT SYSTEMS
          DEBT
          LOANS
          MORTGAGES

CREDIT CONTROL
- 11.02.02
    USE: CREDIT POLICY

CREDIT COOPERATIVES
COOPERATIVES DE CREDIT / COOPERATIVAS DE CREDITO
- 11.02.02
    UF: CREDIT UNIONS
    BT: COOPERATIVES
    RT: CREDIT

CREDIT INSURANCE
ASSURANCE CREDIT / SEGURO DE CREDITO - 11.02.03
    BT: INSURANCE
    RT: CREDIT

CREDIT POLICY
POLITIQUE DU CREDIT / POLITICA CREDITICIA -
11.02.02
    UF: CREDIT CONTROL
    BT: FINANCIAL POLICY
    RT: CREDIT
          MONETARY POLICY

CREDIT SYSTEMS
SYSTEMES DE CREDIT / SISTEMAS DE CREDITOS -
11.02.02
    RT: BANKING SYSTEMS
          CREDIT

CREDIT UNIONS
- 11.02.02
    USE: CREDIT COOPERATIVES

CRIME PREVENTION
PREVENTION DE LA DELINQUANCE / PREVENCION DE LA
DELINCUENCIA - 02.04.03
    RT: CRIMES
          DELINQUENCY
          PENAL SANCTIONS
          POLICE

CRIMES
DELITS / DELITOS - 02.04.02
    BT: SOCIAL PROBLEMS

CRIMES<CONT>
  NT: GENOCIDE
      HOMICIDE
      WAR CRIMES
  RT: CORRUPTION
      CRIME PREVENTION
      DELINQUENCY
      OFFENDERS
      PENAL SANCTIONS
      TERRORISM

CRIMINAL LAW
DROIT PENAL / DERECHO PENAL - 04.01.02
  BT: LAW
  RT: CAPITAL PUNISHMENT
      CRIMINOLOGY
      DELINQUENCY
      PENAL SANCTIONS
      PRISONS

CRIMINOLOGY
CRIMINOLOGIE / CRIMINOLOGIA - 05.01.01
  BT: SOCIAL SCIENCES
  RT: CRIMINAL LAW
      DELINQUENCY

CRITICAL NEEDS
- 05.03.02
  USE: BASIC NEEDS

CRITICAL PATH METHOD
- 12.04.00
  USE: NETWORK ANALYSIS

CROP DIVERSIFICATION
DIVERSIFICATION DES CULTURES / DIVERSIFICACION
DE CULTIVOS - 07.05.04
  BT: CULTIVATION SYSTEMS
  RT: INTERCROPPING
      MULTIPLE CROPPING

CROP PROSPECTS
PERSPECTIVES DE RECOLTE / ESTIMACIONES DE
COSECHA - 07.05.01
  RT: CROP YIELD

CROP ROTATION
ASSOLEMENT / ROTACION DE CULTIVOS - 07.05.04
  BT: CULTIVATION SYSTEMS
  RT: SHIFTING CULTIVATION

CROP YIELD
RENDEMENT DES CULTURES / RENDIMIENTO DE LA
COSECHA - 07.05.01
  RT: CROP PROSPECTS
      HARVESTING
      PLANT PRODUCTION

CROPPING SYSTEMS
- 07.05.04
  USE: CULTIVATION SYSTEMS

CROPS
CULTURES DE PLEIN CHAMP / CULTIVOS - 07.05.04

CROPS<CONT>
  NT: FOOD CROPS
      FORAGE CROPS
      INDUSTRIAL CROPS

CROSS CULTURAL ANALYSIS
ANALYSE TRANSCULTURELLE / ANALISIS TRANSCULTURAL
- 05.01.02
  UF: INTERCULTURAL RESEARCH
  BT: COMPARATIVE ANALYSIS
  RT: CULTURE

CRUSTACEA
CRUSTACES / CRUSTACEOS - 07.10.04
  BT: SHELLFISH
  NT: SHRIMPS

CSTD
CSTD / CCTD - 01.03.02
SN: COMMITTEE ON SCIENCE AND TECHNOLOGY FOR
DEVELOPMENT.
  BT: ECOSOC
  RT: SCIENCE
      TECHNOLOGY

CUBA
CUBA / CUBA - 01.04.03
  BT: CARIBBEAN
      LATIN AMERICA
  RT: CUBAN

CUBAN
CUBAIN / CUBANO - 14.03.02
  RT: CUBA

CULTIVATED LAND
TERRE CULTIVEE / TIERRA CULTIVADA - 07.05.02
  RT: ARABLE LAND

CULTIVATION PRACTICES
PRATIQUES CULTURALES / PRACTICAS DE CULTIVO -
07.05.04
  NT: PLANTING
      SOWING
  RT: CULTIVATION SYSTEMS
      SOIL MANAGEMENT
      WEED CONTROL

CULTIVATION SYSTEMS
SYSTEMES DE CULTURE / SISTEMAS DE CULTIVO -
07.05.04
  UF: CROPPING SYSTEMS
  BT: FARMING SYSTEMS
  NT: CROP DIVERSIFICATION
      CROP ROTATION
      INTERCROPPING
      MULTIPLE CROPPING
      SHIFTING CULTIVATION
  RT: CULTIVATION PRACTICES

CULTURAL AGREEMENTS
ACCORDS CULTURELS / ACUERDOS CULTURALES -
05.02.03
  BT: INTERNATIONAL AGREEMENTS

CULTURAL AGREEMENTS<CONT>
- RT: CULTURAL COOPERATION
  - CULTURE

CULTURAL ANIMATION
ANIMATION CULTURELLE / ANIMACION CULTURAL -
05.02.03
- RT: CULTURAL POLICY
  - CULTURE

CULTURAL CHANGE
CHANGEMENT CULTUREL / CAMBIO CULTURAL - 05.02.02
- RT: CULTURAL INTEGRATION
  - CULTURE
  - MODERNIZATION
  - SOCIAL CHANGE

CULTURAL COOPERATION
COOPERATION CULTURELLE / COOPERACION CULTURAL -
05.02.03
- BT: INTERNATIONAL COOPERATION
- RT: CULTURAL AGREEMENTS
  - CULTURE

CULTURAL DEVELOPMENT
DEVELOPPEMENT CULTUREL / DESARROLLO CULTURAL -
05.02.03
- BT: ECONOMIC AND SOCIAL DEVELOPMENT
- RT: CULTURAL POLICY
  - CULTURE

CULTURAL ENVIRONMENT
MILIEU CULTUREL / MEDIO CULTURAL - 05.02.02
- BT: HUMAN ENVIRONMENT
- RT: CULTURE

CULTURAL EXPENDITURES
DEPENSES CULTURELLES / GASTOS CULTURALES -
05.02.03
- BT: EXPENDITURES
- RT: CULTURE
  - ECONOMICS OF EDUCATION
  - PUBLIC EXPENDITURES

CULTURAL FACTORS
FACTEURS CULTURELS / FACTORES CULTURALES -
05.02.02
- RT: CULTURE

CULTURAL GEOGRAPHY
GEOGRAPHIE CULTURELLE / GEOGRAFIA CULTURAL -
17.03.01
- BT: HUMAN GEOGRAPHY

CULTURAL HERITAGE
PATRIMOINE CULTUREL / PATRIMONIO CULTURAL -
05.02.02
SN: CULTURAL RESOURCES OF A GIVEN COUNTRY.
- RT: CONSERVATION OF CULTURAL HERITAGE
  - CULTURE
  - WORKS OF ART

CULTURAL IDENTITY
IDENTITE CULTURELLE / IDENTIDAD CULTURAL -

CULTURAL IDENTITY<CONT>
05.02.02
- RT: CULTURE

CULTURAL INDUSTRY
INDUSTRIE CULTURELLE / INDUSTRIA CULTURAL -
05.02.03
- RT: CULTURE
  - MASS MEDIA

CULTURAL INFORMATION
INFORMATION CULTURELLE / INFORMACION CULTURAL -
05.02.03
- BT: INFORMATION
- RT: CULTURE

CULTURAL INTEGRATION
INTEGRATION CULTURELLE / INTEGRACION CULTURAL -
05.02.02
- RT: ACCULTURATION
  - CONSERVATION OF CULTURAL HERITAGE
  - CULTURAL CHANGE
  - CULTURAL RELATIONS
  - CULTURE

CULTURAL PLURALISM
PLURALISME CULTUREL / PLURALISMO CULTURAL -
05.02.01
- RT: CULTURE

CULTURAL POLICY
POLITIQUE CULTURELLE / POLITICA CULTURAL -
05.02.03
- BT: GOVERNMENT POLICY
- RT: CULTURAL ANIMATION
  - CULTURAL DEVELOPMENT
  - CULTURE

CULTURAL RELATIONS
RELATIONS CULTURELLES / RELACIONES CULTURALES -
05.02.02
- RT: ACCULTURATION
  - CULTURAL INTEGRATION
  - CULTURE

CULTURE
CULTURE / CULTURA - 05.02.01
- NT: FOLK CULTURE
  - SCIENTIFIC CULTURE
  - SUBCULTURE
  - TRADITIONAL CULTURE

CULTURE<CONT>
　　　RT: ACCESS TO CULTURE
　　　　　ACCULTURATION
　　　　　ALECSO
　　　　　ART
　　　　　CIVILIZATION
　　　　　CROSS CULTURAL ANALYSIS
　　　　　CULTURAL AGREEMENTS
　　　　　CULTURAL ANIMATION
　　　　　CULTURAL CHANGE
　　　　　CULTURAL COOPERATION
　　　　　CULTURAL DEVELOPMENT
　　　　　CULTURAL ENVIRONMENT
　　　　　CULTURAL EXPENDITURES
　　　　　CULTURAL FACTORS
　　　　　CULTURAL HERITAGE
　　　　　CULTURAL IDENTITY
　　　　　CULTURAL INDUSTRY
　　　　　CULTURAL INFORMATION
　　　　　CULTURAL INTEGRATION
　　　　　CULTURAL PLURALISM
　　　　　CULTURAL POLICY
　　　　　CULTURAL RELATIONS
　　　　　DISSEMINATION OF CULTURE
　　　　　ECONOMICS OF CULTURE
　　　　　FOLKLORE
　　　　　RIGHT TO CULTURE
　　　　　SOCIO-CULTURAL FACILITIES
　　　　　UNESCO

CURRENCIES
MONNAIES / MONEDAS - 11.02.01
　　　UF: MONEY
　　　NT: EURODOLLARS
　　　　　LOCAL CURRENCY
　　　　　NON-CONVERTIBLE CURRENCIES
　　　　　PETRODOLLARS
　　　RT: CONVERTIBILITY
　　　　　DEVALUATION
　　　　　FOREIGN EXCHANGE
　　　　　LIQUIDITY
　　　　　MONETARY AGREEMENTS
　　　　　MONETARY AREAS
　　　　　MONETARY CIRCULATION
　　　　　MONETARY CORRECTION
　　　　　MONETARY POLICY
　　　　　MONETARY RELATIONS
　　　　　MONETARY TRANSFERS
　　　　　MONETARY UNIONS
　　　　　MONEY MARKET
　　　　　MONEY SUPPLY

CURRICULUM
PROGRAMME D'ETUDES / PROGRAMA DE ESTUDIOS -
06.05.01
SN: USE TO MEAN THE SUBJECTS TAUGHT AND THE TIME
　　ALLOTTED TO EACH DURING REGULAR COURSES OF
　　STUDY AT AN EDUCATIONAL INSTITUTION.
　　　NT: COURSES
　　　　　INTEGRATED CURRICULUM

CURRICULUM<CONT>
　　　RT: CURRICULUM DEVELOPMENT
　　　　　CURRICULUM SUBJECTS
　　　　　EDUCATION
　　　　　EDUCATIONAL SYSTEMS
　　　　　TEACHING
　　　　　TEACHING PROGRAMMES
　　　　　TRAINING PROGRAMMES

CURRICULUM DEVELOPMENT
ELABORATION DE PROGRAMMES D'ETUDES / DESARROLLO
DE PROGRAMAS DE ESTUDIOS - 06.05.01
　　　RT: CURRICULUM

CURRICULUM SUBJECTS
MATIERES D'ENSEIGNEMENT / MATERIAS DE ENSENANZA
- 06.05.01
　　　RT: CURRICULUM
　　　　　TEACHING

CURRICULUM VITAE
CURRICULUM VITAE / CURRICULUM VITAE - 19.02.02

CUSTOMARY LAW
DROIT COUTUMIER / DERECHO CONSUETUDINARIO -
04.01.02
　　　BT: LAW
　　　RT: TRADITION

CUSTOMS
DOUANE / ADUANA - 09.05.08
　　　RT: TARIFFS

CUSTOMS POLICY
- 09.05.08
　　　USE: TARIFF POLICY

CUSTOMS UNION
UNION DOUANIERE / UNION ADUANERA - 09.05.08
　　　NT: BENELUX
　　　　　CACEU
　　　RT: COMMON MARKET
　　　　　FREE TRADE AREA
　　　　　TARIFFS

CYBERNETICS
CYBERNETIQUE / CIBERNETICA - 18.08.00
　　　UF: SYSTEMS THEORY
　　　NT: SYSTEMS ANALYSIS
　　　　　SYSTEMS DESIGN
　　　RT: COMMUNICATION
　　　　　INFORMATION THEORY

CYCLICAL UNEMPLOYMENT
CHOMAGE CYCLIQUE / DESEMPLEO CICLICO - 13.01.03
SN: PERIODICAL EMPLOYMENT WHICH OCCURS IN
　　REGULAR PHASES, SUCH AS FRUIT PICKING, AND
　　WITH REGULAR EMPLOYMENT VARIATIONS IN THE
　　BUSINESS CYCLE.
　　　BT: UNEMPLOYMENT
　　　NT: SEASONAL UNEMPLOYMENT

CYCLONES
- 17.01.03
　　　USE: STORMS

46

CYPRIOT
CHYPRIOTE / CHIPRIOTA - 14.03.02
    RT: CYPRUS

CYPRUS
CHYPRE / CHIPRE - 01.04.06
    BT: MEDITERRANEAN COUNTRIES
         MIDDLE EAST
         WESTERN EUROPE
    RT: CYPRIOT

CYTOLOGY
CYTOLOGIE / CITOLOGIA - 15.02.01
    BT: HISTOLOGY
    RT: CELLS

CZECHOSLOVAK
TCHECOSLOVAQUE / CHECOSLOVACO - 14.03.02
    RT: CZECHOSLOVAKIA

CZECHOSLOVAKIA
TCHECOSLOVAQUIE / CHECOSLOVAQUIA - 01.04.05
    BT: EASTERN EUROPE
    RT: CZECHOSLOVAK

DAILY
QUOTIDIEN / DIARIO - 19.02.06
    BT: PERIODICALS

DAIRY INDUSTRY
INDUSTRIE LAITIERE / INDUSTRIA LECHERA -
08.06.01
    UF: DAIRY PRODUCTS INDUSTRY
    BT: FOOD INDUSTRY
    RT: DAIRY PRODUCTS
         MILK PROCESSING

DAIRY PRODUCTS
PRODUITS LAITIERS / PRODUCTOS LACTEOS - 07.09.05
    UF: MILK PRODUCTS
    BT: ANIMAL PRODUCTS
         FOOD
    NT: BUTTER
         CHEESE
         MILK
    RT: DAIRY INDUSTRY

DAIRY PRODUCTS INDUSTRY
- 08.06.01
    USE: **DAIRY INDUSTRY**

DAMAGE
DEGATS / DANOS - 16.03.01
    RT: ACCIDENTS
         DAMAGE COMPENSATION
         DEVASTATION
         DISASTERS

DAMAGE COMPENSATION
DEDOMMAGEMENT / INDEMNIZACION - 16.04.01
    RT: DAMAGE
         POLLUTER-PAYS PRINCIPLE

DAMS
BARRAGES / PRESAS - 17.05.04
    RT: ARTIFICIAL LAKES
         HYDROELECTRIC POWER

DANCE
DANSE / DANZA - 05.05.03
    BT: DRAMATIC ART

DANGEROUS SUBSTANCES
SUBSTANCES DANGEREUSES / SUBSTANCIAS PELIGROSAS
- 16.03.04
    UF: HARMFUL SUBSTANCES
    NT: RADIOACTIVE MATERIALS
         TOXIC SUBSTANCES
    RT: POLLUTANTS

DANISH
DANOIS / DANES - 14.03.02
    RT: DENMARK

DATA ACQUISITION
- 18.04.00
    USE: **DATA COLLECTING**

DATA ANALYSIS
ANALYSE DES DONNEES / ANALISIS DE DATOS -

DATA ANALYSIS<CONT>
19.01.02
    BT: DATA PROCESSING
    RT: CONTENT ANALYSIS
        INFORMATION ANALYSIS

DATA BANKS
BANQUES DE DONNEES / BANCOS DE DATOS - 19.01.03
SN: COLLECTION OF RELATED FILES, AVAILABLE UNDER
*   A MULTIPLICITY OF ASPECTS THROUGH COMPUTERS.*
    BT: INFORMATION SERVICES
    RT: DATA PROCESSING
        STATISTICAL DATA

DATA BASES
BASES DE DONNEES / BASES DE DATOS - 19.01.03
SN: COLLECTIONS OF DATA CONSISTING OF AT LEAST
*   ONE FILE SUFFICIENT FOR A GIVEN PURPOSE.*
    BT: INFORMATION SERVICES

DATA COLLECTING
RASSEMBLEMENT DES DONNEES / RECOPILACION DE
DATOS - 18.04.00
    UF: DATA ACQUISITION
        DATA COMPILATION
    BT: RESEARCH METHODS
    NT: CENSUSES
        SURVEYS
    RT: OBSERVATION

DATA COMPILATION
- 18.04.00
    USE: DATA COLLECTING

DATA PROCESSING
TRAITEMENT DES DONNEES / PROCESAMIENTO DE DATOS
- 19.01.02
    BT: INFORMATION PROCESSING
    NT: DATA ANALYSIS
        DATA RETRIEVAL
        DATA STORAGE
        ELECTRONIC DATA PROCESSING
    RT: DATA BANKS
        DATA TRANSMISSION

DATA PROTECTION
PROTECTION DES DONNEES / PROTECCION DE LOS DATOS
- 19.01.01
    RT: ACCESS TO INFORMATION
        INFORMATION POLICY
        PRIVACY PROTECTION

DATA RECORDING
ENREGISTREMENT DES DONNEES / REGISTRO DE DATOS -
19.01.02
    BT: INFORMATION RECORDING
    RT: DATA STORAGE

DATA RETRIEVAL
RAPPEL DES DONNEES / RECUPERACION DE DATOS -
19.01.02
    BT: DATA PROCESSING

DATA STORAGE
EMMAGASINAGE DES DONNEES / ALMACENAMIENTO DE
DATOS - 19.01.02
    BT: DATA PROCESSING
    RT: DATA RECORDING
        INFORMATION RECORDING

DATA TRANSMISSION
TRANSMISSION DES DONNEES / TRANSMISION DE DATOS
- 19.01.02
SN: THE MOVEMENT OF MACHINE-READABLE DATA OVER A
*   DISTANCE.*
    BT: INFORMATION EXCHANGE
    RT: DATA PROCESSING

DATE PALMS
PALMIERS DATIERS / PALMERAS DATILERAS - 07.07.05
    BT: FRUIT TREES
    RT: DATES

DATES
DATTES / DATILES - 07.07.05
    BT: FRUITS
    RT: DATE PALMS

DAY CARE CENTRES
CRECHES / GUARDERIAS - 06.04.02

DE-SCHOOLING
DESCOLARISATION / DESESCOLARIZACION - 06.03.02
    RT: EDUCATIONAL SYSTEMS

DEAF-DUMBNESS
SURDI-MUTITE / SORDOMUDEZ - 15.04.03
    NT: DEAFNESS

DEAFNESS
SURDITE / SORDERA - 15.04.03
    BT: DEAF-DUMBNESS

DEALERS
NEGOCIANTS / COMERCIANTES - 13.09.07
    UF: TRADERS
    RT: COMMERCIAL ENTERPRISES

DEATH
MORT / MUERTE - 14.06.00
    RT: CAUSES OF DEATH
        MORTALITY

DEBENTURES
OBLIGATIONS / OBLIGACIONES - 11.02.07
    UF: BONDS
    BT: SECURITIES

DEBT
DETTE / DEUDA - 11.02.02
    NT: EXTERNAL DEBT
        PUBLIC DEBT

DEBT<CONT>
   RT: BORROWING
       CREDIT
       DEBT CONSOLIDATION
       DEBT RELIEF
       DEBT REPAYMENT
       INDEBTEDNESS
       LOANS

DEBT BURDEN
- 11.02.02
   USE: INDEBTEDNESS

DEBT CONSOLIDATION
CONSOLIDATION DE LA DETTE / CONSOLIDACION DE LA
DEUDA - 11.02.02
   RT: DEBT

DEBT RELIEF
ALLEGEMENT DE LA DETTE / REBAJA DE LA DEUDA -
11.02.02
   RT: DEBT

DEBT REPAYMENT
REMBOURSEMENT / REEMBOLSO - 11.02.02
   RT: DEBT

DECENTRALIZATION
DECENTRALISATION / DESCENTRALIZACION - 04.03.03
   RT: CENTRALIZATION

DECISION MAKING
PRISE DE DECISION / TOMA DE DECISIONES -
12.04.00
   RT: COST-BENEFIT ANALYSIS
       MANAGEMENT TECHNIQUES

DECOLONIZATION
DECOLONISATION / DESCOLONIZACION - 01.02.03
   RT: COLONIAL COUNTRIES
       COLONIALISM
       INDEPENDENCE
       NEOCOLONIALISM

DECONTAMINATION
DECONTAMINATION / DESCONTAMINACION - 16.04.01
   BT: POLLUTION CONTROL

DECORATIVE ARTS
- 05.05.03
   USE: FINE ARTS

DEEP SEA FISHING
PECHE EN HAUTE MER / PESCA EN ALTA MAR -
07.10.03
   BT: MARINE FISHING

DEEP SEA MINING
EXPLOITATION DES FONDS MARINS / EXPLOTACION DE
LOS FONDOS MARINOS - 08.13.00
   BT: MINING
   RT: SEA
       SEABED

DEFENCE
DEFENSE / DEFENSA - 01.02.06
   RT: DEFENCE POLICY

DEFENCE POLICY
POLITIQUE DE DEFENSE / POLITICA DE DEFENSA -
01.02.06
   RT: DEFENCE
       FOREIGN POLICY

DEFICIENCY DISEASES
MALADIES DE CARENCE / ENFERMEDADES POR CARENCIA
- 15.04.02
   RT: MALNUTRITION
       PROTEIN DEFICIENCY
       VITAMIN DEFICIENCY

DEFICIT
DEFICIT / DEFICIT - 11.02.05
   RT: BANKRUPTCY
       DEFICIT FINANCING
       FINANCIAL LOSS

DEFICIT FINANCING
FINANCEMENT DU DEFICIT / FINANCIACION DEL
DEFICIT - 11.02.05
   BT: FINANCING
   NT: COMPENSATORY FINANCING
   RT: DEFICIT

DEFLATION
DEFLATION / DEFLACION - 11.02.01
   RT: INFLATION

DEFORESTATION
DEBOISEMENT / DEFORESTACION - 07.08.03
   RT: DEFORESTED LAND

DEFORESTED LAND
TERRE DEBOISEE / TIERRA DEFORESTADA - 07.08.03
   RT: DEFORESTATION

DEHYDRATED FOOD
ALIMENTS DESHYDRATES / ALIMENTOS DESHIDRATADOS -
08.06.03
   BT: FOOD
   RT: DEHYDRATION
       FOOD PRESERVATION

DEHYDRATION
DESHYDRATATION / DESHIDRATACION - 08.12.03
   RT: DEHYDRATED FOOD
       DRIED FOOD

DELINQUENCY
DELINQUANCE / DELINCUENCIA - 02.04.02
   BT: SOCIAL PROBLEMS
   NT: JUVENILE DELINQUENCY
   RT: CRIME PREVENTION
       CRIMES
       CRIMINAL LAW
       CRIMINOLOGY
       OFFENDERS
       PENAL SANCTIONS

DELIVERY
LIVRAISON / ENTREGA - 10.06.00

DELTAS
DELTAS / DELTAS - 17.03.04

DEMAND
DEMANDE / DEMANDA - 09.01.01
    BT: SUPPLY AND DEMAND
    NT: BASIC NEEDS
        CONSUMER DEMAND
        FINANCIAL NEEDS
        MANPOWER NEEDS
        POWER DEMAND

DEMOCRACY
DEMOCRATIE / DEMOCRACIA - 04.02.02
    BT: POLITICAL SYSTEMS
    RT: DEMOCRATIZATION
        ELECTIONS

DEMOCRATIZATION
DEMOCRATISATION / DEMOCRATIZACION - 04.02.02
    NT: DEMOCRATIZATION OF EDUCATION
    RT: CIVIL LIBERTIES
        DEMOCRACY

DEMOCRATIZATION OF EDUCATION
DEMOCRATISATION DE L'ENSEIGNEMENT /
DEMOCRATIZACION DE LA EDUCACION - 06.02.02
    BT: DEMOCRATIZATION

DEMOGRAPHERS
DEMOGRAPHES / DEMOGRAFOS - 13.09.09
    BT: SCIENTISTS
    RT: DEMOGRAPHY

DEMOGRAPHIC ANALYSIS
ANALYSE DEMOGRAPHIQUE / ANALISIS DEMOGRAFICO -
14.01.01
    RT: DEMOGRAPHY

DEMOGRAPHY
DEMOGRAPHIE / DEMOGRAFIA - 14.01.01
    BT: SOCIAL SCIENCES
    RT: DEMOGRAPHERS
        DEMOGRAPHIC ANALYSIS
        IUSSP
        POPULATION

DEMOTION
RETROGRADATION / DESCENSO - 13.02.02
    SN: THE SHIFTING OF EMPLOYEES DOWNWARD TO
      POSITIONS WHICH REQUIRE A LESSER DEGREE OF
      EXPERIENCE AND SKILL AND ARE LIKELY TO
      COMMAND A LOWER WAGE OR SALARY.
    RT: PERSONNEL MANAGEMENT

DENATIONALIZATION
DENATIONALISATION / DESNACIONALIZACION -
03.03.05
    RT: NATIONALIZATION
        PUBLIC ENTERPRISES
        PUBLIC OWNERSHIP

DENMARK
DANEMARK / DINAMARCA - 01.04.05
    BT: SCANDINAVIA
    RT: DANISH
        FAROE ISLANDS
        GREENLAND

DENSITY
DENSITE / DENSIDAD - 18.06.00
    RT: WEIGHT

DENTISTS
DENTISTES / ODONTOLOGOS - 13.09.10
    BT: MEDICAL PERSONNEL

DEPENDENCE
DEPENDANCE / DEPENDENCIA - 01.02.03
    SN: SITUATION IN WHICH A COUNTRY'S ECONOMY IS
      SUBORDINATED TO THE DEVELOPMENT OF ANOTHER
      COUNTRY'S ECONOMY.
    RT: IMPERIALISM
        INDEPENDENCE
        SELF-RELIANCE

DEPENDENCY BURDEN
CHARGES DE FAMILLE / CARGA FAMILIAR - 14.02.04
    RT: FAMILY

DESALINIZATION
DESALINISATION / DESALINIZACION - 17.05.05
    BT: WATER TREATMENT
    RT: SALT
        SALT WATER

DESEGREGATION
DESEGREGATION / DESEGREGACION - 04.02.04
    BT: RACE RELATIONS
    RT: RACIAL POLICY
        RACIAL SEGREGATION

DESERT
- 17.02.03
    USE: ARID ZONE

DESERTIFICATION
DESERTIFICATION / DESERTIFICACION - 16.03.04
    BT: ENVIRONMENTAL DEGRADATION
    RT: ARID ZONE

DETECTION
- 18.04.00
    USE: OBSERVATION

DETENTE
DETENTE / DISTENSION - 01.02.07
    SN: RELAXING OF TENSIONS BETWEEN POWERS.
    RT: INTERNATIONAL RELATIONS
        PEACEFUL COEXISTENCE

DETERGENTS
DETERGENTS / DETERGENTES - 08.12.08
    BT: CLEANING AGENTS

DEVALUATION
DEVALUATION / DEVALUACION - 11.02.01
    BT: MONETARY POLICY

DEVALUATION<CONT>
>> *RT:* BALANCE OF PAYMENTS
>> CURRENCIES

DEVASTATION
DEVASTATION / DEVASTACION - 16.03.01
>> *RT:* DAMAGE

DEVELOPED COUNTRIES
PAYS DEVELOPPES / PAISES DESARROLLADOS -
03.02.03
>> *UF:* INDUSTRIALIZED COUNTRIES
>> *RT:* OECD

DEVELOPING AREAS
ZONES DE DEVELOPPEMENT / ZONAS EN DESARROLLO -
03.02.03
SN: WITHIN A COUNTRY.
>> *UF:* UNDERDEVELOPED AREAS
>> *RT:* REGIONAL DISPARITY

DEVELOPING COUNTRIES
PAYS EN DEVELOPPEMENT / PAISES EN DESARROLLO -
03.02.03
>> *NT:* LEAST DEVELOPED COUNTRIES

DEVELOPMENT ADMINISTRATION
ADMINISTRATION DU DEVELOPPEMENT / ADMINISTRACION
DEL DESARROLLO - 04.03.02
*SN: PUBLIC ADMINISTRATION DESIGNED TO FOSTER
ECONOMIC AND SOCIAL DEVELOPMENT.*
>> *BT:* PUBLIC ADMINISTRATION
>> *RT:* ACDA
>> CAFRAD
>> DEVELOPMENT PLANNING
>> ECONOMIC AND SOCIAL DEVELOPMENT

DEVELOPMENT AID
AIDE AU DEVELOPPEMENT / AYUDA AL DESARROLLO -
01.01.01
>> *BT:* INTERNATIONAL COOPERATION
>> *NT:* AID IN KIND
>> BILATERAL AID
>> ECONOMIC AID
>> FINANCIAL AID
>> FOOD AID
>> HEALTH AID
>> MULTILATERAL AID
>> PRIVATE AID
>> TECHNICAL ASSISTANCE
>> TRAINING ASSISTANCE
>> *RT:* ABSORPTIVE CAPACITY
>> AID COORDINATION
>> AID EVALUATION
>> AID FINANCING
>> AID INSTITUTIONS
>> AID PROGRAMMES
>> DEVELOPMENT CENTRES
>> DEVELOPMENT PERSONNEL
>> DEVELOPMENT POLICY
>> DEVELOPMENT PROJECTS
>> ECONOMIC AND SOCIAL DEVELOPMENT
>> OECD DAC
>> TERMS OF AID

DEVELOPMENT BANKS
BANQUES DE DEVELOPPEMENT / BANCOS DE DESARROLLO
- 11.02.02
>> *BT:* BANKS
>> *NT:* AFRICAN DEVELOPMENT BANK
>> ASIAN DEVELOPMENT BANK
>> CABEI
>> IBRD
>> IDB
>> *RT:* AGRICULTURAL BANKS
>> AID FINANCING
>> INDUSTRIAL BANKS

DEVELOPMENT CENTRES
CENTRES DE DEVELOPPEMENT / CENTROS DE DESARROLLO
- 01.01.07
>> *NT:* ADC
>> IDCAS
>> IDRC
>> OECD DC
>> *RT:* DEVELOPMENT AID

DEVELOPMENT PERSONNEL
PERSONNEL AFFECTE AU DEVELOPPEMENT / PERSONAL
ADSCRITO AL DESARROLLO - 01.01.07
>> *NT:* CONSULTANTS
>> EXPERTS
>> *RT:* COUNTERPART PERSONNEL
>> DEVELOPMENT AID

DEVELOPMENT PLANNING
PLANIFICATION DU DEVELOPPEMENT / PLANIFICACION
DEL DESARROLLO - 02.01.02
>> *BT:* PLANNING
>> *RT:* CDP
>> DEVELOPMENT ADMINISTRATION
>> ECONOMIC AND SOCIAL DEVELOPMENT
>> SCENARIOS

DEVELOPMENT PLANS
PLANS DE DEVELOPPEMENT / PLANES DE DESARROLLO -
02.01.02
>> *NT:* NATIONAL PLANS
>> REGIONAL PLANS
>> *RT:* DEVELOPMENT POLICY
>> DEVELOPMENT PROJECTS
>> ECONOMIC AND SOCIAL DEVELOPMENT
>> PLAN IMPLEMENTATION

DEVELOPMENT POLICY
POLITIQUE DE DEVELOPPEMENT / POLITICA DE
DESARROLLO - 02.01.01
*SN: USE MORE SPECIFIC DESCRIPTORS SUCH AS
'CULTURAL POLICY', 'ECONOMIC POLICY', ETC.,
IF APPLICABLE.*
>> *BT:* GOVERNMENT POLICY
>> *RT:* BASIC NEEDS
>> DEVELOPMENT AID
>> DEVELOPMENT PLANS
>> DEVELOPMENT STRATEGY
>> ECONOMIC AND SOCIAL DEVELOPMENT
>> SCENARIOS
>> SELF-RELIANCE

DEVELOPMENT POTENTIAL
POTENTIEL DE DEVELOPPEMENT / POTENCIAL DE
DESARROLLO - 02.01.01
SN: OF A REGION, A COUNTRY, OR AN ECONOMIC
    SECTOR.
    NT: INDUSTRIAL POTENTIAL
    RT: AGRICULTURAL POTENTIAL
        ECONOMIC AND SOCIAL DEVELOPMENT
        ECONOMIC INFRASTRUCTURE

DEVELOPMENT PROJECTS
PROJETS DE DEVELOPPEMENT / PROYECTOS DE
DESARROLLO - 01.01.06
SN: USE MORE SPECIFIC DESCRIPTOR, IF APPLICABLE,
    AND INDICATE IF U.N. ASSISTANCE IS INVOLVED.
    NT: AGRICULTURAL PROJECTS
        INDUSTRIAL PROJECTS
        JOINT PROJECTS
        MULTIPURPOSE PROJECTS
        PILOT PROJECTS
    RT: DEVELOPMENT AID
        DEVELOPMENT PLANS
        ECONOMIC AND SOCIAL DEVELOPMENT
        PROJECT APPRAISAL
        PROJECT DESIGN
        PROJECT EVALUATION
        PROJECT IMPLEMENTATION
        PROJECT MANAGEMENT
        PROJECT REPORT
        PROJECT REQUEST
        PROJECT SELECTION

DEVELOPMENT RESEARCH
RECHERCHE SUR LE DEVELOPPEMENT / INVESTIGACION
SOBRE EL DESARROLLO - 02.01.01
    BT: RESEARCH
    RT: ADIPA
        DEVELOPMENT THEORY
        EADI
        ECONOMIC AND SOCIAL DEVELOPMENT

DEVELOPMENT STRATEGY
STRATEGIE DE DEVELOPPEMENT / ESTRATEGIA DEL
DESARROLLO - 02.01.01
    RT: DEVELOPMENT POLICY
        DEVELOPMENT STYLES
        SCENARIOS
        STRATEGIC PLANNING

DEVELOPMENT STYLES
TYPES DE DEVELOPPEMENT / ESTILOS DE DESARROLLO -
02.01.01
    RT: DEVELOPMENT STRATEGY
        DEVELOPMENT THEORY

DEVELOPMENT THEORY
THEORIE DU DEVELOPPEMENT / TEORIA DEL DESARROLLO
- 02.01.01
    BT: THEORY
    RT: DEVELOPMENT RESEARCH
        DEVELOPMENT STYLES

DEVSIS
DEVSIS / DEVSIS - 19.01.02
SN: DEVELOPMENT SCIENCE INFORMATION SYSTEM.
    BT: INFORMATION SYSTEMS
    RT: ECONOMIC AND SOCIAL DEVELOPMENT

DIABETES
DIABETE / DIABETES - 15.04.02

DIAGNOSIS
DIAGNOSTIC / DIAGNOSTICO - 15.04.04

DIAGRAMS
DIAGRAMMES / DIAGRAMAS - 18.08.00
    BT: AUDIOVISUAL MATERIALS
        ILLUSTRATIONS

DIALECTS
DIALECTES / DIALECTOS - 05.06.01
    RT: LANGUAGES
        VERNACULAR LANGUAGES

DIAMOND
DIAMANT / DIAMANTE - 08.13.00
    BT: PRECIOUS STONES

DICTATORSHIP
DICTATURE / DICTADURA - 04.03.01
    BT: POLITICAL SYSTEMS

DICTIONARY
DICTIONNAIRE / DICCIONARIO - 19.03.00
    BT: PRIMARY DOCUMENTS
        REFERENCE MATERIALS
    RT: TERMINOLOGY

DIES AND JIGS
MATRICES ET GABARITS / MOLDES Y MATRICES -
08.14.05

DIESEL ENGINES
MOTEURS DIESEL / MOTORES DIESEL - 08.14.06
    BT: ENGINES

DIET
REGIME ALIMENTAIRE / REGIMEN ALIMENTARIO -
15.03.02

DIFFUSION OF INNOVATIONS
DIFFUSION DES INNOVATIONS / DIFUSION DE
INNOVACIONES - 12.06.00
    RT: INNOVATIONS

DIGESTIVE SYSTEM
SYSTEME DIGESTIF / SISTEMA DIGESTIVO - 15.02.04
    BT: ANATOMY
    NT: LIVER

DIPHTHERIA
DIPHTERIE / DIFTERIA - 15.04.02
    BT: INFECTIOUS DISEASES

DIPLOMACY
DIPLOMATIE / DIPLOMACIA - 01.02.05
    RT: FOREIGN SERVICE

DIPLOMAS
DIPLOMES / DIPLOMAS - 06.04.13
    BT: QUALIFICATIONS

DIPLOMAS<CONT>
> *RT:* EQUIVALENCE BETWEEN DIPLOMAS
>   GRADUATES
>   UNDERGRADUATES

DIRECTIVE PLANNING
**PLANIFICATION DIRECTIVE / PLANIFICACION
DIRECTIVA - 02.01.02**
> *UF:* NORMATIVE PLANNING
> *BT:* PLANNING SYSTEMS

DIRECTORY
REPERTOIRE / DIRECTORIO - 19.02.07
> *BT:* REFERENCE MATERIALS

DISABILITY
INVALIDITE / INCAPACIDAD - 15.04.03
*SN: TEMPORARY OR PERMANENT INCAPACITY FOR WORK
RESULTING FROM A PATHOLOGICAL CONDITION.*
> *RT:* DISABILITY BENEFITS
>   DISABLED CARE
>   PHYSICALLY HANDICAPPED

DISABILITY BENEFITS
**ALLOCATIONS D'INVALIDITE / SUBSIDIOS DE
INVALIDEZ - 02.03.02**
> *BT:* SOCIAL SECURITY
> *RT:* DISABILITY

DISABLED CARE
**SOIN AUX INVALIDES / CUIDADO A LOS INVALIDOS -
02.05.03**
> *BT:* SOCIAL SERVICES
> *RT:* DISABILITY

DISARMAMENT
DESARMEMENT / DESARME - 01.02.06
> *UF:* ARMS LIMITATION

DISASTERS
DESASTRES / DESASTRES - 16.03.01
> *NT:* FIRES
>   MANMADE DISASTERS
>   NATURAL DISASTERS
> *RT:* DAMAGE
>   EMERGENCY RELIEF

DISCHARGE
- 13.05.00
> *USE:* DISMISSAL

DISCOUNT
ESCOMPTE / DESCUENTO - 11.02.07
> *RT:* BANK RATE

DISCRIMINATION
DISCRIMINATION / DISCRIMINACION - 04.02.03
> *NT:* ECONOMIC DISCRIMINATION
>   RACIAL DISCRIMINATION
>   RACISM

DISEASE CONTROL
**LUTTE ANTI-MALADIE / LUCHA CONTRA LAS
ENFERMEDADES - 15.04.04**

DISEASE CONTROL<CONT>
> *RT:* DISEASES
>   MEDICINE

DISEASE TRANSMISSION
**TRANSMISSION DE MALADIE / TRANSMISION DE
ENFERMEDADES - 15.04.04**
> *RT:* DISEASE VECTORS
>   INFECTIOUS DISEASES

DISEASE VECTORS
**VECTEURS DE MALADIES / VECTORES DE ENFERMEDADES
- 15.04.04**
> *RT:* DISEASE TRANSMISSION
>   INFECTIOUS DISEASES

DISEASES
MALADIES / ENFERMEDADES - 15.04.01
> *UF:* PATHOLOGY
> *NT:* ANIMAL DISEASES
>   CHRONIC DISEASES
>   ENDEMIC DISEASES
>   EYE DISEASES
>   IMMUNOLOGIC DISEASES
>   INFECTIOUS DISEASES
>   INTRACTABLE DISEASES
>   MENTAL DISEASES
>   MOUTH DISEASES
>   OCCUPATIONAL DISEASES
>   PLANT DISEASES
>   POISONING
>   WOUNDS AND INJURIES
> *RT:* CAUSES OF DEATH
>   DISEASE CONTROL
>   HEALTH
>   MEDICINE
>   MORBIDITY
>   PATIENTS
>   PHYSICALLY HANDICAPPED
>   SOCIAL PROBLEMS

DISGUISED UNEMPLOYMENT
**CHOMAGE DEGUISE / DESEMPLEO ENCUBIERTO -
13.01.03**
*SN: REFERS TO THE LABOUR FORCE NOT REPORTED AS
UNEMPLOYED BECAUSE IT IS NOT ACTIVELY
SEEKING WORK FOR ONE REASON OR ANOTHER.*
> *BT:* UNEMPLOYMENT

DISMISSAL
LICENCIEMENT / DESPIDO - 13.05.00
*SN: THE TERMINATION OF EMPLOYMENT WHEN IT IS
INITIATED BY THE EMPLOYER.*
> *UF:* DISCHARGE
> *RT:* LABOUR REDUNDANCY
>   PERSONNEL MANAGEMENT
>   RESIGNATION
>   SEVERANCE PAY

DISPERSED HABITAT
HABITAT DISPERSE / HABITAT DISPERSO - 14.04.01
> *BT:* HABITAT

DISPLACEMENT
- 13.05.00
> *USE:* LABOUR MOBILITY

DISPUTE SETTLEMENT
REGLEMENT DE CONFLITS / ARREGLO DE CONFLICTOS -
05.03.06
    UF: CONFLICT RESOLUTION
    NT: ARBITRATION
        CONCILIATION
    RT: CONFLICTS

DISSEMINATION OF CULTURE
DIFFUSION DE LA CULTURE / DIFUSION DE LA CULTURA
- 05.02.03
    RT: CULTURE

DISTANCE
DISTANCE / DISTANCIA - 18.06.00
    RT: DISTANCE STUDY
        REMOTE SENSING
        TELECOMMUNICATIONS

DISTANCE STUDY
ENSEIGNEMENT A DISTANCE / ENSENANZA A DISTANCIA
- 06.05.03
    BT: TEACHING
    NT: CORRESPONDENCE EDUCATION
        EDUCATIONAL RADIO
        EDUCATIONAL TELEVISION
    RT: DISTANCE
        TEACHING METHODS
        TELECOMMUNICATIONS

DISTILLING
DISTILLATION / DESTILACION - 08.12.03
    BT: INDUSTRIAL PROCESSES

DISTRIBUTION
DISTRIBUTION / DISTRIBUCION - 09.04.01
SN: DISTRIBUTION OF GOODS, AS THROUGH A SALES
    NETWORK.
    NT: RETAIL TRADE
        WHOLESALE TRADE
    RT: DISTRIBUTION COSTS
        DISTRIBUTION NETWORK
        DOMESTIC TRADE
        INLAND TRANSPORT

DISTRIBUTION COSTS
COUTS DE DISTRIBUTION / COSTOS DE DISTRIBUCION -
09.04.01
    BT: COSTS
    RT: DISTRIBUTION

DISTRIBUTION NETWORK
CIRCUIT DE DISTRIBUTION / RED DE DISTRIBUCION -
09.04.01
SN: USE ONLY TO DENOTE THE WHOLE DISTRIBUTION
    SYSTEM OF A PARTICULAR PRODUCT IN A
    PARTICULAR COUNTRY AND, FOR EXAMPLE, ITS
    INCIDENCE ON PRICES.
    RT: DISTRIBUTION

DIVIDENDS
- 11.02.07
    USE: INVESTMENT RETURNS

DIVISION OF LABOUR
DIVISION DU TRAVAIL / DIVISION DEL TRABAJO -
03.03.01
    NT: INTERNATIONAL DIVISION OF LABOUR
    RT: ECONOMIC SYSTEMS

DIVORCE
DIVORCE / DIVORCIO - 14.02.05
    RT: FAMILY DISINTEGRATION
        MARRIAGE

DJIBOUTI
DJIBOUTI / DJIBOUTI - 01.04.02
    BT: EAST AFRICA
        FRENCH SPEAKING AFRICA

DOCKERS
DOCKERS / ESTIBADORES - 13.09.08
    BT: TRANSPORT WORKERS
    RT: SEA TRANSPORT

DOCUMENTALISTS
DOCUMENTALISTES / DOCUMENTALISTAS - 13.09.09
    RT: DOCUMENTATION

DOCUMENTARY ANALYSIS
- 19.01.02
    USE: INFORMATION ANALYSIS

DOCUMENTATION
DOCUMENTATION / DOCUMENTACION - 19.01.01
SN: USE FOR MATERIAL ABOUT DOCUMENTATION
    TECHNIQUES. DO NOT USE FOR COLLECTIONS OF
    DOCUMENTS.
    BT: INFORMATION SCIENCES
    NT: CATALOGUING
        INFORMATION ANALYSIS
        INFORMATION RECORDING
    RT: CLADES
        CLASSIFICATION
        DOCUMENTALISTS
        DOCUMENTS
        FID
        ICSSD
        SECONDARY DOCUMENTS

DOCUMENTATION CENTRES
- 19.01.03
    USE: INFORMATION SERVICES

DOCUMENTS
DOCUMENTS / DOCUMENTOS - 19.02.01
    NT: AUDIOVISUAL MATERIALS
        OFFICIAL DOCUMENTS
        PRIMARY DOCUMENTS
        REFERENCE MATERIALS
        RESTRICTED DOCUMENTS
        SECONDARY DOCUMENTS
        UNPUBLISHED DOCUMENTS
    RT: DOCUMENTATION
        LIST OF DOCUMENTS

DOMESTIC ANIMALS
ANIMAUX DOMESTIQUES / ANIMALES DOMESTICOS -

DOMESTIC ANIMALS<CONT>
07.09.01
    BT: ANIMALS
    RT: LIVESTOCK

DOMESTIC CONSUMPTION
CONSOMMATION INTERIEURE / CONSUMO INTERNO -
09.01.03
    BT: CONSUMPTION
    RT: DOMESTIC MARKET

DOMESTIC MARKET
MARCHE INTERIEUR / MERCADO INTERNO - 09.01.02
    BT: MARKET
    RT: DOMESTIC CONSUMPTION
           DOMESTIC TRADE

DOMESTIC TRADE
COMMERCE INTERIEUR / COMERCIO INTERNO - 09.04.01
    UF: HOME TRADE
          INLAND TRADE
    BT: TRADE
    RT: COMMERCIAL POLICY
          DISTRIBUTION
          DOMESTIC MARKET
          HOTEL INDUSTRY

DOMESTIC WASTES
ORDURES MENAGERES / DESPERDICIOS DOMICILIARIOS -
16.03.04
    BT: WASTES
    RT: SANITATION SERVICES

DOMESTIC WORKERS
GENS DE MAISON / TRABAJADORES DOMESTICOS -
13.09.07
    BT: WORKERS

DOMINICA
DOMINIQUE / DOMINICA - 01.04.03
    BT: WEST INDIES ASSOCIATED STATES

DOMINICAN
DOMINICAIN / DOMINICANO - 14.03.02
    RT: DOMINICAN REPUBLIC

DOMINICAN REPUBLIC
REPUBLIQUE DOMINICAINE / REPUBLICA DOMINICANA -
01.04.03
    BT: CARIBBEAN
          LATIN AMERICA
    RT: DOMINICAN

DONKEYS
ANES / ASNOS - 07.09.01
    BT: EQUIDAE
          LIVESTOCK

DOUBLE TAXATION
DOUBLE IMPOSITION / DOBLE TRIBUTACION - 09.05.09
    RT: TAXATION

DRAINAGE
DRAINAGE / DRENAJE - 17.05.03

DRAMATIC ART
ART DRAMATIQUE / ARTE DRAMATICO - 05.05.03
    BT: PERFORMING ARTS
    NT: CINEMA
          DANCE
          THEATRE
    RT: PERFORMERS

DRAUGHTSMEN
DESSINATEURS / DIBUJANTES - 13.09.09
    BT: TECHNICIANS

DREDGING
DRAGAGE / DRAGADO - 17.05.04
    RT: CONTINENTAL SHELVES

DRIED FOOD
ALIMENTS SECHES / ALIMENTOS SECOS - 08.06.03
    BT: FOOD
    NT: DRIED FRUIT
    RT: DEHYDRATION
          DRYING
          FOOD PRESERVATION

DRIED FRUIT
FRUITS SECHES / FRUTAS SECAS - 08.06.04
    BT: DRIED FOOD
    RT: FRUITS

DRILLING
FORAGE / PERFORACION - 17.05.04

DRINKING WATER
EAU POTABLE / AGUA POTABLE - 17.05.05
    BT: WATER

DROPPING OUT
ABANDON EN COURS D'ETUDES / DESERCION ESCOLAR -
06.04.12

DROUGHT
SECHERESSE / SEQUIA - 17.01.03
    BT: NATURAL DISASTERS
    RT: ARID ZONE
          DRY SEASON
          SEMI-ARID ZONE

DRUG ADDICTION
USAGE DE STUPEFIANTS / TOXICOMANIA - 02.04.02
    BT: POISONING
          SOCIAL PROBLEMS
    RT: ALCOHOLISM
          NARCOTICS

DRUGS
MEDICAMENTS / MEDICAMENTOS - 15.05.00
    BT: PHARMACEUTICALS
    NT: ANTIBIOTICS

DRY SEASON
SAISON SECHE / ESTACION SECA - 17.02.02
    BT: SEASONS
    RT: DROUGHT

DRYING
SECHAGE / SECADO - 08.12.03
    BT: INDUSTRIAL PROCESSES
    RT: DRIED FOOD

DUAL ECONOMY
DUALISME ECONOMIQUE / DUALISMO ECONOMICO -
03.03.02
SN: SYSTEM IN WHICH A MODERN CAPITAL-INTENSIVE
SPHERE COEXISTS WITH AN IMPOVERISHED
TRADITIONAL SPHERE.
    BT: ECONOMIC SYSTEMS

DUAL JOBHOLDING
DOUBLE OCCUPATION / EMPLEO DOBLE - 13.02.01
SN: HOLDING OF MORE THAN ONE JOB BY ONE PERSON
IN DIFFERENT ORGANIZATIONS.

DUMPING
DUMPING / DUMPING - 09.05.07
    BT: TRADE BARRIERS
    RT: UNFAIR COMPETITION

DURABLE GOODS
BIENS DURABLES / BIENES DURABLES - 09.01.03
    BT: CONSUMER GOODS

DURATION
DUREE / DURACION - 18.10.00
    RT: TIME FACTOR

DWELLING
- 14.04.01
    USE: HOUSING

DWELLING UNIT
- 14.04.01
    USE: HOUSEHOLD

EAC
CAO / CAO - 01.03.03
SN: EAST AFRICAN COMMUNITY.
    BT: AFRICAN ORGANIZATIONS
        INTERGOVERNMENTAL ORGANIZATIONS
    RT: EAST AFRICA

EADI
AEID / AEID - 01.03.03
SN: EUROPEAN ASSOCIATION OF DEVELOPMENT RESEARCH
AND TRAINING INSTITUTES.
    BT: EUROPEAN ORGANIZATIONS
        NON-GOVERNMENTAL ORGANIZATIONS
    RT: DEVELOPMENT RESEARCH
        RESEARCH CENTRES
        WESTERN EUROPE

EARLY CHILDHOOD
PREMIERE ENFANCE / PRIMERA INFANCIA - 14.02.02
    BT: CHILDHOOD
    RT: INFANTS

EARLY RETIREMENT
RETRAITE ANTICIPEE / JUBILACION ANTICIPADA -
13.05.00
    BT: RETIREMENT

EARTH SCIENCES
SCIENCES DE LA TERRE / CIENCIAS DE LA TIERRA -
17.04.01
    BT: NATURAL SCIENCES
    NT: GEOCHEMISTRY
        GEOLOGY
        GEOMORPHOLOGY
        GEOPHYSICS
        HYDROLOGY
        METEOROLOGY
        MINERALOGY
        OCEANOGRAPHY
        PHYSICAL GEOGRAPHY
        SOIL SCIENCES

EARTHMOVING MACHINERY
MATERIEL DE TERRASSEMENT / MAQUINARIA PARA MOVER
TIERRAS - 08.14.06
    BT: BUILDING MACHINERY

EARTHQUAKES
- 17.04.03
    USE: SEISMS

EAST
EST / ESTE - 17.03.03

EAST AFRICA
AFRIQUE ORIENTALE / AFRICA ORIENTAL - 01.04.02
    BT: AFRICA SOUTH OF SAHARA

EAST AFRICA<CONT>
    NT: BURUNDI
        COMOROS
        DJIBOUTI
        ETHIOPIA
        KENYA
        MALAWI
        MAURITIUS
        MOZAMBIQUE
        REUNION ISLAND
        RHODESIA
        RWANDA
        SEYCHELLES
        SOMALIA
        SUDAN
        TANZANIA
        UGANDA
        ZAMBIA
    RT: EAC

EAST-WEST TRADE
COMMERCE EST-OUEST / COMERCIO ESTE-OESTE -
09.05.02
    BT: INTERNATIONAL TRADE
    RT: TRADE RELATIONS

EASTERN EUROPE
EUROPE ORIENTALE / EUROPA ORIENTAL - 01.04.05
    BT: EUROPE
    NT: ALBANIA
        BULGARIA
        BYELORUSSIAN SSR
        CZECHOSLOVAKIA
        GERMAN DR
        HUNGARY
        POLAND
        ROMANIA
        UKRAINIAN SSR
        USSR
        YUGOSLAVIA
    RT: CMEA

ECA
CEA / CEPA - 01.03.02
SN: ECONOMIC COMMISSION FOR AFRICA.
    BT: AFRICAN ORGANIZATIONS
        ECOSOC
    RT: AFRICA

ECAFE
- 01.03.02
    USE: ESCAP

ECE
CEE (ONU) / CEPE - 01.03.02
SN: ECONOMIC COMMISSION FOR EUROPE.
    BT: ECOSOC
        EUROPEAN ORGANIZATIONS
    RT: EUROPE

ECLA
CEPAL / CEPAL - 01.03.02
SN: ECONOMIC COMMISSION FOR LATIN AMERICA.

ECLA<CONT>
    BT: AMERICAN ORGANIZATIONS
        ECOSOC
    NT: CLADES
    RT: LATIN AMERICA

ECMT
CEMT / CEMT - 01.03.03
SN: EUROPEAN CONFERENCE OF MINISTERS OF
TRANSPORT.
    BT: EUROPEAN ORGANIZATIONS
        INTERGOVERNMENTAL ORGANIZATIONS
    RT: TRANSPORT

ECODEVELOPMENT
ECODEVELOPPEMENT / ECODESARROLLO - 16.01.01
    RT: ECOLOGY

ECOLOGICAL BALANCE
EQUILIBRE ECOLOGIQUE / EQUILIBRIO ECOLOGICO -
16.01.01
    UF: BIOLOGICAL EQUILIBRIUM
        ECOSYSTEM STABILITY
        NATURAL EQUILIBRIUM
    RT: ECOLOGY
        ECOSYSTEMS

ECOLOGICAL RESEARCH
RECHERCHE ECOLOGIQUE / INVESTIGACION ECOLOGICA -
16.01.01
    BT: RESEARCH
    RT: ECOLOGY

ECOLOGY
ECOLOGIE / ECOLOGIA - 16.01.01
SN: USE TO DENOTE THE STUDY OF RELATIONS WITH
THE ENVIRONMENT, ESPECIALLY PHYSICAL OR
GEOGRAPHICAL.
    UF: ENVIRONMENTAL BIOLOGY
    BT: NATURAL SCIENCES
    NT: ANIMAL ECOLOGY
        HUMAN ECOLOGY
        PLANT ECOLOGY
    RT: ECODEVELOPMENT
        ECOLOGICAL BALANCE
        ECOLOGICAL RESEARCH
        ECOSYSTEMS
        ENVIRONMENT
        HABITAT
        INTECOL

ECONOMETRIC MODELS
MODELES ECONOMETRIQUES / MODELOS ECONOMETRICOS -
03.01.02
    BT: ECONOMIC MODELS
    RT: ECONOMETRICS
        ECONOMIC STATISTICS

ECONOMETRICS
ECONOMETRIE / ECONOMETRIA - 03.01.02
SN: USE IN CONNECTION WITH THE APPLICATION OF
MATHEMATICS TO ECONOMIC ANALYSIS.
    BT: ECONOMICS

ECONOMETRICS<CONT>
>> RT: ACTIVITY ANALYSIS
>> ECONOMETRIC MODELS
>> ECONOMIC MODELS
>> INPUT-OUTPUT ANALYSIS
>> MATHEMATICS
>> STATISTICS

ECONOMIC ADMINISTRATION
ADMINISTRATION ECONOMIQUE / ADMINISTRACION DE LA
ECONOMIA - 04.03.02
>> BT: PUBLIC ADMINISTRATION
>> NT: AGRICULTURAL ADMINISTRATION
>> FINANCIAL ADMINISTRATION
>> INDUSTRIAL ADMINISTRATION
>> RT: ECONOMIC PLANNING
>> ECONOMIC POLICY

ECONOMIC AGREEMENTS
ACCORDS ECONOMIQUES / ACUERDOS ECONOMICOS -
09.05.02
SN: TREATIES DESIGNED BY TWO OR MORE GOVERNMENTS
INVOLVING THE SUPPLY AND/OR EXCHANGE OF
GOODS/MATERIALS AND POSSIBLY SERVICES.
>> BT: INTERNATIONAL AGREEMENTS
>> NT: COMPLEMENTARITY AGREEMENTS
>> MONETARY AGREEMENTS
>> PAYMENT AGREEMENTS
>> TARIFF AGREEMENTS
>> TAX AGREEMENTS
>> TRADE AGREEMENTS
>> RT: ECONOMIC POLICY

ECONOMIC AID
AIDE ECONOMIQUE / AYUDA ECONOMICA - 01.01.03
>> BT: DEVELOPMENT AID

ECONOMIC ANALYSIS
ANALYSE ECONOMIQUE / ANALISIS ECONOMICO -
03.01.02
>> NT: ACTIVITY ANALYSIS
>> COST ANALYSIS
>> INPUT-OUTPUT ANALYSIS
>> RT: ECONOMIC POLICY
>> ECONOMIC STATISTICS
>> ECONOMIC THEORY

ECONOMIC AND SOCIAL DEVELOPMENT
DEVELOPPEMENT ECONOMIQUE ET SOCIAL / DESARROLLO
ECONOMICO Y SOCIAL - 02.01.01
>> NT: CULTURAL DEVELOPMENT
>> ECONOMIC DEVELOPMENT
>> INTEGRATED DEVELOPMENT
>> REGIONAL DEVELOPMENT
>> SOCIAL DEVELOPMENT

ECONOMIC AND SOCIAL DEVELOPMENT<CONT>
>> RT: DEVELOPMENT ADMINISTRATION
>> DEVELOPMENT AID
>> DEVELOPMENT PLANNING
>> DEVELOPMENT PLANS
>> DEVELOPMENT POLICY
>> DEVELOPMENT POTENTIAL
>> DEVELOPMENT PROJECTS
>> DEVELOPMENT RESEARCH
>> DEVSIS
>> OBSTACLES TO DEVELOPMENT

ECONOMIC ASPECTS
ASPECTS ECONOMIQUES / ASPECTOS ECONOMICOS -
03.02.01
>> RT: ECONOMIC CONDITIONS
>> ECONOMIC IMPLICATIONS

ECONOMIC BEHAVIOUR
COMPORTEMENT ECONOMIQUE / COMPORTAMIENTO
ECONOMICO - 03.02.01
>> BT: BEHAVIOUR

ECONOMIC CENSUSES
RECENSEMENTS ECONOMIQUES / CENSOS ECONOMICOS -
03.01.02
>> BT: CENSUSES
>> RT: ECONOMIC SURVEYS

ECONOMIC CONCENTRATION
CONCENTRATION ECONOMIQUE / CONCENTRACION
ECONOMICA - 12.02.00
>> NT: CAPITAL CONCENTRATION
>> INDUSTRIAL CONCENTRATION
>> RT: MERGERS

ECONOMIC CONDITIONS
CONDITIONS ECONOMIQUES / CONDICIONES ECONOMICAS
- 03.02.01
>> UF: ECONOMIC SITUATION
>> RT: BUSINESS CYCLE
>> ECONOMIC ASPECTS
>> ECONOMIC INFORMATION

ECONOMIC CONSEQUENCES
- 03.02.01
>> USE: ECONOMIC IMPLICATIONS

ECONOMIC COOPERATION
COOPERATION ECONOMIQUE / COOPERACION ECONOMICA -
01.02.01
>> BT: ECONOMIC RELATIONS
>> NT: BORDER INTEGRATION
>> RT: ECONOMIC INTEGRATION

ECONOMIC CRISIS
- 03.02.04
>> USE: ECONOMIC RECESSION

ECONOMIC DEPRESSION
- 03.02.04
>> USE: ECONOMIC RECESSION

ECONOMIC DEVELOPMENT
DEVELOPPEMENT ECONOMIQUE / DESARROLLO ECONOMICO

ECONOMIC DEVELOPMENT<CONT>
- 03.02.03
SN: USE IN CONNECTION WITH STEPS TO IMPROVE THE
    MATERIAL PROSPERITY OF A REGION, COUNTRY,
    ETC.
    BT: ECONOMIC AND SOCIAL DEVELOPMENT
    NT: AGRICULTURAL DEVELOPMENT
        INDUSTRIAL DEVELOPMENT
    RT: ECONOMIC GROWTH
        ECONOMIC PLANNING
        ECONOMIC POLICY
        ECONOMIC RECONSTRUCTION

ECONOMIC DISCRIMINATION
DISCRIMINATION ECONOMIQUE / DISCRIMINACION
ECONOMICA - 02.01.03
SN: WHEN THE SAME PRODUCT IS SOLD AT DIFFERENT
    PRICES TO DIFFERENT BUYERS AND WHEN FOR THE
    SAME WORK PEOPLE ARE PAID DIFFERENT
    SALARIES.
    BT: DISCRIMINATION
    RT: ECONOMIC POLICY

ECONOMIC DISPARITY
DISPARITE ECONOMIQUE / DESIGUALDAD ECONOMICA -
03.02.03
    NT: REGIONAL DISPARITY

ECONOMIC DOCTRINES
DOCTRINES ECONOMIQUES / DOCTRINAS ECONOMICAS -
03.03.01
    RT: ECONOMIC THOUGHT
        POLITICAL DOCTRINES

ECONOMIC EQUILIBRIUM
EQUILIBRE ECONOMIQUE / EQUILIBRIO ECONOMICO -
03.02.04
    RT: ECONOMIC THEORY

ECONOMIC EVALUATION
EVALUATION ECONOMIQUE / EVALUACION ECONOMICA -
03.01.02
    BT: EVALUATION
    RT: COST-BENEFIT ANALYSIS
        ECONOMIC FORECASTS
        ECONOMIC POLICY
        INPUT-OUTPUT ANALYSIS

ECONOMIC FLUCTUATIONS
- 03.02.04
    USE: BUSINESS CYCLE

ECONOMIC FORECASTS
PREVISIONS ECONOMIQUES / PREDICCIONES ECONOMICAS
- 03.01.02
    BT: FORECASTS
    RT: ECONOMIC EVALUATION

ECONOMIC GEOGRAPHY
GEOGRAPHIE ECONOMIQUE / GEOGRAFIA ECONOMICA -
17.03.01
    BT: HUMAN GEOGRAPHY
    RT: ECONOMICS

ECONOMIC GROWTH
CROISSANCE ECONOMIQUE / CRECIMIENTO ECONOMICO -
03.02.03
SN: USE IN CONNECTION WITH THE INCREASE IN
    WEALTH OF A COUNTRY AS MEASURED IN TERMS OF
    GROSS NATIONAL PRODUCT OR GROSS DOMESTIC
    PRODUCT.
    RT: ECONOMIC DEVELOPMENT
        ECONOMIC POLICY
        GROWTH MODELS
        GROWTH POLICY
        GROWTH RATE
        ZERO GROWTH ECONOMY

ECONOMIC HISTORY
HISTOIRE ECONOMIQUE / HISTORIA ECONOMICA -
05.01.01
    BT: HISTORY
    RT: ECONOMICS

ECONOMIC IMPLICATIONS
IMPLICATIONS ECONOMIQUES / CONSECUENCIAS
ECONOMICAS - 03.02.01
    UF: ECONOMIC CONSEQUENCES
    RT: ECONOMIC ASPECTS

ECONOMIC INDICATORS
INDICATEURS ECONOMIQUES / INDICADORES ECONOMICOS
- 03.01.02
    NT: GROSS DOMESTIC PRODUCT
        GROSS NATIONAL PRODUCT
        GROWTH RATE
        INDEX NUMBERS
    RT: ECONOMIC INFORMATION
        ECONOMIC PLANNING
        ECONOMIC POLICY
        ECONOMIC STATISTICS
        SOCIAL INDICATORS

ECONOMIC INFORMATION
INFORMATION ECONOMIQUE / INFORMACION ECONOMICA -
03.01.02
    BT: INFORMATION
    RT: ECONOMIC CONDITIONS
        ECONOMIC INDICATORS

ECONOMIC INFRASTRUCTURE
INFRASTRUCTURE ECONOMIQUE / INFRAESTRUCTURA
ECONOMICA - 03.02.01
    RT: DEVELOPMENT POTENTIAL
        ECONOMIC RESOURCES

ECONOMIC INTEGRATION
INTEGRATION ECONOMIQUE / INTEGRACION ECONOMICA -
01.02.01
SN: USE ONLY AT THE INTERNATIONAL LEVEL. DO NOT
    CONFUSE WITH 'ECONOMIC CONCENTRATION'.
    BT: ECONOMIC RELATIONS
    NT: HORIZONTAL INTEGRATION
        INDUSTRIAL INTEGRATION
        REGIONAL INTEGRATION
        VERTICAL INTEGRATION
    RT: ECONOMIC COOPERATION
        FREE TRADE AREA

ECONOMIC LEGISLATION
**LEGISLATION ECONOMIQUE / LEGISLACION ECONOMICA -
04.01.02**
    BT: LEGISLATION
    NT: ANTITRUST LEGISLATION
    RT: ECONOMIC POLICY

ECONOMIC LOSS
PERTE ECONOMIQUE / PERDIDA ECONOMICA - 03.02.04
    NT: FINANCIAL LOSS

ECONOMIC MODELS
**MODELES ECONOMIQUES / MODELOS ECONOMICOS -
03.01.02**
    BT: MODELS
    NT: ECONOMETRIC MODELS
        GROWTH MODELS
    RT: ECONOMETRICS
        INPUT-OUTPUT TABLES
        MACROECONOMICS
        MANAGEMENT TECHNIQUES

ECONOMIC PLANNING
**PLANIFICATION ECONOMIQUE / PLANIFICACION
ECONOMICA - 02.01.02**
    BT: PLANNING
    NT: AGRICULTURAL PLANNING
        EXPORT PLANNING
        INDUSTRIAL PLANNING
        MANPOWER PLANNING
        MARKET PLANNING
        PRODUCTION PLANNING
    RT: ECONOMIC ADMINISTRATION
        ECONOMIC DEVELOPMENT
        ECONOMIC INDICATORS
        ECONOMIC POLICY
        ILPES
        PLANNED ECONOMY

ECONOMIC POLICY
**POLITIQUE ECONOMIQUE / POLITICA ECONOMICA -
02.01.03**
    BT: GOVERNMENT POLICY
    NT: AGRICULTURAL POLICY
        AUSTERITY POLICY
        COMMERCIAL POLICY
        FINANCIAL POLICY
        GROWTH POLICY
        INCOMES POLICY
        INDUSTRIAL POLICY
        INVESTMENT POLICY
        PRICE POLICY
        PRODUCTIVITY POLICY
        TRADE POLICY
        TRANSPORT POLICY

ECONOMIC POLICY<CONT>
    RT: ECONOMIC ADMINISTRATION
        ECONOMIC AGREEMENTS
        ECONOMIC ANALYSIS
        ECONOMIC DEVELOPMENT
        ECONOMIC DISCRIMINATION
        ECONOMIC EVALUATION
        ECONOMIC GROWTH
        ECONOMIC INDICATORS
        ECONOMIC LEGISLATION
        ECONOMIC PLANNING
        ECONOMIC REFORM
        LABOUR POLICY
        MACROECONOMICS
        SOCIAL POLICY

ECONOMIC PROJECTIONS
**PERSPECTIVES ECONOMIQUES / PROYECCIONES
ECONOMICAS - 03.01.02**
    BT: PROJECTIONS

ECONOMIC RECESSION
**RECESSION ECONOMIQUE / RECESION ECONOMICA -
03.02.04**
    UF: ECONOMIC CRISIS
        ECONOMIC DEPRESSION
    RT: AUSTERITY POLICY
        BUSINESS CYCLE
        UNEMPLOYMENT

ECONOMIC RECONSTRUCTION
**RECONSTRUCTION ECONOMIQUE / RECONSTRUCCION DE LA
ECONOMIA - 03.02.03**
    RT: ECONOMIC DEVELOPMENT

ECONOMIC RECOVERY
**REPRISE ECONOMIQUE / RECUPERACION ECONOMICA -
03.02.04**
    RT: BUSINESS CYCLE

ECONOMIC REFORM
**REFORME ECONOMIQUE / REFORMA ECONOMICA -
02.01.03**
    RT: ECONOMIC POLICY
        ECONOMIC SYSTEMS

ECONOMIC RELATIONS
**RELATIONS ECONOMIQUES / RELACIONES ECONOMICAS -
01.02.01**
    BT: INTERNATIONAL RELATIONS
    NT: ECONOMIC COOPERATION
        ECONOMIC INTEGRATION
        MONETARY RELATIONS
        TRADE RELATIONS

ECONOMIC RESEARCH
**RECHERCHE ECONOMIQUE / INVESTIGACION ECONOMICA -
03.01.02**
    BT: RESEARCH

ECONOMIC RESOURCES
**RESSOURCES ECONOMIQUES / RECURSOS ECONOMICOS -
03.02.01**

ECONOMIC RESOURCES<CONT>

    NT: BUDGETARY RESOURCES
           FINANCIAL RESOURCES

    RT: ECONOMIC INFRASTRUCTURE
           HUMAN RESOURCES
           NATURAL RESOURCES

ECONOMIC SITUATION
- 03.02.01
    USE: ECONOMIC CONDITIONS

ECONOMIC STAGNATION
STAGNATION ECONOMIQUE / ESTANCAMIENTO ECONOMICO
- 03.02.04

ECONOMIC STATISTICS
STATISTIQUES ECONOMIQUES / ESTADISTICAS
ECONOMICAS - 03.01.02
    BT: STATISTICAL DATA

    NT: AGRICULTURAL STATISTICS
           FINANCIAL STATISTICS
           INDUSTRIAL STATISTICS
           PRODUCTION STATISTICS

    RT: BALANCE OF PAYMENTS
           ECONOMETRIC MODELS
           ECONOMIC ANALYSIS
           ECONOMIC INDICATORS
           INPUT-OUTPUT TABLES
           NATIONAL ACCOUNTS
           SEASONAL FLUCTUATIONS

ECONOMIC STRUCTURE
STRUCTURE ECONOMIQUE / ESTRUCTURA ECONOMICA -
03.02.01
SN: THE RELATIVE IMPORTANCE OF THE VARIOUS
    SECTORS OF THE ECONOMY.
    RT: INPUT-OUTPUT ANALYSIS
           INPUT-OUTPUT TABLES

ECONOMIC SURVEYS
ENQUETES ECONOMIQUES / ESTUDIOS ECONOMICOS -
03.01.02
    BT: SURVEYS
    RT: ECONOMIC CENSUSES

ECONOMIC SYSTEMS
SYSTEMES ECONOMIQUES / SISTEMAS ECONOMICOS -
03.03.01
    NT: CAPITALISM
           COLLECTIVE ECONOMY
           CORPORATISM
           DUAL ECONOMY
           LIBERALISM
           MARGINALISM
           MARKET ECONOMY
           MIXED ECONOMY
           PLANNED ECONOMY

    RT: COOPERATIVES
           DIVISION OF LABOUR
           ECONOMIC REFORM
           NEW INTERNATIONAL ECONOMIC ORDER

ECONOMIC TAKE OFF
DECOLLAGE ECONOMIQUE / DESPEGUE ECONOMICO -

ECONOMIC TAKE OFF<CONT>
03.02.03

ECONOMIC THEORY
THEORIE ECONOMIQUE / TEORIA ECONOMICA - 03.01.02
    BT: THEORY
    RT: COMPARATIVE ADVANTAGE
           ECONOMIC ANALYSIS
           ECONOMIC EQUILIBRIUM
           INTERNATIONAL DIVISION OF LABOUR
           MARXISM
           WELFARE ECONOMICS

ECONOMIC THOUGHT
PENSEE ECONOMIQUE / PENSAMIENTO ECONOMICO -
03.03.01
    RT: ECONOMIC DOCTRINES

ECONOMICS
SCIENCE ECONOMIQUE / ECONOMIA - 03.01.01
    UF: POLITICAL ECONOMY
    BT: SOCIAL SCIENCES
    NT: AGRICULTURAL ECONOMICS
           BUSINESS ECONOMICS
           ECONOMETRICS
           ECONOMICS OF CULTURE
           ECONOMICS OF EDUCATION
           ENERGY ECONOMICS
           ENVIRONMENTAL ECONOMICS
           FOOD ECONOMICS
           INDUSTRIAL ECONOMICS
           LAND ECONOMICS
           MACROECONOMICS
           MICROECONOMICS
           TRANSPORT ECONOMICS
           WELFARE ECONOMICS

    RT: ECONOMIC GEOGRAPHY
           ECONOMIC HISTORY
           ECONOMISTS
           IEA

ECONOMICS OF CULTURE
ECONOMIE DE LA CULTURE / ECONOMIA DE LA CULTURA
- 05.02.03
    BT: ECONOMICS
    RT: CULTURE

ECONOMICS OF EDUCATION
ECONOMIE DE L'EDUCATION / ECONOMIA DE LA
EDUCACION - 06.01.00
    UF: EDUCATIONAL ECONOMICS
    BT: ECONOMICS
           SCIENCES OF EDUCATION
    NT: COST OF EDUCATION
           EDUCATIONAL BUDGET
           EDUCATIONAL FINANCING
           EDUCATIONAL GRANTS
           FREE EDUCATION
    RT: CULTURAL EXPENDITURES

ECONOMISTS
ECONOMISTES / ECONOMISTAS - 13.09.09
    BT: SCIENTISTS
    RT: ECONOMICS

ECONOMY OF SCALE
ECONOMIE D'ECHELLE / ECONOMIA DE ESCALA -
12.09.00
SN: *REDUCTION OF UNIT PRODUCTION COSTS RELATED*
TO A LARGER PRODUCTION CAPACITY.
RT: PRODUCTION CAPACITY
PRODUCTION COSTS
PRODUCTION FUNCTIONS
SIZE OF ENTERPRISE

ECOSOC
ECOSOC / ECOSOC - 01.03.02
SN: *ECONOMIC AND SOCIAL COUNCIL.*
BT: UN
NT: ACAST
CDP
CSTD
ECA
ECE
ECLA
ECWA
ESCAP

ECOSYSTEM STABILITY
- 16.01.01
USE: ECOLOGICAL BALANCE

ECOSYSTEMS
ECOSYSTEMES / ECOSISTEMAS - 16.01.02
RT: ECOLOGICAL BALANCE
ECOLOGY
ENVIRONMENT

ECSC
CECA / CECA - 01.03.03
SN: *EUROPEAN COAL AND STEEL COMMUNITY.*
BT: EUROPEAN COMMUNITIES
RT: COAL
IRON AND STEEL INDUSTRY

ECUADOR
EQUATEUR / ECUADOR - 01.04.03
BT: LATIN AMERICA
SOUTH AMERICA
RT: ECUADORIAN

ECUADORIAN
EQUATORIEN / ECUATORIANO - 14.03.02
RT: ECUADOR

ECWA
CEAO / CEAO - 01.03.02
SN: *ECONOMIC COMMISSION FOR WESTERN ASIA.*
BT: ARAB ORGANIZATIONS
ASIAN ORGANIZATIONS
ECOSOC
RT: MIDDLE EAST

EDIBLE OILS
HUILES COMESTIBLES / ACEITES COMESTIBLES -
08.06.06
BT: FOOD

EDIBLE OILS<CONT>
NT: OLIVE OIL
PALM OIL
PEANUT OIL
RT: MARGARINE

EDITORIAL
EDITORIAL / COMENTARIO EDITORIAL - 19.02.06

EDUCATION
EDUCATION / EDUCACION - 06.02.01
RT: AIMS OF EDUCATION
ALECSO
CURRICULUM
EDUCATIONAL ASPECTS
EDUCATIONAL INSTITUTIONS
EDUCATIONAL SYSTEMS
IBE
LEARNING
SCIENCES OF EDUCATION
TEACHING
TRAINING
UNESCO

EDUCATION OF WOMEN
EDUCATION DES FEMMES / EDUCACION DE LA MUJER -
06.03.05
BT: ADULT EDUCATION
RT: WOMEN

EDUCATIONAL ADMINISTRATION
ADMINISTRATION DE L'ENSEIGNEMENT /
ADMINISTRACION DE LA ENSENANZA - 04.03.02
UF: ADMINISTRATION OF EDUCATION
BT: PUBLIC ADMINISTRATION
RT: EDUCATIONAL PLANNING
EDUCATIONAL POLICY
EDUCATIONAL REFORMS
STUDENT PARTICIPATION

EDUCATIONAL ASPECTS
ASPECTS EDUCATIFS / ASPECTOS EDUCACIONALES -
06.02.01
RT: EDUCATION

EDUCATIONAL ATTENDANCE
ASSISTANCE AUX COURS / ASISTENCIA ESCOLAR -
06.04.12

EDUCATIONAL BUDGET
BUDGET DE L'EDUCATION / PRESUPUESTO DE LA
EDUCACION - 06.02.05
BT: ECONOMICS OF EDUCATION

EDUCATIONAL BUILDINGS
BATIMENTS EDUCATIFS / EDIFICIOS EDUCACIONALES -
06.04.07
BT: BUILDINGS
EDUCATIONAL FACILITIES
NT: SCHOOL BUILDINGS
UNIVERSITY BUILDINGS

EDUCATIONAL CRISIS
CRISE DE L'ENSEIGNEMENT / CRISIS DE LA EDUCACION

EDUCATIONAL CRISIS<CONT>
- 06.02.03
    RT: EDUCATIONAL SYSTEMS

EDUCATIONAL DEVELOPMENT
DEVELOPPEMENT DE L'EDUCATION / DESARROLLO DE LA
EDUCACION - 06.02.03
    UF: ADVANCEMENT OF EDUCATION
    BT: SOCIAL DEVELOPMENT
    RT: EDUCATIONAL PLANNING
        EDUCATIONAL POLICY

EDUCATIONAL ECONOMICS
- 06.01.00
    USE: ECONOMICS OF EDUCATION

EDUCATIONAL EQUIPMENT
EQUIPEMENT EDUCATIF / EQUIPO EDUCATIVO -
06.04.07
    BT: EQUIPMENT
    NT: SCHOOL TRANSPORT
        TEACHING AIDS

EDUCATIONAL EXPENDITURES
- 06.02.05
    USE: COST OF EDUCATION

EDUCATIONAL FACILITIES
INSTALLATIONS EDUCATIVES / INSTALACIONES
EDUCACIONALES - 06.04.07
    NT: EDUCATIONAL BUILDINGS

EDUCATIONAL FILMS
FILMS EDUCATIFS / PELICULAS EDUCATIVAS -
06.05.03
    BT: AUDIOVISUAL AIDS
        FILMS
    RT: TEACHING METHODS

EDUCATIONAL FINANCING
FINANCEMENT DE L'EDUCATION / FINANCIACION DE LA
EDUCACION - 06.02.05
    BT: ECONOMICS OF EDUCATION
        FINANCING
    RT: EDUCATIONAL GRANTS

EDUCATIONAL GRANTS
ALLOCATIONS D'ETUDE / SUBVENCIONES PARA ESTUDIOS
- 06.04.11
    BT: ECONOMICS OF EDUCATION
        GRANTS
    NT: RESEARCH FELLOWSHIPS
        SCHOLARSHIPS
        STUDENT LOANS
        TRAINING ALLOWANCES
    RT: EDUCATIONAL FINANCING

EDUCATIONAL GUIDANCE
ORIENTATION PEDAGOGIQUE / ORIENTACION
PEDAGOGICA - 06.04.09

EDUCATIONAL INNOVATIONS

EDUCATIONAL INNOVATIONS<CONT>
INNOVATIONS PEDAGOGIQUES / INNOVACIONES
PEDAGOGICAS - 06.02.03
    RT: EDUCATIONAL PROJECTS
        EDUCATIONAL SYSTEMS
        TEACHING METHODS

EDUCATIONAL INSTITUTIONS
ETABLISSEMENTS D'ENSEIGNEMENT / ESTABLECIMIENTOS
DE ENSENANZA - 06.04.01
    NT: HIGHER EDUCATION INSTITUTIONS
        SCHOOLS
        TRAINING CENTRES
    RT: EDUCATION
        SCHOOL MANAGEMENT

EDUCATIONAL NEEDS
BESOINS D'EDUCATION / NECESIDADES DE EDUCACION -
06.02.02
*SN: USE IN CONNECTION WITH OVERALL NATIONAL
    EDUCATIONAL REQUIREMENTS.*
    BT: BASIC NEEDS

EDUCATIONAL OPPORTUNITIES
CHANCES D'EDUCATION / OPORTUNIDADES DE EDUCACION
- 06.02.02
    BT: EQUAL OPPORTUNITY
    RT: ACCESS TO EDUCATION

EDUCATIONAL OUTPUT
RENDEMENT DE L'EDUCATION / RENDIMIENTO DE LA
EDUCACION - 06.02.05
    RT: COST OF EDUCATION
        COST-BENEFIT ANALYSIS
        QUALITY OF EDUCATION

EDUCATIONAL PLANNING
PLANIFICATION DE L'EDUCATION / PLANIFICACION DE
LA EDUCACION - 06.02.04
    UF: PLANNING OF EDUCATION
    BT: PLANNING
    RT: EDUCATIONAL ADMINISTRATION
        EDUCATIONAL DEVELOPMENT
        EDUCATIONAL POLICY
        EDUCATIONAL REFORMS
        EDUCATIONAL SYSTEMS
        IIEP

EDUCATIONAL POLICY
POLITIQUE DE L'EDUCATION / POLITICA EDUCACIONAL
- 06.02.04
    BT: GOVERNMENT POLICY
    RT: EDUCATIONAL ADMINISTRATION
        EDUCATIONAL DEVELOPMENT
        EDUCATIONAL PLANNING
        EDUCATIONAL REFORMS
        EDUCATIONAL SYSTEMS
        STUDENT PARTICIPATION

EDUCATIONAL PROJECTS
PROJETS D'EDUCATION / PROYECTOS DE EDUCACION -
06.02.03
    RT: EDUCATIONAL INNOVATIONS

EDUCATIONAL PSYCHOLOGY
- 06.01.00
    USE: **PSYCHOLOGY OF EDUCATION**

EDUCATIONAL RADIO
RADIO EDUCATIVE / RADIO EDUCATIVA - 06.05.03
    UF: INSTRUCTIONAL RADIO
    BT: DISTANCE STUDY
        RADIO
    RT: OUT-OF-SCHOOL EDUCATION

EDUCATIONAL REFORMS
**REFORMES DE L'ENSEIGNEMENT / REFORMAS DE LA
EDUCACION - 06.02.03**
    UF: REFORMS OF EDUCATION
    RT: EDUCATIONAL ADMINISTRATION
        EDUCATIONAL PLANNING
        EDUCATIONAL POLICY
        EDUCATIONAL SYSTEMS

EDUCATIONAL RESEARCH
**RECHERCHE PEDAGOGIQUE / INVESTIGACION PEDAGOGICA
- 06.01.00**
    BT: RESEARCH
    RT: COMPARATIVE EDUCATION
        EDUCATIONAL STATISTICS
        EDUCATIONAL THEORY
        SCIENCES OF EDUCATION

EDUCATIONAL SCIENCES
- 06.01.00
    USE: **SCIENCES OF EDUCATION**

EDUCATIONAL SELECTION
**SELECTION DES ELEVES / SELECCION DE LOS ALUMNOS
- 06.04.09**
    RT: ACCESS TO EDUCATION
        ADMISSION REQUIREMENTS

EDUCATIONAL SOCIOLOGY
- 06.01.00
    USE: **SOCIOLOGY OF EDUCATION**

EDUCATIONAL STATISTICS
**STATISTIQUES DE L'EDUCATION / ESTADISTICAS
EDUCACIONALES - 06.01.00**
    BT: STATISTICAL DATA
    RT: EDUCATIONAL RESEARCH
        SCIENCES OF EDUCATION

EDUCATIONAL SYSTEMS
**SYSTEMES D'ENSEIGNEMENT / SISTEMAS DE ENSENANZA
- 06.03.01**
    UF: SCHOOL SYSTEMS
        SYSTEMS OF EDUCATION
        TEACHING SYSTEMS
    NT: COMPULSORY EDUCATION
        FREE EDUCATION
        GENERAL EDUCATION
        LEVELS OF EDUCATION
        PRIVATE EDUCATION
        PUBLIC EDUCATION
        SPECIAL EDUCATION
        VOCATIONAL EDUCATION

EDUCATIONAL SYSTEMS\<CONT\>
    RT: ACADEMIC FREEDOM
        COURSES
        CURRICULUM
        DE-SCHOOLING
        EDUCATION
        EDUCATIONAL CRISIS
        EDUCATIONAL INNOVATIONS
        EDUCATIONAL PLANNING
        EDUCATIONAL POLICY
        EDUCATIONAL REFORMS
        NON-FORMAL EDUCATION
        OUT-OF-SCHOOL EDUCATION

EDUCATIONAL TECHNOLOGY
**TECHNOLOGIE DE L'EDUCATION / TECNOLOGIA
EDUCATIVA - 06.05.03**
    RT: TEACHING AIDS

EDUCATIONAL TELEVISION
**TELEVISION EDUCATIVE / TELEVISION EDUCATIVA -
06.05.03**
    BT: DISTANCE STUDY
        TELEVISION
    RT: OUT-OF-SCHOOL EDUCATION

EDUCATIONAL THEORY
**THEORIE DE L'EDUCATION / TEORIA DE LA EDUCACION
- 06.01.00**
    BT: THEORY
    RT: EDUCATIONAL RESEARCH
        PHILOSOPHY OF EDUCATION

EEC
CEE / CEE - 01.03.03
SN: EUROPEAN ECONOMIC COMMUNITY.
    BT: COMMON MARKET
        EUROPEAN COMMUNITIES

EFFICIENCY
EFFICACITE / EFICACIA - 12.07.03
    RT: COST ANALYSIS
        MANAGEMENT TECHNIQUES
        RATIONALIZATION
        RESOURCES ALLOCATION

EFTA
AELE / AELC - 01.03.03
SN: EUROPEAN FREE TRADE ASSOCIATION.
    BT: EUROPEAN ORGANIZATIONS
        INTERGOVERNMENTAL ORGANIZATIONS
    RT: FREE TRADE AREA

EGGS
OEUFS / HUEVOS - 07.09.05
    BT: ANIMAL PRODUCTS
    RT: POULTRY

EGYPT
EGYPTE / EGIPTO - 01.04.02
    BT: ARAB COUNTRIES
        ENGLISH SPEAKING AFRICA
        MEDITERRANEAN COUNTRIES
        NORTH AFRICA
    RT: EGYPTIAN

EGYPTIAN
EGYPTIEN / EGIPCIO - 14.03.02
    RT: EGYPT

EIB
BEI / BEI - 01.03.03
SN: EUROPEAN INVESTMENT BANK.
    BT: EUROPEAN COMMUNITIES
        INVESTMENT BANKS

EL SALVADOR
EL SALVADOR / EL SALVADOR - 01.04.03
    BT: CENTRAL AMERICA
    RT: SALVADORIAN

ELECTIONS
ELECTIONS / ELECCIONES - 04.04.02
    RT: DEMOCRACY
        ELECTORAL SYSTEMS
        VOTING

ELECTORAL SYSTEMS
SYSTEMES ELECTORAUX / SISTEMAS ELECTORALES -
04.03.01
    RT: ELECTIONS

ELECTRIC APPLIANCES
APPAREILS ELECTRIQUES / APARATOS ELECTRICOS -
08.15.02
    BT: ELECTRICAL MACHINERY
    NT: HOUSEHOLD APPLIANCES

ELECTRIC LAMPS
LAMPES ELECTRIQUES / LAMPARAS ELECTRICAS -
08.15.02
    RT: ELECTRIC LIGHTING

ELECTRIC LIGHTING
ECLAIRAGE ELECTRIQUE / ALUMBRADO ELECTRICO -
08.15.02
    RT: ELECTRIC LAMPS
        ELECTRICAL MACHINERY

ELECTRIC MOTORS
MOTEURS ELECTRIQUES / MOTORES ELECTRICOS -
08.15.02
    BT: ELECTRICAL MACHINERY
        ENGINES

ELECTRIC POWER
ENERGIE ELECTRIQUE / ENERGIA ELECTRICA -
08.11.02
    BT: ENERGY
    NT: HYDROELECTRIC POWER
    RT: ELECTRICITY
        ELECTRIFICATION

ELECTRIC POWER PLANTS
CENTRALES ELECTRIQUES / CENTRALES ELECTRICAS -
08.11.02
    BT: POWER PLANTS
    NT: HYDROELECTRIC POWER PLANTS
        THERMAL POWER PLANTS

ELECTRICAL ENGINEERING
ELECTROTECHNIQUE / ELECTROTECNIA - 08.11.02
    BT: ENGINEERING
    RT: ELECTRICAL INDUSTRY
        ELECTRONIC ENGINEERING

ELECTRICAL EQUIPMENT
EQUIPEMENT ELECTRIQUE / EQUIPO ELECTRICO -
08.15.02
    BT: EQUIPMENT

ELECTRICAL INDUSTRY
INDUSTRIE ELECTRIQUE / INDUSTRIA ELECTRICA -
08.11.02
    BT: INDUSTRIAL SECTOR
    NT: ELECTRICAL MACHINERY INDUSTRY
    RT: ELECTRICAL ENGINEERING
        ELECTRICITY
        ELECTRIFICATION
        ELECTRONICS INDUSTRY

ELECTRICAL MACHINERY
MATERIEL ELECTRIQUE / MAQUINARIA ELECTRICA -
08.15.02
    BT: MACHINERY
    NT: ELECTRIC APPLIANCES
        ELECTRIC MOTORS
    RT: ELECTRIC LIGHTING
        ELECTRICAL MACHINERY INDUSTRY

ELECTRICAL MACHINERY INDUSTRY
INDUSTRIE ELECTRO-MECANIQUE / INDUSTRIA
ELECTROMECANICA - 08.15.01
    BT: ELECTRICAL INDUSTRY
    RT: ELECTRICAL MACHINERY
        ELECTRONICS INDUSTRY

ELECTRICIANS
ELECTRICIENS / ELECTRICISTAS - 13.09.06
    BT: INDUSTRIAL WORKERS

ELECTRICITY
ELECTRICITE / ELECTRICIDAD - 08.11.02
    RT: ELECTRIC POWER
        ELECTRICAL INDUSTRY

ELECTRIFICATION
ELECTRIFICATION / ELECTRIFICACION - 08.11.02
    RT: ELECTRIC POWER
        ELECTRICAL INDUSTRY

ELECTRONIC COMPUTERS
- 08.15.02
    USE: COMPUTERS

ELECTRONIC DATA PROCESSING
TRAITEMENT ELECTRONIQUE DES DONNEES /
PROCESAMIENTO ELECTRONICO DE DATOS - 19.01.02
    BT: DATA PROCESSING
    RT: COMPUTER CENTRES
        COMPUTERS

ELECTRONIC ENGINEERING

ELECTRONIC ENGINEERING<CONT>
TECHNOLOGIE ELECTRONIQUE / TECNOLOGIA
ELECTRONICA - 08.15.01
> *BT:* ENGINEERING
> *RT:* ELECTRICAL ENGINEERING
> ELECTRONICS

ELECTRONIC EQUIPMENT
EQUIPEMENT ELECTRONIQUE / EQUIPO ELECTRONICO -
08.15.02
> *UF:* HARDWARE
> *BT:* EQUIPMENT
> *NT:* COMPUTERS
> ELECTRONIC TUBES
> RADAR
> TRANSISTORS
> *RT:* COMPUTER PROGRAMMES

ELECTRONIC TUBES
TUBES ELECTRONIQUES / VALVULAS ELECTRONICAS -
08.15.02
> *BT:* ELECTRONIC EQUIPMENT

ELECTRONICS
ELECTRONIQUE / ELECTRONICA - 08.15.01
> *RT:* COMMUNICATION ENGINEERING
> ELECTRONIC ENGINEERING
> ELECTRONICS INDUSTRY

ELECTRONICS INDUSTRY
INDUSTRIE ELECTRONIQUE / INDUSTRIA ELECTRONICA -
08.15.01
> *BT:* INDUSTRIAL SECTOR
> *RT:* ELECTRICAL INDUSTRY
> ELECTRICAL MACHINERY INDUSTRY
> ELECTRONICS
> TELECOMMUNICATION INDUSTRY

ELEMENTARY EDUCATION
- 06.03.06
> *USE:* PRIMARY EDUCATION

ELEMENTARY SCHOOLS
- 06.04.02
> *USE:* PRIMARY SCHOOLS

ELEPHANTS
ELEPHANTS / ELEFANTES - 07.09.01
> *BT:* ANIMALS

ELITE
ELITE / ELITE - 05.03.05
> *RT:* INTELLECTUALS
> POLITICAL LEADERSHIP
> RULING CLASS
> SOCIAL STRATIFICATION
> UPPER CLASS

EMBARGO
EMBARGO / EMBARGO - 09.05.07
> *BT:* TRADE BARRIERS
> *NT:* ARMS EMBARGO
> *RT:* ACCESS TO MARKET

EMBRYO
EMBRYON / EMBRION - 15.02.02
> *RT:* FOETUS

EMERGENCY RELIEF
SECOURS D'URGENCE / AYUDA DE EMERGENCIA -
02.05.03
> *BT:* SOCIAL SERVICES
> *RT:* DISASTERS

EMIGRANTS
EMIGRANTS / EMIGRANTES - 14.07.00
> *BT:* MIGRANTS
> *RT:* EMIGRATION

EMIGRATION
EMIGRATION / EMIGRACION - 14.07.00
> *BT:* INTERNATIONAL MIGRATIONS
> *NT:* BRAIN DRAIN
> *RT:* EMIGRANTS

EMPLOYEE ASSOCIATIONS
ASSOCIATIONS D'EMPLOYES / ASOCIACIONES DE
EMPLEADOS - 13.06.00
*SN: ORGANIZATIONS OTHER THAN THOSE SET UP FOR
COLLECTIVE BARGAINING OR JOINT CONSULTATION
PURPOSES, WHOSE MEMBERSHIP CONSISTS OF
EMPLOYEES OF A SINGLE COMPANY.*
> *BT:* ASSOCIATIONS
> *RT:* EMPLOYEES

EMPLOYEES
EMPLOYES / EMPLEADOS - 13.09.02
> *BT:* WORKERS
> *NT:* OFFICE WORKERS
> PUBLIC SERVANTS
> TRANSPORT WORKERS
> VENDORS
> *RT:* EMPLOYEE ASSOCIATIONS
> EMPLOYEES ATTITUDES
> PROFESSIONALS

EMPLOYEES ATTITUDES
ATTITUDES DES EMPLOYES / ACTITUDES DE LOS
EMPLEADOS - 13.06.00
> *BT:* ATTITUDES
> *RT:* EMPLOYEES
> WORKERS ADAPTATION

EMPLOYERS
EMPLOYEURS / EMPLEADORES - 12.03.00
> *RT:* EMPLOYERS ORGANIZATIONS
> ENTREPRENEURS
> MANAGEMENT ATTITUDES
> PRODUCERS

EMPLOYERS ATTITUDES
- 13.06.00
> *USE:* MANAGEMENT ATTITUDES

EMPLOYERS ORGANIZATIONS
ORGANISATIONS PATRONALES / ORGANIZACIONES
PATRONALES - 13.06.00

EMPLOYERS ORGANIZATIONS<CONT>
- *BT:* ASSOCIATIONS
  - INTEREST GROUPS
- *RT:* EMPLOYERS

EMPLOYMENT
EMPLOI / EMPLEO - 13.01.03
- *NT:* FULL EMPLOYMENT
  - PART TIME EMPLOYMENT
  - TEMPORARY EMPLOYMENT
  - UNEMPLOYMENT
- *RT:* EMPLOYMENT CREATION
  - EMPLOYMENT OPPORTUNITIES
  - EMPLOYMENT POLICY
  - EMPLOYMENT SECURITY
  - EMPLOYMENT SERVICES
  - JOB CLASSIFICATION
  - JOB DESCRIPTION
  - JOB EVALUATION
  - LABOUR MARKET
  - OCCUPATIONAL STRUCTURE
  - TRANSITION FROM SCHOOL TO WORK

EMPLOYMENT CREATION
CREATION D'EMPLOIS / CREACION DE EMPLEOS -
13.01.03
- *RT:* EMPLOYMENT
  - EMPLOYMENT OPPORTUNITIES
  - EMPLOYMENT POLICY

EMPLOYMENT INJURIES BENEFITS
INDEMNITES POUR ACCIDENT DU TRAVAIL / SUBSIDIOS
POR ACCIDENTES DE TRABAJO - 02.03.02
- *BT:* SOCIAL SECURITY
- *RT:* OCCUPATIONAL ACCIDENTS

EMPLOYMENT OPPORTUNITIES
CHANCES D'OBTENIR UN EMPLOI / OPORTUNIDADES DE
EMPLEO - 13.01.02
- *BT:* EQUAL OPPORTUNITY
- *RT:* EMPLOYMENT
  - EMPLOYMENT CREATION
  - EMPLOYMENT POLICY

EMPLOYMENT PLANNING
- 13.01.03
- *USE:* **MANPOWER PLANNING**

EMPLOYMENT POLICY
POLITIQUE DE L'EMPLOI / POLITICA DE EMPLEO -
13.01.03
- *UF:* MANPOWER POLICY
- *BT:* LABOUR POLICY
- *RT:* EMPLOYMENT
  - EMPLOYMENT CREATION
  - EMPLOYMENT OPPORTUNITIES
  - MANPOWER PLANNING
  - WORLD EMPLOYMENT PROGRAMME

EMPLOYMENT SECURITY
SECURITE D'EMPLOI / SEGURIDAD EN EL EMPLEO -
13.01.03
- *RT:* EMPLOYMENT

EMPLOYMENT SERVICES
SERVICES D'EMPLOI / SERVICIOS DE EMPLEO -
13.02.01
- *SN:* *SERVICES PROVIDED OFFICIALLY BY GOVERNMENTS*
  AS WELL AS THOSE RUN ON A PRIVATE FEE-PAYING
  BASIS, WITH A VIEW TO FINDING SUITABLE WORK
  POSITIONS FOR UNEMPLOYED PERSONS.
- *UF:* MANPOWER SERVICES
  - PLACEMENT SERVICES
- *RT:* EMPLOYMENT

ENCYCLOPEDIA
ENCYCLOPEDIE / ENCICLOPEDIA - 19.03.00
- *BT:* PRIMARY DOCUMENTS
  - REFERENCE MATERIALS
- *RT:* TERMINOLOGY

ENDANGERED SPECIES
ESPECES EN DANGER / ESPECIES EN PELIGRO -
16.05.01
- *RT:* PROTECTED SPECIES

ENDEMIC DISEASES
MALADIES ENDEMIQUES / ENFERMEDADES ENDEMICAS -
15.04.02
- *BT:* DISEASES

ENDOCRINE SYSTEM
SYSTEME ENDOCRINIEN / SISTEMA ENDOCRINO -
15.02.04
- *BT:* ANATOMY

ENERGY
ENERGIE / ENERGIA - 08.11.01
- *NT:* ELECTRIC POWER
  - NUCLEAR ENERGY
  - SOLAR ENERGY
  - THERMAL ENERGY
  - TIDAL ENERGY
  - WIND ENERGY
- *RT:* ENERGY CONSERVATION
  - ENERGY CONSUMPTION
  - ENERGY CRISIS
  - ENERGY POLICY
  - ENERGY RESOURCES
  - ENERGY SOURCES
  - ENERGY UTILIZATION
  - OECD IEA

ENERGY CONSERVATION
ECONOMIES D'ENERGIE / CONSERVACION DE LA ENERGIA
- 08.11.01
- *UF:* POWER CONSERVATION
- *BT:* RESOURCES CONSERVATION
- *RT:* ENERGY

ENERGY CONSUMPTION
CONSOMMATION D'ENERGIE / CONSUMO DE ENERGIA -
08.11.01
- *UF:* POWER CONSUMPTION
- *BT:* CONSUMPTION

ENERGY CONSUMPTION<CONT>

> *RT:* ENERGY
> ENERGY ECONOMICS
> ENERGY POLICY
> ENERGY RESOURCES
> ENERGY UTILIZATION
> POWER DEMAND
> POWER DISTRIBUTION

ENERGY CRISIS
CRISE DE L'ENERGIE / CRISIS DE LA ENERGIA -
08.11.01

> *RT:* ENERGY
> POWER DEMAND
> POWER SUPPLY

ENERGY DEMAND
- 08.11.01
> *USE:* POWER DEMAND

ENERGY ECONOMICS
ECONOMIE DE L'ENERGIE / ECONOMIA ENERGETICA -
08.11.01
SN: ECONOMICS AS IT RELATES TO THE ENERGY
SECTOR.

> *BT:* ECONOMICS
> *RT:* ENERGY CONSUMPTION
> ENERGY POLICY
> POWER DEMAND
> POWER DISTRIBUTION
> POWER INDUSTRY

ENERGY POLICY
POLITIQUE ENERGETIQUE / POLITICA ENERGETICA -
08.11.01

> *BT:* GOVERNMENT POLICY
> *RT:* ENERGY
> ENERGY CONSUMPTION
> ENERGY ECONOMICS
> ENERGY RESOURCES
> ENERGY SOURCES

ENERGY REQUIREMENTS
- 08.11.01
> *USE:* POWER DEMAND

ENERGY RESOURCES
RESSOURCES ENERGETIQUES / RECURSOS ENERGETICOS -
16.02.02

> *UF:* POWER RESOURCES
> *BT:* NATURAL RESOURCES
> *NT:* PETROLEUM RESOURCES
> *RT:* ENERGY
> ENERGY CONSUMPTION
> ENERGY POLICY

ENERGY SOURCES
SOURCES D'ENERGIE / FUENTES DE ENERGIA -
08.11.01

ENERGY SOURCES<CONT>

> *NT:* COAL
> COAL GAS
> FUELS
> PETROLEUM
> SOLAR RADIATION
> TIDES
> URANIUM
> WATER
> WIND
> *RT:* ENERGY
> ENERGY POLICY

ENERGY UTILIZATION
UTILISATION DE L'ENERGIE / UTILIZACION DE LA
ENERGIA - 08.11.01
> *RT:* ENERGY
> ENERGY CONSUMPTION

ENGINE FUELS
CARBURANTS / COMBUSTIBLES PARA MOTORES -
08.11.06
> *BT:* FUELS
> *NT:* PETROL

ENGINEERING
INGENIERIE / INGENIERIA - 12.06.00

> *NT:* AGRICULTURAL ENGINEERING
> CHEMICAL ENGINEERING
> CIVIL ENGINEERING
> COMMUNICATION ENGINEERING
> ELECTRICAL ENGINEERING
> ELECTRONIC ENGINEERING
> ENVIRONMENTAL ENGINEERING
> HYDRAULIC ENGINEERING
> INDUSTRIAL ENGINEERING
> MINING ENGINEERING
> NUCLEAR ENGINEERING
> PETROLEUM ENGINEERING
> *RT:* ENGINEERING DESIGN
> ENGINEERS
> TECHNICAL ASPECTS
> TECHNICAL EDUCATION
> TECHNOLOGY

ENGINEERING DESIGN
CONCEPTION TECHNIQUE / DISENO TECNICO - 12.06.00
> *NT:* INDUSTRIAL DESIGN
> PRODUCT DESIGN
> *RT:* ENGINEERING
> SYSTEMS DESIGN

ENGINEERS
INGENIEURS / INGENIEROS - 13.09.09
> *RT:* ENGINEERING

ENGINES
MOTEURS / MOTORES - 08.14.06
SN: INTERNAL COMBUSTION ENGINES, STEAM ENGINES,
ELECTRIC ENGINES.
> *UF:* MOTORS

ENGINES<CONT>
    NT: DIESEL ENGINES
        ELECTRIC MOTORS
        JET ENGINES
        PETROL ENGINES
        STEAM ENGINES
    RT: MOTOR VEHICLE INDUSTRY

ENGLISH LANGUAGE
LANGUE ANGLAISE / LENGUA INGLESA - 05.06.02
    BT: LANGUAGES

ENGLISH SPEAKING AFRICA
AFRIQUE ANGLOPHONE / AFRICA ANGLOFONA - 01.04.02
    BT: AFRICA
    NT: BOTSWANA
        EGYPT
        GAMBIA
        GHANA
        KENYA
        LESOTHO
        LIBERIA
        LIBYA
        MALAWI
        MAURITIUS
        NAMIBIA
        NIGERIA
        RHODESIA
        SIERRA LEONE
        SOUTH AFRICA
        ST HELENA
        SUDAN
        SWAZILAND
        TANZANIA
        UGANDA
        ZAMBIA

ENROLMENT
IMMATRICULATION / MATRICULACION - 06.04.09

ENTERPRISES
ENTREPRISES / EMPRESAS - 12.01.00
    NT: AGRICULTURAL ENTERPRISES
        CAPITALIST ENTERPRISES
        COMMERCIAL ENTERPRISES
        FOREIGN ENTERPRISES
        INDUSTRIAL ENTERPRISES
        JOINT VENTURES
        MIXED ENTERPRISES
        MULTINATIONAL ENTERPRISES
        PILOT ENTERPRISES
        PRIVATE ENTERPRISES
        PUBLIC ENTERPRISES
        SMALL ENTERPRISES
        SOCIALIST ENTERPRISES
    RT: BUSINESS ECONOMICS
        BUSINESS MANAGEMENT
        BUSINESS ORGANIZATION
        ENTREPRENEURS
        SIZE OF ENTERPRISE

ENTOMOLOGY
ENTOMOLOGIE / ENTOMOLOGIA - 07.06.00
    BT: ZOOLOGY
    RT: INSECTS

ENTREPRENEURS
CHEFS D'ENTREPRISE / EMPRESARIOS - 12.03.00
    RT: BUSINESS MANAGEMENT
        EMPLOYERS
        ENTERPRISES
        MANAGEMENT DEVELOPMENT

ENVIRONMENT
ENVIRONNEMENT / MEDIO AMBIENTE - 16.01.02
SN: COVERS PHYSICAL, CHEMICAL AND BIOLOGICAL
    AGENTS AND SOCIAL FACTORS AFFECTING LIVING
    ORGANISMS AND HUMAN ACTIVITIES.
    NT: HUMAN ENVIRONMENT
        PHYSICAL ENVIRONMENT
    RT: ECOLOGY
        ECOSYSTEMS
        ENVIRONMENTAL DEGRADATION
        ENVIRONMENTAL ECONOMICS
        ENVIRONMENTAL EDUCATION
        ENVIRONMENTAL EFFECTS
        ENVIRONMENTAL ENGINEERING
        ENVIRONMENTAL MANAGEMENT
        ENVIRONMENTAL POLICY
        ENVIRONMENTAL PROTECTION
        ENVIRONMENTAL QUALITY
        HABITAT
        UNEP

ENVIRONMENTAL BIOLOGY
- 16.01.01
    USE: ECOLOGY

ENVIRONMENTAL CONTROL
- 19.02.01
    USE: ENVIRONMENTAL MANAGEMENT

ENVIRONMENTAL DEGRADATION
DEGRADATION DE L'ENVIRONNEMENT / DETERIORO DEL
MEDIO AMBIENTE - 16.03.04
    NT: DESERTIFICATION
    RT: ENVIRONMENT
        POLLUTION

ENVIRONMENTAL ECONOMICS
ECONOMIE DE L'ENVIRONNEMENT / ECONOMIA AMBIENTAL
- 16.04.01
    BT: ECONOMICS
    RT: ENVIRONMENT
        POLLUTER-PAYS PRINCIPLE

ENVIRONMENTAL EDUCATION
EDUCATION TOUCHANT L'ENVIRONNEMENT / EDUCACION
AMBIENTAL - 06.03.04
    BT: BASIC EDUCATION
    RT: ENVIRONMENT

ENVIRONMENTAL EFFECTS
EFFETS SUR L'ENVIRONNEMENT / EFECTOS SOBRE EL
MEDIO AMBIENTE - 16.03.04
    UF: ENVIRONMENTAL IMPACT
    RT: ENVIRONMENT
        POLLUTION

ENVIRONMENTAL ENGINEERING

ENVIRONMENTAL ENGINEERING<CONT>
TECHNOLOGIE DE L'ENVIRONNEMENT / INGENIERIA
AMBIENTAL - 16.04.01
    BT: ENGINEERING
    NT: EROSION CONTROL
        FIRE CONTROL
        FLOOD CONTROL
        NOISE CONTROL
        PEST CONTROL
        POLLUTION CONTROL
        WATER TREATMENT
        WEATHER CONTROL
    RT: ENVIRONMENT
        SAFETY

ENVIRONMENTAL IMPACT
- 16.03.04
    USE: ENVIRONMENTAL EFFECTS

ENVIRONMENTAL MANAGEMENT
GESTION DE L'ENVIRONNEMENT / ADMINISTRACION
AMBIENTAL - 16.04.01
    UF: ENVIRONMENTAL CONTROL
        ENVIRONMENTAL MONITORING
    BT: MANAGEMENT
    RT: ENVIRONMENT
        ENVIRONMENTAL POLICY
        ENVIRONMENTAL PROTECTION

ENVIRONMENTAL MONITORING
- 16.04.01
    USE: ENVIRONMENTAL MANAGEMENT

ENVIRONMENTAL POLICY
POLITIQUE DE L'ENVIRONNEMENT / POLITICA
AMBIENTAL - 16.04.01
    BT: GOVERNMENT POLICY
    RT: ENVIRONMENT
        ENVIRONMENTAL MANAGEMENT

ENVIRONMENTAL POLLUTION
- 16.03.04
    USE: POLLUTION

ENVIRONMENTAL PROTECTION
PROTECTION DE L'ENVIRONNEMENT / PROTECCION DEL
MEDIO AMBIENTE - 16.05.01
    BT: NATURE CONSERVATION
    NT: LANDSCAPE PROTECTION
        POLLUTION CONTROL
    RT: ENVIRONMENT
        ENVIRONMENTAL MANAGEMENT

ENVIRONMENTAL QUALITY
QUALITE DE L'ENVIRONNEMENT / CALIDAD AMBIENTAL -
16.01.02
    RT: ENVIRONMENT
        QUALITY OF LIFE

ENZYMES
ENZYMES / ENZIMAS - 15.01.03

EPIDEMIC DISEASES
- 15.04.02
    USE: INFECTIOUS DISEASES

EPIDEMICS
EPIDEMIES / EPIDEMIAS - 15.04.04
    BT: NATURAL DISASTERS
    RT: EPIDEMIOLOGY
        INFECTIOUS DISEASES

EPIDEMIOLOGY
EPIDEMIOLOGIE / EPIDEMIOLOGIA - 15.04.06
    BT: MEDICAL SCIENCES
    RT: EPIDEMICS
        INFECTIOUS DISEASES

EQUAL OPPORTUNITY
EGALITE DE CHANCES / IGUALDAD DE OPORTUNIDADES -
04.02.03
    NT: EDUCATIONAL OPPORTUNITIES
        EMPLOYMENT OPPORTUNITIES

EQUAL PAY
EGALITE DE REMUNERATION / IGUALDAD DE
REMUNERACION - 13.07.00
    RT: WAGE DETERMINATION

EQUATORIAL GUINEA
GUINEE EQUATORIALE / GUINEA ECUATORIAL -
01.04.02
    BT: CENTRAL AFRICA

EQUATORIAL ZONE
ZONE EQUATORIALE / ZONA ECUATORIAL - 17.02.03
    BT: CLIMATIC ZONES

EQUIDAE
EQUIDES / EQUIDOS - 07.09.01
    BT: ANIMALS
    NT: DONKEYS
        HORSES

EQUIPMENT
EQUIPEMENT / EQUIPO - 12.05.00
    NT: AGRICULTURAL EQUIPMENT
        EDUCATIONAL EQUIPMENT
        ELECTRICAL EQUIPMENT
        ELECTRONIC EQUIPMENT
        HYDRAULIC EQUIPMENT
        INDUSTRIAL EQUIPMENT
        OBSOLETE EQUIPMENT
        RESEARCH EQUIPMENT
        SECOND HAND EQUIPMENT
        TRANSPORT EQUIPMENT
    RT: EQUIPMENT COSTS
        EQUIPMENT MANAGEMENT
        MACHINERY
        MAINTENANCE AND REPAIR
        MEANS OF PRODUCTION
        MECHANIZATION
        PRECISION INSTRUMENTS
        SPARE PARTS
        TOOLS

EQUIPMENT COSTS
COUTS D'EQUIPEMENT / COSTOS DEL EQUIPO -
12.09.00
    BT: COSTS
    RT: EQUIPMENT

EQUIPMENT MANAGEMENT
GESTION DU MATERIEL / ADMINISTRACION DEL
MATERIAL - 12.05.00
    BT: MANAGEMENT
    RT: EQUIPMENT

EQUIVALENCE BETWEEN DIPLOMAS
EQUIVALENCE DES DIPLOMES / EQUIVALENCIA DE
ESTUDIOS - 06.04.13
    RT: DIPLOMAS

ERGONOMICS
ERGONOMIE / ERGONOMIA - 13.03.01
*SN: USE IN CONNECTION WITH MOULDING OF WORKING
    ENVIRONMENT TO WORKERS' NEEDS.*
    RT: LABOUR STANDARDS
        WORK STUDY

EROSION
EROSION / EROSION - 16.03.02
    NT: SOIL EROSION
    RT: EROSION CONTROL

EROSION CONTROL
LUTTE ANTI-EROSION / LUCHA CONTRA LA EROSION -
16.04.01
    BT: ENVIRONMENTAL ENGINEERING
    RT: EROSION

ESCAP
CESAP / CESAP - 01.03.02
*SN: ECONOMIC AND SOCIAL COMMISSION FOR ASIA AND
    THE PACIFIC.*
    UF: ECAFE
    BT: ASIAN ORGANIZATIONS
        ECOSOC
    RT: ASIA
        PACIFIC REGION

ESRO
- 01.03.03
    USE: EUROPEAN SPACE AGENCY

ESSENTIAL OILS
HUILES ESSENTIELLES / ACEITES ESENCIALES -
08.06.06
    BT: OILS AND FATS
    RT: PERFUMES

ESTIMATING
- 18.09.00
    USE: EVALUATION

ESTUARIES
ESTUAIRES / ESTUARIOS - 17.03.04

ETHICS
ETHIQUE / ETICA - 05.04.01
    RT: SOCIAL CONTROL
        SOCIAL NORMS
        VALUE SYSTEMS

ETHIOPIA
ETHIOPIE / ETIOPIA - 01.04.02
    BT: EAST AFRICA
    RT: ETHIOPIAN

ETHIOPIAN
ETHIOPIEN / ETIOPE - 14.03.02
    RT: ETHIOPIA

ETHNIC FACTORS
FACTEURS ETHNIQUES / FACTORES ETNICOS - 14.03.01
    RT: ETHNIC GROUPS

ETHNIC GROUPS
GROUPES ETHNIQUES / GRUPOS ETNICOS - 14.03.01
    BT: GROUPS
    NT: ETHNIC MINORITIES
    RT: ETHNIC FACTORS
        ETHNICITY
        GENOCIDE
        INTERETHNIC RELATIONS
        TRIBE

ETHNIC MINORITIES
MINORITES ETHNIQUES / MINORIAS ETNICAS -
14.03.01
    BT: ETHNIC GROUPS
        MINORITY GROUPS
    RT: GENOCIDE

ETHNICITY
ETHNICITE / ETNICIDAD - 14.03.01
    RT: ETHNIC GROUPS

ETHNOGRAPHY
ETHNOGRAPHIE / ETNOGRAFIA - 05.01.01
    BT: ETHNOLOGY

ETHNOLOGY
ETHNOLOGIE / ETNOLOGIA - 05.01.01
    BT: SOCIAL SCIENCES
    NT: ETHNOGRAPHY
        FOLKLORE
    RT: ANTHROPOLOGISTS
        IUAES

EURATOM
EURATOM / EURATOM - 01.03.03
    BT: EUROPEAN COMMUNITIES
    RT: NUCLEAR ENERGY

EURODOLLARS
EURODOLLARS / EURODOLARES - 11.03.01
    BT: CURRENCIES
    RT: FINANCIAL MARKET
        MONETARY RELATIONS

EUROPE
EUROPE / EUROPA - 01.04.05
    NT: EASTERN EUROPE
        WESTERN EUROPE
    RT: ECE
        EUROPEAN
        EUROPEAN ORGANIZATIONS
        MEDITERRANEAN COUNTRIES

EUROPEAN
EUROPEEN / EUROPEO - 14.03.02
    RT: EUROPE

EUROPEAN COMMUNITIES
COMMUNAUTES EUROPEENNES / COMUNIDADES EUROPEAS -
01.03.03
    BT: EUROPEAN ORGANIZATIONS
         INTERGOVERNMENTAL ORGANIZATIONS
    NT: ECSC
         EEC
         EIB
         EURATOM
         EUROPEAN PARLIAMENT

EUROPEAN ORGANIZATIONS
ORGANISATIONS EUROPEENNES / ORGANIZACIONES
EUROPEAS - 01.03.03
    BT: REGIONAL ORGANIZATIONS
    NT: BENELUX
         CERN
         CMEA
         COUNCIL OF EUROPE
         EADI
         ECE
         ECMT
         EFTA
         EUROPEAN COMMUNITIES
         EUROPEAN SPACE AGENCY
         ICEM
         NORDIC COUNCIL
         WEU
    RT: EUROPE
         REGIONAL INTEGRATION

EUROPEAN PARLIAMENT
PARLEMENT EUROPEEN / PARLAMENTO EUROPEO -
01.03.03
    BT: EUROPEAN COMMUNITIES

EUROPEAN SPACE AGENCY
AGENCE SPATIALE EUROPEENNE / AGENCIA ESPACIAL
EUROPEA - 01.03.03
    UF: ESRO
    BT: EUROPEAN ORGANIZATIONS
         INTERGOVERNMENTAL ORGANIZATIONS
    RT: SPACE SCIENCES

EUTHANASIA
EUTHANASIE / EUTANASIA - 15.04.04
    RT: CAUSES OF DEATH

EUTROPHICATION
EUTROPHICATION / EUTROFICACION - 16.03.04
    BT: WATER POLLUTION

EVALUATION
EVALUATION / EVALUACION - 18.09.00
    UF: ESTIMATING
    NT: AID EVALUATION
         AUDIENCE RATING
         ECONOMIC EVALUATION
         PROJECT EVALUATION
         RESOURCES EVALUATION
    RT: EVALUATION TECHNIQUES
         TESTING

EVALUATION TECHNIQUES
TECHNIQUES D'EVALUATION / TECNICAS DE EVALUACION

EVALUATION TECHNIQUES<CONT>
- 18.09.00
    BT: RESEARCH METHODS
    NT: TESTS
    RT: EVALUATION

EVAPORATION
EVAPORATION / EVAPORACION - 08.12.03

EXAMINATIONS
EXAMENS / EXAMENES - 06.04.13
    RT: QUALIFICATIONS

EXCHANGE RATE
TAUX DE CHANGE / TASA DE CAMBIO - 11.03.01
    RT: BALANCE OF PAYMENTS
         FOREIGN EXCHANGE
         INTERNATIONAL MONETARY SYSTEM

EXHIBITIONS
EXPOSITIONS / EXPOSICIONES - 09.03.05
    RT: TRADE FAIRS

EXPATRIATE WORKERS
- 13.09.02
    USE: FOREIGN WORKERS

EXPENDITURES
DEPENSES / GASTOS - 11.02.05
    NT: CAPITAL COSTS
         CONSUMER EXPENDITURES
         CULTURAL EXPENDITURES
         NATIONAL EXPENDITURES
         PUBLIC EXPENDITURES
    RT: COSTS

EXPERIMENTAL CLASSES
CLASSES EXPERIMENTALES / CLASES EXPERIMENTALES -
06.04.10
    BT: CLASSES
    RT: EXPERIMENTAL SCHOOLS

EXPERIMENTAL FARMS
FERMES EXPERIMENTALES / ESTACIONES AGRICOLAS
EXPERIMENTALES - 07.03.01
    BT: FARMS
    RT: AGRICULTURAL RESEARCH
         AGRICULTURAL TRAINING

EXPERIMENTAL SCHOOLS
ECOLES EXPERIMENTALES / ESCUELAS EXPERIMENTALES
- 06.04.03
    BT: SCHOOLS
    RT: EXPERIMENTAL CLASSES

EXPERIMENTAL TEACHING
ENSEIGNEMENT EXPERIMENTAL / ENSENANZA
EXPERIMENTAL - 06.05.02
    BT: TEACHING
    RT: TEACHING METHODS

EXPERIMENTATION
EXPERIMENTATION / EXPERIMENTACION - 18.05.00

EXPERIMENTATION<CONT>
    RT: EXPERIMENTS
         METHODOLOGY
         SIMULATION
         TESTING

EXPERIMENTS
EXPERIENCES / EXPERIMENTOS - 18.05.00
    BT: RESEARCH METHODS
    RT: EXPERIMENTATION
         TESTS

EXPERT REPORT
RAPPORT D'EXPERT / INFORME DE EXPERTO - 19.02.08
    RT: EXPERTS

EXPERTS
EXPERTS / EXPERTOS - 01.01.07
SN: USE ONLY IN CONNECTION WITH TECHNICAL
    COOPERATION EXPERTS.
    BT: DEVELOPMENT PERSONNEL
    RT: EXPERT REPORT

EXPLOITABILITY
EXPLOITABILITE / EXPLOTABILIDAD - 16.02.01
    RT: OVEREXPLOITATION
         RESOURCES DEPLETION
         RESOURCES EVALUATION
         RESOURCES EXPLOITATION

EXPLOSIONS
EXPLOSIONS / EXPLOSIONES - 16.03.02

EXPLOSIVES
EXPLOSIFS / EXPLOSIVOS - 08.12.08

EXPORT CREDIT
CREDIT A L'EXPORTATION / CREDITO A LAS
EXPORTACIONES - 09.05.05
    BT: CREDIT
         EXPORT FINANCING
    RT: EXPORT INSURANCE
         EXPORTS

EXPORT DIVERSIFICATION
DIVERSIFICATION DES EXPORTATIONS /
DIVERSIFICACION DE EXPORTACIONES - 09.05.05
    RT: EXPORTS

EXPORT EARNINGS
RECETTES A L'EXPORTATION / INGRESO POR
EXPORTACIONES - 09.05.05
    RT: COMPENSATORY FINANCING
         EXPORTS

EXPORT FINANCING
FINANCEMENT DES EXPORTATIONS / FINANCIAMIENTO A
LAS EXPORTACIONES - 09.05.05
    BT: FINANCING
    NT: EXPORT CREDIT
         EXPORT SUBSIDIES
    RT: EXPORT PROMOTION
         EXPORTS

EXPORT INSURANCE
ASSURANCE A L'EXPORTATION / SEGURO DE
EXPORTACION - 11.02.03
    BT: INSURANCE
    RT: EXPORT CREDIT
         EXPORT PROMOTION
         EXPORTS

EXPORT OF CAPITAL
EXPORTATION DE CAPITAUX / EXPORTACION DE
CAPITALES - 11.03.03
SN: TRANSFER OF EARNINGS OR ORIGINAL INVESTMENTS
    OUTSIDE THE COUNTRY.
    BT: CAPITAL MOVEMENTS

EXPORT PLANNING
PLANIFICATION DES EXPORTATIONS / PLANIFICACION
DE LA EXPORTACION - 09.05.06
    BT: ECONOMIC PLANNING
    RT: EXPORTS

EXPORT PROMOTION
PROMOTION DES EXPORTATIONS / PROMOCION DE
EXPORTACIONES - 09.05.06
    BT: TRADE PROMOTION
    RT: EXPORT FINANCING
         EXPORT INSURANCE
         EXPORTS

EXPORT RESTRICTIONS
RESTRICTIONS A L'EXPORTATION / RESTRICCIONES A
LA EXPORTACION - 09.05.07
    BT: RESTRICTIVE BUSINESS PRACTICES
    RT: EXPORTS

EXPORT SUBSIDIES
SUBVENTIONS A L'EXPORTATION / SUBSIDIOS A LAS
EXPORTACIONES - 09.05.05
    BT: EXPORT FINANCING
         SUBSIDIES
    RT: EXPORTS

EXPORT VALUE
VALEUR DES EXPORTATIONS / VALOR DE EXPORTACIONES
- 09.05.05
    RT: EXPORTS

EXPORT VOLUME
VOLUME DES EXPORTATIONS / VOLUMEN DE
EXPORTACIONES - 09.05.05
    BT: TRADE VOLUME
    RT: EXPORTS

EXPORT-ORIENTED INDUSTRY
INDUSTRIE EXPORTATRICE / INDUSTRIA DE
EXPORTACION - 08.01.01
    BT: INDUSTRY
    RT: EXPORTS

EXPORTS
EXPORTATIONS / EXPORTACIONES - 09.05.05
    BT: BALANCE OF PAYMENTS
         FOREIGN TRADE

EXPORTS<CONT>
    RT: EXPORT CREDIT
        EXPORT DIVERSIFICATION
        EXPORT EARNINGS
        EXPORT FINANCING
        EXPORT INSURANCE
        EXPORT PLANNING
        EXPORT PROMOTION
        EXPORT RESTRICTIONS
        EXPORT SUBSIDIES
        EXPORT VALUE
        EXPORT VOLUME
        EXPORT-ORIENTED INDUSTRY
        REEXPORT

EXPROPRIATION
EXPROPRIATION / EXPROPIACION - 03.03.05
    RT: NATIONALIZATION
        PUBLIC OWNERSHIP

EXTENSION SERVICES
SERVICES DE VULGARISATION / SERVICIOS DE EXTENSION - 19.01.03
    BT: INFORMATION SERVICES
    NT: AGRICULTURAL EXTENSION
        INDUSTRIAL EXTENSION

EXTENSIVE FARMING
EXPLOITATION AGRICOLE EXTENSIVE / EXPLOTACION AGRICOLA EXTENSIVA - 07.05.03
    BT: FARMING SYSTEMS

EXTERNAL DEBT
DETTE EXTERIEURE / DEUDA EXTERNA - 11.03.01
    BT: DEBT
    RT: BALANCE OF PAYMENTS

EYE DISEASES
MALADIES DES YEUX / ENFERMEDADES DE LOS OJOS - 15.04.02
    BT: DISEASES
    NT: BLINDNESS

FABA BEANS
VICIA FABA / HABAS - 07.07.06
    BT: LEGUMINOSAE

FACTORIES
- 08.03.00
    USE: INDUSTRIAL PLANTS

FACTORY BOATS
BATEAUX USINE / BUQUES FACTORIA - 07.10.03
    BT: FISHING VESSELS

FACTORY LAYOUT
PLANS D'USINE / PLANOS DE FABRICA - 08.03.00
    RT: FACTORY ORGANIZATION
        INDUSTRIAL PLANTS

FACTORY ORGANIZATION
ORGANISATION DE L'USINE / ORGANIZACION DE LA FABRICA - 08.03.00
SN: PLANNING OF WORK WITHIN A PRODUCTION PLANT.
    RT: FACTORY LAYOUT
        INDUSTRIAL PLANTS
        INDUSTRIAL PROFILES

FACTORY WORKERS
- 13.09.06
    USE: INDUSTRIAL WORKERS

FALKLAND ISLANDS
ILES FALKLAND / ISLAS MALVINAS - 01.04.03
    BT: SOUTH AMERICA
    RT: UNITED KINGDOM

FAMILY
FAMILLE / FAMILIA - 14.02.04
    RT: DEPENDENCY BURDEN
        FAMILY ALLOWANCES
        FAMILY BUDGET
        FAMILY DISINTEGRATION
        FAMILY ENVIRONMENT
        FAMILY LAW
        FAMILY PLANNING
        FAMILY POLICY
        FAMILY SIZE
        KINSHIP
        MATERNITY BENEFITS

FAMILY ALLOWANCES
ALLOCATIONS FAMILIALES / SUBSIDIOS FAMILIARES - 02.03.02
    BT: FAMILY POLICY
        SOCIAL SECURITY
    RT: FAMILY
        MATERNITY BENEFITS

FAMILY BUDGET
BUDGET FAMILIAL / PRESUPUESTO FAMILIAR - 03.02.05

FAMILY BUDGET<CONT>
    RT: CONSUMER EXPENDITURES
        CONSUMPTION
        FAMILY
        HOME ECONOMICS
        HOUSEHOLD
        PURCHASING POWER
        STANDARD OF LIVING

FAMILY DISINTEGRATION
DESINTEGRATION DE LA FAMILLE / DESINTEGRACION DE
LA FAMILIA - 14.02.04
    BT: SOCIAL PROBLEMS
    RT: DIVORCE
        FAMILY

FAMILY ENVIRONMENT
MILIEU FAMILIAL / MEDIO FAMILIAR - 14.02.04
    BT: SOCIAL ENVIRONMENT
    RT: FAMILY

FAMILY LAW
DROIT DE LA FAMILLE / DERECHO DE LA FAMILIA -
04.01.02
    BT: CIVIL LAW
    RT: FAMILY

FAMILY PLANNING
PLANIFICATION DE LA FAMILLE / PLANIFICACION
FAMILIAR - 14.05.02
    NT: BIRTH CONTROL
    RT: CONTRACEPTION
        FAMILY
        FAMILY PLANNING AGENCIES
        FAMILY PLANNING PROGRAMMES
        IPPF
        POPULATION POLICY

FAMILY PLANNING AGENCIES
CENTRES DE PLANNING FAMILIAL / AGENCIAS DE
PLANIFICACION FAMILIAR - 14.05.02
    RT: FAMILY PLANNING

FAMILY PLANNING PROGRAMMES
PROGRAMMES DE PLANNING FAMILIAL / PROGRAMAS DE
PLANIFICACION FAMILIAR - 14.05.02
    RT: FAMILY PLANNING

FAMILY POLICY
POLITIQUE FAMILIALE / POLITICA FAMILIAR -
02.05.03
    BT: SOCIAL POLICY
    NT: CHILD CARE
        FAMILY ALLOWANCES
        MATERNITY BENEFITS
    RT: FAMILY

FAMILY SIZE
DIMENSION DE LA FAMILLE / TAMANO DE LA FAMILIA -
14.02.04
    RT: FAMILY

FAMINE
FAMINE / HAMBRE - 15.03.02
    UF: STARVATION
    BT: SOCIAL PROBLEMS

FAMINE<CONT>
    RT: FOOD SHORTAGE
        MALNUTRITION
        NATURAL DISASTERS

FAO
FAO / FAO - 01.03.02
SN: FOOD AND AGRICULTURE ORGANIZATION.
    BT: UN SPECIALIZED AGENCIES
    NT: WORLD FOOD PROGRAMME
    RT: AGRICULTURE
        AGRIS
        FOOD

FAR EAST
EXTREME ORIENT / LEJANO ORIENTE - 01.04.04
    BT: ASIA
    NT: CHINA
        HONG KONG
        JAPAN
        KOREA
        KOREA DPR
        KOREA R
        MACAO
        MONGOLIA PR
        TAIWAN

FARM ANIMALS
- 07.09.02
    USE: LIVESTOCK

FARM BUILDINGS
BATIMENTS DE FERME / CONSTRUCCIONES AGRICOLAS -
07.04.00
    BT: BUILDINGS
    NT: GREENHOUSES
        SILOS

FARM MACHINERY
- 07.04.00
    USE: AGRICULTURAL MACHINERY

FARM MANAGEMENT
GESTION D'ENTREPRISE AGRICOLE / ADMINISTRACION
DE EMPRESA AGRICOLA - 07.03.02
    BT: AGRICULTURAL MANAGEMENT
    RT: AGRICULTURAL ENTERPRISES
        FARMS

FARM SIZE
DIMENSION DE LA FERME / TAMANO DE LA GRANJA -
07.03.02
    BT: SIZE OF ENTERPRISE
    RT: FARMS

FARMER TRAINING
- 06.03.07
    USE: AGRICULTURAL TRAINING

FARMERS
AGRICULTEURS / AGRICULTORES - 13.09.05
    BT: AGRICULTURAL WORKERS
    NT: TENANT FARMERS

FARMERS<CONT>
   RT: AGRICULTURAL ENTERPRISES
        IFAP
        PEASANT MOVEMENTS
        PEASANTS

FARMING
AGRIEXPLOITATION / EXPLOTACION AGRICOLA -
07.05.03
   RT: FARMING SYSTEMS

FARMING SYSTEMS
SYSTEMES D'EXPLOITATION AGRICOLE / SISTEMAS
AGRICOLAS - 07.05.03
   NT: COLLECTIVE FARMING
        COMMERCIAL FARMING
        COOPERATIVE FARMING
        CULTIVATION SYSTEMS
        EXTENSIVE FARMING
        INTENSIVE FARMING ·
        MIXED FARMING
        SUBSISTENCE FARMING
   RT: FARMING

FARMS
FERMES / GRANJAS - 07.03.01
   BT: AGRICULTURAL ENTERPRISES
   NT: EXPERIMENTAL FARMS
        STATE FARMS
   RT: FARM MANAGEMENT
        FARM SIZE

FAROE ISLANDS
ILES FEROE / ISLAS FEROE - 01.04.05
   BT: SCANDINAVIA
   RT: DENMARK

FATHER
PERE / PADRE - 14.02.04
   BT: PARENTS

FATIGUE
FATIGUE / FATIGA - 13.03.04
   RT: REST

FATS
GRAISSES / GRASAS - 08.06.06
   BT: OILS AND FATS
   NT: ANIMAL FATS

FAUNA
FAUNE / FAUNA - 07.09.01
   NT: AQUATIC FAUNA
   RT: ANIMALS

FEASIBILITY STUDIES
ETUDES DE FAISABILITE / ESTUDIOS DE FACTABILIDAD
- 01.01.06

FECUNDITY
FERTILITE / FERTILIDAD - 15.02.02

FEED
ALIMENTS POUR ANIMAUX / ALIMENTOS PARA ANIMALES

FEED<CONT>
- 07.09.03
   BT: FOOD
   RT: UREA

FEEDING
ALIMENTATION / ALIMENTACION - 15.03.01
*SN: THE PROVISION OF FOOD; THE ACT OR PROCESS OF
     ONE THAT FEEDS OR THE ACT OR PROCESS OF
     BEING FED.*
   NT: ANIMAL FEEDING
        BREAST FEEDING

FEES
DROITS DE SCOLARITE / DERECHOS DE INSCRIPCION -
06.04.11
   BT: COST OF EDUCATION

FEMALE MANPOWER
MAIN D'OEUVRE FEMININE / MANO DE OBRA FEMENINA -
13.09.02
   UF: WOMEN WORKERS
   BT: WOMEN
        WORKERS
   RT: MATERNITY LEAVE

FEMALES
FEMELLES / HEMBRAS - 14.02.03
   BT: SEX
   RT: WOMEN

FERMENTATION
FERMENTATION / FERMENTACION - 15.01.03

FERTILITY
FECONDITE / FECUNDIDAD - 14.05.01
   RT: FERTILITY DECLINE
        FERTILIZATION
        POPULATION INCREASE
        PUBERTY
        REPRODUCTION

FERTILITY DECLINE
BAISSE DE LA FECONDITE / DECLINACION DE LA
FECUNDIDAD - 14.05.01
   RT: FERTILITY
        POPULATION DECLINE

FERTILIZATION
FECONDATION / FECUNDACION - 15.02.02
   RT: FERTILITY
        SEMEN

FERTILIZER INDUSTRY
INDUSTRIE DES ENGRAIS / INDUSTRIA DE
FERTILIZANTES - 08.12.05
   BT: CHEMICAL INDUSTRY
   RT: CHEMICAL FERTILIZERS

FERTILIZERS
ENGRAIS / FERTILIZANTES - 08.12.05
   NT: CHEMICAL FERTILIZERS
   RT: FERTILIZING

FERTILIZING
FERTILISATION / FERTILIZACION - 07.05.02
>   RT: FERTILIZERS
>   SOIL FERTILITY

FETISHISM
FETICHISME / FETICHISMO - 05.04.03

FEUDALISM
FEODALISME / FEUDALISMO - 03.03.01

FIBRES
FIBRES / FIBRAS - 08.08.01
>   NT: HARD FIBRES
>   MANMADE FIBRES
>   NATURAL FIBRES
>   SOFT FIBRES
>   RT: TEXTILE INDUSTRY
>   TEXTILES

FID
FID / FID - 01.03.04
SN: INTERNATIONAL FEDERATION FOR DOCUMENTATION.
>   BT: NON-GOVERNMENTAL ORGANIZATIONS
>   RT: DOCUMENTATION

FIELD ACTIVITY
ACTIVITE SUR LE TERRAIN / ACTIVIDADES DE CAMPO -
18.04.00
>   UF: FIELD WORK

FIELD RESEARCH
RECHERCHE SUR LE TERRAIN / INVESTIGACION DE
CAMPO - 18.04.00
>   UF: FIELD STUDY
>   BT: RESEARCH
>   RT: RESEARCH METHODS

FIELD STUDY
- 18.04.00
>   USE: FIELD RESEARCH

FIELD WORK
- 18.04.00
>   USE: FIELD ACTIVITY

FIJI
FIDJI / FIJI - 01.04.07
>   BT: OCEANIA

FILARIASIS
FILARIOSE / FILARIASIS - 15.04.02
>   BT: PARASITIC DISEASES
>   TROPICAL DISEASES

FILIPINO
PHILIPPIN / FILIPINO - 14.03.02
>   RT: PHILIPPINES

FILM INDUSTRY
INDUSTRIE CINEMATOGRAPHIQUE / INDUSTRIA
CINEMATOGRAFICA - 08.16.00
>   BT: COMMUNICATION INDUSTRY
>   RT: FILMS

FILMS
FILMS / PELICULAS - 05.07.03
>   BT: AUDIOVISUAL MATERIALS
>   MASS MEDIA
>   NT: EDUCATIONAL FILMS
>   RT: CINEMA
>   FILM INDUSTRY
>   PROJECTION EQUIPMENT

FINANCIAL ADMINISTRATION
ADMINISTRATION FINANCIERE / ADMINISTRACION
FINANCIERA - 04.03.02
>   BT: ECONOMIC ADMINISTRATION
>   NT: FISCAL ADMINISTRATION
>   RT: FINANCIAL MANAGEMENT
>   FINANCIAL POLICY
>   LOCAL FINANCE
>   PUBLIC FINANCE

FINANCIAL AID
AIDE FINANCIERE / AYUDA FINANCIERA - 01.01.03
>   UF: CAPITAL AID
>   BT: DEVELOPMENT AID
>   RT: CAPITAL
>   FINANCING

FINANCIAL ASPECTS
ASPECTS FINANCIERS / ASPECTOS FINANCIEROS -
11.02.04
>   RT: FINANCIAL TERMS
>   FINANCING

FINANCIAL INSTITUTIONS
INSTITUTIONS FINANCIERES / INSTITUCIONES
FINANCIERAS - 11.02.02
>   NT: BANKS
>   INSURANCE
>   PENSION FUNDS
>   SAVINGS BANKS

FINANCIAL LOSS
PERTE FINANCIERE / PERDIDA FINANCIERA - 12.09.00
>   BT: ECONOMIC LOSS
>   RT: BANKRUPTCY
>   CAPITAL COSTS
>   DEFICIT

FINANCIAL MANAGEMENT
GESTION FINANCIERE / GESTION FINANCIERA -
11.02.04
>   BT: MANAGEMENT
>   RT: FINANCIAL ADMINISTRATION
>   FINANCIAL POLICY

FINANCIAL MARKET
MARCHE FINANCIER / MERCADO FINANCIERO - 11.02.07
>   UF: CAPITAL MARKET
>   STOCK EXCHANGE
>   BT: MARKET
>   RT: COMMERCIAL BANKS
>   EURODOLLARS

FINANCIAL NEEDS
BESOINS FINANCIERS / NECESIDADES FINANCIERAS -

FINANCIAL NEEDS<CONT>
11.02.05
    UF: CAPITAL NEEDS
    BT: DEMAND
    NT: INVESTMENT REQUIREMENTS
    RT: CAPITAL

FINANCIAL POLICY
POLITIQUE FINANCIERE / POLITICA FINANCIERA -
11.02.04
    BT: ECONOMIC POLICY
    NT: BUDGETARY POLICY
        CREDIT POLICY
        FISCAL POLICY
        MONETARY POLICY
    RT: FINANCIAL ADMINISTRATION
        FINANCIAL MANAGEMENT
        PUBLIC FINANCE

FINANCIAL RESOURCES
RESSOURCES FINANCIERES / RECURSOS FINANCIEROS -
11.02.05
    UF: CAPITAL RESOURCES
    BT: ECONOMIC RESOURCES
    RT: CAPITAL

FINANCIAL STATISTICS
STATISTIQUES FINANCIERES / ESTADISTICAS
FINANCIERAS - 11.02.04
    BT: ECONOMIC STATISTICS

FINANCIAL TERMS
CONDITIONS FINANCIERES / CONDICIONES FINANCIERAS
- 11.02.04
    NT: BORROWING
        GRANTS
        LOANS
    RT: FINANCIAL ASPECTS
        TERMS OF AID

FINANCING
FINANCEMENT / FINANCIAMIENTO - 11.02.04
    NT: AID FINANCING
        DEFICIT FINANCING
        EDUCATIONAL FINANCING
        EXPORT FINANCING
        SELF-FINANCING
    RT: FINANCIAL AID
        FINANCIAL ASPECTS
        FINANCING PROGRAMMES

FINANCING PROGRAMMES
PROGRAMMES DE FINANCEMENT / PROGRAMAS DE
FINANCIACION - 11.02.04
    RT: AID PROGRAMMES
        FINANCING

FINE ARTS
BEAUX ARTS / BELLAS ARTES - 05.05.03
    UF: DECORATIVE ARTS
    BT: VISUAL ARTS

FINE ARTS<CONT>
    NT: ARCHITECTURE
        GRAPHIC ARTS
        PLASTIC ARTS

FINISHED PRODUCTS
PRODUITS FINIS / PRODUCTOS TERMINADOS - 08.04.00
SN: USE ONLY IN DISCUSSION OF EXPORT OR IMPORT
OF RAW MATERIALS OR SEMIMANUFACTURED
PRODUCTS AS OPPOSED TO FINISHED PRODUCTS; OR
OF VERTICAL INTEGRATION, REGARDING THE
DECISION TO PROCEED TO THE MANUFACTURE OF
THE FINISHED PRODUCT, RATHER THAN MARKETING
AT AN EARLIER STAGE.
    BT: MANUFACTURED PRODUCTS

FINLAND
FINLANDE / FINLANDIA - 01.04.05
    BT: SCANDINAVIA
    RT: FINNISH

FINNISH
FINLANDAIS / FINLANDES - 14.03.02
    RT: FINLAND

FIRE CONTROL
LUTTE ANTI-INCENDIE / LUCHA CONTRA INCENDIOS -
16.04.01
    BT: ENVIRONMENTAL ENGINEERING
    RT: FIRES

FIRE INSURANCE
ASSURANCE INCENDIE / SEGURO CONTRA INCENDIOS -
11.02.03
    BT: INSURANCE
    RT: FIRES

FIRES
INCENDIES / INCENDIOS - 16.03.02
    BT: DISASTERS
    NT: FOREST FIRES
    RT: FIRE CONTROL
        FIRE INSURANCE

FIRST DEVELOPMENT DECADE
PREMIERE DECENNIE DU DEVELOPPEMENT / PRIMER
DECENIO DEL DESARROLLO - 01.01.01

FISCAL ADMINISTRATION
ADMINISTRATION FISCALE / ADMINISTRACION FISCAL -
04.03.02
    BT: FINANCIAL ADMINISTRATION
    RT: FISCAL POLICY
        TAX COLLECTION
        TAXATION

FISCAL LAW
DROIT FISCAL / DERECHO FISCAL - 04.01.02
    BT: LAW
    RT: FISCAL POLICY
        TAXATION

FISCAL POLICY
POLITIQUE FISCALE / POLITICA FISCAL - 11.01.02
    BT: FINANCIAL POLICY

FISCAL POLICY<CONT>
RT: FISCAL ADMINISTRATION
FISCAL LAW
NATIONAL BUDGET
TAXATION

FISH
POISSON / PEZ - 07.10.04
BT: ANIMALS
NT: FRESHWATER FISH
SALT WATER FISH
RT: FISH BREEDING
FISH CULTURE
FISH MEAL
FISH OILS
FISH PRESERVATION
FISH PRODUCTION
FISH PROTEIN CONCENTRATE
FISH UTILIZATION
FISHERY
FISHERY RESOURCES
PROTEIN RICH FOOD

FISH BREEDING
AMELIORATION GENETIQUE DES POISSONS /
MEJORAMIENTO GENETICO DE PECES - 07.10.04
BT: ANIMAL BREEDING
RT: FISH

FISH CULTURE
PISCICULTURE / PISCICULTURA - 07.10.03
BT: AQUACULTURE
RT: FISH

FISH MEAL
FARINE DE POISSON / HARINA DE PESCADO - 08.06.04
BT: FISHERY PRODUCTS
RT: FISH
FISHERY PRODUCT PROCESSING

FISH OILS
HUILES DE POISSON / ACEITES DE PESCADO -
08.06.06
BT: ANIMAL OILS
RT: FISH
FISHERY PRODUCT PROCESSING

FISH PRESERVATION
CONSERVATION DU POISSON / CONSERVACION DEL
PESCADO - 08.06.02
BT: FOOD PRESERVATION
RT: FISH
FISHERY PRODUCTS

FISH PRODUCTION
PRODUCTION DE POISSON / PRODUCCION PESQUERA -
07.10.04
BT: ANIMAL PRODUCTION
RT: FISH

FISH PROTEIN CONCENTRATE
CONCENTRE DE PROTEINES DE POISSON / CONCENTRADO
DE PROTEINAS DE PESCADO - 08.06.04

FISH PROTEIN CONCENTRATE<CONT>
BT: CONDENSED FOOD
FISHERY PRODUCTS
RT: FISH
FISHERY PRODUCT PROCESSING

FISH UTILIZATION
UTILISATION DU POISSON / UTILIZACION DEL PESCADO
- 07.10.04
RT: FISH

FISHERMEN
PECHEURS / PESCADORES - 13.09.05
BT: AGRICULTURAL WORKERS
RT: FISHERY

FISHERY
PECHE / PESQUERIA - 07.10.01
BT: AGRICULTURE
RT: FISH
FISHERMEN
FISHERY CONSERVATION
FISHERY DEVELOPMENT
FISHERY ECONOMICS
FISHERY INDUSTRY
FISHERY MANAGEMENT
FISHERY PLANNING
FISHERY POLICY
FISHERY PRODUCTS
FISHERY RESEARCH
FISHERY RESOURCES
FISHERY STATISTICS
FISHING

FISHERY CONSERVATION
CONSERVATION DES PECHES / CONTROL DE LA PESCA -
16.05.01
BT: ANIMAL PROTECTION
RT: FISHERY
FISHERY RESOURCES

FISHERY DEVELOPMENT
DEVELOPPEMENT DES PECHES / DESARROLLO PESQUERO -
07.10.02
BT: AGRICULTURAL DEVELOPMENT
RT: FISHERY

FISHERY ECONOMICS
ECONOMIE DES PECHES / ECONOMIA PESQUERA -
07.10.01
SN: ECONOMICS AS IT RELATES TO FISHERY.
BT: AGRICULTURAL ECONOMICS
RT: FISHERY
FISHERY INDUSTRY
FISHERY RESEARCH

FISHERY ENGINEERING
TECHNOLOGIE DE LA PECHE / TECNOLOGIA PESQUERA -
07.10.03
BT: AGRICULTURAL ENGINEERING
RT: FISHING

FISHERY INDUSTRY
INDUSTRIE DE LA PECHE / INDUSTRIA PESQUERA -

FISHERY INDUSTRY<CONT>
07.10.02
  RT: FISHERY
    FISHERY ECONOMICS

FISHERY MANAGEMENT
GESTION DES PECHES / ADMINISTRACION PESQUERA -
07.10.02
  BT: AGRICULTURAL MANAGEMENT
  RT: FISHERY

FISHERY PLANNING
PLANIFICATION DES PECHES / PLANIFICACION
PESQUERA - 07.10.02
  BT: AGRICULTURAL PLANNING
  RT: FISHERY

FISHERY POLICY
POLITIQUE DES PECHES / POLITICA PESQUERA -
07.10.02
  BT: AGRICULTURAL POLICY
  RT: FISHERY

FISHERY PRODUCT PROCESSING
TRAITEMENT DU PRODUIT DE LA PECHE /
PROCESAMIENTO DE PRODUCTOS DE PESCA - 08.06.02
  BT: FOOD PROCESSING
  RT: FISH MEAL
    FISH OILS
    FISH PROTEIN CONCENTRATE

FISHERY PRODUCTS
PRODUITS DE LA PECHE / PRODUCTOS PESQUEROS -
07.10.04
  BT: ANIMAL PRODUCTS
    FOOD
  NT: FISH MEAL
    FISH PROTEIN CONCENTRATE
  RT: FISH PRESERVATION
    FISHERY

FISHERY RESEARCH
RECHERCHE HALIEUTIQUE / INVESTIGACION PESQUERA -
07.10.01
  BT: AGRICULTURAL RESEARCH
  RT: FISHERY
    FISHERY ECONOMICS
    FISHERY STATISTICS

FISHERY RESOURCES
RESSOURCES HALIEUTIQUES / RECURSOS PESQUEROS -
16.02.02
  BT: ANIMAL RESOURCES
  RT: FISH
    FISHERY
    FISHERY CONSERVATION
    SHELLFISH

FISHERY STATISTICS
STATISTIQUES DES PECHES / ESTADISTICAS PESQUERAS
- 07.10.01
  BT: AGRICULTURAL STATISTICS

FISHERY STATISTICS<CONT>
  RT: FISHERY
    FISHERY RESEARCH

FISHING
PRATIQUE DE LA PECHE / PESCA - 07.10.03
  NT: INLAND FISHING
    MARINE FISHING
  RT: FISHERY
    FISHERY ENGINEERING
    FISHING EQUIPMENT
    FISHING GROUNDS
    FISHING PORTS
    FISHING RIGHTS
    FISHING VESSELS

FISHING BOATS
- 07.10.03
  USE: FISHING VESSELS

FISHING EQUIPMENT
MATERIEL DE PECHE / EQUIPO DE PESCA - 07.10.03
  UF: FISHING GEAR
  BT: AGRICULTURAL EQUIPMENT
  RT: FISHING

FISHING FLEET
- 07.10.03
  USE: FISHING VESSELS

FISHING GEAR
- 07.10.03
  USE: FISHING EQUIPMENT

FISHING GROUNDS
LIEUX DE PECHE / ZONAS DE PESCA - 07.10.03
  BT: AGRICULTURAL AREAS
  RT: FISHING
    FISHING RIGHTS

FISHING PORTS
PORTS DE PECHE / PUERTOS PESQUEROS - 07.10.03
  BT: PORTS
  RT: FISHING

FISHING RIGHTS
DROITS DE PECHE / DERECHOS DE PESCA - 07.10.02
  RT: FISHING
    FISHING GROUNDS
    LAW OF THE SEA

FISHING VESSELS
BATEAUX DE PECHE / BUQUES PESQUEROS - 07.10.03
  UF: FISHING BOATS
    FISHING FLEET
  BT: SHIPS
  NT: FACTORY BOATS
    TRAWLERS
  RT: FISHING

FLAGS OF CONVENIENCE
PAVILLONS DE COMPLAISANCE / BANDERAS DE
COMPLACENCIA - 10.05.00
  BT: MARITIME QUESTIONS

FLAGS OF CONVENIENCE<CONT>
> *RT:* SEA TRANSPORT
> SHIPOWNERS

FLAX
LIN / LINO - 07.07.07
> *BT:* INDUSTRIAL CROPS
> OILSEEDS
> PLANT FIBRES

FLEXIBLE HOURS OF WORK
HORAIRE VARIABLE DE TRAVAIL / HORARIO VARIABLE
DE TRABAJO - 13.03.03
> *BT:* HOURS OF WORK

FLOOD CONTROL
LUTTE ANTI-INONDATION / LUCHA CONTRA
INUNDACIONES - 16.04.01
> *BT:* ENVIRONMENTAL ENGINEERING
> *RT:* FLOODS

FLOODS
INONDATIONS / INUNDACIONES - 16.03.02
> *BT:* NATURAL DISASTERS
> *RT:* FLOOD CONTROL

FLORA
FLORE / FLORA - 07.07.01
SN: TAXONOMIC ASPECTS OF PLANT LIFE; FOR
CLIMATIC, GEOLOGICAL OR OTHER ECOLOGICAL
ASPECTS USE «VEGETATION».
> *RT:* PLANTS

FLOUR
FARINE / HARINA - 08.06.04
> *RT:* GRAIN PROCESSING
> MILLING INDUSTRY

FLOW CHART
ORGANIGRAMME / DIAGRAMA DE FLUJO - 12.04.00
SN: DIAGRAMMATIC REPRESENTATION OF THE
RELATIONSHIP OF A SERIES OF PROCESSES.

FLOWERS
FLEURS / FLORES - 07.07.01
> *BT:* PLANTS

FLUORINE
FLUOR / FLUOR - 08.12.04

FODDER
FOURRAGE / FORRAJE - 07.09.03
> *RT:* FORAGE CROPS

FOETUS
FOETUS / FETO - 15.02.02
> *RT:* EMBRYO
> PREGNANCY

FOLK ART
ART POPULAIRE / ARTE POPULAR - 05.05.02
> *BT:* ART
> *RT:* FOLKLORE

FOLK CULTURE
CULTURE POPULAIRE / CULTURA POPULAR - 05.02.01
> *BT:* CULTURE

FOLKLORE
FOLKLORE / FOLKLORE - 05.01.01
> *BT:* ETHNOLOGY
> *RT:* CULTURE
> FOLK ART
> TRADITIONAL CULTURE

FOOD
ALIMENTS / ALIMENTOS - 15.03.01
> *UF:* FOOD PRODUCTS
> *NT:* BAKERY PRODUCTS
> CANNED FOOD
> CEREALS
> CONDENSED FOOD
> DAIRY PRODUCTS
> DEHYDRATED FOOD
> DRIED FOOD
> EDIBLE OILS
> FEED
> FISHERY PRODUCTS
> FROZEN FOOD
> FRUITS
> IRRADIATED FOOD
> MARGARINE
> MEAT PRODUCTS
> PERISHABLE FOOD
> PROTEIN RICH FOOD
> VEGETABLES
> *RT:* FAO
> FOOD ADDITIVES
> FOOD AID
> FOOD CHEMISTRY
> FOOD COMPOSITION
> FOOD CONSUMPTION
> FOOD CONTAMINATION
> FOOD CROPS
> FOOD ECONOMICS
> FOOD HYGIENE
> FOOD INDUSTRY
> FOOD INSPECTION
> FOOD PLANNING
> FOOD POLICY
> FOOD PREPARATION
> FOOD PRESERVATION
> FOOD PROCESSING
> FOOD PRODUCTION
> FOOD REQUIREMENTS
> FOOD RESERVES
> FOOD SCIENCE
> FOOD SHORTAGE
> FOOD SPOILAGE
> FOOD STANDARDS
> FOOD STATISTICS
> FOOD STERILIZATION
> FOOD STORAGE
> FOOD SUPPLY
> FOOD TECHNOLOGY
> PROTEINS
> VITAMINS

FOOD ADDITIVES
ADDITIFS ALIMENTAIRES / ADITIVOS ALIMENTARIOS -
08.06.02
    RT: FOOD
         FOOD ENRICHMENT

FOOD AID
AIDE ALIMENTAIRE / AYUDA ALIMENTARIA - 01.01.03
    BT: DEVELOPMENT AID
    RT: FOOD
         WORLD FOOD PROGRAMME

FOOD ANALYSIS
ANALYSE DES ALIMENTS / ANALISIS DE LOS ALIMENTOS
- 15.03.01

FOOD CHEMISTRY
CHIMIE ALIMENTAIRE / QUIMICA ALIMENTARIA -
15.03.01
    BT: CHEMISTRY
    RT: FOOD

FOOD COMPOSITION
COMPOSITION DES ALIMENTS / COMPOSICION DE LOS
ALIMENTOS - 15.03.01
    RT: FOOD

FOOD CONSUMPTION
CONSOMMATION ALIMENTAIRE / CONSUMO ALIMENTARIO -
15.03.02
    BT: CONSUMPTION
    RT: FOOD
         FOOD HYGIENE

FOOD CONTAMINATION
CONTAMINATION DES ALIMENTS / CONTAMINACION DE
LOS ALIMENTOS - 15.03.01
    RT: FOOD
         FOOD SPOILAGE

FOOD CROPS
CULTURES VIVRIERES / CULTIVOS ALIMENTICIOS -
07.07.02
    BT: CROPS
    NT: CEREALS
         FRUIT CROPS
         VEGETABLE CROPS
    RT: FOOD
         VITICULTURE

FOOD ECONOMICS
ECONOMIE ALIMENTAIRE / ECONOMIA ALIMENTARIA -
15.03.01
    BT: ECONOMICS
    RT: FOOD

FOOD ENGINEERING
- 08.06.02
    USE: FOOD TECHNOLOGY

FOOD ENRICHMENT
ENRICHISSEMENT DES ALIMENTS / ENRIQUECIMIENTO DE
ALIMENTOS - 08.06.02
    RT: FOOD ADDITIVES

FOOD HYGIENE
HYGIENE ALIMENTAIRE / HIGIENE ALIMENTARIA -
15.03.02
*SN: USE IN CONNECTION WITH FOOD CONSUMPTION;
    OTHERWISE USE 'FOOD INSPECTION'.*
    BT: HYGIENE
    RT: FOOD
         FOOD CONSUMPTION

FOOD INDUSTRY
INDUSTRIE ALIMENTAIRE / INDUSTRIA ALIMENTARIA -
08.06.01
    BT: INDUSTRIAL SECTOR
    NT: BEVERAGE INDUSTRY
         CANNING INDUSTRY
         DAIRY INDUSTRY
         MEAT INDUSTRY
         MILLING INDUSTRY
         SUGAR INDUSTRY
    RT: FOOD
         FOOD PROCESSING
         FOOD TECHNOLOGY

FOOD INSPECTION
INSPECTION DES ALIMENTS / INSPECCION DE LOS
ALIMENTOS - 15.03.01
    RT: FOOD

FOOD IRRADIATION
IRRADIATION DES ALIMENTS / IRRADIACION DE
ALIMENTOS - 08.06.02
    BT: IRRADIATION
    RT: FOOD PRESERVATION
         FOOD STERILIZATION
         IRRADIATED FOOD

FOOD PLANNING
PLANIFICATION ALIMENTAIRE / PLANIFICACION
ALIMENTARIA - 15.03.01
    BT: PLANNING
    RT: FOOD
         WORLD FOOD PROGRAMME

FOOD POLICY
POLITIQUE ALIMENTAIRE / POLITICA ALIMENTARIA -
15.03.01
    BT: GOVERNMENT POLICY
    RT: FOOD
         SOCIAL POLICY
         WORLD FOOD PROGRAMME

FOOD PREPARATION
PREPARATION DES ALIMENTS / PREPARACION DE
ALIMENTOS - 15.03.01
    UF: COOKERY
         MEAL PREPARATION
    BT: HOME ECONOMICS
    RT: FOOD

FOOD PRESERVATION
CONSERVATION DES ALIMENTS / CONSERVACION DE
ALIMENTOS - 08.06.02
    BT: FOOD TECHNOLOGY
    NT: FISH PRESERVATION

FOOD PRESERVATION<CONT>
- RT: CANNED FOOD
  DEHYDRATED FOOD
  DRIED FOOD
  FOOD
  FOOD IRRADIATION
  FOOD PROCESSING
  FOOD STERILIZATION
  FROZEN FOOD
  IRRADIATED FOOD

FOOD PROCESSING
TRAITEMENT DES ALIMENTS / PROCESAMIENTO DE ALIMENTOS - 08.06.02
- BT: AGRIPRODUCT PROCESSING
  FOOD TECHNOLOGY
- NT: FISHERY PRODUCT PROCESSING
  GRAIN PROCESSING
  MEAT PROCESSING
  MILK PROCESSING
- RT: FOOD
  FOOD INDUSTRY
  FOOD PRESERVATION
  FOOD STERILIZATION

FOOD PRODUCTION
PRODUCTION ALIMENTAIRE / PRODUCCION ALIMENTARIA - 08.06.01
- BT: PRODUCTION
- RT: FOOD
  FOOD PRODUCTS

FOOD PRODUCTS
- 15.03.01
- USE: FOOD

FOOD REQUIREMENTS
BESOINS ALIMENTAIRES / NECESIDADES ALIMENTARIAS - 15.03.02
- BT: BASIC NEEDS
- RT: FOOD

FOOD RESERVES
RESERVES ALIMENTAIRES / RESERVAS ALIMENTARIAS - 15.03.01
- RT: FOOD
  FOOD STORAGE
  FOOD SUPPLY

FOOD SCIENCE
SCIENCES ALIMENTAIRES / CIENCIAS DE LA ALIMENTACION - 08.06.02
- RT: FOOD
  FOOD TECHNOLOGY

FOOD SHORTAGE
PENURIE ALIMENTAIRE / ESCASEZ DE ALIMENTOS - 15.03.01
- RT: FAMINE
  FOOD
  MALNUTRITION

FOOD SPOILAGE

FOOD SPOILAGE<CONT>
ALTERATION DES ALIMENTS / DETERIORO DE LOS ALIMENTOS - 15.03.01
- RT: FOOD
  FOOD CONTAMINATION
  PERISHABLE FOOD

FOOD STANDARDS
NORMES ALIMENTAIRES / NORMAS ALIMENTARIAS - 15.03.02
- BT: STANDARDS
- RT: FOOD

FOOD STATISTICS
STATISTIQUES ALIMENTAIRES / ESTADISTICAS ALIMENTARIAS - 15.03.02
- BT: STATISTICAL DATA
- RT: FOOD

FOOD STERILIZATION
STERILISATION DES ALIMENTS / ESTERILIZACION DE ALIMENTOS - 08.06.02
- BT: FOOD TECHNOLOGY
- NT: PASTEURIZATION
- RT: FOOD
  FOOD IRRADIATION
  FOOD PRESERVATION
  FOOD PROCESSING

FOOD STORAGE
EMMAGASINAGE DES ALIMENTS / ALMACENAMIENTO DE ALIMENTOS - 08.06.02
- BT: STORAGE
- RT: FOOD
  FOOD RESERVES

FOOD SUPPLY
DISPONIBILITES ALIMENTAIRES / SUMINISTRO DE ALIMENTOS - 15.03.01
- BT: SUPPLY
- RT: FOOD
  FOOD RESERVES

FOOD TECHNOLOGY
TECHNOLOGIE ALIMENTAIRE / TECNOLOGIA DE ALIMENTOS - 08.06.02
- SN: CONCERNS PROCESSES, EQUIPMENT AND TECHNIQUES REQUIRED FOR FOOD PROCESSING.
- UF: FOOD ENGINEERING
- NT: FOOD PRESERVATION
  FOOD PROCESSING
  FOOD STERILIZATION
- RT: CHEMICAL ENGINEERING
  FOOD
  FOOD INDUSTRY
  FOOD SCIENCE

FOOTWEAR
- 08.08.02
- USE: SHOE INDUSTRY

FORAGE CROPS
CULTURES FOURRAGERES / CULTIVOS DE FORRAJE -

FORAGE CROPS<CONT>
07.07.02
    UF: LIVESTOCK CROPS
    BT: CROPS
    NT: GRASSLAND
    RT: FODDER

FORCED LABOUR
TRAVAUX FORCES / TRABAJO FORZADO - 02.04.03
    BT: PENAL SANCTIONS

FORECASTING TECHNIQUES
TECHNIQUES DE PREVISION / TECNICAS DE PREDICCION
- 18.10.00
    BT: RESEARCH METHODS
    RT: FORECASTS
         PROJECTIONS

FORECASTS
PREVISIONS / PREDICCIONES - 18.10.00
    NT: ECONOMIC FORECASTS
         WEATHER FORECASTS
    RT: FORECASTING TECHNIQUES
         PROJECTIONS

FOREIGN AID
AIDE A L'ETRANGER / AYUDA AL EXTERIOR - 01.01.01
SN: AID FROM THE VIEWPOINT OF THE DONOR COUNTRY.
    BT: INTERNATIONAL COOPERATION
    NT: MILITARY AID

FOREIGN CAPITAL
CAPITAUX ETRANGERS / CAPITALES EXTRANJEROS -
11.03.03
    BT: CAPITAL
         FOREIGN OWNERSHIP
    RT: FOREIGN ENTERPRISES
         FOREIGN INVESTMENTS

FOREIGN ENTERPRISES
ENTREPRISES ETRANGERES / EMPRESAS EXTRANJERAS -
03.03.05
*SN: USE WHEN OWNERSHIP IS FOREIGN TO THE COUNTRY
IN WHICH THE ENTERPRISES ARE SITUATED.*
    BT: ENTERPRISES
    RT: FOREIGN CAPITAL
         FOREIGN INVESTMENTS
         FOREIGN OWNERSHIP
         MULTINATIONAL ENTERPRISES

FOREIGN EXCHANGE
DEVISES / DIVISAS - 11.03.01
    RT: CURRENCIES
         EXCHANGE RATE
         FOREIGN EXCHANGE CONTROL
         FOREIGN EXCHANGE RESERVE

FOREIGN EXCHANGE CONTROL
CONTROLE DES CHANGES / CONTROL DE CAMBIOS -
11.03.01
    RT: FOREIGN EXCHANGE
         MONETARY POLICY

FOREIGN EXCHANGE RESERVE
RESERVE DE CHANGE / RESERVA EN DIVISAS -
11.03.01
    RT: FOREIGN EXCHANGE

FOREIGN INTERVENTION
INTERVENTION ETRANGERE / INTERVENCION EXTRANJERA
- 01.02.05
    RT: FOREIGN POLICY
         INTERNATIONAL RELATIONS

FOREIGN INVESTMENTS
INVESTISSEMENTS ETRANGERS / INVERSIONES
EXTRANJERAS - 11.03.03
    BT: INTERNATIONAL INVESTMENTS
    RT: FOREIGN CAPITAL
         FOREIGN ENTERPRISES
         JOINT VENTURES
         MULTINATIONAL ENTERPRISES
         NATIONALIZATION

FOREIGN OWNERSHIP
PROPRIETE ETRANGERE / PROPIEDAD EXTRANJERA -
03.03.05
    BT: OWNERSHIP
    NT: FOREIGN CAPITAL
    RT: FOREIGN ENTERPRISES

FOREIGN POLICY
POLITIQUE ETRANGERE / POLITICA EXTERIOR -
01.02.05
    BT: GOVERNMENT POLICY
    RT: DEFENCE POLICY
         FOREIGN INTERVENTION
         FOREIGN SERVICEEEE
         IMPERIALISM
         ISOLATIONISM

FOREIGN RELATIONS
RELATIONS EXTERIEURES / RELACIONES EXTERIORES -
01.02.01
    BT: INTERNATIONAL RELATIONS

FOREIGN SERVICE
SERVICE DIPLOMATIQUE / SERVICIO DIPLOMATICO -
01.02.05
    BT: CENTRAL GOVERNMENT
    RT: DIPLOMACY
         FOREIGN POLICY

FOREIGN STUDENTS
ETUDIANTS ETRANGERS / ESTUDIANTES EXTRANJEROS -
06.06.01
    BT: COLLEGE STUDENTS
         FOREIGNERS

FOREIGN TRADE
COMMERCE EXTERIEUR / COMERCIO EXTERIOR -
09.05.01
*SN: FROM THE POINT OF VIEW OF A SPECIFIC COUNTRY
OR REGION.*
    BT: INTERNATIONAL TRADE
    NT: EXPORTS
         IMPORTS

FOREIGN TRADE<CONT>
>   *RT:* BALANCE OF TRADE
>   TARIFFS
>   TRADE POLICY
>   TRADE RELATIONS

FOREIGN WORKERS
TRAVAILLEURS ETRANGERS / TRABAJADORES
EXTRANJEROS - 13.09.02
>   *UF:* EXPATRIATE WORKERS
>   *BT:* FOREIGNERS
>   WORKERS
>   *RT:* MIGRANT WORKERS

FOREIGNERS
ETRANGERS / EXTRANJEROS - 14.07.00
>   *NT:* FOREIGN STUDENTS
>   FOREIGN WORKERS
>   *RT:* MIGRANTS

FOREMEN
- 13.09.03
>   *USE:* SUPERVISORS

FOREST AREAS
ZONES FORESTIERES / ZONAS FORESTALES - 07.08.03
>   *BT:* AGRICULTURAL AREAS

FOREST CONSERVATION
CONSERVATION DE LA FORET / PROTECCION FORESTAL -
16.05.01
>   *BT:* PLANT PROTECTION
>   *RT:* FOREST RESOURCES
>   FORESTS

FOREST ENGINEERING
GENIE FORESTIER / INGENIERIA FORESTAL - 07.08.05
>   *BT:* AGRICULTURAL ENGINEERING
>   *RT:* SILVICULTURE

FOREST FIRES
INCENDIES DE FORET / INCENDIOS FORESTALES -
16.03.02
>   *BT:* FIRES
>   NATURAL DISASTERS
>   *RT:* FORESTS

FOREST MANAGEMENT
GESTION FORESTIERE / MANEJO FORESTAL - 07.08.04
>   *BT:* AGRICULTURAL MANAGEMENT
>   *RT:* SILVICULTURE

FOREST NURSERIES
PEPINIERES FORESTIERES / VIVEROS FORESTALES -
07.08.03
>   *RT:* FOREST TREES

FOREST POLICY
POLITIQUE FORESTIERE / POLITICA FORESTAL -
07.08.04
>   *BT:* AGRICULTURAL POLICY

FOREST PRODUCTION
PRODUCTION FORESTIERE / PRODUCCION FORESTAL -

FOREST PRODUCTION<CONT>
07.08.06
>   *BT:* AGRICULTURAL PRODUCTION
>   *NT:* WOOD PRODUCTION

FOREST PRODUCTS
PRODUITS FORESTIERS / PRODUCTOS FORESTALES -
07.08.06
>   *BT:* PLANT PRODUCTS
>   *NT:* GUMS
>   RESINS
>   WOOD
>   WOOD PRODUCTS

FOREST RESOURCES
RESSOURCES FORESTIERES / RECURSOS FORESTALES -
16.02.02
>   *BT:* PLANT RESOURCES
>   *RT:* FOREST CONSERVATION
>   FOREST TREES
>   FORESTRY
>   FORESTS

FOREST TREES
ARBRES FORESTIERS / ARBOLES FORESTALES -
07.08.06
>   *BT:* TREES
>   *RT:* FOREST NURSERIES
>   FOREST RESOURCES
>   FORESTS

FOREST UTILIZATION
UTILISATION DE LA FORET / UTILIZACION FORESTAL -
07.08.03
>   *RT:* LAND USE
>   LOGGING

FORESTRY
FORESTERIE / CIENCIAS FORESTALES - 07.08.01
SN: THE SCIENCE OF DEVELOPING, CARING FOR OR
*   CULTIVATING FORESTS: THE MANAGEMENT OF*
*   GROWING TIMBER.*
>   *BT:* AGRICULTURE
>   *NT:* SILVICULTURE
>   *RT:* FOREST RESOURCES
>   FORESTRY ECONOMICS
>   FORESTRY RESEARCH
>   FORESTRY STATISTICS
>   FORESTS

FORESTRY DEVELOPMENT
DEVELOPPEMENT FORESTIER / DESARROLLO FORESTAL -
07.08.04
>   *BT:* AGRICULTURAL DEVELOPMENT

FORESTRY ECONOMICS
ECONOMIE FORESTIERE / ECONOMIA FORESTAL -
07.08.01
SN: ECONOMICS AS IT RELATES TO FORESTRY.
>   *BT:* AGRICULTURAL ECONOMICS
>   *RT:* FORESTRY
>   FORESTRY INDUSTRY

FORESTRY EQUIPMENT
EQUIPEMENT FORESTIER / EQUIPO FORESTAL -
07.08.05
    BT: AGRICULTURAL EQUIPMENT

FORESTRY INDUSTRY
INDUSTRIE FORESTIERE / INDUSTRIA FORESTAL -
07.08.01
    RT: FORESTRY ECONOMICS

FORESTRY PLANNING
PLANIFICATION FORESTIERE / PLANIFICACION
FORESTAL - 07.08.04
    BT: AGRICULTURAL PLANNING

FORESTRY RESEARCH
RECHERCHE FORESTIERE / INVESTIGACION FORESTAL -
07.08.02
    BT: AGRICULTURAL RESEARCH
    RT: FORESTRY

FORESTRY STATISTICS
STATISTIQUES FORESTIERES / ESTADISTICAS
FORESTALES - 07.08.02
    BT: AGRICULTURAL STATISTICS
    RT: FORESTRY

FORESTS
FORETS / BOSQUES - 07.08.01
    NT: MANMADE FORESTS
    RT: FOREST CONSERVATION
        FOREST FIRES
        FOREST RESOURCES
        FOREST TREES
        FORESTRY

FORGING
FORGEAGE / FORJA - 08.14.03
    BT: MACHINING

FOSSIL FUELS
COMBUSTIBLES FOSSILES / COMBUSTIBLES FOSILES -
08.11.01
    BT: FUELS
    NT: COAL
        COAL GAS
        MINERAL OILS
        NATURAL GAS

FRANCE
FRANCE / FRANCIA - 01.04.05
    BT: MEDITERRANEAN COUNTRIES
        WESTERN EUROPE
    RT: FRENCH
        FRENCH GUIANA
        FRENCH POLYNESIA
        GUADELOUPE
        MARTINIQUE
        NEW CALEDONIA
        PACIFIC ISLANDS FR
        REUNION ISLAND
        ST PIERRE AND MIQUELON

FREE EDUCATION
ENSEIGNEMENT GRATUIT / ENSENANZA GRATUITA -

FREE EDUCATION\<CONT\>
06.03.03
    BT: ECONOMICS OF EDUCATION
        EDUCATIONAL SYSTEMS

FREE PORTS
ZONES FRANCHES / ZONAS FRANCAS - 09.05.08
    RT: TARIFFS

FREE TRADE AREA
ZONE DE LIBRE ECHANGE / ZONA DE LIBRE COMERCIO -
09.05.08
SN: USE THIS DESCRIPTOR IN ITS GENERAL MEANING.
    RT: CARIFTA
        CUSTOMS UNION
        ECONOMIC INTEGRATION
        EFTA
        LAFTA

FREEDOM
LIBERTE / LIBERTAD - 04.02.02
    NT: CIVIL LIBERTIES
    RT: LIBERATION

FREEDOM OF ASSOCIATION
LIBERTE D'ASSOCIATION / LIBERTAD DE ASOCIACION -
04.02.02
SN: THE FREEDOM TO FORM ASSOCIATIONS; APPLIES
    PARTICULARLY TO THE FREEDOM OF WORKERS TO
    FORM TRADE UNIONS WITH A VIEW TO PROTECTING
    THEIR COMMON INTERESTS.
    BT: CIVIL LIBERTIES
    RT: ASSOCIATIONS
        TRADE UNIONS

FREEDOM OF INFORMATION
LIBERTE D'INFORMATION / LIBERTAD DE INFORMACION
- 04.02.02
    BT: CIVIL LIBERTIES
    RT: FREEDOM OF SPEECH

FREEDOM OF OPINION
LIBERTE D'OPINION / LIBERTAD DE OPINION -
04.02.02
    BT: CIVIL LIBERTIES
    RT: FREEDOM OF SPEECH
        PUBLIC OPINION

FREEDOM OF SPEECH
LIBERTE D'EXPRESSION / LIBERTAD DE EXPRESION -
04.02.02
    BT: CIVIL LIBERTIES
    RT: CENSORSHIP
        FREEDOM OF INFORMATION
        FREEDOM OF OPINION

FREEZING
CONGELATION / CONGELACION - 08.12.03
    BT: INDUSTRIAL PROCESSES
    RT: COOLING
        FROZEN FOOD
        REFRIGERATION
        TEMPERATURE

FREIGHT
FRET / FLETE - 10.09.00
UF: TRANSPORT PRICE
RT: FREIGHT MARKET
PRICES

FREIGHT FORWARDING
EXPEDITION / EXPEDICION DE CARGA - 10.06.00

FREIGHT MARKET
MARCHE DU FRET / MERCADO DE FLETE - 10.09.00
BT: MARKET
RT: FREIGHT

FRENCH
FRANCAIS / FRANCES - 14.03.02
RT: FRANCE

FRENCH GUIANA
GUYANE FRANCAISE / GUYANA FRANCESA - 01.04.03
BT: SOUTH AMERICA
RT: FRANCE

FRENCH LANGUAGE
LANGUE FRANCAISE / LENGUA FRANCESA - 05.06.02
BT: LANGUAGES

FRENCH POLYNESIA
POLYNESIE FRANCAISE / POLINESIA FRANCESA -
01.04.07
BT: PACIFIC ISLANDS FR
RT: FRANCE

FRENCH SPEAKING AFRICA
AFRIQUE FRANCOPHONE / AFRICA FRANCOFONA -
01.04.02
BT: AFRICA
NT: ALGERIA
BENIN
BURUNDI
CAMEROON
CENTRAL AFRICAN EMPIRE
CHAD
COMOROS
CONGO
DJIBOUTI
GABON
GUINEA
IVORY COAST
MADAGASCAR
MALAGASY REP
MALI
MAURITANIA
MOROCCO
NIGER
REUNION ISLAND
RWANDA
SENEGAL
TOGO
TUNISIA
UPPER VOLTA
ZAIRE

FRESHWATER
EAU DOUCE / AGUA DULCE - 17.05.05
BT: WATER

FRESHWATER FISH
POISSON D'EAU DOUCE / PEZ DE AGUA DULCE -
07.10.04
BT: FISH

FRIGID ZONE
ZONE GLACIALE / ZONA GLACIAL - 17.02.03
BT: CLIMATIC ZONES
RT: COLD ZONE

FRINGE BENEFITS
AVANTAGES ACCESSOIRES / BENEFICIOS MARGINALES -
13.07.00
SN: INDIVIDUAL COMPENSATION NOT PAID DIRECTLY AS
WAGES OR SALARIES FOR TIME WORKED BUT
COUNTED AS PART OF THE TOTAL COMPENSATION TO
EACH EMPLOYEE.
BT: WAGES

FRONTIER MIGRATIONS
MIGRATIONS FRONTALIERES / MIGRACIONES
FRONTERIZAS - 14.07.00
BT: INTERNATIONAL MIGRATIONS
RT: BOUNDARIES

FRONTIERS
- 01.02.02
USE: BOUNDARIES

FROZEN FOOD
ALIMENTS CONGELES / ALIMENTOS CONGELADOS -
08.06.03
BT: FOOD
RT: FOOD PRESERVATION
FREEZING

FRUIT CROPS
CULTURES FRUITIERES / CULTIVOS DE FRUTALES -
07.07.02
BT: FOOD CROPS
HORTICULTURE
RT: FRUIT TREES
FRUITS

FRUIT JUICES
JUS DE FRUIT / JUGOS DE FRUTA - 08.06.05
BT: NON-ALCOHOLIC BEVERAGES
RT: FRUITS

FRUIT TREES
ARBRES FRUITIERS / ARBOLES FRUTALES - 07.07.05
BT: TREES
NT: BANANA-TREES
COCONUT PALMS
DATE PALMS
RT: FRUIT CROPS
FRUITS

FRUITS
FRUITS / FRUTAS - 07.07.05
BT: FOOD
PLANT PRODUCTS

FRUITS<CONT>
    NT: ALMONDS
        APPLES
        BANANAS
        CASHEW NUTS
        CITRUS FRUITS
        COCONUTS
        DATES
        GRAPES
        GROUNDNUTS
        OLIVES
        PEARS
        PINEAPPLES
        TOMATOES
    RT: DRIED FRUIT
        FRUIT CROPS
        FRUIT JUICES
        FRUIT TREES

FUELS
COMBUSTIBLES / COMBUSTIBLES - 08.11.01
    BT: ENERGY SOURCES
    NT: ENGINE FUELS
        FOSSIL FUELS
        NUCLEAR FUEL
    RT: HYDROCARBONS

FULL EMPLOYMENT
PLEIN EMPLOI / PLENO EMPLEO - 13.01.03
*SN: DENOTES THE SITUATION IN A GIVEN AREA WHERE
    ALL PERSONS SEEKING EMPLOYMENT HAVE BEEN
    PROVIDED WITH PAID POSITIONS.*
    BT: EMPLOYMENT

FULL TIME
PLEIN TEMPS / TIEMPO COMPLETO - 13.03.03

FUNCTIONAL LITERACY
**ALPHABETISATION FONCTIONNELLE / ALFABETIZACION
FUNCIONAL - 06.03.04**
    BT: LITERACY

FUNGI
CHAMPIGNONS / HONGOS - 07.07.01
    BT: PLANTS
    RT: FUNGICIDES

FUNGICIDES
FUNGICIDES / FUNGICIDAS - 08.12.05
    BT: PESTICIDES
    RT: FUNGI

FUNGUS DISEASES
MYCOSES / MICOSIS - 15.04.02
    BT: INFECTIOUS DISEASES

FUR
FOURRURE / PIELES - 08.08.02
    BT: HIDES AND SKINS
    RT: FUR INDUSTRY

FUR INDUSTRY
PELLETERIE / INDUSTRIA PELETERA - 08.08.02
    BT: CLOTHING INDUSTRY

FUR INDUSTRY<CONT>
    RT: FUR
        HIDES AND SKINS

FURNITURE
MEUBLES / MUEBLES - 08.07.03
    RT: FURNITURE INDUSTRY

FURNITURE INDUSTRY
**INDUSTRIE DU MEUBLE / INDUSTRIA DEL MUEBLE -
08.07.03**
    BT: WOODWORKING INDUSTRY
    RT: FURNITURE

FURTHER TRAINING
**FORMATION COMPLEMENTAIRE / PERFECCIONAMIENTO
PROFESIONAL - 06.03.07**
*SN: FOR UP-DATING AND UP-GRADING KNOWLEDGE AND
    SKILLS.*
    BT: VOCATIONAL TRAINING

FUTURE
FUTUR / FUTURO - 18.10.00

GABON
GABON / GABON - 01.04.02
        BT: CENTRAL AFRICA
              FRENCH SPEAKING AFRICA
        RT: GABONESE

GABONESE
GABONAIS / GABONES - 14.03.02
        RT: GABON

GAMBIA
GAMBIE / GAMBIA - 01.04.02
        BT: ENGLISH SPEAKING AFRICA
              WEST AFRICA
        RT: GAMBIAN

GAMBIAN
GAMBIEN / GAMBIANO - 14.03.02
        RT: GAMBIA

GAME PROTECTION
PROTECTION DU GIBIER / CONTROL DE LA CAZA -
16.05.01
        BT: ANIMAL PROTECTION
        RT: BIG GAME
              HUNTING
              SMALL GAME

GARBAGE DISPOSAL
- 16.04.02
        USE: SANITATION SERVICES

GARDENING
JARDINAGE / JARDINERIA - 07.07.02
        BT: HORTICULTURE

GASOLINE
- 08.11.06
        USE: PETROL

GATT
GATT / GATT - 01.03.02
SN: GENERAL AGREEMENT ON TARIFFS AND TRADE.
        BT: TRADE AGREEMENTS
              UN SYSTEM
        RT: INTERNATIONAL TRADE
              ITC
              TARIFF AGREEMENTS
              TRADE AGREEMENTS
              TRADE NEGOTIATIONS

GENEALOGY
GENEALOGIE / GENEALOGIA - 14.02.04

GENERAL EDUCATION
ENSEIGNEMENT GENERAL / EDUCACION GENERAL -
06.03.04
SN: EDUCATION WHICH, IN ITS CHOICE OF SUBJECT
      MATTER, DOES NOT ENVISAGE ANY KIND OF
      SPECIALIZATION WITH A VIEW TO PREPARING
      STUDENTS FOR WORK IN A PARTICULAR SECTOR.
        BT: EDUCATIONAL SYSTEMS
        NT: MASS EDUCATION

GENERAL SYSTEM OF PREFERENCES
SYSTEME GENERAL DE PREFERENCES / SISTEMA GENERAL
DE PREFERENCIAS - 09.05.08
SN: INTERNATIONAL AGREEMENT WHICH PROVIDES LOWER
      TARIFFS FOR GOODS EXPORTED BY DEVELOPING
      COUNTRIES.
        BT: PREFERENTIAL TARIFFS
              TARIFF AGREEMENTS
        RT: IMPORT PROMOTION

GENERATIONS
GENERATIONS / GENERACIONES - 14.02.02
        RT: AGE GROUPS

GENES
GENES / GENES - 15.02.03
        RT: CHROMOSOMES
              GENETIC IMPROVEMENT
              GENETICS

GENETIC IMPROVEMENT
AMELIORATION GENETIQUE / MEJORAMIENTO GENETICO -
15.02.03
        RT: ANIMAL BREEDING
              GENES
              GENETICS
              PLANT BREEDING

GENETICS
GENETIQUE / GENETICA - 15.02.01
        BT: NATURAL SCIENCES
        RT: CHROMOSOMES
              GENES
              GENETIC IMPROVEMENT
              HEREDITY

GENOCIDE
GENOCIDE / GENOCIDIO - 14.03.01
        BT: CRIMES
        RT: ETHNIC GROUPS
              ETHNIC MINORITIES

GEOCHEMISTRY
GEOCHIMIE / GEOQUIMICA - 17.04.01
        BT: CHEMISTRY
              EARTH SCIENCES
        RT: SOIL CHEMISTRY

GEODESY
GEODESIE / GEODESIA - 17.04.01
        BT: GEOPHYSICS

GEOGRAPHERS
GEOGRAPHES / GEOGRAFOS - 13.09.09
        BT: SCIENTISTS
        RT: GEOGRAPHY

GEOGRAPHIC DISTRIBUTION
REPARTITION GEOGRAPHIQUE / DISTRIBUCION
GEOGRAFICA - 17.03.02
        RT: GEOGRAPHY

GEOGRAPHICAL ASPECTS
ASPECTS GEOGRAPHIQUES / ASPECTOS GEOGRAFICOS -

GEOGRAPHICAL ASPECTS<CONT>
17.03.02
   RT: GEOGRAPHY

GEOGRAPHY
GEOGRAPHIE / GEOGRAFIA - 17.03.01
   NT: HUMAN GEOGRAPHY
       PHYSICAL GEOGRAPHY
   RT: GEOGRAPHERS
       GEOGRAPHIC DISTRIBUTION
       GEOGRAPHICAL ASPECTS
       MAPPING
       REGIONAL ANALYSIS

GEOLOGICAL MAPS
CARTES GEOLOGIQUES / MAPAS GEOLOGICOS - 18.07.00
   BT: CHARTS
   RT: GEOLOGY

GEOLOGICAL SURVEYS
ETUDES GEOLOGIQUES / ESTUDIOS GEOLOGICOS -
17.04.04
   BT: SURVEYS
   RT: AERIAL SURVEYS
       GEOLOGY
       REMOTE SENSING

GEOLOGISTS
GEOLOGUES / GEOLOGOS - 13.09.09
   BT: SCIENTISTS
   RT: GEOLOGY

GEOLOGY
GEOLOGIE / GEOLOGIA - 17.04.01
   BT: EARTH SCIENCES
   NT: HYDROGEOLOGY
   RT: GEOLOGICAL MAPS
       GEOLOGICAL SURVEYS
       GEOLOGISTS
       GEOMORPHOLOGY
       PHYSICAL GEOGRAPHY

GEOMORPHOLOGY
GEOMORPHOLOGIE / GEOMORFOLOGIA - 17.04.01
   BT: EARTH SCIENCES
   RT: GEOLOGY
       PHYSICAL GEOGRAPHY

GEOPHYSICS
GEOPHYSIQUE / GEOFISICA - 17.04.01
   BT: EARTH SCIENCES
       PHYSICS
   NT: CLIMATOLOGY
       GEODESY
       SEISMOLOGY
       SOIL PHYSICS
       VULCANOLOGY

GEOTHERMAL ENERGY
ENERGIE GEOTHERMIQUE / ENERGIA GEOTERMICA -
08.11.01
   BT: THERMAL ENERGY

GERMAN
ALLEMAND / ALEMAN - 14.03.02
   RT: GERMAN DR
       GERMANY
       GERMANY FR

GERMAN DR
RD ALLEMANDE / RD ALEMANA - 01.04.05
   BT: EASTERN EUROPE
   RT: GERMAN

GERMANY
ALLEMAGNE / ALEMANIA - 01.04.05
SN: USE FOR HISTORICAL REFERENCES.
   RT: GERMAN

GERMANY FR
ALLEMAGNE RF / ALEMANIA RF - 01.04.05
   BT: WESTERN EUROPE
   RT: GERMAN

GHANA
GHANA / GHANA - 01.04.02
   BT: ENGLISH SPEAKING AFRICA
       WEST AFRICA
   RT: GHANAIAN

GHANAIAN
GHANEEN / GHANES - 14.03.02
   RT: GHANA

GIBRALTAR
GIBRALTAR / GIBRALTAR - 01.04.05
   BT: MEDITERRANEAN COUNTRIES
       WESTERN EUROPE
   RT: UNITED KINGDOM

GIFTED STUDENTS
ELEVES DOUES / ALUMNOS SUPERDOTADOS - 06.06.01
   BT: STUDENTS
   RT: SPECIAL EDUCATION

GLACIERS
GLACIERS / GLACIARES - 17.05.02
   RT: ICE

GLASS
VERRE / VIDRIO - 08.10.04

GLASS INDUSTRY
INDUSTRIE DU VERRE / INDUSTRIA DEL VIDRIO -
08.10.04
   BT: INDUSTRIAL SECTOR

GLOSSARY
GLOSSAIRE / GLOSARIO - 19.03.00
   RT: TERMINOLOGY

GOATS
CHEVRES / CABRAS - 07.09.01
   BT: LIVESTOCK
       RUMINANTS

GOLD
OR / ORO - 08.14.02
   BT: PRECIOUS METALS

GOLD STANDARD
ETALON OR / PATRON ORO - 11.03.01
    RT: CONVERTIBILITY
            INTERNATIONAL MONETARY SYSTEM

GOODS
MARCHANDISES / MERCANCIAS - 10.02.00

GOVERNMENT
GOUVERNEMENT / GOBIERNO - 04.03.02
    NT: CENTRAL GOVERNMENT
            LOCAL GOVERNMENT
            REGIONAL GOVERNMENT
    RT: GOVERNMENT POLICY
            INSTITUTIONAL FRAMEWORK
            OFFICIAL DOCUMENTS
            PUBLIC ADMINISTRATION
            PUBLIC SECTOR

GOVERNMENT POLICY
POLITIQUE GOUVERNEMENTALE / POLITICA
GUBERNAMENTAL - 04.03.02
    NT: COMMUNICATION POLICY
            CULTURAL POLICY
            DEVELOPMENT POLICY
            ECONOMIC POLICY
            EDUCATIONAL POLICY
            ENERGY POLICY
            ENVIRONMENTAL POLICY
            FOOD POLICY
            FOREIGN POLICY
            HEALTH POLICY
            INFORMATION POLICY
            LABOUR POLICY
            POPULATION POLICY
            SCIENCE POLICY
            SOCIAL POLICY
    RT: GOVERNMENT
            NATIONAL POLICY
            POLICY MAKING

GRADUATES
DIPLOMES D'UNIVERSITE / GRADUADOS - 06.06.01
    RT: DIPLOMAS
            HIGHER EDUCATION
            UNIVERSITIES

GRAIN PROCESSING
TRAITEMENT DU GRAIN / PROCESAMIENTO DE CEREALES
- 08.06.02
    BT: FOOD PROCESSING
    RT: FLOUR
            MILLING INDUSTRY

GRAINS
- 07.07.04
    USE: CEREALS

GRANTS
DONS / DONACIONES - 01.01.04
    BT: FINANCIAL TERMS
    NT: EDUCATIONAL GRANTS

GRANTS IN KIND
- 01.01.03
    USE: AID IN KIND

GRAPES
RAISINS / UVAS - 07.07.05
    BT: FRUITS
    RT: VITICULTURE

GRAPHIC ARTS
ARTS GRAPHIQUES / ARTES GRAFICAS - 05.05.03
    BT: FINE ARTS

GRAPHS
GRAPHIQUES / GRAFICOS - 18.08.00
    BT: AUDIOVISUAL MATERIALS
            ILLUSTRATIONS

GRASSES
HERBES / HIERBAS - 07.09.03
    BT: PLANTS
    RT: GRASSLAND
            GRAZING

GRASSLAND
HERBAGE / PASTIZAL - 07.07.02
    BT: FORAGE CROPS
    RT: GRASSES

GRAZING
PATURAGE / PASTOREO - 07.07.02
    RT: GRASSES

GREECE
GRECE / GRECIA - 01.04.05
    BT: MEDITERRANEAN COUNTRIES
            WESTERN EUROPE
    RT: GREEK

GREEK
GREC / GRIEGO - 14.03.02
    RT: GREECE

GREEN REVOLUTION
REVOLUTION VERTE / REVOLUCION VERDE - 07.01.02
SN: PROMOTION OF HIGH YIELD CEREAL CROPS.
    RT: AGRICULTURAL DEVELOPMENT
            CEREALS
            SECOND DEVELOPMENT DECADE

GREENHOUSES
SERRES / INVERNADEROS - 07.04.00
    BT: FARM BUILDINGS

GREENLAND
GROENLAND / GROENLANDIA - 01.04.05
    BT: NORTH AMERICA
            SCANDINAVIA
    RT: DENMARK

GRENADA
GRENADE / GRANADA - 01.04.03
    BT: WEST INDIES ASSOCIATED STATES

GROSS DOMESTIC PRODUCT
PRODUIT INTERIEUR BRUT / PRODUCTO INTERNO BRUTO
- 03.02.02

GROSS DOMESTIC PRODUCT<CONT>
SN: *EQUAL TO GROSS NATIONAL PRODUCT LESS THE NET
    INCOME OF THE PRODUCTION FACTORS RECEIVED
    FROM ABROAD.*
    BT: ECONOMIC INDICATORS
    RT: GROSS NATIONAL PRODUCT
        NATIONAL ACCOUNTING

GROSS NATIONAL PRODUCT
PRODUIT NATIONAL BRUT / PRODUCTO NACIONAL BRUTO
- 03.02.02
SN: *USE IN CONNECTION WITH ALL OUTPUT OF GOODS
    AND SERVICES OF A COUNTRY. TO BE
    DISTINGUISHED FROM 'NATIONAL INCOME'.*
    BT: ECONOMIC INDICATORS
    RT: GROSS DOMESTIC PRODUCT
        NATIONAL ACCOUNTING

GROUNDNUTS
ARACHIDES / CACAHUATES - 07.07.05
    BT: FRUITS
        LEGUMINOSAE
        OILSEEDS
    RT: PEANUT OIL

GROUNDWATER
EAU SOUTERRAINE / AGUA SUBTERRANEA - 17.05.05
    BT: WATER
    RT: HYDROGEOLOGY

GROUP DISCUSSION
DISCUSSION DE GROUPE / DISCUSION EN GRUPO -
05.03.07
    BT: GROUP DYNAMICS
    RT: GROUPS

GROUP DYNAMICS
DYNAMIQUE DE GROUPE / DINAMICA DE GRUPOS -
05.03.07
SN: *USE SPECIALLY IN CONNECTION WITH THE STUDY
    OF GROUP BEHAVIOUR APPLICABLE TO THE
    INDUSTRIAL SITUATION, TO PERSONNEL
    MANAGEMENT, ETC.*
    NT: GROUP DISCUSSION
    RT: GROUPS

GROUP WORK
TRAVAIL EN GROUPE / TRABAJO EN GRUPO - 13.03.02
SN: *WORK UNDERTAKEN IN GROUPS BUT WHICH DOES NOT
    NECESSARILY INVOLVE THE DEPENDENCE OF ONE
    WORKER'S DUTIES ON COMPLETION OF THE DUTIES
    OF ANOTHER MEMBER OF THE GROUP.*
    NT: TEAM WORK
    RT: GROUPS

GROUPS
GROUPES / GRUPOS - 05.03.07
    NT: ETHNIC GROUPS
        INTEREST GROUPS
        MINORITY GROUPS
        RELIGIOUS GROUPS

GROUPS<CONT>
    RT: GROUP DISCUSSION
        GROUP DYNAMICS
        GROUP WORK
        INTERGROUP RELATIONS

GROWTH MODELS
MODELES DE CROISSANCE / MODELOS DE CRECIMIENTO -
03.01.02
    BT: ECONOMIC MODELS
    RT: ECONOMIC GROWTH
        GROWTH POLICY

GROWTH POLES
POLES DE CROISSANCE / POLOS DE CRECIMIENTO -
02.01.02
    RT: REGIONAL PLANNING
        URBAN DEVELOPMENT

GROWTH POLICY
POLITIQUE DE CROISSANCE / POLITICA DE
CRECIMIENTO - 02.01.03
    BT: ECONOMIC POLICY
    RT: ECONOMIC GROWTH
        GROWTH MODELS
        GROWTH RATE

GROWTH RATE
TAUX DE CROISSANCE / TASA DE CRECIMIENTO -
03.01.02
    BT: ECONOMIC INDICATORS
    NT: ZERO GROWTH ECONOMY
    RT: ACCUMULATION RATE
        ECONOMIC GROWTH
        GROWTH POLICY

GUADELOUPE
GUADELOUPE / GUADALUPE - 01.04.03
    BT: CARIBBEAN
    RT: FRANCE

GUARANTEED WAGE
- 13.07.00
    USE: MINIMUM WAGE

GUATEMALA
GUATEMALA / GUATEMALA - 01.04.03
    BT: CENTRAL AMERICA
    RT: GUATEMALAN

GUATEMALAN
GUATEMALTEQUE / GUATEMALTECO - 14.03.02
    RT: GUATEMALA

GUERRILLA
GUERRILLA / GUERRILLA - 01.02.07
    RT: CIVIL WAR
        WAR

GUINEA
GUINEE / GUINEA - 01.04.02
    BT: FRENCH SPEAKING AFRICA
        WEST AFRICA
    RT: GUINEAN

GUINEA-BISSAU
GUINEE-BISSAU / GUINEA-BISSAU - 01.04.02
    BT: WEST AFRICA

GUINEAN
GUINEEN / GUINEO - 14.03.02
    RT: GUINEA

GULFS
GOLFES / GOLFOS - 17.03.04

GUM ARABIC
GOMME ARABIQUE / GOMA ARABIGA - 07.07.08
    BT: GUMS

GUMS
GOMMES / GOMAS - 07.07.08
    BT: FOREST PRODUCTS
    NT: GUM ARABIC
    RT: RESINS

GUYANA
GUYANE / GUYANA - 01.04.03
    BT: SOUTH AMERICA
    RT: GUYANESE

GUYANESE
GUYANAIS / GUYANES - 14.03.02
    RT: GUYANA

GYNAECOLOGY
GYNECOLOGIE / GINECOLOGIA - 15.04.06
    BT: MEDICAL SCIENCES
    RT: WOMEN

HABITAT
HABITAT / HABITAT - 14.04.01
    UF: SETTLEMENT PATTERN
    NT: DISPERSED HABITAT
    RT: BIOSPHERE
        ECOLOGY
        ENVIRONMENT
        HUMAN SETTLEMENTS
        POPULATION DISTRIBUTION

HAITI
HAITI / HAITI - 01.04.03
    BT: CARIBBEAN
        LATIN AMERICA
    RT: HAITIAN

HAITIAN
HAITIEN / HAITIANO - 14.03.02
    RT: HAITI

HAND TOOLS
OUTILS A MAIN / HERRAMIENTAS MANUALES - 08.14.05
    BT: TOOLS

HANDBOOK
- 19.02.09
    USE: MANUAL

HANDICAPPED
HANDICAPES / DEFICIENTES - 15.04.05
    NT: HANDICAPPED STUDENTS
        HANDICAPPED WORKERS
        MENTALLY HANDICAPPED
        PHYSICALLY HANDICAPPED

HANDICAPPED STUDENTS
ELEVES HANDICAPES / ALUMNOS DEFICIENTES -
06.06.01
    BT: HANDICAPPED
        STUDENTS

HANDICAPPED WORKERS
TRAVAILLEURS HANDICAPES / TRABAJADORES IMPEDIDOS
- 13.09.02
    BT: HANDICAPPED
        WORKERS

HANDICRAFT
ARTISANAT / ARTESANIA - 08.02.02
    RT: CRAFTSMEN
        HANDICRAFT PROMOTION
        POTTERY
        WEAVING

HANDICRAFT PROMOTION
PROMOTION DE L'ARTISANAT / PROMOCION DEL
ARTESANADO - 08.01.02
    RT: COTTAGE INDUSTRY
        HANDICRAFT

HANDLING
MANUTENTION / MANIPULACION - 10.06.00
    UF: MATERIALS HANDLING

HARBOURS
- 10.03.00
    USE: PORTS

HARD FIBRES
FIBRES DURES / FIBRAS DURAS - 08.07.01
    BT: FIBRES

HARDWARE
- 08.15.02
    USE: ELECTRONIC EQUIPMENT

HARMFUL SUBSTANCES
- 16.03.04
    USE: DANGEROUS SUBSTANCES

HARVESTING
RECOLTE / COSECHA - 07.05.04
SN: ACTION OF GATHERING ANY CROP, DO NOT CONFUSE
    WITH 'CROP YIELD'.
    RT: CROP YIELD

HAWAII
HAWAI / HAWAI - 01.04.07
    BT: USA

HEALTH
SANTE / SALUD - 15.04.01
    NT: MENTAL HEALTH
        PUBLIC HEALTH
    RT: DISEASES
        HEALTH ADMINISTRATION
        HEALTH AID
        HEALTH EDUCATION
        HEALTH INDICATORS
        HEALTH INSURANCE
        HEALTH PLANNING
        HEALTH POLICY
        HEALTH SERVICES
        MATERNAL AND CHILD HEALTH
        PAHO
        PRENATAL CARE
        WHO

HEALTH ADMINISTRATION
ADMINISTRATION DE LA SANTE / ADMINISTRACION DE
LA SALVO - 04.03.02
    BT: PUBLIC ADMINISTRATION
    NT: HEALTH SERVICES
    RT: HEALTH
        PUBLIC ADMINISTRATION

HEALTH AID
AIDE SANITAIRE / AYUDA SANITARIA - 01.01.03
    BT: DEVELOPMENT AID
    RT: HEALTH

HEALTH CENTRES
DISPENSAIRES / DISPENSARIOS - 02.05.02
    BT: HEALTH SERVICES

HEALTH CONTROL
CONTROLE SANITAIRE / CONTROL SANITARIO -

HEALTH CONTROL<CONT>
15.04.04
    RT: PREVENTIVE MEDICINE
        QUARANTINE

HEALTH EDUCATION
EDUCATION SANITAIRE / EDUCACION SANITARIA -
06.03.04
SN: EDUCATION OF GENERAL POPULATION TO PROMOTE
    HABITS OF HEALTH AND HIGIENE.
    BT: BASIC EDUCATION
    RT: HEALTH
        HYGIENE
        PREVENTIVE MEDICINE
        SAFETY EDUCATION
        SANITATION

HEALTH FACILITIES
EQUIPEMENT SANITAIRE / EQUIPO SANITARIO -
02.05.02
    UF: MEDICAL EQUIPMENT
    RT: HEALTH SERVICES

HEALTH INDICATORS
INDICATEURS DE SANTE / INDICADORES DE SALUD -
02.05.02
    RT: HEALTH
        HEALTH PLANNING
        HEALTH POLICY

HEALTH INSURANCE
ASSURANCE MALADIE / SEGURO DE ENFERMEDAD -
02.03.02
    UF: SICKNESS INSURANCE
    BT: SOCIAL SECURITY
    RT: HEALTH

HEALTH PLANNING
PLANIFICATION DE LA SANTE / PLANIFICACION DE LA
SALUD - 02.05.02
    BT: PLANNING
    RT: HEALTH
        HEALTH INDICATORS
        HEALTH POLICY

HEALTH POLICY
POLITIQUE SANITAIRE / POLITICA DE SALUD -
02.05.02
    BT: GOVERNMENT POLICY
    NT: NUTRITION POLICY
    RT: HEALTH
        HEALTH INDICATORS
        HEALTH PLANNING
        HEALTH SERVICES

HEALTH SERVICES
SERVICES DE SANTE / SERVICIOS DE SALUD -
02.05.02
SN: USE IN CONNECTION WITH FACILITIES TO ENSURE
    PROTECTION OF THE HEALTH OF INDIVIDUALS AND
    THEIR MEDICAL CARE.
    BT: HEALTH ADMINISTRATION
        SOCIAL SERVICES

HEALTH SERVICES<CONT>
  NT: HEALTH CENTRES
      HOSPITALS
  RT: HEALTH
      HEALTH FACILITIES
      HEALTH POLICY
      MEDICAL CARE
      MEDICAL PERSONNEL
      MEDICINE
      PUBLIC HEALTH

HEART
COEUR / CORAZON - 15.02.04
  BT: CARDIOVASCULAR SYSTEM
  RT: CARDIOLOGY

HEATING
CHAUFFAGE / CALEFACCION - 08.12.03
  BT: INDUSTRIAL PROCESSES
  RT: TEMPERATURE

HEAVY INDUSTRY
INDUSTRIE LOURDE / INDUSTRIA PESADA - 08.01.01
  BT: INDUSTRY

HELICOPTERS
HELICOPTERES / HELICOPTEROS - 10.04.00
  BT: AIRCRAFT
  RT: AIR TRANSPORT

HEMP
CHANVRE / CANAMO - 07.07.07
  BT: PLANT FIBRES
  RT: ROPE INDUSTRY

HERBICIDES
DESHERBANTS / HERBICIDAS - 08.12.05
  BT: PESTICIDES
  RT: SULPHATES
      WEED CONTROL

HEREDITARY DEFECTS
TARES HEREDITAIRES / TARAS HEREDITARIAS - 15.02.03
  RT: HEREDITY

HEREDITY
HEREDITE / HERENCIA - 15.02.03
  RT: GENETICS
      HEREDITARY DEFECTS

HEVEAS
HEVEAS / HEVEAS - 07.07.08
  BT: INDUSTRIAL CROPS
      TREES
  RT: LATEX
      RUBBER

HIDES AND SKINS
CUIRS ET PEAUX / CUEROS Y PIELES - 08.08.02
  BT: ANIMAL PRODUCTS
  NT: FUR
      LEATHER

HIDES AND SKINS<CONT>
  RT: FUR INDUSTRY
      LEATHER INDUSTRY
      TANNING INDUSTRY

HIGHER EDUCATION
ENSEIGNEMENT SUPERIEUR / ENSENANZA SUPERIOR - 06.03.06
SN: USE IN CONNECTION WITH EDUCATION AT THE UNIVERSITY OR A SIMILAR LEVEL.
  BT: POST-SECONDARY EDUCATION
  RT: GRADUATES
      HIGHER EDUCATION INSTITUTIONS
      UNIVERSITIES

HIGHER EDUCATION INSTITUTIONS
CENTRES D'ENSEIGNEMENT SUPERIEUR / CENTROS DE ENSENANZA SUPERIOR - 06.04.05
  UF: POST-SECONDARY SCHOOLS
  BT: EDUCATIONAL INSTITUTIONS
  NT: TECHNOLOGICAL INSTITUTES
      UNIVERSITIES
  RT: COLLEGE MANAGEMENT
      HIGHER EDUCATION
      POST-SECONDARY EDUCATION

HILLS
COLLINES / COLINAS - 17.03.04

HINDUISM
HINDOUISME / HINDUISMO - 05.04.03

HIRE PURCHASE
ACHAT A CREDIT / COMPRA A CREDITO - 09.03.02
  BT: PURCHASING
  RT: CONSUMER CREDIT

HISTOLOGY
HISTOLOGIE / HISTOLOGIA - 15.02.01
  BT: ANATOMY
  NT: CYTOLOGY

HISTORICAL ANALYSIS
ANALYSE HISTORIQUE / ANALISIS HISTORICO - 05.01.01
  RT: HISTORY

HISTORY
HISTOIRE / HISTORIA - 05.01.01
  BT: SOCIAL SCIENCES
  NT: ECONOMIC HISTORY
      HISTORY OF EDUCATION
      SOCIAL HISTORY
  RT: ARCHAEOLOGY
      HISTORICAL ANALYSIS

HISTORY OF EDUCATION
HISTOIRE DE L'EDUCATION / HISTORIA DE LA EDUCACION - 06.01.00
  BT: HISTORY
      SCIENCES OF EDUCATION

HOARDING
THESAURISATION / ATESORAMIENTO - 11.02.05
  BT: SAVINGS

HOLIDAYS
VACANCES / VACACIONES - 13.08.00
    NT: SCHOOL HOLIDAYS
    RT: LEISURE
         REST

HOLY SEE
- 01.04.05
    USE: **VATICAN**

HOME ECONOMICS
ECONOMIE DOMESTIQUE / ECONOMIA DOMESTICA -
06.03.04
    BT: BASIC EDUCATION
    NT: CHILD REARING
         FOOD PREPARATION
    RT: FAMILY BUDGET

HOME TRADE
- 09.04.01
    USE: **DOMESTIC TRADE**

HOMICIDE
HOMICIDE / HOMICIDIO - 02.04.02
    BT: CRIMES
    RT: CAPITAL PUNISHMENT
         CAUSES OF DEATH

HONDURAN
HONDURIEN / HONDURENO - 14.03.02
    RT: HONDURAS

HONDURAS
HONDURAS / HONDURAS - 01.04.03
    BT: CENTRAL AMERICA
    RT: HONDURAN

HONEY
MIEL / MIEL - 07.09.05
    BT: ANIMAL PRODUCTS
    RT: APICULTURE

HONG KONG
HONG KONG / HONG KONG - 01.04.04
    BT: FAR EAST
    RT: UNITED KINGDOM

HORIZONTAL COOPERATION
COOPERATION HORIZONTALE / COOPERACION HORIZONTAL
- 01.01.01
*SN: COOPERATION ON EQUAL TERMS BETWEEN COUNTRIES
OR INSTITUTIONS.*
    BT: INTERNATIONAL COOPERATION

HORIZONTAL INTEGRATION
INTEGRATION HORIZONTALE / INTEGRACION HORIZONTAL
- 12.02.00
    BT: ECONOMIC INTEGRATION

HORMONES
HORMONES / HORMONAS - 15.02.04

HORSES
CHEVAUX / CABALLOS - 07.09.01

HORSES<CONT>
    BT: EQUIDAE
         LIVESTOCK

HORTICULTURE
HORTICULTURE / HORTICULTURA - 07.07.02
    NT: FRUIT CROPS
         GARDENING
         VEGETABLE CROPS

HOSPITALIZATION
HOSPITALISATION / HOSPITALIZACION - 15.04.04
    RT: HOSPITALS
         MEDICAL CARE

HOSPITALS
HOPITAUX / HOSPITALES - 02.05.02
    BT: HEALTH SERVICES
    NT: MENTAL HOSPITALS
    RT: HOSPITALIZATION

HOSTAGES
OTAGES / REHENES - 01.02.07
    RT: TERRORISM

HOTEL INDUSTRY
INDUSTRIE HOTELIERE / INDUSTRIA HOTELERA -
09.04.05
    BT: SERVICE INDUSTRY
    RT: DOMESTIC TRADE

HOURS OF WORK
HEURES DE TRAVAIL / HORAS DE TRABAJO - 13.03.03
    BT: ARRANGEMENT OF WORKING TIME
    NT: FLEXIBLE HOURS OF WORK

HOUSEHOLD
MENAGE / HOGAR - 14.04.01
    UF: DWELLING UNIT
    RT: FAMILY BUDGET

HOUSEHOLD APPLIANCES
APPAREILS MENAGERS / APARATOS ELECTRODOMESTICOS
- 08.15.02
*SN: USE FOR FREEZERS, REFRIGERATORS, WASHING
MACHINES, ETC.*
    UF: HOUSEHOLD GOODS
    BT: ELECTRIC APPLIANCES

HOUSEHOLD GOODS
- 08.15.02
    USE: **HOUSEHOLD APPLIANCES**

HOUSING
LOGEMENT / VIVIENDA - 14.04.01
    UF: DWELLING
    NT: COLLECTIVE HOUSING
    RT: HOUSING CENSUSES
         HOUSING COOPERATIVES
         HOUSING NEEDS
         HOUSING POLICY
         IFHP
         LIVING CONDITIONS
         SQUATTERS

HOUSING CENSUSES
RECENSEMENTS DE LOGEMENTS / CENSOS DE VIVIENDA -
14.04.01
    BT: CENSUSES
    RT: HOUSING

HOUSING COOPERATIVES
COOPERATIVES DE LOGEMENT / COOPERATIVAS DE
VIVIENDA - 14.04.01
    BT: COOPERATIVES
    RT: HOUSING

HOUSING NEEDS
BESOINS DE LOGEMENT / NECESIDADES DE VIVIENDA -
14.04.01
    BT: BASIC NEEDS
    RT: HOUSING

HOUSING POLICY
POLITIQUE DU LOGEMENT / POLITICA DE VIVIENDA -
14.04.01
    BT: SOCIAL POLICY
    RT: HOUSING

HUMAN ECOLOGY
ECOLOGIE HUMAINE / ECOLOGIA HUMANA - 16.01.01
    BT: ECOLOGY
    RT: HUMAN ENVIRONMENT

HUMAN ENVIRONMENT
ENVIRONNEMENT HUMAIN / MEDIO AMBIENTE HUMANO -
16.01.02
    BT: ENVIRONMENT
    NT: CULTURAL ENVIRONMENT
        SOCIAL ENVIRONMENT
    RT: HUMAN ECOLOGY
        HUMAN RELATIONS

HUMAN GEOGRAPHY
GEOGRAPHIE HUMAINE / GEOGRAFIA HUMANA - 17.03.01
    BT: GEOGRAPHY
        SOCIAL SCIENCES
    NT: CULTURAL GEOGRAPHY
        ECONOMIC GEOGRAPHY
        POLITICAL GEOGRAPHY

HUMAN NUTRITION
NUTRITION HUMAINE / NUTRICION HUMANA - 15.03.02
    BT: NUTRITION

HUMAN RELATIONS
RELATIONS HUMAINES / RELACIONES HUMANAS -
05.03.01
    RT: HUMAN ENVIRONMENT
        QUALITY OF LIFE

HUMAN RESOURCES
RESSOURCES HUMAINES / RECURSOS HUMANOS -
13.01.02
*SN: THE ACTUAL WORK FORCE (MANPOWER), PLUS THE
    POTENTIAL WORK FORCE.*
    NT: MANPOWER
    RT: ECONOMIC RESOURCES
        NATURAL RESOURCES

HUMAN RIGHTS
DROITS DE L'HOMME / DERECHOS HUMANOS - 04.02.01
    NT: RIGHT TO CULTURE
        RIGHT TO EDUCATION
        RIGHT TO WORK
    RT: CONCENTRATION CAMPS
        TORTURE

HUMAN SETTLEMENTS
ETABLISSEMENTS HUMAINS / ASENTAMIENTOS HUMANOS -
14.04.01
    RT: HABITAT

HUMANIZATION OF WORK
HUMANISATION DU TRAVAIL / HUMANIZACION DEL
TRABAJO - 13.03.01
    RT: JOB SATISFACTION
        WORKING CONDITIONS

HUMID ZONE
ZONE HUMIDE / ZONA HUMEDA - 17.02.03
    BT: CLIMATIC ZONES
    RT: HUMIDITY

HUMIDITY
HUMIDITE / HUMEDAD - 17.01.03
    UF: MOISTURE
    RT: HUMID ZONE

HUNGARIAN
HONGROIS / HUNGARO - 14.03.02
    RT: HUNGARY

HUNGARY
HONGRIE / HUNGRIA - 01.04.05
    BT: EASTERN EUROPE
    RT: HUNGARIAN

HUNTING
CHASSE / CAZA - 07.09.04
    RT: BIG GAME
        GAME PROTECTION
        SMALL GAME

HUSBAND
MARI / ESPOSO - 14.02.05
    BT: MARRIED PERSONS

HYBRIDIZATION
HYBRIDATION / HIBRIDACION - 15.02.03
    RT: PLANT BREEDING

HYDRAULIC ENGINEERING
TECHNOLOGIE HYDRAULIQUE / INGENIERIA HIDRAULICA
- 17.05.04
    BT: ENGINEERING

HYDRAULIC EQUIPMENT
EQUIPEMENT HYDRAULIQUE / EQUIPO HIDRAULICO -
17.05.04
    BT: EQUIPMENT
    NT: PUMPS

HYDROCARBONS
HYDROCARBURES / HIDROCARBUROS - 08.11.06

HYDROCARBONS<CONT>
- BT: CHEMICALS
  POLLUTANTS
- NT: BENZENE
  METHANE
- RT: FUELS
  PETROLEUM PRODUCTS

HYDROELECTRIC POWER
ENERGIE HYDROELECTRIQUE / ENERGIA HIDROELECTRICA - 08.11.02
- BT: ELECTRIC POWER
- RT: DAMS
  HYDROELECTRIC POWER PLANTS

HYDROELECTRIC POWER PLANTS
CENTRALES HYDROELECTRIQUES / CENTRALES HIDROELECTRICAS - 08.11.02
- BT: ELECTRIC POWER PLANTS
- RT: HYDROELECTRIC POWER

HYDROGEN
HYDROGENE / HIDROGENO - 08.12.04

HYDROGEOLOGY
HYDROGEOLOGIE / HIDROGEOLOGIA - 17.05.01
- BT: GEOLOGY
  HYDROLOGY
- RT: GROUNDWATER

HYDROGRAPHY
HYDROGRAPHIE / HIDROGRAFIA - 17.05.01
- BT: HYDROLOGY

HYDROLOGICAL NETWORK
RESEAU HYDROGRAPHIQUE / RED HIDROLOGICA - 17.05.02
- RT: HYDROLOGY
  RIVER BASINS
  RIVERS

HYDROLOGY
HYDROLOGIE / HIDROLOGIA - 17.05.01
- BT: EARTH SCIENCES
- NT: HYDROGEOLOGY
  HYDROGRAPHY
- RT: HYDROLOGICAL NETWORK
  OCEANOGRAPHY
  PHYSICAL GEOGRAPHY
  RIVER BASINS
  RIVERS
  WATER

HYGIENE
HYGIENE / HIGIENE - 15.04.04
- NT: FOOD HYGIENE
  OCCUPATIONAL HYGIENE
  SANITATION
- RT: HEALTH EDUCATION
  PROPHYLAXIS

IAEA
AIEA / OIEA - 01.03.02
- SN: *INTERNATIONAL ATOMIC ENERGY AGENCY.*
  - BT: UN SYSTEM
  - RT: INIS
    NUCLEAR ENERGY

IBE
BIE / OIE - 01.03.02
- SN: *INTERNATIONAL BUREAU OF EDUCATION.*
  - BT: UNESCO
  - RT: EDUCATION

IBRD
BIRD / BIRF - 01.03.02
- SN: *INTERNATIONAL BANK FOR RECONSTRUCTION AND DEVELOPMENT.*
  - UF: WORLD BANK
  - BT: DEVELOPMENT BANKS
    UN SPECIALIZED AGENCIES

ICAO
OACI / OACI - 01.03.02
- SN: *INTERNATIONAL CIVIL AVIATION ORGANIZATION.*
  - BT: UN SPECIALIZED AGENCIES
  - RT: AIR TRANSPORT

ICE
GLACE / HIELO - 17.05.05
- RT: GLACIERS

ICELAND
ISLANDE / ISLANDIA - 01.04.05
- BT: SCANDINAVIA
- RT: ICELANDIC

ICELANDIC
ISLANDAIS / ISLANDES - 14.03.02
- RT: ICELAND

ICEM
CIME / CIME - 01.03.03
- SN: *INTERGOVERNMENTAL COMMITTEE FOR EUROPEAN MIGRATION.*
  - BT: EUROPEAN ORGANIZATIONS
    INTERGOVERNMENTAL ORGANIZATIONS
  - RT: MIGRATIONS

ICFTU
CISL / CIOSL - 01.03.04
- SN: *INTERNATIONAL CONFEDERATION OF FREE TRADE UNIONS.*
  - BT: NON-GOVERNMENTAL ORGANIZATIONS
  - RT: TRADE UNIONS

ICJ
CIJ / CIJ - 01.03.02
- SN: *INTERNATIONAL COURT OF JUSTICE.*
  - BT: UN

ICRISAT
ICRISAT / ICRISAT - 01.03.04
- SN: *INTERNATIONAL CROPS RESEARCH INSTITUTE FOR THE SEMI-ARID TROPICS.*

ICRISAT<CONT>
    BT: NON-GOVERNMENTAL ORGANIZATIONS
        RESEARCH CENTRES
    RT: AGRICULTURAL RESEARCH
        MILLET
        SEMI-ARID ZONE
        SORGHUM
        TROPICAL ZONE

ICSSD
CIDSS / CIDCS - 01.03.04
SN: INTERNATIONAL COMMITTEE FOR SOCIAL SCIENCE INFORMATION AND DOCUMENTATION.
    BT: NON-GOVERNMENTAL ORGANIZATIONS
    RT: DOCUMENTATION
        INFORMATION
        SOCIAL SCIENCES

ICSU
CIUS / CIUC - 01.03.04
SN: INTERNATIONAL COUNCIL OF SCIENTIFIC UNIONS.
    BT: NON-GOVERNMENTAL ORGANIZATIONS
    RT: SCIENCE

ICVA
CIAB / CIAB - 01.03.04
SN: INTERNATIONAL COUNCIL OF VOLUNTARY AGENCIES.
    BT: NON-GOVERNMENTAL ORGANIZATIONS
    RT: VOLUNTARY ORGANIZATIONS

IDA
IDA / AIF - 01.03.02
SN: INTERNATIONAL DEVELOPMENT ASSOCIATION.
    BT: UN SPECIALIZED AGENCIES
    RT: INTERNATIONAL COOPERATION

IDB
BID / BID - 01.03.03
SN: INTER-AMERICAN DEVELOPMENT BANK.
    BT: AMERICAN ORGANIZATIONS
        DEVELOPMENT BANKS
        INTERGOVERNMENTAL ORGANIZATIONS

IDCAS
IDCAS / IDCAS - 01.03.03
SN: INTERNATIONAL DEVELOPMENT CENTRE FOR ARAB STATES.
    BT: DEVELOPMENT CENTRES
        LEAGUE OF ARAB STATES
    RT: ARAB COUNTRIES

IDEOLOGIES
IDEOLOGIES / IDEOLOGIAS - 05.03.02
    RT: BELIEF
        POLITICAL IDEOLOGIES

IDRC
CRDI / CIID - 01.03.04
SN: INTERNATIONAL DEVELOPMENT RESEARCH CENTRE.
    BT: DEVELOPMENT CENTRES
        RESEARCH CENTRES

IEA
AISE / AICE - 01.03.04
SN: INTERNATIONAL ECONOMIC ASSOCIATION.
    BT: NON-GOVERNMENTAL ORGANIZATIONS
    RT: ECONOMICS

IFAP
FIPA / FIPA - 01.03.04
SN: INTERNATIONAL FEDERATION OF AGRICULTURAL PRODUCERS.
    BT: NON-GOVERNMENTAL ORGANIZATIONS
    RT: FARMERS

IFC
SFI / CFI - 01.03.02
SN: INTERNATIONAL FINANCE CORPORATION.
    BT: UN SPECIALIZED AGENCIES

IFHP
FIHUAT / IFHP - 01.03.04
SN: INTERNATIONAL FEDERATION FOR HOUSING AND PLANNING.
    BT: NON-GOVERNMENTAL ORGANIZATIONS
    RT: HOUSING
        URBAN PLANNING

IFIP
IFIP / IFIP - 01.03.04
SN: INTERNATIONAL FEDERATION FOR INFORMATION PROCESSING.
    BT: NON-GOVERNMENTAL ORGANIZATIONS
    RT: INFORMATION PROCESSING

IFLA
FIAB / FIAB - 01.03.04
SN: INTERNATIONAL FEDERATION OF LIBRARY ASSOCIATIONS.
    BT: NON-GOVERNMENTAL ORGANIZATIONS
    RT: LIBRARIANS
        LIBRARY SCIENCE

IIEP
IIPE / IIPE - 01.03.02
SN: INTERNATIONAL INSTITUTE FOR EDUCATIONAL PLANNING.
    BT: UNESCO
    RT: EDUCATIONAL PLANNING

ILLITERACY
ANALPHABETISME / ANALFABETISMO - 06.02.02
    RT: ILLITERATES
        LITERACY

ILLITERATES
ANALPHABETES / ANALFABETOS - 06.06.01
    RT: ILLITERACY

ILLUSTRATIONS
ILLUSTRATIONS / ILUSTRACIONES - 19.02.04
    NT: DIAGRAMS
        GRAPHS
        PHOTOGRAPHS

ILO
OIT / OIT - 01.03.02
SN: USE TO MEAN EITHER THE INTERNATIONAL LABOUR ORGANISATION OR THE INTERNATIONAL LABOUR OFFICE.
    BT: UN SPECIALIZED AGENCIES
    NT: WORLD EMPLOYMENT PROGRAMME

ILO<CONT>
>>RT:<< ISIS
>>>>LABOUR

ILPES
ILPES / ILPES - 01.03.03
SN: LATIN-AMERICAN INSTITUTE FOR ECONOMIC AND
SOCIAL PLANNING.
>>*BT:* AMERICAN ORGANIZATIONS
>>>>NON-GOVERNMENTAL ORGANIZATIONS
>>*RT:* ECONOMIC PLANNING
>>>>LATIN AMERICA
>>>>SOCIAL PLANNING

IMCO
OMCI / OMCI - 01.03.02
SN: INTERGOVERNMENTAL MARITIME CONSULTATIVE
ORGANIZATION.
>>*BT:* UN SPECIALIZED AGENCIES
>>*RT:* SEA TRANSPORT

IMF
FMI / FMI - 01.03.02
SN: INTERNATIONAL MONETARY FUND.
>>*BT:* UN SPECIALIZED AGENCIES
>>*RT:* COMPENSATORY FINANCING
>>>>INTERNATIONAL MONETARY SYSTEM
>>>>SPECIAL DRAWING RIGHTS

IMMIGRANTS
IMMIGRANTS / INMIGRANTES - 14.07.00
>>*BT:* MIGRANTS
>>*RT:* IMMIGRATION

IMMIGRATION
IMMIGRATION / INMIGRACION - 14.07.00
>>*BT:* INTERNATIONAL MIGRATIONS
>>*RT:* IMMIGRANTS
>>>>POPULATION INCREASE

IMMUNIZATION
IMMUNISATION / INMUNIZACION - 15.04.04
>>*RT:* IMMUNOLOGY
>>>>VACCINATION

IMMUNOLOGIC DISEASES
MALADIES IMMUNOLOGIQUES / ENFERMEDADES
INMUNOLOGICAS - 15.04.02
>>*UF:* ALLERGIES
>>*BT:* DISEASES
>>*RT:* IMMUNOLOGY

IMMUNOLOGY
IMMUNOLOGIE / INMUNOLOGIA - 15.04.04
>>*BT:* MEDICAL SCIENCES
>>*RT:* IMMUNIZATION
>>>>IMMUNOLOGIC DISEASES
>>>>VACCINATION

IMPERIALISM
IMPERIALISME / IMPERIALISMO - 01.02.01
SN: POLITICAL, ECONOMIC OR CULTURAL DOMINATION
OF ONE NATION OVER ANOTHER.

IMPERIALISM<CONT>
>>*RT:* DEPENDENCE
>>>>FOREIGN POLICY

IMPORT PROMOTION
PROMOTION DES IMPORTATIONS / PROMOCION DE
IMPORTACIONES - 09.05.06
>>*BT:* TRADE PROMOTION
>>*RT:* GENERAL SYSTEM OF PREFERENCES
>>>>IMPORTS

IMPORT RESTRICTIONS
RESTRICTIONS A L'IMPORTATION / RESTRICCIONES A
LA IMPORTACION - 09.05.07
>>*BT:* PROTECTIONIST MEASURES
>>*NT:* IMPORT TAX
>>*RT:* IMPORTS

IMPORT SUBSTITUTION
REMPLACEMENT DES IMPORTATIONS / SUSTITUCION DE
IMPORTACIONES - 09.05.04
>>*BT:* INDUSTRIALIZATION POLICY
>>>>PROTECTIONIST MEASURES
>>*RT:* IMPORTS

IMPORT TAX
TAXE A L'IMPORTATION / IMPUESTO A LA IMPORTACION
- 11.01.02
>>*BT:* CONSUMPTION TAX
>>>>IMPORT RESTRICTIONS
>>*RT:* IMPORTS
>>>>TARIFFS

IMPORT VOLUME
VOLUME DES IMPORTATIONS / VOLUMEN DE
IMPORTACIONES - 09.05.04
>>*BT:* TRADE VOLUME
>>*RT:* IMPORTS

IMPORTS
IMPORTATIONS / IMPORTACIONES - 09.05.04
>>*BT:* BALANCE OF PAYMENTS
>>>>FOREIGN TRADE
>>*RT:* IMPORT PROMOTION
>>>>IMPORT RESTRICTIONS
>>>>IMPORT SUBSTITUTION
>>>>IMPORT TAX
>>>>IMPORT VOLUME

IMPOVERISHMENT
PAUPERISATION / EMPOBRECIMIENTO - 03.02.05
>>*RT:* POVERTY

IN-PLANT TRAINING
FORMATION EN COURS D'EMPLOI / CAPACITACION EN EL
EMPLEO - 06.03.07
SN: TRAINING GIVEN DURING ACTIVE PAID WORK
PERIODS.
>>*UF:* ON-THE-JOB TRAINING
>>*BT:* VOCATIONAL TRAINING

INBREEDING
CONSANGUINITE / CONSANGUINIDAD - 15.02.03

INCOME
REVENU / INGRESO - 03.02.05
SN: INCOME OF AN INDIVIDUAL OR A FIRM. OTHERWISE
    USE 'NATIONAL INCOME'.
    NT: AGRICULTURAL INCOME
        LAND RENT
        LOW INCOME
        PROFITS
        ROYALTIES
        WAGES
    RT: INCOME TAX
        INCOMES POLICY
        PURCHASING POWER

INCOME DISTRIBUTION
REPARTITION DU REVENU / DISTRIBUCION DEL INGRESO
- 03.02.05
    RT: INCOME REDISTRIBUTION
        INCOMES POLICY
        NATIONAL INCOME
        POVERTY
        SOCIAL JUSTICE
        WEALTH

INCOME REDISTRIBUTION
REDISTRIBUTION DU REVENU / REDISTRIBUCION DEL
INGRESO - 03.02.05
    RT: INCOME DISTRIBUTION
        INCOMES POLICY
        NATIONAL INCOME
        SOCIAL SECURITY
        TAXATION

INCOME TAX
IMPOT SUR LE REVENU / IMPUESTO A LA RENTA -
11.01.02
    BT: TAXES
    NT: CORPORATION TAX
    RT: INCOME
        INCOMES POLICY

INCOMES POLICY
POLITIQUE DES REVENUS / POLITICA DE INGRESOS -
02.01.03
    BT: ECONOMIC POLICY
    NT: WAGE POLICY
    RT: INCOME
        INCOME DISTRIBUTION
        INCOME REDISTRIBUTION
        INCOME TAX
        SOCIAL SECURITY

INDEBTEDNESS
ENDETTEMENT / ENDEUDAMIENTO - 11.02.02
    UF: DEBT BURDEN
    RT: DEBT

INDEPENDENCE
INDEPENDANCE / INDEPENDENCIA - 01.02.03
    RT: DECOLONIZATION
        DEPENDENCE
        LIBERATION
        NATIONAL LIBERATION MOVEMENTS
        SELF-DETERMINATION

INDEPENDENT WORKERS
- 13.09.02
    USE: SELF-EMPLOYED

INDEX
INDEX / INDICE - 19.02.07
    BT: REFERENCE MATERIALS
    RT: INDEXING

INDEX NUMBERS
INDICES / NUMEROS INDICES - 18.08.00
    BT: ECONOMIC INDICATORS
    NT: PRICE INDEX
    RT: SOCIAL INDICATORS

INDEXATION
INDEXATION / INDEXACION - 03.02.05
SN: ADJUSTMENT OF NOMINAL VALUES TO PRICE
    VARIATIONS.
    RT: INFLATION
        TERMS OF TRADE

INDEXING
INDEXAGE / INDIZACION - 19.01.02
    UF: SUBJECT INDEXING
    BT: INFORMATION ANALYSIS
    RT: INDEX

INDIA
INDE / INDIA - 01.04.04
    BT: SOUTH ASIA
        SOUTH EAST ASIA
    RT: INDIAN

INDIAN
INDIEN / INDIO - 14.03.02
SN: USE ONLY IN CONNECTION WITH NATIONALS OF
    INDIA.
    RT: INDIA

INDIAN OCEAN
OCEAN INDIEN / OCEANO INDICO - 17.06.00

INDIGENOUS POPULATION
POPULATION INDIGENE / POBLACION INDIGENA -
14.03.01
SN: DENOTES MEMBERS OF THE ORIGINAL ETHNIC
    GROUPS WHICH POPULATED THE COUNTRY IN WHICH
    THEY ARE LIVING.
    UF: NATIVES
    BT: ABORIGINAL POPULATION
    RT: NATIVE RESERVATION

INDIVIDUALIZED TEACHING
ENSEIGNEMENT INDIVIDUALISE / ENSENANZA
INDIVIDUALIZADA - 06.05.02
    BT: TEACHING

INDIVIDUALS
INDIVIDUS / INDIVIDUOS - 05.03.01
    RT: PERSONALITY

INDOCHINA
INDOCHINE / INDOCHINA - 01.04.04
    BT: SOUTH EAST ASIA

INDOCHINA<CONT>
>>> NT: KAMPUCHEA
>>> LAO PDR
>>> VIETNAM

INDONESIA
INDONESIE / INDONESIA - 01.04.04
>>> BT: SOUTH EAST ASIA
>>> RT: INDONESIAN

INDONESIAN
INDONESIEN / INDONESIO - 14.03.02
>>> RT: INDONESIA

INDUCED MUTATIONS
MUTATIONS PROVOQUEES / MUTACIONES PROVOCADAS -
15.02.03
>>> BT: MUTATIONS

INDUSTRIAL ADAPTATION
ADAPTATION INDUSTRIELLE / ADAPTACION INDUSTRIAL
- 08.01.02
SN: ADAPTATION OF A COUNTRY'S INDUSTRIAL
> STRUCTURE TO CONDITIONS OF INTERNATIONAL
> COMPETITION.
>>> BT: ADAPTATION
>>> RT: INDUSTRIAL STRUCTURE
>>> INDUSTRY

INDUSTRIAL ADMINISTRATION
ADMINISTRATION INDUSTRIELLE / ADMINISTRACION
INDUSTRIAL - 04.03.02
SN: AT THE GOVERNMENT LEVEL. DO NOT CONFUSE WITH
> 'INDUSTRIAL MANAGEMENT'.
>>> BT: ECONOMIC ADMINISTRATION
>>> RT: INDUSTRIAL PLANNING
>>> INDUSTRIAL POLICY

INDUSTRIAL AREAS
ZONES INDUSTRIELLES / ZONAS INDUSTRIALES -
08.02.03
SN: AREAS WITH A RELATIVELY HIGH INDUSTRIAL
> CONCENTRATION, EITHER PLANNED OR UNPLANNED.
>>> RT: INDUSTRIAL CONCENTRATION
>>> INDUSTRY

INDUSTRIAL ASPECTS
ASPECTS INDUSTRIELS / ASPECTOS INDUSTRIALES -
08.01.01
>>> RT: INDUSTRY

INDUSTRIAL BANKS
BANQUES INDUSTRIELLES / BANCOS INDUSTRIALES -
08.02.04
>>> BT: BANKS
>>> RT: DEVELOPMENT BANKS
>>> INDUSTRIAL CREDIT

INDUSTRIAL BUILDINGS
BATIMENTS INDUSTRIELS / CONTRUCCIONES
INDUSTRIALES - 08.03.00
>>> BT: BUILDINGS
>>> RT: INDUSTRIAL PLANTS

INDUSTRIAL CAPITAL
CAPITAL INDUSTRIEL / CAPITAL INDUSTRIAL -
08.02.04
SN: INVESTED AND WORKING CAPITAL OF THE
> INDUSTRIAL SECTOR.
>>> BT: CAPITAL
>>> RT: INDUSTRIAL INVESTMENTS
>>> WORKING CAPITAL

INDUSTRIAL CENSUSES
RECENSEMENTS INDUSTRIELS / CENSOS INDUSTRIALES -
08.01.01
>>> BT: CENSUSES

INDUSTRIAL CONCENTRATION
CONCENTRATION INDUSTRIELLE / CONCENTRACION
INDUSTRIAL - 08.02.03
SN: IN THE GEOGRAPHICAL SENSE, CONCENTRATED IN
> ONE AREA.
>>> BT: ECONOMIC CONCENTRATION
>>> RT: INDUSTRIAL AREAS
>>> INDUSTRY

INDUSTRIAL CREDIT
CREDIT INDUSTRIEL / CREDITO INDUSTRIAL -
08.02.04
>>> BT: CREDIT
>>> RT: INDUSTRIAL BANKS
>>> INDUSTRY

INDUSTRIAL CROPS
CULTURES INDUSTRIELLES / CULTIVOS INDUSTRIALES -
07.07.02
SN: REFERS TO CROPS GROWN ON A LARGE SCALE AND
> PROCESSED WITH MECHANICAL EQUIPMENT.
>>> UF: CASH CROPS
>>> BT: CROPS
>>> NT: COCOA
>>> COCONUTS
>>> COFFEE
>>> COTTON
>>> FLAX
>>> HEVEAS
>>> OIL CROPS
>>> OPIUM
>>> SUGAR BEETS
>>> SUGAR CANE
>>> TEA
>>> TOBACCO
>>> RT: AGROINDUSTRY

INDUSTRIAL DESIGN
ESTHETIQUE INDUSTRIELLE / DISENO INDUSTRIAL -
08.03.00
>>> BT: ENGINEERING DESIGN

INDUSTRIAL DEVELOPMENT
DEVELOPPEMENT INDUSTRIEL / DESARROLLO INDUSTRIAL
- 08.01.02
>>> UF: INDUSTRIAL GROWTH
>>> BT: ECONOMIC DEVELOPMENT
>>> RT: INDUSTRIAL PROMOTION
>>> INDUSTRY
>>> UNIDO

INDUSTRIAL ECONOMICS
ECONOMIE INDUSTRIELLE / ECONOMIA INDUSTRIAL -
08.01.01
SN: *ECONOMICS AS IT RELATES TO THE INDUSTRIAL*
   SECTOR.
    BT: ECONOMICS
    RT: INDUSTRY

INDUSTRIAL ENGINEERING
TECHNOLOGIE INDUSTRIELLE / INGENIERIA INDUSTRIAL
- 08.03.00
    BT: ENGINEERING
    RT: INDUSTRIAL PROCESSES
        INDUSTRY

INDUSTRIAL ENTERPRISES
ENTREPRISES INDUSTRIELLES / EMPRESAS
INDUSTRIALES - 08.02.01
    BT: ENTERPRISES
    RT: INDUSTRIAL MANAGEMENT
        INDUSTRY
        LOCATION OF INDUSTRY

INDUSTRIAL EQUIPMENT
EQUIPEMENT INDUSTRIEL / EQUIPO INDUSTRIAL -
08.03.00
    BT: EQUIPMENT
    RT: INDUSTRY

INDUSTRIAL ESPIONAGE
ESPIONNAGE INDUSTRIEL / ESPIONAJE INDUSTRIAL -
12.08.02
    RT: INDUSTRIAL PROPERTY
        LICENSING
        PATENTS
        TRADE MARKS

INDUSTRIAL EXTENSION
VULGARISATION INDUSTRIELLE / EXTENSION
INDUSTRIAL - 08.01.01
SN: *PROGRAMME FOR BRINGING NEW DEVELOPMENTS AND*
   TECHNIQUES TO THE ATTENTION OF MANAGERS,
   THROUGH SEMINARS, VISITS BY EXPERTS,
   INFORMATION DISSEMINATION, ETC.
    BT: EXTENSION SERVICES
    RT: APPROPRIATE TECHNOLOGY
        INDUSTRIAL TRAINING
        INDUSTRY

INDUSTRIAL GROWTH
- 08.01.02
    USE: INDUSTRIAL DEVELOPMENT

INDUSTRIAL INFORMATION
INFORMATION INDUSTRIELLE / INFORMACION
INDUSTRIAL - 08.01.01
SN: *INFORMATION OF IMMEDIATE USE TO THE*
   INDUSTRIAL ADMINISTRATION. NOT GENERAL
   INFORMATION ON THE INDUSTRIAL CLIMATE OF AN
   AREA.
    BT: TECHNICAL INFORMATION
    RT: INDUSTRIAL STATISTICS
        INDUSTRY
        PATENTS

INDUSTRIAL INTEGRATION
INTEGRATION INDUSTRIELLE / INTEGRACION
INDUSTRIAL - 01.02.01
SN: *MECHANISMS OF COMPLEMENTARITY BETWEEN*
   INDUSTRIES OF VARIOUS COUNTRIES WITHIN A
   PROCESS OF ECONOMIC INTEGRATION.
    BT: ECONOMIC INTEGRATION
    RT: COMPLEMENTARITY AGREEMENTS
        INDUSTRIAL STRUCTURE
        INDUSTRY

INDUSTRIAL INVESTMENTS
INVESTISSEMENTS INDUSTRIELS / INVERSIONES
INDUSTRIALES - 08.02.04
    BT: INVESTMENTS
    RT: INDUSTRIAL CAPITAL
        INDUSTRY

INDUSTRIAL LOCATION
- 08.02.03
    USE: LOCATION OF INDUSTRY

INDUSTRIAL MANAGEMENT
GESTION INDUSTRIELLE / GESTION INDUSTRIAL -
08.02.04
    BT: MANAGEMENT
    RT: INDUSTRIAL ENTERPRISES

INDUSTRIAL PLANNING
PLANIFICATION INDUSTRIELLE / PLANIFICACION
INDUSTRIAL - 08.01.02
    BT: ECONOMIC PLANNING
    RT: INDUSTRIAL ADMINISTRATION
        INDUSTRY

INDUSTRIAL PLANTS
USINES / FABRICAS - 08.03.00
    UF: FACTORIES
    NT: NUCLEAR INSTALLATIONS
        POWER PLANTS
    RT: FACTORY LAYOUT
        FACTORY ORGANIZATION
        INDUSTRIAL BUILDINGS
        INDUSTRIAL WORKERS
        WORKSHOPS

INDUSTRIAL POLICY
POLITIQUE INDUSTRIELLE / POLITICA INDUSTRIAL -
08.01.02
SN: *GOVERNMENT POLICY REGARDING EXISTING*
   INDUSTRY AND THE ESTABLISHMENT OF NEW
   INDUSTRY.
    BT: ECONOMIC POLICY
    NT: INDUSTRIALIZATION POLICY
    RT: INDUSTRIAL ADMINISTRATION
        INDUSTRIAL PROMOTION
        INDUSTRY

INDUSTRIAL POTENTIAL
POTENTIEL INDUSTRIEL / POTENCIAL INDUSTRIAL -
08.01.02
    BT: DEVELOPMENT POTENTIAL

INDUSTRIAL PRICES
PRIX INDUSTRIELS / PRECIOS INDUSTRIALES -

INDUSTRIAL PRICES<CONT>
08.02.04
    BT: PRICES
    RT: INDUSTRY
        TERMS OF TRADE

INDUSTRIAL PROCESSES
OPERATIONS INDUSTRIELLES / PROCESOS INDUSTRIALES
- 08.03.00
    NT: COATING
        COOLING
        DISTILLING
        DRYING
        FREEZING
        HEATING
        MACHINING
        PLATING
        REFINING
        REFRIGERATION
    RT: ASSEMBLY LINES
        INDUSTRIAL ENGINEERING
        INDUSTRY

INDUSTRIAL PRODUCTION
PRODUCTION INDUSTRIELLE / PRODUCCION INDUSTRIAL
- 08.04.00
SN: USE ONLY FOR DISCUSSING THE WHOLE PRODUCTION
    OF THE INDUSTRIAL SECTOR OF A COUNTRY OR
    REGION.
    BT: PRODUCTION
    RT: INDUSTRIAL PRODUCTS
        INDUSTRY

INDUSTRIAL PRODUCTS
PRODUITS INDUSTRIELS / PRODUCTOS INDUSTRIALES -
08.04.00
    BT: PRODUCTS
    NT: MANUFACTURED PRODUCTS
        SEMI-MANUFACTURED PRODUCTS
    RT: INDUSTRIAL PRODUCTION
        INDUSTRY

INDUSTRIAL PROFILES
PROFILS INDUSTRIELS / PERFILES INDUSTRIALES -
08.03.00
    RT: FACTORY ORGANIZATION

INDUSTRIAL PROJECTS
PROJETS INDUSTRIELS / PROYECTOS INDUSTRIALES -
08.01.02
    BT: DEVELOPMENT PROJECTS
    RT: INDUSTRY

INDUSTRIAL PROMOTION
PROMOTION INDUSTRIELLE / PROMOCION INDUSTRIAL -
08.01.02
    RT: INDUSTRIAL DEVELOPMENT
        INDUSTRIAL POLICY

INDUSTRIAL PROPERTY
PROPRIETE INDUSTRIELLE / PROPIEDAD INDUSTRIAL -
08.05.00
    BT: INTELLECTUAL PROPERTY
    NT: PATENTS

INDUSTRIAL PROPERTY<CONT>
    RT: INDUSTRIAL ESPIONAGE
        INDUSTRY
        PATENT LAW

INDUSTRIAL PSYCHOLOGY
PSYCHOLOGIE INDUSTRIELLE / PSICOLOGIA INDUSTRIAL
- 13.03.01
SN: USE IN CONNECTION WITH THE STUDY OF THE
    ATTITUDE OF WORKERS, WITH A VIEW TO
    IMPROVING WORKING CONDITIONS.
    BT: PSYCHOLOGY
    RT: INDUSTRY

INDUSTRIAL RELATIONS
- 13.06.00
    USE: LABOUR RELATIONS

INDUSTRIAL RESEARCH
RECHERCHE INDUSTRIELLE / INVESTIGACION
INDUSTRIAL - 08.05.00
SN: TO DEVELOP NEW OR IMPROVED PRODUCTION
    METHODS AND PRODUCTS.
    BT: RESEARCH
    RT: INDUSTRY

INDUSTRIAL SECTOR
SECTEUR INDUSTRIEL / SECTOR INDUSTRIAL -
08.01.01
SN: INCLUDES MANUFACTURING, MINING, POWER,
    CONSTRUCTION INDUSTRY, ETC.
    UF: SECONDARY SECTOR
    NT: AEROSPACE INDUSTRY
        AIRCRAFT INDUSTRY
        CEMENT INDUSTRY
        CERAMICS INDUSTRY
        CHEMICAL INDUSTRY
        CONSTRUCTION INDUSTRY
        ELECTRICAL INDUSTRY
        ELECTRONICS INDUSTRY
        FOOD INDUSTRY
        GLASS INDUSTRY
        LEATHER INDUSTRY
        PETROLEUM INDUSTRY
        POWER INDUSTRY
        PULP AND PAPER INDUSTRY
        RUBBER INDUSTRY
        SHIPBUILDING
        SHOE INDUSTRY
        TEXTILE INDUSTRY
        WOODWORKING INDUSTRY
    RT: INDUSTRY
        MANUFACTURING

INDUSTRIAL SOCIOLOGY
SOCIOLOGIE INDUSTRIELLE / SOCIOLOGIA INDUSTRIAL
- 13.03.01
SN: USE IN CONNECTION WITH THE LAWS OF HUMAN
    SOCIETY WHICH CONCERN THE INDUSTRIAL
    ELEMENT.
    BT: SOCIOLOGY
    RT: INDUSTRY

INDUSTRIAL STATISTICS

INDUSTRIAL STATISTICS<CONT>
STATISTIQUES INDUSTRIELLES / ESTADISTICAS
INDUSTRIALES - 08.01.01
    BT: ECONOMIC STATISTICS
    RT: INDUSTRIAL INFORMATION
         INDUSTRY
         PRODUCTION STATISTICS

INDUSTRIAL STRUCTURE
STRUCTURE INDUSTRIELLE / ESTRUCTURA INDUSTRIAL -
08.01.02
    RT: INDUSTRIAL ADAPTATION
         INDUSTRIAL INTEGRATION
         INDUSTRY

INDUSTRIAL TRAINING
FORMATION INDUSTRIELLE / CAPACITACION INDUSTRIAL
- 06.03.07
    BT: VOCATIONAL TRAINING
    RT: INDUSTRIAL EXTENSION
         INDUSTRY

INDUSTRIAL WASTES
DECHETS INDUSTRIELS / DESPERDICIOS INDUSTRIALES
- 08.04.00
    BT: WASTES
    NT: METAL SCRAPS
         WOOD WASTES
    RT: INDUSTRY

INDUSTRIAL WORKERS
OUVRIERS INDUSTRIELS / OBREROS INDUSTRIALES -
13.09.06
    UF: FACTORY WORKERS
    BT: WORKERS
    NT: CONSTRUCTION WORKERS
         ELECTRICIANS
         METALWORKERS
         MINERS
         SEMI-SKILLED WORKERS
         SKILLED WORKERS
         TEXTILE WORKERS
         UNSKILLED WORKERS
    RT: INDUSTRIAL PLANTS

INDUSTRIALIZATION
INDUSTRIALISATION / INDUSTRIALIZACION - 08.01.02
*SN: USE ONLY FOR THE INITIAL STAGE OF INDUSTRIAL
DEVELOPMENT.*
    RT: AUTOMATION
         INDUSTRY
         MECHANIZATION

INDUSTRIALIZATION POLICY
POLITIQUE D'INDUSTRIALISATION / POLITICA DE
INDUSTRIALIZACION - 08.01.02
    BT: INDUSTRIAL POLICY
    NT: IMPORT SUBSTITUTION

INDUSTRIALIZED COUNTRIES
- 03.02.03
    USE: DEVELOPED COUNTRIES

INDUSTRY
INDUSTRIE / INDUSTRIA - 08.01.01

INDUSTRY<CONT>
*SN: USE MORE PRECISE DESCRIPTOR AS APPLICABLE:
'CONSTRUCTION INDUSTRY', 'TEXTILE INDUSTRY',
ETC.*
    UF: MANUFACTURING INDUSTRIES
    NT: EXPORT-ORIENTED INDUSTRY
         HEAVY INDUSTRY
         LIGHT INDUSTRY
         MEDIUM-SCALE INDUSTRY
         NATIONALIZED INDUSTRY
         RURAL INDUSTRY
         SMALL-SCALE INDUSTRY
    RT: AGROINDUSTRY
         INDUSTRIAL ADAPTATION
         INDUSTRIAL AREAS
         INDUSTRIAL ASPECTS
         INDUSTRIAL CONCENTRATION
         INDUSTRIAL CREDIT
         INDUSTRIAL DEVELOPMENT
         INDUSTRIAL ECONOMICS
         INDUSTRIAL ENGINEERING
         INDUSTRIAL ENTERPRISES
         INDUSTRIAL EQUIPMENT
         INDUSTRIAL EXTENSION
         INDUSTRIAL INFORMATION
         INDUSTRIAL INTEGRATION
         INDUSTRIAL INVESTMENTS
         INDUSTRIAL PLANNING
         INDUSTRIAL POLICY
         INDUSTRIAL PRICES
         INDUSTRIAL PROCESSES
         INDUSTRIAL PRODUCTION
         INDUSTRIAL PRODUCTS
         INDUSTRIAL PROJECTS
         INDUSTRIAL PROPERTY
         INDUSTRIAL PSYCHOLOGY
         INDUSTRIAL RESEARCH
         INDUSTRIAL SECTOR
         INDUSTRIAL SOCIOLOGY
         INDUSTRIAL STATISTICS
         INDUSTRIAL STRUCTURE
         INDUSTRIAL TRAINING
         INDUSTRIAL WASTES
         INDUSTRIALIZATION

INFANT MORTALITY
MORTALITE INFANTILE / MORTALIDAD INFANTIL -
14.06.00
    BT: MORTALITY
    RT: INFANTS

INFANTS
NOURRISSONS / LACTANTES - 14.02.02
    BT: CHILDREN
    RT: EARLY CHILDHOOD
         INFANT MORTALITY

INFECTIOUS DISEASES
MALADIES INFECTIEUSES / ENFERMEDADES INFECCIOSAS
- 15.04.02
    UF: COMMUNICABLE DISEASES
         CONTAGIOUS DISEASES
         EPIDEMIC DISEASES
    BT: DISEASES

INFECTIOUS DISEASES<CONT>
- *NT:* CHOLERA
  DIPHTHERIA
  FUNGUS DISEASES
  LEPROSY
  MEASLES
  MENINGITIS
  PARASITIC DISEASES
  PLAGUE
  POLIOMYELITIS
  RICKETTSIAL DISEASES
  RUBELLA
  SCARLET FEVER
  SEPTICEMIA
  SMALLPOX
  TROPICAL DISEASES
  TUBERCULOSIS
  TYPHOID
  VENEREAL DISEASES
  YELLOW FEVER
- *RT:* DISEASE TRANSMISSION
  DISEASE VECTORS
  EPIDEMICS
  EPIDEMIOLOGY

INFLATION
INFLATION / INFLACION - 11.02.01
- *RT:* AUSTERITY POLICY
  BUSINESS CYCLE
  DEFLATION
  INDEXATION
  MONETARY CIRCULATION
  MONETARY CORRECTION
  PRICE CONTROL
  PRICE INDEX

INFORMAL SECTOR
SECTEUR INFORMEL / SECTOR INFORMAL - 08.02.02

INFORMATICS
- 18.08.00
  USE: **COMPUTER SCIENCE**

INFORMATION
INFORMATION / INFORMACION - 19.01.01
- *NT:* CULTURAL INFORMATION
  ECONOMIC INFORMATION
  NEWS
  SCIENTIFIC INFORMATION
  SOCIAL INFORMATION
  TECHNICAL INFORMATION
- *RT:* ACCESS TO INFORMATION
  COMMUNICATION
  COMMUNICATION INDUSTRY
  ICSSD
  INFORMATION NEEDS
  INFORMATION POLICY
  INFORMATION SOURCES
  INFORMATION SYSTEMS
  INFORMATION THEORY
  INFORMATION USERS

INFORMATION ANALYSIS

INFORMATION ANALYSIS<CONT>
ANALYSE DE L'INFORMATION / ANALISIS DE LA
INFORMACION - 19.01.02
- *UF:* DOCUMENTARY ANALYSIS
- *BT:* DOCUMENTATION
- *NT:* CONTENT ANALYSIS
  INDEXING
  INFORMATION PROCESSING
- *RT:* DATA ANALYSIS

INFORMATION CENTRES
- 19.01.03
  USE: **INFORMATION SERVICES**

INFORMATION DISSEMINATION
**DIFFUSION DE L'INFORMATION / DISEMINACION DE LA
INFORMACION - 19.01.02**
- *NT:* ADVERTISING
  SDI
- *RT:* ACCESS TO INFORMATION
  INFORMATION SERVICES
  INFORMATION SYSTEMS

INFORMATION EXCHANGE
**ECHANGE D'INFORMATION / INTERCAMBIO DE
INFORMACION - 19.01.02**
- *NT:* DATA TRANSMISSION
  REPORTING SYSTEMS
- *RT:* ACCESS TO INFORMATION
  INFORMATION NETWORK
  INFORMATION SERVICES
  INFORMATION SYSTEMS

INFORMATION NEEDS
**BESOINS D'INFORMATION / NECESIDADES DE
INFORMACION - 19.01.01**
- *BT:* BASIC NEEDS
- *RT:* INFORMATION
  INFORMATION USERS

INFORMATION NETWORK
**RESEAU D'INFORMATION / RED DE INFORMACION -
19.01.01**
- *RT:* INFORMATION EXCHANGE

INFORMATION POLICY
**POLITIQUE DE L'INFORMATION / POLITICA DE
INFORMACION - 19.01.01**
- *BT:* GOVERNMENT POLICY
- *RT:* DATA PROTECTION
  INFORMATION

INFORMATION PROCESSING
**TRAITEMENT DE L'INFORMATION / PROCESAMIENTO DE
LA INFORMACION - 19.01.02**
- *BT:* INFORMATION ANALYSIS
  PROCESSING
- *NT:* DATA PROCESSING
- *RT:* IFIP
  INFORMATION RECORDING

INFORMATION RECORDING
**ENREGISTREMENT DE L'INFORMATION / REGISTRO DE LA
INFORMACION - 19.01.02**
- *BT:* DOCUMENTATION
- *NT:* DATA RECORDING

INFORMATION RECORDING<CONT>
> *RT:* DATA STORAGE
> INFORMATION PROCESSING

INFORMATION SCIENCES
SCIENCES DE L'INFORMATION / CIENCIAS DE LA
INFORMACION - 19.01.01
> *NT:* COMPUTER SCIENCE
> DOCUMENTATION
> LIBRARY SCIENCE
> *RT:* INFORMATION SYSTEMS

INFORMATION SERVICES
SERVICES D'INFORMATION / SERVICIOS DE
INFORMACION - 19.01.03
> *UF:* DOCUMENTATION CENTRES
> INFORMATION CENTRES
> *NT:* ARCHIVES
> AUDIOVISUAL CENTRES
> CLADES
> DATA BANKS
> DATA BASES
> EXTENSION SERVICES
> LIBRARIES
> TRANSLATION SERVICES
> *RT:* INFORMATION DISSEMINATION
> INFORMATION EXCHANGE

INFORMATION SOURCES
SOURCES D'INFORMATION / FUENTES DE INFORMACION -
19.01.01
> *RT:* ACCESS TO INFORMATION
> INFORMATION

INFORMATION SYSTEMS
SYSTEMES D'INFORMATION / SISTEMAS DE INFORMACION
- 19.01.02
> *NT:* AGRIS
> DEVSIS
> INIS
> ISIS
> MANAGEMENT INFORMATION SYSTEM
> REPORTING SYSTEMS
> UNISIST
> *RT:* INFORMATION
> INFORMATION DISSEMINATION
> INFORMATION EXCHANGE
> INFORMATION SCIENCES
> THESAURUS

INFORMATION THEORY
THEORIE DE L'INFORMATION / TEORIA DE LA
INFORMACION - 18.08.00
> *UF:* COMMUNICATION THEORY
> *BT:* THEORY
> *RT:* COMMUNICATION
> CYBERNETICS
> INFORMATION
> PROBABILITY

INFORMATION USERS
UTILISATEURS D'INFORMATION / USUARIOS DE LA
INFORMACION - 19.01.01

INFORMATION USERS<CONT>
> *RT:* ACCESS TO INFORMATION
> INFORMATION
> INFORMATION NEEDS

INIS
INIS / INIS - 19.01.02
SN: INTERNATIONAL NUCLEAR INFORMATION SYSTEM.
> *BT:* INFORMATION SYSTEMS
> *RT:* IAEA
> NUCLEAR ENERGY

INLAND FISHING
PECHE INTERIEURE / PESCA CONTINENTAL - 07.10.03
> *BT:* FISHING

INLAND NAVIGATION
- 10.05.00
> *USE:* INLAND WATER TRANSPORT

INLAND TRADE
- 09.04.01
> *USE:* DOMESTIC TRADE

INLAND TRANSPORT
TRANSPORT INTERIEUR / TRANSPORTE INTERIOR -
10.07.00
SN: TRANSPORT WITHIN THE LIMITS OF A COUNTRY.
> *BT:* TRANSPORT
> *RT:* DISTRIBUTION

INLAND WATER TRANSPORT
TRANSPORT FLUVIAL ET LACUSTRE / TRANSPORTE
FLUVIAL Y LACUSTRE - 10.05.00
> *UF:* INLAND NAVIGATION
> *BT:* MODES OF TRANSPORTATION
> *RT:* INLAND WATERWAYS
> PORTS

INLAND WATERWAYS
VOIES D'EAU INTERIEURES / VIAS DE NAVEGACION
INTERIOR - 10.03.00
> *BT:* WATERWAYS
> *NT:* CANALS
> LAKES
> RIVERS
> *RT:* INLAND WATER TRANSPORT

INNOVATIONS
INNOVATIONS / INNOVACIONES - 12.06.00
> *RT:* DIFFUSION OF INNOVATIONS
> INVENTIONS
> TECHNOLOGICAL CHANGE

INPUT-OUTPUT
INPUT-OUTPUT / INSUMO-PRODUCTO - 03.02.02
> *NT:* INPUT-OUTPUT ANALYSIS
> INPUT-OUTPUT TABLES

INPUT-OUTPUT ANALYSIS
ANALYSE INPUT-OUTPUT / ANALISIS DE
INSUMO-PRODUCTO - 03.02.02

INPUT-OUTPUT ANALYSIS\<S\<CONT\>
SN: ECONOMIC EVALUATION OF LINEAR FORMULAS
CONNECTING LEVELS OF ACTIVITY IN VARIOUS
SECTORS OF AN ECONOMY, AND PREDICTION OF THE
CONSEQUENCES OF CHANGES.
    UF: SECTOR ANALYSIS
    BT: ECONOMIC ANALYSIS
        INPUT-OUTPUT
    RT: ACTIVITY ANALYSIS
        ECONOMETRICS
        ECONOMIC EVALUATION
        ECONOMIC STRUCTURE

INPUT-OUTPUT TABLES
TABLEAUX INPUT-OUTPUT / CUADROS DE
INSUMO-PRODUCTO - 03.02.02
SN: SYSTEM OF DOUBLE ENTRY BOOKKEEPING WHICH
SHOWS, FOR EACH SECTOR OF AN ECONOMY DURING
A GIVEN PERIOD, PURCHASES AND SALES TO OTHER
SECTORS.
    BT: INPUT-OUTPUT
        STATISTICAL TABLES
    RT: ECONOMIC MODELS
        ECONOMIC STATISTICS
        ECONOMIC STRUCTURE

INSECT PESTS
INSECTES PARASITES / INSECTOS PARASITOS -
16.03.03
    BT: INSECTS
    NT: LOCUSTS
    RT: PEST CONTROL

INSECTICIDES
INSECTICIDES / INSECTICIDAS - 08.12.05
    BT: PESTICIDES

INSECTS
INSECTES / INSECTOS - 16.03.03
    BT: ANIMALS
    NT: INSECT PESTS
        SILKWORMS
    RT: ENTOMOLOGY

INSTALMENT CREDIT
- 11.02.02
    USE: CONSUMER CREDIT

INSTITUTIONAL FRAMEWORK
CADRE INSTITUTIONNEL / MARCO INSTITUCIONAL -
04.03.01
    RT: GOVERNMENT
        PUBLIC ADMINISTRATION

INSTRUCTION
- 06.05.02
    USE: TEACHING

INSTRUCTIONAL AIDS
- 06.05.03
    USE: TEACHING AIDS

INSTRUCTIONAL MEDIA
- 06.05.03
    USE: TEACHING AIDS

INSTRUCTIONAL PROGRAMMES
- 06.05.01
    USE: TEACHING PROGRAMMES

INSTRUCTIONAL RADIO
- 06.05.03
    USE: EDUCATIONAL RADIO

INSTRUCTIONAL STAFF
- 06.06.02
    USE: TEACHING PERSONNEL

INSTRUCTORS
INSTRUCTEURS / INSTRUCTORES - 13.09.09
    BT: TEACHING PERSONNEL
    RT: TRAINING

INSTRUMENTATION INDUSTRY
INDUSTRIE D'APPAREILS DE PRECISION / INDUSTRIA
DE APARATOS DE PRECISION - 08.14.08
SN: THE MANUFACTURE OF MEASURING, CONTROLLING,
LABORATORY AND SCIENTIFIC INSTRUMENTS.
    BT: MACHINERY INDUSTRY
    NT: OPTICAL INDUSTRY
        WATCHMAKING INDUSTRY
    RT: PRECISION INSTRUMENTS

INSURANCE
ASSURANCES / SEGUROS - 11.02.03
    BT: FINANCIAL INSTITUTIONS
    NT: ACCIDENT INSURANCE
        AGRICULTURAL INSURANCE
        CREDIT INSURANCE
        EXPORT INSURANCE
        FIRE INSURANCE
        LIFE INSURANCE
    RT: INVESTMENT GUARANTEES
        SOCIAL SECURITY

INTECOL
AIE / AIE - 01.03.04
SN: INTERNATIONAL ASSOCIATION FOR ECOLOGY.
    BT: NON-GOVERNMENTAL ORGANIZATIONS
    RT: ECOLOGY

INTEGRATED APPROACH
APPROCHE INTEGREE / METODO INTEGRADO - 18.03.00
    BT: RESEARCH METHODS

INTEGRATED CURRICULUM
PROGRAMME D'ETUDES INTEGRE / PROGRAMA INTEGRADO
DE ESTUDIOS - 06.05.01
    BT: CURRICULUM

INTEGRATED DEVELOPMENT
DEVELOPPEMENT INTEGRE / DESARROLLO INTEGRADO -
02.01.01
    BT: ECONOMIC AND SOCIAL DEVELOPMENT

INTEGUMENTARY SYSTEM
SYSTEME TEGUMENTAIRE / SISTEMA TEGUMENTARIO -
15.02.04
    BT: ANATOMY
    NT: SKIN

INTELLECTUAL PROPERTY
PROPRIETE INTELLECTUELLE / PROPIEDAD INTELECTUAL
- 19.02.03
    NT: COPYRIGHT
         INDUSTRIAL PROPERTY
    RT: PATENT LAW
         WIPO

INTELLECTUALS
INTELLECTUELS / INTELECTUALES - 05.03.05
    RT: ELITE

INTELLIGENCE QUOTIENT
QUOTIENT INTELLECTUEL / CUOCIENTE DE
INTELIGENCIA - 06.05.04
    RT: APTITUDES

INTENSIVE COURSES
- 06.05.01
    USE: **ACCELERATED COURSES**

INTENSIVE FARMING
EXPLOITATION AGRICOLE INTENSIVE / CULTIVO
INTENSIVO - 07.05.03
    BT: FARMING SYSTEMS

INTERCROPPING
CULTURE INTERCALAIRE / CULTIVO INTERCALADO -
07.05.04
SN: TWO OR MORE CROPS INTERSPERSED ON THE SAME
    PLOT OF LAND AND HARVESTED IN THE SAME
    SEASON.
    BT: CULTIVATION SYSTEMS
    RT: CROP DIVERSIFICATION

INTERCULTURAL RESEARCH
- 05.01.02
    USE: **CROSS CULTURAL ANALYSIS**

INTERDISCIPLINARY RESEARCH
RECHERCHE INTERDISCIPLINAIRE / INVESTIGACION
INTERDISCIPLINARIA - 18.03.00
    BT: RESEARCH METHODS

INTEREST
INTERET / INTERES - 11.02.07
    BT: PROFITS
    RT: INTEREST RATE

INTEREST GROUPS
GROUPES D'INTERET / GRUPOS DE INTERESES -
04.04.02
SN: USE IN CONNECTION WITH BODIES CAPABLE OF
    EXERCISING PRESSURE TO AFFECT DECISION
    MAKING AT THE GOVERNMENT LEVEL.
    UF: PRESSURE GROUPS
    BT: GROUPS
    NT: EMPLOYERS ORGANIZATIONS
         MULTINATIONAL ENTERPRISES
         TRADE UNIONS

INTEREST RATE
TAUX D'INTERET / TASA DE INTERES - 11.02.07

INTEREST RATE<CONT>
    RT: INTEREST
         INVESTMENTS

INTERETHNIC RELATIONS
RELATIONS INTERETHNIQUES / RELACIONES
INTERETNICAS - 14.03.01
SN: RELATIONS BETWEEN ETHNIC GROUPS. DO NOT
    CONFUSE WITH 'RACE RELATIONS'.
    BT: INTERGROUP RELATIONS
    RT: ETHNIC GROUPS

INTERGOVERNMENTAL ORGANIZATIONS
ORGANISATIONS INTERGOUVERNEMENTALES /
ORGANIZACIONES INTERGUBERNAMENTALES - 01.03.01
    BT: INTERNATIONAL ORGANIZATIONS
    NT: ACCT
         AFRICAN DEVELOPMENT BANK
         APO
         APU
         ASEAN
         ASIAN DEVELOPMENT BANK
         ASPAC
         BENELUX
         CABEI
         CACEU
         CACM
         CARICOM
         CARIFTA
         CENTO
         CERN
         CMEA
         COLOMBO PLAN
         COMMONWEALTH
         COUNCIL OF EUROPE
         EAC
         ECMT
         EFTA
         EUROPEAN COMMUNITIES
         EUROPEAN SPACE AGENCY
         ICEM
         IDB
         LAFTA
         LEAGUE OF ARAB STATES
         MPCC
         NATO
         NORDIC COUNCIL
         OAPEC
         OAS
         OAU
         OCAM
         OCAS
         OECD
         OPEC
         SEATO
         SPC
         UN SYSTEM
         WEU

INTERGROUP RELATIONS
RELATIONS INTERGROUPES / RELACIONES ENTRE LOS
GRUPOS - 05.03.06
SN: USE IN CONNECTION WITH THE RELATIONSHIP
    BETWEEN ONE POPULATION GROUP AND ANOTHER.

INTERGROUP RELATIONS<CONT>
- *NT:* CLASS STRUGGLE
  INTERETHNIC RELATIONS
  LABOUR RELATIONS
  RACE RELATIONS
- *RT:* GROUPS

INTERMEDIATE TECHNOLOGY
TECHNOLOGIE INTERMEDIAIRE / TECNOLOGIA
INTERMEDIA - 12.06.00
- *BT:* TECHNOLOGY
- *RT:* ALTERNATIVE TECHNOLOGY
  APPROPRIATE TECHNOLOGY
  TECHNOLOGY TRANSFER

INTERNAL MIGRATIONS
MIGRATIONS INTERNES / MIGRACIONES INTERNAS -
14.07.00
- *BT:* MIGRATIONS
- *NT:* COMMUTING
  RURAL MIGRATIONS

INTERNATIONAL AFFAIRS
- 01.02.01
- *USE:* INTERNATIONAL RELATIONS

INTERNATIONAL AGREEMENTS
ACCORDS INTERNATIONAUX / ACUERDOS
INTERNACIONALES - 01.02.04
- *UF:* TREATIES
- *NT:* CULTURAL AGREEMENTS
  ECONOMIC AGREEMENTS
- *RT:* CONVENTIONS

INTERNATIONAL ASSISTANCE
- 01.01.01
- *USE:* INTERNATIONAL COOPERATION

INTERNATIONAL BORROWING
EMPRUNTS INTERNATIONAUX / EMPRESTITOS
INTERNACIONALES - 11.03.01
- *BT:* BORROWING

INTERNATIONAL CONTROL
REGULATION INTERNATIONALE / CONTROL
INTERNACIONAL - 01.02.04
- *RT:* INTERNATIONAL LAW

INTERNATIONAL COOPERATION
COOPERATION INTERNATIONALE / COOPERACION
INTERNACIONAL - 01.01.01
- *SN: ALL FORMS OF COOPERATION ON AN INTERNATIONAL*
  BASIS.
- *UF:* INTERNATIONAL ASSISTANCE
- *NT:* CULTURAL COOPERATION
  DEVELOPMENT AID
  FOREIGN AID
  HORIZONTAL COOPERATION
  REGIONAL COOPERATION
- *RT:* IDA
  SID

INTERNATIONAL DIVISION OF LABOUR

INTERNATIONAL DIVISION OF LABOUR<CONT>
DIVISION INTERNATIONALE DU TRAVAIL / DIVISION
INTERNACIONAL DEL TRABAJO - 09.05.03
- *SN: THEORY AND PRACTICE OF INTERNATIONAL*
  PLANNING AND AGREEMENTS BY WHICH COUNTRIES
  SPECIALIZE IN THE PRODUCTION OF THOSE
  COMMODITIES FOR WHICH THEY HAVE THE GREATEST
  COMPARATIVE ADVANTAGE.
- *BT:* DIVISION OF LABOUR
- *RT:* COMPARATIVE ADVANTAGE
  ECONOMIC THEORY

INTERNATIONAL ENTERPRISES
- 03.03.05
- *USE:* MULTINATIONAL ENTERPRISES

INTERNATIONAL INVESTMENTS
INVESTISSEMENTS INTERNATIONAUX / INVERSIONES
INTERNACIONALES - 11.03.03
- *BT:* CAPITAL MOVEMENTS
  INVESTMENTS
- *NT:* FOREIGN INVESTMENTS

INTERNATIONAL LAW
DROIT INTERNATIONAL / DERECHO INTERNACIONAL -
01.02.04
- *BT:* LAW
- *NT:* LAW OF THE SEA
- *RT:* INTERNATIONAL CONTROL

INTERNATIONAL LIQUIDITY
LIQUIDITE INTERNATIONALE / LIQUIDEZ
INTERNACIONAL - 11.03.01
- *BT:* LIQUIDITY
- *RT:* INTERNATIONAL MONETARY SYSTEM
  SPECIAL DRAWING RIGHTS

INTERNATIONAL MARKET
MARCHE INTERNATIONAL / MERCADO INTERNACIONAL -
09.05.03
- *BT:* MARKET
- *RT:* INTERNATIONAL TRADE

INTERNATIONAL MIGRATIONS
MIGRATIONS INTERNATIONALES / MIGRACIONES
INTERNACIONALES - 14.07.00
- *BT:* MIGRATIONS
- *NT:* EMIGRATION
  FRONTIER MIGRATIONS
  IMMIGRATION

INTERNATIONAL MONETARY REFORM
REFORME MONETAIRE INTERNATIONALE / REFORMA
MONETARIA INTERNACIONAL - 11.03.01
- *RT:* INTERNATIONAL MONETARY SYSTEM

INTERNATIONAL MONETARY SYSTEM
SYSTEME MONETAIRE INTERNATIONAL / SISTEMA
MONETARIO INTERNACIONAL - 11.03.01

INTERNATIONAL MONETARY SYSTEM<CONT>
    RT: EXCHANGE RATE
        GOLD STANDARD
        IMF
        INTERNATIONAL LIQUIDITY
        INTERNATIONAL MONETARY REFORM
        SPECIAL DRAWING RIGHTS

INTERNATIONAL NEGOTIATION
NEGOCIATION INTERNATIONALE / NEGOCIACION
INTERNACIONAL - 01.02.04

INTERNATIONAL ORGANIZATIONS
ORGANISATIONS INTERNATIONALES / ORGANIZACIONES
INTERNACIONALES - 01.03.01
    NT: INTERGOVERNMENTAL ORGANIZATIONS
        NON-GOVERNMENTAL ORGANIZATIONS
        REGIONAL ORGANIZATIONS
    RT: MULTILATERAL AID

INTERNATIONAL PAYMENTS
PAIEMENTS INTERNATIONAUX / PAGOS INTERNACIONALES
- 11.03.02
    RT: BALANCE OF PAYMENTS
        PAYMENT AGREEMENTS
        PAYMENT SYSTEMS

INTERNATIONAL POLITICS
POLITIQUE INTERNATIONALE / POLITICA
INTERNACIONAL - 01.02.01
    RT: INTERNATIONAL RELATIONS

INTERNATIONAL RELATIONS
RELATIONS INTERNATIONALES / RELACIONES
INTERNACIONALES - 01.02.01
    UF: INTERNATIONAL AFFAIRS
    NT: BILATERAL RELATIONS
        ECONOMIC RELATIONS
        FOREIGN RELATIONS
        MULTILATERAL RELATIONS
    RT: ALLIANCES
        DETENTE
        FOREIGN INTERVENTION
        INTERNATIONAL POLITICS
        NEUTRALISM
        NEUTRALITY
        NEW INTERNATIONAL ECONOMIC ORDER
        PEACEFUL COEXISTENCE

INTERNATIONAL SCHOOLS
ECOLES INTERNATIONALES / ESCUELAS
INTERNACIONALES - 06.04.04
    BT: SCHOOLS

INTERNATIONAL TRADE
COMMERCE INTERNATIONAL / COMERCIO INTERNACIONAL
- 09.05.01
    UF: WORLD TRADE
    BT: TRADE
    NT: EAST-WEST TRADE
        FOREIGN TRADE

INTERNATIONAL TRADE<CONT>
    RT: GATT
        INTERNATIONAL MARKET
        ITC
        TRADE AGREEMENTS
        TRADE BARRIERS
        TRADE DEVELOPMENT
        TRADE LIBERALIZATION
        TRADE NEGOTIATIONS
        TRADE POLICY
        TRADE PROMOTION
        TRADE VOLUME
        UNCTAD

INTERNATIONAL TRANSPORT
TRANSPORT INTERNATIONAL / TRANSPORTE
INTERNACIONAL - 10.07.00
SN: TRANSPORT FROM ONE COUNTRY TO ANOTHER.
    BT: TRANSPORT

INTERNATIONAL WATERWAYS
VOIES D'EAU INTERNATIONALES / VIAS DE AGUA
INTERNACIONALES - 17.05.02
    RT: LAKES
        RIVERS

INTERVIEWS
INTERVIEWS / ENTREVISTAS - 18.04.00
    RT: QUESTIONNAiRES
        SURVEYS

INTRACTABLE DISEASES
MALADIES INCURABLES / ENFERMEDADES INCURABLES -
15.04.02
    BT: DISEASES

INTRAUTERINE DEVICES
DISPOSITIFS INTRA-UTERINS / DISPOSITIVOS
INTRAUTERINOS - 14.05.02
    BT: CONTRACEPTIVES

INTRAUTERINE MORTALITY
MORTALITE FOETALE / MORTALIDAD FETAL - 14.06.00
    BT: MORTALITY

INVENTIONS
INVENTIONS / INVENTOS - 12.06.00
    RT: INNOVATIONS
        INVENTORS
        LICENSING
        PATENTS
        TECHNOLOGICAL CHANGE

INVENTORIES
INVENTAIRES / INVENTARIOS - 09.03.03
    RT: STOCKS

INVENTORS
INVENTEURS / INVENTORES - 12.06.00
    RT: INVENTIONS

INVESTMENT BANKS
BANQUES D'INVESTISSEMENT / BANCOS DE INVERSION -

INVESTMENT BANKS<CONT>
11.02.06
> *BT:* BANKS
> *NT:* EIB
> *RT:* CAPITAL FORMATION
> INVESTMENTS

INVESTMENT GUARANTEES
GARANTIES DES INVESTISSEMENTS / GARANTIAS DE LAS
INVERSIONES - 11.02.06
> *UF:* INVESTMENT INSURANCE
> *RT:* INSURANCE
> INVESTMENTS

INVESTMENT INSURANCE
- 11.02.06
> *USE:* INVESTMENT GUARANTEES

INVESTMENT POLICY
POLITIQUE D'INVESTISSEMENT / POLITICA DE
INVERSIONES - 11.02.06
> *BT:* ECONOMIC POLICY
> *RT:* INVESTMENT PROMOTION
> INVESTMENTS

INVESTMENT PROMOTION
PROMOTION DES INVESTISSEMENTS / FOMENTO DE LAS
INVERSIONES - 11.02.06
> *RT:* INVESTMENT POLICY
> INVESTMENTS
> TAX INCENTIVES

INVESTMENT REQUIREMENTS
BESOINS D'INVESTISSEMENTS / NECESIDADES DE
INVERSIONES - 11.02.06
> *BT:* FINANCIAL NEEDS
> *RT:* INVESTMENTS

INVESTMENT RETURNS
REVENUS D'INVESTISSEMENTS / INGRESOS POR
INVERSIONES - 11.02.07
> *UF:* DIVIDENDS
> RENT
> *BT:* PROFITS
> *RT:* INVESTMENTS

INVESTMENTS
INVESTISSEMENTS / INVERSIONES - 11.02.06
> *UF:* CAPITAL INVESTMENTS
> *NT:* AGRICULTURAL INVESTMENTS
> INDUSTRIAL INVESTMENTS
> INTERNATIONAL INVESTMENTS
> PRIVATE INVESTMENTS
> PUBLIC INVESTMENTS

INVESTMENTS<CONT>
> *RT:* ABSORPTIVE CAPACITY
> ACCUMULATION RATE
> CAPITAL
> CAPITAL FORMATION
> INTEREST RATE
> INVESTMENT BANKS
> INVESTMENT GUARANTEES
> INVESTMENT POLICY
> INVESTMENT PROMOTION
> INVESTMENT REQUIREMENTS
> INVESTMENT RETURNS
> PREINVESTMENT SURVEYS
> RATE OF INVESTMENT
> REINVESTMENTS

INVISIBLE TRANSACTIONS
TRANSACTIONS INVISIBLES / TRANSACCIONES
INVISIBLES - 11.03.03
> *BT:* BALANCE OF PAYMENTS
> *RT:* CAPITAL MOVEMENTS

IONISING RADIATION
RADIATION IONISANTE / RADIACION IONIZANTE -
08.11.04
> *RT:* IRRADIATION

IPPF
IPPF / IPPF - 01.03.04
SN: INTERNATIONAL PLANNED PARENTHOOD FEDERATION.
> *BT:* NON-GOVERNMENTAL ORGANIZATIONS
> *RT:* FAMILY PLANNING

IPSA
AISP / AICP - 01.03.04
SN: INTERNATIONAL POLITICAL SCIENCE ASSOCIATION.
> *BT:* NON-GOVERNMENTAL ORGANIZATIONS
> *RT:* POLITICAL SCIENCE

IRAN
IRAN / IRAN - 01.04.06
> *BT:* MIDDLE EAST
> *RT:* IRANIAN

IRANIAN
IRANIEN / IRANIO - 14.03.02
> *RT:* IRAN

IRAQ
IRAK / IRAQ - 01.04.06
> *BT:* ARAB COUNTRIES
> MIDDLE EAST
> *RT:* IRAQI

IRAQI
IRAKIEN / IRAQUI - 14.03.02
> *RT:* IRAQ

IRELAND
IRLANDE / IRLANDA - 01.04.05
> *BT:* WESTERN EUROPE
> *RT:* IRISH

IRISH
IRLANDAIS / IRLANDES - 14.03.02
> *RT:* IRELAND

IRON
FER / HIERRO - 08.14.02
>> *BT:* METALS
>> *RT:* IRON AND STEEL INDUSTRY
>> IRON ORE

IRON AND STEEL INDUSTRY
INDUSTRIE SIDERURGIQUE / INDUSTRIA SIDERURGICA -
08.14.01
>> *UF:* STEEL INDUSTRY
>> *RT:* ECSC
>> IRON
>> STEEL

IRON ORE
MINERAI DE FER / MINERAL DE HIERRO - 08.13.00
>> *BT:* MINERALS
>> *RT:* IRON

IRRADIATED FOOD
ALIMENTS IRRADIES / ALIMENTOS IRRADIADOS -
08.06.03
>> *BT:* FOOD
>> *RT:* FOOD IRRADIATION
>> FOOD PRESERVATION

IRRADIATION
IRRADIATION / IRRADIACION - 08.12.03
>> *NT:* FOOD IRRADIATION
>> *RT:* IONISING RADIATION

IRRI
IRRI / IRRI - 01.03.04
SN: INTERNATIONAL RICE RESEARCH INSTITUTE.
>> *BT:* NON-GOVERNMENTAL ORGANIZATIONS
>> RESEARCH CENTRES
>> *RT:* AGRICULTURAL RESEARCH
>> RICE

IRRIGATED LAND
TERRE IRRIGUEE / TIERRA DE REGADIO - 07.05.02
>> *RT:* IRRIGATION

IRRIGATION
IRRIGATION / RIEGO - 17.05.03
>> *RT:* IRRIGATED LAND
>> IRRIGATION DEVELOPMENT
>> IRRIGATION SYSTEMS

IRRIGATION DEVELOPMENT
DEVELOPPEMENT DE L'IRRIGATION / DESARROLLO DEL
RIEGO - 17.05.03
>> *RT:* IRRIGATION

IRRIGATION SYSTEMS
SYSTEMES D'IRRIGATION / SISTEMAS DE RIEGO -
17.05.03
>> *RT:* IRRIGATION

ISA
AIS / AIS - 01.03.04
SN: INTERNATIONAL SOCIOLOGICAL ASSOCIATION.
>> *BT:* NON-GOVERNMENTAL ORGANIZATIONS
>> *RT:* SOCIOLOGY

ISIS
ISIS / ISIS - 19.01.02
SN: INTEGRATED SET OF INFORMATION.
>> *BT:* INFORMATION SYSTEMS
>> *RT:* ILO

ISLAM
ISLAM / ISLAMISMO - 05.04.03

ISLANDS
ILES / ISLAS - 17.03.04

ISO
ISO / ISO - 01.03.04
*SN: INTERNATIONAL ORGANIZATION FOR
STANDARDIZATION.*
>> *BT:* NON-GOVERNMENTAL ORGANIZATIONS
>> *RT:* STANDARDIZATION

ISOLATIONISM
ISOLATIONISME / AISLACIONISMO - 01.02.01
>> *RT:* FOREIGN POLICY

ISOTOPES
ISOTOPES / ISOTOPOS - 08.11.04
>> *NT:* RADIOISOTOPES

ISRAEL
ISRAEL / ISRAEL - 01.04.06
>> *BT:* MEDITERRANEAN COUNTRIES
>> MIDDLE EAST
>> *RT:* ISRAELI

ISRAELI
ISRAELIEN / ISRAELI - 14.03.02
>> *RT:* ISRAEL

ISSA
AISS / AISS - 01.03.04
SN: INTERNATIONAL SOCIAL SECURITY ASSOCIATION.
>> *BT:* NON-GOVERNMENTAL ORGANIZATIONS
>> *RT:* SOCIAL SECURITY

ISSC
CISS / CICS - 01.03.04
SN: INTERNATIONAL SOCIAL SCIENCE COUNCIL.
>> *BT:* NON-GOVERNMENTAL ORGANIZATIONS
>> *RT:* SOCIAL SCIENCES

ITALIAN
ITALIEN / ITALIANO - 14.03.02
>> *RT:* ITALY

ITALY
ITALIE / ITALIA - 01.04.05
>> *BT:* MEDITERRANEAN COUNTRIES
>> WESTERN EUROPE
>> *RT:* ITALIAN

ITC
CCI / CCI - 01.03.02
SN: INTERNATIONAL TRADE CENTRE.

ITC<CONT>
  RT: GATT
    INTERNATIONAL TRADE
    UNCTAD

ITU
UIT / UIT - 01.03.02
SN: INTERNATIONAL TELECOMMUNICATION UNION.
  BT: UN SPECIALIZED AGENCIES
  RT: TELECOMMUNICATIONS

IUAES
UISAE / UICAE - 01.03.04
SN: INTERNATIONAL UNION OF ANTHROPOLOGICAL AND
  ETHNOLOGICAL SCIENCES.
    BT: NON-GOVERNMENTAL ORGANIZATIONS
    RT: ANTHROPOLOGY
      ETHNOLOGY

IUSSP
UIESP / UIECP - 01.03.04
SN: INTERNATIONAL UNION FOR THE SCIENTIFIC STUDY
  OF POPULATION.
    BT: NON-GOVERNMENTAL ORGANIZATIONS
    RT: DEMOGRAPHY
      POPULATION

IVORY COAST
COTE D'IVOIRE / COSTA DE MARFIL - 01.04.02
  BT: FRENCH SPEAKING AFRICA
    WEST AFRICA

JAMAICA
JAMAIQUE / JAMAICA - 01.04.03
  BT: CARIBBEAN
  RT: JAMAICAN

JAMAICAN
JAMAIQUAIN / JAMAIQUINO - 14.03.02
  RT: JAMAICA

JAPAN
JAPON / JAPON - 01.04.04
  BT: FAR EAST
  RT: JAPANESE

JAPANESE
JAPONAIS / JAPONES - 14.03.02
  RT: JAPAN

JET ENGINES
MOTEURS A REACTION / MOTORES A REACCION - 08.14.06
  BT: ENGINES

JOB CLASSIFICATION
CLASSIFICATION DES EMPLOIS / CLASIFICACION DE EMPLEOS - 13.02.01
SN: USE TO MEAN THE PROCESS OF ARRANGING JOBS
  INTO VARIOUS CATEGORIES IN A PARTICULAR
  ENTERPRISE OR INDUSTRY; USE ALSO IN
  CONNECTION WITH LISTS OF JOBS SUCH AS THE
  «INTERNATIONAL STANDARD CLASSIFICATION OF
  OCCUPATIONS».
    BT: CLASSIFICATION
    RT: EMPLOYMENT
      PERSONNEL MANAGEMENT

JOB DESCRIPTION
DESCRIPTION D'EMPLOI / DESCRIPCION DEL CARGO - 13.02.01
SN: RECOGNISED LIST OF FUNCTIONS AND TASKS
  INCLUDED IN A PARTICULAR OCCUPATION.
    RT: EMPLOYMENT
      PERSONNEL MANAGEMENT

JOB DISLOCATION
SUPPRESSION D'EMPLOI / SUPRESION DEL PUESTO - 13.05.00
SN: THE DISAPPEARANCE OF PARTICULAR TYPES OF
  WORK AS A RESULT OF THERE BEING NO FURTHER
  NEED OF THE ACTIVITY IN QUESTION.

JOB EVALUATION
EVALUATION DES EMPLOIS / EVALUACION DEL CARGO - 13.02.01
SN: THE DETERMINATION BY LOGICAL PROCEDURES OF
  THE RELATIVE VALUE OF INDIVIDUAL JOBS IN AN
  ORGANIZATION FOR SUCH PURPOSES AS WAGE
  DETERMINATION AND PROMOTION.
    RT: EMPLOYMENT
      PERSONNEL MANAGEMENT

JOB REQUIREMENTS
QUALIFICATION REQUISE POUR L'EMPLOI / CALIFICACION PARA EL EMPLEO - 13.02.01

JOB REQUIREMENTS<CONT>
*SN: APTITUDES, KNOWLEDGE AND/OR SKILLS REQUIRED
TO PERFORM DUTIES ATTACHING TO A PARTICULAR
WORK POSITION.*
    BT: OCCUPATIONAL QUALIFICATION

JOB ROTATION
- 13.05.00
    USE: **REASSIGNMENT**

JOB SATISFACTION
**SATISFACTION AU TRAVAIL / SATISFACCION EN EL
TRABAJO - 13.03.04**
    UF: OCCUPATIONAL SATISFACTION
    RT: HUMANIZATION OF WORK
        WORKERS ADAPTATION

JOB SEARCHING
QUETE D'EMPLOI / BUSQUEDA DE EMPLEO - 13.02.01
    RT: JOB SEEKERS
        LABOUR MARKET

JOB SEEKERS
**DEMANDEURS D'EMPLOI / BUSCADORES DE TRABAJO -
13.02.01**
    RT: JOB SEARCHING
        UNEMPLOYED

JOINT MANAGEMENT
- 13.06.00
    USE: **WORKERS PARTICIPATION**

JOINT PROJECTS
**PROJETS CONJOINTS / PROYECTOS CONJUNTOS -
01.01.06**
*SN: INVOLVING TWO OR MORE TECHNICAL COOPERATION
AGENCIES.*
    BT: DEVELOPMENT PROJECTS

JOINT VENTURES
**ENTREPRISES CONJOINTES / EMPRESAS CONJUNTAS -
03.03.05**
*SN: ENTERPRISES OWNED JOINTLY BY DEVELOPED AND
DEVELOPING COUNTRY INTERESTS.*
    BT: ENTERPRISES
    RT: FOREIGN INVESTMENTS

JORDAN
JORDANIE / JORDANIA - 01.04.06
    BT: ARAB COUNTRIES
        MIDDLE EAST
    RT: JORDANIAN

JORDANIAN
JORDANIEN / JORDANO - 14.03.02
    RT: JORDAN

JOURNAL
- 19.02.06
    USE: **PERIODICALS**

JOURNALISTS
JOURNALISTES / PERIODISTAS - 13.09.09
    RT: PRESS

JUDAISM
JUDAISME / JUDAISMO - 05.04.03

JUDGES
MAGISTRATS / JUECES - 13.09.09
    RT: LEGISLATION

JURIDICAL ASPECTS
- 04.01.01
    USE: **LEGAL ASPECTS**

JURISPRUDENCE
JURISPRUDENCE / JURISPRUDENCIA - 04.01.01
*SN: USE TO DENOTE THE JURISDICTION OF COURTS
ENSUING FROM THEIR INTERPRETATION OF THE
LAW.*
    BT: LEGAL SCIENCES
    RT: ADMINISTRATION OF JUSTICE
        COMMON LAW
        LAW
        LEGISLATION

JUTE
JUTE / YUTE - 07.07.07
    BT: PLANT FIBRES

JUVENILE DELINQUENCY
**DELINQUANCE JUVENILE / DELINCUENCIA JUVENIL -
02.04.02**
    BT: DELINQUENCY
    RT: YOUTH

KAMPUCHEA
KAMPUCHEA / KAMPUCHEA - 01.04.04
     UF: CAMBODIA
     BT: INDOCHINA

KENYA
KENYA / KENIA - 01.04.02
     BT: EAST AFRICA
          ENGLISH SPEAKING AFRICA
     RT: KENYAN

KENYAN
KENYEN / KENIANO - 14.03.02
     RT: KENYA

KINSHIP
PARENTE / PARENTESCO - 14.02.04
     RT: CLAN
          FAMILY

KNOW HOW
SAVOIR-FAIRE / CONOCIMIENTOS TECNOLOGICOS -
12.06.00
SN: INCLUDES TECHNOLOGICAL AND MANAGERIAL
     COMPONENTS.

KOREA
COREE / COREA - 01.04.04
SN: USE FOR HISTORICAL REFERENCES.
     BT: FAR EAST
     RT: KOREAN

KOREA DPR
COREE RPD / COREA RPD - 01.04.04
     UF: KOREA NORTH
     BT: FAR EAST

KOREA NORTH
- 01.04.04
     USE: KOREA DPR

KOREA R
COREE R / COREA R - 01.04.04
     UF: KOREA SOUTH
     BT: FAR EAST

KOREA SOUTH
- 01.04.04
     USE: KOREA R

KOREAN
COREEN / COREANO - 14.03.02
     RT: KOREA

KUWAIT
KOWEIT / KUWAIT - 01.04.06
     BT: PERSIAN GULF STATES
     RT: KUWAITI

KUWAITI
KOWEITIEN / KUWAITI - 14.03.02
     RT: KUWAIT

LABELLING
ETIQUETAGE / ETIQUETAJE - 10.06.00
     RT: PACKAGING

LABORATORIES
LABORATOIRES / LABORATORIOS - 18.02.00
     BT: RESEARCH CENTRES
     RT: RESEARCH EQUIPMENT

LABORATORY EQUIPMENT
- 18.02.00
     USE: RESEARCH EQUIPMENT

LABOUR
TRAVAIL / TRABAJO - 13.01.01
SN: USE FOR DOCUMENTS OF A GENERAL NATURE;
     OTHERWISE USE MORE SPECIFIC DESCRIPTORS.
     NT: CHILD LABOUR
     RT: ILO
          LABOUR ADMINISTRATION
          LABOUR CODE
          LABOUR COSTS
          LABOUR COURTS
          LABOUR INTENSITY
          LABOUR LAW
          LABOUR LEGISLATION
          LABOUR MARKET
          LABOUR MIGRATIONS
          LABOUR MOVEMENTS
          LABOUR POLICY
          LABOUR PRODUCTIVITY
          LABOUR RELATIONS
          MANPOWER
          PRODUCTION FACTORS
          WCL
          WORK ORGANIZATION
          WORKING CONDITIONS

LABOUR ADMINISTRATION
ADMINISTRATION DU TRAVAIL / ADMINISTRACION DEL
TRABAJO - 04.03.02
SN: USE IN CONNECTION WITH THE ORGANIZATION AND
     FUNCTIONING OF A CO-ORDINATED NETWORK OF
     INSTITUTIONS AND ADMINISTRATIVE STRUCTURES
     WITH A VIEW TO ENSURING THAT NATIONAL
     ECONOMIC DEVELOPMENT IS ACCOMPANIED BY AN
     IMPROVEMENT IN SOCIAL CONDITIONS.
     BT: PUBLIC ADMINISTRATION
     RT: LABOUR
          LABOUR POLICY

LABOUR CODE
CODE DU TRAVAIL / CODIGO DEL TRABAJO - 04.01.02
SN: USE ONLY IN CONNECTION WITH A LEGISLATIVE
     TEXT WHICH IS SO NAMED. DO NOT CONFUSE WITH
     A COLLECTION OF LAWS OF A COUNTRY DEALING
     WITH LABOUR MATTERS.
     BT: CODES
          LABOUR LEGISLATION
     RT: LABOUR

LABOUR CONTRACT
CONTRAT DE TRAVAIL / CONTRATO DE TRABAJO -

LABOUR CONTRACT<CONT>
13.02.01
SN: WORK CONTRACT BETWEEN EMPLOYER AND
INDIVIDUAL EMPLOYEE.
    RT: CONTRACT LABOUR
        WORK PERMIT

LABOUR COSTS
COUTS DE MAIN D'OEUVRE / COSTOS DE LA MANO DE
OBRA - 12.09.00
SN: ALL COSTS INVOLVED IN PROVIDING LABOUR, I.E.
WAGES, ALLOWANCES, SOCIAL SERVICES, ETC.
    BT: COSTS
    NT: WAGES
    RT: LABOUR
        MANPOWER

LABOUR COURTS
TRIBUNAUX DU TRAVAIL / TRIBUNALES DEL TRABAJO -
04.01.02
    RT: ADMINISTRATION OF JUSTICE
        LABOUR

LABOUR DISPUTES
CONFLITS DU TRAVAIL / CONFLICTOS LABORALES -
13.06.00
SN: USE MORE SPECIFIC DESCRIPTORS SUCH AS
'STRIKES' OR 'LOCKOUTS', IF APPLICABLE.
    BT: SOCIAL CONFLICTS
    NT: LOCKOUTS
        STRIKES

LABOUR FORCE
- 13.01.02
    USE: MANPOWER

LABOUR INSPECTION
INSPECTION DU TRAVAIL / INSPECCION DEL TRABAJO -
13.02.02
SN: THE SUPERVISION OF CONDITIONS OF WORK TO
ENSURE THAT THEY COMPLY WITH OFFICIAL
REQUIREMENTS.
    RT: PERSONNEL MANAGEMENT

LABOUR INTENSITY
DENSITE DE MAIN D'OEUVRE / INTENSIDAD DE MANO DE
OBRA - 12.06.00
SN: WITH RELATIVELY GREATER LABOUR COSTS THAN
PLANT AND EQUIPMENT COSTS.
    RT: CAPITAL-LABOUR RATIO
        LABOUR

LABOUR LAW
DROIT DU TRAVAIL / DERECHO DEL TRABAJO -
04.01.02
SN: USE FOR WORKS CONCERNING THE SUBJECT AS A
WHOLE.
    BT: LAW
    RT: LABOUR
        RIGHT TO STRIKE

LABOUR LEGISLATION
LEGISLATION DU TRAVAIL / LEGISLACION DEL TRABAJO

LABOUR LEGISLATION<CONT>
- 04.01.02
SN: USE IN CONNECTION WITH THE TEXTS OF LAWS,
DECREES, REGULATIONS, ORDERS, ETC.,
CONCERNING LABOUR MATTERS.
    BT: LEGISLATION
    NT: LABOUR CODE
    RT: LABOUR

LABOUR MARKET
MARCHE DU TRAVAIL / MERCADO DE TRABAJO -
13.01.02
    BT: MARKET
    RT: EMPLOYMENT
        JOB SEARCHING
        LABOUR
        LABOUR MOBILITY
        LABOUR SHORTAGE
        LABOUR SUPPLY
        MANPOWER NEEDS
        UNEMPLOYMENT

LABOUR MIGRATIONS
MIGRATIONS DE TRAVAIL / MIGRACIONES LABORALES -
14.07.00
    BT: MIGRATIONS
    RT: LABOUR
        MIGRANT WORKERS

LABOUR MOBILITY
MOBILITE DE LA MAIN D'OEUVRE / MOVILIDAD DE LA
MANO DE OBRA - 13.05.00
SN: REFERS TO THE ABILITY OF INDIVIDUAL WORKERS
TO MOVE IN AND AMONG LABOUR MARKETS.
    UF: DISPLACEMENT
    BT: SOCIAL MOBILITY
    RT: LABOUR MARKET

LABOUR MOVEMENTS
MOUVEMENTS OUVRIERS / MOVIMIENTOS OBREROS -
13.06.00
SN: USE IN CONNECTION ONLY WITH UNORGANIZED
LABOUR MOVEMENTS, OR WITH A BROAD POLITICAL
MOVEMENT. OTHERWISE USE 'TRADE UNIONS'.
    BT: SOCIAL MOVEMENTS
    RT: LABOUR
        TRADE UNIONS

LABOUR POLICY
POLITIQUE DU TRAVAIL / POLITICA LABORAL -
13.01.01
    BT: GOVERNMENT POLICY
    NT: EMPLOYMENT POLICY
    RT: ECONOMIC POLICY
        LABOUR
        LABOUR ADMINISTRATION
        SOCIAL POLICY

LABOUR PRODUCTIVITY
PRODUCTIVITE DU TRAVAIL / PRODUCTIVIDAD DEL
TRABAJO - 13.02.02

LABOUR PRODUCTIVITY<CONT>
*SN: EFFICIENCY OF PRODUCTION AT THE LEVEL OF THE
INDIVIDUAL, THE ENTERPRISE OR THE SPECIFIC
ECONOMIC SECTOR. LABOUR PRODUCTIVITY IS
USUALLY MEASURED IN TERMS OF OUTPUT PER
WORKER OR PER MAN-HOUR WORKED.*
>   *BT:* PRODUCTIVITY
>   *RT:* LABOUR
>   STANDARD PERFORMANCE
>   WAGE INCENTIVES

LABOUR REDUNDANCY
**SURABONDANCE DE PERSONNEL / EXCESO DE PERSONAL -
13.05.00**
*SN: USE TO MEAN THE DISMISSAL OF EMPLOYEES ON
ACCOUNT OF THE CESSATION OR DIMINUTION OF
THE ACTIVITY FOR THE PURPOSES OF WHICH THEY
WERE EMPLOYED.*
>   *RT:* DISMISSAL
>   SEVERANCE PAY

LABOUR RELATIONS
**RELATIONS INDUSTRIELLES / RELACIONES LABORALES -
13.06.00**
*SN: COVERS BROAD RELATIONS BETWEEN: EMPLOYERS
AND EMPLOYEES; MANAGEMENT AND ORGANIZED
LABOUR; LABOUR, MANAGEMENT AND THE
GOVERNMENT. EXCLUDES SPECIFIC RELATIONSHIPS
BETWEEN AN EMPLOYER AND INDIVIDUAL EMPLOYEES
('PERSONNEL MANAGEMENT').*
>   *UF:* INDUSTRIAL RELATIONS
>   LABOUR-MANAGEMENT RELATIONS
>   *BT:* INTERGROUP RELATIONS
>   *RT:* LABOUR
>   TRADE UNIONS

LABOUR REQUIREMENTS
- 13.01.02
>   *USE:* MANPOWER NEEDS

LABOUR SHORTAGE
**PENURIE DE MAIN D'OEUVRE / ESCASEZ DE MANO DE
OBRA - 13.01.02**
SN: LACK OF PEOPLE TO FILL JOBS.
>   *UF:* OVEREMPLOYMENT
>   *NT:* TEACHER SHORTAGE
>   *RT:* LABOUR MARKET
>   MANPOWER

LABOUR STANDARDS
NORMES DE TRAVAIL / NORMAS DE TRABAJO - 13.03.01
*SN: STANDARDS CONCERNING EMPLOYMENT AND WORKING
CONDITIONS FOUND ACCEPTABLE BY LABOUR AND
MANAGEMENT THROUGH COLLECTIVE BARGAINING AND
BY THE LEGISLATOR THROUGH LABOUR LAWS AND
REGULATIONS.*
>   *BT:* STANDARDS
>   *RT:* ERGONOMICS
>   STANDARD PERFORMANCE
>   WORK STUDY
>   WORKING CONDITIONS

LABOUR SUPPLY
OFFRE DE MAIN D'OEUVRE / OFERTA DE MANO DE OBRA

LABOUR SUPPLY<CONT>
- 13.01.02
*SN: USE TO DENOTE NOT ONLY THE SIZE OF THE WORK
FORCE, BUT ALSO ITS SKILLS AND GEOGRAPHIC
LOCATION AS WELL AS ITS WILLINGNESS AND
ABILITY TO BE PRODUCTIVE.*
>   *BT:* SUPPLY
>   *RT:* LABOUR MARKET

LABOUR UNIONS
- 13.06.00
>   *USE:* TRADE UNIONS

LABOUR-MANAGEMENT RELATIONS
- 13.06.00
>   *USE:* LABOUR RELATIONS

LAFTA
ALALE / ALALC - 01.03.03
SN: LATIN AMERICAN FREE TRADE ASSOCIATION.
>   *BT:* AMERICAN ORGANIZATIONS
>   INTERGOVERNMENTAL ORGANIZATIONS
>   *NT:* ANDEAN GROUP
>   *RT:* FREE TRADE AREA
>   LATIN AMERICA
>   REGIONAL INTEGRATION

LAKES
LACS / LAGOS - 17.05.02
>   *BT:* INLAND WATERWAYS
>   *NT:* ARTIFICIAL LAKES
>   *RT:* INTERNATIONAL WATERWAYS

LAND CAPABILITY
**POTENTIEL DES TERRES / POTENCIAL DE LA TIERRA -
07.05.02**
>   *BT:* AGRICULTURAL POTENTIAL
>   *RT:* PRODUCTION FACTORS

LAND DISTRIBUTION
- 07.02.00
>   *USE:* LAND TENURE

LAND ECONOMICS
**ECONOMIE FONCIERE / ECONOMIA DE LA TIERRA -
07.02.00**
>   *BT:* ECONOMICS
>   *RT:* AGRICULTURAL ECONOMICS

LAND LOCKED COUNTRIES
**PAYS SANS LITTORAL / PAISES SIN LITORAL -
17.03.04**
>   *RT:* LITTORAL ZONES

LAND OWNERSHIP
**PROPRIETE FONCIERE / TENENCIA DE LA TIERRA -
07.02.00**
>   *BT:* OWNERSHIP
>   *RT:* LAND SPECULATION
>   LAND TAX
>   LAND TENURE
>   LANDOWNERS

LAND RECLAMATION
RECUPERATION DU SOL / RECUPERACION DEL SUELO -
07.05.02
> *RT:* SOIL MANAGEMENT

LAND REFORMS
REFORMES FONCIERES / REFORMAS DE TENENCIA DE LA
TIERRA - 07.02.00
SN: INTEGRAL REFORMS OF TENURE, PRODUCTION AND
SUPPORTING SERVICES STRUCTURE TO ELIMINATE
OBSTACLES TO ECONOMIC AND SOCIAL DEVELOPMENT
BY REDISTRIBUTION OF WEALTH, OPPORTUNITY AND
POWER, AS MANIFEST IN THE OWNERSHIP AND
CONTROL OF LAND, WATER AND OTHER RESOURCES.
> *BT:* AGRARIAN REFORMS
> *RT:* LAND TENURE

LAND RENT
RENTE FONCIERE / RENTA DE LA TIERRA - 07.03.03
> *BT:* INCOME

LAND SETTLEMENT
COLONISATION RURALE / COLONIZACION RURAL -
14.04.02
SN: COLONIZATION OF AGRICULTURAL WORKERS AND
THEIR FAMILIES IN VIRGIN TERRITORIES OR
FOLLOWING LAND REDISTRIBUTION.

LAND SPECULATION
SPECULATION FONCIERE / ESPECULACION CON LAS
TIERRAS - 07.02.00
> *RT:* LAND OWNERSHIP

LAND TAX
IMPOT FONCIER / IMPUESTO A LA TIERRA - 11.01.02
> *BT:* TAXES
> *RT:* LAND OWNERSHIP

LAND TENURE
REGIMES FONCIERS / SISTEMAS DE TENENCIA DE LA
TIERRA - 07.02.00
> *UF:* LAND DISTRIBUTION
> *RT:* LAND OWNERSHIP
> LAND REFORMS

LAND USE
UTILISATION DES TERRES / USO DE LA TIERRA -
07.05.02
> *UF:* LAND UTILIZATION
> *RT:* FOREST UTILIZATION
> ZONING

LAND UTILIZATION
- 07.05.02
> *USE:* **LAND USE**

LANDOWNERS
PROPRIETAIRES FONCIERS / PROPIETARIOS RURALES -
07.02.00
> *RT:* LAND OWNERSHIP

LANDSCAPE PROTECTION
PROTECTION DU PAYSAGE / PROTECCION DEL PAISAJE -

LANDSCAPE PROTECTION<CONT>
16.05.01
> *BT:* ENVIRONMENTAL PROTECTION

LANGUAGE BARRIER
BARRIERE LINGUISTIQUE / BARRERA LINGUISTICA -
05.06.01
> *BT:* COMMUNICATION BARRIERS
> *RT:* LANGUAGES

LANGUAGE LABORATORIES
LABORATOIRES DE LANGUES / LABORATORIOS DE
IDIOMAS - 06.04.07
> *RT:* LANGUAGE TEACHING
> LINGUISTICS

LANGUAGE MINORITIES
MINORITES LINGUISTIQUES / MINORIAS LINGUISTICAS
- 05.06.01
> *BT:* MINORITY GROUPS
> *RT:* LANGUAGES

LANGUAGE TEACHING
ENSEIGNEMENT DES LANGUES / ENSENANZA DE IDIOMAS
- 06.03.07
> *RT:* LANGUAGE LABORATORIES
> LINGUISTICS

LANGUAGES
LANGUES / LENGUAS - 05.06.01
> *NT:* ARABIC
> CHINESE LANGUAGE
> ENGLISH LANGUAGE
> FRENCH LANGUAGE
> OFFICIAL LANGUAGES
> RUSSIAN LANGUAGE
> SPANISH LANGUAGE
> VERNACULAR LANGUAGES
> *RT:* DIALECTS
> LANGUAGE BARRIER
> LANGUAGE MINORITIES
> MULTILINGUALISM
> TRANSLATION

LAO
LAO / LAO - 14.03.02
> *RT:* LAO PDR

LAO PDR
RDP LAO / RDP LAO - 01.04.04
> *BT:* INDOCHINA
> *RT:* LAO

LATEX
LATEX / LATEX - 07.07.08
> *RT:* HEVEAS
> RUBBER

LATIN AMERICA
AMERIQUE LATINE / AMERICA LATINA - 01.04.03
> *BT:* AMERICA

LATIN AMERICA<CONT>
NT: ARGENTINA
BOLIVIA
BRAZIL
CENTRAL AMERICA
CHILE
COLOMBIA
CUBA
DOMINICAN REPUBLIC
ECUADOR
HAITI
MEXICO
PARAGUAY
PERU
PUERTO RICO
URUGUAY
VENEZUELA
RT: ANDEAN GROUP
CARIBBEAN
CEMLA
CLACSO
ECLA
ILPES
LAFTA
LATIN AMERICAN
SOUTH AMERICA

LATIN AMERICAN
LATINO-AMERICAIN / LATINOAMERICANO - 14.03.02
RT: LATIN AMERICA

LAW
DROIT / DERECHO - 04.01.01
SN: USE FOR WORKS CONCERNING THE SUBJECT OF
LEGAL SCIENCE. FOR WORKS CONNECTED WITH
INDIVIDUAL LAWS USE 'LEGISLATION', 'LABOUR
LEGISLATION', ETC.
BT: LEGAL SCIENCES
NT: CIVIL LAW
COMMERCIAL LAW
COMMON LAW
CRIMINAL LAW
CUSTOMARY LAW
FISCAL LAW
INTERNATIONAL LAW
LABOUR LAW
MARITIME LAW
PATENT LAW
PUBLIC LAW
RT: JURISPRUDENCE
LAWYERS
LEGAL ASPECTS
LEGAL PROTECTION
LEGISLATION
SOCIAL CONTROL

LAW ENFORCEMENT
- 02.04.03
USE: PENAL SANCTIONS

LAW OF THE SEA
DROIT DE LA MER / DERECHO DEL MAR - 01.02.04
BT: INTERNATIONAL LAW

LAW OF THE SEA<CONT>
RT: FISHING RIGHTS
MARITIME QUESTIONS
SEA
TERRITORIAL WATERS

LAWYERS
AVOCATS / ABOGADOS - 13.09.09
RT: LAW

LAYOFF
MISE A PIED / SUSPENSION LABORAL - 13.05.00
SN: FAILURE, REFUSAL OR INABILITY OF AN EMPLOYER
TO CONTINUE THE EMPLOYMENT OF AN EMPLOYEE ON
ACCOUNT OF SHORTAGE OF RAW MATERIALS, POWER,
OR THE BREAKDOWN OF MACHINERY, ETC. LAYOFF
IS NORMALLY OF A TEMPORARY NATURE AND IS
WITHOUT PREJUDICE TO THE WORKER. DO NOT
CONFUSE WITH 'DISMISSAL'.
RT: PERSONNEL MANAGEMENT

LEAD
PLOMB / PLOMO - 08.14.02
BT: NON-FERROUS METALS
TOXIC METALS

LEADERSHIP
LEADERSHIP / LIDERAZGO - 05.03.05
NT: POLITICAL LEADERSHIP

LEAGUE OF ARAB STATES
LIGUE DES ETATS ARABES / LIGA DE LOS ESTADOS
ARABES - 01.03.03
BT: ARAB ORGANIZATIONS
INTERGOVERNMENTAL ORGANIZATIONS
NT: ALECSO
CAEU
IDCAS

LEARNING
ACQUISITION DE CONNAISSANCES / ADQUISICION DE
CONOCIMIENTOS - 06.05.04
RT: EDUCATION

LEAST DEVELOPED COUNTRIES
PAYS MOINS DEVELOPPES / PAISES MENOS
DESARROLADOS - 03.02.03
BT: DEVELOPING COUNTRIES

LEATHER
CUIR / CUERO - 08.08.02
BT: HIDES AND SKINS
RT: LEATHER GOODS
LEATHER INDUSTRY

LEATHER GOODS
MAROQUINERIE / ARTICULOS DE CUERO - 08.08.02
RT: LEATHER
LEATHER INDUSTRY

LEATHER INDUSTRY
INDUSTRIE DU CUIR / INDUSTRIA DEL CUERO -
08.08.02
BT: INDUSTRIAL SECTOR
NT: TANNING INDUSTRY

LEATHER INDUSTRY<CONT>
    RT: HIDES AND SKINS
        LEATHER
        LEATHER GOODS
        SHOE INDUSTRY

LEAVE OF ABSENCE
AUTORISATION D'ABSENCE / PERMISO - 13.05.00
    RT: ABSENTEEISM

LEAVING SCHOOL
FIN DE SCOLARITE / TERMINO DE LA ESCOLARIDAD - 06.04.12
    RT: SCHOOL LEAVERS
        SCHOOLING

LEBANESE
LIBANAIS / LIBANES - 14.03.02
    RT: LEBANON

LEBANON
LIBAN / LIBANO - 01.04.06
    BT: ARAB COUNTRIES
        MEDITERRANEAN COUNTRIES
        MIDDLE EAST
    RT: LEBANESE

LEGAL ABORTION
AVORTEMENT LEGAL / ABORTO LEGAL - 14.05.02
    BT: ABORTION

LEGAL AID
ASSISTANCE JURIDIQUE / ASESORAMIENTO JURIDICO - 04.02.01

LEGAL ASPECTS
ASPECTS JURIDIQUES / ASPECTOS JURIDICOS - 04.01.01
    UF: JURIDICAL ASPECTS
    RT: LAW
        LEGAL SCIENCES
        LEGISLATION

LEGAL PROTECTION
PROTECTION LEGALE / PROTECCION LEGAL - 04.01.01
    RT: LAW

LEGAL SCIENCES
SCIENCES JURIDIQUES / CIENCIAS JURIDICAS - 04.01.01
    BT: SOCIAL SCIENCES
    NT: JURISPRUDENCE
        LAW
    RT: LEGAL ASPECTS

LEGAL STATUS
STATUT JURIDIQUE / SITUACION JURIDICA - 04.02.01
SN: USE IN CONNECTION WITH THE POSITION IN LAW OF PERSONS OR GROUPS.
    RT: SOCIAL STATUS

LEGISLATION
LEGISLATION / LEGISLACION - 04.01.01

LEGISLATION<CONT>
SN: USE IN CONNECTION WITH THE ACTUAL TEXTS OF LAWS, ORDERS, REGULATIONS, DECREES, ETC., SPECIFYING AND MENTIONING DATE OF ENACTMENT, IF APPLICABLE.
    NT: ECONOMIC LEGISLATION
        LABOUR LEGISLATION
        SOCIAL LEGISLATION
    RT: COMMON LAW
        JUDGES
        JURISPRUDENCE
        LAW
        LEGAL ASPECTS
        PARLIAMENT

LEGUMINOSAE
LEGUMINEUSES / LEGUMINOSAS - 07.07.06
    BT: PLANTS
    NT: BEANS
        CHICKPEAS
        COWPEAS
        FABA BEANS
        GROUNDNUTS
        LENTILS
        PIGEON PEAS
        SOYBEANS
    RT: VEGETABLES

LEISURE
LOISIR / RECREACION - 13.08.00
    RT: HOLIDAYS
        REST
        TOURISM

LENTILS
LENTILLES / LENTEJAS - 07.07.06
    BT: LEGUMINOSAE

LEPROSY
LEPRE / LEPRA - 15.04.02
    BT: INFECTIOUS DISEASES
        TROPICAL DISEASES

LESOTHO
LESOTHO / LESOTHO - 01.04.02
    BT: ENGLISH SPEAKING AFRICA
        SOUTHERN AFRICA

LEVELS OF EDUCATION
NIVEAUX D'ENSEIGNEMENT / NIVELES DE ENSENANZA - 06.03.06
    BT: EDUCATIONAL SYSTEMS
    NT: POST-SECONDARY EDUCATION
        PRESCHOOL EDUCATION
        PRIMARY EDUCATION
        SECONDARY EDUCATION

LIABILITY
RESPONSABILITE LEGALE / RESPONSABILIDAD LEGAL - 04.02.03

LIBERALISM
LIBERALISME / LIBERALISMO - 03.03.01
    BT: ECONOMIC SYSTEMS
    RT: MARKET ECONOMY

LIBERATION
LIBERATION / LIBERACION - 04.02.02
SN: THE PROCESS TOWARDS CULTURAL, SOCIAL,
POLITICAL OR ECONOMIC INDEPENDENCE.
    RT: FREEDOM
        INDEPENDENCE
        NATIONAL LIBERATION MOVEMENTS

LIBERIA
LIBERIA / LIBERIA - 01.04.02
    BT: ENGLISH SPEAKING AFRICA
        WEST AFRICA
    RT: LIBERIAN

LIBERIAN
LIBERIEN / LIBERIANO - 14.03.02
    RT: LIBERIA

LIBRARIANS
BIBLIOTHECAIRES / BIBLIOTECARIOS - 13.09.09
    RT: IFLA
        LIBRARIES

LIBRARIES
BIBLIOTHEQUES / BIBLIOTECAS - 19.01.03
    BT: INFORMATION SERVICES
    RT: LIBRARIANS
        LIBRARY AUTOMATION
        LIBRARY SCIENCE

LIBRARY AUTOMATION
AUTOMATISATION DES BIBLIOTHEQUES /
AUTOMATIZACION DE BIBLIOTECAS - 19.01.03
    BT: AUTOMATION
    RT: COMPUTERS
        LIBRARIES

LIBRARY SCIENCE
BIBLIOTHECONOMIE / BIBLIOTECONOMIA - 19.01.01
    BT: INFORMATION SCIENCES
    RT: IFLA
        LIBRARIES

LIBYA
LIBYE / LIBIA - 01.04.02
    UF: LIBYAN ARAB JAMAHIRIYA
    BT: ARAB COUNTRIES
        ENGLISH SPEAKING AFRICA
        MEDITERRANEAN COUNTRIES
        NORTH AFRICA
    RT: LIBYAN

LIBYAN
LIBYEN / LIBIO - 14.03.02
    RT: LIBYA

LIBYAN ARAB JAMAHIRIYA
- 01.04.02
    USE: LIBYA

LICENSING
ATTRIBUTION DE LICENCE / OTORGAMIENTO DE
LICENCIAS - 08.05.00

LICENSING<CONT>
    RT: INDUSTRIAL ESPIONAGE
        INVENTIONS
        PATENTS
        TRADE MARKS

LIECHTENSTEIN
LIECHTENSTEIN / LIECHTENSTEIN - 01.04.05
    BT: WESTERN EUROPE

LIFE
VIE / VIDA - 15.02.02

LIFE INSURANCE
ASSURANCE VIE / SEGURO DE VIDA - 11.02.03
    BT: INSURANCE

LIFE STYLES
MODES DE VIE / ESTILOS DE VIDA - 05.03.01

LIFE TABLES
TABLES DE MORTALITE / TABLAS DE MORTALIDAD -
14.06.00
    RT: MORTALITY

LIFE-LONG EDUCATION
EDUCATION PERMANENTE / EDUCACION PERMANENTE -
06.03.05
    UF: CONTINUING EDUCATION
        PERMANENT EDUCATION
    BT: ADULT EDUCATION
    RT: RECURRENT EDUCATION

LIGHT INDUSTRY
INDUSTRIE LEGERE / INDUSTRIA LIGERA - 08.01.01
    BT: INDUSTRY

LIME
CHAUX / CAL - 08.10.02
    BT: CONSTRUCTION MATERIALS

LINEAR PROGRAMMING
PROGRAMMATION LINEAIRE / PROGRAMACION LINEAL -
12.04.00
SN: A TECHNIQUE USED TO DETERMINE OPTIMAL
    SOLUTIONS TO PROBLEMS, PARTICULARLY THOSE
    CONCERNING THE ALLOCATION OF RESOURCES.
    BT: MANAGEMENT TECHNIQUES
    RT: ACTIVITY ANALYSIS

LINGUISTICS
LINGUISTIQUE / LINGUISTICA - 05.06.01
    BT: SOCIAL SCIENCES
    RT: LANGUAGE LABORATORIES
        LANGUAGE TEACHING
        LINGUISTS

LINGUISTS
LINGUISTES / LINGUISTAS - 13.09.09
    BT: SCIENTISTS
    RT: LINGUISTICS

LIQUIDITY
LIQUIDITE / LIQUIDEZ - 11.02.01
    NT: INTERNATIONAL LIQUIDITY

LIQUIDITY<CONT>
  RT: CURRENCIES
      MONETARY CIRCULATION
      MONEY SUPPLY

LIST OF DOCUMENTS
LISTE DE DOCUMENTS / LISTA DE DOCUMENTOS -
19.02.05
SN: LIST OF DOCUMENTS DISTRIBUTED TO THE
    PARTICIPANTS IN A MEETING. DO NOT CONFUSE
    WITH 'BIBLIOGRAPHY'.
  RT: DOCUMENTS

LIST OF PARTICIPANTS
LISTE DES PARTICIPANTS / LISTA DE PARTICIPANTES
- 19.02.05

LITERACY
ALPHABETISATION / ALFABETIZACION - 06.03.04
  BT: BASIC EDUCATION
  NT: FUNCTIONAL LITERACY
  RT: ILLITERACY
      READING
      WRITING

LITERATURE
LITTERATURE / LITERATURA - 05.05.03
  BT: ARTS
  RT: WRITERS

LITERATURE SURVEY
ETUDE BIBLIOGRAPHIQUE / ARTICULO BIBLIOGRAFICO -
19.02.07
  RT: BIBLIOGRAPHY

LITTORAL ZONES
ZONES LITTORALES / ZONAS LITORALES - 17.03.04
  UF: COASTAL AREAS
  NT: COASTS
  RT: CONTINENTAL SHELVES
      LAND LOCKED COUNTRIES

LIVER
FOIE / HIGADO - 15.02.04
  BT: DIGESTIVE SYSTEM

LIVESTOCK
CHEPTEL / GANADO - 07.09.02
  UF: FARM ANIMALS
  BT: ANIMALS
  NT: CAMELS
      CATTLE
      DONKEYS
      GOATS
      HORSES
      SHEEP
      SWINE
  RT: DOMESTIC ANIMALS

LIVESTOCK CROPS
- 07.07.02
  USE: FORAGE CROPS

LIVING CONDITIONS
CONDITIONS DE VIE / CONDICIONES DE VIDA -

LIVING CONDITIONS<CONT>
03.02.05
  NT: WORKING CONDITIONS
  RT: BASIC NEEDS
      COST OF LIVING
      HOUSING
      QUALITY OF LIFE

LOADING
CHARGEMENT / CARGUIO - 10.06.00

LOANS
PRETS / PRESTAMOS - 11.02.02
  BT: FINANCIAL TERMS
  NT: STUDENT LOANS
  RT: BORROWING
      CREDIT
      DEBT

LOCAL CURRENCY
MONNAIE LOCALE / MONEDA LOCAL - 11.02.01
  BT: CURRENCIES

LOCAL FINANCE
FINANCES LOCALES / HACIENDA LOCAL - 11.01.01
  BT: PUBLIC FINANCE
  RT: FINANCIAL ADMINISTRATION
      LOCAL GOVERNMENT
      LOCAL TAXES

LOCAL GOVERNMENT
ADMINISTRATION LOCALE / GOBIERNO LOCAL -
04.03.03
  BT: GOVERNMENT
  RT: COMMUNITY
      LOCAL FINANCE
      RURAL PLANNING
      URBAN PLANNING

LOCAL LEVEL
NIVEAU LOCAL / PLANO LOCAL - 04.03.03
SN: AS OPPOSED TO 'NATIONAL LEVEL'.

LOCAL TAXES
IMPOTS LOCAUX / IMPUESTOS LOCALES - 11.01.02
  BT: TAXES
  RT: LOCAL FINANCE

LOCATION FACTORS
CRITERES D'EMPLACEMENT / FACTORES DE
LOCALIZACION - 02.01.02
SN: REFER TO THE POSSIBILITY OF IMPLEMENTING A
    PROJECT IN A SPECIFIC PLACE.
  RT: LOCATION OF INDUSTRY
      REGIONAL PLANNING

LOCATION OF INDUSTRY
LOCALISATION INDUSTRIELLE / LOCALIZACION
INDUSTRIAL - 08.02.03
SN: DECISION MADE IN THE LIGHT OF AVAILABLE
    INFRASTRUCTURE, RAW MATERIALS, LABOUR, ETC.,
    TO LOCATE IN A PARTICULAR AREA.
  UF: INDUSTRIAL LOCATION

LOCATION OF INDUSTRY<CONT>
>   *RT:* INDUSTRIAL ENTERPRISES
>   LOCATION FACTORS

LOCKOUTS
LOCKOUTS / LOCKOUTS - 13.06.00
SN: THE CLOSING OF A PLANT BY AN EMPLOYER TO COMPEL WORKERS TO AGREE TO THE CONDITIONS OF WORK HE PRESCRIBES.
>   *BT:* LABOUR DISPUTES
>   *RT:* PLANT SHUTDOWN

LOCOMOTIVES
LOCOMOTIVES / LOCOMOTORAS - 10.04.00
>   *BT:* TRAINS

LOCUSTS
SAUTERELLES / LANGOSTAS - 16.03.03
>   *BT:* INSECT PESTS

LOGGING
FORESTAGE / EXPLOTACION FORESTAL - 07.08.03
>   *RT:* FOREST UTILIZATION

LOGIC
LOGIQUE / LOGICA - 18.08.00
>   *RT:* MATHEMATICS
>   PHILOSOPHY

LONG TERM
LONG TERME / LARGO PLAZO - 18.10.00

LOW INCOME
FAIBLE REVENU / BAJOS INGRESOS - 03.02.05
>   *BT:* INCOME

LOWER CLASS
CLASSE INFERIEURE / CLASE BAJA - 05.03.05
>   *RT:* PROLETARIAT

LUBRICANTS
LUBRIFIANTS / LUBRICANTES - 08.11.06
>   *RT:* PETROLEUM PRODUCTS

LUXEMBOURG
LUXEMBOURG / LUXEMBURGO - 01.04.05
>   *BT:* WESTERN EUROPE

LYMPHATIC SYSTEM
SYSTEME LYMPHATIQUE / SISTEMA LINFATICO - 15.02.04
>   *BT:* ANATOMY

MACAO
MACAO / MACAO - 01.04.04
>   *BT:* FAR EAST
>   *RT:* PORTUGAL

MACHINE TOOL INDUSTRY
INDUSTRIE DE LA MACHINE OUTIL / INDUSTRIA DE MAQUINAS HERRAMIENTAS - 08.14.05
>   *BT:* MACHINERY INDUSTRY

MACHINE TOOLS
MACHINES OUTILS / MAQUINAS HERRAMIENTAS - 08.14.05
>   *BT:* TOOLS

MACHINERY
MACHINES / MAQUINARIA - 08.14.06
>   *NT:* AGRICULTURAL MACHINERY
>   BUILDING MACHINERY
>   ELECTRICAL MACHINERY
>   *RT:* EQUIPMENT
>   MECHANIZATION

MACHINERY INDUSTRY
INDUSTRIE MECANIQUE / INDUSTRIAS MECANICAS - 08.14.06
>   *BT:* METALWORKING INDUSTRY
>   *NT:* INSTRUMENTATION INDUSTRY
>   MACHINE TOOL INDUSTRY
>   MOTOR VEHICLE INDUSTRY

MACHINING
USINAGE / USINADO - 08.14.03
>   *BT:* INDUSTRIAL PROCESSES
>   *NT:* FORGING
>   METAL CASTING
>   ROLLING
>   WELDING

MACROECONOMICS
MACROECONOMIE / MACROECONOMIA - 03.01.01
>   *BT:* ECONOMICS
>   *RT:* ECONOMIC MODELS
>   ECONOMIC POLICY
>   NATIONAL ACCOUNTING

MADAGASCAR
MADAGASCAR / MADAGASCAR - 01.04.02
>   *BT:* FRENCH SPEAKING AFRICA
>   SOUTHERN AFRICA
>   *RT:* MALAGASY
>   OCAM

MADEIRA
MADERE / MADEIRA - 01.04.05
>   *BT:* WESTERN EUROPE
>   *RT:* PORTUGAL

MAGAZINE
- 19.02.06
>   *USE:* PERIODICALS

MAGIC
MAGIE / MAGIA - 05.04.02

MAGNESIUM
MAGNESIUM / MAGNESIO - 08.12.04

MAIL SURVEYS
ENQUETES PAR CORRESPONDANCE / ENCUESTAS POR
CORREO - 18.04.00
    BT: SURVEYS

MAINTENANCE AND REPAIR
ENTRETIEN ET REPARATION / MANTENIMIENTO Y
REPARACION - 12.05.00
    RT: AUTOMOBILE SERVICE
         EQUIPMENT
         REPAIR SHOPS
         SPARE PARTS

MAIZE
MAIS / MAIZ - 07.07.04
    BT: CEREALS
    RT: CIMMYT

MALADJUSTMENT
INADAPTATION / INADAPTACION - 05.03.03
    RT: ADAPTATION
         MARGINALITY

MALAGASY
MALGACHE / MALGACHE - 14.03.02
    RT: MADAGASCAR

MALARIA
MALARIA / PALUDISMO - 15.04.02
    BT: PARASITIC DISEASES
         TROPICAL DISEASES

MALAWI
MALAWI / MALAWI - 01.04.02
    BT: EAST AFRICA
         ENGLISH SPEAKING AFRICA
         SOUTHERN AFRICA
    RT: MALAWIAN

MALAWIAN
MALAWIEN / MALAWIANO - 14.03.02
    RT: MALAWI

MALAYSIA
MALAISIE / MALASIA - 01.04.04
    BT: SOUTH EAST ASIA
    RT: MALAYSIAN

MALAYSIAN
MALAISIEN / MALASIO - 14.03.02
    RT: MALAYSIA

MALDIVES
MALDIVES / MALDIVAS - 01.04.04
    BT: SOUTH ASIA
         SOUTH EAST ASIA
    RT: MALDIVIAN

MALDIVIAN
MALDIVIEN / MALDIVO - 14.03.02
    RT: MALDIVES

MALES
MALES / MACHOS - 14.02.03
    BT: SEX
    RT: MEN

MALI
MALI / MALI - 01.04.02
    BT: FRENCH SPEAKING AFRICA
         WEST AFRICA
    RT: MALIAN

MALIAN
MALIEN / MALIENSE - 14.03.02
    RT: MALI

MALNUTRITION
MALNUTRITION / MALNUTRICION - 15.03.02
    BT: SOCIAL PROBLEMS
    NT: CALORIE DEFICIENCY
         PROTEIN DEFICIENCY
         VITAMIN DEFICIENCY
    RT: DEFICIENCY DISEASES
         FAMINE
         FOOD SHORTAGE

MALTA
MALTE / MALTA - 01.04.05
    BT: MEDITERRANEAN COUNTRIES
         WESTERN EUROPE
    RT: MALTESE

MALTESE
MALTAIS / MALTES - 14.03.02
    RT: MALTA

MANAGEMENT
GESTION / ADMINISTRACION - 12.04.00
*SN: USE IN CONNECTION WITH THREE MAIN TASKS:
SUPERVISION OF AND RESPONSIBILITY FOR
INCREASING THE PERFORMANCE OF OTHERS;
ALLOCATING LABOUR MATERIAL AND CAPITAL TO
PRODUCE A HIGH RETURN; AND DECISION-MAKING.*
    NT: AGRICULTURAL MANAGEMENT
         BUSINESS MANAGEMENT
         COLLEGE MANAGEMENT
         ENVIRONMENTAL MANAGEMENT
         EQUIPMENT MANAGEMENT
         FINANCIAL MANAGEMENT
         INDUSTRIAL MANAGEMENT
         PERSONNEL MANAGEMENT
         RESOURCES MANAGEMENT
         SCHOOL MANAGEMENT
         SCIENTIFIC MANAGEMENT
         SELF-MANAGEMENT
         WASTE MANAGEMENT
         WATER MANAGEMENT
    RT: MANAGEMENT CONSULTANTS
         MANAGEMENT DEVELOPMENT
         MANAGEMENT INFORMATION SYSTEM
         MANAGEMENT TECHNIQUES
         MANAGERS

MANAGEMENT ATTITUDES
ATTITUDES PATRONALES / ACTITUDES DE LA DIRECCION

MANAGEMENT ATTITUDES<CONT>
- 13.06.00
    UF: EMPLOYERS ATTITUDES
    BT: ATTITUDES
    RT: EMPLOYERS
        MANAGERS

MANAGEMENT BY OBJECTIVES
DIRECTION PAR OBJECTIFS / DIRECCION POR .
OBJETIVOS - 12.04.00
*SN: SETTING TARGETS WITHIN AN ORGANIZATION AS A
    BASIS FOR ACHIEVING GREATER EFFICIENCY AND
    PROVIDING MOTIVATION AND AN INCENTIVE TO
    MANAGERS.*
        BT: MANAGEMENT TECHNIQUES

MANAGEMENT CONSULTANTS
CONSEILLERS DE GESTION / CONSULTORES DE EMPRESAS
- 12.03.00
        RT: BUSINESS ORGANIZATION
            MANAGEMENT

MANAGEMENT DEVELOPMENT
FORMATION A LA GESTION / CAPACITACION DE
EMPRESARIOS - 12.04.00
*SN: DEVELOPING MANAGERIAL SKILLS THROUGH VARIOUS
    PROGRAMMES: MEETINGS, SEMINARS, INFORMATION
    DISSEMINATION, ETC.*
        BT: TRAINING
        RT: ENTREPRENEURS
            MANAGEMENT

MANAGEMENT INFORMATION SYSTEM
SYSTEME D'INFORMATION DE GESTION / SISTEMA
INFORMACION ADMINISTRATIVA - 12.04.00
*SN: A SYSTEM IN WHICH DEFINED DATA ARE
    COLLECTED, PROCESSED AND COMMUNICATED TO
    ASSIST THOSE RESPONSIBLE FOR THE USE OF
    RESOURCES.*
        BT: INFORMATION SYSTEMS
        RT: MANAGEMENT

MANAGEMENT TECHNIQUES
TECHNIQUES DE GESTION / TECNICAS ADMINISTRATIVAS
- 12.04.00
        NT: LINEAR PROGRAMMING
            MANAGEMENT BY OBJECTIVES
            NETWORK ANALYSIS
            OPERATIONAL RESEARCH
        RT: DECISION MAKING
            ECONOMIC MODELS
            EFFICIENCY
            MANAGEMENT
            RESOURCES ALLOCATION
            SCIENTIFIC MANAGEMENT

MANAGERS
CADRES / GERENTES - 12.03.00
        NT: MIDDLE MANAGEMENT
            TOP MANAGEMENT
        RT: MANAGEMENT
            MANAGEMENT ATTITUDES

MANGANESE
MANGANESE / MANGANESO - 08.14.02
        BT: NON-FERROUS METALS

MANMADE DISASTERS
DESASTRES D'ORIGINE HUMAINE / DESASTRES CAUSADOS
POR EL HOMBRE - 16.03.02
        BT: DISASTERS

MANMADE FIBRES
FIBRES ARTIFICIELLES / FIBRAS ARTIFICIALES -
08.08.01
*SN: SYNTHETIC FIBRES PLUS RAYON, GLASS FIBRES,
    MINERAL WOOL, ETC.*
        BT: FIBRES

MANMADE FORESTS
FORETS PLANTEES / BOSQUES ARTIFICIALES -
07.08.03
        BT: FORESTS

MANPOWER
MAIN D'OEUVRE / MANO DE OBRA - 13.01.02
*SN: USE TO MEAN THE ECONOMICALLY ACTIVE
    POPULATION.*
        UF: LABOUR FORCE
        BT: HUMAN RESOURCES
        RT: LABOUR
            LABOUR COSTS
            LABOUR SHORTAGE
            MANPOWER NEEDS
            POPULATION

MANPOWER NEEDS
BESOINS DE MAIN D'OEUVRE / DEMANDA DE MANO DE
OBRA - 13.01.02
*SN: GENERAL DEMAND FOR LABOUR, OR DEMAND IN
    PARTICULAR INDUSTRIES OR SECTORS OF THE
    ECONOMY.*
        UF: LABOUR REQUIREMENTS
        BT: DEMAND
        RT: LABOUR MARKET
            MANPOWER

MANPOWER PLANNING
PLANIFICATION DE LA MAIN D'OEUVRE /
PLANIFICACION DE LA MANO DE OBRA - 13.01.03
        UF: EMPLOYMENT PLANNING
        BT: ECONOMIC PLANNING
        RT: EMPLOYMENT POLICY

MANPOWER POLICY
- 13.01.03
        USE: EMPLOYMENT POLICY

MANPOWER SERVICES
- 13.02.01
        USE: EMPLOYMENT SERVICES

MANUAL
MANUEL / MANUAL - 19.02.09
*SN: BOOK DESIGNED TO GIVE INSTRUCTION IN
    SPECIFIC SUBJECTS AND IN THE USE OF SPECIFIC
    EQUIPMENT AND MATERIAL.*
        UF: HANDBOOK
        BT: TEACHING AIDS

MANUAL WORKERS
TRAVAILLEURS MANUELS / TRABAJADORES MANUALES -
13.09.02
    BT: WORKERS
    RT: PHYSICAL WORK

MANUFACTURED PRODUCTS
PRODUITS MANUFACTURES / PRODUCTOS
MANUFACTURADOS
- 08.04.00
    BT: INDUSTRIAL PRODUCTS
    NT: FINISHED PRODUCTS

MANUFACTURING
FABRICATION INDUSTRIELLE / ELABORACION
INDUSTRIAL - 08.01.01
    RT: INDUSTRIAL SECTOR

MANUFACTURING INDUSTRIES
- 08.01.01
    USE: INDUSTRY

MAPPING
CARTOGRAPHIE / CARTOGRAFIA - 18.07.00
    UF: CARTOGRAPHY
    NT: CHARTING
    RT: GEOGRAPHY
        MAPS

MAPS
CARTES GEOGRAPHIQUES / MAPAS - 18.07.00
    BT: AUDIOVISUAL MATERIALS
    NT: SOIL MAPS
    RT: ATLASES
        MAPPING

MARGARINE
MARGARINE / MARGARINA - 08.06.06
    BT: FOOD
        OILS AND FATS
    RT: BUTTER
        EDIBLE OILS

MARGINALISM
MARGINALISME / MARGINALISMO - 03.03.01
    BT: ECONOMIC SYSTEMS

MARGINALITY
MARGINALITE / MARGINALIDAD - 05.03.03
SN: REFERS TO CERTAIN INDIVIDUALS OR GROUPS
SITUATED OUTSIDE OF THE MAIN STREAMS OF
SOCIAL, POLITICAL OR ECONOMIC LIFE.
    RT: ALIENATION
        MALADJUSTMENT
        POLITICAL PARTICIPATION
        SOCIAL PARTICIPATION

MARINE ENVIRONMENT
ENVIRONNEMENT MARIN / MEDIO AMBIENTE MARINO -
16.01.02
    BT: AQUATIC ENVIRONMENT
    RT: SEA

MARINE FISHING
PECHE EN MER / PESCA MARINA - 07.10.03
    BT: FISHING

MARINE FISHING<CONT>
    NT: COASTAL FISHING
        DEEP SEA FISHING

MARINE POLLUTION
POLLUTION DES MERS / CONTAMINACION DEL MAR -
16.03.04
    BT: WATER POLLUTION
    RT: COASTAL POLLUTION
        SEA
        SEA DUMPING

MARINE RESOURCES
RESSOURCES DE LA MER / RECURSOS DEL MAR -
16.02.02
    BT: NATURAL RESOURCES
    RT: SEA

MARITAL STATUS
SITUATION DE FAMILLE / ESTADO CIVIL - 14.02.05
    RT: CELIBACY
        MARRIED PERSONS

MARITIME LAW
DROIT MARITIME / DERECHO MARITIMO - 04.01.02
    BT: LAW
    RT: SEA TRANSPORT

MARITIME QUESTIONS
QUESTIONS MARITIMES / CUESTIONES MARITIMAS -
10.05.00
SN: USE ONLY IN CASES WHERE A MORE SPECIFIC
DESCRIPTOR CANNOT BE USED.
    NT: FLAGS OF CONVENIENCE
        SEA TRANSPORT
    RT: LAW OF THE SEA
        SEA TRANSPORT

MARITIME TRANSPORT
- 10.05.00
    USE: SEA TRANSPORT

MARKET
MARCHE / MERCADO - 09.01.02
    NT: AGRICULTURAL MARKET
        BLACK MARKET
        COMMODITY MARKET
        DOMESTIC MARKET
        FINANCIAL MARKET
        FREIGHT MARKET
        INTERNATIONAL MARKET
        LABOUR MARKET
        MONEY MARKET
    RT: ACCESS TO MARKET
        MARKET ECONOMY
        MARKET PLANNING
        MARKET STABILIZATION
        MARKET STUDIES
        MARKETING
        MICROECONOMICS
        PRICES
        SUPPLY AND DEMAND

MARKET ECONOMY
ECONOMIE DE MARCHE / ECONOMIA DE MERCADO -

MARKET ECONOMY<CONT>
03.03.01
> *BT:* ECONOMIC SYSTEMS
> *RT:* CAPITALISM
> LIBERALISM
> MARKET

MARKET PLANNING
PLANIFICATION DU MARCHE / PLANIFICACION DEL MERCADO - 09.01.02
> *BT:* ECONOMIC PLANNING
> *RT:* MARKET

MARKET STABILIZATION
STABILISATION DU MARCHE / ESTABILIZACION DEL MERCADO - 09.01.02
> *BT:* STABILIZATION
> *RT:* BUFFER STOCKS
> COMMODITIES
> MARKET
> MARKETING BOARDS
> PRICE STABILIZATION

MARKET STUDIES
ETUDES DE MARCHE / ESTUDIOS DE MERCADO - 09.03.01
> *RT:* CONSUMER BEHAVIOUR
> MARKET
> MARKETING

MARKETING
COMMERCIALISATION / MERCADEO - 09.03.01
> *UF:* SALES PROMOTION
> SELLING
> *NT:* COOPERATIVE MARKETING
> RETAIL MARKETING
> WHOLESALE MARKETING
> *RT:* MARKET
> MARKET STUDIES
> MARKETING BOARDS
> SALESMAN
> VENDORS

MARKETING BOARDS
OFFICES DE VENTE / JUNTAS DE COMERCIALIZACION - 09.03.01
> *RT:* ADMINISTERED PRICES
> MARKET STABILIZATION
> MARKETING
> PRICE STABILIZATION

MARKETING COOPERATIVES
COOPERATIVES DE VENTE / COOPERATIVAS DE VENTAS - 09.03.01
> *BT:* COOPERATIVES
> *RT:* COOPERATIVE MARKETING

MARRIAGE
MARIAGE / MATRIMONIO - 14.02.05

MARRIAGE<CONT>
> *RT:* DIVORCE
> MARRIED PERSONS
> NUPTIALITY
> POLYANDRY
> POLYGAMY

MARRIED PERSONS
PERSONNES MARIEES / PERSONAS CASADAS - 14.02.05
> *NT:* HUSBAND
> WIFE
> *RT:* MARITAL STATUS
> MARRIAGE

MARTINIQUE
MARTINIQUE / MARTINICA - 01.04.03
> *BT:* CARIBBEAN
> *RT:* FRANCE

MARXISM
MARXISME / MARXISMO - 03.03.01
> *RT:* COMMUNISM
> ECONOMIC THEORY
> POLITICAL DOCTRINES

MASS COMMUNICATION
COMMUNICATION DE MASSE / COMUNICACION DE MASAS - 05.07.01
SN: COMMUNICATION BY SUCH MEANS AS NEWSPAPERS, RADIO, TELEVISION, ETC.
> *BT:* COMMUNICATION

MASS EDUCATION
EDUCATION DE MASSE / EDUCACION DE MASAS - 06.03.04
> *BT:* GENERAL EDUCATION

MASS MEDIA
MOYENS DE COMMUNICATION DE MASSE / MEDIOS DE COMUNICACION DE MASAS - 05.07.03
> *BT:* MEDIA
> *NT:* BOOKS
> FILMS
> PRESS
> RADIO
> TELEVISION
> *RT:* AUDIOVISUAL MATERIALS
> CULTURAL INDUSTRY

MASS PRODUCTION
PRODUCTION DE MASSE / PRODUCCION MASIVA - 12.07.01
> *BT:* PRODUCTION

MASTERCRAFTSMEN
MAITRES ARTISANS / MAESTROS ARTESANOS - 13.09.03
SN: USE TO MEAN SKILLED WORKERS WHO HAVE GONE BEYOND THE ORDINARY LEVEL OF SKILLS AND KNOWLEDGE AND HAVE BECOME HIGHLY QUALIFIED WORKERS (BUT NOT TECHNICIANS).
> *BT:* CRAFTSMEN
> *RT:* OCCUPATIONAL QUALIFICATION

MATERIALS HANDLING
- 10.06.00
> *USE:* HANDLING

MATERNAL AND CHILD HEALTH
SANTE DE LA MERE ET DE L'ENFANT / SALUD
MATERNO-INFANTIL - 15.04.04
    BT: PREVENTIVE MEDICINE
    RT: BREAST FEEDING
        HEALTH

MATERNITY BENEFITS
ALLOCATIONS DE MATERNITE / SUBSIDIOS DE
MATERNIDAD - 02.03.02
    BT: FAMILY POLICY
        SOCIAL SECURITY
    RT: FAMILY
        FAMILY ALLOWANCES

MATERNITY LEAVE
CONGE DE MATERNITE / LICENCIA POR MATERNIDAD -
13.05.00
    RT: FEMALE MANPOWER

MATHEMATICAL ANALYSIS
ANALYSE MATHEMATIQUE / ANALISIS MATEMATICO -
18.08.00
    BT: RESEARCH METHODS
    RT: MATHEMATICAL MODELS

MATHEMATICAL MODELS
MODELES MATHEMATIQUES / MODELOS MATEMATICOS -
18.08.00
    BT: MODELS
    RT: MATHEMATICAL ANALYSIS

MATHEMATICIANS
MATHEMATICIENS / MATEMATICOS - 13.09.09
    BT: SCIENTISTS
    RT: MATHEMATICS

MATHEMATICS
MATHEMATIQUES / MATEMATICAS - 18.08.00
    RT: ECONOMETRICS
        LOGIC
        MATHEMATICIANS
        STATISTICS

MAURITANIA
MAURITANIE / MAURITANIA - 01.04.02
    BT: FRENCH SPEAKING AFRICA
        WEST AFRICA
    RT: MAURITANIAN

MAURITANIAN
MAURITANIEN / MAURITANO - 14.03.02
    RT: MAURITANIA

MAURITIAN
MAURICIEN / MAURICIANO - 14.03.02
    RT: MAURITIUS

MAURITIUS
MAURICE / MAURICIO - 01.04.02
    BT: EAST AFRICA
        ENGLISH SPEAKING AFRICA
        SOUTHERN AFRICA
    RT: MAURITIAN

MEAL PREPARATION
- 15.03.01
    USE: FOOD PREPARATION

MEANS OF PRODUCTION
MOYENS DE PRODUCTION / MEDIOS DE PRODUCCION -
12.07.01
    RT: CAPITAL
        EQUIPMENT
        PRODUCTION

MEANS OF TRANSPORT
MOYENS DE TRANSPORT / MEDIOS DE TRANSPORTE -
10.04.00
    NT: MOTOR VEHICLES
        NON-MOTORIZED TRANSPORT

MEASLES
ROUGEOLE / SARAMPION - 15.04.02
    BT: INFECTIOUS DISEASES

MEASUREMENT
MESURE / MEDICION - 18.06.00
    UF: MEASURING
    RT: MEASUREMENT SYSTEMS
        MEASURING INSTRUMENTS
        METROLOGY
        PHOTOGRAMMETRY
        RESEARCH METHODS

MEASUREMENT SYSTEMS
SYSTEMES DE MESURE / SISTEMAS DE MEDICION -
18.06.00
    NT: METRIC SYSTEM
    RT: MEASUREMENT

MEASURING
- 18.06.00
    USE: MEASUREMENT

MEASURING INSTRUMENTS
INSTRUMENTS DE MESURE / INSTRUMENTOS DE MEDICION
- 08.14.08
    BT: PRECISION INSTRUMENTS
    NT: RADAR
    RT: MEASUREMENT

MEAT
VIANDE / CARNE - 07.09.05
    BT: MEAT PRODUCTS
    NT: BEEF
        MUTTON
        PORK
    RT: PROTEIN RICH FOOD

MEAT INDUSTRY
INDUSTRIE DE LA VIANDE / INDUSTRIA DE LA CARNE -
08.06.01
    BT: FOOD INDUSTRY
    RT: MEAT PROCESSING

MEAT PROCESSING
TRAITEMENT DE LA VIANDE / PROCESAMIENTO DE
CARNES - 08.06.02
    BT: FOOD PROCESSING
    RT: MEAT INDUSTRY

MEAT PRODUCTS
PRODUITS CARNES / PRODUCTOS CARNICOS - 07.09.05
    BT: ANIMAL PRODUCTS
        FOOD
    NT: MEAT

MECHANIZATION
MECANISATION / MECANIZACION - 12.05.00
    NT: AGRICULTURAL MECHANIZATION
    RT: EQUIPMENT
        INDUSTRIALIZATION
        MACHINERY

MEDIA
MOYENS DE COMMUNICATION / MEDIOS DE COMUNICACION
- 05.07.03
    UF: COMMUNICATION MEDIA
    NT: MASS MEDIA
    RT: COMMUNICATION

MEDICAL CARE
SOINS MEDICAUX / ATENCION MEDICA - 15.04.04
    UF: MEDICAL TREATMENT
    NT: PRENATAL CARE
    RT: HEALTH SERVICES
        HOSPITALIZATION
        MEDICINE

MEDICAL DOCTORS
- 13.09.10
    USE: PHYSICIANS

MEDICAL EDUCATION
ENSEIGNEMENT MEDICAL / ENSENANZA MEDICA -
06.03.07
    UF: PHYSICIAN EDUCATION
    BT: VOCATIONAL EDUCATION
    RT: MEDICAL PERSONNEL
        MEDICAL SCIENCES
        MEDICINE

MEDICAL EQUIPMENT
- 02.05.02
    USE: HEALTH FACILITIES

MEDICAL EXAMINATION
EXAMEN MEDICAL / EXAMEN MEDICO - 15.04.04

MEDICAL PERSONNEL
PERSONNEL MEDICAL / PERSONAL MEDICO - 13.09.10
    NT: DENTISTS
        PHARMACISTS
        PHYSICIANS
    RT: HEALTH SERVICES
        MEDICAL EDUCATION
        MEDICINE
        PARAMEDICAL PERSONNEL
        SCIENTIFIC PERSONNEL

MEDICAL RESEARCH
RECHERCHE MEDICALE / INVESTIGACION MEDICA -
15.04.06
    BT: RESEARCH

MEDICAL RESEARCH<CONT>
    RT: MEDICAL SCIENCES
        MEDICINE

MEDICAL SCIENCES
SCIENCES MEDICALES / CIENCIAS MEDICAS - 15.04.06
    NT: CARDIOLOGY
        EPIDEMIOLOGY
        GYNAECOLOGY
        IMMUNOLOGY
        PHARMACOLOGY
        RADIOLOGY
    RT: BIOLOGY
        MEDICAL EDUCATION
        MEDICAL RESEARCH
        MEDICINE
        NATURAL SCIENCES

MEDICAL TREATMENT
- 15.04.04
    USE: MEDICAL CARE

MEDICINAL PLANTS
PLANTES MEDICINALES / PLANTAS MEDICINALES -
15.05.00
    BT: PLANTS
    RT: TRADITIONAL MEDICINE

MEDICINE
MEDECINE / MEDICINA - 15.04.06
    NT: ACUPUNCTURE
        OCCUPATIONAL MEDICINE
        PEDIATRICS
        PREVENTIVE MEDICINE
        PSYCHIATRY
        SURGERY
        TRADITIONAL MEDICINE
        VETERINARY MEDICINE
    RT: DISEASE CONTROL
        DISEASES
        HEALTH SERVICES
        MEDICAL CARE
        MEDICAL EDUCATION
        MEDICAL PERSONNEL
        MEDICAL RESEARCH
        MEDICAL SCIENCES
        PHARMACOLOGY

MEDITERRANEAN
MEDITERRANEE / MEDITERRANEO - 17.06.00
    RT: MEDITERRANEAN COUNTRIES

MEDITERRANEAN COUNTRIES
PAYS MEDITERRANEENS / PAISES MEDITERRANEOS -
01.04.05

MEDITERRANEAN COUNTRIES<CONT>
    NT: ALBANIA
        ALGERIA
        CYPRUS
        EGYPT
        FRANCE
        GIBRALTAR
        GREECE
        ISRAEL
        ITALY
        LEBANON
        LIBYA
        MALTA
        MONACO
        MOROCCO
        SAN MARINO
        SPAIN
        SYRIA
        TUNISIA
        TURKEY
        VATICAN
        YUGOSLAVIA
    RT: EUROPE
        MEDITERRANEAN
        MIDDLE EAST
        NORTH AFRICA

MEDIUM TERM
MOYEN TERME / MEDIANO PLAZO - 18.10.00

MEDIUM-SCALE INDUSTRY
MOYENNE INDUSTRIE / INDUSTRIA MEDIANA - 08.02.02
    BT: INDUSTRY
    RT: SIZE OF ENTERPRISE

MEETING PAPER
- 19.02.05
    USE: CONFERENCE PAPER

MEETING REPORT
- 19.02.08
    USE: CONFERENCE REPORT

MELANESIA
- 01.04.07
    USE: OCEANIA

MEMBER STATES
ETATS-MEMBRES / ESTADOS MIEMBROS - 01.03.01

MEMORANDUM
MEMORANDUM / MEMORANDUM - 19.02.05

MEN
HOMMES / HOMBRES - 14.02.03
    RT: MALES

MENINGITIS
MENINGITE / MENINGITIS - 15.04.02
    BT: INFECTIOUS DISEASES

MENTAL DISEASES
MALADIES MENTALES / ENFERMEDADES MENTALES -

MENTAL DISEASES<CONT>
15.04.02
    BT: DISEASES
    RT: MENTAL HEALTH
        MENTAL HOSPITALS
        MENTAL RETARDATION
        MENTALLY HANDICAPPED
        PSYCHIATRY

MENTAL HEALTH
SANTE MENTALE / SALUD MENTAL - 15.04.01
    BT: HEALTH
    RT: MENTAL DISEASES

MENTAL HOSPITALS
HOPITAUX PSYCHIATRIQUES / HOSPITALES
PSIQUIATRICOS - 02.05.02
    BT: HOSPITALS
    RT: MENTAL DISEASES
        PSYCHIATRY

MENTAL RETARDATION
RETARD INTELLECTUEL / RETRASO MENTAL - 06.05.04
    RT: MENTAL DISEASES
        SPECIAL EDUCATION

MENTAL STRESS
TENSION MENTALE / TENSION PSICOLOGICA - 13.03.04
    RT: WORKING CONDITIONS

MENTALLY HANDICAPPED
HANDICAPES MENTAUX / DEFICIENTES MENTALES -
15.04.05
    BT: HANDICAPPED
    RT: MENTAL DISEASES

MERCHANT FLEET
- 10.05.00
    USE: MERCHANT MARINE

MERCHANT MARINE
MARINE MARCHANDE / MARINA MERCANTE - 10.05.00
    UF: MERCHANT FLEET
    RT: CARGO SHIPS
        TANKERS

MERCURY
MERCURE / MERCURIO - 08.14.02
    BT: NON-FERROUS METALS
        TOXIC METALS

MERGERS
FUSIONS D'ENTREPRISES / FUSIONES DE EMPRESAS -
12.02.00
    NT: TRUSTS
    RT: ECONOMIC CONCENTRATION
        SIZE OF ENTERPRISE

MESTIZOS
METIS / MESTIZOS - 14.03.03

METABOLISM
METABOLISME / METABOLISMO - 15.02.04
    RT: NUTRITION

METAL CASTING
FONTE DE METAUX / FUNDICION DE METALES -
08.14.03
    BT: MACHINING

METAL PRODUCTS
PRODUITS METALLIQUES / PRODUCTOS METALICOS -
08.14.01
    NT: CABLES
        CASTINGS
        METAL SHEETS
        PIPES
        WIRE
    RT: METALWORKING INDUSTRY

METAL SCRAPS
FERRAILLE / CHATARRA - 08.14.04
    BT: INDUSTRIAL WASTES

METAL SHEETS
TOLES METALLIQUES / CHAPAS DE METAL - 08.14.04
    BT: METAL PRODUCTS
    RT: SHEET-METAL WORKING

METALLURGY
METALLURGIE / METALURGIA - 08.14.03
SN: THE SCIENCE AND TECHNOLOGY OF METALS.
    RT: METALS
        METALWORKING INDUSTRY

METALS
METAUX / METALES - 08.14.02
    NT: IRON
        NON-FERROUS METALS
        TOXIC METALS
    RT: ALLOYS
        METALLURGY
        METALWORKING INDUSTRY

METALWORKERS
OUVRIERS METALLURGISTES / OBREROS METALURGICOS -
13.09.06
    BT: INDUSTRIAL WORKERS
    RT: METALWORKING INDUSTRY

METALWORKING INDUSTRY
METALLURGIE DE TRANSFORMATION / INDUSTRIA
METALMECANICA - 08.14.01
    NT: BOILERMAKING
        MACHINERY INDUSTRY
        SHEET-METAL WORKING
    RT: METAL PRODUCTS
        METALLURGY
        METALS
        METALWORKERS

METEOROLOGY
METEOROLOGIE / METEOROLOGIA - 17.01.01
    UF: ATMOSPHERIC SCIENCES
    BT: EARTH SCIENCES
    NT: CLIMATOLOGY

METEOROLOGY<CONT>
    RT: METEOROLOGY SERVICES
        PHYSICAL GEOGRAPHY
        PRECIPITATIONS
        STORMS
        WEATHER FORECASTS
        WMO

METEOROLOGY SERVICES
SERVICES DE METEOROLOGIE / SERVICIOS
METEOROLOGICOS - 17.01.01
    RT: METEOROLOGY

METHANE
METHANE / METANO - 08.11.06
    BT: HYDROCARBONS

METHODOLOGY
METHODOLOGIE / METODOLOGIA - 18.03.00
    RT: EXPERIMENTATION
        OBSERVATION
        PLANNING METHODS
        RESEARCH METHODS

METRIC SYSTEM
SYSTEME METRIQUE / SISTEMA METRICO - 18.06.00
    BT: MEASUREMENT SYSTEMS

METROLOGY
METROLOGIE / METROLOGIA - 18.06.00
    RT: MEASUREMENT

MEXICAN
MEXICAIN / MEXICANO - 14.03.02
    RT: MEXICO

MEXICO
MEXIQUE / MEXICO - 01.04.03
    BT: LATIN AMERICA
        NORTH AMERICA
    RT: MEXICAN

MICROBES
MICROBES / MICROBIOS - 15.01.02
    BT: MICROORGANISMS

MICROBIOLOGY
MICROBIOLOGIE / MICROBIOLOGIA - 15.01.01
    BT: BIOLOGY
    NT: BACTERIOLOGY
        VIROLOGY
    RT: MICROORGANISMS

MICROECONOMICS
MICROECONOMIE / MICROECONOMIA - 03.01.01
    BT: ECONOMICS
    RT: MARKET
        SUPPLY AND DEMAND

MICROFICHES
MICROFICHES / MICROFICHAS - 19.01.04

MICROFILMS
MICROFILMS / MICROFILMS - 19.01.04
    BT: AUDIOVISUAL MATERIALS

MICRONESIA
- 01.04.07
  USE: OCEANIA

MICROORGANISMS
MICROORGANISMES / MICROORGANISMOS - 15.01.02
  NT: BACTERIA
  MICROBES
  VIRUSES
  RT: MICROBIOLOGY

MIDDLE CLASS
CLASSE MOYENNE / CLASE MEDIA - 05.03.05
  BT: SOCIAL CLASSES

MIDDLE EAST
MOYEN ORIENT / ORIENTE MEDIO - 01.04.06
  UF: NEAR EAST
  WESTERN ASIA
  NT: AFGHANISTAN
  CYPRUS
  IRAN
  IRAQ
  ISRAEL
  JORDAN
  LEBANON
  OMAN
  PERSIAN GULF STATES
  SAUDI ARABIA
  SYRIA
  TURKEY
  YEMEN
  YEMEN PDR
  RT: ARAB COUNTRIES
  ECWA
  MEDITERRANEAN COUNTRIES

MIDDLE MANAGEMENT
CADRES MOYENS / MANDOS MEDIOS - 12.03.00
*SN: THE WIDE RANGE OF TECHNICAL AND SUPERVISORY
STAFF BETWEEN THE FIRST-LEVEL SUPERVISION
AND TOP MANAGEMENT.*
  BT: MANAGERS
  RT: PROFESSIONALS

MIDDLE-SIZED TOWNS
VILLES MOYENNES / CIUDADES MEDIAS - 14.04.03
  BT: TOWNS

MIDWIVES
SAGES-FEMMES / PARTERAS - 13.09.10
  BT: PARAMEDICAL PERSONNEL

MIGRANT WORKERS
**TRAVAILLEURS MIGRANTS / TRABAJADORES MIGRANTES -
13.09.02**
  BT: MIGRANTS
  WORKERS
  RT: FOREIGN WORKERS
  LABOUR MIGRATIONS
  SEASONAL WORKERS

MIGRANTS
MIGRANTS / MIGRANTES - 14.07.00

MIGRANTS<CONT>
  NT: EMIGRANTS
  IMMIGRANTS
  MIGRANT WORKERS
  NOMADS
  REFUGEES
  RT: FOREIGNERS

MIGRATION POLICY
**POLITIQUE MIGRATOIRE / POLITICA MIGRATORIA -
14.07.00**
  BT: POPULATION POLICY
  RT: MIGRATIONS

MIGRATIONS
MIGRATIONS / MIGRACIONES - 14.07.00
  NT: INTERNAL MIGRATIONS
  INTERNATIONAL MIGRATIONS
  LABOUR MIGRATIONS
  NOMADISM
  POPULATION TRANSFERS
  RETURN MIGRATIONS
  SEASONAL MIGRATIONS
  RT: ICEM
  MIGRATION POLICY

MILITARY
MILITAIRE / MILITAR - 01.02.06
  RT: ARMY

MILITARY AID
AIDE MILITAIRE / AYUDA MILITAR - 01.02.06
  BT: FOREIGN AID
  RT: ARMAMENT

MILITARY BASES
BASES MILITAIRES / BASES MILITARES - 01.02.06

MILITARY EXPENDITURES
**DEPENSES MILITAIRES / GASTOS MILITARES -
01.02.06**
  BT: PUBLIC EXPENDITURES
  RT: ARMAMENT

MILITARY SERVICE
SERVICE MILITAIRE / SERVICIO MILITAR - 01.02.06
  RT: ARMY

MILK
LAIT / LECHE - 07.09.05
  BT: DAIRY PRODUCTS
  NON-ALCOHOLIC BEVERAGES
  NT: MILK POWDER
  RT: COWS

MILK POWDER
LAIT EN POUDRE / LECHE EN POLVO - 07.09.05
  BT: MILK

MILK PROCESSING
**TRAITEMENT DU LAIT / PROCESAMIENTO DE LA LECHE -
08.06.02**
  BT: FOOD PROCESSING
  RT: DAIRY INDUSTRY

MILK PRODUCTS
- 07.09.05
  USE: **DAIRY PRODUCTS**

MILLET
MIL / MIJO - 07.07.04
  BT: CEREALS
  RT: ICRISAT

MILLING INDUSTRY
MINOTERIE / INDUSTRIA HARINERA - 08.06.01
  BT: FOOD INDUSTRY
  RT: FLOUR
     GRAIN PROCESSING

MINERAL OILS
HUILES MINERALES / ACEITES MINERALES - 08.11.06
  BT: FOSSIL FUELS
  NT: PETROLEUM
     SHALE OIL

MINERAL RESOURCES
RESSOURCES MINERALES / RECURSOS MINERALES -
16.02.02
  BT: NATURAL RESOURCES
  RT: MINERALOGY
     MINERALS

MINERAL WATERS
EAUX MINERALES / AGUAS MINERALES - 08.06.05
  BT: NON-ALCOHOLIC BEVERAGES

MINERALOGY
MINERALOGIE / MINERALOGIA - 17.04.01
  BT: EARTH SCIENCES
  RT: MINERAL RESOURCES

MINERALS
MINERAUX / MINERALES - 08.13.00
  UF: ORES
  NT: BAUXITE
     COPPER ORE
     IRON ORE
     PRECIOUS STONES
  RT: MINERAL RESOURCES

MINERS
MINEURS / MINEROS - 13.09.06
  BT: INDUSTRIAL WORKERS
  RT: MINING

MINES
MINES / MINAS - 08.13.00
  RT: MINING

MINIMUM AGE
AGE MINIMUM / EDAD MINIMA - 14.02.02
  BT: AGE

MINIMUM WAGE
SALAIRE MINIMUM / SALARIO MINIMO - 13.07.00
  UF: GUARANTEED WAGE
  BT: WAGES

MINING
INDUSTRIE MINIERE / MINERIA - 08.13.00
  BT: PRIMARY SECTOR
  NT: COAL MINING
     DEEP SEA MINING
  RT: MINERS
     MINES
     MINING ENGINEERING
     PRECIOUS STONES
     QUARRYING

MINING ENGINEERING
TECHNOLOGIE MINIERE / TECNOLOGIA MINERA -
08.13.00
  BT: ENGINEERING
  RT: MINING

MINORITY GROUPS
GROUPES MINORITAIRES / GRUPOS MINORITARIOS -
05.03.07
  BT: GROUPS
  NT: ETHNIC MINORITIES
     LANGUAGE MINORITIES
     RELIGIOUS MINORITIES

MISSION REPORT
RAPPORT DE MISSION / INFORME DE MISION -
19.02.08

MIXED ECONOMY
ECONOMIE MIXTE / ECONOMIA MIXTA - 03.03.02
  BT: ECONOMIC SYSTEMS
  RT: MIXED ENTERPRISES

MIXED ENTERPRISES
ENTREPRISES MIXTES / EMPRESAS MIXTAS - 03.03.05
  BT: ENTERPRISES
  RT: MIXED ECONOMY

MIXED FARMING
AGRIEXPLOITATION MIXTE / EXPLOTACION AGRICOLA
COMBINADA - 07.05.03
  BT: FARMING SYSTEMS

MOBILE SCHOOLS
ECOLES MOBILES / ESCUELAS MOVILES - 06.04.03
  BT: SCHOOLS

MODELS
MODELES / MODELOS - 18.08.00
SN: USE ONLY IN CONNECTION WITH RESEARCH AND
  PLANNING. FOR MODELS OF NEW PRODUCTS, USE
  'PROTOTYPES'.
  NT: ECONOMIC MODELS
     MATHEMATICAL MODELS
  RT: SIMULATION
     THEORY

MODERNIZATION
MODERNISATION / MODERNIZACION - 05.03.04
  RT: CULTURAL CHANGE
     SOCIAL CHANGE
     SOCIAL DEVELOPMENT
     TRADITION

MODES OF PRODUCTION
MODES DE PRODUCTION / MODOS DE PRODUCCION -
12.07.01
> *RT:* CAPITALISM
> PRODUCTION
> SOCIALISM

MODES OF TRANSPORTATION
MODES DE TRANSPORT / MODOS DE TRANSPORTE -
10.05.00
> *NT:* AIR TRANSPORT
> INLAND WATER TRANSPORT
> MULTIMODAL TRANSPORT
> PIPELINE TRANSPORT
> RAILWAY TRANSPORT
> ROAD TRANSPORT
> SEA TRANSPORT
> *RT:* TRANSPORT

MODULAR TRAINING
FORMATION PAR MODULES / CAPACITACION POR MODULOS
- 06.05.02
> *BT:* TRAINING METHODS
> VOCATIONAL TRAINING

MOISTURE
- 17.01.03
> *USE:* HUMIDITY

MOLASSES
MELASSES / MELAZAS - 08.06.04
> *RT:* SUGAR
> SUGAR INDUSTRY

MOLLUSCS
MOLLUSQUES / MOLUSCOS - 07.10.04
> *BT:* SHELLFISH
> *RT:* OYSTER CULTURE

MONACO
MONACO / MONACO - 01.04.05
> *BT:* MEDITERRANEAN COUNTRIES
> WESTERN EUROPE
> *RT:* MONEGASQUE

MONEGASQUE
MONEGASQUE / MONEGASCO - 14.03.02
> *RT:* MONACO

MONETARY AGREEMENTS
ACCORDS MONETAIRES / ACUERDOS MONETARIOS -
11.03.01
> *BT:* ECONOMIC AGREEMENTS
> *NT:* CLEARING AGREEMENTS
> *RT:* CURRENCIES

MONETARY AREAS
ZONES MONETAIRES / ZONAS MONETARIAS - 11.03.01
> *UF:* MONETARY UNIONS
> *RT:* CURRENCIES

MONETARY CIRCULATION
CIRCULATION MONETAIRE / CIRCULACION MONETARIA -

MONETARY CIRCULATION<CONT>
11.02.01
> *RT:* CURRENCIES
> INFLATION
> LIQUIDITY
> MONEY SUPPLY

MONETARY CORRECTION
CORRECTION MONETAIRE / CORRECCION MONETARIA -
11.02.01
> *RT:* CURRENCIES
> INFLATION

MONETARY POLICY
POLITIQUE MONETAIRE / POLITICA MONETARIA -
11.02.01
> *BT:* FINANCIAL POLICY
> *NT:* DEVALUATION
> *RT:* BANK RATE
> CENTRAL BANKS
> CREDIT POLICY
> CURRENCIES
> FOREIGN EXCHANGE CONTROL
> MONEY SUPPLY

MONETARY RELATIONS
RELATIONS MONETAIRES / RELACIONES MONETARIAS -
11.03.01
> *BT:* ECONOMIC RELATIONS
> *RT:* CURRENCIES
> EURODOLLARS
> PETRODOLLARS

MONETARY SYSTEMS
SYSTEMES MONETAIRES / SISTEMAS MONETARIOS -
11.02.01
SN: USE ONLY FOR NATIONAL MONETARY SYSTEMS;
> *OTHERWISE USE 'INTERNATIONAL MONETARY*
> *SYSTEM'.*
> *RT:* CEMLA

MONETARY TRANSFERS
TRANSFERTS MONETAIRES / TRANSFERENCIAS
MONETARIAS - 11.03.01
> *RT:* BORROWING
> CURRENCIES

MONETARY UNIONS
- 11.03.01
> *USE:* MONETARY AREAS
> *RT:* CURRENCIES

MONEY
- 11.02.01
> *USE:* CURRENCIES

MONEY MARKET
MARCHE MONETAIRE / MERCADO MONETARIO - 11.02.07
> *BT:* MARKET
> *RT:* BANK RATE
> CURRENCIES
> MONEY SUPPLY
> TREASURY BONDS

MONEY SUPPLY
DISPONIBILITES MONETAIRES / DISPONIBILIDADES
MONETARIAS - 11.02.01
  BT: SUPPLY
  RT: CURRENCIES
    LIQUIDITY
    MONETARY CIRCULATION
    MONETARY POLICY
    MONEY MARKET

MONGOLIA PR
MONGOLIE RP / MONGOLIA RP - 01.04.04
  BT: FAR EAST
  RT: MONGOLIAN

MONGOLIAN
MONGÔL / MONGOL - 14.03.02
  RT: MONGOLIA PR

MONOGRAPH
MONOGRAPHIE / MONOGRAFIA - 19.02.09
  BT: PRIMARY DOCUMENTS

MONOPOLIES
MONOPOLES / MONOPOLIOS - 12.02.00
  NT: CARTELS
  RT: COMPETITION
    TRUSTS
    UNFAIR COMPETITION

MONSOON
- 17.02.02
  USE: RAINY SEASON

MONTHLY
MENSUEL / PUBLICACION MENSUAL - 19.02.06
  BT: PERIODICALS

MONTSERRAT
MONTSERRAT / MONTSERRAT - 01.04.03
  BT: CARIBBEAN
  RT: UNITED KINGDOM

MORBIDITY
MORBIDITE / MORBILIDAD - 15.04.01
  RT: DISEASES
    MORTALITY

MOROCCAN
MAROCAIN / MARROQUI - 14.03.02
  RT: MOROCCO

MOROCCO
MAROC / MARRUECOS - 01.04.02
  BT: ARAB COUNTRIES
    FRENCH SPEAKING AFRICA
    MEDITERRANEAN COUNTRIES
    NORTH AFRICA
  RT: MOROCCAN

MORTALITY
MORTALITE / MORTALIDAD - 14.06.00

MORTALITY<CONT>
  NT: INFANT MORTALITY
    INTRAUTERINE MORTALITY
    OCCUPATIONAL MORTALITY
  RT: CAUSES OF DEATH
    DEATH
    LIFE TABLES
    MORBIDITY
    MORTALITY DECLINE

MORTALITY DECLINE
BAISSE DE LA MORTALITE / DECLINACION DE LA
MORTALIDAD - 14.06.00
  RT: MORTALITY

MORTGAGES
HYPOTHEQUES / HIPOTECAS - 11.02.02
  RT: CREDIT

MOTHER
MERE / MADRE - 14.02.04
  BT: PARENTS

MOTIVATIONS
MOTIVATIONS / MOTIVACIONES - 05.03.02

MOTOR CARS
- 10.04.00
  USE: AUTOMOBILES

MOTOR VEHICLE INDUSTRY
INDUSTRIE DU VEHICULE A MOTEUR / INDUSTRIA DE
LOS VEHICULOS DE MOTOR - 08.14.07
  BT: MACHINERY INDUSTRY
  NT: AUTOMOBILE INDUSTRY
  RT: ENGINES
    MOTOR VEHICLES

MOTOR VEHICLES
VEHICULES A MOTEUR / VEHICULOS AUTOMOTRICES -
10.04.00
  BT: MEANS OF TRANSPORT
  NT: AIRCRAFT
    AUTOMOBILES
    BUSES
    MOTORCYCLES
    SHIPS
    TRACTORS
    TRAINS
    TRUCKS
  RT: MOTOR VEHICLE INDUSTRY
    ROAD TRANSPORT

MOTORCYCLES
MOTOCYCLETTES / MOTOCICLETAS - 10.04.00
  BT: MOTOR VEHICLES

MOTORS
- 08.14.06
  USE: ENGINES

MOTORWAYS
AUTOROUTES / AUTOPISTAS - 10.03.00
  BT: ROADS

MOUNTAINS
MONTAGNES / MONTANAS - 17.03.04

MOUTH DISEASES
MALADIES DE LA BOUCHE / ENFERMEDADES DE LA BOCA
- 15.04.02
  BT: DISEASES

MOVING EXPENSES
PRIMES DE TRANSFERT / SUBSIDIOS POR TRASLADO -
13.07.00
*SN: PLANS DESIGNED TO AID THE EMPLOYEE
     FINANCIALLY WHEN THE EMPLOYER TRANSFERS HIM
     FROM ONE GEOGRAPHICAL LOCATION TO ANOTHER.*
  BT: WAGES

MOZAMBICAN
MOZAMBICAIN / MOZAMBIQUENO - 14.03.02
  RT: MOZAMBIQUE

MOZAMBIQUE
MOZAMBIQUE / MOZAMBIQUE - 01.04.02
  BT: EAST AFRICA
        SOUTHERN AFRICA
  RT: MOZAMBICAN

MPCC
CPCM / CPCM - 01.03.03
SN: MAGHREB PERMANENT CONSULTATIVE COMMITTEE.
  BT: AFRICAN ORGANIZATIONS
        ARAB ORGANIZATIONS
        INTERGOVERNMENTAL ORGANIZATIONS
  RT: NORTH AFRICA

MULTILATERAL AID
AIDE MULTILATERALE / AYUDA MULTILATERAL -
01.01.02
  BT: DEVELOPMENT AID
        MULTILATERAL RELATIONS
  RT: INTERNATIONAL ORGANIZATIONS

MULTILATERAL RELATIONS
RELATIONS MULTILATERALES / RELACIONES
MULTILATERALES - 01.02.01
  BT: INTERNATIONAL RELATIONS
  NT: MULTILATERAL AID

MULTILINGUALISM
MULTILINGUISME / MULTILINGUISMO - 05.06.01
  NT: BILINGUALISM
  RT: LANGUAGES

MULTIMODAL TRANSPORT
TRANSPORT MULTIMODAL / TRANSPORTE MULTIMODAL -
10.05.00
  BT: MODES OF TRANSPORTATION

MULTINATIONAL ENTERPRISES
ENTREPRISES MULTINATIONALES / EMPRESAS
MULTINACIONALES - 03.03.05
  UF: INTERNATIONAL ENTERPRISES
        TRANSNATIONAL CORPORATIONS
  BT: ENTERPRISES
        INTEREST GROUPS

MULTINATIONAL ENTERPRISES<CONT>
  RT: FOREIGN ENTERPRISES
        FOREIGN INVESTMENTS

MULTIPLE CROPPING
POLYCULTURE / CULTIVO MULTIPLE - 07.05.04
*SN: SIMULTANEOUS CULTIVATION OF DIFFERENT CROPS
     ON SEPARATE PLOTS OR FIELDS OF A FARM.*
  BT: CULTIVATION SYSTEMS
  RT: CROP DIVERSIFICATION

MULTIPURPOSE PROJECTS
PROJETS A FINS MULTIPLES / PROYECTOS
MULTIVALENTES - 01.01.06
  BT: DEVELOPMENT PROJECTS

MUSCULOSKELETAL SYSTEM
SYSTEME LOCOMOTEUR / SISTEMA LOCOMOTOR -
15.02.04
  BT: ANATOMY

MUSEUMS
MUSEES / MUSEOS - 05.05.01

MUSIC
MUSIQUE / MUSICA - 05.05.03
  BT: ARTS
  RT: MUSICAL INSTRUMENTS

MUSICAL INSTRUMENTS
INSTRUMENTS DE MUSIQUE / INSTRUMENTOS MUSICALES
- 05.05.03
  RT: MUSIC

MUTATIONS
MUTATIONS / MUTACIONES - 15.02.03
  NT: INDUCED MUTATIONS

MUTTON
VIANDE DE MOUTON / CARNE DE OVINO - 07.09.05
  UF: SHEEPMEAT
  BT: MEAT
  RT: SHEEP

MYTHOLOGY
MYTHOLOGIE / MITOLOGIA - 05.04.02

NAMIBIA
NAMIBIE / NAMIBIA - 01.04.02
UF: SOUTH WEST AFRICA
BT: ENGLISH SPEAKING AFRICA
SOUTHERN AFRICA
RT: NAMIBIAN

NAMIBIAN
NAMIBIEN / NAMIBIANO - 14.03.02
RT: NAMIBIA

NARCOTICS
STUPEFIANTS / ESTUPEFACIENTES - 15.05.00
BT: PHARMACEUTICALS
NT: OPIUM
RT: DRUG ADDICTION

NATION
NATION / NACION - 04.03.01
RT: NATIONAL POLICY
NATIONALISM
NATIONALIST
POLITICAL INTEGRATION

NATIONAL ACCOUNTING
COMPTABILITE NATIONALE / CONTABILIDAD NACIONAL -
03.02.02
SN: USE IN CONNECTION WITH ALL SECTORS OF AN
ECONOMY IN A GIVEN PERIOD. DO NOT CONFUSE
WITH 'PUBLIC ACCOUNTING'.
BT: ACCOUNTING
RT: GROSS DOMESTIC PRODUCT
GROSS NATIONAL PRODUCT
MACROECONOMICS
NATIONAL ACCOUNTS

NATIONAL ACCOUNTS
COMPTES NATIONAUX / CUENTAS NACIONALES -
03.02.02
RT: ECONOMIC STATISTICS
NATIONAL ACCOUNTING
NATIONAL EXPENDITURES

NATIONAL BUDGET
BUDGET DE L'ETAT / PRESUPUESTO NACIONAL -
11.01.01
BT: PUBLIC FINANCE
NT: BUDGETARY RESOURCES
RT: BUDGETARY POLICY
FISCAL POLICY
PUBLIC EXPENDITURES

NATIONAL EXPENDITURES
DEPENSES NATIONALES / GASTOS NACIONALES -
03.02.02
BT: EXPENDITURES
RT: NATIONAL ACCOUNTS

NATIONAL INCOME
REVENU NATIONAL / INGRESO NACIONAL - 03.02.02
SN: TOTAL NET EARNINGS ASCRIBABLE TO THE VARIOUS
FACTORS EMPLOYED IN THE PRODUCTION OF GOODS
AND SERVICES BY A NATION DURING A PARTICULAR
PERIOD.

NATIONAL INCOME<CONT>
RT: INCOME DISTRIBUTION
INCOME REDISTRIBUTION

NATIONAL LEVEL
NIVEAU NATIONAL / PLANO NACIONAL - 04.03.03

NATIONAL LIBERATION MOVEMENTS
MOUVEMENTS DE LIBERATION NATIONALE / MOVIMIENTOS
DE LIBERACION NACIONAL - 04.04.02
BT: SOCIAL MOVEMENTS
RT: COLONIALISM
INDEPENDENCE
LIBERATION

NATIONAL PARKS
PARCS NATIONAUX / PARQUES NACIONALES - 16.05.02
SN: DELIMITED AREAS FOR THE PROTECTION OF
INDIGENOUS FLORA AND FAUNA.
BT: PROTECTED RESOURCES
RT: NATURE CONSERVATION

NATIONAL PLANNING
PLANIFICATION NATIONALE / PLANIFICACION NACIONAL
- 02.01.02
BT: PLANNING
RT: NATIONAL PLANS

NATIONAL PLANS
PLANS NATIONAUX / PLANES NACIONALES - 02.01.02
BT: DEVELOPMENT PLANS
RT: NATIONAL PLANNING

NATIONAL POLICY
POLITIQUE NATIONALE / POLITICA NACIONAL -
04.03.03
RT: GOVERNMENT POLICY
NATION

NATIONALISM
NATIONALISME / NACIONALISMO - 03.03.01
RT: NATION
NATIONALIST

NATIONALIST
NATIONALISTE / NACIONALISTA - 03.03.01
RT: NATION
NATIONALISM

NATIONALIZATION
NATIONALISATION / NACIONALIZACION - 03.03.05
RT: DENATIONALIZATION
EXPROPRIATION
FOREIGN INVESTMENTS
PUBLIC ENTERPRISES
PUBLIC OWNERSHIP

NATIONALIZED ENTERPRISES
- 03.03.05
USE: PUBLIC ENTERPRISES

NATIONALIZED INDUSTRY
INDUSTRIE NATIONALISEE / INDUSTRIA NACIONALIZADA

NATIONALIZED INDUSTRY<CONT>
- 08.02.01
>> *BT:* INDUSTRY
>> PUBLIC ENTERPRISES

NATIVE RESERVATION
RESERVES INDIGENES / RESERVAS INDIGENAS -
14.03.01
>> *RT:* INDIGENOUS POPULATION

NATIVES
- 14.03.01
>> *USE:* INDIGENOUS POPULATION

NATO
OTAN / OTAN - 01.03.03
SN: NORTH ATLANTIC TREATY ORGANIZATION.
>> *BT:* INTERGOVERNMENTAL ORGANIZATIONS

NATURAL DISASTERS
DESASTRES NATURELS / DESASTRES NATURALES -
16.03.02
>> *BT:* DISASTERS
>> *NT:* DROUGHT
>> EPIDEMICS
>> FLOODS
>> FOREST FIRES
>> SEISMS
>> STORMS
>> TIDAL WAVES
>> VOLCANIC ERUPTIONS
>> *RT:* FAMINE

NATURAL ENVIRONMENT
- 16.01.02
>> *USE:* PHYSICAL ENVIRONMENT

NATURAL EQUILIBRIUM
- 16.01.01
>> *USE:* ECOLOGICAL BALANCE

NATURAL FIBRES
FIBRES NATURELLES / FIBRAS NATURALES - 08.08.01
>> *BT:* FIBRES
>> *NT:* ANIMAL FIBRES
>> PLANT FIBRES

NATURAL GAS
GAZ NATUREL / GAS NATURAL - 08.11.06
>> *BT:* FOSSIL FUELS
>> *RT:* PETROLEUM

NATURAL PRODUCTS
PRODUITS NATURELS / PRODUCTOS NATURALES -
12.08.01
>> *BT:* PRODUCTS

NATURAL RESOURCES
RESSOURCES NATURELLES / RECURSOS NATURALES -
16.02.02

NATURAL RESOURCES<CONT>
>> *NT:* ANIMAL RESOURCES
>> ENERGY RESOURCES
>> MARINE RESOURCES
>> MINERAL RESOURCES
>> NON-RENEWABLE RESOURCES
>> PLANT RESOURCES
>> RENEWABLE RESOURCES
>> SOIL RESOURCES
>> WATER RESOURCES
>> *RT:* COMMODITIES
>> ECONOMIC RESOURCES
>> HUMAN RESOURCES
>> RAW MATERIALS

NATURAL SCIENCES
SCIENCES NATURELLES / CIENCIAS NATURALES -
17.04.01
>> *NT:* ANATOMY
>> ANTHROPOLOGY
>> BIOLOGY
>> BOTANY
>> CHEMISTRY
>> EARTH SCIENCES
>> ECOLOGY
>> GENETICS
>> PHYSICS
>> PHYSIOLOGY
>> SPACE SCIENCES
>> ZOOLOGY
>> *RT:* MEDICAL SCIENCES

NATURE CONSERVATION
CONSERVATION DE LA NATURE / CONSERVACION DE LA
NATURALEZA - 16.05.01
>> *UF:* NATURE PROTECTION
>> WILDLIFE PROTECTION
>> *NT:* ANIMAL PROTECTION
>> ENVIRONMENTAL PROTECTION
>> PLANT PROTECTION
>> *RT:* NATIONAL PARKS
>> NATURE RESERVES
>> RESOURCES CONSERVATION

NATURE PROTECTION
- 16.05.01
>> *USE:* NATURE CONSERVATION

NATURE RESERVES
RESERVES NATURELLES / RESERVAS NATURALES -
16.05.02
SN: AREAS WHERE NATURAL RESOURCES CAN BE
EXPLOITED IN THE SCIENTIFIC AND CONTROLLED
MANNER WHICH ENSURES THEIR CONSERVATION.
>> *BT:* PROTECTED AREAS
>> PROTECTED RESOURCES
>> *RT:* NATURE CONSERVATION

NAURU
NAURU / NAURU - 01.04.07
>> *BT:* OCEANIA
>> *RT:* NAURUAN

NAURUAN
NAURUAN / NAURUANO - 14.03.02
>> *RT:* NAURU

NEAR EAST
- 01.04.06
    USE: MIDDLE EAST

NEIGHBOURHOOD
QUARTIER / BARRIO - 14.04.03
    RT: TOWNS

NEOCOLONIALISM
NEO-COLONIALISME / NEOCOLONIALISMO - 03.03.01
    RT: COLONIALISM
        DECOLONIZATION

NEPAL
NEPAL / NEPAL - 01.04.04
    BT: SOUTH ASIA
        SOUTH EAST ASIA
    RT: NEPALESE

NEPALESE
NEPALAIS / NEPALES - 14.03.02
    RT: NEPAL

NERVOUS SYSTEM
SYSTEME NERVEUX / SISTEMA NERVIOSO - 15.02.04
    BT: ANATOMY
    NT: BRAIN

NETHERLANDER
NEERLANDAIS / NEERLANDES - 14.03.02
    RT: NETHERLANDS

NETHERLANDS
PAYS-BAS / PAISES BAJOS - 01.04.05
    BT: WESTERN EUROPE
    RT: NETHERLANDER
        NETHERLANDS ANTILLES

NETHERLANDS ANTILLES
**ANTILLES NEERLANDAISES / ANTILLAS HOLANDESAS -
01.04.03**
    BT: CARIBBEAN
    RT: NETHERLANDS

NETWORK ANALYSIS
ANALYSE DE RESEAU / ANALISIS DE REDES - 12.04.00
    UF: CRITICAL PATH METHOD
        PERT
    BT: MANAGEMENT TECHNIQUES
    RT: SYSTEMS ANALYSIS

NEUTRALISM
NEUTRALISME / NEUTRALISMO - 01.02.01
    RT: INTERNATIONAL RELATIONS
        NEUTRALISM

NEUTRALITY
NEUTRALITE / NEUTRALIDAD - 01.02.01
    RT: INTERNATIONAL RELATIONS

NEW CALEDONIA
NOUVELLE CALEDONIE / NUEVA CALEDONIA - 01.04.07
    BT: PACIFIC ISLANDS FR
    RT: FRANCE

NEW HEBRIDES
NOUVELLES HEBRIDES / NUEVAS HEBRIDAS - 01.04.07
    BT: PACIFIC ISLANDS UK
        PACIFIC ISLANDS USA

NEW INTERNATIONAL ECONOMIC ORDER
**NOUVEL ORDRE ECON. INTERNATIONAL / NUEVO ORDEN
ECONOMICO INTERNACIONAL - 01.02.01**
    RT: ECONOMIC SYSTEMS
        INTERNATIONAL RELATIONS

NEW PRODUCTS
PRODUITS NOUVEAUX / PRODUCTOS NUEVOS - 12.08.01
    BT: PRODUCTS
    RT: CHOICE OF PRODUCTS
        PRODUCT DESIGN
        PRODUCT DEVELOPMENT
        PROTOTYPES

NEW TOWNS
VILLES NOUVELLES / CIUDADES NUEVAS - 14.04.03
    BT: TOWNS

NEW ZEALAND
NOUVELLE ZELANDE / NUEVA ZELANDIA - 01.04.07
    BT: OCEANIA
    RT: NEW ZELANDER
        PACIFIC ISLANDS NZ

NEW ZELANDER
NEO-ZELANDAIS / NEOZELANDES - 14.03.02
    RT: NEW ZEALAND

NEWS
NOUVELLES / NOTICIAS - 19.01.01
    BT: INFORMATION

NEWS ITEM
COUPURE DE PRESSE / NOTICIA DE PRENSA - 19.02.06
    RT: PRESS

NEWSLETTER
BULLETIN / BOLETIN - 19.02.06
    BT: SERIALS

NICARAGUA
NICARAGUA / NICARAGUA - 01.04.03
    BT: CENTRAL AMERICA
    RT: NICARAGUAN

NICARAGUAN
NICARAGUAYEN / NICARAGUENSE - 14.03.02
    RT: NICARAGUA

NICKEL
NICKEL / NIQUEL - 08.14.02
    BT: NON-FERROUS METALS

NIGER
NIGER / NIGER - 01.04.02
    BT: FRENCH SPEAKING AFRICA
        WEST AFRICA

NIGERIA
NIGERIA / NIGERIA - 01.04.02

NIGERIA<CONT>
  BT: ENGLISH SPEAKING AFRICA
        WEST AFRICA
  RT: NIGERIAN

NIGERIAN
NIGERIAN / NIGERIANO - 14.03.02
  RT: NIGERIA

NIGHT SCHOOLS
COURS DU SOIR / ESCUELAS NOCTURNAS - 06.04.03
  BT: SCHOOLS
  RT: ADULT EDUCATION

NIGHT WORK
TRAVAIL DE NUIT / TRABAJO NOCTURNO - 13.03.03
  BT: ARRANGEMENT OF WORKING TIME

NITRATES
NITRATES / NITRATOS - 08.12.04
  RT: CHEMICAL FERTILIZERS

NITROGEN
AZOTE / NITROGENO - 08.12.04

NITROGEN OXIDES
OXYDES D'AZOTE / OXIDOS NITROGENOS - 08.12.04
  BT: AIR POLLUTANTS

NOISE
BRUIT / RUIDO - 16.03.04
  RT: ACUSTIC POLLUTION
        NOISE CONTROL

NOISE CONTROL
LUTTE ANTI-BRUIT / LUCHA CONTRA EL RUIDO -
16.04.01
  BT: ENVIRONMENTAL ENGINEERING
  RT: NOISE

NOMADISM
NOMADISME / NOMADISMO - 14.07.00
  BT: MIGRATIONS
  RT: NOMADS

NOMADS
NOMADES / NOMADAS - 14.07.00
  BT: MIGRANTS
  RT: NOMADISM

NON-ALCOHOLIC BEVERAGES
BOISSONS NON-ALCOOLISEES / BEBIDAS
NO-ALCOHOLICAS - 08.06.05
  BT: BEVERAGES
  NT: COCOA
        COFFEE
        FRUIT JUICES
        MILK
        MINERAL WATERS
        TEA

NON-CONVERTIBLE CURRENCIES
MONNAIES NON-CONVERTIBLES / DIVISAS
NO-CONVERTIBLES - 11.03.01
  BT: CURRENCIES
  RT: CONVERTIBILITY

NON-FERROUS METALS
METAUX NON-FERREUX / METALES NO-FERROSOS -
08.14.02
  BT: METALS
  NT: ALUMINIUM
        CADMIUM
        CHROMIUM
        COBALT
        COPPER
        LEAD
        MANGANESE
        MERCURY
        NICKEL
        PLUTONIUM
        PRECIOUS METALS
        TIN
        TITANIUM
        TUNGSTEN
        URANIUM
        ZINC

NON-FORMAL EDUCATION
EDUCATION NON-FORMELLE / EDUCACION NO-FORMAL -
06.03.02
  SN: ACTIVITIES OR PROGRAMMES ORGANIZED OUTSIDE
      THE FRAMEWORK OF THE ESTABLISHED EDUCATIONAL
      SYSTEM, BUT DIRECTED TO DEFINITE EDUCATIONAL
      OBJECTIVES.
  RT: EDUCATIONAL SYSTEMS
        OUT-OF-SCHOOL EDUCATION

NON-GOVERNMENTAL ORGANIZATIONS
ORGANISATIONS NON-GOUVERNEMENTALES /
ORGANIZACIONES NO-GUBERNAMENTALES - 01.03.01
  SN: SEE UNDER 01.03.04 FOR ADDITIONAL NARROWER
      TERMS.
  BT: INTERNATIONAL ORGANIZATIONS

NON-GOVERNMENTAL ORGANIZATIONS<CONT>
- *NT:* ACDA
  ADIPA
  AFRASEC
  CAFRAD
  CEMLA
  CIAT
  CIMMYT
  CLACSO
  CODESRIA
  EADI
  FID
  ICFTU
  ICRISAT
  ICSSD
  ICSU
  ICVA
  IEA
  IFAP
  IFHP
  IFIP
  IFLA
  ILPES
  INTECOL
  IPPF
  IPSA
  IRRI
  ISA
  ISO
  ISSA
  ISSC
  IUAES
  IUSSP
  SID
  WARDA
  WCC
  WCL
  WFTU

NON-MOTORIZED TRANSPORT
TRANSPORT NON-MOTORISE / TRANSPORTE
NO-MOTORIZADO - 10.04.00
- *BT:* MEANS OF TRANSPORT
- *NT:* BICYCLES
- *RT:* ANIMALS
  SHIPS

NON-PROFIT ORGANIZATIONS
ORGANISATIONS NON-LUCRATIVES / ORGANIZACIONES
SIN FINES DE LUCRO - 05.03.07
- *RT:* VOLUNTARY ORGANIZATIONS

NON-RENEWABLE RESOURCES
RESSOURCES NON-RENOUVELABLES / RECURSOS
NO-RENOVABLES - 16.02.02
- *BT:* NATURAL RESOURCES
- *RT:* RENEWABLE RESOURCES

NORDIC COUNCIL
CONSEIL SCANDINAVE / CONSEJO ESCANDINAVO -
01.03.03
- *BT:* EUROPEAN ORGANIZATIONS
  INTERGOVERNMENTAL ORGANIZATIONS
- *RT:* SCANDINAVIA

NORMATIVE PLANNING
- 02.01.02
  USE: DIRECTIVE PLANNING

NORTH
NORD / NORTE - 17.03.03

NORTH AFRICA
AFRIQUE DU NORD / AFRICA DEL NORTE - 01.04.02
- *BT:* AFRICA
- *NT:* ALGERIA
  EGYPT
  LIBYA
  MOROCCO
  SUDAN
  TUNISIA
- *RT:* ARAB COUNTRIES
  MEDITERRANEAN COUNTRIES
  MPCC
  NORTH AFRICAN

NORTH AFRICAN
NORD-AFRICAIN / NORTEAFRICANO - 14.03.02
- *RT:* NORTH AFRICA

NORTH AMERICA
AMERIQUE DU NORD / AMERICA DEL NORTE - 01.04.03
- *BT:* AMERICA
- *NT:* BERMUDA
  CANADA
  GREENLAND
  MEXICO
  ST PIERRE AND MIQUELON
  USA

NORTHERN HEMISPHERE
HEMISPHERE NORD / HEMISFERIO NORTE - 01.04.01

NORWAY
NORVEGE / NORUEGA - 01.04.05
- *BT:* SCANDINAVIA
- *RT:* NORWEGIAN

NORWEGIAN
NORVEGIEN / NORUEGO - 14.03.02
- *RT:* NORWAY

NUCLEAR ENERGY
ENERGIE NUCLEAIRE / ENERGIA NUCLEAR - 08.11.03
- *UF:* ATOMIC ENERGY
  NUCLEAR POWER
- *BT:* ENERGY
- *RT:* CERN
  EURATOM
  IAEA
  INIS
  NUCLEAR ENGINEERING
  NUCLEAR INSTALLATIONS
  NUCLEAR REACTORS
  NUCLEAR WEAPONS
  OECD NEA

NUCLEAR ENGINEERING
TECHNOLOGIE NUCLEAIRE / INGENIERIA NUCLEAR -

NUCLEAR ENGINEERING<CONT>
08.11.03
>   *BT:* ENGINEERING
>   *RT:* NUCLEAR ENERGY
>   NUCLEAR FUEL
>   NUCLEAR REACTORS
>   NUCLEAR WEAPONS

NUCLEAR FUEL
COMBUSTIBLE NUCLEAIRE / COMBUSTIBLE NUCLEAR -
08.11.03
>   *BT:* FUELS
>   *RT:* NUCLEAR ENGINEERING
>   NUCLEAR REACTORS
>   PLUTONIUM
>   URANIUM

NUCLEAR INSTALLATIONS
INSTALLATIONS NUCLEAIRES / INSTALACIONES
NUCLEARES - 08.11.03
SN: ANY REACTOR AND ANY OTHER FACLITY IN WHICH
SUBSTANTIAL AMOUNT OF NUCLEAR SUBSTANCES,
NUCLEAR FUELS OR RADIOISOTOPES ARE
MANUFACTURED, PROCESSED, HANDLED, USED OR
STORED; EXCLUDES NUCLEAR PROPULSED VEHICLES.
>   *BT:* INDUSTRIAL PLANTS
>   *NT:* NUCLEAR POWER PLANTS
>   NUCLEAR REACTORS
>   *RT:* NUCLEAR ENERGY

NUCLEAR POWER
- 08.11.03
>   *USE:* NUCLEAR ENERGY

NUCLEAR POWER PLANTS
CENTRALES NUCLEAIRES / CENTRALES NUCLEARES -
08.11.03
>   *BT:* NUCLEAR INSTALLATIONS
>   POWER PLANTS

NUCLEAR REACTORS
REACTEURS NUCLEAIRES / REACTORES NUCLEARES -
08.11.03
>   *BT:* NUCLEAR INSTALLATIONS
>   *RT:* NUCLEAR ENERGY
>   NUCLEAR ENGINEERING
>   NUCLEAR FUEL

NUCLEAR WAR
GUERRE NUCLEAIRE / GUERRA NUCLEAR - 01.02.07
>   *BT:* WAR
>   *RT:* NUCLEAR WEAPONS

NUCLEAR WEAPONS
ARMES NUCLEAIRES / ARMAS NUCLEARES - 01.02.06
>   *UF:* ATOMIC WEAPONS
>   *BT:* WEAPONS
>   *RT:* NUCLEAR ENERGY
>   NUCLEAR ENGINEERING
>   NUCLEAR WAR

NUPTIALITY
NUPTIALITE / NUPCIALIDAD - 14.02.05
>   *RT:* MARRIAGE

NURSERY SCHOOLS
ECOLES MATERNELLES / JARDINES INFANTILES -
06.04.02
>   *BT:* SCHOOLS
>   *RT:* PRESCHOOL EDUCATION

NURSES
INFIRMIERES / ENFERMERAS - 13.09.10
>   *BT:* PARAMEDICAL PERSONNEL

NUTRIENTS
NUTRIMENTS / SUBSTANCIAS NUTRITIVAS - 15.03.02
>   *NT:* PROTEINS
>   VITAMINS
>   *RT:* NUTRITION

NUTRITION
NUTRITION / NUTRICION - 15.03.02
>   *NT:* ANIMAL NUTRITION
>   HUMAN NUTRITION
>   PLANT NUTRITION
>   *RT:* METABOLISM
>   NUTRIENTS
>   NUTRITION POLICY
>   NUTRITION RESEARCH
>   NUTRITIVE VALUE
>   PROTEINS
>   VITAMINS

NUTRITION POLICY
POLITIQUE NUTRITIONNELLE / POLITICA DE LA
NUTRICION - 15.03.02
>   *BT:* HEALTH POLICY
>   *RT:* NUTRITION

NUTRITION RESEARCH
RECHERCHE NUTRITIONNELLE / INVESTIGACION SOBRE
NUTRICION - 15.03.02
>   *BT:* RESEARCH
>   *RT:* NUTRITION

NUTRITIVE VALUE
VALEUR NUTRITIVE / VALOR NUTRITIVO - 15.03.02
>   *RT:* NUTRITION

OAPEC
OPAEP / OPAEP - 01.03.03
SN: *ORGANIZATION OF ARAB PETROLEUM EXPORTING*
COUNTRIES.
    BT: ARAB ORGANIZATIONS
        INTERGOVERNMENTAL ORGANIZATIONS
    RT: ARAB COUNTRIES
        PETROLEUM

OAS
OEA / OEA - 01.03.03
SN: *ORGANIZATION OF AMERICAN STATES.*
    BT: AMERICAN ORGANIZATIONS
        INTERGOVERNMENTAL ORGANIZATIONS
    NT: PAHO
    RT: AMERICA

OASES
OASIS / OASIS - 17.03.04

OAT
AVOINE / AVENA - 07.07.04

OAU
OUA / OUA - 01.03.03
SN: *ORGANIZATION OF AFRICAN UNITY.*
    BT: AFRICAN ORGANIZATIONS
        INTERGOVERNMENTAL ORGANIZATIONS
    RT: AFRICA

OBSERVATION
OBSERVATION / OBSERVACION - 18.04.00
    UF: DETECTION
    NT: REMOTE SENSING
    RT: DATA COLLECTING
        METHODOLOGY

OBSOLETE EQUIPMENT
MATERIEL HORS D'USAGE / EQUIPO EN DESUSO -
12.05.00
    BT: EQUIPMENT
    RT: TECHNOLOGICAL OBSOLESCENCE

OBSTACLES TO DEVELOPMENT
OBSTACLES AU DEVELOPPEMENT / OBSTACULOS AL
DESARROLLO - 03.02.03
    RT: ECONOMIC AND SOCIAL DEVELOPMENT
        RESISTANCE TO CHANGE

OCAM
OCAM / OCAM - 01.03.03
SN: *COMMON AFRO-MALAGASY ORGANIZATION.*
    BT: AFRICAN ORGANIZATIONS
        INTERGOVERNMENTAL ORGANIZATIONS
    RT: AFRICA
        MADAGASCAR

OCAS
OCAS / ODECA - 01.03.03
SN: *ORGANIZATION OF CENTRAL AMERICAN STATES.*
    BT: AMERICAN ORGANIZATIONS
        INTERGOVERNMENTAL ORGANIZATIONS
    RT: CENTRAL AMERICA

OCCUPATIONAL ACCIDENTS
ACCIDENTS DU TRAVAIL / ACCIDENTES DE TRABAJO -
13.04.00
    BT: ACCIDENTS
    RT: EMPLOYMENT INJURIES BENEFITS
        OCCUPATIONS

OCCUPATIONAL CHOICE
CHOIX D'UNE PROFESSION / ELECCION DE UNA
OCUPACION - 13.02.01
    UF: VOCATIONAL CHOICE
    RT: OCCUPATIONS
        VOCATIONAL GUIDANCE

OCCUPATIONAL DISEASES
MALADIES PROFESSIONNELLES / ENFERMEDADES
OCUPACIONALES - 13.04.00
SN: *THE UNHEALTHY RESULTS ON WORKERS OF*
PARTICULAR OCCUPATIONAL ACTIVITIES AND WORK
ENVIRONMENTS.
    UF: STRESS-RELATED DISEASES
    BT: DISEASES
    NT: PNEUMOCONIOSIS
    RT: OCCUPATIONS

OCCUPATIONAL HYGIENE
HYGIENE DU TRAVAIL / HIGIENE DEL TRABAJO -
13.04.00
    BT: HYGIENE

OCCUPATIONAL MEDICINE
MEDECINE DU TRAVAIL / MEDICINA LABORAL -
13.04.00
SN: *IS CONCERNED WITH HEALTH IN ITS RELATION TO*
WORK AND THE WORKING ENVIRONMENT.
    BT: MEDICINE
    RT: OCCUPATIONS

OCCUPATIONAL MOBILITY
MOBILITE PROFESSIONNELLE / MOVILIDAD PROFESIONAL
- 13.02.01
    BT: SOCIAL MOBILITY
    RT: OCCUPATIONS

OCCUPATIONAL MORTALITY
MORTALITE PROFESSIONNELLE / MORTALIDAD
OCUPACIONAL - 14.06.00
    BT: MORTALITY

OCCUPATIONAL ORGANIZATIONS
ORGANISATIONS PROFESSIONNELLES / ORGANIZACIONES
PROFESIONALES - 13.06.00
SN: *ORGANIZED SOCIETIES OF PROFESSIONAL WORKERS*
WHICH ARE NOT CONSIDERED TO BE TRADE UNIONS.
    UF: PROFESSIONAL ASSOCIATIONS
    BT: ASSOCIATIONS
    NT: TEACHER ASSOCIATIONS
    RT: CORPORATISM
        OCCUPATIONS

OCCUPATIONAL QUALIFICATION
QUALIFICATION PROFESSIONNELLE / CALIFICACION
OCUPACIONAL - 13.02.01

144

OCCUPATIONAL QUALIFICATION<CONT>
SN: THE SPECIAL KNOWLEDGE AND SKILLS WHICH ARE
REQUIRED OF THE EMPLOYEE TO CARRY OUT THE
DUTIES ATTACHING TO A PARTICULAR JOB.
    BT: QUALIFICATIONS
    NT: JOB REQUIREMENTS
    RT: MASTERCRAFTSMEN
        OCCUPATIONS
        SEMI-SKILLED WORKERS
        SERVICE CERTIFICATE
        SKILLED WORKERS
        UNSKILLED WORKERS

OCCUPATIONAL SAFETY
SECURITE DU TRAVAIL / SEGURIDAD LABORAL -
13.04.00
SN: REFERS TO POLICIES AND PRACTICES INTENDED TO
PREVENT AND REDUCE INDUSTRIAL ACCIDENTS AND
DISEASES BY MEANS OF TRAINING, REGULATIONS,
ETC.
    UF: ACCIDENT PREVENTION
    BT: SAFETY
    RT: OCCUPATIONS
        SAFETY DEVICES

OCCUPATIONAL SATISFACTION
- 13.03.04
    USE: JOB SATISFACTION

OCCUPATIONAL STRUCTURE
STRUCTURE DE L'EMPLOI / ESTRUCTURA DEL EMPLEO -
13.01.03
    RT: EMPLOYMENT

OCCUPATIONAL TRAINING
- 06.03.07
    USE: VOCATIONAL TRAINING

OCCUPATIONS
PROFESSIONS / OCUPACIONES - 13.09.01
    RT: OCCUPATIONAL ACCIDENTS
        OCCUPATIONAL CHOICE
        OCCUPATIONAL DISEASES
        OCCUPATIONAL MEDICINE
        OCCUPATIONAL MOBILITY
        OCCUPATIONAL ORGANIZATIONS
        OCCUPATIONAL QUALIFICATION
        OCCUPATIONAL SAFETY
        TRANSITION FROM SCHOOL TO WORK
        VOCATIONAL REHABILITATION
        VOCATIONAL TRAINING

OCEANIA
OCEANIE / OCEANIA - 01.04.07
    UF: MELANESIA
        MICRONESIA
        PACIFIC ISLANDS
        POLYNESIA

OCEANIA<CONT>
    NT: AUSTRALIA
        FIJI
        NAURU
        NEW ZEALAND
        PACIFIC ISLANDS AUS
        PACIFIC ISLANDS FR
        PACIFIC ISLANDS NZ
        PACIFIC ISLANDS UK
        PACIFIC ISLANDS USA
        SAMOA
        TONGA

OCEANOGRAPHY
OCEANOGRAPHIE / OCEANOGRAFIA - 17.06.00
    BT: EARTH SCIENCES
    RT: HYDROLOGY
        PHYSICAL GEOGRAPHY

OECD
OCDE / OCDE - 01.03.03
SN: ORGANIZATION FOR ECONOMIC COOPERATION AND
DEVELOPMENT.
    BT: INTERGOVERNMENTAL ORGANIZATIONS
    NT: OECD DAC
        OECD DC
        OECD IEA
        OECD NEA
    RT: DEVELOPED COUNTRIES
        OECD COUNTRIES

OECD COUNTRIES
PAYS DE L'OCDE / PAISES DE LA OCDE - 01.03.03
    RT: OECD

OECD DAC
OCDE CAD / OCDE CAD - 01.03.03
SN: OECD, DEVELOPMENT ASSISTANCE COMMITTEE.
    BT: OECD
    RT: AID COORDINATION
        DEVELOPMENT AID

OECD DC
OCDE CD / OCDE CD - 01.03.03
SN: OECD DEVELOPMENT CENTRE.
    BT: DEVELOPMENT CENTRES
        OECD

OECD IEA
OCDE AIE / OCDE AIE - 01.03.03
SN: OECD, INTERNATIONAL ENERGY AGENCY.
    BT: OECD
    RT: ENERGY

OECD NEA
OCDE AEN / OCDE AEN - 01.03.03
SN: OECD NUCLEAR ENERGY AGENCY.
    BT: OECD
    RT: NUCLEAR ENERGY

OFFENDERS
CONTREVENANTS / TRANSGRESORES - 02.04.02
    RT: CRIMES
        DELINQUENCY

OFFICE MACHINES
MACHINES DE BUREAU / MAQUINAS DE OFICINA -
08.14.06

OFFICE WORKERS
EMPLOYES DE BUREAU / EMPLEADOS DE OFICINA -
13.09.07
    UF: CLERICAL WORKERS
    BT: EMPLOYEES
    NT: ACCOUNTANTS

OFFICIAL DOCUMENTS
DOCUMENTS OFFICIELS / DOCUMENTOS OFICIALES -
19.02.01
    BT: DOCUMENTS
    RT: GOVERNMENT

OFFICIAL LANGUAGES
LANGUES OFFICIELLES / LENGUAS OFICIALES -
05.06.01
    BT: LANGUAGES

OFFPRINTS
TIRES A PART / SEPARATAS - 19.02.04

OIL CROPS
CULTURES OLEAGINEUSES / CULTIVOS OLEAGINOSOS -
07.07.02
    BT: INDUSTRIAL CROPS
    NT: OIL PALMS
        OILSEEDS
        OLIVES
    RT: VEGETABLE OILS

OIL PALMS
PALMIERS A HUILE / PALMERAS ACEITERAS - 07.07.05
    BT: OIL CROPS
        TREES
    RT: PALM OIL

OILS AND FATS
MATIERES GRASSES / ACEITES Y GRASAS - 08.06.06
    NT: ANIMAL OILS
        ESSENTIAL OILS
        FATS
        MARGARINE
        VEGETABLE OILS

OILSEEDS
GRAINES OLEAGINEUSES / SEMILLAS OLEAGINOSAS -
07.07.05
    BT: OIL CROPS
        SEEDS
    NT: COTTON
        FLAX
        GROUNDNUTS
        RAPE
        SOYBEANS
    RT: VEGETABLE OILS

OLD AGE
VIEILLESSE / VEJEZ - 14.02.02
    BT: AGE GROUPS

OLD AGE\<CONT\>
    RT: AGED
        AGEING
        OLD AGE BENEFITS

OLD AGE BENEFITS
ALLOCATIONS VIEILLESSE / SUBSIDIOS DE VEJEZ -
02.03.02
    BT: PENSION SCHEMES
        SOCIAL SECURITY
    RT: AGED
        OLD AGE
        RETIREMENT PENSIONS

OLDER PEOPLE
- 14.02.02
    USE: AGED

OLDER WORKERS
TRAVAILLEURS AGES / TRABAJADORES DE EDAD
AVANZADA - 13.09.02
    BT: AGED
        WORKERS

OLIVE OIL
HUILE D'OLIVE / ACEITE DE OLIVA - 08.06.06
    BT: EDIBLE OILS
        VEGETABLE OILS
    RT: OLIVES

OLIVES
OLIVES / ACEITUNAS - 07.07.05
    BT: FRUITS
        OIL CROPS
    RT: OLIVE OIL

OMAN
OMAN / OMAN - 01.04.06
    BT: ARAB COUNTRIES
        MIDDLE EAST
    RT: OMANI

OMANI
OMANAIS / OMANI - 14.03.02
    RT: OMAN

OMBUDSMAN
OMBUDSMAN / OMBUDSMAN - 04.03.02
*SN: USE FOR NATIONAL MECHANISMS INVOLVING THE
    APPOINTMENT OF AN ADMINISTRATOR TO EXAMINE
    COMPLAINTS RELATING TO UNFAIR DECISIONS
    TAKEN WITHIN THE FRAMEWORK OF PUBLIC
    ADMINISTRATION.*
    RT: CIVIL LIBERTIES
        PUBLIC ADMINISTRATION

ON-THE-JOB TRAINING
- 06.03.07
    USE: IN-PLANT TRAINING

ONCHOCERCIASIS
ONCHOCERCOSE / ONCHOCERCOSIS - 15.04.02
*SN: CAUSED BY NEMATODE SPREAD BY BLACKFLY; MAY
    RESULT IN BLINDNESS.*
    UF: RIVER BLINDNESS

ONCHOCERCIASIS<CONT>
- *BT:* PARASITIC DISEASES
  TROPICAL DISEASES
- *RT:* BLINDNESS

ONIONS
OIGNONS / CEBOLLAS - 07.07.06
- *BT:* VEGETABLES

OPEC
OPEP / OPEP - 01.03.03
*SN: ORGANIZATION OF PETROLEUM EXPORTING
COUNTRIES.*
- *BT:* INTERGOVERNMENTAL ORGANIZATIONS
- *RT:* PETRODOLLARS
  PETROLEUM

OPERATIONAL RESEARCH
**RECHERCHE OPERATIONNELLE / INVESTIGACION
OPERATIVA - 12.04.00**
*SN: APPLICATION OF SCIENTIFIC METHOD TO PROBLEMS
INVOLVING THE OPERATION OF A SYSTEM SO AS TO
PROVIDE THOSE IN CONTROL OF THE SYSTEM WITH
OPTIMUM SOLUTIONS TO THE PROBLEM ON THE
BASIS OF WHICH DECISIONS MAY BE TAKEN.*
- *BT:* MANAGEMENT TECHNIQUES
  RESEARCH METHODS
- *NT:* SCENARIOS

OPINION
OPINION / OPINION - 05.03.02
- *RT:* BELIEF
  PUBLIC OPINION

OPIUM
OPIUM / OPIO - 07.07.09
- *BT:* INDUSTRIAL CROPS
  NARCOTICS

OPTICAL INDUSTRY
**INDUSTRIE OPTIQUE / FABRICACION DE INSTRUMENTOS
OPTICOS - 08.14.08**
- *BT:* INSTRUMENTATION INDUSTRY

OPTICAL INSTRUMENTS
**INSTRUMENTS D'OPTIQUE / INSTRUMENTOS OPTICOS -
08.14.08**
- *BT:* PRECISION INSTRUMENTS

OPTICS
OPTIQUE / OPTICA - 08.14.08
- *BT:* PHYSICS

ORAL CONTRACEPTIVES
**CONTRACEPTIFS ORAUX / ANTICONCEPTIVOS ORALES -
14.05.02**
- *BT:* CONTRACEPTIVES

ORES
- 08.13.00
- *USE:* MINERALS

ORGANIC CHEMISTRY
CHIMIE ORGANIQUE / QUIMICA ORGANICA - 08.12.02
- *BT:* CHEMISTRY

ORGANIZATION OF RESEARCH
**ORGANISATION DE LA RECHERCHE / ORGANIZACION DE
LA INVESTIGACION - 18.02.00**
- *RT:* RESEARCH
  RESEARCH POLICY

ORPHANAGES
ORPHELINATS / ORFELINATOS - 02.05.03
- *BT:* SOCIAL SERVICES
- *RT:* CHILDREN

OUT-OF-SCHOOL EDUCATION
**EDUCATION EXTRA-SCOLAIRE / EDUCACION
EXTRAESCOLAR - 06.03.02**
- *RT:* EDUCATIONAL RADIO
  EDUCATIONAL SYSTEMS
  EDUCATIONAL TELEVISION
  NON-FORMAL EDUCATION

OUTER SPACE
**ESPACE COSMIQUE / ESPACIO EXTRATERRESTRE -
17.07.00**
- *BT:* SPACE
- *RT:* AEROSPACE INDUSTRY
  SPACE SCIENCES

OVEREMPLOYMENT
- 13.01.02
- *USE:* LABOUR SHORTAGE

OVEREXPLOITATION
SUREXPLOITATION / SOBREEXPLOTACION - 16.02.01
- *RT:* EXPLOITABILITY
  RESOURCES DEPLETION
  RESOURCES EXPLOITATION

OVERHEAD COSTS
FRAIS GENERAUX / GASTOS GENERALES - 12.09.00
- *BT:* COSTS

OVERPOPULATION
SURPEUPLEMENT / SUPERPOBLACION - 14.01.02
- *RT:* POPULATION

OVERPRODUCTION
SURPRODUCTION / SOBREPRODUCCION - 12.07.01
- *BT:* PRODUCTION
- *RT:* PRODUCTION CAPACITY
  SURPLUSES

OVERSEAS TERRITORIES
**TERRITOIRES D'OUTRE-MER / TERRITORIOS DE
ULTRAMAR - 01.02.03**

OVERTIME
HEURES SUPPLEMENTAIRES / HORAS EXTRAS - 13.03.03

OVIDAE
OVIDES / OVIDOS - 07.09.01
- *BT:* RUMINANTS
- *NT:* SHEEP

OWNERSHIP
PROPRIETE / PROPIEDAD - 03.03.05

OWNERSHIP\<CONT>
- *NT:* COLLECTIVE OWNERSHIP
  FOREIGN OWNERSHIP
  LAND OWNERSHIP
  PRIVATE OWNERSHIP
  PUBLIC OWNERSHIP

OXYGEN
OXYGENE / OXIGENO - 08.12.04
- *RT:* OZONE

OYSTER CULTURE
OSTREICULTURE / OSTRICULTURA - 07.10.03
- *BT:* AQUACULTURE
- *RT:* MOLLUSCS

OZONE
OZONE / OZONO - 08.12.04
- *RT:* OXYGEN

PACIFIC ISLANDS
- 01.04.07
- *USE:* OCEANIA

PACIFIC ISLANDS AUS
ILES DU PACIFIQUE AUS / ISLAS DEL PACIFICO AUS - 01.04.07
- *BT:* OCEANIA
- *NT:* PAPUA NEW GUINEA
- *RT:* AUSTRALIA

PACIFIC ISLANDS FR
ILES DU PACIFIQUE FR / ISLAS DEL PACIFICO FR - 01.04.07
- *BT:* OCEANIA
- *NT:* FRENCH POLYNESIA
  NEW CALEDONIA
- *RT:* FRANCE

PACIFIC ISLANDS NZ
ILES DU PACIFIQUE NZ / ISLAS DEL PACIFICO NZ - 01.04.07
- *BT:* OCEANIA
- *RT:* NEW ZEALAND

PACIFIC ISLANDS UK
ILES DU PACIFIQUE RU / ISLAS DEL PACIFICO RU - 01.04.07
- *BT:* OCEANIA
- *NT:* NEW HEBRIDES
- *RT:* UNITED KINGDOM

PACIFIC ISLANDS USA
ILES DU PACIFIQUE EU / ISLAS DEL PACIFICO EU - 01.04.07
- *SN: INCLUDES PACIFIC ISLAND TRUST TERRITORIES CONTROLLED BY USA.*
- *BT:* OCEANIA
- *NT:* NEW HEBRIDES
- *RT:* USA

PACIFIC OCEAN
OCEAN PACIFIQUE / OCEANO PACIFICO - 17.06.00
- *RT:* PACIFIC REGION

PACIFIC REGION
REGION DU PACIFIQUE / REGION DEL PACIFICO - 01.04.07
- *RT:* ADIPA
  ASPAC
  ESCAP
  PACIFIC OCEAN
  SPC

PACKAGING
EMBALLAGE / EMBALAJE - 10.06.00
- *RT:* BAGS
  BOXES
  CANNING INDUSTRY
  LABELLING

PAHO
OPS / OPS - 01.03.03
- *SN: PAN AMERICAN HEALTH ORGANIZATION.*
- *BT:* OAS

PAHO<CONT>
    RT: AMERICA
        HEALTH

PAINTS AND VARNISHES
PEINTURES ET VERNIS / PINTURAS Y BARNICES -
08.12.08
    RT: COATING

PAKISTAN
PAKISTAN / PAKISTAN - 01.04.04
    BT: SOUTH ASIA
        SOUTH EAST ASIA
    RT: PAKISTANI

PAKISTANI
PAKISTANAIS / PAKISTANI - 14.03.02
    RT: PAKISTAN

PALM OIL
HUILE DE PALME / ACEITE DE PALMA - 08.06.06
    BT: EDIBLE OILS
        VEGETABLE OILS
    RT: OIL PALMS

PAMPA
PAMPA / PAMPA - 17.03.04

PANAMA
PANAMA / PANAMA - 01.04.03
    BT: CENTRAL AMERICA
    RT: PANAMANIAN

PANAMA CANAL ZONE
ZONE DU CANAL DE PANAMA / ZONA DEL CANAL DE
PANAMA - 01.04.03
    BT: CENTRAL AMERICA

PANAMANIAN
PANAMEEN / PANAMENO - 14.03.02
    RT: PANAMA

PAPER
PAPIER / PAPEL - 08.07.02
    BT: WOOD PRODUCTS
    RT: PULP AND PAPER INDUSTRY

PAPUA NEW GUINEA
PAPOUASIE-NOUVELLE-GUINEE / PAPUA NUEVA GUINEA -
01.04.07
    BT: PACIFIC ISLANDS AUS

PARAGUAY
PARAGUAY / PARAGUAY - 01.04.03
    BT: LATIN AMERICA
        SOUTH AMERICA
    RT: PARAGUAYAN

PARAGUAYAN
PARAGUAYEN / PARAGUAYO - 14.03.02
    RT: PARAGUAY

PARAMEDICAL PERSONNEL
PERSONNEL PARAMEDICAL / PERSONAL PARAMEDICO -

PARAMEDICAL PERSONNEL<CONT>
13.09.10
    UF: AUXILIARY HEALTH WORKERS
    NT: BAREFOOT DOCTORS
        MIDWIVES
        NURSES
        SOCIAL WORKERS
    RT: MEDICAL PERSONNEL

PARASITES
PARASITES / PARASITOS - 15.01.02
    RT: PARASITIC DISEASES
        PARASITOLOGY
        PEST CONTROL

PARASITIC DISEASES
MALADIES PARASITAIRES / ENFERMEDADES
PARASITARIAS - 15.04.02
    BT: INFECTIOUS DISEASES
    NT: FILARIASIS
        MALARIA
        ONCHOCERCIASIS
        SCHISTOSOMIASIS
        TRYPANOSOMIASIS
    RT: PARASITES

PARASITOLOGY
PARASITOLOGIE / PARASITOLOGIA - 15.01.01
    RT: PARASITES

PARENTS
PARENTS / PADRES - 14.02.04
    NT: FATHER
        MOTHER

PARLIAMENT
PARLEMENT / PARLAMENTO - 04.03.01
    RT: APU
        LEGISLATION
        PARLIAMENTARY PROCEDURE

PARLIAMENTARY PROCEDURE
PROCEDURE PARLEMENTAIRE / PRACTICA PARLAMENTARIA
- 04.03.01
    RT: PARLIAMENT

PART TIME
TEMPS PARTIEL / TIEMPO PARCIAL - 13.03.03
    RT: PART TIME EMPLOYMENT

PART TIME EMPLOYMENT
EMPLOI A TEMPS PARTIEL / EMPLEO A TIEMPO PARCIAL
- 13.01.03
    BT: EMPLOYMENT
    RT: PART TIME

PARTICIPATION IN CULTURAL LIFE
PARTICIPATION A LA VIE CULTURELLE /
PARTICIPACION EN LA VIDA CULTURAL - 05.02.02
    RT: SOCIAL PARTICIPATION

PARTICLE BOARDS
PANNEAUX DE PARTICULES / MADERA PRENSADA -

PARTICLE BOARDS<CONT>
08.07.01
    BT: CONSTRUCTION MATERIALS
        WOOD PRODUCTS

PASSENGER RATE
TARIF VOYAGEURS / TARIFA DE PASAJEROS - 10.09.00
    RT: PASSENGERS

PASSENGERS
VOYAGEURS / PASAJEROS - 10.02.00
    RT: PASSENGER RATE
        TRAVELS

PASTEURIZATION
PASTEURISATION / PASTEURIZACION - 08.06.02
    BT: FOOD STERILIZATION

PATENT LAW
DROIT DES BREVETS / DERECHO DE PATENTES -
04.01.02
    BT: LAW
    RT: INDUSTRIAL PROPERTY
        INTELLECTUAL PROPERTY
        PATENTS

PATENTS
BREVETS / PATENTES - 08.05.00
    BT: INDUSTRIAL PROPERTY
    RT: INDUSTRIAL ESPIONAGE
        INDUSTRIAL INFORMATION
        INVENTIONS
        LICENSING
        PATENT LAW
        TRADE MARKS

PATHOLOGY
- 15.04.01
    USE: DISEASES

PATIENTS
MALADES / ENFERMOS - 15.04.05
    RT: DISEASES
        PHYSICALLY HANDICAPPED
        WOUNDED

PAYMENT AGREEMENTS
ACCORDS DE PAIEMENT / CONVENIOS DE PAGOS -
11.03.02
    BT: ECONOMIC AGREEMENTS
    RT: INTERNATIONAL PAYMENTS

PAYMENT BY RESULT
REMUNERATION AU RENDEMENT / PAGO A DESTAJO -
13.07.00
*SN: PAYMENT IS MADE ACCORDING TO THE QUANTITY OF
    GOODS PRODUCED.*
    UF: PIECE WORK
    BT: WAGE PAYMENT SYSTEMS

PAYMENT SYSTEMS
SYSTEMES DE PAIEMENT / SISTEMAS DE PAGOS -

PAYMENT SYSTEMS<CONT>
11.03.02
    RT: INTERNATIONAL PAYMENTS

PAYROLL TAX
IMPOT SUR LES SALAIRES / IMPUESTO A LOS SALARIOS
- 11.01.02
*SN: PAID BY EMPLOYERS ACCORDING TO TOTAL AMOUNT
    OF WAGES.*
    BT: TAXES
    RT: WAGES

PEACE
PAIX / PAZ - 01.02.07
    RT: ARMISTICE
        PEACE KEEPING
        PEACE RESEARCH
        PEACEFUL COEXISTENCE

PEACE CORPS
VOLONTAIRES DE LA PAIX / CUERPOS DE PAZ -
01.01.08
*SN: USE IN CONNECTION WITH OPERATIONS OF THE
    PEACE CORPS OF THE USA, AND OF SIMILAR
    ORGANIZATIONS EXISTING ELSEWHERE, SPECIFYING
    AS NECESSARY.*

PEACE KEEPING
MAINTIEN DE LA PAIX / MANTENIMIENTO DE LA PAZ -
01.02.07
    RT: PEACE

PEACE RESEARCH
RECHERCHE SUR LA PAIX / INVESTIGACION SOBRE LA
PAZ - 01.02.07
    BT: RESEARCH
    RT: PEACE

PEACEFUL COEXISTENCE
COEXISTENCE PACIFIQUE / COEXISTENCIA PACIFICA -
01.02.07
    RT: DETENTE
        INTERNATIONAL RELATIONS
        PEACE

PEANUT OIL
HUILE D'ARACHIDE / ACEITE DE CACAHUATE -
08.06.06
    BT: EDIBLE OILS
        VEGETABLE OILS
    RT: GROUNDNUTS

PEARS
POIRES / PERAS - 07.07.05
    BT: FRUITS

PEASANT MOVEMENTS
MOUVEMENTS PAYSANS / MOVIMIENTOS CAMPESINOS -
05.03.07
    BT: SOCIAL MOVEMENTS
    RT: FARMERS
        PEASANTS

PEASANTS
PAYSANS / CAMPESINOS - 05.03.05
    BT: AGRICULTURAL POPULATION
    RT: FARMERS
        PEASANT MOVEMENTS

PEDAGOGY
- 06.01.00
    USE: SCIENCES OF EDUCATION

PEDESTRIANS
PIETONS / PEATONES - 10.02.00

PEDIATRICIANS
PEDIATRES / PEDIATRAS - 13.09.10
    BT: PHYSICIANS
    RT: CHILD CARE
        CHILD DEVELOPMENT

PEDIATRICS
PEDIATRIE / PEDIATRIA - 15.04.06
    BT: MEDICINE
    RT: CHILD DEVELOPMENT

PEDOLOGY
- 17.04.04
    USE: SOIL SCIENCES

PEER TEACHING
ENSEIGNEMENT MUTUEL / ENSENANZA MUTUA - 06.05.02
    BT: TEACHING

PENAL SANCTIONS
SANCTIONS PENALES / SANCIONES PENALES - 02.04.03
    UF: LAW ENFORCEMENT
    NT: CAPITAL PUNISHMENT
        FORCED LABOUR
        PRISONS
    RT: CRIME PREVENTION
        CRIMES
        CRIMINAL LAW
        DELINQUENCY
        SOCIAL CONTROL

PENSION FUNDS
CAISSES DE RETRAITE / CAJAS DE JUBILACIONES - 11.02.02
    BT: FINANCIAL INSTITUTIONS
    RT: PENSION SCHEMES

PENSION SCHEMES
PLANS DE RETRAITE / SISTEMAS DE JUBILACION - 02.03.02
    NT: OLD AGE BENEFITS
    RT: PENSION FUNDS
        RETIREMENT PENSIONS

PEPPER
POIVRE / PIMIENTA - 07.07.09
    BT: SPICES

PERFORMERS
ARTISTES INTERPRETES / ARTISTAS INTERPRETES -

PERFORMERS<CONT>
13.09.09
    RT: DRAMATIC ART

PERFORMING ARTS
ARTS DU SPECTACLE / ARTES DEL ESPECTACULO - 05.05.03
    BT: ARTS
    NT: DRAMATIC ART

PERFUMES
PARFUMS / PERFUMES - 08.12.08
    BT: TOILET PREPARATIONS
    RT: ESSENTIAL OILS

PERIODICALS
PERIODIQUES / PUBLICACIONES PERIODICAS - 19.02.06
    UF: JOURNAL
        MAGAZINE
    BT: SERIALS
    NT: DAILY
        MONTHLY
        QUARTERLY
        WEEKLY
        YEARBOOK
    RT: ARTICLE
        PRESS

PERISHABLE FOOD
ALIMENTS PERISSABLES / ALIMENTOS PERECEDEROS - 15.03.01
    BT: FOOD
    RT: FOOD SPOILAGE

PERMANENT EDUCATION
- 06.03.05
    USE: LIFE-LONG EDUCATION

PERSIAN GULF STATES
ETATS DU GOLFE PERSIQUE / ESTADOS DEL GOLFO PERSICO - 01.04.06
    BT: ARAB COUNTRIES
        MIDDLE EAST
    NT: BAHRAIN
        KUWAIT
        QATAR
        UNITED ARAB EMIRATES

PERSONALITY
PERSONNALITE / PERSONALIDAD - 05.03.01
    RT: ALIENATION
        INDIVIDUALS
        PERSONALITY DEVELOPMENT

PERSONALITY DEVELOPMENT
DEVELOPPEMENT DE LA PERSONNALITE / DESARROLLO DE LA PERSONALIDAD - 05.03.01
    RT: PERSONALITY

PERSONNEL ADMINISTRATION
- 13.02.02
    USE: PERSONNEL MANAGEMENT

PERSONNEL MANAGEMENT
GESTION DU PERSONNEL / ADMINISTRACION DEL
PERSONAL - 13.02.02
- *UF:* PERSONNEL ADMINISTRATION
- *BT:* MANAGEMENT
- *RT:* DEMOTION
  DISMISSAL
  JOB CLASSIFICATION
  JOB DESCRIPTION
  JOB EVALUATION
  LABOUR INSPECTION
  LAYOFF
  PROMOTION
  RECRUITMENT
  STAFF REGULATION
  WORK ORGANIZATION

PERT
- 12.04.00
- *USE:* NETWORK ANALYSIS

PERU
PEROU / PERU - 01.04.03
- *BT:* LATIN AMERICA
  SOUTH AMERICA
- *RT:* PERUVIAN

PERUVIAN
PERUVIEN / PERUANO - 14.03.02
- *RT:* PERU

PEST CONTROL
LUTTE ANTI-PARASITE / CONTROL DE PLAGAS -
16.04.01
- *BT:* ENVIRONMENTAL ENGINEERING
- *RT:* INSECT PESTS
  PARASITES
  PESTICIDES
  PESTS OF ANIMALS
  PESTS OF PLANTS

PESTICIDE RESIDUES
RESIDUS DE PESTICIDES / RESIDUOS DE PESTICIDAS -
08.12.05
- *RT:* PESTICIDES

PESTICIDES
PESTICIDES / PESTICIDAS - 08.12.05
- *NT:* FUNGICIDES
  HERBICIDES
  INSECTICIDES
- *RT:* PEST CONTROL
  PESTICIDE RESIDUES
  SULPHATES

PESTS OF ANIMALS
PARASITES DES ANIMAUX / PARASITOS DE ANIMALES -
16.03.03
- *RT:* ANIMAL DISEASES
  PEST CONTROL

PESTS OF PLANTS
ENNEMIS DES CULTURES / PARASITOS DE PLANTAS -

PESTS OF PLANTS\<CONT\>
16.03.03
- *RT:* PEST CONTROL
  PLANT DISEASES

PETROCHEMICAL INDUSTRY
INDUSTRIE PETROCHIMIQUE / INDUSTRIA PETROQUIMICA
- 08.12.01
- *BT:* CHEMICAL INDUSTRY
  PETROLEUM INDUSTRY
- *RT:* PETROCHEMICALS
  PETROCHEMISTRY

PETROCHEMICALS
PRODUITS PETROCHIMIQUES / PRODUCTOS
PETROQUIMICOS - 08.12.04
- *BT:* CHEMICALS
- *RT:* PETROCHEMICAL INDUSTRY
  PETROCHEMISTRY
  PETROLEUM PRODUCTS

PETROCHEMISTRY
PETROCHIMIE / PETROQUIMICA - 08.12.02
- *BT:* CHEMISTRY
- *RT:* PETROCHEMICAL INDUSTRY
  PETROCHEMICALS

PETRODOLLARS
PETRODOLLARS / PETRODOLARES - 11.03.01
- *BT:* CURRENCIES
- *RT:* MONETARY RELATIONS
  OPEC
  PETROLEUM

PETROL
ESSENCE / GASOLINA - 08.11.06
- *UF:* GASOLINE
- *BT:* ENGINE FUELS
- *RT:* PETROL ENGINES

PETROL ENGINES
MOTEURS A ESSENCE / MOTORES A GASOLINA -
08.14.06
- *BT:* ENGINES
- *RT:* PETROL

PETROLEUM
PETROLE / PETROLEO - 08.11.06
- *BT:* ENERGY SOURCES
  MINERAL OILS
- *RT:* NATURAL GAS
  OAPEC
  OPEC
  PETRODOLLARS
  PETROLEUM ENGINEERING
  PETROLEUM EXTRACTION
  PETROLEUM INDUSTRY
  PETROLEUM PRODUCTS
  PETROLEUM REFINERIES
  PETROLEUM RESOURCES
  TANKERS

PETROLEUM ENGINEERING
TECHNOLOGIE PETROLIERE / TECNOLOGIA DEL PETROLEO

PETROLEUM ENGINEERING<CONT>
- 08.11.06
>   BT: ENGINEERING
>   RT: PETROLEUM
>   PETROLEUM INDUSTRY

PETROLEUM EXTRACTION
EXTRACTION DU PETROLE / EXTRACCION PETROLERA -
08.13.00
>   RT: PETROLEUM
>   PETROLEUM INDUSTRY

PETROLEUM INDUSTRY
INDUSTRIE PETROLIERE / INDUSTRIA DEL PETROLEO -
08.11.06
>   BT: INDUSTRIAL SECTOR
>   NT: PETROCHEMICAL INDUSTRY
>   RT: PETROLEUM
>   PETROLEUM ENGINEERING
>   PETROLEUM EXTRACTION
>   PETROLEUM PRODUCTS
>   PETROLEUM REFINERIES

PETROLEUM PRODUCTS
PRODUITS PETROLIERS / PRODUCTOS PETROLEROS -
08.11.06
>   RT: HYDROCARBONS
>   LUBRICANTS
>   PETROCHEMICALS
>   PETROLEUM
>   PETROLEUM INDUSTRY

PETROLEUM REFINERIES
RAFFINERIES DE PETROLE / REFINERIAS DE PETROLEO
- 08.11.06
>   RT: PETROLEUM
>   PETROLEUM INDUSTRY
>   REFINING

PETROLEUM RESOURCES
RESSOURCES PETROLIERES / RECURSOS PETROLIFEROS -
16.02.02
>   BT: ENERGY RESOURCES
>   RT: PETROLEUM

PHARMACEUTICAL INDUSTRY
INDUSTRIE PHARMACEUTIQUE / INDUSTRIA
FARMACEUTICA - 08.12.06
>   BT: CHEMICAL INDUSTRY
>   RT: PHARMACEUTICALS
>   PHARMACOLOGY

PHARMACEUTICALS
PRODUITS PHARMACEUTIQUES / PRODUCTOS
FARMACEUTICOS - 08.12.06
>   BT: CHEMICALS
>   NT: DRUGS
>   NARCOTICS
>   SERUMS
>   VACCINES

PHARMACEUTICALS<CONT>
>   RT: CONTRACEPTIVES
>   PHARMACEUTICAL INDUSTRY
>   PHARMACOLOGY
>   POISONS

PHARMACISTS
PHARMACIENS / QUIMICOS FARMACEUTICOS - 13.09.10
>   BT: MEDICAL PERSONNEL

PHARMACOLOGY
PHARMACOLOGIE / FARMACOLOGIA - 15.05.00
>   BT: MEDICAL SCIENCES
>   RT: MEDICINE
>   PHARMACEUTICAL INDUSTRY
>   PHARMACEUTICALS

PHILIPPINES
PHILIPPINES / FILIPINAS - 01.04.04
>   BT: SOUTH EAST ASIA
>   RT: FILIPINO

PHILOSOPHY
PHILOSOPHIE / FILOSOFIA - 05.01.01
>   NT: AESTHETICS
>   PHILOSOPHY OF EDUCATION
>   RT: LOGIC

PHILOSOPHY OF EDUCATION
PHILOSOPHIE DE L'EDUCATION / FILOSOFIA DE LA
EDUCACION - 06.01.00
>   BT: PHILOSOPHY
>   SCIENCES OF EDUCATION
>   RT: EDUCATIONAL THEORY

PHOSPHATES
PHOSPHATES / FOSFATOS - 08.12.04
>   RT: CHEMICAL FERTILIZERS

PHOSPHORUS
PHOSPHORE / FOSFORO - 08.12.04

PHOTOGRAMMETRY
PHOTOGRAMMETRIE / FOTOGRAMETRIA - 18.07.00
>   RT: AERIAL SURVEYS
>   MEASUREMENT

PHOTOGRAPHS
PHOTOS / FOTOS - 19.02.04
>   BT: AUDIOVISUAL MATERIALS
>   ILLUSTRATIONS
>   RT: SLIDES

PHYSICAL CAPACITY
CAPACITE PHYSIQUE / CAPACIDAD FISICA - 13.02.01
>   RT: PHYSICAL WORK

PHYSICAL EDUCATION
EDUCATION PHYSIQUE / EDUCACION FISICA - 06.03.04
>   BT: BASIC EDUCATION
>   RT: SPORT

PHYSICAL ENVIRONMENT
ENVIRONNEMENT PHYSIQUE / MEDIO AMBIENTE FISICO -

PHYSICAL ENVIRONMENT<CONT>
16.01.02
    UF: NATURAL ENVIRONMENT
    BT: ENVIRONMENT
    NT: AQUATIC ENVIRONMENT
        ATMOSPHERE
        BIOSPHERE
        TERRESTRIAL ENVIRONMENT
    RT: PHYSICAL GEOGRAPHY

PHYSICAL GEOGRAPHY
GEOGRAPHIE PHYSIQUE / GEOGRAFIA FISICA -
17.03.01
    BT: EARTH SCIENCES
        GEOGRAPHY
    RT: GEOLOGY
        GEOMORPHOLOGY
        HYDROLOGY
        METEOROLOGY
        OCEANOGRAPHY
        PHYSICAL ENVIRONMENT
        SEISMOLOGY
        TOPOGRAPHY
        VULCANOLOGY

PHYSICAL PROPERTIES
PROPRIETES PHYSIQUES / PROPIEDADES FISICAS -
18.06.00
    RT: PHYSICS

PHYSICAL WORK
TRAVAIL PHYSIQUE / TRABAJO FISICO - 13.03.02
    RT: MANUAL WORKERS
        PHYSICAL CAPACITY

PHYSICALLY HANDICAPPED
HANDICAPES PHYSIQUES / DEFICIENTES FISICOS -
15.04.05
    BT: HANDICAPPED
    RT: DISABILITY
        DISEASES
        PATIENTS
        WOUNDED

PHYSICIAN EDUCATION
- 06.03.07
    USE: MEDICAL EDUCATION

PHYSICIANS
MEDECINS / MEDICOS - 13.09.10
    UF: MEDICAL DOCTORS
    BT: MEDICAL PERSONNEL
    NT: PEDIATRICIANS

PHYSICISTS
PHYSICIENS / FISICOS - 13.09.09
    BT: SCIENTISTS
    RT: PHYSICS

PHYSICS
PHYSIQUE / FISICA - 17.04.01
    BT: NATURAL SCIENCES

PHYSICS<CONT>
    NT: ACOUSTICS
        GEOPHYSICS
        OPTICS
    RT: PHYSICAL PROPERTIES
        PHYSICISTS

PHYSIOLOGY
PHYSIOLOGIE / FISIOLOGIA - 15.02.01
    BT: NATURAL SCIENCES

PHYTOPATHOLOGY
- 15.04.01
    USE: PLANT DISEASES

PIECE WORK
- 13.07.00
    USE: PAYMENT BY RESULT

PIGEON PEAS
POIS D'ANGOLA / GUANDUS - 07.07.06
    BT: LEGUMINOSAE

PIGS
- 07.09.01
    USE: SWINE

PILOT PROJECTS
PROJETS PILOTES / PROYECTOS EXPERIMENTALES -
01.01.06
    BT: DEVELOPMENT PROJECTS

PILOTS
PILOTES / PILOTOS - 13.09.08
    BT: TRANSPORT WORKERS
    RT: AIRCRAFT

PINEAPPLES
ANANAS / PINAS - 07.07.05
    BT: FRUITS

PIPELINE TRANSPORT
TRANSPORT PAR CONDUITE / TRANSPORTE POR DUCTO -
10.05.00
    BT: MODES OF TRANSPORTATION
    RT: PIPELINES

PIPELINES
PIPELINES / DUCTOS - 10.03.00
    BT: TRANSPORT INFRASTRUCTURE
    RT: PIPELINE TRANSPORT

PIPES
TUYAUX / TUBOS - 08.14.04
    BT: METAL PRODUCTS

PLACEMENT SERVICES
- 13.02.01
    USE: EMPLOYMENT SERVICES

PLAGUE
PESTE / PESTE - 15.04.02
    BT: INFECTIOUS DISEASES

PLAINS
PLAINES / LLANURAS - 17.03.04

PLAN IMPLEMENTATION
REALISATION DU PLAN / IMPLEMENTACION DEL PLAN -
02.01.02
    RT: DEVELOPMENT PLANS

PLANNED ECONOMY
ECONOMIE PLANIFIEE / ECONOMIA PLANIFICADA -
03.03.02
    BT: ECONOMIC SYSTEMS
    RT: ECONOMIC PLANNING

PLANNERS
PLANIFICATEURS / PLANIFICADORES - 02.01.02
    RT: PLANNING

PLANNING
PLANIFICATION / PLANIFICACION - 02.01.02
    NT: COMMUNICATION PLANNING
        DEVELOPMENT PLANNING
        ECONOMIC PLANNING
        EDUCATIONAL PLANNING
        FOOD PLANNING
        HEALTH PLANNING
        NATIONAL PLANNING
        PROGRAMME PLANNING
        REGIONAL PLANNING
        RURAL PLANNING
        SOCIAL PLANNING
        TRANSPORT PLANNING
        URBAN PLANNING
    RT: PLANNERS
        PLANNING METHODS
        PLANNING SYSTEMS

PLANNING METHODS
METHODES DE PLANIFICATION / METODOS DE
PLANIFICACION - 02.01.02
    RT: METHODOLOGY
        PLANNING
        PLANNING SYSTEMS

PLANNING OF EDUCATION
- 06.02.04
    USE: EDUCATIONAL PLANNING

PLANNING SYSTEMS
SYSTEMES DE PLANIFICATION / SISTEMAS DE
PLANIFICACION - 02.01.02
    NT: DIRECTIVE PLANNING
        SECTORAL PLANNING
        STRATEGIC PLANNING
    RT: PLANNING
        PLANNING METHODS

PLANS OF OPERATION
PLANS D'OPERATION / PLANES DE OPERACIONES -
01.01.06
SN: USE IN CONNECTION WITH U.N. PROJECTS.

PLANT BREEDING
AMELIORATION DES PLANTES / FITOMEJORAMIENTO -

PLANT BREEDING<CONT>
07.07.01
    RT: GENETIC IMPROVEMENT
        HYBRIDIZATION
        PLANTS
        REPRODUCTION

PLANT DISEASES
MALADIES DES PLANTES / ENFERMEDADES DE LAS
PLANTAS - 15.04.01
    UF: PHYTOPATHOLOGY
    BT: DISEASES
    RT: PESTS OF PLANTS
        PLANT PATHOLOGY
        PLANTS

PLANT ECOLOGY
PHYTOECOLOGIE / FITOECOLOGIA - 16.01.01
    BT: ECOLOGY
    RT: PLANT RESOURCES
        PLANTS

PLANT FIBRES
FIBRES VEGETALES / FIBRAS VEGETALES - 07.07.07
    BT: NATURAL FIBRES
        PLANT PRODUCTS
    NT: COIR
        COTTON
        FLAX
        HEMP
        JUTE
        SISAL
        WOOD FIBRES

PLANT NUTRITION
NUTRITION DES PLANTES / NUTRICION DE LAS PLANTAS
- 07.07.01
    BT: NUTRITION
    RT: PLANTS

PLANT PATHOLOGY
PATHOLOGIE VEGETALE / FITOPATOLOGIA - 07.07.01
    RT: PLANT DISEASES
        PLANTS

PLANT PRODUCTION
PRODUCTION VEGETALE / PRODUCCION VEGETAL -
07.07.03
    BT: AGRICULTURAL PRODUCTION
    RT: CROP YIELD
        PLANTS

PLANT PRODUCTS
PRODUITS VEGETAUX / PRODUCTOS VEGETALES -
07.07.03
    BT: AGRICULTURAL PRODUCTS
    NT: CEREALS
        FOREST PRODUCTS
        FRUITS
        PLANT FIBRES
        VEGETABLE OILS
    RT: PLANTS

PLANT PROTECTION
PROTECTION DES PLANTES / PROTECCION DE LAS
PLANTAS - 16.05.01
    BT: NATURE CONSERVATION
    NT: FOREST CONSERVATION
    RT: PLANT RESOURCES
        PLANTS
        PROTECTED SPECIES
        WEED CONTROL

PLANT RESOURCES
RESSOURCES VEGETALES / RECURSOS VEGETALES -
16.02.02
    BT: NATURAL RESOURCES
    NT: FOREST RESOURCES
    RT: PLANT ECOLOGY
        PLANT PROTECTION
        PLANTS

PLANT SHUTDOWN
FERMETURE D'USINE / CIERRE DE EMPRESA - 13.05.00
    RT: LOCKOUTS

PLANTATIONS
PLANTATIONS / PLANTACIONES - 07.03.01
*SN: AREAS PLANTED WITH CROPS, USUALLY LARGE
    ESTATES. DO NOT USE FOR FOREST PLANTATIONS,
    SEE 'MANMADE FORESTS'.*
    BT: AGRICULTURAL ENTERPRISES

PLANTING
PLANTAGE / PLANTILLO - 07.05.04
    BT: CULTIVATION PRACTICES
    RT: REFORESTATION

PLANTS
PLANTES / PLANTAS - 07.07.01
    NT: AQUATIC PLANTS
        FLOWERS
        FUNGI
        GRASSES
        LEGUMINOSAE
        MEDICINAL PLANTS
        SEEDS
        TREES
        VEGETABLES
        WILD PLANTS
    RT: BOTANICAL GARDENS
        BOTANY
        FLORA
        PLANT BREEDING
        PLANT DISEASES
        PLANT ECOLOGY
        PLANT NUTRITION
        PLANT PATHOLOGY
        PLANT PRODUCTION
        PLANT PRODUCTS
        PLANT PROTECTION
        PLANT RESOURCES
        VEGETATION

PLASTIC ARTS
ARTS PLASTIQUES / ARTES PLASTICAS - 05.05.03
    BT: FINE ARTS

PLASTICS
MATIERES PLASTIQUES / PLASTICOS - 08.12.07
    BT: POLYMERS
    NT: POLYESTER
    RT: PLASTICS INDUSTRY

PLASTICS INDUSTRY
INDUSTRIE DES MATIERES PLASTIQUES / INDUSTRIA
DEL PLASTICO - 08.12.07
    BT: CHEMICAL INDUSTRY
    RT: PLASTICS

PLATEAUS
PLATEAUX / ALTIPLANICIES - 17.03.04

PLATING
PLACAGE / PLACACION - 08.12.03
    BT: INDUSTRIAL PROCESSES
    RT: COATING

PLATINUM
PLATINE / PLATINO - 08.14.02
    BT: PRECIOUS METALS

PLUTONIUM
PLUTONIUM / PLUTONIO - 08.14.02
    BT: NON-FERROUS METALS
    RT: NUCLEAR FUEL

PLYWOOD
CONTREPLAQUE / CONTRACHAPADO - 08.07.01
    BT: CONSTRUCTION MATERIALS
        WOOD PRODUCTS

PNEUMOCONIOSIS
PNEUMOCONIOSE / NEUMOCONIOSIS - 15.04.02
    BT: OCCUPATIONAL DISEASES

PNEUMONIA
PNEUMONIE / NEUMONIA - 15.04.02

POISONING
INTOXICATION / INTOXICACION - 15.04.02
    BT: DISEASES
    NT: ALCOHOLISM
        DRUG ADDICTION
    RT: TOXINS

POISONS
POISONS / VENENOS - 15.05.00
    NT: TOXINS
    RT: PHARMACEUTICALS

POLAND
POLOGNE / POLONIA - 01.04.05
    BT: EASTERN EUROPE
    RT: POLISH

POLICE
POLICE / POLICIA - 04.03.02
    RT: CRIME PREVENTION

POLICY MAKING

POLICY MAKING<CONT>
ELABORATION D'UNE POLITIQUE / ELABORACION DE
POLITICA - 04.03.02
    RT: GOVERNMENT POLICY

POLIOMYELITIS
POLIOMYELITE / POLIOMIELITIS - 15.04.02
    BT: INFECTIOUS DISEASES

POLISH
POLONAIS / POLACO - 14.03.02
    RT: POLAND

POLITICAL AFFILIATION
AFFILIATION POLITIQUE / AFILIACION POLITICA -
04.04.02
    RT: POLITICAL IDEOLOGIES
        POLITICAL PARTICIPATION
        POLITICAL PARTIES
        POLITICS

POLITICAL ASPECTS
ASPECTS POLITIQUES / ASPECTOS POLITICOS -
04.04.02
    RT: POLITICS

POLITICAL BEHAVIOUR
COMPORTEMENT POLITIQUE / COMPORTAMIENTO POLITICO
- 04.04.02
    BT: BEHAVIOUR
    RT: POLITICAL PARTICIPATION
        RADICALISM
        VOTING

POLITICAL DEVELOPMENT
DEVELOPPEMENT POLITIQUE / DESARROLLO POLITICO -
04.04.02
*SN: THE WAY IN WHICH POLICY AND EVENTS AFFECT
THE EVOLUTION OF THE POLITICAL SYSTEM.*
    RT: POLITICAL STABILITY
        POLITICAL SYSTEMS
        POLITICS

POLITICAL DOCTRINES
DOCTRINES POLITIQUES / DOCTRINAS POLITICAS -
04.04.02
    RT: ECONOMIC DOCTRINES
        MARXISM

POLITICAL ECONOMY
- 03.01.01
    USE: ECONOMICS

POLITICAL EDUCATION
EDUCATION POLITIQUE / EDUCACION POLITICA -
06.03.04
    BT: BASIC EDUCATION
    RT: CIVIC EDUCATION
        POLITICAL PARTICIPATION

POLITICAL GEOGRAPHY
GEOGRAPHIE POLITIQUE / GEOGRAFIA POLITICA -
17.03.01

POLITICAL GEOGRAPHY<CONT>
    BT: HUMAN GEOGRAPHY
        SOCIAL SCIENCES
    RT: POLITICAL SCIENCE

POLITICAL IDEOLOGIES
IDEOLOGIES POLITIQUES / IDEOLOGIAS POLITICAS -
04.04.02
    RT: IDEOLOGIES
        POLITICAL AFFILIATION
        RADICALISM

POLITICAL INTEGRATION
INTEGRATION POLITIQUE / INTEGRACION POLITICA -
04.04.02
    RT: NATION

POLITICAL LEADERSHIP
LEADERSHIP POLITIQUE / LIDERAZGO POLITICO -
04.04.02
    BT: LEADERSHIP
    RT: ELITE
        RULING CLASS

POLITICAL OPPOSITION
OPPOSITION POLITIQUE / OPOSICION POLITICA -
04.04.02
    RT: POLITICAL PARTICIPATION

POLITICAL PARTICIPATION
PARTICIPATION POLITIQUE / PARTICIPACION POLITICA
- 04.04.02
    RT: MARGINALITY
        POLITICAL AFFILIATION
        POLITICAL BEHAVIOUR
        POLITICAL EDUCATION
        POLITICAL OPPOSITION
        SOCIAL PARTICIPATION
        VOTING

POLITICAL PARTIES
PARTIS POLITIQUES / PARTIDOS POLITICOS -
04.04.02
    RT: POLITICAL AFFILIATION

POLITICAL POWER
POUVOIR POLITIQUE / PODER POLITICO - 04.03.01
    RT: BUREAUCRACY
        TECHNOCRACY

POLITICAL PROBLEMS
PROBLEMES POLITIQUES / PROBLEMAS POLITICOS -
04.04.02
    RT: TERRORISM

POLITICAL SCIENCE
SCIENCE POLITIQUE / CIENCIAS POLITICAS -
04.04.01
    BT: SOCIAL SCIENCES
    RT: IPSA
        POLITICAL GEOGRAPHY
        POLITICAL SCIENTISTS

POLITICAL SCIENTISTS
POLITOLOGUES / POLITOLOGOS - 13.09.09
    BT: SCIENTISTS
    RT: POLITICAL SCIENCE

POLITICAL STABILITY
STABILITE POLITIQUE / ESTABILIDAD POLITICA -
04.04.02
  RT: POLITICAL DEVELOPMENT
    POLITICS

POLITICAL SYSTEMS
REGIMES POLITIQUES / SISTEMAS POLITICOS -
04.03.01
  NT: DEMOCRACY
    DICTATORSHIP
  RT: POLITICAL DEVELOPMENT

POLITICAL THEORY
THEORIE POLITIQUE / TEORIA POLITICA - 04.04.01
  BT: THEORY

POLITICS
POLITIQUE / POLITICA - 04.04.02
SN: USE IN CONNECTION WITH POLITICAL LIFE AS A
  WHOLE. DO NOT CONFUSE WITH 'POLITICAL
  SCIENCE'.
  RT: POLITICAL AFFILIATION
    POLITICAL ASPECTS
    POLITICAL DEVELOPMENT
    POLITICAL STABILITY
    REVOLUTION

POLLUTANT BURDEN
- 16.03.04
  USE: POLLUTION LEVEL

POLLUTANTS
POLLUANTS / CONTAMINANTES - 16.03.04
  UF: CONTAMINANTS
  NT: AIR POLLUTANTS
    HYDROCARBONS
    SOIL POLLUTANTS
    WASTES
    WATER POLLUTANTS
  RT: DANGEROUS SUBSTANCES
    POLLUTION
    POLLUTION SOURCES

POLLUTED AREAS
ZONES POLLUEES / ZONAS CONTAMINADAS - 16.03.04
  RT: POLLUTION

POLLUTER-PAYS PRINCIPLE
PRINCIPE POLLUEUR-PAYEUR / PRINCIPIO
CONTAMINADOR-PAGADOR - 16.04.01
  BT: POLLUTION CONTROL
  RT: DAMAGE COMPENSATION
    ENVIRONMENTAL ECONOMICS

POLLUTION
POLLUTION / CONTAMINACION - 16.03.04
  UF: ENVIRONMENTAL POLLUTION

POLLUTION<CONT>
  NT: ACUSTIC POLLUTION
    AIR POLLUTION
    CHEMICAL POLLUTION
    COASTAL POLLUTION
    RADIOACTIVE POLLUTION
    SOIL POLLUTION
    THERMAL POLLUTION
    TRANSFRONTIER POLLUTION
    WATER POLLUTION
  RT: ENVIRONMENTAL DEGRADATION
    ENVIRONMENTAL EFFECTS
    POLLUTANTS
    POLLUTED AREAS
    POLLUTION CONTROL
    POLLUTION INDEX
    POLLUTION LEVEL
    POLLUTION SOURCES

POLLUTION CONTROL
LUTTE ANTI-POLLUTION / LUCHA CONTRA LA
CONTAMINACION - 16.04.01
  BT: ENVIRONMENTAL ENGINEERING
    ENVIRONMENTAL PROTECTION
  NT: DECONTAMINATION
    POLLUTER-PAYS PRINCIPLE
    WARNING DEVICES
  RT: POLLUTION

POLLUTION INDEX
INDICE DE POLLUTION / INDICE DE CONTAMINACION -
16.04.01
  RT: POLLUTION
    WARNING DEVICES

POLLUTION LEVEL
NIVEAU DE POLLUTION / NIVEL DE CONTAMINACION -
16.03.04
  UF: CONCENTRATION OF POLLUTANTS
    POLLUTANT BURDEN
  RT: POLLUTION

POLLUTION SOURCES
SOURCES DE POLLUTION / FUENTES DE CONTAMINACION
- 16.03.04
  RT: POLLUTANTS
    POLLUTION

POLYANDRY
POLYANDRIE / POLIANDRIA - 14.02.05
  RT: MARRIAGE

POLYESTER
POLYESTER / POLIESTERES - 08.12.07
  BT: PLASTICS

POLYGAMY
POLYGAMIE / POLIGAMIA - 14.02.05
  RT: MARRIAGE

POLYMERS
POLYMERES / POLIMEROS - 08.12.04
  NT: PLASTICS

POLYNESIA
- 01.04.07
  USE: OCEANIA

POPULATION
POPULATION / POBLACION - 14.01.02
  NT: ABORIGINAL POPULATION
    RURAL POPULATION
    URBAN POPULATION

  RT: DEMOGRAPHY
    IUSSP
    MANPOWER
    OVERPOPULATION
    POPULATION CENSUSES
    POPULATION COMPOSITION
    POPULATION DECLINE
    POPULATION DENSITY
    POPULATION DISTRIBUTION
    POPULATION DYNAMICS
    POPULATION INCREASE
    POPULATION OPTIMUM
    POPULATION POLICY
    POPULATION SIZE
    POPULATION THEORY

POPULATION CENSUSES
RECENSEMENTS DE POPULATION / CENSOS DE POBLACION
- 14.01.01
  BT: CENSUSES
  RT: POPULATION

POPULATION COMPOSITION
COMPOSITION DE LA POPULATION / COMPOSICION DE LA
POBLACION - 14.02.01
  RT: AGE-SEX DISTRIBUTION
    POPULATION

POPULATION DECLINE
DEPEUPLEMENT / DESPOBLACION - 14.01.02
  RT: FERTILITY DECLINE
    POPULATION
    POPULATION DYNAMICS

POPULATION DENSITY
DENSITE DE POPULATION / DENSIDAD DE POBLACION -
14.01.02
  RT: POPULATION
    POPULATION SIZE

POPULATION DISTRIBUTION
REPARTITION DE LA POPULATION / DISTRIBUCION DE
LA POBLACION - 14.04.01
  RT: HABITAT
    POPULATION

POPULATION DYNAMICS
DYNAMIQUE DE LA POPULATION / DINAMICA DE LA
POBLACION - 14.01.02
  RT: POPULATION
    POPULATION DECLINE
    POPULATION INCREASE
    STATIONARY POPULATION

POPULATION INCREASE

POPULATION INCREASE<CONT>
ACCROISSEMENT DE POPULATION / CRECIMIENTO
DEMOGRAFICO - 14.01.02
  RT: FERTILITY
    IMMIGRATION
    POPULATION
    POPULATION DYNAMICS

POPULATION OPTIMUM
OPTIMUM DE PEUPLEMENT / OPTIMO DE POBLACION -
14.01.02
  RT: POPULATION
    POPULATION SIZE

POPULATION POLICY
POLITIQUE DEMOGRAPHIQUE / POLITICA DE POBLACION
- 14.01.02
  BT: GOVERNMENT POLICY
  NT: MIGRATION POLICY
  RT: FAMILY PLANNING
    POPULATION
    SOCIAL POLICY

POPULATION SIZE
DIMENSION DE LA POPULATION / TAMANO DE LA
POBLACION - 14.01.02
  RT: POPULATION
    POPULATION DENSITY
    POPULATION OPTIMUM

POPULATION THEORY
THEORIE DE LA POPULATION / TEORIA DE LA
POBLACION - 14.01.02
  BT: THEORY
  RT: POPULATION

POPULATION TRANSFERS
TRANSFERTS DE POPULATION / TRANSFERENCIAS DE
POBLACION - 14.07.00
  BT: MIGRATIONS

PORK
VIANDE DE PORC / CARNE DE CERDO - 07.09.05
  BT: MEAT
  RT: SWINE

PORTS
PORTS / PUERTOS - 10.03.00
  UF: HARBOURS
  BT: TRANSPORT INFRASTRUCTURE
  NT: FISHING PORTS
  RT: INLAND WATER TRANSPORT
    SEA TRANSPORT

PORTUGAL
PORTUGAL / PORTUGAL - 01.04.05
  BT: WESTERN EUROPE
  RT: AZORES
    MACAO
    MADEIRA
    PORTUGUESE
    PORTUGUESE TIMOR

PORTUGUESE
PORTUGAIS / PORTUGUES - 14.03.02
  RT: PORTUGAL

PORTUGUESE TIMOR
TIMOR PORTUGAIS / TIMOR PORTUGUESA - 01.04.04
    BT: SOUTH EAST ASIA
    RT: PORTUGAL

POST-SECONDARY EDUCATION
ENSEIGNEMENT POST-SECONDAIRE / ENSENANZA
POSTSECUNDARIA - 06.03.06
    BT: LEVELS OF EDUCATION
    NT: HIGHER EDUCATION
    RT: HIGHER EDUCATION INSTITUTIONS

POST-SECONDARY SCHOOLS
- 06.04.05
    USE: HIGHER EDUCATION INSTITUTIONS

POSTAL SERVICES
SERVICE POSTAL / SERVICIO POSTAL - 08.16.00
    RT: TELEGRAPH
         TELEPHONE
         UPU

POTASH
POTASSE / POTASA - 08.12.04
    RT: CHEMICAL FERTILIZERS
         CLEANING AGENTS

POTASSIUM
POTASSIUM / POTASIO - 08.12.04

POTATOES
POMMES DE TERRE / PAPAS - 07.07.06
    BT: ROOT CROPS

POTTERY
POTERIE / ALFARERIA - 08.10.03
    RT: CERAMICS INDUSTRY
         HANDICRAFT

POULTRY
VOLAILLE / AVES DE CORRAL - 07.09.01
    BT: BIRDS
    RT: EGGS

POVERTY
PAUVRETE / POBREZA - 03.02.05
    BT: SOCIAL PROBLEMS
    RT: BASIC NEEDS
         IMPOVERISHMENT
         INCOME DISTRIBUTION
         SOCIAL JUSTICE

POWER CONSERVATION
- 08.11.01
    USE: ENERGY CONSERVATION

POWER CONSUMPTION
- 08.11.01
    USE: ENERGY CONSUMPTION

POWER DEMAND
DEMANDE ENERGETIQUE / DEMANDA DE ENERGIA -
08.11.01

POWER DEMAND<CONT>
    UF: ENERGY DEMAND
         ENERGY REQUIREMENTS
    BT: DEMAND
    RT: ENERGY CONSUMPTION
         ENERGY CRISIS
         ENERGY ECONOMICS
         POWER GENERATION
         POWER SUPPLY

POWER DISTRIBUTION
DISTRIBUTION D'ENERGIE / DISTRIBUCION DE ENERGIA
- 08.11.01
    RT: ENERGY CONSUMPTION
         ENERGY ECONOMICS
         POWER GENERATION
         POWER INDUSTRY

POWER GENERATION
PRODUCTION D'ENERGIE / GENERACION DE ENERGIA -
08.11.01
    UF: POWER PRODUCTION
    BT: PRODUCTION
    RT: POWER DEMAND
         POWER DISTRIBUTION
         POWER INDUSTRY
         POWER PLANTS

POWER INDUSTRY
INDUSTRIE ENERGETIQUE / INDUSTRIA ENERGETICA -
08.11.01
    BT: INDUSTRIAL SECTOR
    RT: ENERGY ECONOMICS
         POWER DISTRIBUTION
         POWER GENERATION
         POWER PLANTS

POWER PLANTS
STATIONS ENERGETIQUES / CENTRALES DE ENERGIA -
08.11.01
    BT: INDUSTRIAL PLANTS
    NT: ELECTRIC POWER PLANTS
         NUCLEAR POWER PLANTS
    RT: POWER GENERATION
         POWER INDUSTRY

POWER PRODUCTION
- 08.11.01
    USE: POWER GENERATION

POWER RESOURCES
- 16.02.02
    USE: ENERGY RESOURCES

POWER SUPPLY
DISPONIBILITES ENERGETIQUES / ABASTECIMIENTO DE
ENERGIA - 08.11.01
    BT: SUPPLY
    RT: ENERGY CRISIS
         POWER DEMAND

POWER UTILIZATION
- 08.11.01

PRAIRIE
PRAIRIE / PRADERA - 17.03.04

PRECIOUS METALS
METAUX PRECIEUX / METALES PRECIOSOS - 08.14.02
    BT: NON-FERROUS METALS
    NT: GOLD
        PLATINUM
        SILVER

PRECIOUS STONES
PIERRES PRECIEUSES / PIEDRAS PRECIOSAS -
08.13.00
    BT: MINERALS
    NT: DIAMOND
    RT: MINING

PRECIPITATIONS
PRECIPITATIONS / PRECIPITACIONES - 17.01.03
    NT: RAIN
        SNOW
    RT: METEOROLOGY
        WEATHER

PRECISION INSTRUMENTS
INSTRUMENTS DE PRECISION / INSTRUMENTOS DE
PRECISION - 08.14.08
    NT: MEASURING INSTRUMENTS
        OPTICAL INSTRUMENTS
    RT: EQUIPMENT
        INSTRUMENTATION INDUSTRY

PREFABRICATED BUILDINGS
BATIMENTS PREFABRIQUES / CONSTRUCCIONES
PREFABRICADAS - 08.10.01
    BT: BUILDINGS
    RT: CONSTRUCTION TECHNIQUES

PREFERENTIAL TARIFFS
TARIFS PREFERENTIELS / ARANCELES PREFERENCIALES
- 09.05.08
    BT: TARIFFS
    NT: GENERAL SYSTEM OF PREFERENCES

PREGNANCY
GROSSESSE / EMBARAZO - 14.05.01
    RT: FOETUS

PREINVESTMENT SURVEYS
ENQUETES DE PREINVESTISSEMENT / ESTUDIOS DE
PREINVERSION - 11.02.06
    RT: INVESTMENTS

PRENATAL CARE
SOINS PRENATAUX / ATENCION PRENATAL - 15.04.04
    BT: MEDICAL CARE
        PREVENTIVE MEDICINE
    RT: HEALTH

PRESCHOOL EDUCATION
EDUCATION PRESCOLAIRE / EDUCACION PREESCOLAR -
06.03.06
    BT: LEVELS OF EDUCATION
    RT: NURSERY SCHOOLS

PRESIDENCY
PRESIDENCE / PRESIDENCIA - 04.03.01

PRESS
PRESSE / PRENSA - 05.07.03
    BT: MASS MEDIA
    RT: JOURNALISTS
        NEWS ITEM
        PERIODICALS
        PRESS RELEASE

PRESS RELEASE
COMMUNIQUE DE PRESSE / COMUNICADO DE PRENSA -
19.02.06
    RT: PRESS

PRESSURE GROUPS
- 04.04.02
    USE: INTEREST GROUPS

PREVENTIVE MEDICINE
MEDECINE PREVENTIVE / MEDICINA PREVENTIVA -
15.04.04
    BT: MEDICINE
    NT: MATERNAL AND CHILD HEALTH
        PRENATAL CARE
        PROPHYLAXIS
        VACCINATION
    RT: HEALTH CONTROL
        HEALTH EDUCATION

PRICE CONTROL
CONTROLE DES PRIX / CONTROL DE PRECIOS -
09.02.00
    RT: INFLATION
        PRICE POLICY
        PRICES

PRICE INDEX
INDICE DES PRIX / INDICE DE PRECIOS - 09.02.00
    BT: INDEX NUMBERS
    RT: COST OF LIVING
        INFLATION
        PRICES

PRICE LIST
LISTE DE PRIX / LISTA DE PRECIOS - 09.02.00
    RT: PRICES

PRICE POLICY
POLITIQUE DES PRIX / POLITICA DE PRECIOS -
09.02.00
    BT: ECONOMIC POLICY
    RT: PRICE CONTROL
        PRICES

PRICE STABILIZATION
STABILISATION DES PRIX / ESTABILIZACION DE LOS
PRECIOS - 09.02.00
    BT: STABILIZATION

PRICE STABILIZATION<CONT>
    RT: BUFFER STOCKS
         COMMON FUND
         MARKET STABILIZATION
         MARKETING BOARDS
         PRICES

PRICE SUPPORT
**SOUTIEN DES PRIX / MANTENIMIENTO DE PRECIOS -
09.02.00**
    RT: PRICES
         SUBSIDIES

PRICES
PRIX / PRECIOS - 09.02.00
    NT: ADMINISTERED PRICES
         COMMODITY PRICES
         CONSUMER PRICES
         INDUSTRIAL PRICES
         RETAIL PRICES
         WHOLESALE PRICES
    RT: FREIGHT
         MARKET
         PRICE CONTROL
         PRICE INDEX
         PRICE LIST
         PRICE POLICY
         PRICE STABILIZATION
         PRICE SUPPORT
         PRICING
         PURCHASING POWER
         SUPPLY AND DEMAND

PRICING
**FIXATION DU PRIX / FIJACION DEL PRECIO -
12.09.00**
    RT: PRICES

PRIMARY DOCUMENTS
**DOCUMENTS PRIMAIRES / DOCUMENTOS PRIMARIOS -
19.02.01**
*SN: ORIGINAL DOCUMENTS WHICH ARE NOT THE RESULT
    OF A DOCUMENTATION PROCESS.*
    BT: DOCUMENTS
    NT: BIOGRAPHIES
         CORRESPONDENCE
         DICTIONARY
         ENCYCLOPEDIA
         MONOGRAPH
         SERIALS
         THESAURUS
         THESIS

PRIMARY EDUCATION
**ENSEIGNEMENT PRIMAIRE / ENSENANZA PRIMARIA -
06.03.06**
*SN: ELEMENTARY EDUCATION GIVEN TO CHILDREN FROM
    THE TIME THEY FIRST ATTEND SCHOOL UNTIL THEY
    PASS TO SECONDARY EDUCATION OR LEAVE SCHOOL
    TO WORK.*
    UF: ELEMENTARY EDUCATION
    BT: LEVELS OF EDUCATION
    RT: PRIMARY SCHOOLS

PRIMARY PRODUCTS
- 12.08.01
    USE: COMMODITIES

PRIMARY SCHOOLS
ECOLES PRIMAIRES / ESCUELAS PRIMARIAS - 06.04.02
    UF: ELEMENTARY SCHOOLS
    BT: SCHOOLS
    RT: PRIMARY EDUCATION

PRIMARY SECTOR
SECTEUR PRIMAIRE / SECTOR PRIMARIO - 07.01.01
    NT: AGRICULTURAL SECTOR
         MINING

PRINTING INDUSTRY
IMPRIMERIE / INDUSTRIAS GRAFICAS - 08.16.00
    BT: COMMUNICATION INDUSTRY

PRISONERS
PRISONNIERS / PRISIONEROS - 02.04.03
    RT: PRISONS
         TORTURE

PRISONS
PRISONS / PRISIONES - 02.04.03
    BT: PENAL SANCTIONS
    RT: CRIMINAL LAW
         PRISONERS

PRIVACY PROTECTION
**PROTECTION DE LA VIE PRIVEE / PROTECCION DE LA
VIDA PRIVADA - 05.03.01**
    RT: DATA PROTECTION

PRIVATE AID
AIDE PRIVEE / AYUDA PRIVADA - 01.01.02
SN: AID PROVIDED BY CHURCHES, FOUNDATIONS, ETC.
    UF: AID BY RELIGIOUS BODIES
    BT: DEVELOPMENT AID

PRIVATE EDUCATION
**ENSEIGNEMENT PRIVE / ENSENANZA PRIVADA -
06.03.03**
    BT: EDUCATIONAL SYSTEMS
    RT: PRIVATE SCHOOLS

PRIVATE ENTERPRISES
**ENTREPRISES PRIVEES / EMPRESAS PRIVADAS -
03.03.05**
    BT: ENTERPRISES
    RT: PRIVATE OWNERSHIP
         PRIVATE SECTOR

PRIVATE INVESTMENTS
**INVESTISSEMENTS PRIVES / INVERSIONES PRIVADAS -
11.02.06**
    BT: INVESTMENTS

PRIVATE OWNERSHIP
PROPRIETE PRIVEE / PROPIEDAD PRIVADA - 03.03.05
    BT: OWNERSHIP

PRIVATE OWNERSHIP<CONT>
    RT: CAPITALIST ENTERPRISES
       PRIVATE ENTERPRISES
       PRIVATE SECTOR

PRIVATE SCHOOLS
ECOLES PRIVEES / ESCUELAS PRIVADAS - 06.04.04
    BT: SCHOOLS
    RT: PRIVATE EDUCATION

PRIVATE SECTOR
SECTEUR PRIVE / SECTOR PRIVADO - 03.03.05
    RT: PRIVATE ENTERPRISES
       PRIVATE OWNERSHIP

PROBABILITY
PROBABILITE / PROBABILIDAD - 18.08.00
    RT: INFORMATION THEORY
       STATISTICAL ANALYSIS

PROBATION PERIOD
PERIODE D'ESSAI / PERIODO DE PRUEBA - 13.02.01
SN: PERIOD OF TRAINING OR OF WORK IN EMPLOYMENT,
INTENDED FOR TESTING THE VALIDITY OF
OCCUPATIONAL CHOICE OR THE APTITUDE FOR THE
JOB.
    RT: RECRUITMENT

PROCESSING
TRAITEMENT / PROCESAMIENTO - 12.07.02
    NT: AGRIPRODUCT PROCESSING
       INFORMATION PROCESSING
       REPROCESSING

PRODUCERS
PRODUCTEURS / PRODUCTORES - 12.03.00
    RT: EMPLOYERS
       PRODUCERS ASSOCIATIONS
       PRODUCTION

PRODUCERS ASSOCIATIONS
ASSOCIATIONS DE PRODUCTEURS / ASOCIACIONES DE
PRODUCTORES - 12.02.00
SN: USE TO DENOTE GROUPS OF COUNTRIES PRODUCING
THE SAME COMMODITY.
    RT: CARTELS
       COMMODITY AGREEMENTS
       COMMODITY PRICES
       PRODUCERS

PRODUCT DESIGN
CONCEPTION DE PRODUITS / DISENO DE PRODUCTOS -
12.08.02
    BT: ENGINEERING DESIGN
    RT: CHOICE OF PRODUCTS
       NEW PRODUCTS
       PRODUCT DEVELOPMENT
       PRODUCTS

PRODUCT DEVELOPMENT
MISE AU POINT DE PRODUITS / DESARROLLO DE
PRODUCTOS - 12.08.02

PRODUCT DEVELOPMENT<CONT>
    RT: CHOICE OF PRODUCTS
       NEW PRODUCTS
       PRODUCT DESIGN
       PRODUCTS
       PROTOTYPES

PRODUCTION
PRODUCTION / PRODUCCION - 12.07.01
SN: THE TOTAL AMOUNT OF GOODS OR THE VOLUME OF
SERVICES WHICH AN ENTERPRISE, A COUNTRY, A
REGION, ETC., PRODUCES IN A GIVEN PERIOD OF
TIME.
    NT: AGRICULTURAL PRODUCTION
       FOOD PRODUCTION
       INDUSTRIAL PRODUCTION
       MASS PRODUCTION
       OVERPRODUCTION
       POWER GENERATION
    RT: MEANS OF PRODUCTION
       MODES OF PRODUCTION
       PRODUCERS
       PRODUCTION CAPACITY
       PRODUCTION CONTROL
       PRODUCTION COSTS
       PRODUCTION DIVERSIFICATION
       PRODUCTION FACTORS
       PRODUCTION FUNCTIONS
       PRODUCTION INCREASE
       PRODUCTION PLANNING
       PRODUCTION SPECIALIZATION
       PRODUCTION STANDARDS
       PRODUCTION STATISTICS
       PRODUCTION TARGETS
       PRODUCTIVITY
       PRODUCTS

PRODUCTION CAPACITY
CAPACITE DE PRODUCTION / CAPACIDAD DE PRODUCCION
- 12.07.01
    RT: ECONOMY OF SCALE
       OVERPRODUCTION
       PRODUCTION

PRODUCTION CONTROL
REGULATION DE LA PRODUCTION / REGULACION DE LA
PRODUCCION - 12.07.02
    NT: AUTOMATIC CONTROL
    RT: PRODUCTION
       PRODUCTION PLANNING
       PRODUCTION STANDARDS

PRODUCTION COOPERATIVES
COOPERATIVES DE PRODUCTION / COOPERATIVAS DE
PRODUCCION - 12.01.00
    BT: COOPERATIVES
    RT: WORKERS SELF-MANAGEMENT

PRODUCTION COSTS
COUTS DE PRODUCTION / COSTOS DE PRODUCCION -
12.09.00
    BT: COSTS
    RT: ECONOMY OF SCALE
       PRODUCTION

PRODUCTION DIVERSIFICATION
DIVERSIFICATION DE LA PRODUCTION /
DIVERSIFICACION DE LA PRODUCCION - 12.07.01
    RT: PRODUCTION
          PRODUCTION SPECIALIZATION

PRODUCTION FACTORS
FACTEURS DE PRODUCTION / FACTORES DE PRODUCCION
- 12.07.01
    RT: CAPITAL
          LABOUR
          LAND CAPABILITY
          PRODUCTION

PRODUCTION FUNCTIONS
FONCTIONS DE PRODUCTION / FUNCIONES DE
PRODUCCION - 12.07.01
SN: USE TO MEAN THE VARIOUS COMBINATIONS OF THE
    FACTORS OF PRODUCTION WHICH ARE NEEDED TO
    PRODUCE A GIVEN QUANTITY OF OUTPUT.
    NT: CAPITAL-LABOUR RATIO
          CAPITAL-OUTPUT RATIO
    RT: ECONOMY OF SCALE
          PRODUCTION
          PRODUCTION INCREASE
          PRODUCTION STATISTICS
          PRODUCTIVITY

PRODUCTION GOODS
BIENS DE PRODUCTION / BIENES DE PRODUCCION -
11.02.05
    RT: CAPITAL

PRODUCTION INCREASE
ACCROISSEMENT DE PRODUCTION / CRECIMIENTO DE LA
PRODUCCION - 12.07.01
    RT: PRODUCTION
          PRODUCTION FUNCTIONS

PRODUCTION PLANNING
PLANIFICATION DE LA PRODUCTION / PLANIFICACION
DE LA PRODUCCION - 12.07.01
    BT: ECONOMIC PLANNING
    RT: PRODUCTION
          PRODUCTION CONTROL
          PRODUCTION TARGETS

PRODUCTION SPECIALIZATION
SPECIALISATION DE LA PRODUCTION /
ESPECIALIZACION DE LA PRODUCCION - 12.07.01
    RT: PRODUCTION
          PRODUCTION DIVERSIFICATION

PRODUCTION STANDARDS
NORMES DE PRODUCTION / NORMAS DE PRODUCCION -
12.07.02
    BT: STANDARDS
    RT: PRODUCTION
          PRODUCTION CONTROL

PRODUCTION STATISTICS
STATISTIQUES DE PRODUCTION / ESTADISTICAS DE
PRODUCCION - 12.07.01
    BT: ECONOMIC STATISTICS

PRODUCTION STATISTICS<CONT>
    RT: AGRICULTURAL STATISTICS
          INDUSTRIAL STATISTICS
          PRODUCTION
          PRODUCTION FUNCTIONS

PRODUCTION TARGETS
OBJECTIFS DE PRODUCTION / METAS DE PRODUCCION -
12.07.02
    RT: PRODUCTION
          PRODUCTION PLANNING

PRODUCTIVITY
PRODUCTIVITE / PRODUCTIVIDAD - 12.07.03
SN: THE RATIO OF THE OUTPUT TO THE EFFORT AND
    INVESTMENT PUT IN.
    NT: LABOUR PRODUCTIVITY
    RT: APO
          PRODUCTION
          PRODUCTION FUNCTIONS
          PRODUCTIVITY POLICY

PRODUCTIVITY POLICY
POLITIQUE DE PRODUCTIVITE / POLITICA DE LA
PRODUCTIVIDAD - 12.07.03
    BT: ECONOMIC POLICY
    RT: PRODUCTIVITY

PRODUCTS
PRODUITS / PRODUCTOS - 12.08.01
    NT: BY-PRODUCTS
          COMMODITIES
          COMPETITIVE PRODUCTS
          INDUSTRIAL PRODUCTS
          NATURAL PRODUCTS
          NEW PRODUCTS
          SUBSTITUTE PRODUCTS
    RT: CHOICE OF PRODUCTS
          PRODUCT DESIGN
          PRODUCT DEVELOPMENT
          PRODUCTION

PROFESSIONAL ASSOCIATIONS
- 13.06.00
    USE: **OCCUPATIONAL ORGANIZATIONS**

PROFESSIONAL EDUCATION
- 06.03.07
    USE: **VOCATIONAL EDUCATION**

PROFESSIONALS
PROFESSIONNELS / PROFESIONALES - 13.09.03
    RT: EMPLOYEES
          MIDDLE MANAGEMENT
          TOP MANAGEMENT
          WAGE EARNERS

PROFESSORS
- 13.09.09
    USE: **TEACHERS**

PROFIT SHARING
PARTICIPATION AUX BENEFICES / PARTICIPACION EN
LOS BENEFICIOS - 13.07.00
    BT: WAGES
    RT: WORKERS STOCK OWNERSHIP

PROFITABILITY
RENTABILITE / RENTABILIDAD - 12.09.00
    RT: PROFITS

PROFITS
PROFITS / GANANCIAS - 12.09.00
    BT: INCOME
    NT: CAPITAL GAINS
        CASH FLOW
        INTEREST
        INVESTMENT RETURNS
    RT: CAPITALIST ENTERPRISES
        PROFITABILITY
        REINVESTMENTS

PROGRAMME PLANNING
PLANIFICATION DE PROGRAMME / PLANIFICACION DE
PROGRAMAS - 12.04.00
    BT: PLANNING
    RT: COST-BENEFIT ANALYSIS

PROGRAMMED INSTRUCTION
ENSEIGNEMENT PROGRAMME / ENSENANZA PROGRAMADA -
06.05.03
SN: INSTRUCTION USING PROGRAMMED MATERIAL,
    EITHER IN TEXTBOOK OR TEACHING MACHINE
    USABLE FORM.
    UF: PROGRAMMED LEARNING
    BT: TEACHING METHODS

PROGRAMMED LEARNING
- 06.05.03
    USE: PROGRAMMED INSTRUCTION

PROGRESS REPORT
RAPPORT D'ACTIVITE / INFORME DE ACTIVIDADES -
19.02.08

PROJECT APPRAISAL
APPRECIATION DE PROJET / ESTIMACION DE PROYECTOS
- 01.01.06
SN: REFERS TO TECHNIQUES APPLIED FOR ASSESSMENT
    BEFORE A PROJECT IS APPROVED.
    RT: DEVELOPMENT PROJECTS

PROJECT DESIGN
ELABORATION DE PROJET / ELABORACION DE PROYECTOS
- 01.01.06
    UF: PROJECT PLANNING
    RT: DEVELOPMENT PROJECTS

PROJECT EVALUATION
EVALUATION DE PROJET / EVALUACION DE PROYECTOS -
01.01.06
SN: REFERS TO TECHNIQUES APPLIED FOR ASSESSMENT
    AFTER A PROJECT IS APPROVED, UNDERWAY OR
    COMPLETED.
    BT: EVALUATION
    RT: AID EVALUATION
        COST-BENEFIT ANALYSIS
        DEVELOPMENT PROJECTS

PROJECT IMPLEMENTATION

PROJECT IMPLEMENTATION\<CONT\>
MISE EN OEUVRE DE PROJET / IMPLEMENTACION DE
PROYECTOS - 01.01.06
    RT: DEVELOPMENT PROJECTS

PROJECT MANAGEMENT
GESTIOOOON DE PROJET / ADMINISTRACION DE PROYECTOS
- 01.01.06
    RT: DEVELOPMENT PROJECTS

PROJECT PLANNING
- 01.01.06
    USE: PROJECT DESIGN

PROJECT REPORT
RAPPORT DE PROJET / INFORME SOBRE PROYECTO -
19.02.08
SN: USE FOR REPORTS OF TECHNICAL COOPERATION
    PROJECTS, INCLUDING OF THE U.N. AND
    SPECIALIZED AGENCIES AS WELL AS THOSE OF
    BILATERALLLL PROGRAMMES.
    RT: DEVELOPMENT PROJECTS

PROJECT REQUEST
DEMANDE DE PROJET / SOLICITUD PARA REALIZAR
PROYECTOS - 01.01.06
    RT: DEVELOPMENT PROJECTS

PROJECT SELECTION
CHOIX DE PROJET / ELECCION DE PROYECTOS -
01.01.06
    RT: DEVELOPMENT PROJECTS

PROJECTION EQUIPMENT
APPAREILS DE PROJECTION / APARATOS DE PROYECCION
- 08.15.02
    RT: FILMS
        SLIDES

PROJECTIONS
PERSPECTIVES / PROYECCIONES - 18.10.00
SN: USE ONLY IN CONNECTION WITH STATISTICAL
    DATA; OTHERWISE USE 'FORECASTS' OR 'TRENDS'
    AS APPLICABLE.
    NT: ECONOMIC PROJECTIITIONS
    RT: FORECASTING TECHNIQUES
        FORECASTS

PROLETARIAN INTERNATIONALISM
INTERNATIONALISME PROLETARIEN /
INTERNACIONALISMO PROLETARIO - 01.02.01
    RT: PROLETARIAT
        TRADE UNIONISM

PROLETARIAT
PROLETARIAT / PROLETARIADO - 05.03.05
    RT: LOWER CLASS
        PROLETARIAN INTERNATIONALISM
        WORKING CLASS

PROMOTION
PROMOTION / ASCENSO - 13.02.02
    UF: ADVANCEMENT
    RT: PERSONNEL MANAGEMENT

PROPAGANDA
PROPAGANDE / PROPAGANDA - 04.04.02
    RT: PUBLIC OPINION

PROPHYLAXIS
PROPHYLAXIE / PROFILAXIS - 15.04.04
    BT: PREVENTIVE MEDICINE
    RT: HYGIENE

PROSTITUTION
PROSTITUTION / PROSTITUCION - 02.04.02
    BT: SOCIAL PROBLEMS

PROTECTED AREAS
ZONES PROTEGEES / ZONAS PROTEGIDAS - 16.05.01
    NT: NATURE RESERVES
    RT: PROTECTED RESOURCES

PROTECTED RESOURCES
RESSOURCES PROTEGEES / RECURSOS PROTEGIDOS -
16.05.01
    NT: BOTANICAL GARDENS
          NATIONAL PARKS
          NATURE RESERVES
          ZOOLOGICAL GARDENS
    RT: PROTECTED AREAS
          RESOURCES CONSERVATION

PROTECTED SPECIES
ESPECES PROTEGEES / ESPECIES PROTEGIDAS -
16.05.01
    RT: ANIMAL PROTECTION
          BOTANICAL GARDENS
          ENDANGERED SPECIES
          PLANT PROTECTION
          ZOOLOGICAL GARDENS

PROTECTIONISM
PROTECTIONNISME / PROTECCIONISMO - 09.05.07
    RT: PROTECTIONIST MEASURES

PROTECTIONIST MEASURES
MESURES PROTECTIONNISTES / MEDIDAS
PROTECCIONISTAS - 09.05.07
    BT: RESTRICTIVE BUSINESS PRACTICES
          TRADE POLICY
    NT: IMPORT RESTRICTIONS
          IMPORT SUBSTITUTION
          QUOTA SYSTEM
    RT: PROTECTIONISM
          TARIFFS

PROTEIN DEFICIENCY
DEFICIENCE PROTEIQUE / CARENCIA PROTEICA -
15.03.02
    BT: MALNUTRITION
    RT: DEFICIENCY DISEASES
          PROTEINS

PROTEIN RICH FOOD
ALIMENTS RICHES EN PROTEINES / ALIMENTOS RICOS
EN PROTEINAS - 15.03.01
    BT: FOOD

PROTEIN RICH FOOD<CONT>
    RT: FISH
          MEAT
          PROTEINS

PROTEINS
PROTEINES / PROTEINAS - 15.01.03
    BT: NUTRIENTS
    NT: AMINO ACIDS
    RT: FOOD
          NUTRITION
          PROTEIN DEFICIENCY
          PROTEIN RICH FOOD

PROTOTYPES
PROTOTYPES / PROTOTIPOS - 12.08.02
*SN: WORKING MODELS OF PROPOSED PRODUCTS, WHICH
    CAN BE TESTED, AND IF NECESSARY MODIFIED,
    BEFORE PRODUCTION BEGINS.*
    RT: NEW PRODUCTS
          PRODUCT DEVELOPMENT

PSYCHIATRY
PSYCHIATRIE / PSIQUIATRIA - 15.04.06
    BT: MEDICINE
    RT: MENTAL DISEASES
          MENTAL HOSPITALS

PSYCHOLOGICAL ASPECTS
ASPECTS PSYCHOLOGIQUES / ASPECTOS PSICOLOGICOS -
05.03.02
    RT: PSYCHOLOGY
          SOCIAL PSYCHOLOGY

PSYCHOLOGISTS
PSYCHOLOGUES / PSICOLOGOS - 13.09.09
    BT: SCIENTISTS
    RT: PSYCHOLOGY

PSYCHOLOGY
PSYCHOLOGIE / PSICOLOGIA - 05.01.01
    BT: BEHAVIOURAL SCIENCES
    NT: INDUSTRIAL PSYCHOLOGY
          PSYCHOLOGY OF EDUCATION
    RT: PSYCHOLOGICAL ASPECTS
          PSYCHOLOGISTS

PSYCHOLOGY OF EDUCATION
PSYCHOLOGIE DE L'EDUCATION / PSICOLOGIA DE LA
EDUCACION - 06.01.00
    UF: EDUCATIONAL PSYCHOLOGY
    BT: PSYCHOLOGY
          SCIENCES OF EDUCATION

PUBERTY
PUBERTE / PUBERTAD - 15.02.02
    RT: FERTILITY

PUBLIC ACCOUNTING
COMPTABILITE PUBLIQUE / CONTABILIDAD PUBLICA -
11.01.01
*SN: USE IN CONNECTION WITH THE NATIONAL (STATE)
    BUDGET AND PUBLIC EXPENDITURE. DO NOT
    CONFUSE WITH 'NATIONAL ACCOUNTING'.*

PUBLIC ACCOUNTING<CONT>
> *BT:* ACCOUNTING
> PUBLIC FINANCE
> *RT:* BUDGETARY RESOURCES

PUBLIC ADMINISTRATION
**ADMINISTRATION PUBLIQUE / ADMINISTRACION PUBLICA
- 04.03.02**
> *NT:* ADMINISTRATION OF JUSTICE
> DEVELOPMENT ADMINISTRATION
> ECONOMIC ADMINISTRATION
> EDUCATIONAL ADMINISTRATION
> HEALTH ADMINISTRATION
> LABOUR ADMINISTRATION
> SOCIAL ADMINISTRATION
> *RT:* ADMINISTRATIVE ASPECTS
> ADMINISTRATIVE LAW
> ADMINISTRATIVE REFORMS
> BUREAUCRACY
> CIVIL SERVANTS
> CIVIL SERVICE
> CORRUPTION
> GOVERNMENT
> HEALTH ADMINISTRATION
> INSTITUTIONAL FRAMEWORK
> OMBUDSMAN
> TECHNOCRACY

PUBLIC BORROWING
**EMPRUNTS PUBLICS / EMPRESTITOS PUBLICOS -
11.01.01**
> *BT:* BORROWING
> PUBLIC FINANCE
> *RT:* TREASURY BONDS

PUBLIC DEBT
DETTE PUBLIQUE / DEUDA PUBLICA - 11.01.01
> *BT:* DEBT
> PUBLIC FINANCE

PUBLIC EDUCATION
**ENSEIGNEMENT PUBLIC / ENSENANZA PUBLICA -
06.03.03**
> *BT:* EDUCATIONAL SYSTEMS

PUBLIC ENTERPRISES
**ENTREPRISES PUBLIQUES / EMPRESAS PUBLICAS -
03.03.05**
> *UF:* NATIONALIZED ENTERPRISES
> *BT:* ENTERPRISES
> *NT:* NATIONALIZED INDUSTRY
> *RT:* DENATIONALIZATION
> NATIONALIZATION
> PUBLIC OWNERSHIP
> PUBLIC SECTOR

PUBLIC EXPENDITURES
DEPENSES PUBLIQUES / GASTOS PUBLICOS - 11.01.01
> *BT:* EXPENDITURES
> PUBLIC FINANCE
> *NT:* MILITARY EXPENDITURES
> *RT:* BUDGETARY RESOURCES
> CULTURAL EXPENDITURES
> NATIONAL BUDGET

PUBLIC FINANCE
FINANCES PUBLIQUES / HACIENDA PUBLICA - 11.01.01
*SN: THE FINANCES OF THE STATE, INCLUDING FISCAL
POLICY, TAXATION, ETC.*
> *NT:* LOCAL FINANCE
> NATIONAL BUDGET
> PUBLIC ACCOUNTING
> PUBLIC BORROWING
> PUBLIC DEBT
> PUBLIC EXPENDITURES
> TAXES
> *RT:* FINANCIAL ADMINISTRATION
> FINANCIAL POLICY

PUBLIC HEALTH
SANTE PUBLIQUE / SALUD PUBLICA - 15.04.01
> *BT:* HEALTH
> *RT:* HEALTH SERVICES

PUBLIC INVESTMENTS
**INVESTISSEMENTS PUBLICS / INVERSIONES PUBLICAS -
11.02.06**
> *BT:* INVESTMENTS
> *RT:* PUBLIC WORKS

PUBLIC LAND
TERRES DOMANIALES / TIERRAS ESTATALES - 07.02.00
> *NT:* COMMUNAL LAND
> *RT:* PUBLIC OWNERSHIP

PUBLIC LAW
DROIT PUBLIC / DERECHO PUBLICO - 04.01.02
> *BT:* LAW
> *NT:* ADMINISTRATIVE LAW
> CONSTITUTIONAL LAW

PUBLIC OPINION
OPINION PUBLIQUE / OPINION PUBLICA - 04.04.02
> *RT:* FREEDOM OF OPINION
> OPINION
> PROPAGANDA

PUBLIC OWNERSHIP
**PROPRIETE PUBLIQUE / PROPIEDAD PUBLICA -
03.03.05**
> *BT:* OWNERSHIP
> *RT:* COLLECTIVE OWNERSHIP
> DENATIONALIZATION
> EXPROPRIATION
> NATIONALIZATION
> PUBLIC ENTERPRISES
> PUBLIC LAND
> SOCIALIST ENTERPRISES

PUBLIC RELATIONS
**RELATIONS PUBLIQUES / RELACIONES PUBLICAS -
09.03.04**
> *RT:* ADVERTISING

PUBLIC SECTOR
SECTEUR PUBLIC / SECTOR PUBLICO - 03.03.05

PUBLIC SECTOR<CONT>
>   RT: BUREAUCRACY
           GOVERNMENT
           PUBLIC ENTERPRISES
           STATE INTERVENTION

PUBLIC SERVANTS
EMPLOYES DES SERVICES PUBLICS / EMPLEADOS
PUBLICOS - 13.09.04
SN: USE TO DENOTE EMPLOYEES OF SERVICES
       CONTROLLED BY THE NATIONAL OR LOCAL
       GOVERNMENT, SUCH AS ELECTRICITY, GAS, WATER,
       ETC.
       BT: EMPLOYEES
       RT: PUBLIC SERVICES

PUBLIC SERVICES
SERVICES PUBLICS / SERVICIOS PUBLICOS - 04.03.06
SN: USE IN CONNECTION WITH SERVICES SUPPLIED TO
       THE POPULATION AS A WHOLE AND CONTROLLED BY
       THE NATIONAL OR LOCAL GOVERNMEMT, SUCH AS
       WATER, GAS, ELECTRICITY, ETC.
       UF: PUBLIC UTILITIES
       NT: SANITATION SERVICES
       RT: PUBLIC SERVANTS

PUBLIC TRANSPORT
TRANSPORT PUBLIC / TRANSPORTE PUBLICO - 10.01.00
       UF: COLLECTIVE TRANSPORT
       BT: TRANSPORT

PUBLIC UTILITIES
- 04.03.06
       USE: PUBLIC SERVICES

PUBLIC WORKS
TRAVAUX PUBLICS / OBRAS PUBLICAS - 04.03.06
SN: CONSTRUCTION OF PUBLIC BUILDINGS, UTILITIES,
       ETC.
       RT: CIVIL ENGINEERING
           CONSTRUCTION INDUSTRY
           PUBLIC INVESTMENTS
           TRANSPORT INFRASTRUCTURE

PUBLISHING
EDITION / EDICION - 08.16.00
       BT: BOOK INDUSTRY

PUERTO RICAN
PORTORICAIN / PUERTORRIQUENO - 14.03.02
       RT: PUERTO RICO

PUERTO RICO
PORTO RICO / PUERTO RICO - 01.04.03
       BT: CARIBBEAN
           LATIN AMERICA
       RT: PUERTO RICAN
           USA

PULP
PATE A PAPIER / PULPA - 08.07.02
SN: MADE FROM VARIOUS AGRICULTURAL OR FORESTRY
       PRODUCTS OR BY-PRODUCTS.
       BT: WOOD PRODUCTS

PULP AND PAPER INDUSTRY
INDUSTRIE DE PATE ET PAPIER / INDUSTRIA DE PULPA
Y PAPEL - 08.07.02
       BT: INDUSTRIAL SECTOR
       RT: CARDBOARD
           PAPER
           WOOD PROCESSING

PUMPING PLANTS
STATIONS DE POMPAGE / ESTACIONES DE BOMBEO -
17.05.04

PUMPS
POMPES / BOMBAS - 17.05.04
       BT: HYDRAULIC EQUIPMENT

PUNCHED CARDS
FICHES PERFOREES / TARJETAS PERFORADAS -
19.01.04
       BT: CARDS

PUPILS
- 06.06.01
       USE: STUDENTS

PURCHASING
ACHAT / COMPRA - 09.03.02
       UF: BUYING
       NT: HIRE PURCHASE

PURCHASING POWER
POUVOIR D'ACHAT / PODER DE COMPRA - 03.02.05
       RT: COST OF LIVING
           FAMILY BUDGET
           INCOME
           PRICES

QATAR
QATAR / QATAR - 01.04.06
   BT: PERSIAN GULF STATES

QUALIFICATIONS
QUALIFICATIONS / CALIFICACIONES - 06.04.13
   NT: CERTIFICATES
       DIPLOMAS
       OCCUPATIONAL QUALIFICATION
       UNIVERSITY DEGREES
   RT: EXAMINATIONS

QUALITY CONTROL
CONTROLE DE QUALITE / CONTROL DE CALIDAD -
12.07.02
*SN: THE PROCESS OF CHECKING INDUSTRIAL PRODUCTS
   AT VARIOUS STAGES OF MANUFACTURE TO ENSURE
   THAT THEY CONFORM TO SET STANDARDS.*
   RT: QUALITY STANDARDS
       TESTING

QUALITY OF EDUCATION
QUALITE DE L'EDUCATION / CALIDAD DE LA EDUCACION
- 06.02.03
   RT: EDUCATIONAL OUTPUT

QUALITY OF LIFE
QUALITE DE LA VIE / CALIDAD DE VIDA - 05.03.01
   RT: BASIC NEEDS
       ENVIRONMENTAL QUALITY
       HUMAN RELATIONS
       LIVING CONDITIONS

QUALITY STANDARDS
NORMES DE QUALITE / NORMAS DE CALIDAD - 12.07.02
   BT: STANDARDS
   RT: APPELLATION OF ORIGIN
       QUALITY CONTROL

QUARANTINE
QUARANTAINE / CUARENTENA - 15.04.04
   RT: HEALTH CONTROL

QUARRYING
EXPLOITATION DE CARRIERES / EXPLOTACION DE
CANTERAS - 08.10.01
   RT: MINING

QUARTERLY
PUBLICATION TRIMESTRIELLE / PUBLICACION
TRIMESTRAL - 19.02.06
   BT: PERIODICALS

QUATERNARY
QUATERNAIRE / CUATERNARIO - 17.04.02

QUESTIONNAIRES
QUESTIONNAIRES / CUESTIONARIOS - 18.04.00
   RT: INTERVIEWS
       SURVEYS

QUOTA SYSTEM
CONTINGENTEMENT / SISTEMA DE CONTINGENTES -

QUOTA SYSTEM<CONT>
09.05.07
   BT: PROTECTIONIST MEASURES

RACE RELATIONS
RELATIONS RACIALES / RELACIONES RACIALES -
04.02.04
SN: WITH RACE DISCRIMINATION.
   OTHERWISE USE 'INTERETHNIC RELATIONS'.
      BT: INTERGROUP RELATIONS
      NT: DESEGREGATION
         RACIAL CONFLICTS
         RACISM
      RT: RACIAL DISCRIMINATION

RACIAL CONFLICTS
CONFLITS RACIAUX / CONFLICTOS RACIALES -
04.02.04
      BT: CONFLICTS
         RACE RELATIONS

RACIAL DISCRIMINATION
DISCRIMINATION RACIALE / DISCRIMINACION RACIAL
- 04.02.04
      BT: DISCRIMINATION
      RT: RACE RELATIONS

RACIAL POLICY
POLITIQUE RACIALE / POLITICA RACIAL - 04.02.04
      RT: DESEGREGATION
         RACISM

RACIAL SEGREGATION
SEGREGATION RACIALE / SEGREGACION RACIAL -
04.02.04
      NT: APARTHEID
      RT: DESEGREGATION

RACISM
RACISME / RACISMO - 04.02.04
      BT: DISCRIMINATION
         RACE RELATIONS
      RT: RACIAL POLICY

RADAR
RADAR / RADAR - 08.15.02
      BT: ELECTRONIC EQUIPMENT
         MEASURING INSTRUMENTS

RADIATION PROTECTION
PROTECTION CONTRE LES RADIATIONS / PROTECCION
CONTRA LAS RADIACIONES - 16.04.01
      RT: RADIOACTIVITY

RADICALISM
EXTREMISME / EXTREMISMO - 04.04.02
      RT: POLITICAL BEHAVIOUR
         POLITICAL IDEOLOGIES

RADIO
RADIO / RADIO - 05.07.03
      BT: MASS MEDIA
         TELECOMMUNICATIONS
      NT: EDUCATIONAL RADIO
      RT: BROADCASTING
         RADIO RECEIVERS

RADIO RECEIVERS
RECEPTEURS DE RADIO / RADIO RECEPTORES -

RADIO RECEIVERS<CONT>
08.16.00
      RT: RADIO

RADIOACTIVE MATERIALS
MATIERES RADIOACTIVES / MATERIAS RADIACTIVAS -
08.11.04
      BT: DANGEROUS SUBSTANCES
      NT: RADIOACTIVE WASTES
      RT: RADIOACTIVITY
         RADIOISOTOPES

RADIOACTIVE POLLUTION
POLLUTION RADIOACTIVE / CONTAMINACION RADIACTIVA
- 16.03.04
      BT: POLLUTION
      RT: RADIOACTIVE WASTES
         RADIOACTIVITY

RADIOACTIVE WASTES
DECHETS RADIOACTIFS / DESPERDICIOS RADIACTIVOS -
08.11.04
      BT: RADIOACTIVE MATERIALS
         WASTES
      RT: RADIOACTIVE POLLUTION

RADIOACTIVITY
RADIOACTIVITE / RADIACTIVIDAD - 08.11.04
      RT: RADIATION PROTECTION
         RADIOACTIVE MATERIALS
         RADIOACTIVE POLLUTION

RADIOISOTOPES
RADIOISOTOPES / RADIOISOTOPOS - 08.11.04
      BT: ISOTOPES
      RT: RADIOACTIVE MATERIALS

RADIOLOGY
RADIOLOGIE / RADIOLOGIA - 15.04.06
      BT: MEDICAL SCIENCES

RAILWAY NETWORK
RESEAU FERROVIAIRE / RED FERROVIARIA - 10.03.00
      RT: RAILWAY TRANSPORT

RAILWAY TRAFFIC
CIRCULATION FERROVIAIRE / TRAFICO FERROVIARIO -
10.08.00
      BT: TRAFFIC

RAILWAY TRANSPORT
TRANSPORT FERROVIAIRE / TRANSPORTE FERROVIARIO -
10.05.00
      BT: MODES OF TRANSPORTATION
      RT: RAILWAY NETWORK
         RAILWAYS
         TRAINS

RAILWAYS
CHEMINS DE FER / FERROCARRILES - 10.03.00
      BT: TRANSPORT INFRASTRUCTURE
      RT: RAILWAY TRANSPORT
         TRAINS

RAIN
PLUIE / LLUVIA - 17.01.03
    BT: PRECIPITATIONS
    RT: RAINY SEASON

RAINY SEASON
SAISON DES PLUIES / ESTACION DE LLUVIAS -
17.02.02
    UF: MONSOON
    BT: SEASONS
    RT: RAIN

RAPE
COLZA / COLZA - 07.07.06
    BT: OILSEEDS

RATE OF INVESTMENT
TAUX D'INVESTISSEMENT / TASA DE INVERSION -
11.02.06
    RT: INVESTMENTS

RATIONALIZATION
RATIONALISATION / RACIONALIZACION - 12.04.00
    RT: EFFICIENCY
        RESOURCES ALLOCATION

RATIONING
RATIONNEMENT / RACIONAMIENTO - 03.02.05
    BT: RESOURCES ALLOCATION
    RT: SUPPLY

RAW MATERIALS
MATIERES PREMIERES / MATERIAS PRIMAS - 12.08.01
    BT: COMMODITIES
    RT: NATURAL RESOURCES

READING
LECTURE / LECTURA - 06.03.04
    RT: LITERACY

REASSIGNMENT
REAFFECTATION / REASIGNACION FUNCIONAL -
13.05.00
SN: CHANGES OF JOB WITHIN THE SAME FIRM.
    UF: JOB ROTATION

RECOMMENDATION
RECOMMANDATION / RECOMENDACION - 19.02.05
SN: FORMAL RECOMMENDATIONS FROM A MEETING OR AN
    EXPERT.

RECORD INDUSTRY
INDUSTRIE DU DISQUE / INDUSTRIA DEL DISCO -
08.16.00
    BT: COMMUNICATION INDUSTRY

RECOVERY
RECUPERATION / RECUPERACION - 12.07.02
    RT: WASTES

RECRUITMENT
RECRUTEMENT / CONTRATACION - 13.02.01
SN: POLICIES AND PROCEDURES FOR SEEKING
    QUALIFIED EMPLOYEES.
    NT: TEACHER RECRUITMENT

RECRUITMENT<CONT>
    RT: PERSONNEL MANAGEMENT
        PROBATION PERIOD

RECURRENT EDUCATION
EDUCATION RECURRENTE / EDUCACION RECURRENTE -
06.03.05
    BT: ADULT EDUCATION
    RT: LIFE-LONG EDUCATION

REEXPORT
REEXPORTATION / REEXPORTACION - 09.05.05
    RT: EXPORTS

REFERENCE MATERIALS
INSTRUMENTS DE REFERENCE / MATERIAL DE
REFERENCIA - 19.02.07
    BT: DOCUMENTS
    NT: BIBLIOGRAPHY
        DICTIONARY
        DIRECTORY
        ENCYCLOPEDIA
        INDEX
        THESAURUS
        YEARBOOK
    RT: SECONDARY DOCUMENTS

REFINING
RAFFINAGE / REFINACION - 08.12.03
    BT: INDUSTRIAL PROCESSES
    RT: PETROLEUM REFINERIES

REFORESTATION
REBOISEMENT / REFORESTACION - 07.08.03
    BT: AFFORESTATION
    RT: PLANTING

REFORMS OF EDUCATION
- 06.02.03
    USE: EDUCATIONAL REFORMS

REFRACTORY MATERIALS
MATERIAUX REFRACTAIRES / MATERIALES
REFRACTARIOS - 08.10.03
    BT: CONSTRUCTION MATERIALS
    NT: ASBESTOS
    RT: CERAMICS

REFRIGERATION
REFRIGERATION / REFRIGERACION - 08.12.03
    BT: INDUSTRIAL PROCESSES
    RT: COOLING
        FREEZING
        TEMPERATURE

REFUGEES
REFUGIES / REFUGIADOS - 14.07.00
SN: POPULATION FLEEING THE NORMAL AREA OF
    HABITATION FOR POLITICAL OR OTHER REASONS.
    BT: MIGRANTS
    RT: UNHCR
        UNRWA

REGIONAL AGENCIES
AGENCES REGIONALES / ORGANISMOS REGIONALES -

REGIONAL AGENCIES<CONT>
01.01.07
    BT: AID INSTITUTIONS
          REGIONAL ORGANIZATIONS
    RT: REGIONAL COOPERATION

REGIONAL ANALYSIS
ANALYSE REGIONALE / ANALISIS REGIONAL - 17.03.01
SN: EVALUATION OF THE CHARACTERISTICS OF A
    REGION AND THEIR ECONOMIC, ECOLOGICAL, OR
    SOCIAL IMPLICATIONS.
    UF: AREA STUDY
          REGIONAL SCIENCE
    RT: GEOGRAPHY

REGIONAL COOPERATION
COOPERATION REGIONALE / COOPERACION REGIONAL -
01.01.01
SN: IN A MULTI-COUNTRY REGION.
    BT: INTERNATIONAL COOPERATION
    RT: REGIONAL AGENCIES
          REGIONAL ORGANIZATIONS

REGIONAL DEVELOPMENT
DEVELOPPEMENT REGIONAL / DESARROLLO REGIONAL -
03.02.03
SN: USE IN CONNECTION WITH STEPS TO IMPROVE THE
    MATERIAL PROSPERITY OF A REGION AT BOTH
    SUBNATIONAL AND MULTINATIONAL LEVELS.
    BT: ECONOMIC AND SOCIAL DEVELOPMENT
    RT: REGIONAL PLANNING
          REGIONAL POLICY
          REGIONALIZATION

REGIONAL DISPARITY
DISPARITE REGIONALE / DESIGUALDAD REGIONAL -
03.02.03
    BT: ECONOMIC DISPARITY
    RT: DEVELOPING AREAS

REGIONAL GOVERNMENT
ADMINISTRATION REGIONALE / GOBIERNO REGIONAL -
04.03.03
SN: WITHIN A COUNTRY.
    BT: GOVERNMENT

REGIONAL INTEGRATION
INTEGRATION REGIONALE / INTEGRACION REGIONAL -
01.02.01
    BT: ECONOMIC INTEGRATION
    RT: AFRICAN ORGANIZATIONS
          ARAB ORGANIZATIONS
          ASIAN ORGANIZATIONS
          COMMON MARKET
          EUROPEAN ORGANIZATIONS
          LAFTA
          REGIONALIZATION

REGIONAL ORGANIZATIONS
ORGANISATIONS REGIONALES / ORGANIZACIONES
REGIONALES - 01.03.01
    BT: INTERNATIONAL ORGANIZATIONS

REGIONAL ORGANIZATIONS<CONT>
    NT: AFRICAN ORGANIZATIONS
          AMERICAN ORGANIZATIONS
          ARAB ORGANIZATIONS
          ASIAN ORGANIZATIONS
          EUROPEAN ORGANIZATIONS
          REGIONAL AGENCIES
    RT: REGIONAL COOPERATION

REGIONAL PLANNING
PLANIFICATION REGIONALE / PLANIFICACION REGIONAL
- 02.01.02
SN: USE TO MEAN PLANNING AT BOTH THE
    SUB-NATIONAL AND MULTI-NATIONAL LEVELS.
    BT: PLANNING
    RT: GROWTH POLES
          LOCATION FACTORS
          REGIONAL DEVELOPMENT
          REGIONAL PLAN
          REGIONAL PLANS
          REGIONAL POLICY
          REGIONALIZATION

REGIONAL PLANS
PLANS REGIONAUX / PLANES REGIONALES - 02.01.02
SN: USE IN REFERENCE TO THE SCOPE NOTE PROVIDED
    FOR 'REGIONAL PLANNING'.
    BT: DEVELOPMENT PLANS
    RT: REGIONAL PLANNING
          REGIONAL POLICY
          REGIONALIZATION

REGIONAL POLICY
POLITIQUE REGIONALE / POLITICA REGIONAL -
02.01.02
    RT: REGIONAL DEVELOPMENT
          REGIONAL PLANNING
          REGIONAL PLANS

REGIONAL SCIENCE
- 17.03.01
    USE: REGIONAL ANALYSIS

REGIONALIZATION
REGIONALISATION / REGIONALIZACION - 02.01.02
    RT: REGIONAL DEVELOPMENT
          REGIONAL INTEGRATION
          REGIONAL PLAN
          REGIONAL PLANNING
          REGIONAL PLANS

REGULATIONS
REGLEMENTATIONS / REGLAMENTACIONES - 04.01.01

REHABILITATION
READAPTATION / REHABILITACION - 15.04.04
    NT: VOCATIONAL REHABILITATION

REINSURANCE
REASSURANCE / REASEGURO - 11.02.03

REINVESTMENTS
REINVESTISSEMENTS / REINVERSIONES - 11.02.06

REINVESTMENTS<CONT>
    RT: INVESTMENTS
        PROFITS

RELIGION
RELIGION / RELIGION - 05.04.02
    RT: RELIGIOUS FREEDOM
        RELIGIOUS INSTITUTIONS
        RELIGIOUS MINORITIES
        RELIGIOUS PRACTICE
        SOCIAL CONTROL
        WORSHIP

RELIGIOUS FREEDOM
LIBERTE RELIGIEUSE / LIBERTAD RELIGIOSA -
04.02.02
    BT: CIVIL LIBERTIES
    RT: RELIGION

RELIGIOUS GROUPS
GROUPES RELIGIEUX / GRUPOS RELIGIOSOS - 05.04.02
    BT: GROUPS

RELIGIOUS INSTITUTIONS
INSTITUTIONS RELIGIEUSES / INSTITUCIONES
RELIGIOSAS - 05.04.04
    NT: RELIGIOUS MISSIONS
    RT: RELIGION

RELIGIOUS MINORITIES
MINORITES RELIGIEUSES / MINORIAS RELIGIOSAS -
05.04.02
    BT: MINORITY GROUPS
    RT: RELIGION

RELIGIOUS MISSIONS
MISSIONS RELIGIEUSES / MISIONES RELIGIOSAS -
05.04.04
SN: USE ONLY TO DENOTE A MISSION STATION.
    BT: RELIGIOUS INSTITUTIONS
    RT: CHRISTIANITY

RELIGIOUS PRACTICE
PRATIQUE RELIGIEUSE / PRACTICA RELIGIOSA -
05.04.02
    RT: RELIGION
        WORSHIP

REMEDIAL TEACHING
ENSEIGNEMENT CORRECTIF / ENSENANZA CORRECTIVA -
06.05.02
    BT: TEACHING

REMOTE SENSING
TELEDETECTION / PERCEPCION REMOTA - 18.04.00
    BT: OBSERVATION
    RT: AERIAL SURVEYS
        COMMUNICATION SATELLITES
        DISTANCE
        GEOLOGICAL SURVEYS

RENEWABLE RESOURCES
RESSOURCES RENOUVELABLES / RECURSOS RENOVABLES -

RENEWABLE RESOURCES<CONT>
16.02.02
    BT: NATURAL RESOURCES
    RT: NON-RENEWABLE RESOURCES

RENT
- 11.02.07
    USE: INVESTMENT RETURNS

REPAIR SHOPS
ATELIERS DE REPARATION / TALLERES DE REPARACION
- 08.03.00
    BT: WORKSHOPS
    RT: MAINTENANCE AND REPAIR

REPATRIATION OF CAPITAL
RAPATRIEMENT DE CAPITAUX / REPATRIACION DE
CAPITALES - 11.03.03
    BT: CAPITAL MOVEMENTS

REPORTING SYSTEMS
SYSTEMES DE NOTIFICATION / SISTEMAS DE
NOTIFICACION - 19.01.02
    BT: INFORMATION EXCHANGE
        INFORMATION SYSTEMS

REPROCESSING
RETRAITEMENT / REPROCESAMIENTO - 12.07.02
    BT: PROCESSING

REPRODUCTION
REPRODUCTION / REPRODUCCION - 15.02.02
    RT: ANIMAL BREEDING
        FERTILITY
        PLANT BREEDING

REPTILES
REPTILES / REPTILES - 07.09.01
    BT: ANIMALS

RESEARCH
RECHERCHE / INVESTIGACION - 18.01.00
    UF: SCIENTIFIC RESEARCH
    NT: AGRICULTURAL RESEARCH
        APPLIED RESEARCH
        BASIC RESEARCH
        COMMUNICATION RESEARCH
        DEVELOPMENT RESEARCH
        ECOLOGICAL RESEARCH
        ECONOMIC RESEARCH
        EDUCATIONAL RESEARCH
        FIELD RESEARCH
        INDUSTRIAL RESEARCH
        MEDICAL RESEARCH
        NUTRITION RESEARCH
        PEACE RESEARCH
        RESEARCH AND DEVELOPMENT
        SOCIAL RESEARCH

RESEARCH<CONT>
RT: ORGANIZATION OF RESEARCH
RESEARCH FELLOWSHIPS
RESEARCH METHODS
RESEARCH POLICY
RESEARCH PROGRAMMES
RESEARCH PROJECTS
RESEARCH REPORT
RESEARCH RESULTS
RESEARCH WORKERS

RESEARCH AND DEVELOPMENT
RECHERCHE ET DEVELOPPEMENT / INVESTIGACION Y
DESARROLLO - 18.01.00
BT: RESEARCH
RT: APPLIED RESEARCH
SCIENCE

RESEARCH CENTRES
CENTRES DE RECHERCHE / CENTROS DE INVESTIGACION
- 18.02.00
UF: RESEARCH INSTITUTES
NT: CAFRAD
CIMMYT
ICRISAT
IDRC
IRRI
LABORATORIES
UNITAR
UNRISD
RT: ADIPA
EADI

RESEARCH EQUIPMENT
EQUIPEMENT DE RECHERCHE / EQUIPO DE
INVESTIGACION - 18.02.00
UF: LABORATORY EQUIPMENT
BT: EQUIPMENT
RT: LABORATORIES

RESEARCH FELLOWSHIPS
BOURSES DE RECHERCHE / BECAS DE INVESTIGACION -
06.04.11
BT: EDUCATIONAL GRANTS
RT: RESEARCH

RESEARCH INSTITUTES
- 18.02.00
USE: RESEARCH CENTRES

RESEARCH METHODS
METHODES DE RECHERCHE / METODOS DE INVESTIGACION
- 18.03.00
NT: COMPARATIVE ANALYSIS
DATA COLLECTING
EVALUATION TECHNIQUES
EXPERIMENTS
FORECASTING TECHNIQUES
INTEGRATED APPROACH
INTERDISCIPLINARY RESEARCH
MATHEMATICAL ANALYSIS
OPERATIONAL RESEARCH
SIMULATION
STATISTICAL ANALYSIS

RESEARCH METHODS<CONT>
RT: FIELD RESEARCH
MEASUREMENT
METHODOLOGY
RESEARCH

RESEARCH POLICY
POLITIQUE DE LA RECHERCHE / POLITICA DE
INVESTIGACION - 18.01.00
BT: SCIENCE POLICY
RT: ORGANIZATION OF RESEARCH
RESEARCH

RESEARCH PROGRAMMES
PROGRAMMES DE RECHERCHE / PROGRAMAS DE
INVESTIGACION - 18.01.00
NT: RESEARCH PROJECTS
RT: RESEARCH

RESEARCH PROJECTS
PROJETS DE RECHERCHE / PROYECTOS DE
INVESTIGACION - 18.01.00
BT: RESEARCH PROGRAMMES
RT: RESEARCH

RESEARCH REPORT
RAPPORT DE RECHERCHE / INFORME DE INVESTIGACION
- 19.02.08
RT: RESEARCH

RESEARCH RESULTS
RESULTATS DE RECHERCHE / RESULTADOS DE
INVESTIGACION - 18.03.00
RT: RESEARCH

RESEARCH WORKERS
CHERCHEURS / INVESTIGADORES - 13.09.09
UF: SCIENTIFIC RESEARCHERS
RT: RESEARCH
SCIENTISTS

RESERVOIRS
RESERVOIRS / EMBALSES - 17.05.04

RESIGNATION
DEMISSION / RENUNCIA - 13.05.00
RT: DISMISSAL

RESINS
RESINES / RESINAS - 07.07.08
BT: FOREST PRODUCTS
RT: GUMS

RESISTANCE TO CHANGE
RESISTANCE AU CHANGEMENT / RESISTENCIA AL CAMBIO
- 05.03.04
RT: ADAPTATION TO CHANGE
CONSERVATISM
OBSTACLES TO DEVELOPMENT
SOCIAL CHANGE

RESOLUTION
RESOLUTION / RESOLUCION - 19.02.05

RESOLUTION<CONT>
SN: DECISION MADE BY AN ASSEMBLY TO ORIENT
    FUTURE ACTION.

RESOURCES ALLOCATION
AFFECTATION DES RESSOURCES / ASIGNACION DE
RECURSOS - 02.01.02
    NT: RATIONING
    RT: EFFICIENCY
        MANAGEMENT TECHNIQUES
        RATIONALIZATION
        WELFARE ECONOMICS

RESOURCES APPRAISAL
- 16.02.01
    USE: RESOURCES INVENTORY

RESOURCES CENTRES
CENTRES DE MATERIEL DIDACTIQUE / CENTROS DE
MATERIAL DIDACTICO - 06.05.03
    RT: TEACHING AIDS

RESOURCES CONSERVATION
CONSERVATION DES RESSOURCES / CONSERVACION DE
LOS RECURSOS - 16.05.01
    NT: ENERGY CONSERVATION
        SOIL CONSERVATION
        WATER CONSERVATION
    RT: NATURE CONSERVATION
        PROTECTED RESOURCES

RESOURCES DEPLETION
EPUISEMENT DES RESSOURCES / AGOTAMIENTO DE
RECURSOS - 16.02.01
    RT: EXPLOITABILITY
        OVEREXPLOITATION
        RESOURCES EXPLOITATION

RESOURCES EVALUATION
EVALUATION DES RESSOURCES / EVALUACION DE
RECURSOS - 16.02.01
    BT: EVALUATION
    RT: EXPLOITABILITY
        RESOURCES EXPLOITATION
        RESOURCES MANAGEMENT

RESOURCES EXPLOITATION
EXPLOITATION DES RESSOURCES / EXPLOTACION DE
RECURSOS - 16.02.01
    RT: EXPLOITABILITY
        OVEREXPLOITATION
        RESOURCES DEPLETION
        RESOURCES EVALUATION

RESOURCES EXPLORATION
- 16.02.01
    USE: RESOURCES INVENTORY

RESOURCES INVENTORY
INVENTAIRE DES RESSOURCES / INVENTARIO DE
RECURSOS - 16.02.01
    UF: RESOURCES APPRAISAL
        RESOURCES EXPLORATION

RESOURCES MANAGEMENT
GESTION DES RESSOURCES / ADMINISTRACION DE
RECURSOS - 16.02.01
    BT: MANAGEMENT
    RT: RESOURCES EVALUATION

RESPIRATORY SYSTEM
SYSTEME RESPIRATOIRE / SISTEMA RESPIRATORIO -
15.02.04
    BT: ANATOMY

RESPONSIBILITY
RESPONSABILITE / RESPONSABILIDAD - 05.04.01
    RT: SOCIAL NORMS
        VALUE SYSTEMS

REST
REPOS / DESCANSO - 13.03.04
    RT: FATIGUE
        HOLIDAYS
        LEISURE
        REST PERIOD

REST PERIOD
TEMPS DE REPOS / PERIODO DE DESCANSO - 13.03.03
    BT: ARRANGEMENT OF WORKING TIME
    NT: WEEKLY REST
    RT: REST

RESTRICTED DOCUMENTS
DOCUMENTS A DIFFUSION RESTREINTE / DOCUMENTOS
RESTRINGIDOS - 19.02.01
SN: FOR DOCUMENTS ACCESS TO WHICH HAS BEEN
    RESTRICTED BY THE ISSUING BODY.
    BT: DOCUMENTS

RESTRICTIVE BUSINESS PRACTICES
PRATIQUES COMMERCIALES RESTRICTIVES / PRACTICAS
COMERCIALES RESTRICTIVAS - 09.05.07
    BT: TRADE BARRIERS
    NT: CARTELS
        EXPORT RESTRICTIONS
        PROTECTIONIST MEASURES
    RT: ANTITRUST LEGISLATION
        COMPETITION
        CONSUMER PROTECTION

RETAIL MARKETING
VENTE AU DETAIL / VENTA AL POR MENOR - 09.03.01
    BT: MARKETING
    RT: RETAIL TRADE

RETAIL PRICES
PRIX DE DETAIL / PRECIOS AL POR MENOR - 09.02.00
SN: USE ONLY BY OPPOSITION TO 'WHOLESALE
    PRICES', OTHERWISE USE 'CONSUMER PRICES'.
    BT: PRICES
    RT: RETAIL TRADE

RETAIL TRADE
COMMERCE DE DETAIL / COMERCIO MINORISTA -
09.04.04
    BT: DISTRIBUTION
        TRADE

RETAIL TRADE<CONT>
    RT: RETAIL MARKETING
           RETAIL PRICES

RETIREMENT
RETRAITE / JUBILACION - 13.05.00
    NT: EARLY RETIREMENT
    RT: RETIREMENT PENSIONS

RETIREMENT PENSIONS
PENSIONS DE RETRAITE / PENSIONES DE RETIRO -
02.03.02
    RT: OLD AGE BENEFITS
           PENSION SCHEMES
           RETIREMENT

RETRAINING
FORMATION DE RECYCLAGE / RECAPACITATION -
06.03.07
SN: TRAINING DESIGNED TO PROVIDE WORKERS
    RENDERED OBSOLETE BY TECHNOLOGICAL CHANGE
    WITH NEW SKILLS FOR WHICH THERE IS A DEMAND
    IN THE LABOUR MARKET.
    BT: VOCATIONAL TRAINING

RETURN MIGRATIONS
MIGRATIONS DE RETOUR / MIGRACIONES DE RETORNO -
14.07.00
    BT: MIGRATIONS

REUNION ISLAND
ILE DE LA REUNION / ISLA DE LA REUNION -
01.04.02
    BT: EAST AFRICA
           FRENCH SPEAKING AFRICA
           SOUTHERN AFRICA
    RT: FRANCE

REVOLUTION
REVOLUTION / REVOLUCION - 05.03.04
    RT: CIVIL WAR
           POLITICS
           SOCIAL CHANGE
           SOCIAL MOVEMENTS

RHODESIA
RHODESIE / RODESIA - 01.04.02
    BT: EAST AFRICA
           ENGLISH SPEAKING AFRICA
           SOUTHERN AFRICA

RICE
RIZ / ARROZ - 07.07.04
    BT: CEREALS
    RT: IRRI
           WARDA

RICKETTSIAL DISEASES
RICKETTSIOSES / RICKETTSIOSAS - 15.04.02
    BT: INFECTIOUS DISEASES
    NT: TYPHUS

RIGHT TO CULTURE
DROIT A LA CULTURE / DERECHO A LA CULTURA -

RIGHT TO CULTURE<CONT>
05.02.03
    BT: HUMAN RIGHTS
    RT: CULTURE

RIGHT TO EDUCATION
DROIT A L'EDUCATION / DERECHO A LA EDUCACION -
06.02.02
    BT: HUMAN RIGHTS
    RT: ACCESS TO CULTURE
           ACCESS TO EDUCATION

RIGHT TO STRIKE
DROIT DE GREVE / DERECHO DE HUELGA - 13.06.00
    RT: LABOUR LAW
           STRIKES

RIGHT TO WORK
DROIT AU TRAVAIL / DERECHO AL TRABAJO - 13.02.01
    BT: HUMAN RIGHTS

RIVER BASINS
BASSINS FLUVIAUX / CUENCAS FLUVIALES - 17.05.02
    RT: HYDROLOGICAL NETWORK
           HYDROLOGY
           RIVERS

RIVER BLINDNESS
- 15.04.02
    USE: ONCHOCERCIASIS

RIVER POLLUTION
POLLUTION DES COURS D'EAU / CONTAMINACION
FLUVIAL - 16.03.04
    BT: WATER POLLUTION
    RT: RIVERS

RIVERS
COURS D'EAU / RIOS - 17.05.02
    BT: INLAND WATERWAYS
    RT: HYDROLOGICAL NETWORK
           HYDROLOGY
           INTERNATIONAL WATERWAYS
           RIVER BASINS
           RIVER POLLUTION

ROAD CONSTRUCTION
CONSTRUCTION DE ROUTE / CONSTRUCCION VIAL -
10.03.00
    RT: ROAD TRANSPORT

ROAD NETWORK
RESEAU ROUTIER / RED VIAL - 10.03.00
    RT: ROAD TRANSPORT

ROAD SAFETY
SECURITE ROUTIERE / SEGURIDAD EN LAS CARRETERAS
- 10.08.00
    BT: SAFETY
    RT: ROAD TRAFFIC
           ROADS

ROAD TRAFFIC
CIRCULATION ROUTIERE / TRAFICO POR CARRETERA -

ROAD TRAFFIC<CONT>
10.08.00
>   *BT:* TRAFFIC
>   *RT:* ROAD SAFETY
>   ROAD TRANSPORT

ROAD TRANSPORT
TRANSPORT ROUTIER / TRANSPORTE POR CARRETERA -
10.05.00
>   *BT:* MODES OF TRANSPORTATION
>   *RT:* AUTOMOBILE INDUSTRY
>   AUTOMOBILE SERVICE
>   MOTOR VEHICLES
>   ROAD CONSTRUCTION
>   ROAD NETWORK
>   ROAD TRAFFIC
>   ROADS

ROADS
ROUTES / CARRETERAS - 10.03.00
>   *BT:* TRANSPORT INFRASTRUCTURE
>   *NT:* MOTORWAYS
>   *RT:* ROAD SAFETY
>   ROAD TRANSPORT

RODENTS
RONGEURS / ROEDORES - 16.03.03
>   *BT:* ANIMALS

ROLLING
LAMINAGE / LAMINADO - 08.14.03
>   *BT:* MACHINING

ROLLING STOCK
MATERIEL ROULANT / MATERIAL RODANTE - 10.04.00
>   *BT:* TRAINS

ROMANIA
ROUMANIE / RUMANIA - 01.04.05
>   *BT:* EASTERN EUROPE
>   *RT:* ROMANIAN

ROMANIAN
ROUMAIN / RUMANO - 14.03.02
>   *RT:* ROMANIA

ROOT CROPS
PLANTES-RACINES / CULTIVOS DE TUBEROSAS -
07.07.02
>   *NT:* CASSAVA
>   POTATOES
>   SUGAR BEETS
>   SWEET POTATOES
>   *RT:* VEGETABLE CROPS

ROPE INDUSTRY
CORDERIE / CORDELERIA - 08.08.01
>   *BT:* TEXTILE INDUSTRY
>   *RT:* HEMP

ROYALTIES
REDEVANCES / DERECHOS DE PATENTE - 11.02.07
>   *BT:* INCOME

RUBBER
CAOUTCHOUC / CAUCHO - 08.09.00
>   *NT:* SYNTHETIC RUBBER
>   *RT:* HEVEAS
>   LATEX
>   RUBBER INDUSTRY

RUBBER INDUSTRY
INDUSTRIE DU CAOUTCHOUC / INDUSTRIA DEL CAUCHO -
08.09.00
>   *BT:* INDUSTRIAL SECTOR
>   *RT:* RUBBER
>   TYRES

RUBELLA
RUBEOLE / RUBEOLA - 15.04.02
>   *BT:* INFECTIOUS DISEASES

RULING CLASS
CLASSE DIRIGEANTE / CLASE DIRIGENTE - 05.03.05
>   *BT:* SOCIAL CLASSES
>   *RT:* ELITE
>   POLITICAL LEADERSHIP
>   UPPER CLASS

RUMINANTS
RUMINANTS / RUMIANTES - 07.09.01
>   *BT:* ANIMALS
>   *NT:* BOVIDAE
>   CAMELS
>   GOATS
>   OVIDAE

RURAL
RURAL / RURAL - 14.04.02

RURAL AREAS
ZONES RURALES / ZONAS RURALES - 14.04.02
>   *RT:* RURAL INDUSTRY
>   RURAL SCHOOLS
>   RURAL WORKERS

RURAL COMMUNITIES
COLLECTIVITES RURALES / COMUNIDADES RURALES -
14.04.02
>   *RT:* VILLAGES

RURAL DEVELOPMENT
DEVELOPPEMENT RURAL / DESARROLLO RURAL -
14.04.02
>   *RT:* RURAL PLANNING

RURAL ENVIRONMENT
MILIEU RURAL / MEDIO RURAL - 14.04.02
>   *BT:* SOCIAL ENVIRONMENT

RURAL EXODUS
- 14.07.00
>   *USE:* RURAL MIGRATIONS

RURAL INDUSTRY
INDUSTRIE RURALE / INDUSTRIA RURAL - 08.02.02
>   *BT:* INDUSTRY
>   *NT:* COTTAGE INDUSTRY
>   *RT:* RURAL AREAS

RURAL MIGRATIONS
MIGRATIONS RURALES / MIGRACIONES RURALES -
14.07.00
*SN: THE MIGRATION OF RURAL WORKERS TO URBAN
AREAS.*
    UF: RURAL EXODUS
    BT: INTERNAL MIGRATIONS
    RT: RURAL POPULATION

RURAL PLANNING
AMENAGEMENT RURAL / PLANIFICACION RURAL -
14.04.02
    BT: PLANNING
    RT: LOCAL GOVERNMENT
        RURAL DEVELOPMENT

RURAL POPULATION
POPULATION RURALE / POBLACION RURAL - 14.04.02
    BT: POPULATION
    NT: AGRICULTURAL POPULATION
    RT: RURAL MIGRATIONS

RURAL SCHOOLS
ECOLES RURALES / ESCUELAS RURALES - 06.04.04
    BT: SCHOOLS
    RT: RURAL AREAS

RURAL SOCIOLOGY
SOCIOLOGIE RURALE / SOCIOLOGIA RURAL - 14.04.02
    BT: SOCIOLOGY

RURAL WORKERS
TRAVAILLEURS RURAUX / TRABAJADORES RURALES -
13.09.05
    BT: WORKERS
    NT: AGRICULTURAL WORKERS
    RT: RURAL AREAS

RURAL YOUTH
JEUNESSE RURALE / JUVENTUD RURAL - 14.04.02
    BT: YOUTH

RUSSIAN
RUSSE / RUSO - 14.03.02
    RT: USSR

RUSSIAN LANGUAGE
LANGUE RUSSE / LENGUA RUSA - 05.06.02
    BT: LANGUAGES

RWANDA
RWANDA / RWANDA - 01.04.02
    BT: CENTRAL AFRICA
        EAST AFRICA
        FRENCH SPEAKING AFRICA
    RT: RWANDESE

RWANDESE
RWANDAIS / RWANDES - 14.03.02
    RT: RWANDA

RYE
SEIGLE / CENTENO - 07.07.04
    BT: CEREALS

SAFETY
SECURITE / SEGURIDAD - 16.04.01
    NT: OCCUPATIONAL SAFETY
        ROAD SAFETY
    RT: ACCIDENTS
        ENVIRONMENTAL ENGINEERING
        SAFETY EDUCATION
        WARNING DEVICES

SAFETY DEVICES
DISPOSITIFS DE PROTECTION / DISPOSITIVOS DE
PROTECCION - 13.04.00
    RT: OCCUPATIONAL SAFETY

SAFETY EDUCATION
ENSEIGNEMENT RELATIF A LA SECURITE / EDUCACION
SOBRE SEGURIDAD - 06.03.04
    BT: BASIC EDUCATION
    RT: HEALTH EDUCATION
        SAFETY

SAHARA
SAHARA / SAHARA - 01.04.02
    BT: AFRICA
    RT: ARID ZONE

SAHEL
SAHEL / SAHEL - 01.04.02
    BT: CENTRAL AFRICA
        WEST AFRICA

SALARY
- 13.07.00
    USE: WAGES

SALES
VENTES / VENTAS - 09.03.02
SN: USE TO MEAN THE AMOUNT OF COMMODITIES SOLD.
    RT: TURNOVER

SALES PROMOTION
- 09.03.01
    USE: MARKETING

SALES TAX
- 11.01.02
    USE: CONSUMPTION TAX

SALESMEN
- 13.09.07
    USE: VENDORS
    RT: MARKETING

SALT
SEL / SAL - 08.12.04
    RT: DESALINIZATION

SALT WATER
EAU SALEE / AGUA SALADA - 17.05.05
    BT: WATER
    RT: DESALINIZATION

SALT WATER FISH
POISSON DE MER / PEZ DE MAR - 07.10.04
    BT: FISH

SALVADORIAN
SALVADORIEN / SALVADORENO - 14.03.02
    RT: EL SALVADOR

SAMOA
SAMOA / SAMOA - 01.04.07
    BT: OCEANIA
    RT: SAMOAN

SAMOAN
SAMOAN / SAMOANO - 14.03.02
    RT: SAMOA

SAMPLE
ECHANTILLON / MUESTRA - 18.04.00

SAN MARINO
SAINT-MARIN / SAN MARINO - 01.04.05
    BT: MEDITERRANEAN COUNTRIES
          WESTERN EUROPE

SAND
SABLE / ARENA - 08.10.02
    BT: CONSTRUCTION MATERIALS

SANDWICH TRAINING
FORMATION EN ALTERNANCE / CAPACITACION ALTERNADA
- 06.03.07
*SN: TRAINING IN SCHOOL AND IN A WORKING
    SITUATION.*
    BT: VOCATIONAL TRAINING

SANITATION
ASSAINISSEMENT / SANEAMIENTO AMBIENTAL -
16.04.02
    BT: HYGIENE
    RT: HEALTH EDUCATION
          SANITATION SERVICES

SANITATION SERVICES
SERVICES DE VOIRIE / SERVICIOS DE SANEAMIENTO -
16.04.02
    UF: SEWAGE DISPOSAL
    BT: PUBLIC SERVICES
    RT: DOMESTIC WASTES
          SANITATION
          WASTE MANAGEMENT

SAO TOME AND PRINCIPE
SAO TOME ET PRINCIPE / SANTO TOME Y PRINCIPE -
01.04.02
    BT: CENTRAL AFRICA

SATELLITE TOWNS
VILLES SATELLITES / CIUDADES SATELITES -
14.04.03
    BT: TOWNS

SAUDI ARABIA
ARABIE SAOUDITE / ARABIA SAUDITA - 01.04.06
    BT: ARAB COUNTRIES
          MIDDLE EAST
    RT: SAUDI ARABIAN

SAUDI ARABIAN
SAOUDIEN / ARABE SAUDITA - 14.03.02
    RT: SAUDI ARABIA

SAVANNA
SAVANE / SABANA - 17.03.04

SAVINGS
EPARGNE / AHORROS - 11.02.05
    NT: HOARDING
    RT: SAVINGS BANKS

SAVINGS BANKS
CAISSES D'EPARGNE / CAJAS DE AHORROS - 11.02.02
    BT: FINANCIAL INSTITUTIONS
    RT: SAVINGS

SCANDINAVIA
SCANDINAVIE / ESCANDINAVIA - 01.04.05
    BT: WESTERN EUROPE
    NT: DENMARK
          FAROE ISLANDS
          FINLAND
          GREENLAND
          ICELAND
          NORWAY
          SWEDEN
    RT: NORDIC COUNCIL
          SCANDINAVIAN

SCANDINAVIAN
SCANDINAVE / ESCANDINAVO - 14.03.02
    RT: SCANDINAVIA

SCARLET FEVER
SCARLATINE / ESCARLATINA - 15.04.02
    BT: INFECTIOUS DISEASES

SCENARIOS
SCENARIOS / ESCENARIOS - 02.01.01
    BT: OPERATIONAL RESEARCH
    RT: DEVELOPMENT PLANNING
          DEVELOPMENT POLICY
          DEVELOPMENT STRATEGY

SCHISTOSOMIASIS
SCHISTOSOMIASE / ESQUISTOSOMIASIS - 15.04.02
    UF: BILHARZIASIS
    BT: PARASITIC DISEASES
          TROPICAL DISEASES

SCHOLARSHIP HOLDERS
BOURSIERS / BECARIOS - 06.06.01
    RT: SCHOLARSHIPS

SCHOLARSHIPS
BOURSES D'ETUDE / BECAS - 06.04.11
    BT: EDUCATIONAL GRANTS
    RT: SCHOLARSHIP HOLDERS

SCHOOL ADAPTATION
ADAPTATION SCOLAIRE / ADAPTACION ESCOLAR -
06.04.12
    BT: SOCIAL ADAPTATION
    RT: SCHOOL ENVIRONMENT

SCHOOL AGE POPULATION
POPULATION D'AGE SCOLAIRE / POBLACION EN EDAD
ESCOLAR - 14.02.02
    BT: AGE GROUPS

SCHOOL BUILDINGS
BATIMENTS SCOLAIRES / EDIFICIOS ESCOLARES -
06.04.07
    BT: EDUCATIONAL BUILDINGS
    RT: SCHOOLS

SCHOOL DISCIPLINE
DISCIPLINE SCOLAIRE / DISCIPLINA ESCOLAR -
06.04.08

SCHOOL ENVIRONMENT
MILIEU SCOLAIRE / MEDIO ESCOLAR - 06.04.12
    BT: SOCIAL ENVIRONMENT
    NT: SCHOOL-COMMUNITY RELATIONSHIPS
        TEACHER-STUDENT RELATIONSHIPS
    RT: SCHOOL ADAPTATION
        SCHOOLS

SCHOOL HOLIDAYS
VACANCES SCOLAIRES / VACACIONES ESCOLARES -
06.04.12
    BT: HOLIDAYS

SCHOOL LEAVERS
ELEVES SORTANTS / ALUMNOS EGRESADOS - 06.06.01
*SN: PERSONS WHO LEAVE SCHOOL AT THE REGULAR END
    OF A TRAINING PERIOD. DO NOT CONFUSE WITH
    'DROPOUTS'.*
    RT: LEAVING SCHOOL

SCHOOL MANAGEMENT
ADMINISTRATION SCOLAIRE / ADMINISTRACION ESCOLAR
- 06.04.08
    BT: MANAGEMENT
    RT: EDUCATIONAL INSTITUTIONS
        SCHOOLS

SCHOOL SEGREGATION
SEGREGATION SCOLAIRE / SEGREGACION ESCOLAR -
06.04.12

SCHOOL SYSTEMS
- 06.03.01
    USE: EDUCATIONAL SYSTEMS

SCHOOL TRANSPORT
TRANSPORT SCOLAIRE / TRANSPORTE ESCOLAR -
06.04.07
    BT: EDUCATIONAL EQUIPMENT
        TRANSPORT

SCHOOL-COMMUNITY RELATIONSHIPS
RELATIONS ECOLE-COLLECTIVITE / RELACIONES
ESCUELA-COMUNIDAD - 06.04.12
    BT: SCHOOL ENVIRONMENT
    RT: COMMUNITY
        SCHOOLS

SCHOOLING
SCOLARITE / ESCOLARIDAD - 06.03.02

SCHOOLING<CONT>
    RT: COMPULSORY EDUCATION
        LEAVING SCHOOL

SCHOOLS
ECOLES / ESCUELAS - 06.04.02
*SN: USE ONLY IN CASES WHERE A DESCRIPTOR
    CONCERNING A TYPE OF EDUCATION CANNOT BE
    USED.*
    BT: EDUCATIONAL INSTITUTIONS
    NT: BOARDING SCHOOLS
        COEDUCATIONAL SCHOOLS
        COMMERCIAL SCHOOLS
        COMPREHENSIVE SCHOOLS
        EXPERIMENTAL SCHOOLS
        INTERNATIONAL SCHOOLS
        MOBILE SCHOOLS
        NIGHT SCHOOLS
        NURSERY SCHOOLS
        PRIMARY SCHOOLS
        PRIVATE SCHOOLS
        RURAL SCHOOLS
        SECONDARY SCHOOLS
        SPECIAL SCHOOLS
        SUMMER SCHOOLS
        TECHNICAL SCHOOLS
        VOCATIONAL SCHOOLS
    RT: SCHOOL BUILDINGS
        SCHOOL ENVIRONMENT
        SCHOOL MANAGEMENT
        SCHOOL-COMMUNITY RELATIONSHIPS

SCIENCE
SCIENCE / CIENCIA - 18.01.00
    RT: ACAST
        ALECSO
        CSTD
        ICSU
        RESEARCH AND DEVELOPMENT
        SCIENCE POLICY
        SCIENTIFIC COOPERATION
        SCIENTIFIC CULTURE
        SCIENTIFIC INFORMATION
        SCIENTIFIC PROGRESS
        SCIENTISTS
        TECHNOLOGY
        UNESCO

SCIENCE AND TECHNOLOGY POLICY
- 18.01.00
    USE: SCIENCE POLICY

SCIENCE POLICY
POLITIQUE SCIENTIFIQUE / POLITICA CIENTIFICA -
18.01.00
    UF: SCIENCE AND TECHNOLOGY POLICY
    BT: GOVERNMENT POLICY
    NT: RESEARCH POLICY
    RT: SCIENCE

SCIENCES OF EDUCATION
SCIENCES DE L'EDUCATION / CIENCIAS DE LA
EDUCACION - 06.01.00

SCIENCES OF EDUCATION<CONT>
>*UF:* EDUCATIONAL SCIENCES
>PEDAGOGY
>*NT:* ECONOMICS OF EDUCATION
>HISTORY OF EDUCATION
>PHILOSOPHY OF EDUCATION
>PSYCHOLOGY OF EDUCATION
>SOCIOLOGY OF EDUCATION
>*RT:* COMPARATIVE EDUCATION
>EDUCATION
>EDUCATIONAL RESEARCH
>EDUCATIONAL STATISTICS

SCIENTIFIC COOPERATION
**COOPERATION SCIENTIFIQUE / COOPERACION
CIENTIFICA - 18.01.00**
>*RT:* SCIENCE

SCIENTIFIC CULTURE
**CULTURE SCIENTIFIQUE / CULTURA CIENTIFICA -
05.02.01**
>*BT:* CULTURE
>*RT:* SCIENCE

SCIENTIFIC DISCOVERIES
**DECOUVERTES SCIENTIFIQUES / DESCUBRIMIENTOS
CIENTIFICOS - 12.06.00**

SCIENTIFIC INFORMATION
**INFORMATION SCIENTIFIQUE / INFORMACION
CIENTIFICA - 19.01.01**
>*BT:* INFORMATION
>*RT:* SCIENCE

SCIENTIFIC MANAGEMENT
**GESTION SCIENTIFIQUE / ADMINISTRACION CIENTIFICA
- 12.04.00**
*SN: MANAGEMENT BASED ON DATA PROVIDED THROUGH
OPERATIONAL RESEARCH.*
>*BT:* MANAGEMENT
>*RT:* MANAGEMENT TECHNIQUES

SCIENTIFIC PERSONNEL
**PERSONNEL SCIENTIFIQUE / PERSONAL CIENTIFICO -
13.09.03**
>*RT:* MEDICAL PERSONNEL
>SCIENTISTS
>TEACHING PERSONNEL

SCIENTIFIC PROGRESS
**PROGRES SCIENTIFIQUE / PROGRESO CIENTIFICO -
18.01.00**
>*RT:* SCIENCE
>TECHNOLOGICAL CHANGE

SCIENTIFIC RESEARCH
- 18.01.00
>*USE:* **RESEARCH**

SCIENTIFIC RESEARCHERS
- 13.09.09
>*USE:* **RESEARCH WORKERS**

SCIENTISTS
SCIENTIFIQUES / CIENTIFICOS - 13.09.09

SCIENTISTS<CONT>
>*NT:* AGRONOMISTS
>ANTHROPOLOGISTS
>BIOLOGISTS
>BOTANISTS
>CHEMISTS
>DEMOGRAPHERS
>ECONOMISTS
>GEOGRAPHERS
>GEOLOGISTS
>LINGUISTS
>MATHEMATICIANS
>PHYSICISTS
>POLITICAL SCIENTISTS
>PSYCHOLOGISTS
>SOCIOLOGISTS
>STATISTICIANS
>*RT:* RESEARCH WORKERS
>SCIENCE
>SCIENTIFIC PERSONNEL

SDI
DSI / DSI - 19.01.02
SN: SELECTIVE DISSEMINATION OF INFORMATION.
>*BT:* INFORMATION DISSEMINATION

SEA
MER / MAR - 17.06.00
>*RT:* DEEP SEA MINING
>LAW OF THE SEA
>MARINE ENVIRONMENT
>MARINE POLLUTION
>MARINE RESOURCES
>SEA DUMPING
>SEABED

SEA DUMPING
**IMMERSION DE DECHETS EN MER / DEPOSITO DE
DESPERDICIOS EN EL MAR - 16.04.02**
>*BT:* WASTE DISPOSAL
>*RT:* MARINE POLLUTION
>SEA

SEA TRAFFIC
**CIRCULATION MARITIME / TRAFICO MARITIMO -
10.08.00**
>*BT:* TRAFFIC
>*RT:* SEA TRANSPORT

SEA TRANSPORT
**TRANSPORT MARITIME / TRANSPORTE MARITIMO -
10.05.00**
>*UF:* MARITIME TRANSPORT
>SHIPPING
>*BT:* MARITIME QUESTIONS
>MODES OF TRANSPORTATION

SEA TRANSPORT<CONT>
    RT: DOCKERS
        FLAGS OF CONVENIENCE
        IMCO
        MARITIME LAW
        MARITIME QUESTIONS
        PORTS
        SEA TRAFFIC
        SEAFARERS
        SHIPBUILDING
        SHIPOWNERS
        SHIPS

SEABED
FONDS MARINS / FONDOS MARINOS - 17.06.00
    RT: DEEP SEA MINING
        SEA

SEAFARERS
MARINS / MARINEROS - 13.09.08
    BT: TRANSPORT WORKERS
    RT: SEA TRANSPORT

SEASONAL FLUCTUATIONS
VARIATIONS SAISONNIERES / VARIACIONES
ESTACIONALES - 03.02.04
    BT: BUSINESS CYCLE
    RT: ECONOMIC STATISTICS
        SEASONS

SEASONAL MIGRATIONS
MIGRATIONS SAISONNIERES / MIGRACIONES
ESTACIONALES - 14.07.00
    BT: MIGRATIONS

SEASONAL UNEMPLOYMENT
CHOMAGE SAISONNIER / DESEMPLEO ESTACIONAL -
13.01.03
    BT: CYCLICAL UNEMPLOYMENT
    RT: SEASONAL WORKERS

SEASONAL WORKERS
TRAVAILLEURS SAISONNIERS / TRABAJADORES DE
TEMPORADA - 13.09.02
    RT: MIGRANT WORKERS
        SEASONAL UNEMPLOYMENT
        TEMPORARY EMPLOYMENT

SEASONS
SAISONS / ESTACIONES DEL ANO - 17.02.02
    NT: COLD SEASON
        DRY SEASON
        RAINY SEASON
        WARM SEASON
    RT: CLIMATE
        CLIMATOLOGY
        SEASONAL FLUCTUATIONS
        WEATHER

SEATO
OTASE / OTASE - 01.03.03
SN: SOUTH-EAST ASIA TREATY ORGANIZATION.
    BT: ASIAN ORGANIZATIONS
        INTERGOVERNMENTAL ORGANIZATIONS
    RT: SOUTH EAST ASIA

SEAWEEDS
- 07.10.04
    USE: ALGAE

SECOND DEVELOPMENT DECADE
DEUXIEME DECENNIE DU DEVELOPPEMENT / SEGUNDO
DECENIO DEL DESARROLLO - 01.01.01
    RT: GREEN REVOLUTION

SECOND HAND EQUIPMENT
MATERIEL D'OCCASION / EQUIPO DE SEGUNDA MANO -
12.05.00
    BT: EQUIPMENT

SECONDARY DOCUMENTS
DOCUMENTS SECONDAIRES / DOCUMENTOS SECUNDARIOS -
19.02.01
SN: DOCUMENTS CONTAINING DATA OR INFORMATON
    ABOUT PRIMARY DOCUMENTS.
    BT: DOCUMENTS
    NT: ABSTRACT
        BIBLIOGRAPHY
        BOOK REVIEW
        CATALOGUE
        COMMENT
    RT: DOCUMENTATION
        REFERENCE MATERIALS

SECONDARY EDUCATION
ENSEIGNEMENT SECONDAIRE / ENSENANZA SECUNDARIA -
06.03.06
SN: THE STAGE OF EDUCATION WHICH FOLLOWS PRIMARY
    EDUCATION AND CONTINUES UNTIL SUCH
    EXAMINATIONS AS THE ABITUR (GERMANY) AND THE
    BACCALAUREAT (FRANCE), THE PASSING OF WHICH
    WOULD ENABLE THE STUDENT TO ENTER HIGHER
    EDUCATION.
    BT: LEVELS OF EDUCATION
    RT: SECONDARY SCHOOLS

SECONDARY SCHOOLS
ECOLES SECONDAIRES / ESCUELAS SECUNDARIAS -
06.04.02
    BT: SCHOOLS
    RT: SECONDARY EDUCATION

SECONDARY SECTOR
- 08.01.01
    USE: INDUSTRIAL SECTOR

SECTOR ANALYSIS
- 03.02.02
    USE: INPUT-OUTPUT ANALYSIS

SECTORAL PLANNING
PLANIFICATION SECTORIELLE / PLANIFICACION
SECTORIAL - 02.01.02
    BT: PLANNING SYSTEMS

SECULARIZATION
SECULARISATION / SECULARIZACION - 05.04.04

SECURITIES
VALEURS MOBILIERES / TITULOS - 11.02.07

SECURITIES<CONT>
>   *NT:* DEBENTURES
>   SHARES
>   TREASURY BONDS

SEEDS
GRAINES / SEMILLAS - 07.07.01
>   *BT:* PLANTS
>   *NT:* OILSEEDS

SEISMOLOGY
SISMOLOGIE / SISMOLOGIA - 17.04.03
>   *BT:* GEOPHYSICS
>   *RT:* PHYSICAL GEOGRAPHY

SEISMS
SEISMES / SISMOS - 17.04.03
>   *BT:* NATURAL DISASTERS
>   *RT:* TIDAL WAVES

SELF-DETERMINATION
AUTODETERMINATION / AUTODETERMINACION - 01.02.03
>   *RT:* INDEPENDENCE

SELF-EMPLOYED
**TRAVAILLEURS INDEPENDANTS / TRABAJADORES
INDEPENDIENTES - 13.09.02**
>   *UF:* INDEPENDENT WORKERS
>   *BT:* WORKERS

SELF-FINANCING
AUTOFINANCEMENT / AUTOFINANCIAMIENTO - 11.02.05
>   *BT:* FINANCING

SELF-HELP
AUTOASSISTANCE / ESFUERZO PROPIO - 14.04.01

SELF-INSTRUCTION
AUTOENSEIGNEMENT / AUTOAPRENDIZAJE - 06.05.02
>   *BT:* TEACHING

SELF-MANAGEMENT
AUTOGESTION / AUTOGESTION - 12.04.00
>   *BT:* MANAGEMENT
>   *NT:* WORKERS SELF-MANAGEMENT

SELF-RELIANCE
AUTODEVELOPPEMENT / AUTODESARROLLO - 02.01.01
>   *SN: RELIANCE PRIMARILY ON A COUNTRY'S OWN
>   RESOURCES, HUMAN AND NATURAL, AND THE
>   CAPACITY FOR AUTONOMOUS GOAL-SETTING AND
>   DECISION-MAKING.*
>   *RT:* DEPENDENCE
>   DEVELOPMENT POLICY

SELLING
- 09.03.01
>   *USE:* **MARKETING**

SEMEN
SPERME / SEMEN - 15.02.02
>   *RT:* FERTILIZATION

SEMI-ARID ZONE
ZONE SEMI-ARIDE / ZONA SEMIARIDA - 17.02.03
>   *BT:* CLIMATIC ZONES

SEMI-ARID ZONE<E<CONT>
>   *RT:* DROUGHT
>   ICRISAT

SEMI-MANUFACTURED PRODUCTS
**PRODUITS SEMI-MANUFACTURES / PRODUCTOS
SEMIMANUFACTURADOS - 08.04.00**
>   *BT:* INDUSTRIAL PRODUCTS

SEMI-SKILLED WORKERS
**OUVRIERS SPECIALISES / TRABAJADORES
SEMICALIFICADOS - 13.09.03**
*SN: WORKERS WHO HAVE UNDERGONE A PERIOD OF
   TRAINING WHICH IS SHORTER THAN A FULL
   APPRENTICESHIP FOR A TRADE OR WHO HAVE
   LEARNED ONLY A LIMITED PART OF A TRADE.*
>   *BT:* INDUSTRIAL WORKERS
>   *RT:* OCCUPATIONAL QUALIFICATION

SEMINAR
SEMINAIRE / SEMINARIO - 19.04.00

SENEGAL
SENEGAL / SENEGAL - 01.04.02
>   *BT:* FRENCH SPEAKING AFRICA
>   WEST AFRICA
>   *RT:* SENEGALESE

SENEGALESE
SENEGALAIS / SENEGALES - 14.03.02
>   *RT:* SENEGAL

SENIORITY BENEFITS
**AVANTAGES POUR ANCIENNETE / BENEFICIOS POR
ANTIGUEDAD - 13.07.00**
*SN: PREFERENCES GRANTED EMPLOYEES ON THE BASIS
   OF THEIR RELATIVE LENGTH OF SERVICE WITH THE
   COMPANY.*
>   *BT:* WAGES

SEPTICEMIA
SEPTICEMIE / SEPTICEMIA - 15.04.02
>   *BT:* INFECTIOUS DISEASES

SERIALS
**PUBLICATIONS EN SERIE / PUBLICACIONES SERIADAS -
19.02.06**
>   *BT:* PRIMARY DOCUMENTS
>   *NT:* NEWSLETTER
>   PERIODICALS

SERUMS
SERUMS / SUEROS - 15.05.00
>   *BT:* PHARMACEUTICALS
>   *RT:* VACCINES

SERVICE CERTIFICATE
**CERTIFICAT DE TRAVAIL / CERTIFICADO DE TRABAJO -
13.02.01**
>   *RT:* OCCUPATIONAL QUALIFICATION

SERVICE INDUSTRY
SECTEUR TERTIAIRE / SECTOR TERCIARIO - 09.01.01
>   *UF:* TERTIARY SECTOR

SERVICE INDUSTRY<CONT>
    NT: AUTOMOBILE SERVICE
        BANKING SYSTEMS
        HOTEL INDUSTRY
        TOURISM
        TRADE
        TRANSPORT

SETTLEMENT PATTERN
- 14.04.01
    USE: HABITAT

SEVERANCE PAY
INDEMNITE DE LICENCIEMENT / INDEMNIZACION POR
CESANTIA - 13.07.00
    BT: WAGES
    RT: DISMISSAL
        LABOUR REDUNDANCY

SEWAGE
- 16.03.04
    USE: WASTE WATERS

SEWAGE DISPOSAL
- 16.04.02
    USE: SANITATION SERVICES

SEX
SEXE / SEXO - 14.02.03
    NT: FEMALES
        MALES
    RT: SEX DISTRIBUTION
        SEXUAL BEHAVIOUR
        SEXUALITY

SEX DISTRIBUTION
REPARTITION PAR SEXE / DISTRIBUCION POR SEXO -
14.02.03
    BT: AGE-SEX DISTRIBUTION
    RT: SEX

SEX EDUCATION
EDUCATION SEXUELLE / EDUCACION SEXUAL - 06.03.04
    BT: BASIC EDUCATION
    RT: SEXUALITY

SEXUAL BEHAVIOUR
COMPORTEMENT SEXUEL / COMPORTAMIENTO SEXUAL -
14.02.03
    BT: BEHAVIOUR
    RT: SEX
        SEXUALITY

SEXUALITY
SEXUALITE / SEXUALIDAD - 14.02.03
    RT: SEX
        SEX EDUCATION
        SEXUAL BEHAVIOUR

SEYCHELLES
SEYCHELLES / SEYCHELLES - 01.04.02
    BT: EAST AFRICA

SHALE OIL
HUILE DE SCHISTE / ACEITE DE ESQUISTO - 08.11.06
    BT: MINERAL OILS

SHARE FARMERS
- 07.02.00
    USE: TENANT FARMERS

SHAREHOLDERS
ACTIONNAIRES / ACCIONISTAS - 11.02.07
    RT: SHARES

SHARES
ACTIONS / ACCIONES - 11.02.07
    BT: SECURITIES
    RT: SHAREHOLDERS
        WORKERS STOCK OWNERSHIP

SHEEP
MOUTONS / OVEJAS - 07.09.01
    BT: LIVESTOCK
        OVIDAE
    RT: MUTTON

SHEEPMEAT
- 07.09.05
    USE: MUTTON

SHEET-METAL WORKING
TOLERIE / CHAPISTERIA - 08.14.01
    BT: METALWORKING INDUSTRY
    RT: METAL SHEETS

SHIFT WORK
TRAVAIL PAR ROULEMENT / TRABAJO EN TURNOS -
13.03.03
    BT: ARRANGEMENT OF WORKING TIME

SHIFTING CULTIVATION
AGRICULTURE ITINERANTE / AGRICULTURA MIGRATORIA
- 07.05.04
*SN: TEMPORARY USE OF AGRICULTURAL LAND FOR
    CULTIVATION AS LONG AS IT IS FERTILE.*
    BT: CULTIVATION SYSTEMS
    RT: CROP ROTATION

SHINTOISM
SHINTOISME / SINTOISMO - 05.04.03

SHIPBUILDING
CONSTRUCTION NAVALE / CONSTRUCCION NAVAL -
08.14.07
    BT: INDUSTRIAL SECTOR
    RT: SEA TRANSPORT
        SHIPS

SHIPOWNERS
ARMATEURS / ARMADORES - 10.05.00
    RT: FLAGS OF CONVENIENCE
        SEA TRANSPORT
        SHIPS

SHIPPING
- 10.05.00
    USE: SEA TRANSPORT

SHIPS
NAVIRES / BUQUES - 10.04.00
    UF: BOATS
    BT: MOTOR VEHICLES

SHIPS<CONT>
- NT: CARGO SHIPS
  FISHING VESSELS
  TANKERS
- RT: NON-MOTORIZED TRANSPORT
  SEA TRANSPORT
  SHIPBUILDING
  SHIPOWNERS

SHOE INDUSTRY
INDUSTRIE DE LA CHAUSSURE / INDUSTRIA DEL
CALZADO - 08.08.02
- UF: FOOTWEAR
- BT: INDUSTRIAL SECTOR
- RT: LEATHER INDUSTRY

SHOP STEWARDS
DELEGUES DU PERSONNEL / DELEGADOS DEL PERSONAL -
13.06.00
- SN: WORKERS ELECTED BY TRADE UNION MEMBERS TO
  MAKE DIRECT CONTACTS WITH MANAGEMENT
  REGARDING LABOUR PROBLEMS AT THE PLANT OR
  UNIT LEVEL.
- RT: WORKERS REPRESENTATION

SHOPS
MAGASINS / TIENDAS - 09.04.04

SHORT TERM
COURT TERME / CORTO PLAZO - 18.10.00

SHRIMPS
CREVETTES / CAMARONES - 07.10.04
- BT: CRUSTACEA

SICKNESS INSURANCE
- 02.03.02
- USE: HEALTH INSURANCE

SID
SID / SID - 01.03.04
- SN: SOCIETY FOR INTERNATIONAL DEVELOPMENT.
- BT: NON-GOVERNMENTAL ORGANIZATIONS
- RT: INTERNATIONAL COOPERATION

SIECA
SIECA / SIECA - 01.03.03
- SN: GENERAL TREATY ON CENTRAL AMERICAN ECONOMIC
  INTEGRATION.
- BT: CACM
- RT: CENTRAL AMERICA

SIERRA LEONE
SIERRA LEONE / SIERRA LEONA - 01.04.02
- BT: ENGLISH SPEAKING AFRICA
  WEST AFRICA
- RT: SIERRA LEONEAN

SIERRA LEONEAN
SIERRA-LEONIEN / SIERRALEONES - 14.03.02
- RT: SIERRA LEONE

SIKKIM
SIKKIM / SIKKIM - 01.04.04
- BT: SOUTH EAST ASIA

SILICON
SILICIUM / SILICIO - 08.12.04

SILK
SOIE / SEDA - 07.09.05
- BT: ANIMAL FIBRES
- RT: SILKWORMS

SILKWORMS
VERS A SOIE / GUSANOS DE SEDA - 07.09.01
- BT: INSECTS
- RT: SILK

SILOS
SILOS / SILOS - 07.04.00
- BT: FARM BUILDINGS
- RT: STORAGE
  WAREHOUSES

SILVER
ARGENT / PLATA - 08.14.02
- BT: PRECIOUS METALS

SILVICULTURE
SYLVICULTURE / SILVICULTURA - 07.08.01
- SN: A PHASE OF FORESTRY THAT DEALS WITH THE
  ESTABLISHMENT, DEVELOPMENT, REPRODUCTION AND
  CARE OF FOREST TREES.
- BT: FORESTRY
- RT: FOREST ENGINEERING
  FOREST MANAGEMENT

SIMULATION
SIMULATION / SIMULACION - 18.08.00
- BT: RESEARCH METHODS
- RT: EXPERIMENTATION
  MODELS

SINGAPORE
SINGAPOUR / SINGAPUR - 01.04.04
- BT: SOUTH EAST ASIA
- RT: SINGAPOREAN

SINGAPOREAN
SINGAPOURIEN / SINGAPURENSE - 14.03.02
- RT: SINGAPORE

SISAL
SISAL / SISAL - 07.07.07
- BT: PLANT FIBRES

SIZE OF ENTERPRISE
DIMENSION DE L'ENTREPRISE / TAMANO DE LA EMPRESA
- 12.02.00
- NT: FARM SIZE
- RT: ECONOMY OF SCALE
  ENTERPRISES
  MEDIUM-SCALE INDUSTRY
  MERGERS
  SMALL ENTERPRISES
  SMALL-SCALE INDUSTRY

SKILLED WORKERS
OUVRIERS QUALIFIES / TRABAJADORES CALIFICADOS -

SKILLED WORKERS\<CONT\>
13.09.03
    BT: INDUSTRIAL WORKERS
    RT: OCCUPATIONAL QUALIFICATION

SKIN
PEAU / PIEL - 15.02.04
    BT: INTEGUMENTARY SYSTEM

SLAUGHTERHOUSES
ABATTOIRS / MATADEROS - 07.09.04

SLAUGHTERING
ABATTAGE DE BETAIL / BENEFICIO DE GANADO -
07.09.04

SLAVERY
ESCLAVAGE / ESCLAVITUD - 05.03.05

SLEEPING SICKNESS
- 15.04.02
    USE: TRYPANOSOMIASIS

SLIDES
DIAPOSITIVES / DIAPOSITIVAS - 19.02.04
    BT: AUDIOVISUAL MATERIALS
    RT: PHOTOGRAPHS
        PROJECTION EQUIPMENT

SLUMS
BIDONVILLES / BARRIOS DE TUGURIOS - 14.04.03

SMALL ENTERPRISES
PETITES ENTREPRISES / PEQUENAS EMPRESAS -
12.01.00
    BT: ENTERPRISES
    RT: SIZE OF ENTERPRISE

SMALL GAME
MENU GIBIER / CAZA MENOR - 07.09.01
    BT: WILD ANIMALS
    RT: GAME PROTECTION
        HUNTING

SMALL TOWNS
PETITES VILLES / CIUDADES PEQUENAS - 14.04.03
    BT: TOWNS

SMALL-SCALE INDUSTRY
PETITE INDUSTRIE / PEQUENA INDUSTRIA - 08.02.02
    BT: INDUSTRY
    NT: COTTAGE INDUSTRY
    RT: SIZE OF ENTERPRISE

SMALLPOX
VARIOLE / VIRUELA - 15.04.02
    BT: INFECTIOUS DISEASES

SNOW
NEIGE / NIEVE - 17.01.03
    BT: PRECIPITATIONS

SOAP
SAVON / JABON - 08.12.08

SOAP\<CONT\>
    BT: CLEANING AGENTS
        TOILET PREPARATIONS

SOCIAL ADAPTATION
ADAPTATION SOCIALE / ADAPTACION SOCIAL -
05.03.03
    BT: ADAPTATION
    NT: SCHOOL ADAPTATION
        WORKERS ADAPTATION
    RT: SOCIAL INFLUENCE
        SOCIALIZATION

SOCIAL ADMINISTRATION
ADMINISTRATION SOCIALE / ADMINISTRACION SOCIAL -
04.03.02
    BT: PUBLIC ADMINISTRATION
    NT: SOCIAL SERVICES
    RT: SOCIAL LEGISLATION
        SOCIAL PLANNING
        SOCIAL POLICY

SOCIAL ASPECTS
ASPECTS SOCIAUX / ASPECTOS SOCIALES - 05.03.04

SOCIAL ASSIMILATION
- 05.03.03
    USE: SOCIAL INTEGRATION

SOCIAL ASSISTANCE
- 02.05.01
    USE: SOCIAL SERVICES

SOCIAL BEHAVIOUR
COMPORTEMENT SOCIAL / COMPORTAMIENTO SOCIAL -
05.03.03
    BT: BEHAVIOUR

SOCIAL CHANGE
CHANGEMENT SOCIAL / CAMBIO SOCIAL - 05.03.04
SN: USE IN CONNECTION WITH CHANGES IN COMMUNITY
    LIFE BROUGHT ABOUT, FOR EXAMPLE, BY
    MODERNIZATION.
    RT: ADAPTATION TO CHANGE
        CULTURAL CHANGE
        MODERNIZATION
        RESISTANCE TO CHANGE
        REVOLUTION
        SOCIAL DEVELOPMENT
        SOCIAL HISTORY
        SOCIAL POLICY
        SOCIAL REFORM

SOCIAL CLASSES
CLASSES SOCIALES / CLASES SOCIALES - 05.03.05
    NT: BOURGEOISIE
        MIDDLE CLASS
        RULING CLASS
        UPPER CLASS
        WORKING CLASS
    RT: CLASS CONSCIOUSNESS
        CLASS STRUGGLE
        SOCIAL STRATIFICATION

SOCIAL CONDITIONS
CONDITIONS SOCIALES / CONDICIONES SOCIALES -
05.03.04

SOCIAL CONFLICTS
CONFLITS SOCIAUX / CONFLICTOS SOCIALES -
05.03.06
  BT: CONFLICTS
    SOCIAL PROBLEMS
  NT: LABOUR DISPUTES
  RT: CLASS STRUGGLE

SOCIAL CONSEQUENCES
- 05.03.04
  USE: SOCIAL IMPLICATIONS

SOCIAL CONTROL
REGULATION SOCIALE / CONTROL SOCIAL - 05.03.04
  RT: ETHICS
    LAW
    PENAL SANCTIONS
    RELIGION
    SOCIAL INFLUENCE
    SOCIAL NORMS
    VALUE SYSTEMS

SOCIAL COSTS
COUTS SOCIAUX / COSTOS SOCIALES - 02.02.01
  RT: SOCIAL PROBLEMS

SOCIAL DEVELOPMENT
DEVELOPPEMENT SOCIAL / DESARROLLO SOCIAL -
05.03.04
  UF: SOCIAL PROGRESS
  BT: ECONOMIC AND SOCIAL DEVELOPMENT
  NT: COMMUNITY DEVELOPMENT
    EDUCATIONAL DEVELOPMENT
  RT: MODERNIZATION
    SOCIAL CHANGE
    SOCIAL REFORM
    UNRISD

SOCIAL ENVIRONMENT
MILIEU SOCIAL / MEDIO SOCIAL - 05.03.03
  BT: HUMAN ENVIRONMENT
  NT: FAMILY ENVIRONMENT
    RURAL ENVIRONMENT
    SCHOOL ENVIRONMENT
    URBAN ENVIRONMENT
  RT: SOCIAL INFLUENCE
    SOCIETY

SOCIAL HISTORY
HISTOIRE SOCIALE / HISTORIA SOCIAL - 05.01.01
  BT: HISTORY
  RT: SOCIAL CHANGE
    SOCIETY
    SOCIOLOGY

SOCIAL IMPLICATIONS
IMPLICATIONS SOCIALES / CONSECUENCIAS SOCIALES -
05.03.04
  UF: SOCIAL CONSEQUENCES

SOCIAL INDICATORS
INDICATEURS SOCIAUX / INDICADORES SOCIALES -
05.01.02
  RT: ECONOMIC INDICATORS
    INDEX NUMBERS
    SOCIAL INFORMATION

SOCIAL INEQUALITY
INEGALITE SOCIALE / DESIGUALDAD SOCIAL -
05.03.05
  RT: SOCIAL JUSTICE
    SOCIAL STRATIFICATION

SOCIAL INFLUENCE
INFLUENCE SOCIALE / INFLUENCIA SOCIAL - 05.03.03
  RT: SOCIAL ADAPTATION
    SOCIAL CONTROL
    SOCIAL ENVIRONMENT
    SOCIALIZATION

SOCIAL INFORMATION
INFORMATION SOCIALE / INFORMACION SOCIAL -
05.01.02
  BT: INFORMATION
  RT: SOCIAL INDICATORS

SOCIAL INSURANCE
- 02.03.01
  USE: SOCIAL SECURITY

SOCIAL INTEGRATION
INTEGRATION SOCIALE / INTEGRACION SOCIAL -
05.03.03
*SN: PROCESS LEADING TO THE UNIFICATION OF THE
    VARIOUS ELEMENTS OF A SOCIETY AND TO THE
    BUILDING-UP OF A SOCIAL SYSTEM.*
  UF: SOCIAL ASSIMILATION
  RT: SOCIAL SYSTEM

SOCIAL JUSTICE
JUSTICE SOCIALE / JUSTICIA SOCIAL - 02.02.01
  RT: INCOME DISTRIBUTION
    POVERTY
    SOCIAL INEQUALITY

SOCIAL LEGISLATION
LEGISLATION SOCIALE / LEGISLACION SOCIAL -
02.02.01
  BT: LEGISLATION
  RT: SOCIAL ADMINISTRATION
    SOCIAL POLICY
    SOCIAL PROBLEMS
    SOCIAL REFORM
    SOCIAL SECURITY

SOCIAL MOBILITY
MOBILITE SOCIALE / MOVILIDAD SOCIAL - 05.03.05
  NT: LABOUR MOBILITY
    OCCUPATIONAL MOBILITY

SOCIAL MOVEMENTS
MOUVEMENTS SOCIAUX / MOVIMIENTOS SOCIALES -
05.03.07

SOCIAL MOVEMENTS<CONT>
SN: USE IN CONNECTION WITH COLLECTIVE EFFORTS TO
    TRANSFORM SOME GIVEN AREA OF ESTABLISHED
    SOCIAL RELATIONS.
    NT: COOPERATIVE MOVEMENTS
        LABOUR MOVEMENTS
        NATIONAL LIBERATION MOVEMENTS
        PEASANT MOVEMENTS
        STUDENT MOVEMENTS
    RT: REVOLUTION
        WOMEN'S ORGANIZATIONS

SOCIAL NORMS
NORMES SOCIALES / NORMAS SOCIALES - 05.04.01
    RT: ETHICS
        RESPONSIBILITY
        SOCIAL CONTROL
        VALUE SYSTEMS

SOCIAL PARTICIPATION
PARTICIPATION SOCIALE / PARTICIPACION SOCIAL -
05.03.03
    NT: STUDENT PARTICIPATION
    RT: COMMUNITY DEVELOPMENT
        MARGINALITY
        PARTICIPATION IN CULTURAL LIFE
        POLITICAL PARTICIPATION

SOCIAL PLANNING
PLANIFICATION SOCIALE / PLANIFICACION SOCIAL -
02.02.01
    BT: PLANNING
    RT: ILPES
        SOCIAL ADMINISTRATION
        SOCIAL POLICY
        SOCIAL PROBLEMS

SOCIAL POLICY
POLITIQUE SOCIALE / POLITICA SOCIAL - 02.02.01
    BT: GOVERNMENT POLICY
    NT: FAMILY POLICY
        HOUSING POLICY
    RT: ECONOMIC POLICY
        FOOD POLICY
        LABOUR POLICY
        POPULATION POLICY
        SOCIAL ADMINISTRATION
        SOCIAL CHANGE
        SOCIAL LEGISLATION
        SOCIAL PLANNING
        SOCIAL PROBLEMS
        SOCIAL REFORM

SOCIAL PROBLEMS
PROBLEMES SOCIAUX / PROBLEMAS SOCIALES -
02.04.01

SOCIAL PROBLEMS<CONT>
    NT: ACCIDENTS
        ALCOHOLISM
        CORRUPTION
        CRIMES
        DELINQUENCY
        DRUG ADDICTION
        FAMILY DISINTEGRATION
        FAMINE
        MALNUTRITION
        POVERTY
        PROSTITUTION
        SOCIAL CONFLICTS
        UNEMPLOYMENT
    RT: DISEASES
        SOCIAL COSTS
        SOCIAL LEGISLATION
        SOCIAL PLANNING
        SOCIAL POLICY
        SOCIAL SECURITY
        SOCIAL SERVICES
        TERRORISM

SOCIAL PROGRESS
- 05.03.04
    USE: SOCIAL DEVELOPMENT

SOCIAL PROTECTION
- 02.03.01
    USE: SOCIAL SECURITY

SOCIAL PSYCHOLOGY
PSYCHOLOGIE SOCIALE / PSICOLOGIA SOCIAL -
05.01.01
    BT: BEHAVIOURAL SCIENCES
        SOCIAL SCIENCES
    RT: PSYCHOLOGICAL ASPECTS

SOCIAL REFORM
REFORME SOCIALE / REFORMA SOCIAL - 02.02.01
    RT: SOCIAL CHANGE
        SOCIAL DEVELOPMENT
        SOCIAL LEGISLATION
        SOCIAL POLICY

SOCIAL RESEARCH
RECHERCHE SOCIALE / INVESTIGACION SOCIAL -
05.01.02
    BT: RESEARCH
    RT: SOCIOLOGY

SOCIAL ROLE
ROLE SOCIAL / PAPEL SOCIAL - 05.03.03
    RT: SOCIAL STATUS

SOCIAL SCIENCES
SCIENCES SOCIALES / CIENCIAS SOCIALES - 05.01.01

SOCIAL SCIENCES<CONT>
　　NT: ANTHROPOLOGY
　　　　CRIMINOLOGY
　　　　DEMOGRAPHY
　　　　ECONOMICS
　　　　ETHNOLOGY
　　　　HISTORY
　　　　HUMAN GEOGRAPHY
　　　　LEGAL SCIENCES
　　　　LINGUISTICS
　　　　POLITICAL GEOGRAPHY
　　　　POLITICAL SCIENCE
　　　　SOCIAL PSYCHOLOGY
　　　　SOCIOLOGY
　　RT: BEHAVIOURAL SCIENCES
　　　　CLACSO
　　　　ICSSD
　　　　ISSC

SOCIAL SECURITY
SECURITE SOCIALE / SEGURIDAD SOCIAL - 02.03.01
　　UF: SOCIAL INSURANCE
　　　　SOCIAL PROTECTION
　　NT: DISABILITY BENEFITS
　　　　EMPLOYMENT INJURIES BENEFITS
　　　　FAMILY ALLOWANCES
　　　　HEALTH INSURANCE
　　　　MATERNITY BENEFITS
　　　　OLD AGE BENEFITS
　　　　SURVIVORS BENEFITS
　　　　UNEMPLOYMENT INSURANCE
　　RT: BENEFIT PLANS
　　　　CONTINGENCY FUNDS
　　　　INCOME REDISTRIBUTION
　　　　INCOMES POLICY
　　　　INSURANCE
　　　　ISSA
　　　　SOCIAL LEGISLATION
　　　　SOCIAL PROBLEMS

SOCIAL SERVICES
SERVICES SOCIAUX / SERVICIOS SOCIALES - 02.05.01
SN: USE IN CONNECTION WITH ADMINISTRATION OF
　　SOCIAL ASPECTS OF COMMUNITY LIFE.
　　UF: SOCIAL ASSISTANCE
　　　　WELFARE INSTITUTIONS
　　BT: SOCIAL ADMINISTRATION
　　NT: CARE OF THE AGED
　　　　CHILD CARE
　　　　DISABLED CARE
　　　　EMERGENCY RELIEF
　　　　HEALTH SERVICES
　　　　ORPHANAGES
　　RT: SOCIAL PROBLEMS

SOCIAL STATUS
STATUT SOCIAL / CONDICION SOCIAL - 05.03.05
SN: USE IN CONNECTION WITH THE RELATIVE POSITION
　　IN A COMMUNITY OF THE VARIOUS MEMBERS OF THE
　　COMMUNITY.
　　RT: LEGAL STATUS
　　　　SOCIAL ROLE
　　　　TEACHER STATUS

SOCIAL STRATIFICATION
STRATIFICATION SOCIALE / ESTRATIFICACION SOCIAL
- 05.03.05
　　RT: CASTES
　　　　ELITE
　　　　SOCIAL CLASSES
　　　　SOCIAL INEQUALITY
　　　　SOCIAL STRUCTURE
　　　　SOCIAL SYSTEM

SOCIAL STRUCTURE
STRUCTURE SOCIALE / ESTRUCTURA SOCIAL - 05.03.04
　　RT: SOCIAL STRATIFICATION

SOCIAL SURVEYS
ENQUETES SOCIALES / ENCUESTAS SOCIALES -
05.01.02
　　BT: SURVEYS
　　RT: SOCIOLOGY

SOCIAL SYSTEM
SYSTEME SOCIAL / SISTEMA SOCIAL - 05.03.01
　　RT: SOCIAL INTEGRATION
　　　　SOCIAL STRATIFICATION
　　　　SOCIETY

SOCIAL THEORY
THEORIE SOCIALE / TEORIA SOCIAL - 02.02.02
SN: THEORY USED AS A BASIS FOR SOCIAL POLICY.
　　BT: THEORY

SOCIAL WORK
TRAVAIL SOCIAL / TRABAJO SOCIAL - 02.05.01
　　RT: SOCIAL WORKERS

SOCIAL WORKERS
TRAVAILLEURS SOCIAUX / TRABAJADORES SOCIALES -
13.09.10
　　BT: PARAMEDICAL PERSONNEL
　　RT: SOCIAL WORK

SOCIALISM
SOCIALISME / SOCIALISMO - 03.03.01
　　RT: COLLECTIVISM
　　　　MODES OF PRODUCTION
　　　　SOCIALIST
　　　　SOCIALIST COUNTRIES
　　　　SOCIALIST ENTERPRISES

SOCIALIST
SOCIALISTE / SOCIALISTA - 03.03.01
　　RT: SOCIALISM
　　　　SOCIALIST COUNTRIES

SOCIALIST COUNTRIES
PAYS SOCIALISTES / PAISES SOCIALISTAS - 03.03.03
　　RT: SOCIALISM
　　　　SOCIALIST
　　　　SOCIALIST ENTERPRISES

SOCIALIST ENTERPRISES
ENTREPRISES SOCIALISTES / EMPRESAS SOCIALISTAS -
12.01.00
　　BT: ENTERPRISES

SOCIALIST ENTERPRISES<CONT>
  RT: PUBLIC OWNERSHIP
      SOCIALISM
      SOCIALIST COUNTRIES

SOCIALIZATION
SOCIALISATION / SOCIALIZACION - 05.03.03
  RT: SOCIAL ADAPTATION
      SOCIAL INFLUENCE

SOCIETY
SOCIETE / SOCIEDAD - 05.03.01
  NT: AFFLUENT SOCIETY
  RT: SOCIAL ENVIRONMENT
      SOCIAL HISTORY
      SOCIAL SYSTEM

SOCIO-CULTURAL FACILITIES
EQUIPEMENT SOCIO-CULTUREL / EQUIPO
SOCIO-CULTURAL - 05.02.03
  RT: CULTURE

SOCIOLOGICAL ANALYSIS
ANALYSE SOCIOLOGIQUE / ANALISIS SOCIOLOGICO -
05.01.02
  RT: SOCIOLOGY

SOCIOLOGISTS
SOCIOLOGUES / SOCIOLOGOS - 13.09.09
  BT: SCIENTISTS
  RT: SOCIOLOGY

SOCIOLOGY
SOCIOLOGIE / SOCIOLOGIA - 05.01.01
  BT: SOCIAL SCIENCES
  NT: INDUSTRIAL SOCIOLOGY
      RURAL SOCIOLOGY
      SOCIOLOGY OF EDUCATION
      URBAN SOCIOLOGY
  RT: ISA
      SOCIAL HISTORY
      SOCIAL RESEARCH
      SOCIAL SURVEYS
      SOCIOLOGICAL ANALYSIS
      SOCIOLOGISTS

SOCIOLOGY OF EDUCATION
SOCIOLOGIE DE L'EDUCATION / SOCIOLOGIA DE LA
EDUCACION - 06.01.00
  UF: EDUCATIONAL SOCIOLOGY
  BT: SCIENCES OF EDUCATION
      SOCIOLOGY

SODA
SOUDE / SODA - 08.12.04
  NT: CAUSTIC SODA

SODIUM
SODIUM / SODIO - 08.12.04

SOFT FIBRES
FIBRES SOUPLES / FIBRAS BLANDAS - 08.08.01
  BT: FIBRES

SOFTWARE
- 08.15.02
  USE: COMPUTER PROGRAMMES

SOIL ANALYSIS
ANALYSE DU SOL / ANALISIS DEL SUELO - 17.04.04
  RT: SOIL SCIENCES
      SOIL SURVEYS
      SOILS

SOIL CHEMISTRY
CHIMIE DU SOL / QUIMICA DEL SUELO - 17.04.04
  BT: CHEMISTRY
      SOIL SCIENCES
  RT: GEOCHEMISTRY
      SOILS

SOIL CLASSIFICATION
CLASSIFICATION DES SOLS / CLASIFICACION DE
SUELOS - 17.04.04
  BT: CLASSIFICATION
  RT: SOIL SCIENCES
      SOIL TYPES
      SOILS

SOIL CONSERVATION
CONSERVATION DU SOL / CONSERVACION DEL SUELO -
16.05.01
  BT: RESOURCES CONSERVATION
  RT: SOIL MANAGEMENT
      SOIL RESOURCES
      SOILS

SOIL CULTIVATION
- 07.05.02
  USE: SOIL MANAGEMENT

SOIL EROSION
EROSION DU SOL / EROSION DEL SUELO - 16.03.02
  BT: EROSION
  RT: SOILS

SOIL FERTILITY
FERTILITE DU SOL / FERTILIDAD DEL SUELO -
07.05.02
  RT: FERTILIZING

SOIL IMPROVEMENT
AMELIORATION DES SOLS / MEJORAMIENTO DE SUELOS -
07.05.02
  RT: SOIL MANAGEMENT

SOIL MANAGEMENT
MISE EN VALEUR DU SOL / APROVECHAMIENTO DEL
SUELO - 07.05.02
  UF: SOIL CULTIVATION
  RT: CULTIVATION PRACTICES
      LAND RECLAMATION
      SOIL CONSERVATION
      SOIL IMPROVEMENT

SOIL MAPS
CARTES PEDOLOGIQUES / MAPAS EDAFOLOGICOS -

SOIL MAPS<CONT>
18.07.00
    BT: MAPS
    RT: SOILS

SOIL PHYSICS
PHYSIQUE DU SOL / FISICA DEL SUELO - 17.04.04
    BT: GEOPHYSICS
        SOIL SCIENCES
    RT: SOILS

SOIL POLLUTANTS
POLLUANTS DU SOL / CONTAMINANTES DEL SUELO -
16.03.04
    BT: POLLUTANTS
    RT: SOIL POLLUTION
        SOILS

SOIL POLLUTION
POLLUTION DU SOL / CONTAMINACION DEL SUELO -
16.03.04
    BT: POLLUTION
    RT: SOIL POLLUTANTS
        SOILS

SOIL RESOURCES
RESSOURCES EN SOL / RECURSOS DE SUELO - 16.02.02
SN: USE TO DENOTE THE AVAILABILITY OF SOIL,
    MAINLY FOR CULTIVATION PURPOSES. TO MEAN
    RESOURCES FROM THE SOIL, USE 'MINERAL
    RESOURCES', 'PETROLEUM RESOURCES', ETC.
    BT: NATURAL RESOURCES
    RT: SOIL CONSERVATION
        SOILS

SOIL SCIENCES
SCIENCES DU SOL / CIENCIAS DEL SUELO - 17.04.04
    UF: PEDOLOGY
    BT: EARTH SCIENCES
    NT: SOIL CHEMISTRY
        SOIL PHYSICS
    RT: SOIL ANALYSIS
        SOIL CLASSIFICATION
        SOIL SURVEYS
        SOILS

SOIL SURVEYS
ETUDES PEDOLOGIQUES / ESTUDIOS DEL SUELO -
17.04.04
    BT: SURVEYS
    RT: SOIL ANALYSIS
        SOIL SCIENCES
        SOILS

SOIL TYPES
TYPES DE SOL / TIPOS DE SUELO - 17.04.04
    RT: SOIL CLASSIFICATION
        SOILS

SOILS
SOLS / SUELOS - 17.04.04

SOILS<CONT>
    RT: SOIL ANALYSIS
        SOIL CHEMISTRY
        SOIL CLASSIFICATION
        SOIL CONSERVATION
        SOIL EROSION
        SOIL MAPS
        SOIL PHYSICS
        SOIL POLLUTANTS
        SOIL POLLUTION
        SOIL RESOURCES
        SOIL SCIENCES
        SOIL SURVEYS
        SOIL TYPES

SOLAR ENERGY
ENERGIE SOLAIRE / ENERGIA SOLAR - 08.11.01
    BT: ENERGY
    RT: SOLAR RADIATION

SOLAR RADIATION
RADIATION SOLAIRE / RADIACION SOLAR - 17.01.03
    BT: ENERGY SOURCES
    RT: SOLAR ENERGY

SOLVENTS
DISSOLVANTS / SOLVENTES - 08.12.08

SOMALI
SOMALI / SOMALI - 14.03.02
    RT: SOMALIA

SOMALIA
SOMALIE / SOMALIA - 01.04.02
    BT: EAST AFRICA
    RT: SOMALI

SORGHUM
SORGHO / SORGO - 07.07.04
    BT: CEREALS
    RT: ICRISAT

SOUTH
SUD / SUR - 17.03.03

SOUTH AFRICA
AFRIQUE DU SUD / SUDAFRICA - 01.04.02
    BT: ENGLISH SPEAKING AFRICA
        SOUTHERN AFRICA
    RT: APARTHEID
        SOUTH AFRICAN

SOUTH AFRICAN
SUD-AFRICAIN / SUDAFRICANO - 14.03.02
    RT: SOUTH AFRICA

SOUTH AMERICA
AMERIQUE DU SUD / AMERICA DEL SUR - 01.04.03
    BT: AMERICA

SOUTH AMERICA<CONT>
NT: ANDEAN REGION
BOLIVIA
BRAZIL
COLOMBIA
ECUADOR
FALKLAND ISLANDS
FRENCH GUIANA
GUYANA
PARAGUAY
PERU
SOUTHERN CONE
SURINAM
VENEZUELA
RT: LATIN AMERICA

SOUTH ASIA
ASIE DU SUD / ASIA DEL SUR - 01.04.04
BT: ASIA
NT: BANGLADESH
BHUTAN
INDIA
MALDIVES
NEPAL
PAKISTAN
SRI LANKA

SOUTH EAST ASIA
ASIE DU SUD-EST / ASIA SUDORIENTAL - 01.04.04
BT: ASIA
NT: BANGLADESH
BHUTAN
BRUNEI
BURMA
INDIA
INDOCHINA
INDONESIA
MALAYSIA
MALDIVES
NEPAL
PAKISTAN
PHILIPPINES
PORTUGUESE TIMOR
SIKKIM
SINGAPORE
SRI LANKA
THAILAND
RT: ASEAN
SEATO

SOUTH WEST AFRICA
- 01.04.02
USE: NAMIBIA

SOUTH YEMEN
- 01.04.06
USE: YEMEN PDR

SOUTHERN AFRICA
AFRIQUE MERIDIONALE / AFRICA MERIDIONAL -
01.04.02
BT: AFRICA SOUTH OF SAHARA

SOUTHERN AFRICA<CONT>
NT: ANGOLA
BOTSWANA
COMOROS
LESOTHO
MADAGASCAR
MALAGASY REP
MALAWI
MAURITIUS
MOZAMBIQUE
NAMIBIA
REUNION ISLAND
RHODESIA
SOUTH AFRICA
ST HELENA
SWAZILAND
ZAMBIA

SOUTHERN CONE
CONE SUD / CONO SUR - 01.04.03
BT: SOUTH AMERICA
NT: ARGENTINA
CHILE
URUGUAY

SOUTHERN HEMISPHERE
HEMISPHERE SUD / HEMISFERIO SUR - 01.04.01

SOVIET
SOVIETIQUE / SOVIETICO - 14.03.02
RT: USSR

SOWING
ENSEMENCEMENT / SIEMBRA - 07.05.04
BT: CULTIVATION PRACTICES

SOYBEANS
SOJA / SOYA - 07.07.06
BT: LEGUMINOSAE
OILSEEDS

SPACE
ESPACE / ESPACIO - 17.07.00
NT: OUTER SPACE
RT: SPACE SCIENCES

SPACE SCIENCES
SCIENCES DE L'ESPACE / CIENCIAS DEL ESPACIO -
17.07.00
BT: NATURAL SCIENCES
NT: ASTRONAUTICS
ASTRONOMY
RT: EUROPEAN SPACE AGENCY
OUTER SPACE
SPACE

SPAIN
ESPAGNE / ESPANA - 01.04.05
BT: MEDITERRANEAN COUNTRIES
WESTERN EUROPE
RT: CANARY ISLANDS
SPANISH

SPANISH
ESPAGNOL / ESPANOL - 14.03.02
RT: SPAIN

SPANISH LANGUAGE
LANGUE ESPAGNOLE / LENGUA ESPANOLA - 05.06.02
    BT: LANGUAGES

SPARE PARTS
PIECES DE RECHANGE / PIEZAS DE REPUESTO -
12.05.00
    RT: EQUIPMENT
        MAINTENANCE AND REPAIR

SPATIAL ANALYSIS
ANALYSE SPATIALE / ANALISIS ESPACIAL - 17.03.01

SPC
CPS / CPS - 01.03.03
SN: SOUTH PACIFIC COMMISSION
    BT: ASIAN ORGANIZATIONS
        INTERGOVERNMENTAL ORGANIZATIONS
    RT: PACIFIC REGION

SPECIAL DRAWING RIGHTS
DROITS DE TIRAGE SPECIAUX / DERECHOS ESPECIALES
DE GIRO - 11.03.01
    RT: IMF
        INTERNATIONAL LIQUIDITY
        INTERNATIONAL MONETARY SYSTEM

SPECIAL EDUCATION
EDUCATION SPECIALE / EDUCACION ESPECIAL -
06.03.03
SN: SPECIAL TYPES OF EDUCATION FOR EXCEPTIONAL
    (GIFTED OR HANDICAPPED) CHILDREN.
    BT: EDUCATIONAL SYSTEMS
    NT: COMPENSATORY EDUCATION
        CORRECTIONAL EDUCATION
    RT: GIFTED STUDENTS
        MENTAL RETARDATION
        SPECIAL SCHOOLS

SPECIAL SCHOOLS
CENTRES D'EDUCATION SPECIALE / CENTROS DE
EDUCACION ESPECIAL - 06.04.03
    BT: SCHOOLS
    NT: CORRECTIONAL INSTITUTIONS
    RT: SPECIAL EDUCATION

SPECIFICATIONS
SPECIFICATIONS / ESPECIFICACIONES - 12.07.02
    RT: APPELLATION OF ORIGIN
        STANDARDIZATION

SPICES
EPICES / ESPECIAS - 07.07.09
    NT: PEPPER

SPINNING
FILAGE / HILADO - 08.08.01
    RT: TEXTILE INDUSTRY

SPORT
SPORT / DEPORTE - 13.08.00
    RT: PHYSICAL EDUCATION
        SPORTS FACILITIES

SPORTS FACILITIES
INSTALLATIONS SPORTIVES / INSTALACIONES
DEPORTIVAS - 13.08.00
    RT: SPORT

SQUATTERS
SQUATTERS / COLONOS USURPADORES - 14.04.01
    RT: HOUSING

SRI LANKA
SRI LANKA / SRI LANKA - 01.04.04
    UF: CEYLON
    BT: SOUTH ASIA
        SOUTH EAST ASIA
    RT: SRI LANKAN

SRI LANKAN
SRI-LANKAIS / SRI LANKANO - 14.03.02
    RT: SRI LANKA

ST HELENA
SAINTE HELENE / SANTA HELENA - 01.04.02
    BT: ENGLISH SPEAKING AFRICA
        SOUTHERN AFRICA
        WEST AFRICA
    RT: UNITED KINGDOM

ST KITTS-NEVIS-ANGUILLA
ST CHRISTOPHE ET NIEVES ET ANGUILLA / SAN
CRISTOBAL NIEVES Y ANGUILA - 01.04.03
    BT: WEST INDIES ASSOCIATED STATES

ST LUCIA
SAINTE LUCIE / SANTA LUCIA - 01.04.03
    BT: WEST INDIES ASSOCIATED STATES

ST PIERRE AND MIQUELON
SAINT PIERRE ET MIQUELON / SAN PEDRO Y MIQUELON
- 01.04.03
    BT: NORTH AMERICA
    RT: FRANCE

ST VINCENT
SAINT VINCENT / SAN VICENTE - 01.04.03
    BT: WEST INDIES ASSOCIATED STATES

STABILIZATION
STABILISATION / ESTABILIZACION - 03.02.04
    NT: MARKET STABILIZATION
        PRICE STABILIZATION

STAFF
PERSONNEL / PERSONAL - 13.02.02
SN: THE WHOLE PERSONNEL OF AN ENTERPRISE OR AN
    ORGANIZATION.
    RT: STAFF REGULATION

STAFF REGULATION
REGLEMENT DU PERSONNEL / REGLAMENTO DEL PERSONAL
- 13.02.02
    RT: PERSONNEL MANAGEMENT
        STAFF

STANDARD OF LIVING
NIVEAU DE VIE / NIVEL DE VIDA - 03.02.05

STANDARD OF LIVING<CONT>
SN: THE LEVEL OF GOODS AND SERVICES OBTAINABLE
AS A RESULT OF A GIVEN INCOME. DO NOT
CONFUSE WITH 'COST OF LIVING'.
    RT: CONSUMPTION PER CAPITA
       FAMILY BUDGET

STANDARD PERFORMANCE
RENDEMENT TYPE / RENDIMIENTO NORMAL - 13.02.02
SN: THE RATE OF OUTPUT WHICH SKILLED WORKERS
WILL NATURALLY ACHIEVE.
    RT: LABOUR PRODUCTIVITY
       LABOUR STANDARDS
       WORK STUDY

STANDARDIZATION
NORMALISATION / NORMALIZACION - 12.07.02
    RT: ISO
       SPECIFICATIONS
       STANDARDS

STANDARDS
NORMES / NORMAS - 12.07.02
    NT: FOOD STANDARDS
       LABOUR STANDARDS
       PRODUCTION STANDARDS
       QUALITY STANDARDS
    RT: STANDARDIZATION

STARCH
AMIDON / ALMIDON - 08.06.04
    BT: CARBOHYDRATES

STARVATION
- 15.03.02
    USE: FAMINE

STATE
ETAT / ESTADO - 04.03.01
    RT: STATE AID
       STATE INTERVENTION
       STATE PARTICIPATION

STATE AID
AIDE DE L'ETAT / AYUDA ESTATAL - 11.01.01
    NT: SUBSIDIES
       TAX EXEMPTION
    RT: STATE
       STATE INTERVENTION

STATE FARMS
FERMES D'ETAT / GRANJAS ESTATALES - 07.03.02
    BT: FARMS
    RT: COLLECTIVE FARMING

STATE INTERVENTION
INTERVENTION DE L'ETAT / INTERVENCION DEL ESTADO
- 04.03.01
    RT: PUBLIC SECTOR
       STATE
       STATE AID
       STATE PARTICIPATION

STATE PARTICIPATION
PARTICIPATION DE L'ETAT / PARTICIPACION ESTATAL

STATE PARTICIPATION<CONT>
- 11.01.01
    RT: STATE
       STATE INTERVENTION

STATEMENT
EXPOSE / DECLARACION - 19.02.05

STATIONARY POPULATION
POPULATION STATIONNAIRE / POBLACION ESTACIONARIA
- 14.01.02
    RT: POPULATION DYNAMICS

STATIONS
GARES / ESTACIONES - 10.03.00
    BT: TRANSPORT INFRASTRUCTURE

STATISTICAL ANALYSIS
ANALYSE STATISTIQUE / ANALISIS ESTADISTICO -
18.08.00
    BT: RESEARCH METHODS
    RT: PROBABILITY
       STATISTICAL TABLES
       STATISTICS

STATISTICAL DATA
DONNEES STATISTIQUES / DATOS ESTADISTICOS -
18.08.00
    NT: ECONOMIC STATISTICS
       EDUCATIONAL STATISTICS
       FOOD STATISTICS
       VITAL STATISTICS
    RT: DATA BANKS
       STATISTICAL TABLES
       STATISTICS

STATISTICAL SERVICES
SERVICES STATISTIQUES / SERVICIOS ESTADISTICOS -
18.02.00
    RT: STATISTICS

STATISTICAL TABLES
TABLEAUX STATISTIQUES / CUADROS ESTADISTICOS -
18.08.00
    NT: INPUT-OUTPUT TABLES
    RT: STATISTICAL ANALYSIS
       STATISTICAL DATA
       STATISTICS

STATISTICIANS
STATISTICIENS / ESTADISTICOS - 13.09.09
    BT: SCIENTISTS
    RT: STATISTICS

STATISTICS
STATISTIQUE / ESTADISTICA - 18.08.00
SN: USE WHEN REFERRING TO THE SCIENCE OF
STATISTICS.

STATISTICS<CONT>
  RT: ECONOMETRICS
      MATHEMATICS
      STATISTICAL ANALYSIS
      STATISTICAL DATA
      STATISTICAL SERVICES
      STATISTICAL TABLES
      STATISTICIANS

STEAM ENGINES
MACHINES A VAPEUR / MAQUINAS DE VAPOR - 08.14.06
  BT: ENGINES

STEEL
ACIER / ACERO - 08.14.02
  BT: ALLOYS
  RT: IRON AND STEEL INDUSTRY

STEEL CONSTRUCTION
CONSTRUCTION EN ACIER / CONSTRUCCION EN ACERO -
08.10.01
  BT: CONSTRUCTION TECHNIQUES

STEEL INDUSTRY
- 08.14.01
  USE: IRON AND STEEL INDUSTRY

STEPPES
STEPPES / ESTEPAS - 17.03.04

STERILITY
STERILITE / ESTERILIDAD - 15.02.02
  RT: VASECTOMY

STOCK EXCHANGE
- 11.02.07
  USE: FINANCIAL MARKET

STOCKS
STOCKS / EXISTENCIAS - 09.03.03
SN: DO NOT CONFUSE WITH SHARES, SECURITIES,
    BONDS, ETC.
  NT: BUFFER STOCKS
  RT: INVENTORIES

STONE
PIERRE / PIEDRA - 08.10.02
  BT: CONSTRUCTION MATERIALS
  RT: STONE CONSTRUCTION

STONE CONSTRUCTION
CONSTRUCTION EN PIERRE / CONSTRUCCION EN PIEDRA
- 08.10.01
  BT: CONSTRUCTION TECHNIQUES
  RT: STONE

STORAGE
STOCKAGE / ALMACENAMIENTO - 09.03.03
  NT: FOOD STORAGE
      WATER STORAGE
  RT: SILOS
      STORAGE CAPACITY
      WAREHOUSES

STORAGE CAPACITY
CAPACITE DE STOCKAGE / CAPACIDAD DE
ALMACENAMIENTO - 09.03.03
  RT: STORAGE

STORMS
TEMPETES / TEMPORALES - 17.01.03
  UF: CYCLONES
      TYPHOONS
  BT: NATURAL DISASTERS
  RT: METEOROLOGY
      WIND

STRAITS
DETROITS / ESTRECHOS - 17.03.04

STRATEGIC PLANNING
PLANIFICATION STRATEGIQUE / PLANIFICACION
ESTRATEGICA - 02.01.02
  BT: PLANNING SYSTEMS
  RT: DEVELOPMENT STRATEGY

STREAMING
- 06.04.10
  USE: ABILITY GROUPING

STRESS-RELATED DISEASES
- 13.04.00
  USE: OCCUPATIONAL DISEASES

STRIKERS
GREVISTES / HUELGUISTAS - 13.06.00
  RT: STRIKES

STRIKES
GREVES / HUELGAS - 13.06.00
SN: CONCERTED CESSATIONS OF WORK BY WORKERS WHO
    HAVE GRIEVANCES TO SETTLE, STANDARDS TO BE
    DEFENDED, OR GOALS TO BE ATTAINED.
  BT: LABOUR DISPUTES
  NT: WILDCAT STRIKES
  RT: RIGHT TO STRIKE
      STRIKERS

STRUCTURAL UNEMPLOYMENT
CHOMAGE STRUCTUREL / DESEMPLEO ESTRUCTURAL -
13.01.03
SN: UNEMPLOYMENT CAUSED BY CHANGES IN THE
    STRUCTURE OF THE ECONOMY RESULTING FROM SUCH
    FACTORS AS TECHNOLOGICAL CHANGE OR
    RELOCATION OF INDUSTRY, OR BY CHANGES IN THE
    COMPOSTION OF THE LABOUR FORCE.
  BT: UNEMPLOYMENT

STUDENT BEHAVIOUR
COMPORTEMENT DE L'ETUDIANT / COMPORTAMIENTO
ESTUDIANTIL - 06.06.01
  BT: BEHAVIOUR
  NT: STUDENT PARTICIPATION
  RT: COLLEGE STUDENTS

STUDENT EXCHANGE
ECHANGE D'ETUDIANTS / INTERCAMBIO DE ESTUDIANTES

STUDENT EXCHANGE<CONT>
- 06.05.02

STUDENT LOANS
PRETS D'ETUDE / PRESTAMOS PARA ESTUDIOS -
06.04.11
      BT: EDUCATIONAL GRANTS
             LOANS

STUDENT MOVEMENTS
MOUVEMENTS ETUDIANTS / MOVIMIENTOS ESTUDIANTILES
- 06.06.01
      BT: SOCIAL MOVEMENTS
             YOUTH ORGANIZATIONS
      RT: COLLEGE STUDENTS

STUDENTTTT PARTICIPATION
PARTICIPATION DES ETUDIANTS / PARTICIPACION
ESTUDIANTIL - 06.06.01
      BT: SOCIAL PARTICIPATION
             STUDENT BEHAVIOUR
      RT: EDUCATIONAL ADMINISTRATION
             EDUCATIONAL POLICY

STUDENTS
ELEVES / ALUMNOS - 06.06.01
      UF: PUPILS
      NT: COLLEGE STUDENTS
             GIFTED STUDENTS
             HANDICAPPED STUDENTS
      RT: TEACHER-STUDENT RELATIONSHIPS

STUDY TOURS
VOYAGES D'ETUDE / VIAJES DE ESTUDIOS - 06.05.02
      BT: TRAVELS

SUBCONTRACTING
SOUS-TRAITANCE / SUBCONTRATACION - 12.07.02
      BT: CONTRACTING

SUBCULTURE
SUBCULTURE / SUBCULTURA - 05.02.01
      BT: CULTURE

SUBJECT INDEXING
- 19.01.02
      USE: INDEXING

SUBSIDIES
SUBVENTIONS / SUBSIDIOS - 11.02.02
      BT: STATE AID
      NT: EXPORT SUBSIDIES
      RT: PRICE SUPPORT

SUBSISTENCE FARMING
AGRICULTURE DE SUBSISTANCE / AGRICULTURA DE
SUBSISTENCIA - 07.05.03
      BT: FARMING SYSTEMS

SUBSTITUTE PRODUCTS
PRODUITS DE REMPLACEMENT / PRODUCTOS
SUBSTITUTIVOS - 12.08.01
      BT: PRODUCTS

SUBTROPICAL ZONE
ZONE SUBTROPICALE / ZONA SUBTROPICAL - 17.02.03
      BT: CLIMATIC ZONES

SUBURBAN AREAS
ZONES SUBURBAINES / AREAS SUBURBANAS - 14.04.03
      UF: SUBURBS
      RT: TOWNS
             URBAN AREAS

SUBURBS
- 14.04.03
      USE: SUBURBAN AREAS

SUDAN
SOUDAN / SUDAN - 01.04.02
      BT: ARAB COUNTRIES
             EAST AFRICA
             ENGLISH SPEAKING AFRICA
             NORTH AFRICA
      RT: SUDANESE

SUDANESE
SOUDANAIS / SUDANES - 14.03.02
      RT: SUDAN

SUGAR
SUCRE / AZUCAR - 08.06.04
      BT: CARBOHYDRATES
      NT: BEET SUGAR
             CANE SUGAR
      RT: MOLASSES
             SUGAR INDUSTRY

SUGAR BEETS
BETTERAVES SUCRIERES / REMOLACHAS AZUCARERAS -
07.07.06
      BT: INDUSTRIAL CROPS
             ROOT CROPS
      RT: BEET SUGAR
             SUGAR INDUSTRY

SUGAR CANE
CANNE A SUCRE / CANA DE AZUCAR - 07.07.06
      BT: INDUSTRIAL CROPS
      RT: CANE SUGAR
             SUGAR INDUSTRY

SUGAR INDUSTRY
INDUSTRIE DU SUCRE / INDUSTRIA AZUCARERA -
08.06.01
      BT: FOOD INDUSTRY
      RT: MOLASSES
             SUGAR
             SUGAR BEETS
             SUGAR CANE

SULPHATES
SULFATES / SULFATOS - 08.12.04
      RT: HERBICIDES
             PESTICIDES

SULPHUR
SOUFRE / AZUFRE - 08.12.04

SULPHUR DIOXIDE
ANHYDRIDE SULFUREUX / ANHIDRIDO SULFUROSO -
08.12.04
    BT: AIR POLLUTANTS

SUMMER SCHOOLS
ECOLES D'ETE / CURSOS DE VERANO - 06.04.03
    BT: SCHOOLS

SUPERMARKETS
SUPERMARCHES / SUPERMERCADOS - 09.04.04

SUPERSTITION
SUPERSTITION / SUPERSTICION - 05.04.02

SUPERVISORS
CONTREMAITRES / SUPERVISORES - 13.09.03
    UF: FOREMEN

SUPPLIERS
FOURNISSEURS / PROVEEDORES - 09.03.02
    RT: CATERING

SUPPLY
OFFRE / OFERTA - 09.01.01
    BT: SUPPLY AND DEMAND
    NT: FOOD SUPPLY
        LABOUR SUPPLY
        MONEY SUPPLY
        POWER SUPPLY
        WATER SUPPLY
    RT: RATIONING

SUPPLY AND DEMAND
OFFRE ET DEMANDE / OFERTA Y DEMANDA - 09.01.01
    NT: DEMAND
        SUPPLY
    RT: MARKET
        MICROECONOMICS
        PRICES

SURGERY
CHIRURGIE / CIRUGIA - 15.04.06
    BT: MEDICINE

SURINAM
SURINAM / SURINAM - 01.04.03
    BT: SOUTH AMERICA
    RT: SURINAMESE

SURINAMESE
SURINAMAIS / SURINAMES - 14.03.02
    RT: SURINAM

SURPLUSES
EXCEDENTS / EXCEDENTES - 12.08.01
    NT: AGRICULTURAL SURPLUSES
    RT: OVERPRODUCTION

SURVEY AREA
ZONE D'ENQUETE / ZONA DE ESTUDIO - 18.04.00
    RT: SURVEYS

SURVEYORS
METREURS / AGRIMENSORES - 13.09.09

SURVEYS
ENQUETES / ENCUESTAS - 18.04.00
SN: COLLECTING DATA ON A GIVEN TOPIC, MAINLY
    THROUGH INTERVIEWS, QUESTIONNAIRES, ETC.
    BT: DATA COLLECTING
    NT: AERIAL SURVEYS
        CADASTRAL SURVEYS
        ECONOMIC SURVEYS
        GEOLOGICAL SURVEYS
        MAIL SURVEYS
        SOCIAL SURVEYS
        SOIL SURVEYS
    RT: INTERVIEWS
        QUESTIONNAIRES
        SURVEY AREA

SURVIVORS BENEFITS
PENSIONS DE SURVIE / SUBSIDIOS DE SOBREVIVIENTE
- 02.03.02
    BT: SOCIAL SECURITY

SWAMPS
MARAIS / PANTANOS - 17.05.02

SWAZI
SOUAZI / SWAZI - 14.03.02
    RT: SWAZILAND

SWAZILAND
SOUAZILAND / SWAZILANDIA - 01.04.02
    BT: ENGLISH SPEAKING AFRICA
        SOUTHERN AFRICA
    RT: SWAZI

SWEDEN
SUEDE / SUECIA - 01.04.05
    BT: SCANDINAVIA
    RT: SWEDISH

SWEDISH
SUEDOIS / SUECO - 14.03.02
    RT: SWEDEN

SWEET POTATOES
PATATES DOUCES / CAMOTES - 07.07.06
    BT: ROOT CROPS

SWINE
PORCS / CERDOS - 07.09.01
    UF: PIGS
    BT: ANIMALS
        LIVESTOCK
    RT: PORK

SWISS
SUISSES / SUIZO - 14.03.02
    RT: SWITZERLAND

SWITZERLAND
SUISSE / SUIZA - 01.04.05
    BT: WESTERN EUROPE
    RT: SWISS

SYNTHETIC RUBBER
CAOUTCHOUC SYNTHETIQUE / CAUCHO SINTETICO -

SYNTHETIC RUBBER<CONT>
08.09.00
>> *BT:* RUBBER

SYRIA
SYRIE / SIRIA - 01.04.06
>> *BT:* ARAB COUNTRIES
>>> MEDITERRANEAN COUNTRIES
>>> MIDDLE EAST
>> *RT:* SYRIAN

SYRIAN
SYRIEN / SIRIO - 14.03.02
>> *RT:* SYRIA

SYSTEMS ANALYSIS
ANALYSE DE SYSTEMES / ANALISIS DE SISTEMAS -
18.08.00
>> *BT:* CYBERNETICS
>> *RT:* NETWORK ANALYSIS
>>> SYSTEMS DESIGN

SYSTEMS DESIGN
CONCEPTION DE SYSTEMES / DISENO DE SISTEMAS -
12.04.00
SN: THE DEVELOPMENT OF AN INTEGRATED METHOD FOR
PRODUCING A REQUIRED ARTICLE OR PERFORMING A
DESIRED OPERATION.
>> *BT:* CYBERNETICS
>> *RT:* COMPUTER PROGRAMMES
>>> ENGINEERING DESIGN
>>> SYSTEMS ANALYSIS

SYSTEMS OF EDUCATION
- 06.03.01
>> *USE:* EDUCATIONAL SYSTEMS

SYSTEMS THEORY
- 18.08.00
>> *USE:* CYBERNETICS

TAIWAN
TAIWAN / TAIWAN - 01.04.04
>> *BT:* FAR EAST

TANKERS
PETROLIERS / BUQUES CISTERNAS - 10.04.00
>> *BT:* SHIPS
>> *RT:* MERCHANT MARINE
>>> PETROLEUM

TANNING INDUSTRY
TANNERIE / INDUSTRIA DEL CURTIDO - 08.08.02
>> *BT:* LEATHER INDUSTRY
>> *RT:* HIDES AND SKINS

TANZANIA
TANZANIE / TANZANIA - 01.04.02
>> *BT:* EAST AFRICA
>>> ENGLISH SPEAKING AFRICA
>> *RT:* TANZANIAN

TANZANIAN
TANZANIEN / TANZANIANO - 14.03.02
>> *RT:* TANZANIA

TAOISM
TAOISME / TAOISMO - 05.04.03

TARIFF AGREEMENTS
ACCORDS TARIFAIRES / ACUERDOS ARANCELARIOS -
09.05.08
>> *BT:* ECONOMIC AGREEMENTS
>> *NT:* GENERAL SYSTEM OF PREFERENCES
>> *RT:* GATT
>>> TARIFF NEGOTIATIONS
>>> TARIFFS
>>> TRADE AGREEMENTS

TARIFF NEGOTIATIONS
NEGOCIATIONS TARIFAIRES / NEGOCIACIONES
ARANCELARIAS - 09.05.08
>> *RT:* TARIFF AGREEMENTS
>>> TARIFFS
>>> TRADE NEGOTIATIONS

TARIFF POLICY
POLITIQUE TARIFAIRE / POLITICA ARANCELARIA -
09.05.08
>> *UF:* CUSTOMS POLICY
>> *BT:* TRADE POLICY
>> *RT:* TARIFFS

TARIFF REDUCTIONS
REDUCTIONS TARIFAIRES / REDUCCIONES ARANCELARIAS
- 09.05.08
>> *RT:* TARIFFS
>>> TRADE LIBERALIZATION

TARIFF REFORMS
REFORMES TARIFAIRES / REFORMAS ARANCELARIAS -
09.05.08
>> *RT:* TARIFFS

TARIFFS
TARIFS DOUANIERS / ARANCELES - 09.05.08
>> *BT:* TRADE BARRIERS
>> *NT:* PREFERENTIAL TARIFFS

TARIFFS<CONT>
RT: CUSTOMS
CUSTOMS UNION
FOREIGN TRADE
FREE PORT
FREE PORTS
IMPORT TAX
PROTECTIONIST MEASURES
TARIFF AGREEMENTS
TARIFF NEGOTIATIONS
TARIFF POLICY
TARIFF REDUCTIONS
TARIFF REFORMS

TAX AGREEMENTS
ACCORDS FISCAUX / ACUERDOS TRIBUTARIOS -
09.05.09
BT: ECONOMIC AGREEMENTS
RT: TAXATION

TAX COLLECTION
COLLECTE DES IMPOTS / RECAUDACION DE IMPUESTOS -
11.01.02
RT: FISCAL ADMINISTRATION
TAXES

TAX DEDUCTION
DEDUCTION FISCALE / DEDUCCION TRIBUTARIA -
11.01.02
RT: TAXES

TAX EVASION
FRAUDE FISCALE / EVASION TRIBUTARIA - 11.01.02
RT: TAXES

TAX EXEMPTION
EXONERATION FISCALE / EXENCION TRIBUTARIA -
11.01.02
BT: STATE AID
RT: TAX HAVENS
TAXES

TAX HAVENS
PARADIS FISCAUX / PARAISOS FISCALES - 11.01.02
SN: COUNTRIES GRANTING HIGH TAX EXEMPTION.
RT: TAX EXEMPTION
TAX SYSTEMS

TAX INCENTIVES
STIMULANTS FISCAUX / ESTIMULOS TRIBUTARIOS -
11.01.02
RT: INVESTMENT PROMOTION
TAXES

TAX REFORMS
REFORMES FISCALES / REFORMAS TRIBUTARIAS -
11.01.02
RT: TAX SYSTEMS
TAXATION

TAX REVENUES
RECETTES FISCALES / INGRESOS FISCALES - 11.01.02
BT: BUDGETARY RESOURCES
RT: TAXES

TAX SYSTEMS
SYSTEMES FISCAUX / SISTEMAS TRIBUTARIOS -
11.01.02
RT: TAX HAVENS
TAX REFORMS
TAXATION
TAXPAYERS

TAXATION
FISCALITE / TRIBUTACION - 11.01.02
RT: DOUBLE TAXATION
FISCAL ADMINISTRATION
FISCAL LAW
FISCAL POLICY
INCOME REDISTRIBUTION
TAX AGREEMENTS
TAX REFORMS
TAX SYSTEMS
TAXES
TAXPAYERS

TAXES
IMPOTS / IMPUESTOS - 11.01.02
BT: PUBLIC FINANCE
NT: CAPITAL TAX
CONSUMPTION TAX
INCOME TAX
LAND TAX
LOCAL TAXES
PAYROLL TAX
RT: TAX COLLECTION
TAX DEDUCTION
TAX EVASION
TAX EXEMPTION
TAX INCENTIVES
TAX REVENUES
TAXATION

TAXPAYERS
CONTRIBUABLES / CONTRIBUYENTES - 11.01.02
RT: TAX SYSTEMS
TAXATION

TEA
THE / TE - 07.07.09
BT: INDUSTRIAL CROPS
NON-ALCOHOLIC BEVERAGES

TEACHER ASSOCIATIONS
ASSOCIATIONS D'ENSEIGNANTS / ASOCIACIONES DE
DOCENTES - 06.06.02
BT: OCCUPATIONAL ORGANIZATIONS
RT: TEACHERS

TEACHER RECRUITMENT
RECRUTEMENT D'ENSEIGNANTS / RECLUTAMIENTO DE
DOCENTES - 06.06.02
BT: RECRUITMENT
RT: TEACHERS

TEACHER SHORTAGE
PENURIE D'ENSEIGNANTS / ESCASEZ DE DOCENTES -
06.06.02
BT: LABOUR SHORTAGE
RT: TEACHERS

TEACHER STATUS
**STATUT DE L'ENSEIGNANT / STATUS DE LOS DOCENTES
- 06.06.02**
    RT: SOCIAL STATUS
        TEACHERS

TEACHER TRAINING
**FORMATION DES ENSEIGNANTS / FORMACION DE
DOCENTES - 06.06.02**
    BT: TRAINING
    RT: COLLEGES OF EDUCATION
        TEACHERS

TEACHER TRAINING COLLEGES
- 06.04.05
    USE: **COLLEGES OF EDUCATION**

TEACHER-STUDENT RELATIONSHIPS
**RELATIONS ENSEIGNANTS-ENSEIGNES / RELACIONES
DOCENTES-ALUMNOS - 06.06.02**
    BT: SCHOOL ENVIRONMENT
    RT: STUDENTS
        TEACHERS

TEACHERS
ENSEIGNANTS / DOCENTES - 13.09.09
    UF: PROFESSORS
    BT: TEACHING PERSONNEL
    RT: TEACHER ASSOCIATIONS
        TEACHER RECRUITMENT
        TEACHER SHORTAGE
        TEACHER STATUS
        TEACHER TRAINING
        TEACHER-STUDENT RELATIONSHIPS
        TEACHING
        TEACHING PERSONNEL

TEACHING
ENSEIGNEMENT / ENSENANZA - 06.05.02
    UF: INSTRUCTION
    NT: DISTANCE STUDY
        EXPERIMENTAL TEACHING
        INDIVIDUALIZED TEACHING
        PEER TEACHING
        REMEDIAL TEACHING
        SELF-INSTRUCTION
        TEAM TEACHING
    RT: COURSES
        CURRICULUM
        CURRICULUM SUBJECTS
        EDUCATION
        TEACHERS
        TEACHING AIDS
        TEACHING METHODS
        TEACHING PERSONNEL
        TEACHING PRACTICE
        TEACHING PROGRAMMES
        TRAINING

TEACHING AIDS
**MOYENS D'ENSEIGNEMENT / MEDIOS DE ENSENANZA -
06.05.03**

TEACHING AIDS<CONT>
    UF: INSTRUCTIONAL AIDS
        INSTRUCTIONAL MEDIA
        TEACHING MATERIALS
    BT: EDUCATIONAL EQUIPMENT
    NT: AUDIOVISUAL AIDS
        MANUAL
        TEXTBOOK
    RT: EDUCATIONAL TECHNOLOGY
        RESOURCES CENTRES
        TEACHING

TEACHING MATERIALS
- 06.05.03
    USE: **TEACHING AIDS**

TEACHING METHODS
**METHODES PEDAGOGIQUES / METODOS PEDAGOGICOS -
06.05.02**
    NT: PROGRAMMED INSTRUCTION
    RT: DISTANCE STUDY
        EDUCATIONAL FILMS
        EDUCATIONAL INNOVATIONS
        EXPERIMENTAL TEACHING
        TEACHING
        TEACHING PRACTICE

TEACHING PERSONNEL
CORPS ENSEIGNANT / PERSONAL DOCENTE - 06.06.02
    UF: INSTRUCTIONAL STAFF
    NT: INSTRUCTORS
        TEACHERS
    RT: SCIENTIFIC PERSONNEL
        TEACHERS
        TEACHING

TEACHING PRACTICE
**PRATIQUE PEDAGOGIQUE / PRACTICA PEDAGOGICA -
06.05.02**
    RT: TEACHING
        TEACHING METHODS

TEACHING PROGRAMMES
**PROGRAMMES D'ENSEIGNEMENT / PROGRAMAS DE
ENSENANZA - 06.05.01**
    UF: INSTRUCTIONAL PROGRAMMES
    RT: CURRICULUM
        TEACHING

TEACHING SYSTEMS
- 06.03.01
    USE: **EDUCATIONAL SYSTEMS**

TEAM TEACHING
**ENSEIGNEMENT EN EQUIPE / ENSENANZA EN EQUIPO -
06.05.02**
    BT: TEACHING

TEAM WORK
TRAVAIL D'EQUIPE / TRABAJO EN EQUIPO - 13.03.02
*SN: WORK UNDERTAKEN IN GROUPS WHICH INVOLVES THE
    DEPENDENCE OF ONE WORKER'S DUTIES ON
    COMPLETION OF THE DUTIES OF ANOTHER MEMBER
    OF THE GROUP.*
    BT: GROUP WORK

TECHNICAL ASPECTS
ASPECTS TECHNIQUES / ASPECTOS TECNICOS -
12.06.00
    RT: ENGINEERING
        TECHNOLOGY

TECHNICAL ASSISTANCE
ASSISTANCE TECHNIQUE / ASISTENCIA TECNICA -
01.01.03
    BT: DEVELOPMENT AID
    RT: TECHNOLOGY TRANSFER

TECHNICAL EDUCATION
ENSEIGNEMENT TECHNIQUE / ENSENANZA TECNICA -
06.03.07
    BT: VOCATIONAL EDUCATION
    RT: ENGINEERING
        TECHNICAL SCHOOLS
        TECHNOLOGICAL INSTITUTES
        TECHNOLOGY

TECHNICAL INFORMATION
INFORMATION TECHNIQUE / INFORMACION TECNICA -
19.01.01
    UF: TECHNOLOGICAL INFORMATION
    BT: INFORMATION
    NT: INDUSTRIAL INFORMATION
    RT: TECHNOLOGY

TECHNICAL PERSONNEL
PERSONNEL TECHNIQUE / PERSONAL TECNICO -
13.09.03
    NT: TECHNICIANS
    RT: WORKERS

TECHNICAL PROGRESS
- 12.06.00
    USE: TECHNOLOGICAL CHANGE

TECHNICAL REPORT
RAPPORT TECHNIQUE / INFORME TECNICO - 19.02.08

TECHNICAL SCHOOLS
ECOLES TECHNIQUES / ESCUELAS TECNICAS - 06.04.06
    BT: SCHOOLS
    RT: TECHNICAL EDUCATION
        VOCATIONAL EDUCATION
        VOCATIONAL SCHOOLS

TECHNICAL UNEMPLOYMENT
CHOMAGE TECHNOLOGIQUE / DESEMPLEO TECNICO -
13.01.03
    BT: UNEMPLOYMENT
    RT: TECHNOLOGICAL CHANGE

TECHNICIANS
TECHNICIENS / TECNICOS - 13.09.03
*SN: WITH MORE TECHNICAL KNOWLEDGE THAN A SKILLED
WORKER, BUT LESS THAN AN ENGINEER.*
    BT: TECHNICAL PERSONNEL
    NT: DRAUGHTSMEN

TECHNIQUE
- 12.06.00
    USE: TECHNOLOGY

TECHNOCRACY
TECHNOCRATIE / TECNOCRACIA - 04.03.05
    RT: CIVIL SERVICE
        POLITICAL POWER
        PUBLIC ADMINISTRATION

TECHNOLOGICAL CHANGE
CHANGEMENT TECHNOLOGIQUE / CAMBIO TECNOLOGICO -
12.06.00
    UF: TECHNICAL PROGRESS
    RT: AUTOMATION
        INNOVATIONS
        INVENTIONS
        SCIENTIFIC PROGRESS
        TECHNICAL UNEMPLOYMENT
        TECHNOLOGY

TECHNOLOGICAL FORECASTING
PREVISION TECHNOLOGIQUE / PREDICCION TECNOLOGICA
- 12.06.00
    RT: TECHNOLOGY

TECHNOLOGICAL INFORMATION
- 19.01.01
    USE: **TECHNICAL INFORMATION**

TECHNOLOGICAL INSTITUTES
INSTITUTS DE TECHNOLOGIE / INSTITUTOS DE
TECNOLOGIA - 06.04.06
*SN: USE IN CONNECTION WITH ESTABLISHMENTS GIVING
HIGH-LEVEL INSTRUCTION IN A PARTICULAR ART
OR SCIENCE.*
    BT: HIGHER EDUCATION INSTITUTIONS
    RT: TECHNICAL EDUCATION

TECHNOLOGICAL OBSOLESCENCE
OBSOLESCENCE TECHNOLOGIQUE / OBSOLESCENCIA
TECNOLOGICA - 12.06.00
    RT: OBSOLETE EQUIPMENT
        TECHNOLOGY

TECHNOLOGY
TECHNOLOGIE / TECNOLOGIA - 12.06.00
*SN: THE STATE OF TECHNOLOGY AS A WHOLE OR IN A
PARTICULAR INDUSTRIAL BRANCH; SEE ALSO
«ENGINEERING».*
    UF: TECHNIQUE
    NT: ALTERNATIVE TECHNOLOGY
        APPROPRIATE TECHNOLOGY
        INTERMEDIATE TECHNOLOGY
        TRADITIONAL TECHNOLOGY
    RT: ACAST
        CHOICE OF TECHNOLOGY
        CSTD
        ENGINEERING
        SCIENCE
        TECHNICAL ASPECTS
        TECHNICAL EDUCATION
        TECHNICAL INFORMATION
        TECHNOLOGICAL CHANGE
        TECHNOLOGICAL FORECASTING
        TECHNOLOGICAL OBSOLESCENCE
        TECHNOLOGY TRANSFER

TECHNOLOGY TRANSFER
TRANSFERT DE TECHNOLOGIE / TRANSFERENCIA DE
TECNOLOGIAS - 12.06.00
SN: *TRANSFER TO DEVELOPING COUNTRIES OF
    TECHNOLOGICAL KNOWHOW, PRODUCTION TECHNIQUES
    AND EQUIPMENT TO BE USED IN THE PRODUCTION
    PROCESS.*
    RT: APPROPRIATE TECHNOLOGY
        INTERMEDIATE TECHNOLOGY
        TECHNICAL ASSISTANCE
        TECHNOLOGY

TELECOMMUNICATION INDUSTRY
INDUSTRIE DES TELECOMMUNICATIONS / INDUSTRIA DE
TELECOMUNICACIONES - 08.16.00
    BT: COMMUNICATION INDUSTRY
    NT: BROADCASTING
    RT: ELECTRONICS INDUSTRY
        TELECOMMUNICATIONS

TELECOMMUNICATIONS
TELECOMMUNICATIONS / TELECOMUNICACIONES -
05.07.03
    BT: COMMUNICATION
    NT: RADIO
        TELEGRAPH
        TELEPHONE
        TELEVISION
        TELEX
    RT: DISTANCE
        DISTANCE STUDY
        ITU
        TELECOMMUNICATION INDUSTRY

TELEGRAPH
TELEGRAPHE / TELEGRAFO - 08.16.00
    BT: TELECOMMUNICATIONS
    RT: POSTAL SERVICES

TELEPHONE
TELEPHONE / TELEFONO - 08.16.00
    BT: TELECOMMUNICATIONS
    RT: POSTAL SERVICES

TELEVISION
TELEVISION / TELEVISION - 05.07.03
    BT: MASS MEDIA
        TELECOMMUNICATIONS
    NT: EDUCATIONAL TELEVISION
    RT: BROADCASTING
        TELEVISION RECEIVERS

TELEVISION RECEIVERS
RECEPTEURS DE TELEVISION / RECEPTORES DE
TELEVISION - 08.16.00
    RT: TELEVISION

TELEX
TELEX / TELEX - 08.16.00
    BT: TELECOMMUNICATIONS

TEMPERATE ZONE
ZONE TEMPEREE / ZONA TEMPLADA - 17.02.03
    BT: CLIMATIC ZONES

TEMPERATURE
TEMPERATURE / TEMPERATURA - 18.06.00
    RT: CALORIES
        COOLING
        FREEZING
        HEATING
        REFRIGERATION
        THERMAL POLLUTION

TEMPORARY EMPLOYMENT
EMPLOI TEMPORAIRE / EMPLEO TEMPORAL - 13.01.03
    BT: EMPLOYMENT
    RT: CASUAL WORKERS
        SEASONAL WORKERS

TENANT FARMERS
FERMIERS / ARRENDATARIOS AGRICOLAS - 07.02.00
SN: *USE IN CONNECTION WITH GRANTING LAND FOR
    CULTIVATION IN RETURN FOR A CERTAIN
    CONSIDERATION (RENT).*
    UF: SHARE FARMERS
    BT: FARMERS

TERMINOLOGY
TERMINOLOGIE / TERMINOLOGIA - 19.03.00
    RT: DICTIONARY
        ENCYCLOPEDIA
        GLOSSARY
        THESAURUS

TERMS OF AID
CONDITIONS DE L'AIDE / CONDICIONES DE LA AYUDA -
01.01.04
    UF: TIED AID
    RT: DEVELOPMENT AID
        FINANCIAL TERMS

TERMS OF TRADE
TERMES DE L'ECHANGE / TERMINOS DE INTERCAMBIO -
09.05.03
    RT: COMMODITY PRICES
        INDEXATION
        INDUSTRIAL PRICES

TERRESTRIAL ENVIRONMENT
ENVIRONNEMENT TERRESTRE / MEDIO AMBIENTE
TERRESTRE - 16.01.02
    BT: PHYSICAL ENVIRONMENT

TERRITORIAL WATERS
EAUX TERRITORIALES / AGUAS JURISDICCIONALES -
17.06.00
    RT: COASTAL WATERS
        LAW OF THE SEA

TERRORISM
TERRORISME / TERRORISMO - 01.02.07
    RT: AIR PIRACY
        CRIMES
        HOSTAGES
        POLITICAL PROBLEMS
        SOCIAL PROBLEMS
        VIOLENCE

TERTIARY
TERTIAIRE / TERCIARIO - 17.04.02

TERTIARY SECTOR
- 09.01.01
    USE: SERVICE INDUSTRY

TESTING
MISE A L'EPREUVE / ENSAYO - 18.09.00
    RT: EVALUATION
          EXPERIMENTATION
          QUALITY CONTROL
          TESTS

TESTS
TESTS / PRUEBAS - 18.09.00
    BT: EVALUATION TECHNIQUES
    RT: EXPERIMENTS
          TESTING

TEXTBOOK
MANUEL SCOLAIRE / LIBRO DE TEXTO - 19.02.09
    BT: TEACHING AIDS

TEXTILE INDUSTRY
INDUSTRIE TEXTILE / INDUSTRIA TEXTIL - 08.08.01
    BT: INDUSTRIAL SECTOR
    NT: CLOTHING INDUSTRY
          ROPE INDUSTRY
    RT: CARPETS
          FIBRES
          SPINNING
          TEXTILE WORKERS
          TEXTILES
          WEAVING

TEXTILE WORKERS
OUVRIERS DU TEXTILE / OBREROS TEXTILES -
13.09.06
    BT: INDUSTRIAL WORKERS
    RT: TEXTILE INDUSTRY

TEXTILES
TEXTILES / TEXTILES - 08.08.01
    RT: FIBRES
          TEXTILE INDUSTRY

THAI
THAILANDAIS / TAILANDES - 14.03.02
    RT: THAILAND

THAILAND
THAILANDE / TAILANDIA - 01.04.04
    BT: SOUTH EAST ASIA
    RT: THAI

THEATRE
THEATRE / TEATRO - 05.05.03
    BT: DRAMATIC ART

THEORY
THEORIE / TEORIA - 18.03.00

THEORY<CONT>
    NT: DEVELOPMENT THEORY
          ECONOMIC THEORY
          EDUCATIONAL THEORY
          INFORMATION THEORY
          POLITICAL THEORY
          POPULATION THEORY
          SOCIAL THEORY
    RT: MODELS

THERMAL ENERGY
ENERGIE THERMIQUE / ENERGIA TERMICA - 08.11.01
    BT: ENERGY
    NT: GEOTHERMAL ENERGY
    RT: THERMAL POWER PLANTS

THERMAL POLLUTION
POLLUTION THERMIQUE / CONTAMINACION TERMICA -
16.03.04
    BT: POLLUTION
    RT: TEMPERATURE
          WATER POLLUTION

THERMAL POWER PLANTS
CENTRALES THERMIQUES / CENTRALES TERMICAS -
08.11.02
    BT: ELECTRIC POWER PLANTS
    RT: THERMAL ENERGY

THESAURUS
THESAURUS / TESAURO - 19.03.00
    BT: PRIMARY DOCUMENTS
          REFERENCE MATERIALS
    RT: INFORMATION SYSTEMS
          TERMINOLOGY

THESIS
THESE / TESIS - 19.02.09
    BT: PRIMARY DOCUMENTS

TIDAL ENERGY
ENERGIE MAREMOTRICE / ENERGIA DE LAS MAREAS -
08.11.01
    BT: ENERGY
    RT: TIDES

TIDAL WAVES
RAZ DE MAREE / MAREMOTOS - 17.04.03
    BT: NATURAL DISASTERS
    RT: SEISMS
          VOLCANIC ERUPTIONS

TIDES
MAREES / MAREAS - 17.06.00
    BT: ENERGY SOURCES
    RT: TIDAL ENERGY

TIED AID
- 01.01.04
    USE: TERMS OF AID

TIMBER
BOIS DE CONSTRUCTION / MADERA DE CONSTRUCCION -

TIMBER<CONT>
08.07.01
      BT: CONSTRUCTION MATERIALS
           WOOD

TIME BUDGET
BUDGET TEMPS / DISTRIBUCION DEL TIEMPO -
13.03.03

TIME FACTOR
FACTEUR TEMPS / FACTOR TIEMPO - 18.10.00
      RT: CHRONOLOGY
           DURATION

TIME STUDY
- 13.03.01
      USE: WORK STUDY

TIN
ETAIN / ESTANO - 08.14.02
      BT: NON-FERROUS METALS

TIN PLATE
FER BLANC / HOJALATA - 08.14.04

TITANIUM
TITANE / TITANIO - 08.14.02
      BT: NON-FERROUS METALS

TOBACCO
TABAC / TABACO - 07.07.09
      BT: INDUSTRIAL CROPS
      RT: TOBACCO INDUSTRY

TOBACCO INDUSTRY
INDUSTRIE DU TABAC / INDUSTRIA TABACALERA -
08.06.01
      RT: TOBACCO

TOGO
TOGO / TOGO - 01.04.02
      BT: FRENCH SPEAKING AFRICA
           WEST AFRICA
      RT: TOGOLESE

TOGOLESE
TOGOLAIS / TOGOLES - 14.03.02
      RT: TOGO

TOILET PREPARATIONS
PRODUITS DE TOILETTE / PRODUCTOS DE TOCADOR -
08.12.08
      NT: COSMETICS
           PERFUMES
           SOAP

TOMATOES
TOMATES / TOMATES - 07.07.05
      BT: FRUITS

TONGA
TONGA / TONGA - 01.04.07
      BT: OCEANIA
      RT: TONGAN

TONGAN
TONGAN / TONGANO - 14.03.02
      RT: TONGA

TONNAGE
TONNAGE / TONELAJE - 10.06.00

TOOLS
OUTILS / HERRAMIENTAS - 08.14.05
      NT: HAND TOOLS
           MACHINE TOOLS
      RT: EQUIPMENT

TOP MANAGEMENT
CADRES SUPERIEURS / MANDOS SUPERIORES - 12.03.00
SN: MANAGEMENT RESPONSIBLE FOR THE OVERALL
*   RUNNING OF AN ORGANIZATION.*
      BT: MANAGERS
      RT: PROFESSIONALS

TOPOGRAPHY
TOPOGRAPHIE / TOPOGRAFIA - 18.07.00
      RT: PHYSICAL GEOGRAPHY

TORTURE
TORTURE / TORTURA - 02.04.03
      RT: HUMAN RIGHTS
           PRISONERS
           VIOLENCE

TOURISM
TOURISME / TURISMO - 09.04.05
      BT: SERVICE INDUSTRY
      RT: LEISURE
           TRAVELS

TOWN CENTRE
CENTRE VILLE / CENTRO CIUDAD - 14.04.03
      RT: TOWNS

TOWN PLANNING
- 14.04.03
      USE: URBAN PLANNING

TOWNS
VILLES / CIUDADES - 14.04.03
      UF: CITIES
      NT: MIDDLE-SIZED TOWNS
           NEW TOWNS
           SATELLITE TOWNS
           SMALL TOWNS

TOWNS<CONT>

    RT: NEIGHBOURHOOD
        SUBURBAN AREAS
        TOWN CENTRE
        URBAN
        URBAN AREAS
        URBAN ATTRACTION
        URBAN COMMUNITIES
        URBAN CONCENTRATION
        URBAN DEVELOPMENT
        URBAN ENVIRONMENT
        URBAN PLANNING
        URBAN POPULATION
        URBAN RENEWAL
        URBAN SOCIOLOGY
        URBAN TRAFFIC
        URBAN TRANSPORT
        URBANIZATION

TOXIC METALS
METAUX TOXIQUES / METALES TOXICOS - 15.05.00
    BT: METALS
        TOXIC SUBSTANCES
    NT: CADMIUM
        LEAD
        MERCURY
        ZINC

TOXIC SUBSTANCES
**SUBSTANCES TOXIQUES / SUBSTANCIAS TOXICAS -
15.05.00**
    BT: DANGEROUS SUBSTANCES
    NT: TOXIC METALS
    RT: TOXICITY

TOXICITY
TOXICITE / TOXICIDAD - 15.05.00
    RT: TOXIC SUBSTANCES

TOXINS
TOXINES / TOXINAS - 15.03.02
    BT: POISONS
    RT: POISONING

TOYS
JOUETS / JUGUETES - 08.07.03

TRACTORS
TRACTEURS / TRACTORES - 07.04.00
    BT: AGRICULTURAL MACHINERY
        MOTOR VEHICLES

TRADE
COMMERCE / COMERCIO - 09.01.01
*SN: THE BUYING AND SELLING OF GOODS AND
    SERVICES.*
    BT: SERVICE INDUSTRY
    NT: BARTER
        DOMESTIC TRADE
        INTERNATIONAL TRADE
        RETAIL TRADE
        WHOLESALE TRADE

TRADE<CONT>
    RT: COMMERCIAL BANKS
        COMMERCIAL CREDIT
        COMMERCIAL ENTERPRISES
        COMMERCIAL LAW

TRADE AGREEMENTS
**ACCORDS COMMERCIAUX / CONVENIOS COMERCIALES -
09.05.02**
    BT: ECONOMIC AGREEMENTS
    NT: COMMODITY AGREEMENTS
        GATT
    RT: ACCESS TO MARKET
        COMMON MARKET
        GATT
        INTERNATIONAL TRADE
        TARIFF AGREEMENTS
        TRADE NEGOTIATIONS

TRADE BARRIERS
**BARRIERES COMMERCIALES / BARRERAS COMERCIALES -
09.05.07**
    NT: BOYCOTT
        DUMPING
        EMBARGO
        RESTRICTIVE BUSINESS PRACTICES
        TARIFFS
    RT: INTERNATIONAL TRADE
        TRADE POLICY
        UNFAIR COMPETITION

TRADE DEVELOPMENT
**DEVELOPPEMENT DU COMMERCE INTERNAT. / DESARROLLO
DEL COMERCIO INTERNAC. - 09.05.06**
    RT: INTERNATIONAL TRADE
        TRADE POLICY
        TRADE PROMOTION

TRADE FAIRS
**FOIRES COMMERCIALES / FERIAS COMERCIALES -
09.03.05**
    RT: EXHIBITIONS
        TRADE PROMOTION

TRADE LIBERALIZATION
**LIBERALISATION DES ECHANGES / LIBERALIZACION DEL
INTERCAMBIO - 09.05.07**
    BT: TRADE POLICY
    RT: INTERNATIONAL TRADE
        TARIFF REDUCTIONS

TRADE MARKS
**MARQUES COMMERCIALES / MARCAS REGISTRADAS -
09.03.04**
    RT: INDUSTRIAL ESPIONAGE
        LICENSING
        PATENTS

TRADE MISSIONS
**MISSIONS COMMERCIALES / MISIONES COMERCIALES -
09.05.06**
    RT: TRADE PROMOTION

TRADE NEGOTIATIONS

TRADE NEGOTIATIONS<CONT>
NEGOCIATIONS COMMERCIALES / NEGOCIACIONES
COMERCIALES - 09.05.02
    RT: GATT
        INTERNATIONAL TRADE
        TARIFF NEGOTIATIONS
        TRADE AGREEMENTS

TRADE POLICY
POLITIQUE DU COMMERCE INTERNATIONAL / POLITICA
COMERCIAL INTERNACIONAL - 09.05.06
    BT: ECONOMIC POLICY
    NT: PROTECTIONIST MEASURES
        TARIFF POLICY
        TRADE LIBERALIZATION
    RT: COMMON MARKET
        FOREIGN TRADE
        INTERNATIONAL TRADE
        TRADE BARRIERS
        TRADE DEVELOPMENT

TRADE PROMOTION
PROMOTION DU COMMERCE INTERNATIONAL / PROMOCION
DEL COMERCIO INTERNAC. - 09.05.06
    NT: EXPORT PROMOTION
        IMPORT PROMOTION
    RT: INTERNATIONAL TRADE
        TRADE DEVELOPMENT
        TRADE FAIRS
        TRADE MISSIONS

TRADE RELATIONS
RELATIONS COMMERCIALES / RELACIONES COMERCIALES
- 09.05.02
*SN: EXPORT-IMPORT RELATIONS WITH OTHER
    COUNTRIES.*
    BT: ECONOMIC RELATIONS
    RT: EAST-WEST TRADE
        FOREIGN TRADE

TRADE UNIONISM
SYNDICALISME / SINDICALISMO - 13.06.00
    RT: PROLETARIAN INTERNATIONALISM
        TRADE UNIONS

TRADE UNIONS
SYNDICATS / SINDICATOS - 13.06.00
*SN: ORGANIZATIONS OF EMPLOYEES, USUALLY
    ASSOCIATED BEYOND THE CONFINES OF ONE
    ENTERPRISE, ESTABLISHED FOR PROTECTING OR
    IMPROVING, THROUGH COLLECTIVE ACTION, THE
    ECONOMIC AND SOCIAL STATUS OF THEIR MEMBERS.*
    UF: LABOUR UNIONS
    BT: INTEREST GROUPS

TRADE UNIONS<CONT>
    RT: ASSOCIATIONS
        FREEDOM OF ASSOCIATION
        ICFTU
        LABOUR MOVEMENTS
        LABOUR RELATIONS
        TRADE UNIONISM
        WCL
        WFTU
        WORKERS EDUCATION
        WORKERS PARTICIPATION
        WORKERS REPRESENTATION

TRADE VOLUME
VOLUME DU COMMERCE INTERNATIONAL / VOLUMEN DEL
COMERCIO INTERNACIONAL - 09.05.03
    NT: EXPORT VOLUME
        IMPORT VOLUME
    RT: INTERNATIONAL TRADE

TRADERS
- 13.09.07
    USE: DEALERS

TRADITION
TRADITION / TRADICION - 05.02.01
    RT: CONSERVATISM
        CUSTOMARY LAW
        MODERNIZATION
        TRADITIONAL CULTURE

TRADITIONAL CULTURE
CULTURE TRADITIONNELLE / CULTURA TRADICIONAL -
05.02.01
    BT: CULTURE
    RT: FOLKLORE
        TRADITION

TRADITIONAL MEDICINE
MEDECINE TRADITIONNELLE / MEDICINA TRADICIONAL -
15.04.06
    BT: MEDICINE
    RT: MEDICINAL PLANTS

TRADITIONAL TECHNOLOGY
TECHNOLOGIE TRADITIONNELLE / TECNOLOGIA
TRADICIONAL - 12.06.00
    BT: TECHNOLOGY

TRAFFIC
CIRCULATION / TRAFICO - 10.08.00
    NT: AIR TRAFFIC
        RAILWAY TRAFFIC
        ROAD TRAFFIC
        SEA TRAFFIC
        URBAN TRAFFIC
    RT: TRAFFIC CONTROL

TRAFFIC CONTROL
REGULATION DE LA CIRCULATION / REGULACION DÈL
TRAFICO - 10.08.00
    RT: TRAFFIC

TRAINEES
STAGIAIRES / ALUMNOS PRACTICANTES - 06.06.01

TRAINEES<CONT>
SN: USE TO MEAN PERSONS UNDERGOING TRAINING OR
EDUCATION UNDER SUPERVISION AND WITH AN
OCCUPATIONAL BIAS.
RT: VOCATIONAL TRAINING

TRAINING
FORMATION / CAPACITACION - 06.02.01
NT: MANAGEMENT DEVELOPMENT
TEACHER TRAINING
TRAINING ABROAD
VOCATIONAL TRAINING

RT: EDUCATION
INSTRUCTORS
TEACHING
TRAINING ALLOWANCES
TRAINING ASSISTANCE
TRAINING COURSES
TRAINING METHODS
TRAINING PROGRAMMES

TRAINING ABROAD
FORMATION A L'ETRANGER / CAPACITACION EN EL
EXTRANJERO - 06.05.02
BT: TRAINING

TRAINING ALLOWANCES
INDEMNITES DE FORMATION / BECAS DE FORMACION
PROFESIONAL - 06.04.11
SN: COMPENSATION ALLOTTED BY EMPLOYERS TO
EMPLOYEES PICKED TO UNDERGO SPECIAL TRAINING
FOR A CERTAIN PERIOD, USUALLY OUTSIDE THEIR
NORMAL PLACE OF WORK.
BT: EDUCATIONAL GRANTS
RT: TRAINING
VOCATIONAL TRAINING

TRAINING ASSISTANCE
ASSISTANCE EN MATIERE DE FORMATION / ASISTENCIA
EN FORMACION PROFESIONAL - 01.01.03
BT: DEVELOPMENT AID
RT: TRAINING

TRAINING CENTRES
CENTRES DE FORMATION / CENTROS DE CAPACITACION -
06.04.06
UF: TRAINING WORKSHOPS
BT: EDUCATIONAL INSTITUTIONS
RT: VOCATIONAL EDUCATION
VOCATIONAL TRAINING

TRAINING COURSES
COURS DE FORMATION / CURSOS DE CAPACITACION -
06.05.01
BT: COURSES
RT: TRAINING

TRAINING METHODS
METHODES DE FORMATION / METODOS DE CAPACITACION
- 06.05.02
NT: MODULAR TRAINING
RT: TRAINING

TRAINING PROGRAMMES

TRAINING PROGRAMMES<CONT>
PROGRAMMES DE FORMATION / PROGRAMAS DE
CAPACITACION - 06.05.01
RT: CURRICULUM
TRAINING

TRAINING WORKSHOPS
- 06.04.06
USE: TRAINING CENTRES

TRAINS
TRAINS / TRENES - 10.04.00
BT: MOTOR VEHICLES
NT: LOCOMOTIVES
ROLLING STOCK
RT: RAILWAY TRANSPORT
RAILWAYS

TRANSFRONTIER POLLUTION
POLLUTION TRANSFRONTIERE / CONTAMINACION
TRANSFRONTERA - 16.03.04
BT: POLLUTION
RT: BOUNDARIES

TRANSISTORS
TRANSISTORS / TRANSISTORES - 08.15.02
BT: ELECTRONIC EQUIPMENT

TRANSIT
TRANSIT / TRANSITO - 10.07.00
SN: TRANSPORT IN A COUNTRY OUTSIDE OF WHICH ARE
SITUATED THE DEPARTURE AND DESTINATION
POINTS.
RT: TRANSPORT

TRANSITION FROM SCHOOL TO WORK
PASSAGE A LA VIE ACTIVE / TRANSICION A LA VIDA
PROFESIONAL - 06.03.07
RT: EMPLOYMENT
OCCUPATIONS
WORKING LIFE

TRANSLATION
TRADUCTION / TRADUCCION - 05.06.01
RT: LANGUAGES
TRANSLATION SERVICES
TRANSLATORS

TRANSLATION SERVICES
SERVICES DE TRADUCTION / SERVICIOS DE TRADUCCION
- 19.01.03
BT: INFORMATION SERVICES
RT: TRANSLATION

TRANSLATORS
TRADUCTEURS / TRADUCTORES - 13.09.09
RT: TRANSLATION

TRANSNATIONAL CORPORATIONS
- 03.03.05
USE: MULTINATIONAL ENTERPRISES

TRANSPORT
TRANSPORT / TRANSPORTE - 10.01.00
UF: TRANSPORTATION
BT: SERVICE INDUSTRY

TRANSPORT<CONT>
> NT: INLAND TRANSPORT
>   INTERNATIONAL TRANSPORT
>   PUBLIC TRANSPORT
>   SCHOOL TRANSPORT
>   URBAN TRANSPORT
> RT: CARRIERS
>   ECMT
>   MODES OF TRANSPORTATION
>   TRANSIT
>   TRANSPORT ECONOMICS
>   TRANSPORT EQUIPMENT
>   TRANSPORT INFRASTRUCTURE
>   TRANSPORT PLANNING
>   TRANSPORT POLICY
>   TRANSPORT WORKERS
>   TRAVELS

TRANSPORT CONTAINERS
CONTENEURS / CONTENEDORES - 10.06.00
> BT: CONTAINERS

TRANSPORT ECONOMICS
ECONOMIE DES TRANSPORTS / ECONOMIA DEL TRANSPORTE - 10.01.00
> SN: *ECONOMICS AS IT RELATES TO THE TRANSPORT SECTOR.*
> BT: ECONOMICS
> RT: TRANSPORT

TRANSPORT EQUIPMENT
MATERIEL DE TRANSPORT / EQUIPO DE TRANSPORTE - 10.04.00
> BT: EQUIPMENT
> RT: TRANSPORT

TRANSPORT INFRASTRUCTURE
INFRASTRUCTURE DE TRANSPORT / INFRAESTRUCTURA DE TRANSPORTE - 10.03.00
> SN: *USE IN CONNECTION WITH THE CONSTRUCTION OF ROADS, RAILWAYS, ETC., AS A BASIS FOR TRANSPORT AND FURTHER DEVELOPMENT.*
> NT: BRIDGES
>   CANALS
>   PIPELINES
>   PORTS
>   RAILWAYS
>   ROADS
>   STATIONS
>   TUNNELS
> RT: CIVIL ENGINEERING
>   CONSTRUCTION INDUSTRY
>   PUBLIC WORKS
>   TRANSPORT

TRANSPORT PLANNING
PLANIFICATION DES TRANSPORTS / PLANIFICACION DEL TRANSPORTE - 10.01.00
> BT: PLANNING
> RT: TRANSPORT

TRANSPORT POLICY
POLITIQUE DES TRANSPORTS / POLITICA DE TRANSPORTE - 10.01.00
> BT: ECONOMIC POLICY
> RT: TRANSPORT

TRANSPORT PRICE
- 10.09.00
> *USE:* **FREIGHT**

TRANSPORT WORKERS
EMPLOYES DES TRANSPORTS / EMPLEADOS DEL TRANSPORTE - 13.09.08
> BT: EMPLOYEES
> NT: DOCKERS
>   PILOTS
>   SEAFARERS
> RT: TRANSPORT

TRANSPORTATION
- 10.01.00
> *USE:* **TRANSPORT**

TRAVELS
VOYAGES / VIAJES - 09.04.05
> NT: STUDY TOURS
> RT: PASSENGERS
>   TOURISM
>   TRANSPORT

TRAWLERS
CHALUTIERS / BUQUES ARRASTREROS - 07.10.03
> BT: FISHING VESSELS

TREASURY BONDS
BONS DU TRESOR / BONOS DEL TESORO - 11.02.07
> BT: SECURITIES
> RT: MONEY MARKET
>   PUBLIC BORROWING

TREATIES
- 01.02.04
> *USE:* **INTERNATIONAL AGREEMENTS**

TREES
ARBRES / ARBOLES - 07.07.01
> BT: PLANTS
> NT: FOREST TREES
>   FRUIT TREES
>   HEVEAS
>   OIL PALMS

TRENDS
TENDANCES / TENDENCIAS - 18.10.00
> SN: *DISTINGUISH BETWEEN TRENDS (TENDENCIES), PROJECTIONS (FROM STATISTICAL DATA), AND FORECASTS (ESTIMATES).*
> RT: BUSINESS CYCLE

TRIBE
TRIBU / TRIBU - 14.03.01
> RT: ETHNIC GROUPS

TRINIDAD AND TOBAGO
TRINITE ET TOBAGO / TRINIDAD Y TABAGO - 01.04.03
> BT: CARIBBEAN

TRITICALE
TRITICALE / TRITICAL - 07.07.04
> BT: CEREALS
> RT: CIMMYT

TROPICAL DISEASES
MALADIES TROPICALES / ENFERMEDADES TROPICALES -
15.04.02
    BT: INFECTIOUS DISEASES
    NT: CHOLERA
      · · FILARIASIS
      LEPROSY
      MALARIA
      ONCHOCERCIASIS
      SCHISTOSOMIASIS
      TRYPANOSOMIASIS
      TYPHUS
      YELLOW FEVER
    RT: TROPICAL ZONE

TROPICAL ZONE
ZONE TROPICALE / ZONA TROPICAL - 17.02.03
    BT: CLIMATIC ZONES
    RT: CIAT
      ICRISAT
      TROPICAL DISEASES

TRUCIAL STATES
- 01.04.06
    USE: **UNITED ARAB EMIRATES**

TRUCKS
CAMIONS / CAMIONES - 10.04.00
    BT: MOTOR VEHICLES

TRUST TERRITORIES
TERRITOIRES SOUS TUTELLE / TERRITORIOS EN
FIDEICOMISO - 01.02.03
    RT: TRUSTEESHIP COUNCIL

TRUSTEESHIP COUNCIL
CONSEIL DE TUTELLE / CONSEJO DE ADMIN.
FIDUCIARIA - 01.03.02
    BT: UN
    RT: TRUST TERRITORIES

TRUSTS
TRUSTS / TRUSTS - 12.02.00
    BT: MERGERS
    RT: ANTITRUST LEGISLATION
      MONOPOLIES

TRYPANOSOMIASIS
TRYPANOSOMIASE / TRIPANOSOMIASIS - 15.04.02
    UF: SLEEPING SICKNESS
    BT: PARASITIC DISEASES
      TROPICAL DISEASES

TUBERCULOSIS
TUBERCULOSE / TUBERCULOSIS - 15.04.02
    BT: INFECTIOUS DISEASES

TUNDRA
TOUNDRA / TUNDRA - 17.03.04

TUNGSTEN
TUNGSTENE / TUNGSTENO - 08.14.02
    BT: NON-FERROUS METALS

TUNISIA
TUNISIE / TUNEZ - 01.04.02 •
    BT: ARAB COUNTRIES
      FRENCH SPEAKING AFRICA
      MEDITERRANEAN COUNTRIES
      NORTH AFRICA
    RT: TUNISIAN

TUNISIAN
TUNISIEN / TUNECINO - 14.03.02
    RT: TUNISIA

TUNNELS
TUNNELS / TUNELES - 10.03.00
    BT: TRANSPORT INFRASTRUCTURE

TURBINES
TURBINES / TURBINAS - 08.14.06

TURKEY
TURQUIE / TURQUIA - 01.04.06
    BT: MEDITERRANEAN COUNTRIES
      MIDDLE EAST
      WESTERN EUROPE
    RT: TURKISH

TURKISH
TURC / TURCO - 14.03.02
    RT: TURKEY

TURKS AND CAICOS ISLANDS
ILES TURQUES ET CAIQUES / ISLAS TURCAS Y CAICOS
- 01.04.03
    BT: CARIBBEAN
    RT: UNITED KINGDOM

TURNOVER
CHIFFRE D'AFFAIRES / MONTO DE VENTAS - 09.03.02
    RT: SALES

TYPHOID
TYPHOIDE / TIFOIDEA - 15.04.02
    BT: INFECTIOUS DISEASES

TYPHOONS
- 17.01.03
    USE: **STORMS**

TYPHUS
TYPHUS / TIFUS - 15.04.02
    BT: RICKETTSIAL DISEASES
      TROPICAL DISEASES

TYRES
PNEUS / NEUMATICOS - 08.09.00
    RT: RUBBER INDUSTRY

UGANDA
OUGANDA / UGANDA - 01.04.02
    BT: EAST AFRICA
          ENGLISH SPEAKING AFRICA
    RT: UGANDAN

UGANDAN
OUGANDAIS / UGANDES - 14.03.02
    RT: UGANDA

UKRAINIAN
UKRAINIEN / UCRANIO - 14.03.02
    RT: UKRAINIAN SSR

UKRAINIAN SSR
RSS D'UKRAINE / RSS DE UCRANIA - 01.04.05
    BT: EASTERN EUROPE
    RT: UKRAINIAN

UN
ONU / NU - 01.03.02
SN: UNITED NATIONS.
    BT: UN SYSTEM
    NT: CCAQ
        ECOSOC
        ICJ
        TRUSTEESHIP COUNCIL
        UN SECRETARIAT
        UN SECURITY COUNCIL
        UNCRD
        UNCTAD
        UNDP
        UNEP
        UNHCR
        UNICEF
        UNITAR
        UNRISD
        UNRWA

UN AND SPECIALIZED AGENCIES
- 01.03.02
    USE: UN SYSTEM

UN GENERAL ASSEMBLY
ASSEMBLEE GENERALE DE L'ONU / ASAMBLEA GENERAL
DE LAS NU - 01.03.02

UN SECRETARIAT
SECRETARIAT DE L'ONU / SECRETARIADO DE LAS NU -
01.03.02
    BT: UN

UN SECURITY COUNCIL
CONSEIL DE SECURITE DE L'ONU / CONSEJO DE
SEGURIDAD DE LAS NU - 01.03.02
    BT: UN

UN SPECIALIZED AGENCIES
INSTITUTIONS SPECIALISEES DE L'ONU / ORGANISMOS
ESPECIALIZADOS DE LAS NU - 01.03.02
    BT: UN SYSTEM

UN SPECIALIZED AGENCIES<CONT>
    NT: FAO
        IBRD
        ICAO
        IDA
        IFC
        ILO
        IMCO
        IMF
        ITU
        UNESCO
        UNIDO
        UPU
        WHO
        WIPO
        WMO

UN SYSTEM
SYSTEME DES NATIONS-UNIES / SISTEMA DE LAS NU -
01.03.02
    UF: UN AND SPECIALIZED AGENCIES
    BT: INTERGOVERNMENTAL ORGANIZATIONS
    NT: GATT
        IAEA
        UN
        UN SPECIALIZED AGENCIES

UNCRD
UNCRD / UNCRD - 01.03.02
SN: UNITED NATIONS CENTRE FOR REGIONAL
    DEVELOPMENT.
    BT: UN

UNCTAD
CNUCED / UNCTAD - 01.03.02
SN: UNITED NATIONS CONFERENCE ON TRADE AND
    DEVELOPMENT.
    BT: UN
    RT: INTERNATIONAL TRADE
        ITC

UNDERDEVELOPED AREAS
- 03.02.03
    USE: DEVELOPING AREAS

UNDERDEVELOPMENT
SOUS-DEVELOPPEMENT / SUBDESARROLLO - 03.02.03

UNDEREMPLOYMENT
SOUS-EMPLOI / SUBEMPLEO - 13.01.03
SN: USE IN CONNECTION WITH THE REDUCTION OF
    WORKING HOURS OF ALL WORKERS IN AN
    ENTERPRISE OF WHICH THE OUTPUT HAS HAD TO BE
    REDUCED TEMPORARILY, OR WITH THE ECONOMIC
    SITUATION OF A COUNTRY WHICH IS NOT
    SUFFICIENTLY DEVELOPED TO PERMIT FULL
    EMPLOYMENT OF AVAILABLE MANPOWER.
    BT: UNEMPLOYMENT

UNDERGRADUATES
ETUDIANTS NON DIPLOMES / ESTUDIANTES NO
GRADUADOS - 06.06.01
    BT: COLLEGE STUDENTS
    RT: DIPLOMAS

UNDP
PNUD / PNUD - 01.03.02
SN: UNITED NATIONS DEVELOPMENT PROGRAMME.
    BT: UN

UNEMPLOYED
CHOMEURS / DESEMPLEADOS - 13.01.02
    RT: JOB SEEKERS
        UNEMPLOYMENT

UNEMPLOYMENT
CHOMAGE / DESEMPLEO - 13.01.03
    BT: EMPLOYMENT
        SOCIAL PROBLEMS
    NT: CYCLICAL UNEMPLOYMENT
        DISGUISED UNEMPLOYMENT
        STRUCTURAL UNEMPLOYMENT
        TECHNICAL UNEMPLOYMENT
        UNDEREMPLOYMENT
        YOUTH UNEMPLOYMENT
    RT: BUSINESS CYCLE
        ECONOMIC RECESSION
        LABOUR MARKET
        UNEMPLOYED
        UNEMPLOYMENT INSURANCE

UNEMPLOYMENT BENEFITS
- 02.03.02
    USE: UNEMPLOYMENT INSURANCE

UNEMPLOYMENT INSURANCE
ASSURANCE CHOMAGE / SUBSIDIOS DE DESEMPLEO -
02.03.02
    UF: UNEMPLOYMENT BENEFITS
    BT: SOCIAL SECURITY
    RT: UNEMPLOYMENT

UNEP
PNUE / PNUMA - 01.03.02
SN: UNITED NATIONS ENVIRONMENT PROGRAMME.
    BT: UN
    RT: ENVIRONMENT

UNESCO
UNESCO / UNESCO - 01.03.02
*SN: UNITED NATIONS EDUCATIONAL, SCIENTIFIC AND
CULTURAL ORGANIZATION.*
    BT: UN SPECIALIZED AGENCIES
    NT: IBE
        IIEP
    RT: CULTURE
        EDUCATION
        SCIENCE
        UNISIST

UNFAIR COMPETITION
CONCURRENCE DELOYALE / COMPETENCIA DESLEAL -
09.01.02
    BT: COMPETITION
    RT: DUMPING
        MONOPOLIES
        TRADE BARRIERS

UNHCR
UNHCR / UNHCR - 01.03.02

UNHCR<CONT>
*SN: UNITED NATIONS OFFICE OF THE HIGH
COMMISSIONER FOR REFUGEES.*
    BT: UN
    RT: REFUGEES

UNICEF
UNICEF / UNICEF - 01.03.02
SN: UNITED NATIONS CHILDREN'S FUND.
    BT: UN
    RT: CHILDHOOD

UNIDO
ONUDI / ONUDI - 01.03.02
*SN: UNITED NATIONS INDUSTRIAL DEVELOPMENT
ORGANIZATION.*
    BT: UN SPECIALIZED AGENCIES
    RT: INDUSTRIAL DEVELOPMENT

UNION OF SOVIET SOCIALIST REPUBLICS
- 01.04.05
    USE: USSR

UNISIST
UNISIST / UNISIST - 19.01.02
    BT: INFORMATION SYSTEMS
    RT: UNESCO

UNITAR
UNITAR / UNITAR - 01.03.02
*SN: UNITED NATIONS INSTITUTE FOR TRAINING AND
RESEARCH.*
    BT: RESEARCH CENTRES
        UN

UNITED ARAB EMIRATES
EMIRATS ARABES UNIS / EMIRATOS ARABES UNIDOS -
01.04.06
    UF: TRUCIAL STATES
    BT: PERSIAN GULF STATES

UNITED KINGDOM
ROYAUME-UNI / REINO UNIDO - 01.04.05
    BT: WESTERN EUROPE
    RT: BAHAMAS
        BERMUDA
        BRITISH
        BRITISH VIRGIN ISLANDS
        BRUNEI
        CAYMAN ISLANDS
        FALKLAND ISLANDS
        GIBRALTAR
        HONG KONG
        MONTSERRAT
        PACIFIC ISLANDS UK
        ST HELENA
        TURKS AND CAICOS ISLANDS
        WEST INDIES ASSOCIATED STATES

UNITED STATES OF AMERICA
- 01.04.03
    USE: USA

UNITED STATES VIRGIN ISLANDS
ILES VIERGES AMERICAINES / ISLAS VIRGENES EU -

UNITED STATES VIRGIN ISLANDS<CONT>
01.04.03
>> BT: CARIBBEAN
>> RT: USA

UNIVERSITIES
UNIVERSITES / UNIVERSIDADES - 06.04.05
>> BT: HIGHER EDUCATION INSTITUTIONS
>> RT: GRADUATES
>> HIGHER EDUCATION
>> UNIVERSITY BUILDINGS

UNIVERSITY BUILDINGS
BATIMENTS UNIVERSITAIRES / EDIFICIOS
UNIVERSITARIOS - 06.04.07
>> BT: EDUCATIONAL BUILDINGS
>> RT: UNIVERSITIES

UNIVERSITY DEGREES
GRADES UNIVERSITAIRES / GRADOS UNIVERSITARIOS -
06.04.13
>> BT: QUALIFICATIONS

UNPUBLISHED DOCUMENTS
DOCUMENTS NON PUBLIES / DOCUMENTOS INEDITOS -
19.02.01
>> BT: DOCUMENTS

UNRISD
IRNU / UNRISD - 01.03.02
SN: UNITED NATIONS RESEARCH INSTITUTE FOR SOCIAL
>> DEVELOPMENT.
>> BT: RESEARCH CENTRES
>> UN
>> RT: SOCIAL DEVELOPMENT

UNRWA
UNRWA / UNRWA - 01.03.02
SN: UNITED NATIONS RELIEF AND WORK AGENCY FOR
>> PALESTINE REFUGEES IN THE NEAR EAST.
>> BT: UN
>> RT: REFUGEES

UNSKILLED WORKERS
OUVRIERS NON-QUALIFIES / TRABAJADORES
NO-CALIFICADOS - 13.09.03
>> BT: INDUSTRIAL WORKERS
>> RT: OCCUPATIONAL QUALIFICATION

UPPER CLASS
CLASSE SUPERIEURE / CLASE ALTA - 05.03.05
>> BT: SOCIAL CLASSES
>> RT: ELITE
>> RULING CLASS

UPPER VOLTA
HAUTE VOLTA / ALTO VOLTA - 01.04.02
>> BT: FRENCH SPEAKING AFRICA
>> WEST AFRICA

UPU
UPU / UPU - 01.03.02
SN: UNIVERSAL POSTAL UNION.
>> BT: UN SPECIALIZED AGENCIES
>> RT: POSTAL SERVICES

URANIUM
URANIUM / URANIO - 08.14.02
>> BT: ENERGY SOURCES
>> NON-FERROUS METALS
>> RT: NUCLEAR FUEL

URBAN
URBAIN / URBANO - 14.04.03
>> RT: TOWNS

URBAN AREAS
ZONES URBAINES / ZONAS URBANAS - 14.04.03
>> RT: SUBURBAN AREAS
>> TOWNS

URBAN ATTRACTION
ATTRACTION URBAINE / ATRACCION URBANA - 14.04.03
>> RT: TOWNS

URBAN COMMUNITIES
COLLECTIVITES URBAINES / COMUNIDADES URBANAS -
14.04.03
>> RT: TOWNS

URBAN CONCENTRATION
CONCENTRATION URBAINE / CONCENTRACION URBANA -
14.04.03
>> NT: CONURBATION
>> RT: TOWNS

URBAN DEVELOPMENT
DEVELOPPEMENT URBAIN / DESARROLLO URBANO -
14.04.03
>> RT: GROWTH POLES
>> TOWNS
>> URBAN PLANNING

URBAN ENVIRONMENT
MILIEU URBAIN / MEDIO URBANO - 14.04.03
>> BT: SOCIAL ENVIRONMENT
>> RT: TOWNS

URBAN PLANNING
AMENAGEMENT URBAIN / PLANIFICACION URBANA -
14.04.03
>> UF: TOWN PLANNING
>> BT: PLANNING
>> NT: ZONING
>> RT: IFHP
>> LOCAL GOVERNMENT
>> TOWNS
>> URBAN DEVELOPMENT
>> URBANISM

URBAN POPULATION
POPULATION URBAINE / POBLACION URBANA - 14.04.03
>> BT: POPULATION
>> RT: TOWNS

URBAN RENEWAL
RENOVATION URBAINE / RENOVACION URBANA -
14.04.03
>> RT: TOWNS
>> URBANISM

URBAN SOCIOLOGY
SOCIOLOGIE URBAINE / SOCIOLOGIA URBANA -
14.04.03
    BT: SOCIOLOGY
    RT: TOWNS

URBAN TRAFFIC
CIRCULATION URBAINE / TRAFICO URBANO - 10.08.00
    BT: TRAFFIC
    RT: TOWNS
        URBAN TRANSPORT

URBAN TRANSPORT
TRANSPORT URBAIN / TRANSPORTE URBANO - 10.07.00
    BT: TRANSPORT
    RT: BUSES
        TOWNS
        URBAN TRAFFIC

URBANISM
URBANISME / URBANISMO - 14.04.03
    RT: URBAN PLANNING
        URBAN RENEWAL

URBANIZATION
URBANISATION / URBANIZACION - 14.04.03
    RT: TOWNS

UREA
UREE / UREA - 08.12.04
    RT: FEED

UROGENITAL SYSTEM
SYSTEME UROGENITAL / SISTEMA UROGENITAL -
15.02.04
    BT: ANATOMY

URUGUAY
URUGUAY / URUGUAY - 01.04.03
    BT: LATIN AMERICA
        SOUTHERN CONE
    RT: URUGUAYAN

URUGUAYAN
URUGUAYEN / URUGUAYO - 14.03.02
    RT: URUGUAY

USA
ETATS-UNIS / ESTADOS UNIDOS - 01.04.03
    UF: UNITED STATES OF AMERICA
    BT: NORTH AMERICA
    NT: HAWAII
    RT: AMERICAN
        PACIFIC ISLANDS USA
        PUERTO RICO
        UNITED STATES VIRGIN ISLANDS

USSR
URSS / URSS - 01.04.05
    UF: UNION OF SOVIET SOCIALIST REPUBLICS
    BT: EASTERN EUROPE
    RT: RUSSIAN
        SOVIET

VACCINATION
VACCINATION / VACUNACION - 15.04.04
    BT: PREVENTIVE MEDICINE
    RT: IMMUNIZATION
        IMMUNOLOGY
        VACCINES

VACCINES
VACCINS / VACUNAS - 15.05.00
    BT: PHARMACEUTICALS
    RT: SERUMS
        VACCINATION

VALLEYS
VALLEES / VALLES - 17.03.04

VALUE ADDED
VALEUR AJOUTEE / VALOR AGREGADO - 12.09.00
    RT: VALUE ADDED TAX

VALUE ADDED TAX
TAXE A LA VALEUR AJOUTEE / IMPUESTO AL VALOR
AGREGADO - 11.01.02
    BT: CONSUMPTION TAX
    RT: VALUE ADDED

VALUE SYSTEMS
SYSTEMES DE VALEURS / SISTEMAS DE VALORES -
05.04.01
    RT: ETHICS
        RESPONSIBILITY
        SOCIAL CONTROL
        SOCIAL NORMS

VASECTOMY
VASECTOMIE / VASECTOMIA - 14.05.02
    RT: STERILITY

VATICAN
VATICAN / VATICANO - 01.04.05
    UF: HOLY SEE
    BT: MEDITERRANEAN COUNTRIES
        WESTERN EUROPE

VEGETABLE CROPS
CULTURES MARAICHERES / CULTIVOS DE HORTALIZAS -
07.07.02
    BT: FOOD CROPS
        HORTICULTURE
    RT: ROOT CROPS
        VEGETABLES

VEGETABLE OILS
HUILES VEGETALES / ACEITES VEGETALES - 08.06.06
    BT: OILS AND FATS
        PLANT PRODUCTS
    NT: OLIVE OIL
        PALM OIL
        PEANUT OIL
    RT: OIL CROPS
        OILSEEDS

VEGETABLES
LEGUMES / HORTALIZAS - 07.07.06

VEGETABLES<CONT>
    BT: FOOD
        PLANTS
    NT: ONIONS
    RT: LEGUMINOSAE
        VEGETABLE CROPS

VEGETATION
VEGETATION / VEGETACION - 07.07.01
SN: PLANT LIFE OF CLIMATIC, GEOLOGICAL OR OTHER ECOLOGICAL AREAS; FOR TAXONOMIC ASPECTS USE «FLORA«.
    RT: PLANTS

VENDORS
VENDEURS / VENDEDORES - 13.09.07
    UF: SALESMEN
    BT: EMPLOYEES
    RT: MARKETING

VENEREAL DISEASES
MALADIES VENERIENNES / ENFERMEDADES VENEREAS - 15.04.02
    BT: INFECTIOUS DISEASES

VENEZUELA
VENEZUELA / VENEZUELA - 01.04.03
    BT: LATIN AMERICA
        SOUTH AMERICA
    RT: VENEZUELAN

VENEZUELAN
VENEZUELIEN / VENEZOLANO - 14.03.02
    RT: VENEZUELA

VERNACULAR LANGUAGES
LANGUES VERNACULAIRES / LENGUAS VERNACULAS - 05.06.01
    BT: LANGUAGES
    RT: DIALECTS

VERTICAL INTEGRATION
INTEGRATION VERTICALE / INTEGRACION VERTICAL - 12.02.00
    BT: ECONOMIC INTEGRATION

VETERINARIANS
VETERINAIRES / MEDICOS VETERINARIOS - 13.09.10
    NT: ZOOTECHNICIANS
    RT: VETERINARY MEDICINE

VETERINARY MEDICINE
MEDECINE VETERINAIRE / MEDICINA VETERINARIA - 15.04.06
    BT: MEDICINE
    RT: ANIMAL DISEASES
        VETERINARIANS

VIETNAM
VIETNAM / VIETNAM - 01.04.04
    BT: INDOCHINA
    RT: VIETNAMESE

VIETNAMESE
VIETNAMIEN / VIETNAMITA - 14.03.02
    RT: VIETNAM

VILLAGES
VILLAGES / PUEBLOS - 14.04.02
    RT: RURAL COMMUNITIES

VIOLENCE
VIOLENCE / VIOLENCIA - 01.02.07
    RT: CONCENTRATION CAMPS
        CONFLICTS
        TERRORISM
        TORTURE

VIROLOGY
VIROLOGIE / VIROLOGIA - 15.01.01
    BT: MICROBIOLOGY
    RT: VIRUSES

VIRUSES
VIRUS / VIRUS - 15.01.02
    BT: MICROORGANISMS
    RT: VIROLOGY

VISUAL ARTS
ARTS VISUELS / ARTES VISUALES - 05.05.03
    BT: ARTS
    NT: FINE ARTS

VITAL STATISTICS
STATISTIQUES DE L'ETAT CIVIL / ESTADISTICAS VITALES - 14.01.01
SN: VITAL REGISTRATION. PROBLEMS OF COMPILING VITAL STATISTICS.
    BT: STATISTICAL DATA

VITAMIN DEFICIENCY
CARENCE VITAMINIQUE / CARENCIA VITAMINICA - 15.03.02
    BT: MALNUTRITION
    RT: DEFICIENCY DISEASES
        VITAMINS

VITAMINS
VITAMINES / VITAMINAS - 15.01.03
    BT: NUTRIENTS
    RT: FOOD
        NUTRITION
        VITAMIN DEFICIENCY

VITICULTURE
VITICULTURE / VITICULTURA - 07.07.02
    RT: FOOD CROPS
        GRAPES
        WINE

VOCATIONAL CHOICE
- 13.02.01
    USE: OCCUPATIONAL CHOICE

VOCATIONAL EDUCATION
ENSEIGNEMENT PROFESSIONNEL / ENSENANZA PROFESIONAL - 06.03.07
    UF: PROFESSIONAL EDUCATION
    BT: EDUCATIONAL SYSTEMS

VOCATIONAL EDUCATION<CONT>
- *NT:* AGRICULTURAL EDUCATION
  ART EDUCATION
  COMMERCIAL EDUCATION
  MEDICAL EDUCATION
  TECHNICAL EDUCATION
- *RT:* TECHNICAL SCHOOLS
  TRAINING CENTRES
  VOCATIONAL SCHOOLS
  VOCATIONAL TRAINING

VOCATIONAL GUIDANCE
ORIENTATION PROFESSIONNELLE / ORIENTACION
PROFESIONAL - 06.03.07
*SN: HELP GIVEN INSIDE OR OUTSIDE THE SCHOOL
SYSTEM IN CHOOSING A CAREER OR OCCUPATION.*
- *RT:* OCCUPATIONAL CHOICE

VOCATIONAL REHABILITATION
READAPTATION PROFESSIONNELLE / READAPTACION
PROFESIONAL - 13.05.00
- *BT:* REHABILITATION
- *RT:* OCCUPATIONS

VOCATIONAL SCHOOLS
ECOLES PROFESSIONNELLES / ESCUELAS PROFESIONALES
- 06.04.06
- *BT:* SCHOOLS
- *RT:* COMMERCIAL SCHOOLS
  TECHNICAL SCHOOLS
  VOCATIONAL EDUCATION

VOCATIONAL TRAINING
FORMATION PROFESSIONNELLE / FORMACION
PROFESIONAL - 06.03.07
*SN: USE TO DENOTE ACTIVITIES AIMED AT PROVIDING
THE SKILLS, KNOWLEDGE AND ATTITUDES REQUIRED
FOR EMPLOYMENT IN A PARTICULAR OCCUPATION
(OR A GROUP OF RELATED OCCUPATIONS) IN ANY
FIELD OF ECONOMIC ACTIVITY.*
- *UF:* OCCUPATIONAL TRAINING
- *BT:* TRAINING
- *NT:* AGRICULTURAL TRAINING
  APPRENTICESHIP
  BASIC TRAINING
  FURTHER TRAINING
  IN-PLANT TRAINING
  INDUSTRIAL TRAINING
  MODULAR TRAINING
  RETRAINING
  SANDWICH TRAINING
- *RT:* APPRENTICES
  OCCUPATIONS
  TRAINEES
  TRAINING ALLOWANCES
  TRAINING CENTRES
  VOCATIONAL EDUCATION

VOLCANIC ERUPTIONS
ERUPTIONS VOLCANIQUES / ERUPCIONES VOLCANICAS -
17.04.03
- *BT:* NATURAL DISASTERS
- *RT:* TIDAL WAVES
  VULCANOLOGY

VOLUME
VOLUME / VOLUMEN - 18.06.00

VOLUNTARY ORGANIZATIONS
ORGANISATIONS VOLONTAIRES / ORGANIZACIONES
VOLUNTARIAS - 05.03.07
- *RT:* ICVA
  NON-PROFIT ORGANIZATIONS

VOLUNTARY SERVICES
SERVICES BENEVOLES / SERVICIOS VOLUNTARIOS -
01.01.08

VOLUNTEERS
VOLONTAIRES / VOLUNTARIOS - 01.01.08

VOTING
VOTE / VOTACION - 04.04.02
- *RT:* ELECTIONS
  POLITICAL BEHAVIOUR
  POLITICAL PARTICIPATION

VULCANOLOGY
VULCANOLOGIE / VULCANOLOGIA - 17.04.03
- *BT:* GEOPHYSICS
- *RT:* PHYSICAL GEOGRAPHY
  VOLCANIC ERUPTIONS

WAGE DETERMINATION
FIXATION DU SALAIRE / DETERMINACION DEL SALARIO
- 13.07.00
SN: THE PROCESS OF SETTING WAGE RATES OR
ESTABLISHING WAGE STRUCTURES IN PARTICULAR
SITUATIONS.
      RT: EQUAL PAY
           WAGES

WAGE EARNERS
SALARIES / ASALARIADOS - 13.07.00
      BT: WORKERS
      RT: PROFESSIONALS
           WAGES

WAGE INCENTIVES
PRIMES DE SALAIRE / INCENTIVOS MONETARIOS -
13.07.00
SN: ADDITIONAL WAGE PAYMENTS INTENDED TO
STIMULATE PRODUCTION.
      UF: BONUSES
      BT: WAGES
      RT: LABOUR PRODUCTIVITY

WAGE PAYMENT SYSTEMS
SYSTEMES DE REMUNERATION / SISTEMAS DE
REMUNERACION - 13.07.00
SN: REFERS TO THE VARIOUS METHODS OF CALCULATING
THE AMOUNT OF REMUNERATION DUE TO AN
EMPLOYEE FOR WORK PERFORMED DURING A
SPECIFIC PERIOD OF TIME.
      NT: PAYMENT BY RESULT
      RT: WAGES

WAGE POLICY
POLITIQUE DES SALAIRES / POLITICA SALARIAL -
13.07.00
      BT: INCOMES POLICY
      RT: WAGES

WAGE RATE
TAUX DE SALAIRE / TASA DE SALARIO - 13.07.00
      RT: WAGES

WAGE SCALE
ECHELLE DES SALAIRES / ESCALA DE SUELDOS -
13.07.00
      RT: WAGES

WAGES
SALAIRES / SALARIOS - 13.07.00
SN: PAYMENT MADE FOR WORK PERFORMED.
      UF: COMPENSATION
           SALARY
      BT: INCOME
           LABOUR COSTS
      NT: FRINGE BENEFITS
           MINIMUM WAGE
           MOVING EXPENSES
           PROFIT SHARING
           SENIORITY BENEFITS
           SEVERANCE PAY
           WAGE INCENTIVES

WAGES<CONT>
      RT: PAYROLL TAX
           WAGE DETERMINATION
           WAGE EARNERS
           WAGE PAYMENT SYSTEMS
           WAGE POLICY
           WAGE RATE
           WAGE SCALE

WAR
GUERRE / GUERRA - 01.02.07
      BT: CONFLICTS
      NT: CIVIL WAR
           NUCLEAR WAR
      RT: AGGRESSION
           ARMISTICE
           GUERRILLA
           WAR CRIMES

WAR CRIMES
CRIMES DE GUERRE / CRIMENES DE GUERRA - 01.02.07
      BT: CRIMES
      RT: WAR

WARDA
ADRAO / WARDA - 01.03.03
SN: WEST AFRICA RICE DEVELOPMENT ASSOCIATION.
      BT: AFRICAN ORGANIZATIONS
           NON-GOVERNMENTAL ORGANIZATIONS
      RT: RICE
           WEST AFRICA

WAREHOUSES
ENTREPOTS / ALMACENES - 09.03.03
      RT: SILOS
           STORAGE

WARM SEASON
SAISON CHAUDE / ESTACION CALIDA - 17.02.02
      BT: SEASONS

WARNING DEVICES
DISPOSITIFS D'ALARME / SISTEMAS DE ALARMA -
16.04.01
      BT: POLLUTION CONTROL
      RT: POLLUTION INDEX
           SAFETY

WASTE DISPOSAL
ELIMINATION DES DECHETS / ELIMINACION DE
DESPERDICIOS - 16.04.02
      BT: WASTE MANAGEMENT
      NT: SEA DUMPING
      RT: BIODEGRADATION
           WASTES

WASTE MANAGEMENT
GESTION DES DECHETS / ADMINISTRACION DE
DESPERDICIOS - 16.04.02
      BT: MANAGEMENT
      NT: WASTE DISPOSAL
           WASTE RECYCLING
           WASTE TREATMENT
           WASTE UTILIZATION

WASTE MANAGEMENT<CONT>
    RT: SANITATION SERVICES
        WASTES

WASTE RECYCLING
RECYCLAGE DES DECHETS / RECICLAJE DE
DESPERDICIOS - 16.04.02
    BT: WASTE MANAGEMENT
    RT: WASTE TREATMENT
        WASTE UTILIZATION

WASTE TREATMENT
TRAITEMENT DES DECHETS / TRATAMIENTO DE
DESPERDICIOS - 16.04.02
    BT: WASTE MANAGEMENT
    RT: WASTE RECYCLING

WASTE UTILIZATION
UTILISATION DES DECHETS / UTILIZACION DE
DESPERDICIOS - 16.04.02
    BT: WASTE MANAGEMENT
    RT: WASTE RECYCLING

WASTE WATERS
EAUX RESIDUAIRES / AGUAS RESIDUALES - 16.03.04
    UF: SEWAGE
    BT: WASTES
    RT: WATER POLLUTION

WASTES
DECHETS / DESPERDICIOS - 12.08.01
    BT: POLLUTANTS
    NT: AGRICULTURAL WASTES
        DOMESTIC WASTES
        INDUSTRIAL WASTES
        RADIOACTIVE WASTES
        WASTE WATERS
    RT: RECOVERY
        WASTE DISPOSAL
        WASTE MANAGEMENT

WATCHMAKING INDUSTRY
INDUSTRIE HORLOGERE / FABRICACION DE RELOJES -
08.14.08
    BT: INSTRUMENTATION INDUSTRY

WATER
EAU / AGUA - 17.05.05
    BT: ENERGY SOURCES
    NT: DRINKING WATER
        FRESHWATER
        GROUNDWATER
        SALT WATER

WATER<CONT>
    RT: HYDROLOGY
        WATER CONSERVATION
        WATER CONSUMPTION
        WATER DISTRIBUTION
        WATER MANAGEMENT
        WATER POLLUTANTS
        WATER POLLUTION
        WATER QUALITY
        WATER REQUIREMENTS
        WATER RESOURCES
        WATER STORAGE
        WATER SUPPLY
        WATER TREATMENT
        WATER UTILIZATION

WATER BUFFALOES
BUFFLES D'EAU / BUFALOS DEL AGUA - 07.09.01
    BT: BOVIDAE

WATER CONSERVATION
CONSERVATION DE L'EAU / CONSERVACION DEL AGUA -
16.05.01
    BT: RESOURCES CONSERVATION
    RT: WATER
        WATER RESOURCES

WATER CONSUMPTION
CONSOMMATION D'EAU / CONSUMO DE AGUA - 17.05.05
    BT: CONSUMPTION
    RT: WATER

WATER DISTRIBUTION
DISTRIBUTION DE L'EAU / DISTRIBUCION DEL AGUA -
17.05.05
    BT: WATER MANAGEMENT
    RT: WATER
        WATER SUPPLY

WATER MANAGEMENT
AMENAGEMENT HYDRAULIQUE / APROVECHAMIENTO
HIDROLOGICO - 17.05.05
    BT: MANAGEMENT
    NT: WATER DISTRIBUTION
        WATER STORAGE
        WATER TREATMENT
        WATER UTILIZATION
    RT: WATER

WATER POLLUTANTS
POLLUANTS DE L'EAU / CONTAMINANTES DEL AGUA -
16.03.04
    BT: POLLUTANTS
    RT: WATER
        WATER POLLUTION

WATER POLLUTION
POLLUTION DE L'EAU / CONTAMINACION DEL AGUA -
16.03.04
    BT: POLLUTION
    NT: EUTROPHICATION
        MARINE POLLUTION
        RIVER POLLUTION

WATER POLLUTION<CONT>
>>>RT: THERMAL POLLUTION
>>>>WASTE WATERS
>>>>WATER
>>>>WATER POLLUTANTS
>>>>WATER RESOURCES

WATER QUALITY
QUALITE DE L'EAU / CALIDAD DEL AGUA - 17.05.05
>>>RT: WATER

WATER REQUIREMENTS
BESOINS EN EAU / NECESIDADES DE AGUA - 17.05.05
>>>BT: BASIC NEEDS
>>>RT: WATER

WATER RESOURCES
RESSOURCES EN EAU / RECURSOS HIDRICOS - 16.02.02
>>>BT: NATURAL RESOURCES
>>>RT: WATER
>>>>WATER CONSERVATION
>>>>WATER POLLUTION

WATER STORAGE
STOCKAGE D'EAU / ALMACENAMIENTO DE AGUA -
17.05.05
>>>BT: STORAGE
>>>>WATER MANAGEMENT
>>>RT: WATER

WATER SUPPLY
ALIMENTATION EN EAU / ABASTECIMIENTO DE AGUA -
17.05.05
>>>BT: SUPPLY
>>>RT: WATER
>>>>WATER DISTRIBUTION

WATER TREATMENT
TRAITEMENT DE L'EAU / TRATAMIENTO DEL AGUA -
17.05.05
>>>BT: ENVIRONMENTAL ENGINEERING
>>>>WATER MANAGEMENT
>>>NT: DESALINIZATION
>>>RT: WATER

WATER UTILIZATION
UTILISATION DE L'EAU / UTILIZACION DEL AGUA -
17.05.05
>>>BT: WATER MANAGEMENT
>>>RT: WATER

WATERWAYS
VOIES NAVIGABLES / VIAS NAVEGABLES - 10.03.00
>>>NT: INLAND WATERWAYS

WAX
CIRE / CERA - 08.12.08

WCC
COE / WCC - 01.03.04
SN: WORLD COUNCIL OF CHURCHES.
>>>BT: NON-GOVERNMENTAL ORGANIZATIONS

WCL
CMT / CMT - 01.03.04
SN: WORLD CONFEDERATION OF LABOUR.
>>>BT: NON-GOVERNMENTAL ORGANIZATIONS

WCL<CONT>
>>>RT: LABOUR
>>>>TRADE UNIONS

WEALTH
RICHESSE / RIQUEZA - 03.02.05
>>>RT: ABUNDANCE
>>>>INCOME DISTRIBUTION

WEAPON PROCUREMENT
ACHAT D'ARMES / COMPRA DE ARMAS - 01.02.06
>>>RT: ARMAMENT
>>>>WEAPONS

WEAPONS
ARMES / ARMAS - 01.02.06
>>>NT: BACTERIOLOGICAL WEAPONS
>>>>CONVENTIONAL WEAPONS
>>>>NUCLEAR WEAPONS
>>>RT: ARMAMENT
>>>>ARMS EMBARGO
>>>>WEAPON PROCUREMENT

WEATHER
CONDITIONS ATMOSPHERIQUES / CONDICIONES
ATMOSFERICAS - 17.01.02
>>>RT: ATMOSPHERE
>>>>PRECIPITATIONS
>>>>SEASONS
>>>>WEATHER CONTROL
>>>>WEATHER FORECASTS
>>>>WIND

WEATHER CONTROL
CONTROLE METEOROLOGIQUE / CONTROL METEOROLOGICO
- 16.04.01
>>>BT: ENVIRONMENTAL ENGINEERING
>>>RT: WEATHER
>>>>WEATHER FORECASTS

WEATHER FORECASTS
PREVISIONS METEOROLOGIQUES / PREDICCIONES
METEOROLOGICAS - 17.01.01
>>>BT: FORECASTS
>>>RT: METEOROLOGY
>>>>WEATHER
>>>>WEATHER CONTROL

WEAVING
TISSAGE / TEJIDO - 08.08.01
>>>RT: COTTAGE INDUSTRY
>>>>HANDICRAFT
>>>>TEXTILE INDUSTRY

WEED CONTROL
LUTTE CONTRE LES PLANTES ADVENTICES / CONTROL DE
MALEZAS - 07.05.04
>>>RT: CULTIVATION PRACTICES
>>>>HERBICIDES
>>>>PLANT PROTECTION

WEEKLY
HEBDOMADAIRE / SEMANARIO - 19.02.06
>>>BT: PERIODICALS

WEEKLY REST
REPOS HEBDOMADAIRE / DESCANSO SEMANAL - 13.03.03
    BT: REST PERIOD

WEIGHT
POIDS / PESO - 18.06.00
    RT: DENSITY

WELDING
SOUDAGE / SOLDADURA - 08.14.03
    BT: MACHINING

WELFARE
BIEN-ETRE / BIENESTAR - 02.02.02
    RT: WELFARE ECONOMICS

WELFARE ECONOMICS
ECONOMIE DE BIEN-ETRE / ECONOMIA DE BIENESTAR -
02.02.02
    BT: ECONOMICS
    RT: ECONOMIC THEORY
        RESOURCES ALLOCATION
        WELFARE

WELFARE INSTITUTIONS
- 02.05.01
    USE: SOCIAL SERVICES

WELLS
PUITS / POZOS - 17.05.04

WEST
OUEST / OESTE - 17.03.03

WEST AFRICA
AFRIQUE OCCIDENTALE / AFRICA OCCIDENTAL -
01.04.02
    BT: AFRICA SOUTH OF SAHARA
    NT: BENIN
        CAMEROON
        CAPE VERDE
        GAMBIA
        GHANA
        GUINEA
        GUINEA-BISSAU
        IVORY COAST
        LIBERIA
        MALI
        MAURITANIA
        NIGER
        NIGERIA
        SAHEL
        SENEGAL
        SIERRA LEONE
        ST HELENA
        TOGO
        UPPER VOLTA
    RT: WARDA

WEST INDIAN
ANTILLAIS / ANTILLANO - 14.03.02
    RT: CARIBBEAN

WEST INDIES
- 01.04.03
    USE: CARIBBEAN

WEST INDIES ASSOCIATED STATES
ETATS ASSOCIES DES ANTILLES / ESTADOS ASOC.
INDIAS OCCIDENTALES - 01.04.03
    BT: CARIBBEAN
    NT: ANTIGUA
        DOMINICA
        GRENADA
        ST KITTS-NEVIS-ANGUILLA
        ST LUCIA
        ST VINCENT
    RT: UNITED KINGDOM

WESTERN ASIA
- 01.04.06
    USE: MIDDLE EAST

WESTERN EUROPE
EUROPE OCCIDENTALE / EUROPA OCCIDENTAL -
01.04.05
    BT: EUROPE
    NT: ANDORRA
        AUSTRIA
        AZORES
        BELGIUM
        CANARY ISLANDS
        CYPRUS
        FRANCE
        GERMANY FR
        GIBRALTAR
        GREECE
        IRELAND
        ITALY
        LIECHTENSTEIN
        LUXEMBOURG
        MADEIRA
        MALTA
        MONACO
        NETHERLANDS
        PORTUGAL
        SAN MARINO
        SCANDINAVIA
        SPAIN
        SWITZERLAND
        TURKEY
        UNITED KINGDOM
        VATICAN
    RT: COUNCIL OF EUROPE
        EADI
        WEU

WEU
UEO / UEO - 01.03.03
SN: WESTERN EUROPEAN UNION.
    BT: EUROPEAN ORGANIZATIONS
        INTERGOVERNMENTAL ORGANIZATIONS
    RT: WESTERN EUROPE

WFTU
FSM / FSM - 01.03.04
SN: WORLD FEDERATION OF TRADE UNIONS.
    BT: NON-GOVERNMENTAL ORGANIZATIONS
    RT: TRADE UNIONS

WHEAT
BLE / TRIGO - 07.07.04
    BT: CEREALS
    RT: CIMMYT

WHITES
BLANCS / BLANCOS - 14.03.03

WHO
OMS / OMS - 01.03.02
SN: WORLD HEALTH ORGANIZATION.
    BT: UN SPECIALIZED AGENCIES
    RT: HEALTH

WHOLESALE MARKETING
VENTE EN GROS / VENTA AL POR MAYOR - 09.03.01
    BT: MARKETING
    RT: WHOLESALE TRADE

WHOLESALE PRICES
PRIX DE GROS / PRECIOS AL POR MAYOR - 09.02.00
    BT: PRICES
    RT: WHOLESALE TRADE

WHOLESALE TRADE
COMMERCE DE GROS / COMERCIO MAYORISTA - 09.04.04
    BT: DISTRIBUTION
        TRADE
    RT: WHOLESALE MARKETING
        WHOLESALE PRICES

WIFE
EPOUSE / ESPOSA - 14.02.05
    BT: MARRIED PERSONS

WILD ANIMALS
ANIMAUX SAUVAGES / ANIMALES SALVAJES - 07.09.01
    BT: ANIMALS
    NT: BIG GAME
        SMALL GAME
    RT: WILDLIFE PROTECTION

WILD PLANTS
PLANTES SAUVAGES / PLANTAS SILVESTRES - 07.07.01
    BT: PLANTS
    RT: WILDLIFE PROTECTION

WILDCAT STRIKES
GREVES SAUVAGES / HUELGAS ILEGALES - 13.06.00
    BT: STRIKES

WILDLIFE PROTECTION
- 16.05.01
    USE: NATURE CONSERVATION
    RT: WILD ANIMALS
        WILD PLANTS

WIND
VENT / VIENTO - 17.01.03
    BT: ENERGY SOURCES
    RT: STORMS
        WEATHER
        WIND ENERGY

WIND ENERGY
ENERGIE EOLIENNE / ENERGIA EOLICA - 08.11.01
    BT: ENERGY
    RT: WIND

WINE
VIN / VINO - 08.06.05
    BT: ALCOHOLIC BEVERAGES
    RT: VITICULTURE

WIPO
OMPI / OMPI - 01.03.02
SN: WORLD INTELLECTUAL PROPERTY ORGANIZATION.
    BT: UN SPECIALIZED AGENCIES
    RT: INTELLECTUAL PROPERTY

WIRE
FIL METALLIQUE / ALAMBRE - 08.14.04
    BT: METAL PRODUCTS

WMO
OMM / OMM - 01.03.02
SN: WORLD METEOROLOGICAL ORGANIZATION.
    BT: UN SPECIALIZED AGENCIES
    RT: ATMOSPHERIC SCIENCE
        METEOROLOGY

WOMEN
FEMMES / MUJERES - 14.02.03
    NT: FEMALE MANPOWER
    RT: EDUCATION OF WOMEN
        FEMALES
        GYNAECOLOGY
        WOMEN'S ORGANIZATIONS
        WOMEN'S RIGHTS

WOMEN WORKERS
- 13.09.02
    USE: FEMALE MANPOWER

WOMEN'S ORGANIZATIONS
ORGANISATIONS FEMININES / ORGANIZACIONES
FEMENINAS - 05.03.07
    RT: SOCIAL MOVEMENTS
        WOMEN

WOMEN'S RIGHTS
DROITS DE LA FEMME / DERECHOS DE LA MUJER -
04.02.01
    RT: WOMEN

WOOD
BOIS / MADERA - 08.07.01
    BT: FOREST PRODUCTS
    NT: CORK
        TIMBER
    RT: CELLULOSE
        WOOD CONSTRUCTION
        WOOD PROCESSING
        WOOD PRODUCTION
        WOOD PRODUCTS
        WOOD TECHNOLOGY
        WOOD WASTES
        WOODWORKING INDUSTRY

WOOD CONSTRUCTION
CONSTRUCTION EN BOIS / CONSTRUCCION EN MADERA -
08.10.01
    BT: CONSTRUCTION TECHNIQUES
    RT: WOOD

WOOD FIBRES
FIBRES DE BOIS / FIBRAS DE MADERA - 08.07.01
    BT: PLANT FIBRES
        WOOD PRODUCTS

WOOD PROCESSING
TRAITEMENT DU BOIS / PROCESAMIENTO DE LA MADERA
- 08.07.01
    RT: PULP AND PAPER INDUSTRY
        WOOD
        WOOD TECHNOLOGY
        WOODWORKING INDUSTRY

WOOD PRODUCTION
PRODUCTION DE BOIS / PRODUCCION DE MADERA -
07.08.06
    BT: FOREST PRODUCTION
    RT: WOOD

WOOD PRODUCTS
PRODUITS DE BOIS / ARTICULOS DE MADERA -
08.07.01
    BT: FOREST PRODUCTS
    NT: CARDBOARD
        PAPER
        PARTICLE BOARDS
        PLYWOOD
        PULP
        WOOD FIBRES
    RT: WOOD

WOOD TECHNOLOGY
TECHNOLOGIE DU BOIS / TECNOLOGIA DE LA MADERA -
08.07.01
    RT: WOOD
        WOOD PROCESSING
        WOODWORKING INDUSTRY

WOOD WASTES
DECHETS DE BOIS / DESPERDICIOS DE MADERA -
08.07.01
    BT: INDUSTRIAL WASTES
    RT: WOOD

WOODWORKING INDUSTRY
INDUSTRIE DU BOIS / INDUSTRIA DE LA MADERA -
08.07.01
    BT: INDUSTRIAL SECTOR
    NT: FURNITURE INDUSTRY
    RT: WOOD
        WOOD PROCESSING
        WOOD TECHNOLOGY

WOOL
LAINE / LANA - 07.09.05
    BT: ANIMAL FIBRES

WORK AT HOME
TRAVAIL A DOMICILE / TRABAJO A DOMICILIO -
13.03.02
SN: REMUNERATED WORK PERFORMED AT HOME.

WORK ENVIRONMENT
MILIEU DE TRAVAIL / AMBIENTE DE TRABAJO -

WORK ENVIRONMENT\<CONT\>
13.03.01
    RT: WORKERS ADAPTATION

WORK ORGANIZATION
ORGANISATION DU TRAVAIL / ORGANIZACION DEL
TRABAJO - 13.03.01
    RT: LABOUR
        PERSONNEL MANAGEMENT
        WORK RULES

WORK PERMIT
PERMIS DE TRAVAIL / PERMISO DE TRABAJO -
13.02.01
    RT: LABOUR CONTRACT

WORK PROGRAMME
PROGRAMME DE TRAVAIL / PROGRAMA DE TRABAJO -
19.02.05

WORK RULES
REGLEMENTS D'ENTREPRISE / REGLAMENTOS DE EMPRESA
- 13.03.01
*SN: RULES WHICH STIPULATE THE CONDITIONS WHICH
THE EMPLOYER AND EMPLOYEES MUST OBSERVE IN
CARRYING OUT THE WORK.*
    RT: BUSINESS ORGANIZATION
        WORK ORGANIZATION

WORK STUDY
ETUDE DU TRAVAIL / ESTUDIO DEL TRABAJO -
13.03.01
*SN: DETAILED EXAMINATION OF THE MANNER IN WHICH
A PARTICULAR JOB IS PERFORMED, WITH A VIEW
TO RATIONALIZING THE PERFORMANCE AND SO
INCREASING PRODUCTIVITY.*
    UF: TIME STUDY
    RT: ERGONOMICS
        LABOUR STANDARDS
        STANDARD PERFORMANCE

WORKERS
TRAVAILLEURS / TRABAJADORES - 13.09.02
*SN: USE, WHERE APPLICABLE, MORE SPECIFIC
DESCRIPTORS.*
    NT: AUXILIARY WORKERS
        CASUAL WORKERS
        DOMESTIC WORKERS
        EMPLOYEES
        FEMALE MANPOWER
        FOREIGN WORKERS
        HANDICAPPED WORKERS
        INDUSTRIAL WORKERS
        MANUAL WORKERS
        MIGRANT WORKERS
        OLDER WORKERS
        RURAL WORKERS
        SELF-EMPLOYED
        WAGE EARNERS
        YOUNG WORKERS

WORKERS<CONT>
- RT: TECHNICAL PERSONNEL
  WORKERS ADAPTATION
  WORKERS EDUCATION
  WORKERS PARTICIPATION
  WORKERS REPRESENTATION
  WORKING CLASS

WORKERS ADAPTATION
ADAPTATION DES TRAVAILLEURS / ADAPTACION DE LOS TRABAJADORES - 13.02.02
- BT: SOCIAL ADAPTATION
- RT: EMPLOYEES ATTITUDES
  JOB SATISFACTION
  WORK ENVIRONMENT
  WORKERS

WORKERS EDUCATION
EDUCATION SYNDICALE / EDUCACION SINDICAL - 06.03.05
SN: *THE EDUCATION OF WORKER MEMBERS OF TRADE UNIONS IN MATTERS WHICH WILL AID THEM TO MAINTAIN FAIR BARGAINING RELATIONSHIPS WITH EMPLOYERS. DO NOT CONFUSE WITH 'ADULT EDUCATION'.*
- RT: TRADE UNIONS
  WORKERS

WORKERS PARTICIPATION
PARTICIPATION DES TRAVAILLEURS / PARTICIPACION DE LOS TRABAJADORES - 13.06.00
- UF: JOINT MANAGEMENT
- RT: TRADE UNIONS
  WORKERS
  WORKERS SELF-MANAGEMENT

WORKERS REPRESENTATION
REPRESENTATION DES TRAVAILLEURS / REPRESENTACION OBRERA - 13.06.00
SN: *USE IN CONNECTION WITH THE FUNCTION OF REPRESENTING THE INTERESTS OF, OR SPEAKING FOR, THE WORKERS OF A GIVEN ENTERPRISE.*
- RT: SHOP STEWARDS
  TRADE UNIONS
  WORKERS

WORKERS SELF-MANAGEMENT
AUTOGESTION OUVRIERE / AUTOGESTION OBRERA - 13.06.00
- BT: SELF-MANAGEMENT
- RT: PRODUCTION COOPERATIVES
  WORKERS PARTICIPATION

WORKERS STOCK OWNERSHIP
ACTIONNARIAT OUVRIER / PARTICIPACION OBRERA EN ACCIONES - 13.07.00
- RT: PROFIT SHARING
  SHARES

WORKING CAPITAL
FONDS DE ROULEMENT / CAPITAL DE GIRO - 12.09.00
- BT: CAPITAL
- RT: INDUSTRIAL CAPITAL

WORKING CLASS
CLASSE OUVRIERE / CLASE OBRERA - 05.03.05
- BT: SOCIAL CLASSES
- RT: PROLETARIAT
  WORKERS

WORKING CONDITIONS
CONDITIONS DE TRAVAIL / CONDICIONES DE TRABAJO - 13.03.01
SN: *THE PHYSICAL, SOCIAL AND MANAGERIAL FACTORS AFFECTING A WORKER'S JOB ENVIRONMENT.*
- BT: LIVING CONDITIONS
- RT: ASSEMBLY-LINE WORK
  COLLECTIVE AGREEMENTS
  CONTRACT LABOUR
  HUMANIZATION OF WORK
  LABOUR
  LABOUR STANDARDS
  MENTAL STRESS

WORKING LIFE
VIE ACTIVE / VIDA ACTIVA - 13.03.03
- RT: TRANSITION FROM SCHOOL TO WORK

WORKS OF ART
OEUVRES D'ART / OBRAS DE ARTE - 05.05.02
- RT: ART
  CULTURAL HERITAGE

WORKSHOPS
ATELIERS / TALLERES - 08.03.00
- NT: REPAIR SHOPS
- RT: INDUSTRIAL PLANTS

WORLD BANK
- 01.03.02
- USE: IBRD

WORLD EMPLOYMENT PROGRAMME
PROGRAMME MONDIAL DE L'EMPLOI / PROGRAMA MUNDIAL DEL EMPLEO - 01.03.02
SN: *I.L.O. PROGRAMME FOR EMPLOYMENT PLANNING AND PROMOTION.*
- BT: ILO
- RT: EMPLOYMENT POLICY

WORLD FOOD PROGRAMME
PROGRAMME ALIMENTAIRE MONDIAL / PROGRAMA MUNDIAL DE ALIMENTOS - 01.03.02
- BT: FAO
- RT: FOOD AID
  FOOD PLANNING
  FOOD POLICY

WORLD TRADE
- 09.05.01
- USE: INTERNATIONAL TRADE

WORSHIP
CULTE / CULTO - 05.04.02
- RT: RELIGION
  RELIGIOUS PRACTICE

WOUNDED
BLESSES / HERIDOS - 15.04.04

WOUNDED<CONT>
    RT: PATIENTS
        PHYSICALLY HANDICAPPED
        WOUNDS AND INJURIES

WOUNDS AND INJURIES
BLESSURES ET LESIONS / HERIDAS Y LESIONES -
15.04.02
    BT: DISEASES
    NT: BURNS
    RT: WOUNDED

WRITERS
ECRIVAINS / ESCRITORES - 13.09.09
    RT: LITERATURE

WRITING
ECRITURE / ESCRITURA - 06.03.04
    RT: LITERACY

YEARBOOK
ANNUAIRE / ANUARIO - 19.02.06
    BT: PERIODICALS
        REFERENCE MATERIALS

YEAST
LEVURE / LEVADURA - 15.01.03

YELLOW FEVER
FIEVRE JAUNE / FIEBRE AMARILLA - 15.04.02
    BT: INFECTIOUS DISEASES
        TROPICAL DISEASES

YEMEN
YEMEN / YEMEN - 01.04.06
    UF: YEMEN ARAB REPUBLIC
    BT: ARAB COUNTRIES
        MIDDLE EAST
    RT: YEMENI

YEMEN ARAB REPUBLIC
- 01.04.06
    USE: YEMEN

YEMEN PDR
YEMEN RDP / YEMEN RDP - 01.04.06
    UF: SOUTH YEMEN
    BT: ARAB COUNTRIES
        MIDDLE EAST

YEMENI
YEMENITE / YEMENITA - 14.03.02
    RT: YEMEN

YOUNG WORKERS
JEUNES TRAVAILLEURS / TRABAJADORES JOVENES -
13.09.02
    BT: WORKERS
    RT: YOUTH
        YOUTH UNEMPLOYMENT

YOUTH
JEUNESSE / JUVENTUD - 14.02.02
    UF: ADOLESCENCE
    BT: AGE GROUPS
    NT: RURAL YOUTH
    RT: JUVENILE DELINQUENCY
        YOUNG WORKERS
        YOUTH CENTRES
        YOUTH ORGANIZATIONS
        YOUTH UNEMPLOYMENT

YOUTH CENTRES
CENTRES DE JEUNESSE / CENTROS JUVENILES -
05.03.07
    RT: YOUTH

YOUTH ORGANIZATIONS
ORGANISATIONS DE JEUNESSE / ORGANIZACIONES
JUVENILES - 05.03.07
    NT: STUDENT MOVEMENTS
    RT: YOUTH

YOUTH UNEMPLOYMENT
CHOMAGE DES JEUNES / DESEMPLEO JUVENIL -

YOUTH UNEMPLOYMENT<CONT>
13.01.03
    BT: UNEMPLOYMENT
    RT: YOUNG WORKERS
        YOUTH

YUGOSLAV
YOUGOSLAVE / YUGOSLAVO - 14.03.02
    RT: YUGOSLAVIA

YUGOSLAVIA
YOUGOSLAVIE / YUGOSLAVIA - 01.04.05
    BT: EASTERN EUROPE
        MEDITERRANEAN COUNTRIES
    RT: YUGOSLAV

ZAIRE
ZAIRE / ZAIRE - 01.04.02
    UF: CONGO (KINSHASA)
    BT: CENTRAL AFRICA
        FRENCH SPEAKING AFRICA
    RT: ZAIRIAN

ZAIRIAN
ZAIROIS / ZAIRENSE - 14.03.02
    RT: ZAIRE

ZAMBIA
ZAMBIE / ZAMBIA - 01.04.02
    BT: EAST AFRICA
        ENGLISH SPEAKING AFRICA
        SOUTHERN AFRICA
    RT: ZAMBIAN

ZAMBIAN
ZAMBIEN / ZAMBIANO - 14.03.02
    RT: ZAMBIA

ZERO GROWTH ECONOMY
CROISSANCE ZERO DE L'ECONOMIE / CRECIMIENTO ECONOMICO NULO - 03.02.03
SN: PLANNED ZERO GROWTH IN ORDER TO CONSERVE RESOURCES AND TO PRESERVE QUALITY OF LIFE.
    BT: GROWTH RATE
    RT: ECONOMIC GROWTH

ZINC
ZINC / ZINC - 08.14.02
    BT: NON-FERROUS METALS
        TOXIC METALS

ZONING
ZONAGE / ZONIFICACION - 14.04.03
    BT: URBAN PLANNING
    RT: LAND USE

ZOOLOGICAL GARDENS
JARDINS ZOOLOGIQUES / JARDINES ZOOLOGICOS - 16.05.02
    BT: PROTECTED RESOURCES
    RT: ANIMALS
        PROTECTED SPECIES
        ZOOLOGY

ZOOLOGY
ZOOLOGIE / ZOOLOGIA - 07.06.00
    BT: NATURAL SCIENCES
    NT: ENTOMOLOGY
    RT: ANIMALS
        ZOOLOGICAL GARDENS

ZOOTECHNICIANS
ZOOTECHNICIENS / ZOOTECNISTAS - 13.09.10
    BT: VETERINARIANS
    RT: ANIMAL HUSBANDRY

III. DESCRIPTOR GROUP DISPLAY

Subject category fields

01. INTERNATIONAL COOPERATION. INTERNATIONAL RELATIONS.

01.01 INTERNATIONAL COOPERATION.
01.02 INTERNATIONAL RELATIONS.
01.03 INTERNATIONAL ORGANIZATIONS.
01.04 COUNTRIES AND REGIONS.

02. ECONOMIC POLICY. SOCIAL POLICY. PLANNING.

02.01 ECONOMIC POLICY. PLANNING.
02.02 SOCIAL POLICY.
02.03 SOCIAL SECURITY.
02.04 SOCIAL PROBLEMS.
02.05 SOCIAL SERVICES.

03. ECONOMIC CONDITIONS. ECONOMIC RESEARCH. ECONOMIC SYSTEMS.

03.01 ECONOMIC RESEARCH. ECONOMICS.
03.02 ECONOMIC CONDITIONS.
03.03 ECONOMIC SYSTEMS.

04. INSTITUTIONAL FRAMEWORK.

04.01 LAW. LEGISLATION.
04.02 HUMAN RIGHTS.
04.03 GOVERNMENT. PUBLIC ADMINISTRATION.
04.04 POLITICS.

05. CULTURE. SOCIETY.

05.01 SOCIAL SCIENCES.
05.02 CULTURE.
05.03 SOCIETY.
05.04 ETHICS. RELIGION.
05.05 ART.
05.06 LANGUAGES.
05.07 COMMUNICATION.

06. EDUCATION. TRAINING.

06.01 SCIENCES OF EDUCATION.
06.02 EDUCATIONAL DEVELOPMENT. EDUCATIONAL POLICY.
06.03 EDUCATIONAL SYSTEMS.
06.04 EDUCATIONAL INSTITUTIONS.
06.05 CURRICULUM. TEACHING. LEARNING.
06.06 STUDENTS. TEACHING PERSONNEL.

07. AGRICULTURE.

07.01 AGRICULTURAL ECONOMICS.
07.02 LAND ECONOMICS.
07.03 AGRICULTURAL ENTERPRISES.
07.04 AGRICULTURAL EQUIPMENT.
07.05 AGRICULTURAL PRODUCTION.
07.06 AGRICULTURAL RESEARCH.
07.07 PLANT PRODUCTION.
07.08 FORESTS.
07.09 ANIMAL PRODUCTION.
07.10 FISHERY.

08. INDUSTRY.

08.01 INDUSTRIAL ECONOMICS.
08.02 INDUSTRIAL ENTERPRISES.
08.03 INDUSTRIAL ENGINEERING. INDUSTRIAL EQUIPMENT.
08.04 INDUSTRIAL PRODUCTION. INDUSTRIAL PRODUCTS.
08.05 INDUSTRIAL RESEARCH.
08.06 FOOD INDUSTRY.
08.07 WOODWORKING INDUSTRY. PULP AND PAPER INDUSTRY.
08.08 TEXTILE INDUSTRY. LEATHER INDUSTRY.
08.09 RUBBER INDUSTRY.
08.10 CONSTRUCTION INDUSTRY. CERAMICS. GLASS.
08.11 ENERGY.
08.12 CHEMICAL INDUSTRY.
08.13 MINING.
08.14 METALWORKING INDUSTRY.
08.15 ELECTRONICS. ELECTRICAL EQUIPMENT.
08.16 COMMUNICATION INDUSTRY.

09. TRADE.

09.01 DEMAND. MARKET. CONSUMPTION.
09.02 PRICES.
09.03 MARKETING.
09.04 DOMESTIC TRADE.
09.05 INTERNATIONAL TRADE.

10. TRANSPORT.

10.01 TRANSPORT ECONOMICS.
10.02 GOODS. PASSENGERS.
10.03 TRANSPORT INFRASTRUCTURE.
10.04 MEANS OF TRANSPORT.
10.05 MODES OF TRANSPORTATION.
10.06 LOADING. PACKAGING.
10.07 INTERNATIONAL TRANSPORT. URBAN TRANSPORT.
10.08 TRAFFIC.
10.09 FREIGHT.

11. PUBLIC FINANCE. BANKING. INTERNATIONAL MONETARY RELATIONS.

11.01 PUBLIC FINANCE. TAXATION.
11.02 CURRENCIES. FINANCING.
11.03 INTERNATIONAL MONETARY SYSTEM.

12. MANAGEMENT. PRODUCTIVITY.

12.01 ENTERPRISES.
12.02 ECONOMIC CONCENTRATION.
12.03 ENTREPRENEURS.
12.04 MANAGEMENT.
12.05 EQUIPMENT.
12.06 TECHNOLOGY.
12.07 PRODUCTION. PRODUCTIVITY.
12.08 PRODUCTS. PRODUCT DEVELOPMENT.
12.09 COST ACCOUNTING. PROFITS.

13. LABOUR.

13.01 HUMAN RESOURCES.
13.02 EMPLOYMENT SERVICES. OCCUPATIONAL QUALIFICATION. PERSONNEL MANAGEMENT.
13.03 WORKING CONDITIONS.
13.04 OCCUPATIONAL SAFETY.
13.05 DISMISSAL. LABOUR MOBILITY.
13.06 LABOUR RELATIONS.
13.07 WAGES. WAGE INCENTIVES.
13.08 LEISURE.
13.09 OCCUPATIONS.

14. DEMOGRAPHY. POPULATION.

14.01 POPULATION DYNAMICS.
14.02 AGE GROUPS.
14.03 ETHNIC GROUPS.
14.04 HABITAT. RURAL. URBAN.
14.05 FERTILITY. FAMILY PLANNING.
14.06 MORTALITY.
14.07 MIGRATIONS.

15. BIOLOGY. FOOD. HEALTH.

15.01 BIOLOGY. PARASITOLOGY. BIOCHEMISTRY.
15.02 ANATOMY. GENETICS. PHYSIOLOGY.
15.03 FOOD. NUTRITION.
15.04 MEDICINE. DISEASES.
15.05 PHARMACOLOGY. TOXICOLOGY.

16. ENVIRONMENT. NATURAL RESOURCES.

16.01 ECOLOGY.
16.02 NATURAL RESOURCES.
16.03 DISASTERS. POLLUTION.
16.04 POLLUTION CONTROL. ENVIRONMENTAL ENGINEERING.
16.05 RESOURCES CONSERVATION.

17. EARTH SCIENCES. SPACE SCIENCES.

17.01 METEOROLOGY.
17.02 CLIMATE.
17.03 GEOGRAPHY.
17.04 GEOPHYSICS. GEOLOGY. SOIL SCIENCES.
17.05 HYDROLOGY. WATER.
17.06 OCEANOGRAPHY.
17.07 SPACE SCIENCES.

18. SCIENCE. RESEARCH. METHODOLOGY.

18.01 RESEARCH. SCIENCE.
18.02 ORGANIZATION OF RESEARCH.
18.03 RESEARCH METHODS. THEORY.
18.04 DATA COLLECTING.
18.05 EXPERIMENTS.
18.06 MEASUREMENT.
18.07 MAPPING.
18.08 MATHEMATICS. STATISTICAL ANALYSIS.
18.09 COMPARISON. EVALUATION.
18.10 FORECASTS. TIME FACTOR.

19. INFORMATION. DOCUMENTATION.

19.01   INFORMATION.
19.02   DOCUMENTS.
19.03   TERMINOLOGY.
19.04   CONFERENCE.

Descriptor groups

01.

INTERNATIONAL COOPERATION. INTERNATIONAL RELATIONS.

01.01

INTERNATIONAL COOPERATION.

01.01.01

DEVELOPMENT AID
FIRST DEVELOPMENT DECADE
FOREIGN AID
HORIZONTAL COOPERATION
INTERNATIONAL ASSISTANCE
  USE: INTERNATIONAL COOPERATION
INTERNATIONAL COOPERATION
REGIONAL COOPERATION
SECOND DEVELOPMENT DECADE

01.01.02

AID BY RELIGIOUS BODIES
  USE: PRIVATE AID
BILATERAL AID
MULTILATERAL AID
PRIVATE AID

01.01.03

AID IN KIND
CAPITAL AID
  USE: FINANCIAL AID
ECONOMIC AID
FINANCIAL AID
FOOD AID
GRANTS IN KIND
  USE: AID IN KIND
HEALTH AID
TECHNICAL ASSISTANCE
TRAINING ASSISTANCE

01.01.04

AID COORDINATION
AID EVALUATION
AID FINANCING
AID PROGRAMMES
GRANTS
TERMS OF AID
TIED AID
  USE: TERMS OF AID

01.01.05

COUNTERPART
COUNTERPART FUNDS
COUNTERPART PERSONNEL

01.01.06

DEVELOPMENT PROJECTS
FEASIBILITY STUDIES
JOINT PROJECTS
MULTIPURPOSE PROJECTS
PILOT PROJECTS

01.01.06<CONT>

PLANS OF OPERATION
PROJECT APPRAISAL
PROJECT DESIGN
PROJECT EVALUATION
PROJECT IMPLEMENTATION
PROJECT MANAGEMENT
PROJECT PLANNING
  USE: PROJECT DESIGN
PROJECT REQUEST
PROJECT SELECTION

01.01.07

AID INSTITUTIONS
CONSULTANTS
DEVELOPMENT CENTRES
DEVELOPMENT PERSONNEL
EXPERTS
REGIONAL AGENCIES

01.01.08

PEACE CORPS
VOLUNTARY SERVICES
VOLUNTEERS

01.02

INTERNATIONAL RELATIONS.

01.02.01

ALLIANCES
BILATERAL RELATIONS
BORDER INTEGRATION
COMMON MARKET
COMPLEMENTARITY AGREEMENTS
ECONOMIC COOPERATION
ECONOMIC INTEGRATION
ECONOMIC RELATIONS
FOREIGN RELATIONS
IMPERIALISM
INDUSTRIAL INTEGRATION
INTERNATIONAL AFFAIRS
  USE: INTERNATIONAL RELATIONS
INTERNATIONAL POLITICS
INTERNATIONAL RELATIONS
ISOLATIONISM
MULTILATERAL RELATIONS
NEUTRALISM
NEUTRALITY
NEW INTERNATIONAL ECONOMIC ORDER
PROLETARIAN INTERNATIONALISM
REGIONAL INTEGRATION

01.02.02

BORDERS
  USE: BOUNDARIES

01.02.02<CONT>

    BOUNDARIES

    FRONTIERS
      USE: BOUNDARIES

01.02.03

    COLONIAL COUNTRIES

    DECOLONIZATION

    DEPENDENCE

    INDEPENDENCE

    OVERSEAS TERRITORIES

    SELF-DETERMINATION

    TRUST TERRITORIES

01.02.04

    CONVENTIONS

    INTERNATIONAL AGREEMENTS

    INTERNATIONAL CONTROL

    INTERNATIONAL LAW

    INTERNATIONAL NEGOTIATION

    LAW OF THE SEA

    TREATIES
      USE: INTERNATIONAL AGREEMENTS

01.02.05

    DIPLOMACY

    FOREIGN INTERVENTION

    FOREIGN POLICY

    FOREIGN SERVICE

01.02.06

    ARMAMENT

    ARMS EMBARGO

    ARMS LIMITATION
      USE: DISARMAMENT

    ARMS RACE
      USE: ARMAMENT

    ARMY

    ATOMIC WEAPONS
      USE: NUCLEAR WEAPONS

    BACTERIOLOGICAL WEAPONS

    CONVENTIONAL WEAPONS

    DEFENCE

    DEFENCE POLICY

    DISARMAMENT

    MILITARY

    MILITARY AID

    MILITARY BASES

    MILITARY EXPENDITURES

    MILITARY SERVICE

    NUCLEAR WEAPONS

    WEAPON PROCUREMENT

    WEAPONS

01.02.07

    AGGRESSION

01.02.07<CONT>

    AIR PIRACY

    ARMISTICE

    BLOCKADE

    CIVIL WAR

    DETENTE

    GUERRILLA

    HOSTAGES

    NUCLEAR WAR

    PEACE001

    PEACE KEEPING

    PEACE RESEARCH

    PEACEFUL COEXISTENCE

    TERRORISM

    VIOLENCE

    WAR

    WAR CRIMES

01.03

INTERNATIONAL ORGANIZATIONS.

01.03.01

    INTERGOVERNMENTAL ORGANIZATIONS

    INTERNATIONAL ORGANIZATIONS

    MEMBER STATES

    NON-GOVERNMENTAL ORGANIZATIONS

    REGIONAL ORGANIZATIONS

01.03.02

    ACAST

    CCAQ

    CDP

    CLADES

    CSTD

    ECA

    ECAFE
      USE: ESCAP

    ECE

    ECLA

    ECOSOC

    ECWA

    ESCAP

    FAO

    GATT

    IAEA

    IBE

    IBRD

    ICAO

    ICJ

    IDA

    IFC

NATO
NORDIC COUNCIL
OAPEC
OAS
OAU
OCAM
OCAS
OECD
OECD COUNTRIES
OECD DAC
OECD DC
OECD IEA
OECD NEA
OPEC
PAHO
SEATO
SIECA
SPC
WARDA
WEU

01.03.04

CAB
CEMLA
CIAT
CIMMYT
FID
ICFTU
ICRISAT
ICSSD
ICSU
ICVA
IDRC
IEA
IFAP
IFHP
IFIP
IFLA
INTECOL
IPPF
IPSA
IRRI
ISA
ISO
ISSA
ISSC

IUAES
IUSSP
SID
WCC
WCL
WFTU

01.04

COUNTRIES AND REGIONS.

01.04.01

ANTARCTICA
NORTHERN HEMISPHERE
SOUTHERN HEMISPHERE

01.04.02

AFRICA
AFRICA SOUTH OF SAHARA
ALGERIA
ANGOLA
BENIN
BOTSWANA
BURUNDI
CAMEROON
CAPE VERDE
CENTRAL AFRICA
CENTRAL AFRICAN EMPIRE
CHAD
COMOROS
CONGO
DJIBOUTI
EAST AFRICA
EGYPT
ENGLISH SPEAKING AFRICA
EQUATORIAL GUINEA
ETHIOPIA
FRENCH SPEAKING AFRICA
GABON
GAMBIA
GHANA
GUINEA
GUINEA-BISSAU
IVORY COAST
KENYA
LESOTHO
LIBERIA
LIBYA
LIBYAN ARAB JAMAHIRIYA
    USE: LIBYA
MADAGASCAR

01.04.02<CONT>

MALAWI
MALI
MAURITANIA
MAURITIUS
MOROCCO
MOZAMBIQUE
NAMIBIA
NIGER
NIGERIA
NORTH AFRICA
REUNION ISLAND
RHODESIA
RWANDA
SAHARA
SAHEL
SAO TOME AND PRINCIPE
SENEGAL
SEYCHELLES
SIERRA LEONE
SOMALIA
SOUTH AFRICA
SOUTH WEST AFRICA
    USE: NAMIBIA
SOUTHERN AFRICA
ST HELENA
SUDAN
SWAZILAND
TANZANIA
TOGO
TUNISIA
UGANDA
UPPER VOLTA
WEST AFRICA
ZAIRE
ZAMBIA

01.04.03

AMERICA
ANDEAN REGION
ANTIGUA
ANTILLES
    USE: CARIBBEAN
ARGENTINA
BAHAMAS
BARBADOS
BELIZE
BERMUDA

01.04.03<CONT>

BOLIVIA
BRAZIL
BRITISH HONDURAS
    USE: BELIZE
BRITISH VIRGIN ISLANDS
CANADA
CARIBBEAN
CAYMAN ISLANDS
CENTRAL AMERICA
CHILE
COLOMBIA
COSTA RICA
CUBA
DOMINICA
DOMINICAN REPUBLIC
ECUADOR
EL SALVADOR
FALKLAND ISLANDS
FRENCH GUIANA
GRENADA
GUADELOUPE
GUATEMALA
GUYANA
HAITI
HONDURAS
JAMAICA
LATIN AMERICA
MARTINIQUE
MEXICO
MONTSERRAT
NETHERLANDS ANTILLES
NICARAGUA
NORTH AMERICA
PANAMA
PANAMA CANAL ZONE
PARAGUAY
PERU
PUERTO RICO
SOUTH AMERICA
SOUTHERN CONE
ST KITTS-NEVIS-ANGUILLA
ST LUCIA
ST PIERRE AND MIQUELON
ST VINCENT
SURINAM

01.04.03<CONT>

TRINIDAD AND TOBAGO

TURKS AND CAICOS ISLANDS

UNITED STATES OF AMERICA
    USE: USA

UNITED STATES VIRGIN ISLANDS

URUGUAY

USA

VENEZUELA

WEST INDIES
    USE: CARIBBEAN

WEST INDIES ASSOCIATED STATES

01.04.04

ASIA

BANGLADESH

BHUTAN

BRUNEI

BURMA

CAMBODIA
    USE: KAMPUCHEA

CEYLON
    USE: SRI LANKA

CHINA

FAR EAST

HONG KONG

INDIA

INDOCHINA

INDONESIA

JAPAN

KAMPUCHEA

KOREA

KOREA DPR

KOREA NORTH
    USE: KOREA DPR

KOREA R

KOREA SOUTH
    USE: KOREA R

LAO PDR

MACAO

MALAYSIA

MALDIVES

MONGOLIA PR

NEPALLLL

PAKISTAN

PHILIPPINES

PORTUGUESE TIMOR

SIKKIM

SINGAPORE

SOUTH   ASIA

01.04.04<CONT>

SOUTH EAST ASIA

SRI LANKA

TAIWAN

THAILAND

01.04.05

ALBANIA

ANDORRA

AUSTRIA

AZORES

BELGIUM

BULGARIA

BYELORUSSIAN SSR

CANARY ISLANDS

CZECHOSLOVAKIA

DENMARK

EASTERN EUROPE

EUROPE

FAROE ISLANDS

FINLAND

FRANCE

GERMAN DR

GERMANY

GERMANY FR

GIBRALTAR

GREECE

GREENLAND

HOLY SEE
    USE: VATICAN

HUNGARY

ICELAND

IRELAND

ITALY

LIECHTENSTEIN

LUXEMBOURG

MADEIRA

MALTA

MEDITERRANEAN COUNTRIES

MONACO

NETHERLANDS

NORWAY

POLAND

PORTUGAL

ROMANIA

SAN MARINO

SCANDINAVIA

01.04.05<CONT>

SPAIN

SWEDEN

SWITZERLAND

UKRAINIAN SSR

UNION OF SOVIET SOCIALIST REPUBLICS
  USE: USSR

UNITED KINGDOM

USSR

VATICAN

WESTERN EUROPE

YUGOSLAVIA

01.04.06

AFGHANISTAN

ARAB COUNTRIES

BAHRAIN

CYPRUS

IRAN

IRAQ

ISRAEL

JORDAN

KUWAIT

LEBANON

MIDDLE EAST

NEAR EAST
  USE: MIDDLE EAST

OMAN

PERSIAN GULF STATES

QATAR

SAUDI ARABIA

SOUTH YEMEN
  USE: YEMEN PDR

SYRIA

TRUCIAL STATES
  USE: UNITED ARAB EMIRATES

TURKEY

UNITED ARAB EMIRATES

WESTERN ASIA
  USE: MIDDLE EAST

YEMEN

YEMEN ARAB REPUBLIC
  USE: YEMEN

YEMEN PDR

01.04.07

AUSTRALIA

FIJI

FRENCH POLYNESIA

HAWAII

MELANESIA
  USE: OCEANIA

01.04.07<CONT>

MICRONESIA
  USE: OCEANIA

NAURU

NEW CALEDONIA

NEW HEBRIDES

NEW ZEALAND

OCEANIA

PACIFIC ISLANDS
  USE: OCEANIA

PACIFIC ISLANDS AUS

PACIFIC ISLANDS FR

PACIFIC ISLANDS NZ

PACIFIC ISLANDS UK

PACIFIC ISLANDS USA

PACIFIC REGION

PAPUA NEW GUINEA

POLYNESIA
  USE: OCEANIA

SAMOA

TONGA

02.

ECONOMIC POLICY. SOCIAL POLICY. PLANNING.

02.01

ECONOMIC POLICY. PLANNING.

02.01.01

BASIC NEEDS
DEVELOPMENT POLICY
DEVELOPMENT POTENTIAL
DEVELOPMENT RESEARCH
DEVELOPMENT STRATEGY
DEVELOPMENT STYLES
DEVELOPMENT THEORY
ECONOMIC AND SOCIAL DEVELOPMENT
INTEGRATED DEVELOPMENT
SCENARIOS
SELF-RELIANCE

02.01.02

DEVELOPMENT PLANNING
DEVELOPMENT PLANS
DIRECTIVE PLANNING
ECONOMIC PLANNING
GROWTH POLES
LOCATION FACTORS
NATIONAL PLANNING
NATIONAL PLANS
NORMATIVE PLANNING
   USE: DIRECTIVE PLANNING
PLAN IMPLEMENTATION
PLANNERS
PLANNING
PLANNING METHODS
PLANNING SYSTEMS
REGIONAL PLANNING
REGIONAL PLANS
REGIONAL POLICY
REGIONALIZATION
RESOURCES ALLOCATION
SECTORAL PLANNING
STRATEGIC PLANNING

02.01.03

AUSTERITY POLICY
ECONOMIC DISCRIMINATION
ECONOMIC POLICY
ECONOMIC REFORM
GROWTH POLICY
INCOMES POLICY

02.02

SOCIAL POLICY.

02.02.01

SOCIAL COSTS

02.02.01<CONT>

SOCIAL JUSTICE
SOCIAL LEGISLATION
SOCIAL PLANNING
SOCIAL POLICY
SOCIAL REFORM

02.02.02

SOCIAL THEORY
WELFARE
WELFARE ECONOMICS

02.03

SOCIAL SECURITY.

02.03.01

SOCIAL INSURANCE
   USE: SOCIAL SECURITY
SOCIAL PROTECTION
   USE: SOCIAL SECURITY
SOCIAL SECURITY

02.03.02

BENEFIT PLANS
CONTINGENCY FUNDS
DISABILITY BENEFITS
EMPLOYMENT INJURIES BENEFITS
FAMILY ALLOWANCES
HEALTH INSURANCE
MATERNITY BENEFITS
OLD AGE BENEFITS
PENSION SCHEMES
RETIREMENT PENSIONS
SICKNESS INSURANCE
   USE: HEALTH INSURANCE
SURVIVORS BENEFITS
UNEMPLOYMENT BENEFITS
   USE: UNEMPLOYMENT INSURANCE
UNEMPLOYMENT INSURANCE

02.04

SOCIAL PROBLEMS.

02.04.01

SOCIAL PROBLEMS

02.04.02

ACCIDENTS
ALCOHOLISM
CORRUPTION
CRIMES
DELINQUENCY
DRUG ADDICTION
HOMICIDE
JUVENILE DELINQUENCY
OFFENDERS
PROSTITUTION

02.04.03

CAPITAL PUNISHMENT

02.04.03<CONT>

   CONCENTRATION CAMPS
   CRIME PREVENTION
   FORCED LABOUR
   LAW ENFORCEMENT
      USE: PENAL SANCTIONS
   PENAL SANCTIONS
   PRISONERS
   PRISONS
   TORTURE

02.05

SOCIAL SERVICES.

02.05.01

   SOCIAL ASSISTANCE
      USE: SOCIAL SERVICES
   SOCIAL SERVICES
   SOCIAL WORK
   WELFARE INSTITUTIONS
      USE: SOCIAL SERVICES

02.05.02

   HEALTH CENTRES
   HEALTH FACILITIES
   HEALTH INDICATORS
   HEALTH PLANNING
   HEALTH POLICY
   HEALTH SERVICES
   HOSPITALS
   MEDICAL EQUIPMENT
      USE: HEALTH FACILITIES
   MENTAL HOSPITALS

02.05.03

   CARE OF THE AGED
   CHILD CARE
   DISABLED CARE
   EMERGENCY RELIEF
   FAMILY POLICY
   ORPHANAGES

03.

ECONOMIC CONDITIONS. ECONOMIC RESEARCH.
ECONOMIC SYSTEMS.

03.01

ECONOMIC RESEARCH. ECONOMICS.

03.01.01

   ECONOMICS
   MACROECONOMICS
   MICROECONOMICS
   POLITICAL ECONOMY
      USE: ECONOMICS

03.01.02

   ACCUMULATION RATE
   ECONOMETRIC MODELS
   ECONOMETRICS
   ECONOMIC ANALYSIS
   ECONOMIC CENSUSES
   ECONOMIC EVALUATION
   ECONOMIC FORECASTS
   ECONOMIC INDICATORS
   ECONOMIC INFORMATION
   ECONOMIC MODELS
   ECONOMIC PROJECTIONS
   ECONOMIC RESEARCH
   ECONOMIC STATISTICS
   ECONOMIC SURVEYS
   ECONOMIC THEORY
   GROWTH MODELS
   GROWTH RATE

03.02

ECONOMIC CONDITIONS.

03.02.01

   ECONOMIC ASPECTS
   ECONOMIC BEHAVIOUR
   ECONOMIC CONDITIONS
   ECONOMIC CONSEQUENCES
      USE: ECONOMIC IMPLICATIONS
   ECONOMIC IMPLICATIONS
   ECONOMIC INFRASTRUCTURE
   ECONOMIC RESOURCES
   ECONOMIC SITUATION
      USE: ECONOMIC CONDITIONS
   ECONOMIC STRUCTURE

03.02.02

   GROSS DOMESTIC PRODUCT
   GROSS NATIONAL PRODUCT
   INPUT-OUTPUT
   INPUT-OUTPUT ANALYSIS
   INPUT-OUTPUT TABLES
   NATIONAL ACCOUNTING
   NATIONAL ACCOUNTS

03.02.02<CONT>

SECTOR ANALYSIS
    USE: INPUT-OUTPUT ANALYSIS
NATIONAL EXPENDITURES
NATIONAL INCOME
SECTOR ANALYSIS
    USE: INPUT-OUTPUT ANALYSIS

03.02.03

DEVELOPED COUNTRIES
DEVELOPING AREAS
DEVELOPING COUNTRIES
ECONOMIC DEVELOPMENT
ECONOMIC DISPARITY
ECONOMIC GROWTH
ECONOMIC RECONSTRUCTION
ECONOMIC TAKE OFF
INDUSTRIALIZED COUNTRIES
    USE: DEVELOPED COUNTRIES
LEAST DEVELOPED COUNTRIES
OBSTACLES TO DEVELOPMENT
REGIONAL DEVELOPMENT
REGIONAL DISPARITY
UNDERDEVELOPED AREAS
    USE: DEVELOPING AREAS
UNDERDEVELOPMENT
ZERO GROWTH ECONOMY

03.02.04

BUSIIIINESS CYCLE
ECONOMIC CRISIS
    USE: ECONOMIC RECESSION
ECONOMIC DEPRESSION
    USE: ECONOMIC RECESSION
ECONOMIC EQUILIBRIUM
ECONOMIC FLUCTUATIONS
    USE: BUSINESS CYCLE
ECONOMIC LOSS
ECONOMIC RECESSION
ECONOMIC RECOVERY
ECONOMIC STAGNATION
SEASONAL FLUCTUATIONS
STABILIZATION

03.02.05

ABUNDANCE
AFFLUENT SOCIETY
COST OF LIVING
FAMILY BUDGET
IMPOVERISHMENT
INCOME
INCOME DISTRIBUTION
INCOME REDISTRIBUTION
INDEXATION
LIVING CONDITIONS

03.02.05<CONT>

LOW INCOME
POVERTY
PURCHASING POWER
RATIONING
STANDARD OF LIVING
WEALTH

03.03

ECONOMIC SYSTEMS.

03.03.01

CAPITALISM
CAPITALIST
COLLECTIVISM
COLONIALISM
COMMUNISM
COMMUNIST
CORPORATISM
DIVISION OF LABOUR
ECONOMIC DOCTRINES
ECONOMIC SYSTEMS
ECONOMIC THOUGHT
FEUDALISM
LIBERALISM
MARGINALISM
MARKET ECONOMY
MARXISM
NATIONALISM
NATIONALIST
NEOCOLONIALISM
SOCIALISM
SOCIALIST

03.03.02

COLLECTIVE ECONOMY
DUAL ECONOMY
MIXED ECONOMY
PLANNED ECONOMY

03.03.03

CAPITALIST COUNTRIES
SOCIALIST COUNTRIES

03.03.04

COOPERATIVE MOVEMENTS
COOPERATIVES

03.03.05

COLLECTIVE OWNERSHIP
DENATIONALIZATION
EXPROPRIATION
FOREIGN ENTERPRISES
FOREIGN OWNERSHIP
INTERNATIONAL ENTERPRISES
    USE: MULTINATIONAL ENTERPRISES

03.03.05<CONT>

JOINT VENTURES

MIXED ENTERPRISES

MULTINATIONAL ENTERPRISES

NATIONALIZATION

NATIONALIZED ENTERPRISES
  USE: PUBLIC ENTERPRISES

OWNERSHIP

PRIVATE ENTERPRISES

PRIVATE OWNERSHIP

PRIVATE SECTOR

PUBLIC ENTERPRISES

PUBLIC OWNERSHIP

PUBLIC SECTOR

TRANSNATIONAL CORPORATIONS
  USE: MULTINATIONAL ENTERPRISES

04.

INSTITUTIONAL FRAMEWORK.

04.01

LAW. LEGISLATION.

04.01.01

CODES

JURIDICAL ASPECTS
  USE: LEGAL ASPECTS

JURISPRUDENCE

LAW

LEGAL ASPECTS

LEGAL PROTECTION

LEGAL SCIENCES

LEGISLATION

REGULATIONS

04.01.02

ADMINISTRATIVE LAW

CIVIL LAW

COMMERCIAL LAW

COMMON LAW

CONSTITUTIONAL LAW

CRIMINAL LAW

CUSTOMARY LAW

ECONOMIC LEGISLATION

FAMILY LAW

FISCAL LAW

LABOUR CODE

LABOUR COURTS

LABOUR LAW

LABOUR LEGISLATION

MARITIME LAW

PATENT LAW

PUBLIC LAW

04.02

HUMAN RIGHTS.

04.02.01

CIVIL RIGHTS

HUMAN RIGHTS

LEGAL AID

LEGAL STATUS

WOMEN'S RIGHTS

04.02.02

ACADEMIC FREEDOM

CIVIL LIBERTIES

DEMOCRACY

DEMOCRATIZATION

FREEDOM

FREEDOM OF ASSOCIATION

FREEDOM OF INFORMATION

04.04.02<CONT>

POLITICS
PRESSURE GROUPS
   USE: INTEREST GROUPS
PROPAGANDA
PUBLIC OPINION
RADICALISM
VOTING

05.

CULTURE. SOCIETY.

05.01

SOCIAL SCIENCES.

05.01.01

ANTHROPOLOGY
BEHAVIOURAL SCIENCES
CRIMINOLOGY
ECONOMIC HISTORY
ETHNOGRAPHY
ETHNOLOGY
FOLKLORE
HISTORICAL ANALYSIS
HISTORY
PHILOSOPHY
PSYCHOLOGY
SOCIAL HISTORY
SOCIAL PSYCHOLOGY
SOCIAL SCIENCES
SOCIOLOGY

05.01.02

CROSS CULTURAL ANALYSIS
INTERCULTURAL RESEARCH
   USE: CROSS CULTURAL ANALYSIS
SOCIAL INDICATORS
SOCIAL INFORMATION
SOCIAL RESEARCH
SOCIAL SURVEYS
SOCIOLOGICAL ANALYSIS

05.02

CULTURE.

05.02.01

CIVILIZATION
CULTURAL PLURALISM
CULTURE
FOLK CULTURE
SCIENTIFIC CULTURE
SUBCULTURE
TRADITION
TRADITIONAL CULTURE

05.02.02

ACCULTURATION
CONSERVATION OF CULTURAL HERITAGE
CULTURAL CHANGE
CULTURAL ENVIRONMENT
CULTURAL FACTORS
CULTURAL HERITAGE
CULTURAL IDENTITY
CULTURAL INTEGRATION

05.02.02<CONT>

CULTURAL RELATIONS

PARTICIPATION IN CULTURAL LIFE

05.02.03

ACCESS TO CULTURE

CULTURAL AGREEMENTS

CULTURAL ANIMATION

CULTURAL COOPERATION

CULTURAL DEVELOPMENT

CULTURAL EXPENDITURES

CULTURAL INDUSTRY

CULTURAL INFORMATION

CULTURAL POLICY

DISSEMINATION OF CULTURE

ECONOMICS OF CULTURE

RIGHT TO CULTURE

SOCIO-CULTURAL FACILITIES

05.03

SOCIETY.

05.03.01

HUMAN RELATIONS

INDIVIDUALS

LIFE STYLES

PERSONALITY

PERSONALITY DEVELOPMENT

PRIVACY PROTECTION

QUALITY OF LIFE

SOCIAL SYSTEM

SOCIETY

05.03.02

ATTITUDES

BEHAVIOUR

BELIEF

CONSERVATISM

CREATIVITY

CRITICAL NEEDS
  USE: BASIC NEEDS

IDEOLOGIES

MOTIVATIONS

OPINION

PSYCHOLOGICAL ASPECTS

05.03.03

ADAPTATION

ADJUSTMENT
  USE: ADAPTATION

ALIENATION

MALADJUSTMENT

MARGINALITY

SOCIAL ADAPTATION

05.03.03<CONT>

SOCIAL ASSIMILATION
  USE: SOCIAL INTEGRATION

SOCIAL BEHAVIOUR

SOCIAL ENVIRONMENT

SOCIAL INFLUENCE

SOCIAL INTEGRATION

SOCIAL PARTICIPATION

SOCIAL ROLE

SOCIALIZATION

05.03.04

ADAPTATION TO CHANGE

MODERNIZATION

RESISTANCE TO CHANGE

REVOLUTION

SOCIAL ASPECTS

SOCIAL CHANGE

SOCIAL CONDITIONS

SOCIAL CONSEQUENCES
  USE: SOCIAL IMPLICATIONS

SOCIAL CONTROL

SOCIAL DEVELOPMENT

SOCIAL IMPLICATIONS

SOCIAL PROGRESS
  USE: SOCIAL DEVELOPMENT

SOCIAL STRUCTURE

05.03.05

BOURGEOISIE

CASTES

CLASS CONSCIOUSNESS

ELITE

INTELLECTUALS

LEADERSHIP

LOWER CLASS

MIDDLE CLASS

PEASANTS

PROLETARIAT

RULING CLASS

SLAVERY

SOCIAL CLASSES

SOCIAL INEQUALITY

SOCIAL MOBILITY

SOCIAL STATUS

SOCIAL STRATIFICATION

UPPER CLASS

WORKING CLASS

05.03.06

ARBITRATION

CLASS STRUGGLE

05.03.06<CONT>

CONCILIATION
CONFLICT RESOLUTION
   USE: DISPUTE SETTLEMENT
CONFLICTS
DISPUTE SETTLEMENT
INTERGROUP RELATIONS
SOCIAL CONFLICTS

05.03.07

ASSOCIATIONS
GROUP DISCUSSION
GROUP DYNAMICS
GROUPS
MINORITY GROUPS
NON-PROFIT ORGANIZATIONS
PEASANT MOVEMENTS
SOCIAL MOVEMENTS
VOLUNTARY ORGANIZATIONS
WOMEN'S ORGANIZATIONS
YOUTH CENTRES
YOUTH ORGANIZATIONS

05.04

ETHICS. RELIGION.

05.04.01

ETHICS
RESPONSIBILITY
SOCIAL NORMS
VALUE SYSTEMS

05.04.02

ATHEISM
MAGIC
MYTHOLOGY
RELIGION
RELIGIOUS GROUPS
RELIGIOUS MINORITIES
RELIGIOUS PRACTICE
SUPERSTITION
WORSHIP

05.04.03

ANIMISM
BUDDHISM
CHRISTIANITY
CONFUCIANISM
FETISHISM
HINDUISM
ISLAM
JUDAISM
SHINTOISM
TAOISM

05.04.04

CLERGY
RELIGIOUS INSTITUTIONS
RELIGIOUS MISSIONS
SECULARIZATION

05.05

ART.

05.05.01

ARCHAEOLOGICAL SITES
ARCHAEOLOGY
MUSEUMS

05.05.02

AESTHETICS
ART
ARTISTIC CREATION
FOLK ART
WORKS OF ART

05.05.03

ARCHITECTURE
ARTS
CINEMA
DANCE
DECORATIVE ARTS
   USE: FINE ARTS
DRAMATIC ART
FINE ARTS
GRAPHIC ARTS
LITERATURE
MUSIC
MUSICAL INSTRUMENTS
PERFORMING ARTS
PLASTIC ARTS
THEATRE
VISUAL ARTS

05.06

LANGUAGES.

05.06.01

BILINGUALISM
DIALECTS
LANGUAGE BARRIER
LANGUAGE MINORITIES
LANGUAGES
LINGUISTICS
MULTILINGUALISM
OFFICIAL LANGUAGES
TRANSLATION
VERNACULAR LANGUAGES

05.06.02

ARABIC
CHINESE LANGUAGE

05.06.02<CONT>
ENGLISH LANGUAGE
FRENCH LANGUAGE
RUSSIAN LANGUAGE
SPANISH LANGUAGE

05.07

COMMUNICATION.

05.07.01
CENSORSHIP
COMMUNICATION
COMMUNICATION BARRIERS
COMMUNICATION PLANNING
COMMUNICATION POLICY
COMMUNICATION RESEARCH
COMMUNICATION SYSTEMS
MASS COMMUNICATION

05.07.02
AUDIENCE
AUDIENCE RATING
COMMUNICATION USERS
   USE: AUDIENCE

05.07.03
BOOKS
COMMUNICATION MEDIA
   USE: MEDIA
FILMS
MASS MEDIA
MEDIA
PRESS
RADIO
TELECOMMUNICATIONS
TELEVISION

06.

EDUCATION. TRAINING.

06.01

SCIENCES OF EDUCATION.

06.01.00
COMPARATIVE EDUCATION
ECONOMICS OF EDUCATION
EDUCATIONAL ECONOMICS
   USE: ECONOMICS OF EDUCATION
EDUCATIONAL PSYCHOLOGY
   USE: PSYCHOLOGY OF EDUCATION
EDUCATIONAL RESEARCH
EDUCATIONAL SCIENCES
   USE: SCIENCES OF EDUCATION
EDUCATIONAL SOCIOLOGY
   USE: SOCIOLOGY OF EDUCATION
EDUCATIONAL STATISTICS
EDUCATIONAL THEORY
HISTORY OF EDUCATION
PEDAGOGY
   USE: SCIENCES OF EDUCATION
PHILOSOPHY OF EDUCATION
PSYCHOLOGY OF EDUCATION
SCIENCES OF EDUCATION
SOCIOLOGY OF EDUCATION

06.02

EDUCATIONAL DEVELOPMENT. EDUCATIONAL POLICY.

06.02.01
AIMS OF EDUCATION
EDUCATION
EDUCATIONAL ASPECTS
TRAINING

06.02.02
ACCESS TO EDUCATION
DEMOCRATIZATION OF EDUCATION
EDUCATIONAL NEEDS
EDUCATIONAL OPPORTUNITIES
ILLITERACY
RIGHT TO EDUCATION

06.02.03
ADVANCEMENT OF EDUCATION
   USE: EDUCATIONAL DEVELOPMENT
EDUCATIONAL CRISIS
EDUCATIONAL DEVELOPMENT
EDUCATIONAL INNOVATIONS
EDUCATIONAL PROJECTS
EDUCATIONAL REFORMS
QUALITY OF EDUCATION
REFORMS OF EDUCATION
   USE: EDUCATIONAL REFORMS

06.02.04
EDUCATIONAL PLANNING
EDUCATIONAL POLICY

06.02.04<CONT>

PLANNING OF EDUCATION
USE: EDUCATIONAL PLANNING

06.02.05

COST OF EDUCATION

EDUCATIONAL BUDGET

EDUCATIONAL EXPENDITURES
USE: COST OF EDUCATION

EDUCATIONAL FINANCING

EDUCATIONAL OUTPUT

06.03

EDUCATIONAL SYSTEMS.

06.03.01

EDUCATIONAL SYSTEMS

SCHOOL SYSTEMS
USE: EDUCATIONAL SYSTEMS

SYSTEMS OF EDUCATION
USE: EDUCATIONAL SYSTEMS

TEACHING SYSTEMS
USE: EDUCATIONAL SYSTEMS

06.03.02

DE-SCHOOLING

NON-FORMAL EDUCATION

OUT-OF-SCHOOL EDUCATION

SCHOOLING

06.03.03

COMPENSATORY EDUCATION

COMPULSORY EDUCATION

CORRECTIONAL EDUCATION

FREE EDUCATION

PRIVATE EDUCATION

PUBLIC EDUCATION

SPECIAL EDUCATION

06.03.04

BASIC EDUCATION

CIVIC EDUCATION

CONSUMER EDUCATION

ENVIRONMENTAL EDUCATION

FUNCTIONAL LITERACY

GENERAL EDUCATION

HEALTH EDUCATION

HOME ECONOMICS

LITERACY

MASS EDUCATION

PHYSICAL EDUCATION

POLITICAL EDUCATION

READING

SAFETY EDUCATION

SEX EDUCATION

WRITING

06.03.05

ADULT EDUCATION

06.03.05<CONT>

CONTINUING EDUCATION
USE: LIFE-LONG EDUCATION

EDUCATION OF WOMEN

LIFE-LONG EDUCATION

PERMANENT EDUCATION
USE: LIFE-LONG EDUCATION

RECURRENT EDUCATION

WORKERS EDUCATION

06.03.06

ELEMENTARY EDUCATION
USE: PRIMARY EDUCATION

HIGHER EDUCATION

LEVELS OF EDUCATION

POST-SECONDARY EDUCATION

PRESCHOOL EDUCATION

PRIMARY EDUCATION

SECONDARY EDUCATION

06.03.07

AGRICULTURAL EDUCATION

AGRICULTURAL TRAINING

APPRENTICESHIP

ART EDUCATION

BASIC TRAINING

COMMERCIAL EDUCATION

FARMER TRAINING
USE: AGRICULTURAL TRAINING

FURTHER TRAINING

IN-PLANT TRAINING

INDUSTRIAL TRAINING

LANGUAGE TEACHING

MEDICAL EDUCATION

OCCUPATIONAL TRAINING
USE: VOCATIONAL TRAINING

ON-THE-JOB TRAINING
USE: IN-PLANT TRAINING

PHYSICIAN EDUCATION
USE: MEDICAL EDUCATION

PROFESSIONAL EDUCATION
USE: VOCATIONAL EDUCATION

RETRAINING

SANDWICH TRAINING

TECHNICAL EDUCATION

TRANSITION FROM SCHOOL TO WORK

VOCATIONAL EDUCATION

VOCATIONAL GUIDANCE

VOCATIONAL TRAINING

06.04

EDUCATIONAL INSTITUTIONS.

06.04.01

EDUCATIONAL INSTITUTIONS

06.04.02

DAY CARE CENTRES

06.04.02<CONT>

ELEMENTARY SCHOOLS
    USE: PRIMARY SCHOOLS
NURSERY SCHOOLS
PRIMARY SCHOOLS
SCHOOLS
SECONDARY SCHOOLS

06.04.03

BOARDING SCHOOLS
COEDUCATIONAL SCHOOLS
COMPREHENSIVE SCHOOLS
CORRECTIONAL INSTITUTIONS
EXPERIMENTAL SCHOOLS
MOBILE SCHOOLS
NIGHT SCHOOLS
SPECIAL SCHOOLS
SUMMER SCHOOLS

06.04.04

INTERNATIONAL SCHOOLS
PRIVATE SCHOOLS
RURAL SCHOOLS

06.04.05

COLLEGES OF EDUCATION
HIGHER EDUCATION INSTITUTIONS
POST-SECONDARY SCHOOLS
    USE: HIGHER EDUCATION INSTITUTIONS
TEACHER TRAINING COLLEGES
    USE: COLLEGES OF EDUCATION
UNIVERSITIES

06.04.06

AGRICULTURAL INSTITUTES
COMMERCIAL SCHOOLS
TECHNICAL SCHOOLS
TECHNOLOGICAL INSTITUTES
TRAINING CENTRES
TRAINING WORKSHOPS
    USE: TRAINING CENTRES
VOCATIONAL SCHOOLS

06.04.07

EDUCATIONAL BUILDINGS
EDUCATIONAL EQUIPMENT
EDUCATIONAL FACILITIES
LANGUAGE LABORATORIES
SCHOOL BUILDINGS
SCHOOL TRANSPORT
UNIVERSITY BUILDINGS

06.04.08

COLLEGE MANAGEMENT
SCHOOL DISCIPLINE
SCHOOL MANAGEMENT

06.04.09

ADMISSION REQUIREMENTS

06.04.09<CONT>

EDUCATIONAL GUIDANCE
EDUCATIONAL SELECTION
ENROLMENT

06.04.10

ABILITY GROUPING
CLASSES
EXPERIMENTAL CLASSES
STREAMING
    USE: ABILITY GROUPING

06.04.11

EDUCATIONAL GRANTS
FEES
RESEARCH FELLOWSHIPS
SCHOLARSHIPS
STUDENT LOANS
TRAINING ALLOWANCES

06.04.12

DROPPING OUT
EDUCATIONAL ATTENDANCE
LEAVING SCHOOL
SCHOOL ADAPTATION
SCHOOL ENVIRONMENT
SCHOOL HOLIDAYS
SCHOOL SEGREGATION
SCHOOL-COMMUNITY RELATIONSHIPS

06.04.13

CERTIFICATES
DIPLOMAS
EQUIVALENCE BETWEEN DIPLOMAS
EXAMINATIONS
QUALIFICATIONS
UNIVERSITY DEGREES

06.05

CURRICULUM. TEACHING. LEARNING.

06.05.01

ACCELERATED COURSES
COURSES
CURRICULUM
CURRICULUM DEVELOPMENT
CURRICULUM SUBJECTS
INSTRUCTIONAL PROGRAMMES
    USE: TEACHING PROGRAMMES
INTEGRATED CURRICULUM
INTENSIVE COURSES
    USE: ACCELERATED COURSES
TEACHING PROGRAMMES
TRAINING COURSES
TRAINING PROGRAMMES

06.05.02

EXPERIMENTAL TEACHING

06.05.02<CONT>

INDIVIDUALIZED TEACHING

INSTRUCTION
  USE: TEACHING

MODULAR TRAINING

PEER TEACHING

REMEDIAL TEACHING

SELF-INSTRUCTION

STUDENT EXCHANGE

STUDY TOURS

TEACHING

TEACHING METHODS

TEACHING PRACTICE

TEAM TEACHING

TRAINING ABROAD

TRAINING METHODS

06.05.03

AUDIOVISUAL AIDS

CORRESPONDENCE EDUCATION

DISTANCE STUDY

EDUCATIONAL FILMS

EDUCATIONAL RADIO

EDUCATIONAL TECHNOLOGY

EDUCATIONAL TELEVISION

INSTRUCTIONAL AIDS
  USE: TEACHING AIDS

INSTRUCTIONAL MEDIA
  USE: TEACHING AIDS

INSTRUCTIONAL RADIO
  USE: EDUCATIONAL RADIO

PROGRAMMED INSTRUCTION

PROGRAMMED LEARNING
  USE: PROGRAMMED INSTRUCTION

RESOURCES CENTRES

TEACHING AIDS

TEACHING MATERIALS
  USE: TEACHING AIDS

06.05.04

APTITUDES

CHILD DEVELOPMENT

INTELLIGENCE QUOTIENT

LEARNING

MENTAL RETARDATION

06.06

STUDENTS. TEACHING PERSONNEL.

06.06.01

COLLEGE STUDENTS

FOREIGN STUDENTS

GIFTED STUDENTS

GRADUATES

HANDICAPPED STUDENTS

06.06.01<CONT>

ILLITERATES

PUPILS
  USE: STUDENTS

SCHOLARSHIP HOLDERS

SCHOOL LEAVERS

STUDENT BEHAVIOUR

STUDENT MOVEMENTS

STUDENT PARTICIPATION

STUDENTS

TRAINEES

UNDERGRADUATES

06.06.02

INSTRUCTIONAL STAFF
  USE: TEACHING PERSONNEL

TEACHER ASSOCIATIONS

TEACHER RECRUITMENT

TEACHER SHORTAGE

TEACHER STATUS

TEACHER TRAINING

TEACHER-STUDENT RELATIONSHIPS

TEACHING PERSONNEL

07.
AGRICULTURE.

07.01
AGRICULTURAL ECONOMICS.

07.01.01
AGRICULTURAL ASPECTS
AGRICULTURAL ECONOMICS
AGRICULTURAL ECONOMY
AGRICULTURAL INDUSTRY
   USE: AGROINDUSTRY
AGRICULTURAL SECTOR
AGRICULTURE
AGROINDUSTRIAL COMPLEX
   USE: AGROINDUSTRY
AGROINDUSTRY
PRIMARY SECTOR

07.01.02
AGRICULTURAL DEVELOPMENT
AGRICULTURAL EXTENSION
AGRICULTURAL MANAGEMENT
AGRICULTURAL PLANNING
AGRICULTURAL POLICY
AGRICULTURAL POTENTIAL
AGRICULTURAL PROJECTS
GREEN REVOLUTION

07.01.03
AGRICULTURAL MARKET
AGRICULTURAL PRICES
AGRICULTURAL SURPLUSES

07.02
LAND ECONOMICS.

07.02.00
AGRARIAN REFORMS
AGRARIAN STRUCTURE
AGRARIAN SYSTEMS
   USE: AGRARIAN STRUCTURE
COMMUNAL LAND
LAND DISTRIBUTION
   USE: LAND TENURE
LAND ECONOMICS
LAND OWNERSHIP
LAND REFORMS
LAND SPECULATION
LAND TENURE
LANDOWNERS
PUBLIC LAND
SHARE FARMERS
   USE: TENANT FARMERS
TENANT FARMERS

07.03
AGRICULTURAL ENTERPRISES.

07.03.01
AGRICULTURAL ENTERPRISES

07.03.01<CONT>
EXPERIMENTAL FARMS
FARMS
PLANTATIONS

07.03.02
AGRICULTURAL COOPERATIVES
FARM MANAGEMENT
FARM SIZE
STATE FARMS

07.03.03
AGRICULTURAL BANKS
AGRICULTURAL CREDIT
AGRICULTURAL INCOME
AGRICULTURAL INSURANCE
AGRICULTURAL INVESTMENTS
LAND RENT

07.04
AGRICULTURAL EQUIPMENT.

07.04.00
AGRICULTURAL ENGINEERING
AGRICULTURAL EQUIPMENT
AGRICULTURAL MACHINERY
AGRICULTURAL MECHANIZATION
AGRICULTURAL TECHNOLOGY
   USE: AGRICULTURAL ENGINEERING
FARM BUILDINGS
FARM MACHINERY
   USE: AGRICULTURAL MACHINERY
GREENHOUSES
SILOS
TRACTORS

07.05
AGRICULTURAL PRODUCTION.

07.05.01
AGRICULTURAL CENSUSES
AGRICULTURAL PRODUCTION
AGRICULTURAL STATISTICS
CROP PROSPECTS
CROP YIELD

07.05.02
AGRICULTURAL AREAS
ARABLE LAND
CULTIVATED LAND
FERTILIZING
IRRIGATED LAND
LAND CAPABILITY
LAND RECLAMATION
LAND USE
LAND UTILIZATION
   USE: LAND USE
SOIL CULTIVATION
   USE: SOIL MANAGEMENT

07.05.02<CONT>
SOIL FERTILITY
SOIL IMPROVEMENT
SOIL MANAGEMENT

07.05.03
COLLECTIVE FARMING
COMMERCIAL FARMING
COOPERATIVE FARMING
EXTENSIVE FARMING
FARMING
FARMING SYSTEMS
INTENSIVE FARMING
MIXED FARMING
SUBSISTENCE FARMING

07.05.04
CROP DIVERSIFICATION
CROP ROTATION
CROPPING SYSTEMS
    USE: CULTIVATION SYSTEMS
CROPS
CULTIVATION PRACTICES
CULTIVATION SYSTEMS
HARVESTING
INTERCROPPING
MULTIPLE CROPPING
PLANTING
SHIFTING CULTIVATION
SOWING
WEED CONTROL

07.05.05
AGRICULTURAL COMMODITIES
    USE: AGRICULTURAL PRODUCTS
AGRICULTURAL PRODUCTS
AGRICULTURAL WASTES

07.06
AGRICULTURAL RESEARCH.

07.06.00
AGRICULTURAL RESEARCH
AGRONOMY
BOTANY
ENTOMOLOGY
ZOOLOGY

07.07
PLANT PRODUCTION.

07.07.01
AQUATIC PLANTS
FLORA
FLOWERS
FUNGI
PLANT BREEDING

07.07.01<CONT>
PLANT NUTRITION
PLANT PATHOLOGY
PLANTS
SEEDS
TREES
VEGETATION
WILD PLANTS

07.07.02
CASH CROPS
    USE: INDUSTRIAL CROPS
FOOD CROPS
FORAGE CROPS
FRUIT CROPS
GARDENING
GRASSLAND
GRAZING
HORTICULTURE
INDUSTRIAL CROPS
LIVESTOCK CROPS
    USE: FORAGE CROPS
OIL CROPS
ROOT CROPS
VEGETABLE CROPS
VITICULTURE

07.07.03
PLANT PRODUCTION
PLANT PRODUCTS

07.07.04
BARLEY
CEREALS
GRAINS
    USE: CEREALS
MAIZE
MILLET
OAT
RICE
RYE
SORGHUM
TRITICALE
WHEAT

07.07.05
ALMONDS
APPLES
BANANA-TREES
BANANAS
CASHEW NUTS
CITRUS FRUITS
COCONUT PALMS

07.07.05<CONT>
COCONUTS
DATE PALMS
DATES
FRUIT TREES
FRUITS
GRAPES
GROUNDNUTS
OIL PALMS
OILSEEDS
OLIVES
PEARS
PINEAPPLES
TOMATOES

07.07.06
BEANS
CASSAVA
CHICKPEAS
COWPEAS
FABA BEANS
LEGUMINOSAE
LENTILS
ONIONS
PIGEON PEAS
POTATOES
RAPE
SOYBEANS
SUGAR BEETS
SUGAR CANE
SWEET POTATOES
VEGETABLES

07.07.07
COIR
COTTON
FLAX
HEMP
JUTE
PLANT FIBRES
SISAL

07.07.08
GUM ARABIC
GUMS
HEVEAS
LATEX
RESINS

07.07.09
COCOA
COFFEE

07.07.09<CONT>
OPIUM
PEPPER
SPICES
TEA
TOBACCO

07.08
FORESTS.

07.08.01
FORESTRY
FORESTRY ECONOMICS
FORESTRY INDUSTRY
FORESTS
SILVICULTURE

07.08.02
FORESTRY RESEARCH
FORESTRY STATISTICS

07.08.03
AFFORESTATION
DEFORESTATION
DEFORESTED LAND
FOREST AREAS
FOREST NURSERIES
FOREST UTILIZATION
LOGGING
MANMADE FORESTS
REFORESTATION

07.08.04
FOREST MANAGEMENT
FOREST POLICY
FORESTRY DEVELOPMENT
FORESTRY PLANNING

07.08.05
FOREST ENGINEERING
FORESTRY EQUIPMENT

07.08.06
FOREST PRODUCTION
FOREST PRODUCTS
FOREST TREES
WOOD PRODUCTION

07.09
ANIMAL PRODUCTION.

07.09.01
ANIMALS
BIG GAME
BIRDS
BOVIDAE
CALVES
CAMELS
CATTLE

07.09.01<CONT>

COWS
DOMESTIC ANIMALS
DONKEYS
ELEPHANTS
EQUIDAE
FAUNA
GOATS
HORSES
OVIDAE
PIGS
    USE: SWINE
POULTRY
REPTILES
RUMINANTS
SHEEP
SILKWORMS
SMALL GAME
SWINE
WATER BUFFALOES
WILD ANIMALS

07.09.02

ANIMAL BREEDING
ANIMAL HUSBANDRY
ANIMAL PRODUCTION
APICULTURE
CATTLE PRODUCTION
FARM ANIMALS
    USE: LIVESTOCK
LIVESTOCK

07.09.03

ANIMAL FEEDING
ANIMAL NUTRITION
FEED
FODDER
GRASSES

07.09.04

HUNTING
SLAUGHTERHOUSES
SLAUGHTERING

07.09.05

ANIMAL FIBRES
ANIMAL PRODUCTS
BEEF
BUTTER
CHEESE
DAIRY PRODUCTS
EGGS
HONEY

07.09.05<CONT>

MEAT
MEAT PRODUCTS
MILK
MILK POWDER
MILK PRODUCTS
    USE: DAIRY PRODUCTS
MUTTON
PORK
SHEEPMEAT
    USE: MUTTON
SILK
WOOL

07.10

FISHERY.

07.10.01

FISHERY
FISHERY ECONOMICS
FISHERY RESEARCH
FISHERY STATISTICS

07.10.02

FISHERY DEVELOPMENT
FISHERY INDUSTRY
FISHERY MANAGEMENT
FISHERY PLANNING
FISHERY POLICY
FISHING RIGHTS

07.10.03

AQUACULTURE
COASTAL FISHING
DEEP SEA FISHING
FACTORY BOATS
FISH CULTURE
FISHERY ENGINEERING
FISHING
FISHING BOATS
    USE: FISHING VESSELS
FISHING EQUIPMENT
FISHING FLEET
    USE: FISHING VESSELS
FISHING GEAR
    USE: FISHING EQUIPMENT
FISHING GROUNDS
FISHING PORTS
FISHING VESSELS
INLAND FISHING
MARINE FISHING
OYSTER CULTURE
TRAWLERS

07.10.04

ALGAE

257

07.10.04<CONT>

AQUATIC FAUNA

CRUSTACEA

FISH

FISH BREEDING

FISH PRODUCTION

FISH UTILIZATION

FISHERY PRODUCTS

FRESHWATER FISH

MOLLUSCS

SALT WATER FISH

SEAWEEDS
USE: ALGAE

SHRIMPS

08.

INDUSTRY.

08.01

INDUSTRIAL ECONOMICS.

08.01.01

EXPORT-ORIENTED INDUSTRY

HEAVY INDUSTRY

INDUSTRIAL ASPECTS

INDUSTRIAL CENSUSES

INDUSTRIAL ECONOMICS

INDUSTRIAL EXTENSION

INDUSTRIAL INFORMATION

INDUSTRIAL SECTOR

INDUSTRIAL STATISTICS

INDUSTRY

LIGHT INDUSTRY

MANUFACTURING

MANUFACTURING INDUSTRIES
USE: INDUSTRY

SECONDARY SECTOR
USE: INDUSTRIAL SECTOR

08.01.02

HANDICRAFT PROMOTION

INDUSTRIAL ADAPTATION

INDUSTRIAL DEVELOPMENT

INDUSTRIAL GROWTH
USE: INDUSTRIAL DEVELOPMENT

INDUSTRIAL PLANNING

INDUSTRIAL POLICY

INDUSTRIAL POTENTIAL

INDUSTRIAL PROJECTS

INDUSTRIAL PROMOTION

INDUSTRIAL STRUCTURE

INDUSTRIALIZATION

INDUSTRIALIZATION POLICY

08.02

INDUSTRIAL ENTERPRISES.

08.02.01

INDUSTRIAL ENTERPRISES

NATIONALIZED INDUSTRY

08.02.02

COTTAGE INDUSTRY

HANDICRAFT

INFORMAL SECTOR

MEDIUM-SCALE INDUSTRY

RURAL INDUSTRY

SMALL-SCALE INDUSTRY

08.02.03

INDUSTRIAL AREAS

INDUSTRIAL CONCENTRATION

INDUSTRIAL LOCATION
USE: LOCATION OF INDUSTRY

08.02.03<CONT>

    LOCATION OF INDUSTRY

08.02.04

    INDUSTRIAL BANKS
    INDUSTRIAL CAPITAL
    INDUSTRIAL CREDIT
    INDUSTRIAL INVESTMENTS
    INDUSTRIAL MANAGEMENT
    INDUSTRIAL PRICES

08.03

INDUSTRIAL ENGINEERING. INDUSTRIAL EQUIPMENT.

08.03.00

    FACTORIES
        USE: INDUSTRIAL PLANTS
    FACTORY LAYOUT
    FACTORY ORGANIZATION
    INDUSTRIAL BUILDINGS
    INDUSTRIAL DESIGN
    INDUSTRIAL ENGINEERING
    INDUSTRIAL EQUIPMENT
    INDUSTRIAL PLANTS
    INDUSTRIAL PROCESSES
    INDUSTRIAL PROFILES
    REPAIR SHOPS
    WORKSHOPS

08.04

INDUSTRIAL PRODUCTION. INDUSTRIAL PRODUCTS.

08.04.00

    FINISHED PRODUCTS
    INDUSTRIAL PRODUCTION
    INDUSTRIAL PRODUCTS
    INDUSTRIAL WASTES
    MANUFACTURED PRODUCTS
    SEMI-MANUFACTURED PRODUCTS

08.05

INDUSTRIAL RESEARCH.

08.05.00

    INDUSTRIAL PROPERTY
    INDUSTRIAL RESEARCH
    LICENSING
    PATENTS

08.06

FOOD INDUSTRY.

08.06.01

    CANNING INDUSTRY
    DAIRY INDUSTRY
    DAIRY PRODUCTS INDUSTRY
        USE: DAIRY INDUSTRY
    FOOD INDUSTRY
    FOOD PRODUCTION
    MEAT INDUSTRY

08.06.01<CONT>

    MILLING INDUSTRY
    SUGAR INDUSTRY
    TOBACCO INDUSTRY

08.06.02

    AGRIPRODUCT PROCESSING
    FISH PRESERVATION
    FISHERY PRODUCT PROCESSING
    FOOD ADDITIVES
    FOOD ENGINEERING
        USE: FOOD TECHNOLOGY
    FOOD ENRICHMENT
    FOOD IRRADIATION
    FOOD PRESERVATION
    FOOD PROCESSING
    FOOD SCIENCE
    FOOD STERILIZATION
    FOOD STORAGE
    FOOD TECHNOLOGY
    GRAIN PROCESSING
    MEAT PROCESSING
    MILK PROCESSING
    PASTEURIZATION

08.06.03

    CANNED FOOD
    CONDENSED FOOD
    DEHYDRATED FOOD
    DRIED FOOD
    FROZEN FOOD
    IRRADIATED FOOD

08.06.04

    BAKERY PRODUCTS
    BEET SUGAR
    BREAD
    CANE SUGAR
    CARBOHYDRATES
    CHOCOLATE
    DRIED FRUIT
    FISH MEAL
    FISH PROTEIN CONCENTRATE
    FLOUR
    MOLASSES
    STARCH
    SUGAR

08.06.05

    ALCOHOLIC BEVERAGES
    BEER
    BEVERAGE INDUSTRY

08.06.05<CONT>

    BEVERAGES
    BREWERY
    FRUIT JUICES
    MINERAL WATERS
    NON-ALCOHOLIC BEVERAGES
    WINE

08.06.06

    ANIMAL FATS
    ANIMAL OILS
    EDIBLE OILS
    ESSENTIAL OILS
    FATS
    FISH OILS
    MARGARINE
    OILS AND FATS
    OLIVE OIL
    PALM OIL
    PEANUT OIL
    VEGETABLE OILS

08.07

WOODWORKING INDUSTRY. PULP AND PAPER INDUSTRY.

08.07.01

    CELLULOSE
    CORK
    HARD FIBRES
    PARTICLE BOARDS
    PLYWOOD
    TIMBER
    WOOD
    WOOD FIBRES
    WOOD PROCESSING
    WOOD PRODUCTS
    WOOD TECHNOLOGY
    WOOD WASTES
    WOODWORKING INDUSTRY

08.07.02

    CARDBOARD
    PAPER
    PULP
    PULP AND PAPER INDUSTRY

08.07.03

    FURNITURE
    FURNITURE INDUSTRY
    TOYS

08.08

TEXTILE INDUSTRY. LEATHER INDUSTRY.

08.08.01

    CARPETS

08.08.01<CONT>

    CLOTHING INDUSTRY
    FIBRES
    MANMADE FIBRES
    NATURAL FIBRES
    ROPE INDUSTRY
    SOFT FIBRES
    SPINNING
    TEXTILE INDUSTRY
    TEXTILES
    WEAVING

08.08.02

    FOOTWEAR
       USE: SHOE INDUSTRY
    FUR
    FUR INDUSTRY
    HIDES AND SKINS
    LEATHER
    LEATHER GOODS
    LEATHER INDUSTRY
    SHOE INDUSTRY
    TANNING INDUSTRY

08.09

RUBBER INDUSTRY.

08.09.00

    RUBBER
    RUBBER INDUSTRY
    SYNTHETIC RUBBER
    TYRES

08.10

CONSTRUCTION INDUSTRY. CERAMICS. GLASS.

08.10.01

    BUILDING INDUSTRY
       USE: CONSTRUCTION INDUSTRY
    BUILDINGS
    CONCRETE CONSTRUCTION
    CONSTRUCTION INDUSTRY
    CONSTRUCTION TECHNIQUES
    PREFABRICATED BUILDINGS
    QUARRYING
    STEEL CONSTRUCTION
    STONE CONSTRUCTION
    WOOD CONSTRUCTION

08.10.02

    AGGLOMERATES
    ASBESTOS
    BITUMENS
    BUILDING MATERIALS
       USE: CONSTRUCTION MATERIALS
    CEMENT

08.10.02<CONT>

CEMENT INDUSTRY
CONCRETE
CONSTRUCTION MATERIALS
LIME
SAND
STONE

08.10.03

BRICKS
CERAMICS
CERAMICS INDUSTRY
CLAY
POTTERY
REFRACTORY MATERIALS

08.10.04

GLASS
GLASS INDUSTRY

08.11

ENERGY.

08.11.01

ENERGY
ENERGY CONSERVATION
ENERGY CONSUMPTION
ENERGY CRISIS
ENERGY DEMAND
    USE: POWER DEMAND
ENERGY ECONOMICS
ENERGY POLICY
ENERGY REQUIREMENTS
    USE: POWER DEMAND
ENERGY SOURCES
ENERGY UTILIZATION
FOSSIL FUELS
FUELS
GEOTHERMAL ENERGY
POWER CONSERVATION
    USE: ENERGY CONSERVATION
POWER CONSUMPTION
    USE: ENERGY CONSUMPTION
POWER DEMAND
POWER DISTRIBUTION
POWER GENERATION
POWER INDUSTRY
POWER PLANTS
POWER PRODUCTION
    USE: POWER GENERATION
POWER SUPPLY
POWER UTILIZATION
SOLAR ENERGY
THERMAL ENERGY

08.11.01<CONT>

TIDAL ENERGY
WIND ENERGY

08.11.02

ELECTRIC POWER
ELECTRIC POWER PLANTS
ELECTRICAL ENGINEERING
ELECTRICAL INDUSTRY
ELECTRICITY
ELECTRIFICATION
HYDROELECTRIC POWER
HYDROELECTRIC POWER PLANTS
THERMAL POWER PLANTS

08.11.03

ATOMIC ENERGY
    USE: NUCLEAR ENERGY
NUCLEAR ENERGY
NUCLEAR ENGINEERING
NUCLEAR FUEL
NUCLEAR INSTALLATIONS
NUCLEAR POWER
    USE: NUCLEAR ENERGY
NUCLEAR POWER PLANTS
NUCLEAR REACTORS

08.11.04

IONISING RADIATION
ISOTOPES
RADIOACTIVE MATERIALS
RADIOACTIVE WASTES
RADIOACTIVITY
RADIOISOTOPES

08.11.05

COAL
COAL GAS
COKE

08.11.06

BENZENE
ENGINE FUELS
GASOLINE
    USE: PETROL
HYDROCARBONS
LUBRICANTS
METHANE
MINERAL OILS
NATURAL GAS
PETROL
PETROLEUM
PETROLEUM ENGINEERING
PETROLEUM INDUSTRY
PETROLEUM PRODUCTS

08.11.06<CONT>

    PETROLEUM REFINERIES
    SHALE OIL

08.12

CHEMICAL INDUSTRY.

08.12.01

    CHEMICAL INDUSTRY
    PETROCHEMICAL INDUSTRY

08.12.02

    CHEMICAL ANALYSIS
    CHEMICAL ENGINEERING
    CHEMISTRY
    ORGANIC CHEMISTRY
    PETROCHEMISTRY

08.12.03

    COATING
    COOLING
    CORROSION
    DEHYDRATION
    DISTILLING
    DRYING
    EVAPORATION
    FREEZING
    HEATING
    IRRADIATION
    PLATING
    REFINING
    REFRIGERATION

08.12.04

    ACIDS
    ALCOHOL
    AMMONIA
    CALCIUM
    CAUSTIC SODA
    CHEMICALS
    CHLORINE
    FLUORINE
    HYDROGEN
    MAGNESIUM
    NITRATES
    NITROGEN
    NITROGEN OXIDES
    OXYGEN
    OZONE
    PETROCHEMICALS
    PHOSPHATES
    PHOSPHORUS
    POLYMERS

08.12.04<CONT>

    POTASH
    POTASSIUM
    SALT
    SILICON
    SODA
    SODIUM
    SULPHATES
    SULPHUR
    SULPHUR DIOXIDE
    UREA

08.12.05

    CHEMICAL FERTILIZERS
    FERTILIZER INDUSTRY
    FERTILIZERS
    FUNGICIDES
    HERBICIDES
    INSECTICIDES
    PESTICIDE RESIDUES
    PESTICIDES

08.12.06

    PHARMACEUTICAL INDUSTRY
    PHARMACEUTICALS

08.12.07

    PLASTICS
    PLASTICS INDUSTRY
    POLYESTER

08.12.08

    ABRASIVES
    ADHESIVES
    CLEANING AGENTS
    COSMETICS
    DETERGENTS
    EXPLOSIVES
    PAINTS AND VARNISHES
    PERFUMES
    SOAP
    SOLVENTS
    TOILET PREPARATIONS
    WAX

08.13

MINING.

08.13.00

    ALUMINIUM ORE
      USE: BAUXITE
    BAUXITE
    COAL MINING
    COPPER ORE
    DEEP SEA MINING

08.13.00<CONT>
DIAMOND
IRON ORE
MINERALS
MINES
MINING
MINING ENGINEERING
ORES
  USE: MINERALS
PETROLEUM EXTRACTION
PRECIOUS STONES

08.14

METALWORKING INDUSTRY.

08.14.01
ALUMINIUM INDUSTRY
BOILERMAKING
IRON AND STEEL INDUSTRY
METAL PRODUCTS
METALWORKING INDUSTRY
SHEET-METAL WORKING
STEEL INDUSTRY
  USE: IRON AND STEEL INDUSTRY

08.14.02
ALLOYS
ALUMINIUM
CADMIUM
CHROMIUM
COBALT
COPPER
GOLD
IRON
LEAD
MANGANESE
MERCURY
METALS
NICKEL
NON-FERROUS METALS
PLATINUM
PLUTONIUM
PRECIOUS METALS
SILVER
STEEL
TIN
TITANIUM
TUNGSTEN
URANIUM
ZINC

08.14.03
FORGING

08.14.03<CONT>
MACHINING
METAL CASTING
METALLURGY
ROLLING
WELDING

08.14.04
CABLES
CASTINGS
METAL SCRAPS
METAL SHEETS
PIPES
TIN PLATE
WIRE

08.14.05
DIES AND JIGS
HAND TOOLS
MACHINE TOOL INDUSTRY
MACHINE TOOLS
TOOLS

08.14.06
BUILDING MACHINERY
CONSTRUCTION EQUIPMENT
  USE: BUILDING MACHINERY
DIESEL ENGINES
EARTHMOVING MACHINERY
ENGINES
JET ENGINES
MACHINERY
MACHINERY INDUSTRY
MOTORS
  USE: ENGINES
OFFICE MACHINES
PETROL ENGINES
STEAM ENGINES
TURBINES

08.14.07
AEROSPACE INDUSTRY
AIRCRAFT INDUSTRY
ASSEMBLY LINES
AUTOMOBILE INDUSTRY
MOTOR VEHICLE INDUSTRY
SHIPBUILDING

08.14.08
ACOUSTICS
INSTRUMENTATION INDUSTRY
MEASURING INSTRUMENTS
OPTICAL INDUSTRY
OPTICAL INSTRUMENTS

08.14.08<CONT>
   OPTICS
   PRECISION INSTRUMENTS
   WATCHMAKING INDUSTRY

08.15

ELECTRONICS. ELECTRICAL EQUIPMENT.

08.15.01
   ELECTRICAL MACHINERY INDUSTRY
   ELECTRONIC ENGINEERING
   ELECTRONICS
   ELECTRONICS INDUSTRY

08.15.02
   COMPUTER PROGRAMMES
   COMPUTERS
   ELECTRIC APPLIANCES
   ELECTRIC LAMPS
   ELECTRIC LIGHTING
   ELECTRIC MOTORS
   ELECTRICAL EQUIPMENT
   ELECTRICAL MACHINERY
   ELECTRONIC COMPUTERS
      USE: COMPUTERS
   ELECTRONIC EQUIPMENT
   ELECTRONIC TUBES
   HARDWARE
      USE: ELECTRONIC EQUIPMENT
   HOUSEHOLD APPLIANCES
   HOUSEHOLD GOODS
      USE: HOUSEHOLD APPLIANCES
   PROJECTION EQUIPMENT
   RADAR
   SOFTWARE
      USE: COMPUTER PROGRAMMES
   TRANSISTORS

08.16

COMMUNICATION INDUSTRY.

08.16.00
   BOOK INDUSTRY
   BOOKSELLING
   BROADCASTING
   COMMUNICATION ENGINEERING
   COMMUNICATION INDUSTRY
   COMMUNICATION SATELLITES
   FILM INDUSTRY
   POSTAL SERVICES
   PRINTING INDUSTRY
   PUBLISHING
   RADIO RECEIVERS
   RECORD INDUSTRY
   TELECOMMUNICATION INDUSTRY

08.16.00<CONT>
   TELEGRAPH
   TELEPHONE
   TELEVISION RECEIVERS
   TELEX

09.

TRADE.

09.01

DEMAND. MARKET. CONSUMPTION.

09.01.01

BARTER
DEMAND
SERVICE INDUSTRY
SUPPLY
SUPPLY AND DEMAND
TERTIARY SECTOR
  USE: SERVICE INDUSTRY
TRADE

09.01.02

BLACK MARKET
COMMODITY MARKET
COMPETITION
DOMESTIC MARKET
MARKET
MARKET PLANNING
MARKET STABILIZATION
UNFAIR COMPETITION

09.01.03

CONSUMER BEHAVIOUR
CONSUMER DEMAND
CONSUMER EXPENDITURES
CONSUMER GOODS
CONSUMER PROTECTION
CONSUMERS
CONSUMPTION
CONSUMPTION FUNCTIONS
CONSUMPTION PER CAPITA
DOMESTIC CONSUMPTION
DURABLE GOODS

09.02

PRICES.

09.02.00

ADMINISTERED PRICES
COMMODITY PRICES
CONSUMER PRICES
PRICE CONTROL
PRICE INDEX
PRICE LIST
PRICE POLICY
PRICE STABILIZATION
PRICE SUPPORT
PRICES
RETAIL PRICES
WHOLESALE PRICES

09.03

MARKETING.

09.03.01

ACCESS TO MARKET
CONSUMERS COOPERATIVES
COOPERATIVE MARKETING
MARKET STUDIES
MARKETING
MARKETING BOARDS
MARKETING COOPERATIVES
RETAIL MARKETING
SALES PROMOTION
  USE: MARKETING
SELLING
  USE: MARKETING
WHOLESALE MARKETING

09.03.02

BUYING
  USE: PURCHASING
CATERING
HIRE PURCHASE
PURCHASING
SALES
SUPPLIERS
TURNOVER

09.03.03

INVENTORIES
STOCKS
STORAGE
STORAGE CAPACITY
WAREHOUSES

09.03.04

ADVERTISING
PUBLIC RELATIONS
TRADE MARKS

09.03.05

EXHIBITIONS
TRADE FAIRS

09.04

DOMESTIC TRADE.

09.04.01

DISTRIBUTION
DISTRIBUTION COSTS
DISTRIBUTION NETWORK
DOMESTIC TRADE
HOME TRADE
  USE: DOMESTIC TRADE
INLAND TRADE
  USE: DOMESTIC TRADE

09.04.02

COMMERCIAL POLICY

09.04.03

COMMERCIAL BANKS

09.04.03<CONT>
    COMMERCIAL CREDIT
    COMMERCIAL ENTERPRISES

09.04.04
    RETAIL TRADE
    SHOPS
    SUPERMARKETS
    WHOLESALE TRADE

09.04.05
    HOTEL INDUSTRY
    TOURISM
    TRAVELS

09.05
INTERNATIONAL TRADE.

09.05.01
    FOREIGN TRADE
    INTERNATIONAL TRADE
    WORLD TRADE
      USE: INTERNATIONAL TRADE

09.05.02
    BUFFER STOCKS
    COMMODITY AGREEMENTS
    COMMON FUND
    EAST-WEST TRADE
    ECONOMIC AGREEMENTS
    TRADE AGREEMENTS
    TRADE NEGOTIATIONS
    TRADE RELATIONS

09.05.03
    BALANCE OF TRADE
    COMPARATIVE ADVANTAGE
    INTERNATIONAL DIVISION OF LABOUR
    INTERNATIONAL MARKET
    TERMS OF TRADE
    TRADE VOLUME

09.05.04
    IMPORT SUBSTITUTION
    IMPORT VOLUME
    IMPORTS

09.05.05
    EXPORT CREDIT
    EXPORT DIVERSIFICATION
    EXPORT EARNINGS
    EXPORT FINANCING
    EXPORT SUBSIDIES
    EXPORT VALUE
    EXPORT VOLUME
    EXPORTS
    REEXPORT

09.05.06
    EXPORT PLANNING

09.05.06<CONT>
    EXPORT PROMOTION
    IMPORT PROMOTION
    TRADE DEVELOPMENT
    TRADE MISSIONS
    TRADE POLICY
    TRADE PROMOTION

09.05.07
    BOYCOTT
    DUMPING
    EMBARGO
    EXPORT RESTRICTIONS
    IMPORT RESTRICTIONS
    PROTECTIONISM
    PROTECTIONIST MEASURES
    QUOTA SYSTEM
    RESTRICTIVE BUSINESS PRACTICES
    TRADE BARRIERS
    TRADE LIBERALIZATION

09.05.08
    CUSTOMS
    CUSTOMS POLICY
      USE: TARIFF POLICY
    CUSTOMS UNION
    FREE PORTS
    FREE TRADE AREA
    GENERAL SYSTEM OF PREFERENCES
    PREFERENTIAL TARIFFS
    TARIFF AGREEMENTS
    TARIFF NEGOTIATIONS
    TARIFF POLICY
    TARIFF REDUCTIONS
    TARIFF REFORMS
    TARIFFS

09.05.09
    DOUBLE TAXATION
    TAX AGREEMENTS

10.

TRANSPORT.

10.01

TRANSPORT ECONOMICS.

10.01.00

COLLECTIVE TRANSPORT
    USE: PUBLIC TRANSPORT
PUBLIC TRANSPORT
TRANSPORT
TRANSPORT ECONOMICS
TRANSPORT PLANNING
TRANSPORT POLICY
TRANSPORTATION
    USE: TRANSPORT

10.02

GOODS. PASSENGERS.

10.02.00

CARRIERS
GOODS
PASSENGERS
PEDESTRIANS

10.03

TRANSPORT INFRASTRUCTURE.

10.03.00

AIRPORTS
AUTOMOBILE SERVICE
BRIDGES
CANALS
HARBOURS
    USE: PORTS
INLAND WATERWAYS
MOTORWAYS
PIPELINES
PORTS
RAILWAY NETWORK
RAILWAYS
ROAD CONSTRUCTION
ROAD NETWORK
ROADS
STATIONS
TRANSPORT INFRASTRUCTURE
TUNNELS
WATERWAYS

10.04

MEANS OF TRANSPORT.

10.04.00

AIRCRAFT
AUTOMOBILES
BICYCLES
BOATS
    USE: SHIPS
BUSES

10.04.00 \<CONT\>

CARGO SHIPS
HELICOPTERS
LOCOMOTIVES
MEANS OF TRANSPORT
MOTOR CARS
    USE: AUTOMOBILES
MOTOR VEHICLES
MOTORCYCLES
NON-MOTORIZED TRANSPORT
ROLLING STOCK
SHIPS
TANKERS
TRAINS
TRANSPORT EQUIPMENT
TRUCKS

10.05

MODES OF TRANSPORTATION.

10.05.00

AIR TRANSPORT
FLAGS OF CONVENIENCE
INLAND NAVIGATION
    USE: INLAND WATER TRANSPORT
INLAND WATER TRANSPORT
MARITIME QUESTIONS
MARITIME TRANSPORT
    USE: SEA TRANSPORT
MERCHANT FLEET
    USE: MERCHANT MARINE
MERCHANT MARINE
MODES OF TRANSPORTATION
MULTIMODAL TRANSPORT
PIPELINE TRANSPORT
RAILWAY TRANSPORT
ROAD TRANSPORT
SEA TRANSPORT
SHIPOWNERS
SHIPPING
    USE: SEA TRANSPORT

10.06

LOADING. PACKAGING.

10.06.00

BAGS
BOXES
CARGO
CONTAINERS
DELIVERY
FREIGHT FORWARDING
HANDLING
LABELLING

10.06.00<CONT>
  LOADING
  MATERIALS HANDLING
    USE: HANDLING
  PACKAGING
  TONNAGE
  TRANSPORT CONTAINERS

10.07

INTERNATIONAL TRANSPORT. URBAN TRANSPORT.

10.07.00
  INLAND TRANSPORT
  INTERNATIONAL TRANSPORT
  TRANSIT
  URBAN TRANSPORT

10.08

TRAFFIC.

10.08.00
  AIR TRAFFIC
  RAILWAY TRAFFIC
  ROAD SAFETY
  ROAD TRAFFIC
  SEA TRAFFIC
  TRAFFIC
  TRAFFIC CONTROL
  URBAN TRAFFIC

10.09

FREIGHT.

10.09.00
  FREIGHT
  FREIGHT MARKET
  PASSENGER RATE
  TRANSPORT PRICE
    USE: FREIGHT

11.

PUBLIC FINANCE. BANKING. INTERNATIONAL MONETARY RELATIONS.

11.01

PUBLIC FINANCE. TAXATION.

11.01.01
  BUDGETARY POLICY
  BUDGETARY RESOURCES
  LOCAL FINANCE
  NATIONAL BUDGET
  PUBLIC ACCOUNTING
  PUBLIC BORROWING
  PUBLIC DEBT
  PUBLIC EXPENDITURES
  PUBLIC FINANCE
  STATE AID
  STATE PARTICIPATION

11.01.02
  CAPITAL TAX
  CONSUMPTION TAX
  CORPORATION TAX
  FISCAL POLICY
  IMPORT TAX
  INCOME TAX
  LAND TAX
  LOCAL TAXES
  PAYROLL TAX
  SALES TAX
    USE: CONSUMPTION TAX
  TAX COLLECTION
  TAX DEDUCTION
  TAX EVASION
  TAX EXEMPTION
  TAX HAVENS
  TAX INCENTIVES
  TAX REFORMS
  TAX REVENUES
  TAX SYSTEMS
  TAXATION
  TAXES
  TAXPAYERS
  VALUE ADDED TAX

11.02

CURRENCIES. FINANCING.

11.02.01
  CURRENCIES
  DEFLATION
  DEVALUATION
  INFLATION

11.02.01<CONT>

LIQUIDITY
LOCAL CURRENCY
MONETARY CIRCULATION
MONETARY CORRECTION
MONETARY POLICY
MONETARY SYSTEMS
MONEY
   USE: CURRENCIES
MONEY SUPPLY

11.02.02

BANKING
BANKING SYSTEMS
BANKS
BORROWING
CENTRAL BANKS
CONSUMER CREDIT
CREDIT
CREDIT CONTROL
   USE: CREDIT POLICY
CREDIT COOPERATIVES
CREDIT POLICY
CREDIT SYSTEMS
CREDIT UNIONS
   USE: CREDIT COOPERATIVES
DEBT
DEBT BURDEN
   USE: INDEBTEDNESS
DEBT CONSOLIDATION
DEBT RELIEF
DEBT REPAYMENT
DEVELOPMENT BANKS
FINANCIAL INSTITUTIONS
INDEBTEDNESS
INSTALMENT CREDIT
   USE: CONSUMER CREDIT
LOANS
MORTGAGES
PENSION FUNDS
SAVINGS BANKS
SUBSIDIES

11.02.03

ACCIDENT INSURANCE
CREDIT INSURANCE
EXPORT INSURANCE
FIRE INSURANCE
INSURANCE
LIFE INSURANCE
REINSURANCE

11.02.04

COMPENSATORY FINANCING
FINANCIAL ASPECTS
FINANCIAL MANAGEMENT
FINANCIAL POLICY
FINANCIAL STATISTICS
FINANCIAL TERMS
FINANCING
FINANCING PROGRAMMES

11.02.05

AMORTIZATION
CAPITAL
CAPITAL CONCENTRATION
CAPITAL DEPRECIATION
CAPITAL FORMATION
CAPITAL NEEDS
   USE: FINANCIAL NEEDS
CAPITAL RESOURCES
   USE: FINANCIAL RESOURCES
DEFICIT
DEFICIT FINANCING
EXPENDITURES
FINANCIAL NEEDS
FINANCIAL RESOURCES
HOARDING
PRODUCTION GOODS
SAVINGS
SELF-FINANCING

11.02.06

ABSORPTIVE CAPACITY
CAPITAL INVESTMENTS
   USE: INVESTMENTS
INVESTMENT BANKS
INVESTMENT GUARANTEES
INVESTMENT INSURANCE
   USE: INVESTMENT GUARANTEES
INVESTMENT POLICY
INVESTMENT PROMOTION
INVESTMENT REQUIREMENTS
INVESTMENTS
PREINVESTMENT SURVEYS
PRIVATE INVESTMENTS
PUBLIC INVESTMENTS
RATE OF INVESTMENT
REINVESTMENTS

11.02.07

BANK RATE
BONDS
   USE: DEBENTURES
CAPITAL MARKET
   USE: FINANCIAL MARKET

11.02.07<CONT>

- DEBENTURES
- DISCOUNT
- DIVIDENDS
    - *USE:* INVESTMENT RETURNS
- FINANCIAL MARKET
- INTEREST
- INTEREST RATE
- INVESTMENT RETURNS
- MONEY MARKET
- RENT
    - *USE:* INVESTMENT RETURNS
- ROYALTIES
- SECURITIES
- SHAREHOLDERS
- SHARES
- STOCK EXCHANGE
    - *USE:* FINANCIAL MARKET
- TREASURY BONDS

11.03

INTERNATIONAL MONETARY SYSTEM.

11.03.01

- CLEARING AGREEMENTS
- CLEARING SYSTEMS
- CONVERTIBILITY
- EURODOLLARS
- EXCHANGE RATE
- EXTERNAL DEBT
- FOREIGN EXCHANGE
- FOREIGN EXCHANGE CONTROL
- FOREIGN EXCHANGE RESERVE
- GOLD STANDARD
- INTERNATIONAL BORROWING
- INTERNATIONAL LIQUIDITY
- INTERNATIONAL MONETARY REFORM
- INTERNATIONAL MONETARY SYSTEM
- MONETARY AGREEMENTS
- MONETARY AREAS
- MONETARY RELATIONS
- MONETARY TRANSFERS
- MONETARY UNIONS
    - *USE:* MONETARY AREAS
- NON-CONVERTIBLE CURRENCIES
- PETRODOLLARS
- SPECIAL DRAWING RIGHTS

11.03.02

- BALANCE OF PAYMENTS
- INTERNATIONAL PAYMENTS
- PAYMENT AGREEMENTS

11.03.02<CONT>

- PAYMENT SYSTEMS

11.03.03

- CAPITAL FLOWS
    - *USE:* CAPITAL MOVEMENTS
- CAPITAL MOVEMENTS
- CAPITAL TRANSFERS
- EXPORT OF CAPITAL
- FOREIGN CAPITAL
- FOREIGN INVESTMENTS
- INTERNATIONAL INVESTMENTS
- INVISIBLE TRANSACTIONS
- REPATRIATION OF CAPITAL

12.

MANAGEMENT. PRODUCTIVITY.

12.01

ENTERPRISES.

12.01.00

BUSINESS ECONOMICS
CAPITALIST ENTERPRISES
ENTERPRISES
PRODUCTION COOPERATIVES
SMALL ENTERPRISES
SOCIALIST ENTERPRISES

12.02

ECONOMIC CONCENTRATION.

12.02.00

ANTITRUST LEGISLATION
CARTELS
ECONOMIC CONCENTRATION
HORIZONTAL INTEGRATION
MERGERS
MONOPOLIES
PRODUCERS ASSOCIATIONS
SIZE OF ENTERPRISE
TRUSTS
VERTICAL INTEGRATION

12.03

ENTREPRENEURS.

12.03.00

EMPLOYERS
ENTREPRENEURS
MANAGEMENT CONSULTANTS
MANAGERS
MIDDLE MANAGEMENT
PRODUCERS
TOP MANAGEMENT

12.04

MANAGEMENT.

12.04.00

ACTIVITY ANALYSIS
BUSINESS MANAGEMENT
BUSINESS ORGANIZATION
CRITICAL PATH METHOD
    USE: NETWORK ANALYSIS
DECISION MAKING
FLOW CHART
LINEAR PROGRAMMING
MANAGEMENT
MANAGEMENT BY OBJECTIVES
MANAGEMENT DEVELOPMENT
MANAGEMENT INFORMATION SYSTEM
MANAGEMENT TECHNIQUES

12.04.00<CONT>

NETWORK ANALYSIS
OPERATIONAL RESEARCH
PERT
    USE: NETWORK ANALYSIS
PROGRAMME PLANNING
RATIONALIZATION
SCIENTIFIC MANAGEMENT
SELF-MANAGEMENT
SYSTEMS DESIGN

12.05

EQUIPMENT.

12.05.00

EQUIPMENT
EQUIPMENT MANAGEMENT
MAINTENANCE AND REPAIR
MECHANIZATION
OBSOLETE EQUIPMENT
SECOND HAND EQUIPMENT
SPARE PARTS

12.06

TECHNOLOGY.

12.06.00

ALTERNATIVE TECHNOLOGY
APPROPRIATE TECHNOLOGY
CAPITAL INTENSITY
CHOICE OF TECHNOLOGY
CIVIL ENGINEERING
DIFFUSION OF INNOVATIONS
ENGINEERING
ENGINEERING DESIGN
INNOVATIONS
INTERMEDIATE TECHNOLOGY
INVENTIONS
INVENTORS
KNOW HOW
LABOUR INTENSITY
SCIENTIFIC DISCOVERIES
TECHNICAL ASPECTS
TECHNICAL PROGRESS
    USE: TECHNOLOGICAL CHANGE
TECHNIQUE
    USE: TECHNOLOGY
TECHNOLOGICAL CHANGE
TECHNOLOGICAL FORECASTING
TECHNOLOGICAL OBSOLESCENCE
TECHNOLOGY
TECHNOLOGY TRANSFER
TRADITIONAL TECHNOLOGY

12.07

PRODUCTION. PRODUCTIVITY.

12.07.01

MASS PRODUCTION
MEANS OF PRODUCTION
MODES OF PRODUCTION
OVERPRODUCTION
PRODUCTION
PRODUCTION CAPACITY
PRODUCTION DIVERSIFICATION
PRODUCTION FACTORS
PRODUCTION FUNCTIONS
PRODUCTION INCREASE
PRODUCTION PLANNING
PRODUCTION SPECIALIZATION
PRODUCTION STATISTICS

12.07.02

APPELLATION OF ORIGIN
AUTOMATIC CONTROL
AUTOMATION
CONTRACTING
PROCESSING
PRODUCTION CONTROL
PRODUCTION STANDARDS
PRODUCTION TARGETS
QUALITY CONTROL
QUALITY STANDARDS
RECOVERY
REPROCESSING
SPECIFICATIONS
STANDARDIZATION
STANDARDS
SUBCONTRACTING

12.07.03

CAPITAL-LABOUR RATIO
CAPITAL-OUTPUT RATIO
EFFICIENCY
PRODUCTIVITY
PRODUCTIVITY POLICY

12.08

PRODUCTS. PRODUCT DEVELOPMENT.

12.08.01

BY-PRODUCTS
COMMODITIES
NATURAL PRODUCTS
NEW PRODUCTS
PRIMARY PRODUCTS
    USE: COMMODITIES
PRODUCTS

12.08.01<CONT>

RAW MATERIALS
SUBSTITUTE PRODUCTS
SURPLUSES
WASTES

12.08.02

CHOICE OF PRODUCTS
COMPETITIVE PRODUCTS
INDUSTRIAL ESPIONAGE
PRODUCT DESIGN
PRODUCT DEVELOPMENT
PROTOTYPES

12.09

COST ACCOUNTING. PROFITS.

12.09.00

ACCOUNTING
AUDITING
BANKRUPTCY
BUDGET
BUDGETING
BUDGETING METHODS
CAPITAL COSTS
CAPITAL EXPENDITURES
    USE: CAPITAL COSTS
CAPITAL GAINS
CASH FLOW
CASH INCOME
    USE: CASH FLOW
COST ACCOUNTING
COST ANALYSIS
COST-BENEFIT ANALYSIS
COSTS
ECONOMY OF SCALE
EQUIPMENT COSTS
FINANCIAL LOSS
LABOUR COSTS
OVERHEAD COSTS
PRICING
PRODUCTION COSTS
PROFITABILITY
PROFITS
VALUE ADDED
WORKING CAPITAL

13.

LABOUR.

13.01

HUMAN RESOURCES.

13.01.01
LABOUR
LABOUR POLICY

13.01.02
EMPLOYMENT OPPORTUNITIES
HUMAN RESOURCES
LABOUR FORCE
  USE: MANPOWER
LABOUR MARKET
LABOUR REQUIREMENTS
  USE: MANPOWER NEEDS
LABOUR SHORTAGE
LABOUR SUPPLY
MANPOWER
MANPOWER NEEDS
OVEREMPLOYMENT
  USE: LABOUR SHORTAGE
UNEMPLOYED

13.01.03
CYCLICAL UNEMPLOYMENT
DISGUISED UNEMPLOYMENT
EMPLOYMENT
EMPLOYMENT CREATION
EMPLOYMENT PLANNING
  USE: MANPOWER PLANNING
EMPLOYMENT POLICY
EMPLOYMENT SECURITY
FULL EMPLOYMENT
MANPOWER PLANNING
MANPOWER POLICY
  USE: EMPLOYMENT POLICY
OCCUPATIONAL STRUCTURE
PART TIME EMPLOYMENT
SEASONAL UNEMPLOYMENT
STRUCTURAL UNEMPLOYMENT
TECHNICAL UNEMPLOYMENT
TEMPORARY EMPLOYMENT
UNDEREMPLOYMENT
UNEMPLOYMENT
YOUTH UNEMPLOYMENT

13.02

EMPLOYMENT SERVICES. OCCUPATIONAL QUALIFICATION. PERSONNEL MANAGEMENT.

13.02.01
CONTRACT LABOUR
CRAFTSMANSHIP
DUAL JOBHOLDING
EMPLOYMENT SERVICES

13.02.01<CONT>
JOB CLASSIFICATION
JOB DESCRIPTION
JOB EVALUATION
JOB REQUIREMENTS
JOB SEARCHING
JOB SEEKERS
LABOUR CONTRACT
MANPOWER SERVICES
  USE: EMPLOYMENT SERVICES
OCCUPATIONAL CHOICE
OCCUPATIONAL MOBILITY
OCCUPATIONAL QUALIFICATION
PHYSICAL CAPACITY
PLACEMENT SERVICES
  USE: EMPLOYMENT SERVICES
PROBATION PERIOD
RECRUITMENT
RIGHT TO WORK
SERVICE CERTIFICATE
VOCATIONAL CHOICE
  USE: OCCUPATIONAL CHOICE
WORK PERMIT

13.02.02
ADVANCEMENT
  USE: PROMOTION
DEMOTION
LABOUR INSPECTION
LABOUR PRODUCTIVITY
PERSONNEL ADMINISTRATION
  USE: PERSONNEL MANAGEMENT
PERSONNEL MANAGEMENT
PROMOTION
STAFF
STAFF REGULATION
STANDARD PERFORMANCE
WORKERS ADAPTATION

13.03

WORKING CONDITIONS.

13.03.01
ERGONOMICS
HUMANIZATION OF WORK
INDUSTRIAL PSYCHOLOGY
INDUSTRIAL SOCIOLOGY
LABOUR STANDARDS
TIME STUDY
  USE: WORK STUDY
WORK ENVIRONMENT
WORK ORGANIZATION
WORK RULES

13.03.01<CONT>

WORK STUDY

WORKING CONDITIONS

13.03.02

ASSEMBLY-LINE WORK

GROUP WORK

PHYSICAL WORK

TEAM WORK

WORK AT HOME

13.03.03

ARRANGEMENT OF WORKING TIME

CONTINUOUS WORKING DAY

FLEXIBLE HOURS OF WORK

FULL TIME

HOURS OF WORK

NIGHT WORK

OVERTIME

PART TIME

REST PERIOD

SHIFT WORK

TIME BUDGET

WEEKLY REST

WORKING LIFE

13.03.04

FATIGUE

JOB SATISFACTION

MENTAL STRESS

OCCUPATIONAL SATISFACTION
USE: JOB SATISFACTION

REST

13.04

OCCUPATIONAL SAFETY.

13.04.00

ACCIDENT PREVENTION
USE: OCCUPATIONAL SAFETY

OCCUPATIONAL ACCIDENTS

OCCUPATIONAL DISEASES

OCCUPATIONAL HYGIENE

OCCUPATIONAL MEDICINE

OCCUPATIONAL SAFETY

SAFETY DEVICES

STRESS-RELATED DISEASES
USE: OCCUPATIONAL DISEASES

13.05

DISMISSAL. LABOUR MOBILITY.

13.05.00

ABSENTEEISM

DISCHARGE
USE: DISMISSAL

DISMISSAL

DISPLACEMENT
USE: LABOUR MOBILITY

13.05.00<CONT>

EARLY RETIREMENT

JOB DISLOCATION

JOB ROTATION
USE: REASSIGNMENT

LABOUR MOBILITY

LABOUR REDUNDANCY

LAYOFF

LEAVE OF ABSENCE

MATERNITY LEAVE

PLANT SHUTDOWN

REASSIGNMENT

RESIGNATION

RETIREMENT

VOCATIONAL REHABILITATION

13.06

LABOUR RELATIONS.

13.06.00

COLLECTIVE AGREEMENTS

COLLECTIVE BARGAINING

EMPLOYEE ASSOCIATIONS

EMPLOYEES ATTITUDES

EMPLOYERS ATTITUDES
USE: MANAGEMENT ATTITUDES

EMPLOYERS ORGANIZATIONS

INDUSTRIAL RELATIONS
USE: LABOUR RELATIONS

JOINT MANAGEMENT
USE: WORKERS PARTICIPATION

LABOUR DISPUTES

LABOUR MOVEMENTS

LABOUR RELATIONS

LABOUR UNIONS
USE: TRADE UNIONS

LABOUR-MANAGEMENT RELATIONS
USE: LABOUR RELATIONS

LOCKOUTS

MANAGEMENT ATTITUDES

OCCUPATIONAL ORGANIZATIONS

PROFESSIONAL ASSOCIATIONS
USE: OCCUPATIONAL ORGANIZATIONS

RIGHT TO STRIKE

SHOP STEWARDS

STRIKERS

STRIKES

TRADE UNIONISM

TRADE UNIONS

WILDCAT STRIKES

WORKERS PARTICIPATION

WORKERS REPRESENTATION

13.06.00<CONT>

WORKERS SELF-MANAGEMENT

13.07

WAGES. WAGE INCENTIVES.

13.07.00

BONUSES
    USE: WAGE INCENTIVES
COMPENSATION
    USE: WAGES
EQUAL PAY
FRINGE BENEFITS
GUARANTEED WAGE
    USE: MINIMUM WAGE
MINIMUM WAGE
MOVING EXPENSES
PAYMENT BY RESULT
PIECE WORK
    USE: PAYMENT BY RESULT
PROFIT SHARING
SALARY
    USE: WAGES
SENIORITY BENEFITS
SEVERANCE PAY
WAGE DETERMINATION
WAGE EARNERS
WAGE INCENTIVES
WAGE PAYMENT SYSTEMS
WAGE POLICY
WAGE RATE
WAGE SCALE
WAGES
WORKERS STOCK OWNERSHIP

13.08

LEISURE.

13.08.00

HOLIDAYS
LEISURE
SPORT
SPORTS FACILITIES

13.09

OCCUPATIONS.

13.09.01

OCCUPATIONS

13.09.02

AUXILIARY WORKERS
CASUAL WORKERS
CHILD LABOUR
EMPLOYEES
EXPATRIATE WORKERS
    USE: FOREIGN WORKERS
FEMALE MANPOWER
FOREIGN WORKERS

13.09.02<CONT>

HANDICAPPED WORKERS
INDEPENDENT WORKERS
    USE: SELF-EMPLOYED
MANUAL WORKERS
MIGRANT WORKERS
OLDER WORKERS
SEASONAL WORKERS
SELF-EMPLOYED
WOMEN WORKERS
    USE: FEMALE MANPOWER
WORKERS
YOUNG WORKERS

13.09.03

APPRENTICES
FOREMEN
    USE: SUPERVISORS
MASTERCRAFTSMEN
PROFESSIONALS
SCIENTIFIC PERSONNEL
SEMI-SKILLED WORKERS
SKILLED WORKERS
SUPERVISORS
TECHNICAL PERSONNEL
TECHNICIANS
UNSKILLED WORKERS

13.09.04

CIVIL SERVANTS
PUBLIC SERVANTS

13.09.05

AGRICULTURAL WORKERS
FARMERS
FISHERMEN
RURAL WORKERS

13.09.06

CONSTRUCTION WORKERS
CRAFTSMEN
ELECTRICIANS
FACTORY WORKERS
    USE: INDUSTRIAL WORKERS
INDUSTRIAL WORKERS
METALWORKERS
MINERS
TEXTILE WORKERS

13.09.07

CLERICAL WORKERS
    USE: OFFICE WORKERS
DEALERS
DOMESTIC WORKERS
OFFICE WORKERS
SALESMEN
    USE: VENDORS

13.09.07<CONT>

TRADERS
USE: DEALERS

VENDORS

13.09.08

DOCKERS

PILOTS

SEAFARERS

TRANSPORT WORKERS

13.09.09

ACCOUNTANTS

ACTUARIES

AGRONOMISTS

ANTHROPOLOGISTS

ARCHITECTS

ARTISTS

BIOLOGISTS

BOTANISTS

CHEMISTS

DEMOGRAPHERS

DOCUMENTALISTS

DRAUGHTSMEN

ECONOMISTS

ENGINEERS

GEOGRAPHERS

GEOLOGISTS

INSTRUCTORS

JOURNALISTS

JUDGES

LAWYERS

LIBRARIANS

LINGUISTS

MATHEMATICIANS

PERFORMERS

PHYSICISTS

POLITICAL SCIENTISTS

PROFESSORS
USE: TEACHERS

PSYCHOLOGISTS

RESEARCH WORKERS

SCIENTIFIC RESEARCHERS
USE: RESEARCH WORKERS

SCIENTISTS

SOCIOLOGISTS

STATISTICIANS

SURVEYORS

TEACHERS

TRANSLATORS

13.09.09<CONT>

WRITERS

13.09.10

AUXILIARY HEALTH WORKERS
USE: PARAMEDICAL PERSONNEL

BAREFOOT DOCTORS

DENTISTS

MEDICAL DOCTORS
USE: PHYSICIANS

MEDICAL PERSONNEL

MIDWIVES

NURSES

PARAMEDICAL PERSONNEL

PEDIATRICIANS

PHARMACISTS

PHYSICIANS

SOCIAL WORKERS

VETERINARIANS

ZOOTECHNICIANS

276

14.

DEMOGRAPHY. POPULATION.

14.01

POPULATION DYNAMICS.

14.01.01

DEMOGRAPHIC ANALYSIS
DEMOGRAPHY
POPULATION CENSUSES
VITAL STATISTICS

14.01.02

OVERPOPULATION
POPULATION
POPULATION DECLINE
POPULATION DENSITY
POPULATION DYNAMICS
POPULATION INCREASE
POPULATION OPTIMUM
POPULATION POLICY
POPULATION SIZE
POPULATION THEORY
STATIONARY POPULATION

14.02

AGE GROUPS.

14.02.01

AGE-SEX DISTRIBUTION
POPULATION COMPOSITION

14.02.02

ADOLESCENCE
   USE: YOUTH
ADULTS
AGE
AGE DISTRIBUTION
AGE GROUPS
AGED
AGEING
CHILDHOOD
CHILDREN
EARLY CHILDHOOD
GENERATIONS
INFANTS
MINIMUM AGE
OLD AGE
OLDER PEOPLE
   USE: AGED
SCHOOL AGE POPULATION
YOUTH

14.02.03

FEMALES
MALES
MEN

14.02.03<CONT>

SEX
SEX DISTRIBUTION
SEXUAL BEHAVIOUR
SEXUALITY
WOMEN

14.02.04

CLAN
DEPENDENCY BURDEN
FAMILY
FAMILY DISINTEGRATION
FAMILY ENVIRONMENT
FAMILY SIZE
FATHER
GENEALOGY
KINSHIP
MOTHER
PARENTS

14.02.05

CELIBACY
DIVORCE
HUSBAND
MARITAL STATUS
MARRIAGE
MARRIED PERSONS
NUPTIALITY
POLYANDRY
POLYGAMY
WIFE

14.03

ETHNIC GROUPS.

14.03.01

ABORIGINAL POPULATION
ETHNIC FACTORS
ETHNIC GROUPS
ETHNIC MINORITIES
ETHNICITY
GENOCIDE
INDIGENOUS POPULATION
INTERETHNIC RELATIONS
NATIVE RESERVATION
NATIVES
   USE: INDIGENOUS POPULATION
TRIBE

14.03.02

AFGHAN
AFRICAN
ALBANIAN
ALGERIAN

AMERICAN
ANGOLAN
ARABS
ARGENTINIAN
ASIAN
AUSTRALIAN
AUSTRIAN
BAHAMIAN
BARBADIAN
BELGIAN
BENGALI
BENINESE
BHUTANESE
BOLIVIAN
BRAZILIAN
BRITISH
BULGARIAN
BURMESE
BYELORUSSIAN
CAMEROONIAN
CANADIAN
CAPE VERDEAN
CHILEAN
CHINESE
COLOMBIAN
COMORIAN
CONGOLESE
COSTA RICAN
CUBAN
CYPRIOT
CZECHOSLOVAK
DANISH
DOMINICAN
ECUADORIAN
EGYPTIAN
ETHIOPIAN
EUROPEAN
FILIPINO
FINNISH
FRENCH
GABONESE
GAMBIAN
GERMAN
GHANAIAN
GREEK

GUATEMALAN
GUINEAN
GUYANESE
HAITIAN
HONDURAN
HUNGARIAN
ICELANDIC
INDIAN
INDONESIAN
IRANIAN
IRAQI
IRISH
ISRAELI
ITALIAN
JAMAICAN
JAPANESE
JORDANIAN
KENYAN
KOREAN
KUWAITI
LAO
LATIN AMERICAN
LEBANESE
LIBERIAN
LIBYAN
MALAGASY
MALAWIAN
MALAYSIAN
MALDIVIAN
MALIAN
MALTESE
MAURITANIAN
MAURITIAN
MEXICAN
MONEGASQUE
MONGOLIAN
MOROCCAN
MOZAMBICAN
NAMIBIAN
NAURUAN
NEPALESE
NETHERLANDER
NEW ZELANDER
NICARAGUAN
NIGERIAN

14.03.02<CONT>

NORTH AFRICAN

NORWEGIAN

OMANI

PAKISTANI

PANAMANIAN

PARAGUAYAN

PERUVIAN

POLISH

PORTUGUESE

PUERTO RICAN

ROMANIAN

RUSSIAN

RWANDESE

SALVADORIAN

SAMOAN

SAUDI ARABIAN

SCANDINAVIAN

SENEGALESE

SIERRA LEONEAN

SINGAPOREAN

SOMALI

SOUTH AFRICAN

SOVIET

SPANISH

SRI LANKAN

SUDANESE

SURINAMESE

SWAZI

SWEDISH

SWISS

SYRIAN

TANZANIAN

THAI

TOGOLESE

TONGAN

TUNISIAN

TURKISH

UGANDAN

UKRAINIAN

URUGUAYAN

VENEZUELAN

VIETNAMESE

WEST INDIAN

YEMENI

YUGOSLAV

14.03.02<CONT>

ZAIRIAN

ZAMBIAN

14.03.03

AMERINDIANS

ANDEAN INDIANS
USE: AMERINDIANS

BLACKS

MESTIZOS

WHITES

14.04

HABITAT. RURAL. URBAN.

14.04.01

COLLECTIVE HOUSING

COMMUNITY

COMMUNITY DEVELOPMENT

COMMUNITY RELATIONS

DISPERSED HABITAT

DWELLING
USE: HOUSING

DWELLING UNIT
USE: HOUSEHOLD

HABITAT

HOUSEHOLD

HOUSING

HOUSING CENSUSES

HOUSING COOPERATIVES

HOUSING NEEDS

HOUSING POLICY

HUMAN SETTLEMENTS

POPULATION DISTRIBUTION

SELF-HELP

SETTLEMENT PATTERN
USE: HABITAT

SQUATTERS

14.04.02

AGRICULTURAL POPULATION

LAND SETTLEMENT

RURAL

RURAL AREAS

RURAL COMMUNITIES

RURAL DEVELOPMENT

RURAL ENVIRONMENT

RURAL PLANNING

RURAL POPULATION

RURAL SOCIOLOGY

RURAL YOUTH

VILLAGES

14.04.03

CITIES
USE: TOWNS

14.04.03<CONT>

  CONURBATION
  MIDDLE-SIZED TOWNS
  NEIGHBOURHOOD
  NEW TOWNS
  SATELLITE TOWNS
  SLUMS
  SMALL TOWNS
  SUBURBAN AREAS
  SUBURBS
    USE: SUBURBAN AREAS
  TOWN CENTRE
  TOWN PLANNING
    USE: URBAN PLANNING
  TOWNS
  URBAN
  URBAN AREAS
  URBAN ATTRACTION
  URBAN COMMUNITIES
  URBAN CONCENTRATION
  URBAN DEVELOPMENT
  URBAN ENVIRONMENT
  URBAN PLANNING
  URBAN POPULATION
  URBAN RENEWAL
  URBAN SOCIOLOGY
  URBANISM
  URBANIZATION
  ZONING

14.05

FERTILITY. FAMILY PLANNING.

14.05.01

  BIRTH
  BIRTH RATE
  FERTILITY
  FERTILITY DECLINE
  PREGNANCY

14.05.02

  ABORTION
  BIRTH CONTROL
  BIRTH SPACING
  CHEMICAL CONTRACEPTIVES
  CONDOMS
  CONTRACEPTION
  CONTRACEPTIVE METHODS
  CONTRACEPTIVES
  FAMILY PLANNING
  FAMILY PLANNING AGENCIES

14.05.02<CONT>

  FAMILY PLANNING PROGRAMMES
  INTRAUTERINE DEVICES
  LEGAL ABORTION
  ORAL CONTRACEPTIVES
  VASECTOMY

14.06

MORTALITY.

14.06.00

  CAUSES OF DEATH
  DEATH
  INFANT MORTALITY
  INTRAUTERINE MORTALITY
  LIFE TABLES
  MORTALITY
  MORTALITY DECLINE
  OCCUPATIONAL MORTALITY

14.07

MIGRATIONS.

14.07.00

  BRAIN DRAIN
  COMMUTING
  EMIGRANTS
  EMIGRATION
  FOREIGNERS
  FRONTIER MIGRATIONS
  IMMIGRANTS
  IMMIGRATION
  INTERNAL MIGRATIONS
  INTERNATIONAL MIGRATIONS
  LABOUR MIGRATIONS
  MIGRANTS
  MIGRATION POLICY
  MIGRATIONS
  NOMADISM
  NOMADS
  POPULATION TRANSFERS
  REFUGEES
  RETURN MIGRATIONS
  RURAL EXODUS
    USE: RURAL MIGRATIONS
  RURAL MIGRATIONS
  SEASONAL MIGRATIONS

15.
BIOLOGY. FOOD. HEALTH.

15.01
BIOLOGY. PARASITOLOGY. BIOCHEMISTRY.

15.01.01
BACTERIOLOGY
BIOLOGY
MICROBIOLOGY
PARASITOLOGY
VIROLOGY

15.01.02
BACTERIA
MICROBES
MICROORGANISMS
PARASITES
VIRUSES

15.01.03
AMINO ACIDS
BIOCHEMISTRY
BIODEGRADATION
BIODETERIORATION
   USE: BIODEGRADATION
ENZYMES
FERMENTATION
PROTEINS
VITAMINS
YEAST

15.02
ANATOMY. GENETICS. PHYSIOLOGY.

15.02.01
ANATOMY
CYTOLOGY
GENETICS
HISTOLOGY
PHYSIOLOGY

15.02.02
ARTIFICIAL INSEMINATION
EMBRYO
FECUNDITY
FERTILIZATION
FOETUS
LIFE
PUBERTY
REPRODUCTION
SEMEN
STERILITY

15.02.03
CHROMOSOMES
GENES
GENETIC IMPROVEMENT

15.02.03<CONT>
HEREDITARY DEFECTS
HEREDITY
HYBRIDIZATION
INBREEDING
INDUCED MUTATIONS
MUTATIONS

15.02.04
BLOOD
BRAIN
CARDIOVASCULAR SYSTEM
CELLS
DIGESTIVE SYSTEM
ENDOCRINE SYSTEM
HEART
HORMONES
INTEGUMENTARY SYSTEM
LIVER
LYMPHATIC SYSTEM
METABOLISM
MUSCULOSKELETAL SYSTEM
NERVOUS SYSTEM
RESPIRATORY SYSTEM
SKIN
UROGENITAL SYSTEM

15.03

FOOD. NUTRITION.

15.03.01
COOKERY
   USE: FOOD PREPARATION
FEEDING
FOOD
FOOD ANALYSIS
FOOD CHEMISTRY
FOOD COMPOSITION
FOOD CONTAMINATION
FOOD ECONOMICS
FOOD INSPECTION
FOOD PLANNING
FOOD POLICY
FOOD PREPARATION
FOOD PRODUCTS
   USE: FOOD
FOOD RESERVES
FOOD SHORTAGE
FOOD SPOILAGE
FOOD SUPPLY
MEAL PREPARATION
   USE: FOOD PREPARATION

15.03.01<CONT>

PERISHABLE FOOD

PROTEIN RICH FOOD

15.03.02

BREAST FEEDING

CALORIE DEFICIENCY

CALORIES

CHILD REARING

DIET

FAMINE

FOOD CONSUMPTION

FOOD HYGIENE

FOOD REQUIREMENTS

FOOD STANDARDS

FOOD STATISTICS

HUMAN NUTRITION

MALNUTRITION

NUTRIENTS

NUTRITION

NUTRITION POLICY

NUTRITION RESEARCH

NUTRITIVE VALUE

PROTEIN DEFICIENCY

STARVATION
  USE: FAMINE

TOXINS

VITAMIN DEFICIENCY

15.04

MEDICINE. DISEASES.

15.04.01

ANIMAL DISEASES

DISEASES

HEALTH

MENTAL HEALTH

MORBIDITY

PATHOLOGY
  USE: DISEASES

PHYTOPATHOLOGY
  USE: PLANT DISEASES

PLANT DISEASES

PUBLIC HEALTH

15.04.02

ALLERGIES
  USE: IMMUNOLOGIC DISEASES

ASTHMA

BILHARZIASIS
  USE: SCHISTOSOMIASIS

BURNS

CANCER

CHOLERA

15.04.02<CONT>

CHRONIC DISEASES

COMMUNICABLE DISEASES
  USE: INFECTIOUS DISEASES

CONTAGIOUS DISEASES
  USE: INFECTIOUS DISEASES

DEFICIENCY DISEASES

DIABETES

DIPHTHERIA

ENDEMIC DISEASES

EPIDEMIC DISEASES
  USE: INFECTIOUS DISEASES

EYE DISEASES

FILARIASIS

FUNGUS DISEASES

IMMUNOLOGIC DISEASES

INFECTIOUS DISEASES

INTRACTABLE DISEASES

LEPROSY

MALARIA

MEASLES

MENINGITIS

MENTAL DISEASES

MOUTH DISEASES

ONCHOCERCIASIS

PARASITIC DISEASES

PLAGUE

PNEUMOCONIOSIS

PNEUMONIA

POISONING

POLIOMYELITIS

RICKETTSIAL DISEASES

RIVER BLINDNESS
  USE: ONCHOCERCIASIS

RUBELLA

SCARLET FEVER

SCHISTOSOMIASIS

SEPTICEMIA

SLEEPING SICKNESS
  USE: TRYPANOSOMIASIS

SMALLPOX

TROPICAL DISEASES

TRYPANOSOMIASIS

TUBERCULOSIS

TYPHOID

TYPHUS

VENEREAL DISEASES

WOUNDS AND INJURIES

15.04.02<CONT>
  YELLOW FEVER

15.04.03
  BLINDNESS
  DEAF-DUMBNESS
  DEAFNESS
  DISABILITY

15.04.04
  ACUPUNCTURE
  DIAGNOSIS
  DISEASE CONTROL
  DISEASE TRANSMISSION
  DISEASE VECTORS
  EPIDEMICS
  EUTHANASIA
  HEALTH CONTROL
  HOSPITALIZATION
  HYGIENE
  IMMUNIZATION
  IMMUNOLOGY
  MATERNAL AND CHILD HEALTH
  MEDICAL CARE
  MEDICAL EXAMINATION
  MEDICAL TREATMENT
    USE: MEDICAL CARE
  PRENATAL CARE
  PREVENTIVE MEDICINE
  PROPHYLAXIS
  QUARANTINE
  REHABILITATION
  VACCINATION
  WOUNDED

15.04.05
  HANDICAPPED
  MENTALLY HANDICAPPED
  PATIENTS
  PHYSICALLY HANDICAPPED

15.04.06
  CARDIOLOGY
  EPIDEMIOLOGY
  GYNAECOLOGY
  MEDICAL RESEARCH
  MEDICAL SCIENCES
  MEDICINE
  PEDIATRICS
  PSYCHIATRY
  RADIOLOGY
  SURGERY

15.04.06<CONT>
  TRADITIONAL MEDICINE
  VETERINARY MEDICINE

15.05

PHARMACOLOGY. TOXICOLOGY.

15.05.00
  ANTIBIOTICS
  DRUGS
  MEDICINAL PLANTS
  NARCOTICS
  PHARMACOLOGY
  POISONS
  SERUMS
  TOXIC METALS
  TOXIC SUBSTANCES
  TOXICITY
  VACCINES

16.

ENVIRONMENT. NATURAL RESOURCES.

16.01

ECOLOGY.

16.01.01

ANIMAL ECOLOGY
BIOLOGICAL EQUILIBRIUM
    USE: ECOLOGICAL BALANCE
ECODEVELOPMENT
ECOLOGICAL BALANCE
ECOLOGICAL RESEARCH
ECOLOGY
ECOSYSTEM STABILITY
    USE: ECOLOGICAL BALANCE
ENVIRONMENTAL BIOLOGY
    USE: ECOLOGY
HUMAN ECOLOGY
NATURAL EQUILIBRIUM
    USE: ECOLOGICAL BALANCE
PLANT ECOLOGY

16.01.02

AQUATIC ENVIRONMENT
BIOMASS
BIOSPHERE
ECOSYSTEMS
ENVIRONMENT
ENVIRONMENTAL QUALITY
HUMAN ENVIRONMENT
MARINE ENVIRONMENT
NATURAL ENVIRONMENT
    USE: PHYSICAL ENVIRONMENT
PHYSICAL ENVIRONMENT
TERRESTRIAL ENVIRONMENT

16.02

NATURAL RESOURCES.

16.02.01

EXPLOITABILITY
OVEREXPLOITATION
RESOURCES APPRAISAL
    USE: RESOURCES INVENTORY
RESOURCES DEPLETION
RESOURCES EVALUATION
RESOURCES EXPLOITATION
RESOURCES EXPLORATION
    USE: RESOURCES INVENTORY
RESOURCES INVENTORY
RESOURCES MANAGEMENT

16.02.02

ANIMAL RESOURCES
ENERGY RESOURCES
FISHERY RESOURCES
FOREST RESOURCES

16.02.02<CONT>

MARINE RESOURCES
MINERAL RESOURCES
NATURAL RESOURCES
NON-RENEWABLE RESOURCES
PETROLEUM RESOURCES
PLANT RESOURCES
POWER RESOURCES
    USE: ENERGY RESOURCES
RENEWABLE RESOURCES
SOIL RESOURCES
WATER RESOURCES

16.03

DISASTERS. POLLUTION.

16.03.01

DAMAGE
DEVASTATION
DISASTERS

16.03.02

EROSION
EXPLOSIONS
FIRES
FLOODS
FOREST FIRES
MANMADE DISASTERS
NATURAL DISASTERS
SOIL EROSION

16.03.03

INSECT PESTS
INSECTS
LOCUSTS
PESTS OF ANIMALS
PESTS OF PLANTS
RODENTS

16.03.04

ACUSTIC POLLUTION
AEROSOLS
AIR POLLUTANTS
AIR POLLUTION
ATMOSPHERIC POLLUTION
    USE: AIR POLLUTION
CHEMICAL POLLUTION
COASTAL POLLUTION
CONCENTRATION OF POLLUTANTS
    USE: POLLUTION LEVEL
CONTAMINANTS
    USE: POLLUTANTS
DANGEROUS SUBSTANCES
DESERTIFICATION
DOMESTIC WASTES

16.03.04<CONT>

ENVIRONMENTAL DEGRADATION

ENVIRONMENTAL EFFECTS

ENVIRONMENTAL IMPACT
   USE: ENVIRONMENTAL EFFECTS

ENVIRONMENTAL POLLUTION
   USE: POLLUTION

EUTROPHICATION

HARMFUL SUBSTANCES
   USE: DANGEROUS SUBSTANCES

MARINE POLLUTION

NOISE

POLLUTANT BURDEN
   USE: POLLUTION LEVEL

POLLUTANTS

POLLUTED AREAS

POLLUTION

POLLUTION LEVEL

POLLUTION SOURCES

RADIOACTIVE POLLUTION

RIVER POLLUTION

SEWAGE
   USE: WASTE WATERS

SOIL POLLUTANTS

SOIL POLLUTION

THERMAL POLLUTION

TRANSFRONTIER POLLUTION

WASTE WATERS

WATER POLLUTANTS

WATER POLLUTION

16.04

POLLUTION CONTROL. ENVIRONMENTAL ENGINEERING.

16.04.01

DAMAGE COMPENSATION

DECONTAMINATION

ENVIRONMENTAL ECONOMICS

ENVIRONMENTAL ENGINEERING

ENVIRONMENTAL MANAGEMENT

ENVIRONMENTAL MONITORING
   USE: ENVIRONMENTAL MANAGEMENT

ENVIRONMENTAL POLICY

EROSION CONTROL

FIRE CONTROL

FLOOD CONTROL

NOISE CONTROL

PEST CONTROL

POLLUTER-PAYS PRINCIPLE

POLLUTION CONTROL

POLLUTION INDEX

RADIATION PROTECTION

16.04.01<CONT>

SAFETY

WARNING DEVICES

WEATHER CONTROL

16.04.02

GARBAGE DISPOSAL
   USE: SANITATION SERVICES

SANITATION

SANITATION SERVICES

SEA DUMPING

SEWAGE DISPOSAL
   USE: SANITATION SERVICES

WASTE DISPOSAL

WASTE MANAGEMENT

WASTE RECYCLING

WASTE TREATMENT

WASTE UTILIZATION

16.05

RESOURCES CONSERVATION.

16.05.01

ANIMAL PROTECTION

ENDANGERED SPECIES

ENVIRONMENTAL PROTECTION

FISHERY CONSERVATION

FOREST CONSERVATION

GAME PROTECTION

LANDSCAPE PROTECTION

NATURE CONSERVATION

NATURE PROTECTION
   USE: NATURE CONSERVATION

PLANT PROTECTION

PROTECTED AREAS

PROTECTED RESOURCES

PROTECTED SPECIES

RESOURCES CONSERVATION

SOIL CONSERVATION

WATER CONSERVATION

WILDLIFE PROTECTION
   USE: NATURE CONSERVATION

16.05.02

BOTANICAL GARDENS

NATIONAL PARKS

NATURE RESERVES

ZOOLOGICAL GARDENS

17.

EARTH SCIENCES. SPACE SCIENCES.

17.01

METEOROLOGY.

17.01.01

ATMOSPHERIC SCIENCES
  USE: METEOROLOGY
BIOCLIMATOLOGY
CLIMATOLOGY
METEOROLOGY
METEOROLOGY SERVICES
WEATHER FORECASTS

17.01.02

AIR
  USE: ATMOSPHERE
ATMOSPHERE
BAROMETRIC PRESSURE
WEATHER

17.01.03

CYCLONES
  USE: STORMS
DROUGHT
HUMIDITY
MOISTURE
  USE: HUMIDITY
PRECIPITATIONS
RAIN
SNOW
SOLAR RADIATION
STORMS
TYPHOONS
  USE: STORMS
WIND

17.02

CLIMATE.

17.02.01

ACCLIMATIZATION
CLIMATE
CLIMATIC INFLUENCE

17.02.02

COLD SEASON
DRY SEASON
MONSOON
  USE: RAINY SEASON
RAINY SEASON
SEASONS
WARM SEASON

17.02.03

ARID ZONE
CLIMATIC REGIONS
  USE: CLIMATIC ZONES
CLIMATIC ZONES
COLD ZONE

17.02.03<CONT>

DESERT
  USE: ARID ZONE
EQUATORIAL ZONE
FRIGID ZONE
HUMID ZONE
SEMI-ARID ZONE
SUBTROPICAL ZONE
TEMPERATE ZONE
TROPICAL ZONE

17.03

GEOGRAPHY.

17.03.01

AREA STUDY
  USE: REGIONAL ANALYSIS
CULTURAL GEOGRAPHY
ECONOMIC GEOGRAPHY
GEOGRAPHY
HUMAN GEOGRAPHY
PHYSICAL GEOGRAPHY
POLITICAL GEOGRAPHY
REGIONAL ANALYSIS
REGIONAL SCIENCE
  USE: REGIONAL ANALYSIS
SPATIAL ANALYSIS

17.03.02

GEOGRAPHIC DISTRIBUTION
GEOGRAPHICAL ASPECTS

17.03.03

EAST
NORTH
SOUTH
WEST

17.03.04

COASTAL AREAS
  USE: LITTORAL ZONES
COASTS
CONTINENTAL SHELVES
CONTINENTS
DELTAS
ESTUARIES
GULFS
HILLS
ISLANDS
LAND LOCKED COUNTRIES
LITTORAL ZONES
MOUNTAINS
OASES
PAMPA
PLAINS

17.03.04<CONT>

    PLATEAUS
    PRAIRIE
    SAVANNA
    STEPPES
    STRAITS
    TUNDRA
    VALLEYS

17.04

GEOPHYSICS. GEOLOGY. SOIL SCIENCES.

17.04.01

    EARTH SCIENCES
    GEOCHEMISTRY
    GEODESY
    GEOLOGY
    GEOMORPHOLOGY
    GEOPHYSICS
    MINERALOGY
    NATURAL SCIENCES
    PHYSICS

17.04.02

    QUATERNARY
    TERTIARY

17.04.03

    EARTHQUAKES
      USE: SEISMS
    SEISMOLOGY
    SEISMS
    TIDAL WAVES
    VOLCANIC ERUPTIONS
    VULCANOLOGY

17.04.04

    GEOLOGICAL SURVEYS
    PEDOLOGY
      USE: SOIL SCIENCES
    SOIL ANALYSIS
    SOIL CHEMISTRY
    SOIL CLASSIFICATION
    SOIL PHYSICS
    SOIL SCIENCES
    SOIL SURVEYS
    SOIL TYPES
    SOILS

17.05

HYDROLOGY. WATER.

17.05.01

    HYDROGEOLOGY
    HYDROGRAPHY
    HYDROLOGY

17.05.02

    GLACIERS

17.05.02<CONT>

    HYDROLOGICAL NETWORK
    INTERNATIONAL WATERWAYS
    LAKES
    RIVER BASINS
    RIVERS
    SWAMPS

17.05.03

    DRAINAGE
    IRRIGATION
    IRRIGATION DEVELOPMENT
    IRRIGATION SYSTEMS

17.05.04

    AQUEDUCTS
    ARTIFICIAL LAKES
    DAMS
    DREDGING
    DRILLING
    HYDRAULIC ENGINEERING
    HYDRAULIC EQUIPMENT
    PUMPING PLANTS
    PUMPS
    RESERVOIRS
    WELLS

17.05.05

    DESALINIZATION
    DRINKING WATER
    FRESHWATER
    GROUNDWATER
    ICE
    SALT WATER
    WATER
    WATER CONSUMPTION
    WATER DISTRIBUTION
    WATER MANAGEMENT
    WATER QUALITY
    WATER REQUIREMENTS
    WATER STORAGE
    WATER SUPPLY
    WATER TREATMENT
    WATER UTILIZATION

17.06

OCEANOGRAPHY.

17.06.00

    ATLANTIC OCEAN
    COASTAL WATERS
    INDIAN OCEAN
    MEDITERRANEAN

17.06.00<CONT>

OCEANOGRAPHY
PACIFIC OCEAN
SEA
SEABED
TERRITORIAL WATERS
TIDES

17.07

SPACE SCIENCES.

17.07.00

ASTRONAUTICS
ASTRONOMY
OUTER SPACE
SPACE
SPACE SCIENCES

18.

SCIENCE. RESEARCH. METHODOLOGY.

18.01

RESEARCH. SCIENCE.

18.01.00

APPLIED RESEARCH
BASIC RESEARCH
RESEARCH
RESEARCH AND DEVELOPMENT
RESEARCH POLICY
RESEARCH PROGRAMMES
RESEARCH PROJECTS
SCIENCE
SCIENCE AND TECHNOLOGY POLICY
   USE: SCIENCE POLICY
SCIENCE POLICY
SCIENTIFIC COOPERATION
SCIENTIFIC PROGRESS
SCIENTIFIC RESEARCH
   USE: RESEARCH

18.02

ORGANIZATION OF RESEARCH.

18.02.00

COMPUTER CENTRES
LABORATORIES
LABORATORY EQUIPMENT
   USE: RESEARCH EQUIPMENT
ORGANIZATION OF RESEARCH
RESEARCH CENTRES
RESEARCH EQUIPMENT
RESEARCH INSTITUTES
   USE: RESEARCH CENTRES
STATISTICAL SERVICES

18.03

RESEARCH METHODS. THEORY.

18.03.00

INTEGRATED APPROACH
INTERDISCIPLINARY RESEARCH
METHODOLOGY
RESEARCH METHODS
RESEARCH RESULTS
THEORY

18.04

DATA COLLECTING.

18.04.00

AERIAL SURVEYS
CADASTRAL SURVEYS
CASE STUDIES
CENSUSES
DATA ACQUISITION
   USE: DATA COLLECTING
DATA COLLECTING

18.04.00<CONT>

DATA COMPILATION
USE: DATA COLLECTING

DETECTION
USE: OBSERVATION

FIELD ACTIVITY

FIELD RESEARCH

FIELD STUDY
USE: FIELD RESEARCH

FIELD WORK
USE: FIELD ACTIVITY

INTERVIEWS

MAIL SURVEYS

OBSERVATION

QUESTIONNAIRES

REMOTE SENSING

SAMPLE

SURVEY AREA

SURVEYS

18.05

EXPERIMENTS.

18.05.00

EXPERIMENTATION

EXPERIMENTS

18.06

MEASUREMENT.

18.06.00

ALTITUDE

DENSITY

DISTANCE

MEASUREMENT

MEASUREMENT SYSTEMS

MEASURING
USE: MEASUREMENT

METRIC SYSTEM

METROLOGY

PHYSICAL PROPERTIES

TEMPERATURE

VOLUME

WEIGHT

18.07

MAPPING.

18.07.00

ATLASES

CARTOGRAPHY
USE: MAPPING

CHARTING

CHARTS

GEOLOGICAL MAPS

MAPPING

MAPS

PHOTOGRAMMETRY

18.07.00<CONT>

SOIL MAPS

TOPOGRAPHY

18.08

MATHEMATICS. STATISTICAL ANALYSIS.

18.08.00

COMMUNICATION THEORY
USE: INFORMATION THEORY

COMPUTATION

COMPUTER SCIENCE

CYBERNETICS

DIAGRAMS

GRAPHS

INDEX NUMBERS

INFORMATICS
USE: COMPUTER SCIENCE

INFORMATION THEORY

LOGIC

MATHEMATICAL ANALYSIS

MATHEMATICAL MODELS

MATHEMATICS

MODELS

PROBABILITY

SIMULATION

STATISTICAL ANALYSIS

STATISTICAL DATA

STATISTICAL TABLES

STATISTICS

SYSTEMS ANALYSIS

SYSTEMS THEORY
USE: CYBERNETICS

18.09

COMPARISON. EVALUATION.

18.09.00

COMPARATIVE ANALYSIS

COMPARATIVE STUDY
USE: COMPARATIVE ANALYSIS

COMPARISON

ESTIMATING
USE: EVALUATION

EVALUATION

EVALUATION TECHNIQUES

TESTING

TESTS

18.10

FORECASTS. TIME FACTOR.

18.10.00

CHRONOLOGY

DURATION

FORECASTING TECHNIQUES

FORECASTS

18.10.00<CONT>
    FUTURE
    LONG TERM
    MEDIUM TERM
    PROJECTIONS
    SHORT TERM
    TIME FACTOR
    TRENDS

19.

INFORMATION. DOCUMENTATION.

19.01

INFORMATION.

19.01.01
    ACCESS TO INFORMATION
    DATA PROTECTION
    DOCUMENTATION
    INFORMATION
    INFORMATION NEEDS
    INFORMATION NETWORK
    INFORMATION POLICY
    INFORMATION SCIENCES
    INFORMATION SOURCES
    INFORMATION USERS
    LIBRARY SCIENCE
    NEWS
    SCIENTIFIC INFORMATION
    TECHNICAL INFORMATION
    TECHNOLOGICAL INFORMATION
        USE: TECHNICAL INFORMATION

19.01.02
    AGRIS
    CATALOGUING
    CLASSIFICATION
    CONTENT ANALYSIS
    DATA ANALYSIS
    DATA PROCESSING
    DATA RECORDING
    DATA RETRIEVAL
    DATA STORAGE
    DATA TRANSMISSION
    DEVSIS
    DOCUMENTARY ANALYSIS
        USE: INFORMATION ANALYSIS
    ELECTRONIC DATA PROCESSING
    INDEXING
    INFORMATION ANALYSIS
    INFORMATION DISSEMINATION
    INFORMATION EXCHANGE
    INFORMATION PROCESSING
    INFORMATION RECORDING
    INFORMATION SYSTEMS
    INIS
    ISIS
    REPORTING SYSTEMS
    SDI
    SUBJECT INDEXING
        USE: INDEXING

19.01.02<CONT>
UNISIST

19.01.03
ARCHIVES
AUDIOVISUAL CENTRES
DATA BANKS
DATA BASES
DOCUMENTATION CENTRES
   USE: INFORMATION SERVICES
EXTENSION SERVICES
INFORMATION CENTRES
   USE: INFORMATION SERVICES
INFORMATION SERVICES
LIBRARIES
LIBRARY AUTOMATION
TRANSLATION SERVICES

19.01.04
CARD FILES
CARDS
MICROFICHES
MICROFILMS
PUNCHED CARDS

19.02
DOCUMENTS.

19.02.01
AUDIOVISUAL MATERIALS
DOCUMENTS
ENVIRONMENTAL CONTROL
   USE: ENVIRONMENTAL MANAGEMENT
OFFICIAL DOCUMENTS
PRIMARY DOCUMENTS
RESTRICTED DOCUMENTS
SECONDARY DOCUMENTS
UNPUBLISHED DOCUMENTS

19.02.02
BIOGRAPHIES
CURRICULUM VITAE

19.02.03
AUTHORS
COPYRIGHT
INTELLECTUAL PROPERTY

19.02.04
ILLUSTRATIONS
OFFPRINTS
PHOTOGRAPHS
SLIDES

19.02.05
CONFERENCE PAPER
LIST OF DOCUMENTS
LIST OF PARTICIPANTS
MEETING PAPER
   USE: CONFERENCE PAPER

19.02.05<CONT>
MEMORANDUM
RECOMMENDATION
RESOLUTION
STATEMENT
WORK PROGRAMME

19.02.06
ARTICLE
DAILY
EDITORIAL
JOURNAL
   USE: PERIODICALS
MAGAZINE
   USE: PERIODICALS
MONTHLY
NEWS ITEM
NEWSLETTER
PERIODICALS
PRESS RELEASE
QUARTERLY
SERIALS
WEEKLY
YEARBOOK

19.02.07
ABSTRACT
ANNOTATED BIBLIOGRAPHY
BIBLIOGRAPHY
BOOK REVIEW
CATALOGUE
COMMENT
DIRECTORY
INDEX
LITERATURE SURVEY
REFERENCE MATERIALS

19.02.08
ANNUAL REPORT
CONFERENCE REPORT
CONSULTANT REPORT
EXPERT REPORT
MEETING REPORT
   USE: CONFERENCE REPORT
MISSION REPORT
PROGRESS REPORT
PROJECT REPORT
RESEARCH REPORT
TECHNICAL REPORT

19.02.09
CORRESPONDENCE
HANDBOOK
   USE: MANUAL

19.02.09<CONT>
  MANUAL
  MONOGRAPH
  TEXTBOOK
  THESIS

19.03

TERMINOLOGY.

19.03.00
  DICTIONARY
  ENCYCLOPEDIA
  GLOSSARY
  TERMINOLOGY
  THESAURUS

19.04

CONFERENCE.

19.04.00
  CONF
  CONFERENCE
  SEMINAR

IV. HIERARCHICAL DISPLAY

ABORTION
. LEGAL ABORTION

ACCOUNTING
. COST ACCOUNTING
. NATIONAL ACCOUNTING
. PUBLIC ACCOUNTING

ADAPTATION
. ADAPTATION TO CHANGE
. INDUSTRIAL ADAPTATION
. SOCIAL ADAPTATION
. . SCHOOL ADAPTATION
. . WORKERS ADAPTATION

ADULT EDUCATION
. EDUCATION OF WOMEN
. LIFE-LONG EDUCATION
. RECURRENT EDUCATION

AFFORESTATION
. REFORESTATION

AFRICA
. AFRICA SOUTH OF SAHARA
. . CENTRAL AFRICA
. . . BURUNDI
. . . CAMEROON
. . . CENTRAL AFRICAN EMPIRE
. . . CHAD
. . . CONGO
. . . EQUATORIAL GUINEA
. . . GABON
. . . RWANDA
. . . SAHEL
. . . SAO TOME AND PRINCIPE
. . . ZAIRE
. . EAST AFRICA
. . . BURUNDI
. . . COMOROS
. . . DJIBOUTI
. . . ETHIOPIA
. . . KENYA
. . . MALAWI
. . . MAURITIUS
. . . MOZAMBIQUE
. . . REUNION ISLAND
. . . RHODESIA
. . . RWANDA
. . . SEYCHELLES
. . . SOMALIA
. . . SUDAN
. . . TANZANIA
. . . UGANDA
. . . ZAMBIA
. . SOUTHERN AFRICA
. . . ANGOLA
. . . BOTSWANA
. . . COMOROS
. . . LESOTHO
. . . MADAGASCAR
. . . MALAWI
. . . MAURITIUS
. . . MOZAMBIQUE
. . . NAMIBIA
. . . REUNION ISLAND
. . . RHODESIA
. . . SOUTH AFRICA

AFRICA<CONT>
. . . ST HELENA
. . . SWAZILAND
. . . ZAMBIA
. . WEST AFRICA
. . . BENIN
. . . CAMEROON
. . . CAPE VERDE
. . . GAMBIA
. . . GHANA
. . . GUINEA
. . . GUINEA-BISSAU
. . . IVORY COAST
. . . LIBERIA
. . . MALI
. . . MAURITANIA
. . . NIGER
. . . NIGERIA
. . . SAHEL
. . . SENEGAL
. . . SIERRA LEONE
. . . ST HELENA
. . . TOGO
. . . UPPER VOLTA
. ENGLISH SPEAKING AFRICA
. . BOTSWANA
. . EGYPT
. . GAMBIA
. . GHANA
. . KENYA
. . LESOTHO
. . LIBERIA
. . LIBYA
. . MALAWI
. . MAURITIUS
. . NAMIBIA
. . NIGERIA
. . RHODESIA
. . SIERRA LEONE
. . SOUTH AFRICA
. . ST HELENA
. . SUDAN
. . SWAZILAND
. . TANZANIA
. . UGANDA
. . ZAMBIA
. FRENCH SPEAKING AFRICA
. . ALGERIA
. . BENIN
. . BURUNDI
. . CAMEROON
. . CENTRAL AFRICAN EMPIRE
. . CHAD
. . COMOROS
. . CONGO
. . DJIBOUTI
. . GABON
. . GUINEA
. . IVORY COAST
. . MADAGASCAR
. . MALI
. . MAURITANIA
. . MOROCCO
. . NIGER
. . REUNION ISLAND
. . RWANDA
. . SENEGAL
. . TOGO

ANIMALS
. BIRDS
. . POULTRY
. DOMESTIC ANIMALS
. ELEPHANTS
. EQUIDAE
. . DONKEYS
. . HORSES
. FISH
. . FRESHWATER FISH
. . SALT WATER FISH
. INSECTS
. . INSECT PESTS
. . . LOCUSTS
. . SILKWORMS
. LIVESTOCK
. . CAMELS
. . CATTLE
. . DONKEYS
. . GOATS
. . HORSES
. . SHEEP
. . SWINE
. REPTILES
. RODENTS
. RUMINANTS
. . BOVIDAE
. . . CALVES
. . . COWS
. . . WATER BUFFALOES
. . CAMELS
. . GOATS
. . OVIDAE
. . . SHEEP
. SWINE
. WILD ANIMALS
. . BIG GAME
. . SMALL GAME

AQUACULTURE
. FISH CULTURE
. OYSTER CULTURE

ARAB COUNTRIES
. ALGERIA
. EGYPT
. IRAQ
. JORDAN
. LEBANON
. LIBYA
. MOROCCO
. OMAN
. PERSIAN GULF STATES
. . BAHRAIN
. . KUWAIT
. . QATAR
. . UNITED ARAB EMIRATES
. SAUDI ARABIA
. SUDAN
. SYRIA
. TUNISIA
. YEMEN
. YEMEN PDR

ARRANGEMENT OF WORKING TIME
. CONTINUOUS WORKING DAY
. HOURS OF WORK
. . FLEXIBLE HOURS OF WORK

ARRANGEMENT OF WORKING TIME<CONT>
. NIGHT WORK
. REST PERIOD
. . WEEKLY REST
. SHIFT WORK

ART
. FOLK ART

ARTS
. LITERATURE
. MUSIC
. PERFORMING ARTS
. . DRAMATIC ART
. . . CINEMA
. . . DANCE
. . . THEATRE
. VISUAL ARTS
. FINE ARTS
. . . ARCHITECTURE
. . . GRAPHIC ARTS
. . . PLASTIC ARTS

ASIA
. FAR EAST
. . CHINA
. . HONG KONG
. . JAPAN
. . KOREA
. . KOREA DPR
. . KOREA R
. . MACAO
. . MONGOLIA PR
. . TAIWAN
. SOUTH ASIA
. . BANGLADESH
. . BHUTAN
. . INDIA
. . MALDIVES
. . NEPAL
. . PAKISTAN
. . SRI LANKA
. SOUTH EAST ASIA
. . BANGLADESH
. . BHUTAN
. . BRUNEI
. . BURMA
. . INDIA
. . INDOCHINA
. . . KAMPUCHEA
. . . LAO PDR
. . . VIETNAM
. . INDONESIA
. . MALAYSIA
. . MALDIVES
. . NEPAL
. . PAKISTAN
. . PHILIPPINES
. . PORTUGUESE TIMOR
. . SIKKIM
. . SINGAPORE
. . SRI LANKA
. . THAILAND

ASSOCIATIONS
. EMPLOYEE ASSOCIATIONS
. EMPLOYERS ORGANIZATIONS
. OCCUPATIONAL ORGANIZATIONS

ASSOCIATIONS<CONT>
. . TEACHER ASSOCIATIONS

ATTITUDES
. EMPLOYEES ATTITUDES
. MANAGEMENT ATTITUDES

AUTOMATION
. LIBRARY AUTOMATION

BALANCE OF PAYMENTS
. BALANCE OF TRADE
. CAPITAL MOVEMENTS
. . CAPITAL TRANSFERS
. . EXPORT OF CAPITAL
. . INTERNATIONAL INVESTMENTS
. . . FOREIGN INVESTMENTS
. . REPATRIATION OF CAPITAL
. EXPORTS
. IMPORTS
. INVISIBLE TRANSACTIONS

BASIC EDUCATION
. CIVIC EDUCATION
. CONSUMER EDUCATION
. ENVIRONMENTAL EDUCATION
. HEALTH EDUCATION
. HOME ECONOMICS
. . CHILD REARING
. . FOOD PREPARATION
. LITERACY
. . FUNCTIONAL LITERACY
. PHYSICAL EDUCATION
. POLITICAL EDUCATION
. SAFETY EDUCATION
. SEX EDUCATION

BEHAVIOUR
. CONSUMER BEHAVIOUR
. ECONOMIC BEHAVIOUR
. POLITICAL BEHAVIOUR
. SEXUAL BEHAVIOUR
. SOCIAL BEHAVIOUR
. STUDENT BEHAVIOUR
. . STUDENT PARTICIPATION

BEHAVIOURAL SCIENCES
. PSYCHOLOGY
. . INDUSTRIAL PSYCHOLOGY
. . PSYCHOLOGY OF EDUCATION
. SOCIAL PSYCHOLOGY

BEVERAGES
. ALCOHOLIC BEVERAGES
. . BEER
. . WINE
. NON-ALCOHOLIC BEVERAGES
. . COCOA
. . COFFEE
. . FRUIT JUICES
. . MILK
. . . MILK POWDER
. . MINERAL WATERS
. . TEA

BUILDINGS
. EDUCATIONAL BUILDINGS
. . SCHOOL BUILDINGS

BUILDINGS<CONT>
. . UNIVERSITY BUILDINGS
. FARM BUILDINGS
. . GREENHOUSES
. . SILOS
. INDUSTRIAL BUILDINGS
. PREFABRICATED BUILDINGS

BUSINESS CYCLE
. SEASONAL FLUCTUATIONS

CAPITAL
. FOREIGN CAPITAL
. INDUSTRIAL CAPITAL
. WORKING CAPITAL

CARBOHYDRATES
. CELLULOSE
. STARCH
. SUGAR
. . BEET SUGAR
. . CANE SUGAR

CARDS
. PUNCHED CARDS

CHEMICALS
. HYDROCARBONS
. . BENZENE
. . METHANE
. PETROCHEMICALS
. PHARMACEUTICALS
. . DRUGS
. . . ANTIBIOTICS
. . NARCOTICS
. . . OPIUM
. . SERUMS
. . VACCINES

CHILDREN
. INFANTS

CLASSES
. EXPERIMENTAL CLASSES

CLASSIFICATION
. JOB CLASSIFICATION
. SOIL CLASSIFICATION

CLEANING AGENTS
. DETERGENTS
. SOAP

CLIMATIC ZONES
. ARID ZONE
. COLD ZONE
. EQUATORIAL ZONE
. FRIGID ZONE
. HUMID ZONE
. SEMI-ARID ZONE
. SUBTROPICAL ZONE
. TEMPERATE ZONE
. TROPICAL ZONE

CODES
. LABOUR CODE

CROPS<CONT>
. FORAGE CROPS
. . GRASSLAND
. INDUSTRIAL CROPS
. . COCOA
. . COCONUTS
. . COFFEE
. . COTTON
. . FLAX
. . HEVEAS
. . OIL CROPS
. . . OIL PALMS
. . . OILSEEDS
. . . . COTTON
. . . . FLAX
. . . . GROUNDNUTS
. . . . RAPE
. . . . SOYBEANS
. . . OLIVES
. . OPIUM
. . SUGAR BEETS
. . SUGAR CANE
. . TEA
. . TOBACCO

CULTIVATION PRACTICES
. PLANTING
. SOWING

CULTURE
. FOLK CULTURE
. SCIENTIFIC CULTURE
. SUBCULTURE
. TRADITIONAL CULTURE

CURRENCIES
. EURODOLLARS
. LOCAL CURRENCY
. NON-CONVERTIBLE CURRENCIES
. PETRODOLLARS

CURRICULUM
. COURSES
. . ACCELERATED COURSES
. . TRAINING COURSES
. INTEGRATED CURRICULUM

CUSTOMS UNION
. BENELUX
. CACEU

CYBERNETICS
. SYSTEMS ANALYSIS
. SYSTEMS DESIGN

DANGEROUS SUBSTANCES
. RADIOACTIVE MATERIALS
. . RADIOACTIVE WASTES
. TOXIC SUBSTANCES
. . TOXIC METALS
. . . CADMIUM
. . . LEAD
. . . MERCURY
. . . ZINC

DEAF-DUMBNESS
. DEAFNESS

DEBT
. EXTERNAL DEBT
. PUBLIC DEBT

DEMOCRATIZATION
. DEMOCRATIZATION OF EDUCATION

DEVELOPING COUNTRIES
. LEAST DEVELOPED COUNTRIES

DEVELOPMENT CENTRES
. ADC
. IDCAS
. IDRC
. OECD DC

DEVELOPMENT PERSONNEL
. CONSULTANTS
. EXPERTS

DEVELOPMENT PLANS
. NATIONAL PLANS
. REGIONAL PLANS

DEVELOPMENT POTENTIAL
. INDUSTRIAL POTENTIAL

DEVELOPMENT PROJECTS
. AGRICULTURAL PROJECTS
. INDUSTRIAL PROJECTS
. JOINT PROJECTS
. MULTIPURPOSE PROJECTS
. PILOT PROJECTS

DISASTERS
. FIRES
. . FOREST FIRES
. MANMADE DISASTERS
. NATURAL DISASTERS
. . DROUGHT
. . EPIDEMICS
. . FLOODS
. . FOREST FIRES
. . SEISMS
. . STORMS
. . TIDAL WAVES
. . VOLCANIC ERUPTIONS

DISCRIMINATION
. ECONOMIC DISCRIMINATION
. RACIAL DISCRIMINATION
. RACISM

DISEASES
. ANIMAL DISEASES
. CHRONIC DISEASES
. ENDEMIC DISEASES
. EYE DISEASES
. . BLINDNESS
. IMMUNOLOGIC DISEASES
. INFECTIOUS DISEASES
. . CHOLERA
. . DIPHTHERIA
. . FUNGUS DISEASES
. . LEPROSY
. . MEASLES
. . MENINGITIS
. . PARASITIC DISEASES

DISEASES\<CONT\>
. . . FILARIASIS
. . . MALARIA
. . . ONCHOCERCIASIS
. . . SCHISTOSOMIASIS
. . . TRYPANOSOMIASIS
. . PLAGUE
. . POLIOMYELITIS
. . RICKETTSIAL DISEASES
. . . TYPHUS
. . RUBELLA
. . SCARLET FEVER
. . SEPTICEMIA
. . SMALLPOX
. . TROPICAL DISEASES
. . . CHOLERA
. . . FILARIASIS
. . . LEPROSY
. . . MALARIA
. . . ONCHOCERCIASIS
. . . SCHISTOSOMIASIS
. . . TRYPANOSOMIASIS
. . . TYPHUS
. . . YELLOW FEVER
. . TUBERCULOSIS
. . TYPHOID
. . VENEREAL DISEASES
. . YELLOW FEVER
. INTRACTABLE DISEASES
. MENTAL DISEASES
. MOUTH DISEASES
. OCCUPATIONAL DISEASES
. . PNEUMOCONIOSIS
. PLANT DISEASES
. POISONING
. . ALCOHOLISM
. . DRUG ADDICTION
. WOUNDS AND INJURIES
. . BURNS

DISPUTE SETTLEMENT
. ARBITRATION
. CONCILIATION

DISTRIBUTION
. RETAIL TRADE
. WHOLESALE TRADE

DIVISION OF LABOUR
. INTERNATIONAL DIVISION OF LABOUR

DOCUMENTS
. AUDIOVISUAL MATERIALS
. . CHARTS
. . . GEOLOGICAL MAPS
. . DIAGRAMS
. . FILMS
. . . EDUCATIONAL FILMS
. . GRAPHS
. . MAPS
. . . SOIL MAPS
. . MICROFILMS
. . PHOTOGRAPHS
. . SLIDES
. OFFICIAL DOCUMENTS
. PRIMARY DOCUMENTS
. . BIOGRAPHIES
. . CORRESPONDENCE

DOCUMENTS\<CONT\>
. . DICTIONARY
. . ENCYCLOPEDIA
. . MONOGRAPH
. . SERIALS
. . . NEWSLETTER
. . . PERIODICALS
. . . . DAILY
. . . . MONTHLY
. . . . QUARTERLY
. . . . WEEKLY
. . . . YEARBOOK
. . THESAURUS
. . THESIS
. REFERENCE MATERIALS
. . BIBLIOGRAPHY
. . . ANNOTATED BIBLIOGRAPHY
. . DICTIONARY
. . DIRECTORY
. . ENCYCLOPEDIA
. . INDEX
. . THESAURUS
. . YEARBOOK
. RESTRICTED DOCUMENTS
. SECONDARY DOCUMENTS
. . ABSTRACT
. . BIBLIOGRAPHY
. . . ANNOTATED BIBLIOGRAPHY
. . BOOK REVIEW
. . CATALOGUE
. . COMMENT
. UNPUBLISHED DOCUMENTS

ECONOMIC ANALYSIS
. ACTIVITY ANALYSIS
. COST ANALYSIS
. INPUT-OUTPUT ANALYSIS

ECONOMIC AND SOCIAL DEVELOPMENT
. CULTURAL DEVELOPMENT
. ECONOMIC DEVELOPMENT
. . AGRICULTURAL DEVELOPMENT
. . . FISHERY DEVELOPMENT
. . . FORESTRY DEVELOPMENT
. . INDUSTRIAL DEVELOPMENT
. INTEGRATED DEVELOPMENT
. REGIONAL DEVELOPMENT
. SOCIAL DEVELOPMENT
. . COMMUNITY DEVELOPMENT
. . EDUCATIONAL DEVELOPMENT

ECONOMIC CONCENTRATION
. CAPITAL CONCENTRATION
. INDUSTRIAL CONCENTRATION

ECONOMIC DISPARITY
. REGIONAL DISPARITY

ECONOMIC INDICATORS
. GROSS DOMESTIC PRODUCT
. GROSS NATIONAL PRODUCT
. GROWTH RATE
. . ZERO GROWTH ECONOMY
. INDEX NUMBERS
. . PRICE INDEX

ECONOMIC LOSS
. FINANCIAL LOSS

ENGINEERING<CONT>
. . . DESALINIZATION
. . WEATHER CONTROL
. HYDRAULIC ENGINEERING
. INDUSTRIAL ENGINEERING
. MINING ENGINEERING
. NUCLEAR ENGINEERING
. PETROLEUM ENGINEERING

ENGINEERING DESIGN
. INDUSTRIAL DESIGN
. PRODUCT DESIGN

ENGINES
. DIESEL ENGINES
. ELECTRIC MOTORS
. JET ENGINES
. PETROL ENGINES
. STEAM ENGINES

ENTERPRISES
. AGRICULTURAL ENTERPRISES
. . AGRICULTURAL COOPERATIVES
. . FARMS
. . . EXPERIMENTAL FARMS
. . . STATE FARMS
. . PLANTATIONS
. CAPITALIST ENTERPRISES
. COMMERCIAL ENTERPRISES
. FOREIGN ENTERPRISES
. INDUSTRIAL ENTERPRISES
. JOINT VENTURES
. MIXED ENTERPRISES
. MULTINATIONAL ENTERPRISES
. PRIVATE ENTERPRISES
. PUBLIC ENTERPRISES
. . NATIONALIZED INDUSTRY
. SMALL ENTERPRISES
. SOCIALIST ENTERPRISES

ENVIRONMENT
. HUMAN ENVIRONMENT
. . CULTURAL ENVIRONMENT
. . SOCIAL ENVIRONMENT
. . . FAMILY ENVIRONMENT
. . . RURAL ENVIRONMENT
. . . SCHOOL ENVIRONMENT
. . . . SCHOOL-COMMUNITY RELATIONSHIPS
. . . . TEACHER-STUDENT RELATIONSHIPS
. . . URBAN ENVIRONMENT
. PHYSICAL ENVIRONMENT
. . AQUATIC ENVIRONMENT
. . . MARINE ENVIRONMENT
. . ATMOSPHERE
. . BIOSPHERE
. . TERRESTRIAL ENVIRONMENT

ENVIRONMENTAL DEGRADATION
. DESERTIFICATION

EQUAL OPPORTUNITY
. EDUCATIONAL OPPORTUNITIES
. EMPLOYMENT OPPORTUNITIES

EQUIPMENT
. AGRICULTURAL EQUIPMENT
. . AGRICULTURAL MACHINERY
. . . TRACTORS

EQUIPMENT<CONT>
. . FISHING EQUIPMENT
. . FORESTRY EQUIPMENT
. EDUCATIONAL EQUIPMENT
. . SCHOOL TRANSPORT
. . TEACHING AIDS
. . . AUDIOVISUAL AIDS
. . . . EDUCATIONAL FILMS
. . . MANUAL
. . . TEXTBOOK
. ELECTRICAL EQUIPMENT
. ELECTRONIC EQUIPMENT
. . COMPUTERS
. . ELECTRONIC TUBES
. . RADAR
. . TRANSISTORS
. HYDRAULIC EQUIPMENT
. . PUMPS
. INDUSTRIAL EQUIPMENT
. OBSOLETE EQUIPMENT
. RESEARCH EQUIPMENT
. SECOND HAND EQUIPMENT
. TRANSPORT EQUIPMENT

EROSION
. SOIL EROSION

EUROPE
. EASTERN EUROPE
. . ALBANIA
. . BULGARIA
. . BYELORUSSIAN SSR
. . CZECHOSLOVAKIA
. . GERMAN DR
. . HUNGARY
. . POLAND
. . ROMANIA
. . UKRAINIAN SSR
. . USSR
. . YUGOSLAVIA
. WESTERN EUROPE
. . ANDORRA
. . AUSTRIA
. . AZORES
. . BELGIUM
. . CANARY ISLANDS
. . CYPRUS
. . FRANCE
. . GERMANY FR
. . GIBRALTAR
. . GREECE
. . IRELAND
. . ITALY
. . LIECHTENSTEIN
. . LUXEMBOURG
. . MADEIRA
. . MALTA
. . MONACO
. . NETHERLANDS
. . PORTUGAL
. . SAN MARINO
. . SCANDINAVIA
. . . DENMARK
. . . FAROE ISLANDS
. . . FINLAND
. . . GREENLAND
. . . ICELAND
. . . NORWAY

303

EUROPE<CONT>
. . . SWEDEN
. . SPAIN
. . SWITZERLAND
. . TURKEY
. . UNITED KINGDOM
. . VATICAN

EVALUATION
. AID EVALUATION
. AUDIENCE RATING
. ECONOMIC EVALUATION
. PROJECT EVALUATION
. RESOURCES EVALUATION

EXPENDITURES
. CAPITAL COSTS
. CONSUMER EXPENDITURES
. CULTURAL EXPENDITURES
. NATIONAL EXPENDITURES
. PUBLIC EXPENDITURES
. . MILITARY EXPENDITURES

FAMILY PLANNING
. BIRTH CONTROL
. . BIRTH SPACING

FARMING SYSTEMS
. COLLECTIVE FARMING
. COMMERCIAL FARMING
. COOPERATIVE FARMING
. CULTIVATION SYSTEMS
. . CROP DIVERSIFICATION
. . CROP ROTATION
. . INTERCROPPING
. . MULTIPLE CROPPING
. . SHIFTING CULTIVATION
. EXTENSIVE FARMING
. INTENSIVE FARMING
. MIXED FARMING
. SUBSISTENCE FARMING

FAUNA
. AQUATIC FAUNA

FEEDING
. ANIMAL FEEDING
. BREAST FEEDING

FERTILIZERS
. CHEMICAL FERTILIZERS

FIBRES
. HARD FIBRES
. MANMADE FIBRES
. NATURAL FIBRES
. . ANIMAL FIBRES
. . . SILK
. . . WOOL
. . PLANT FIBRES
. . . COIR
. . . COTTON
. . . FLAX
. . . HEMP
. . . JUTE
. . . SISAL
. . . WOOD FIBRES
. SOFT FIBRES

FINANCIAL INSTITUTIONS
. BANKS
. . AGRICULTURAL BANKS
. . CENTRAL BANKS
. . COMMERCIAL BANKS
. . DEVELOPMENT BANKS
. . . AFRICAN DEVELOPMENT BANK
. . . ASIAN DEVELOPMENT BANK
. . . CABEI
. . . IBRD
. . . IDB
. . INDUSTRIAL BANKS
. . INVESTMENT BANKS
. . . EIB
. INSURANCE
. . ACCIDENT INSURANCE
. . AGRICULTURAL INSURANCE
. . CREDIT INSURANCE
. . EXPORT INSURANCE
. . FIRE INSURANCE
. . LIFE INSURANCE
. PENSION FUNDS
. SAVINGS BANKS

FINANCIAL TERMS
. BORROWING
. . PUBLIC BORROWING
. GRANTS
. . EDUCATIONAL GRANTS
. . . RESEARCH FELLOWSHIPS
. . . SCHOLARSHIPS
. . . STUDENT LOANS
. . . TRAINING ALLOWANCES
. LOANS
. . STUDENT LOANS

FINANCING
. AID FINANCING
. DEFICIT FINANCING
. . COMPENSATORY FINANCING
. EDUCATIONAL FINANCING
. EXPORT FINANCING
. . EXPORT CREDIT
. . EXPORT SUBSIDIES
. SELF-FINANCING

FISHING
. INLAND FISHING
. MARINE FISHING
. . COASTAL FISHING
. . DEEP SEA FISHING

FOOD
. BAKERY PRODUCTS
. . BREAD
. CANNED FOOD
. CEREALS
. . BARLEY
. . MAIZE
. . MILLET
. . RICE
. . RYE
. . SORGHUM
. . TRITICALE
. . WHEAT
. CONDENSED FOOD
. . FISH PROTEIN CONCENTRATE
. DAIRY PRODUCTS

FOOD<CONT>
. . BUTTER
. . CHEESE
. . MILK
. . . MILK POWDER
. DEHYDRATED FOOD
. DRIED FOOD
. . DRIED FRUIT
. EDIBLE OILS
. . OLIVE OIL
. . PALM OIL
. . PEANUT OIL
. FEED
. FISHERY PRODUCTS
. . FISH MEAL
. . FISH PROTEIN CONCENTRATE
. FROZEN FOOD
. FRUITS
. . ALMONDS
. . APPLES
. . BANANAS
. . CASHEW NUTS
. . CITRUS FRUITS
. . COCONUTS
. . DATES
. . GRAPES
. . GROUNDNUTS
. . OLIVES
. . PEARS
. . PINEAPPLES
. . TOMATOES
. IRRADIATED FOOD
. MARGARINE
. MEAT PRODUCTS
. . MEAT
. . . BEEF
. . . MUTTON
. . . PORK
. PERISHABLE FOOD
. PROTEIN RICH FOOD
. VEGETABLES
. . ONIONS

FOOD TECHNOLOGY
. FOOD PRESERVATION
. . FISH PRESERVATION
. FOOD PROCESSING
. . FISHERY PRODUCT PROCESSING
. . GRAIN PROCESSING
. . MEAT PROCESSING
. . MILK PROCESSING
. FOOD STERILIZATION
. . PASTEURIZATION

FORECASTS
. ECONOMIC FORECASTS
. WEATHER FORECASTS

FOREIGNERS
. FOREIGN STUDENTS
. FOREIGN WORKERS

FORESTS
. MANMADE FORESTS

FREEDOM
. CIVIL LIBERTIES
. . ACADEMIC FREEDOM

FREEDOM<CONT>
. . FREEDOM OF ASSOCIATION
. . FREEDOM OF INFORMATION
. . FREEDOM OF OPINION
. . FREEDOM OF SPEECH
. . RELIGIOUS FREEDOM

GEOGRAPHY
. HUMAN GEOGRAPHY
. . CULTURAL GEOGRAPHY
. . ECONOMIC GEOGRAPHY
. . POLITICAL GEOGRAPHY
. PHYSICAL GEOGRAPHY

GOVERNMENT
. CENTRAL GOVERNMENT
. . FOREIGN SERVICE
. LOCAL GOVERNMENT
. REGIONAL GOVERNMENT

GOVERNMENT POLICY
. COMMUNICATION POLICY
. . CENSORSHIP
. CULTURAL POLICY
. DEVELOPMENT POLICY
. ECONOMIC POLICY
. . AGRICULTURAL POLICY
. . . FISHERY POLICY
. . . FOREST POLICY
. . AUSTERITY POLICY
. . COMMERCIAL POLICY
. . FINANCIAL POLICY
. . . BUDGETARY POLICY
. . . CREDIT POLICY
. . . FISCAL POLICY
. . . MONETARY POLICY
. . . . DEVALUATION
. . GROWTH POLICY
. . INCOMES POLICY
. . . WAGE POLICY
. . INDUSTRIAL POLICY
. . . INDUSTRIALIZATION POLICY
. . . . IMPORT SUBSTITUTION
. . INVESTMENT POLICY
. . PRICE POLICY
. . PRODUCTIVITY POLICY
. . TRADE POLICY
. . . PROTECTIONIST MEASURES
. . . . IMPORT RESTRICTIONS
. . . . . IMPORT TAX
. . . . IMPORT SUBSTITUTION
. . . . QUOTA SYSTEM
. . . TARIFF POLICY
. . . TRADE LIBERALIZATION
. . TRANSPORT POLICY
. EDUCATIONAL POLICY
. ENERGY POLICY
. ENVIRONMENTAL POLICY
. FOOD POLICY
. FOREIGN POLICY
. HEALTH POLICY
. . NUTRITION POLICY
. INFORMATION POLICY
. LABOUR POLICY
. . EMPLOYMENT POLICY
. POPULATION POLICY
. . MIGRATION POLICY
. SCIENCE POLICY

INDUSTRIAL SECTOR<CONT>
.. MILLING INDUSTRY
.. SUGAR INDUSTRY
. GLASS INDUSTRY
. LEATHER INDUSTRY
.. TANNING INDUSTRY
. PETROLEUM INDUSTRY
.. PETROCHEMICAL INDUSTRY
. POWER INDUSTRY
. PULP AND PAPER INDUSTRY
. RUBBER INDUSTRY
. SHIPBUILDING
. SHOE INDUSTRY
. TEXTILE INDUSTRY
.. CLOTHING INDUSTRY
... FUR INDUSTRY
.. ROPE INDUSTRY
. WOODWORKING INDUSTRY
.. FURNITURE INDUSTRY

INDUSTRY
. EXPORT-ORIENTED INDUSTRY
. HEAVY INDUSTRY
. LIGHT INDUSTRY
. MEDIUM-SCALE INDUSTRY
. NATIONALIZED INDUSTRY
. RURAL INDUSTRY
.. COTTAGE INDUSTRY
. SMALL-SCALE INDUSTRY
.. COTTAGE INDUSTRY

INFORMATION
. CULTURAL INFORMATION
. ECONOMIC INFORMATION
. NEWS
. SCIENTIFIC INFORMATION
. SOCIAL INFORMATION
. TECHNICAL INFORMATION
.. INDUSTRIAL INFORMATION

INFORMATION DISSEMINATION
. ADVERTISING
. SDI

INFORMATION EXCHANGE
. DATA TRANSMISSION
. REPORTING SYSTEMS

INFORMATION SCIENCES
. COMPUTER SCIENCE
. DOCUMENTATION
.. CATALOGUING
.. INFORMATION ANALYSIS
... CONTENT ANALYSIS
... INDEXING
... INFORMATION PROCESSING
.... DATA PROCESSING
..... DATA ANALYSIS
..... DATA RETRIEVAL
..... DATA STORAGE
..... ELECTRONIC DATA PROCESSING
.. INFORMATION RECORDING
... DATA RECORDING
. LIBRARY SCIENCE

INFORMATION SERVICES
. ARCHIVES
. AUDIOVISUAL CENTRES

INFORMATION SERVICES<CONT>
. CLADES
. DATA BANKS
. DATA BASES
. EXTENSION SERVICES
.. AGRICULTURAL EXTENSION
.. INDUSTRIAL EXTENSION
. LIBRARIES
. TRANSLATION SERVICES

INFORMATION SYSTEMS
. AGRIS
. DEVSIS
. INIS
. ISIS
. MANAGEMENT INFORMATION SYSTEM
. REPORTING SYSTEMS
. UNISIST

INPUT-OUTPUT
. INPUT-OUTPUT ANALYSIS
. INPUT-OUTPUT TABLES

INTELLECTUAL PROPERTY
. COPYRIGHT
. INDUSTRIAL PROPERTY
.. PATENTS

INTERGROUP RELATIONS
. CLASS STRUGGLE
. INTERETHNIC RELATIONS
. LABOUR RELATIONS
. RACE RELATIONS
.. DESEGREGATION
.. RACIAL CONFLICTS
.. RACISM

INTERNATIONAL AGREEMENTS
. CULTURAL AGREEMENTS
. ECONOMIC AGREEMENTS
.. COMPLEMENTARITY AGREEMENTS
.. MONETARY AGREEMENTS
... CLEARING AGREEMENTS
.. PAYMENT AGREEMENTS
.. TARIFF AGREEMENTS
... GENERAL SYSTEM OF PREFERENCES
.. TAX AGREEMENTS
.. TRADE AGREEMENTS
... COMMODITY AGREEMENTS
.... COMMON FUND
... GATT

INTERNATIONAL COOPERATION
. CULTURAL COOPERATION
. DEVELOPMENT AID
.. AID IN KIND
.. BILATERAL AID
.. ECONOMIC AID
.. FINANCIAL AID
.. FOOD AID
.. HEALTH AID
.. MULTILATERAL AID
.. PRIVATE AID
.. TECHNICAL ASSISTANCE
.. TRAINING ASSISTANCE
. FOREIGN AID
.. MILITARY AID
. HORIZONTAL COOPERATION

INTERNATIONAL COOPERATION<CONT>
. REGIONAL COOPERATION

INTERNATIONAL ORGANIZATIONS
. INTERGOVERNMENTAL ORGANIZATIONS
. . ACCT
. . AFRICAN DEVELOPMENT BANK
. . APO
. . APU
. . . ADC
. . ASEAN
. . ASIAN DEVELOPMENT BANK
. . ASPAC
. . BENELUX
. . CABEI
. . CACEU
. . CACM
. . . SIECA
. . CARICOM
. . CARIFTA
. . CENTO
. . CERN
. . CMEA
. . COLOMBO PLAN
. . COMMONWEALTH
. . COUNCIL OF EUROPE
. . EAC
. . ECMT
. . EFTA
. . EUROPEAN COMMUNITIES
. . . ECSC
. . . EEC
. . . EIB
. . . EURATOM
. . . EUROPEAN PARLIAMENT
. . EUROPEAN SPACE AGENCY
. . ICEM
. . IDB
. . LAFTA
. . . ANDEAN GROUP
. . LEAGUE OF ARAB STATES
. . . ALECSO
. . . CAEU
. . . IDCAS
. . MPCC
. . NATO
. . NORDIC COUNCIL
. . OAPEC
. . OAS
. . . PAHO
. . OAU
. . OCAM
. . OCAS
. . OECD
. . . OECD DAC
. . . OECD DC
. . . OECD IEA
. . . OECD NEA
. . OPEC
. . SEATO
. . SPC
. . UN SYSTEM
. . . GATT
. . . IAEA
. . . UN
. . . . CCAQ
. . . . ECOSOC
. . . . . ACAST

INTERNATIONAL ORGANIZATIONS<CONT>
. . . . . CDP
. . . . . CSTD
. . . . . ECA
. . . . . ECE
. . . . . ECLA
. . . . . . CLADES
. . . . . ECWA
. . . . . ESCAP
. . . . ICJ
. . . . TRUSTEESHIP COUNCIL
. . . . UN SECRETARIAT
. . . . UN SECURITY COUNCIL
. . . . UNCRD
. . . . UNCTAD
. . . . UNDP
. . . . UNEP
. . . . UNHCR
. . . . UNICEF
. . . . UNITAR
. . . . UNRISD
. . . . UNRWA
. . . UN SPECIALIZED AGENCIES
. . . . FAO
. . . . . WORLD FOOD PROGRAMME
. . . . IBRD
. . . . ICAO
. . . . IDA
. . . . IFC
. . . . ILO
. . . . . WORLD EMPLOYMENT PROGRAMME
. . . . IMCO
. . . . IMF
. . . . ITU
. . . . UNESCO
. . . . . IBE
. . . . . IIEP
. . . . UNIDO
. . . . UPU
. . . . WHO
. . . . WIPO
. . . . WMO
. . WEU
. NON-GOVERNMENTAL ORGANIZATIONS
. . ACDA
. . ADIPA
. . AFRASEC
. . CAFRAD
. . CEMLA
. . CIAT
. . CIMMYT
. . CLACSO
. . CODESRIA
. . EADI
. . FID
. . ICFTU
. . ICRISAT
. . ICSSD
. . ICSU
. . ICVA
. . IEA
. . IFAP
. . IFHP
. . IFIP
. . IFLA
. . ILPES
. . INTECOL
. . IPPF

LEADERSHIP
. POLITICAL LEADERSHIP

LEGISLATION
. ECONOMIC LEGISLATION
. . ANTITRUST LEGISLATION
. LABOUR LEGISLATION
. . LABOUR CODE
. SOCIAL LEGISLATION

LIQUIDITY
. INTERNATIONAL LIQUIDITY

LITTORAL ZONES
. COASTS

LIVING CONDITIONS
. WORKING CONDITIONS

MACHINERY
. AGRICULTURAL MACHINERY
. . TRACTORS
. BUILDING MACHINERY
. . EARTHMOVING MACHINERY
. ELECTRICAL MACHINERY
. . ELECTRIC APPLIANCES
. . . HOUSEHOLD APPLIANCES
. . ELECTRIC MOTORS

MANAGEMENT
. AGRICULTURAL MANAGEMENT
. . FARM MANAGEMENT
. . FISHERY MANAGEMENT
. . FOREST MANAGEMENT
. BUSINESS MANAGEMENT
. COLLEGE MANAGEMENT
. ENVIRONMENTAL MANAGEMENT
. EQUIPMENT MANAGEMENT
. FINANCIAL MANAGEMENT
. INDUSTRIAL MANAGEMENT
. PERSONNEL MANAGEMENT
. RESOURCES MANAGEMENT
. SCHOOL MANAGEMENT
. SCIENTIFIC MANAGEMENT
. SELF-MANAGEMENT
. . WORKERS SELF-MANAGEMENT
. WASTE MANAGEMENT
. . WASTE DISPOSAL
. . . SEA DUMPING
. . WASTE RECYCLING
. . WASTE TREATMENT
. . WASTE UTILIZATION
. WATER MANAGEMENT
. . WATER DISTRIBUTION
. . WATER STORAGE
. . WATER TREATMENT
. . . DESALINIZATION
. . WATER UTILIZATION

MANAGEMENT TECHNIQUES
. LINEAR PROGRAMMING
. MANAGEMENT BY OBJECTIVES
. NETWORK ANALYSIS
. OPERATIONAL RESEARCH
. . SCENARIOS

MANAGERS
. MIDDLE MANAGEMENT

MANAGERS<CONT>
. TOP MANAGEMENT

MAPPING
. CHARTING

MARITIME QUESTIONS
. FLAGS OF CONVENIENCE
. SEA TRANSPORT

MARKET
. AGRICULTURAL MARKET
. BLACK MARKET
. COMMODITY MARKET
. DOMESTIC MARKET
. FINANCIAL MARKET
. FREIGHT MARKET
. INTERNATIONAL MARKET
. LABOUR MARKET
. MONEY MARKET

MARKETING
. COOPERATIVE MARKETING
. RETAIL MARKETING
. WHOLESALE MARKETING

MARRIED PERSONS
. HUSBAND
. WIFE

MEANS OF TRANSPORT
. MOTOR VEHICLES
. . AIRCRAFT
. . . HELICOPTERS
. . AUTOMOBILES
. . BUSES
. . MOTORCYCLES
. . SHIPS
. . . CARGO SHIPS
. . . FISHING VESSELS
. . . . FACTORY BOATS
. . . . TRAWLERS
. . . TANKERS
. . TRACTORS
. . TRAINS
. . . LOCOMOTIVES
. . . ROLLING STOCK
. . TRUCKS
. NON-MOTORIZED TRANSPORT
. . BICYCLES

MEASUREMENT SYSTEMS
. METRIC SYSTEM

MECHANIZATION
. AGRICULTURAL MECHANIZATION

MEDIA
. MASS MEDIA
. . BOOKS
. . FILMS
. . . EDUCATIONAL FILMS
. . PRESS
. . RADIO
. . . EDUCATIONAL RADIO
. . TELEVISION
. . . EDUCATIONAL TELEVISION

MEDICAL CARE
. PRENATAL CARE

MEDICAL PERSONNEL
. DENTISTS
. PHARMACISTS
. PHYSICIANS
. . PEDIATRICIANS

MEDICAL SCIENCES
. CARDIOLOGY
. EPIDEMIOLOGY
. GYNAECOLOGY
. IMMUNOLOGY
. PHARMACOLOGY
. RADIOLOGY

MEDICINE
. ACUPUNCTURE
. OCCUPATIONAL MEDICINE
. PEDIATRICS
. PREVENTIVE MEDICINE
. . MATERNAL AND CHILD HEALTH
. . PRENATAL CARE
. . PROPHYLAXIS
. . VACCINATION
. PSYCHIATRY
. SURGERY
. TRADITIONAL MEDICINE
. VETERINARY MEDICINE

MEDITERRANEAN COUNTRIES
. ALBANIA
. ALGERIA
. CYPRUS
. EGYPT
. FRANCE
. GIBRALTAR
. GREECE
. ISRAEL
. ITALY
. LEBANON
. LIBYA
. MALTA
. MONACO
. MOROCCO
. SAN MARINO
. SPAIN
. SYRIA
. TUNISIA
. TURKEY
. VATICAN
. YUGOSLAVIA

MERGERS
. TRUSTS

METAL PRODUCTS
. CABLES
. CASTINGS
. METAL SHEETS
. PIPES
. WIRE

METALS
. IRON
. NON-FERROUS METALS
. . ALUMINIUM

METALS<CONT>
. . CADMIUM
. . CHROMIUM
. . COBALT
. . COPPER
. . LEAD
. . MANGANESE
. . MERCURY
. . NICKEL
. . PLUTONIUM
. . PRECIOUS METALS
. . . GOLD
. . . PLATINUM
. . . SILVER
. . TIN
. . TITANIUM
. . TUNGSTEN
. . URANIUM
. . ZINC
. TOXIC METALS
. . CADMIUM
. . LEAD
. . MERCURY
. . ZINC

METALWORKING INDUSTRY
. BOILERMAKING
. MACHINERY INDUSTRY
. . INSTRUMENTATION INDUSTRY
. . . OPTICAL INDUSTRY
. . . WATCHMAKING INDUSTRY
. . MACHINE TOOL INDUSTRY
. . MOTOR VEHICLE INDUSTRY
. . . AUTOMOBILE INDUSTRY
. SHEET-METAL WORKING

MICROORGANISMS
. BACTERIA
. MICROBES
. VIRUSES

MIDDLE EAST
. AFGHANISTAN
. CYPRUS
. IRAN
. IRAQ
. ISRAEL
. JORDAN
. LEBANON
. OMAN
. PERSIAN GULF STATES
. . BAHRAIN
. . KUWAIT
. . QATAR
. . UNITED ARAB EMIRATES
. SAUDI ARABIA
. SYRIA
. TURKEY
. YEMEN
. YEMEN PDR

MIGRANTS
. EMIGRANTS
. IMMIGRANTS
. MIGRANT WORKERS
. NOMADS
. REFUGEES

MIGRATIONS
. INTERNAL MIGRATIONS
. . COMMUTING
. . RURAL MIGRATIONS
. INTERNATIONAL MIGRATIONS
. . EMIGRATION
. . . BRAIN DRAIN
. . FRONTIER MIGRATIONS
. . IMMIGRATION
. LABOUR MIGRATIONS
. NOMADISM
. POPULATION TRANSFERS
. RETURN MIGRATIONS
. SEASONAL MIGRATIONS

MINERALS
. BAUXITE
. COPPER ORE
. IRON ORE
. PRECIOUS STONES
. . DIAMOND

MODELS
. ECONOMIC MODELS
. . ECONOMETRIC MODELS
. . GROWTH MODELS
. MATHEMATICAL MODELS

MODES OF TRANSPORTATION
. AIR TRANSPORT
. INLAND WATER TRANSPORT
. MULTIMODAL TRANSPORT
. PIPELINE TRANSPORT
. RAILWAY TRANSPORT
. ROAD TRANSPORT
. SEA TRANSPORT

MONOPOLIES
. CARTELS

MORTALITY
. INFANT MORTALITY
. INTRAUTERINE MORTALITY
. OCCUPATIONAL MORTALITY

MULTILINGUALISM
. BILINGUALISM

MUTATIONS
. INDUCED MUTATIONS

NATURAL RESOURCES
. ANIMAL RESOURCES
. . FISHERY RESOURCES
. ENERGY RESOURCES
. . PETROLEUM RESOURCES
. MARINE RESOURCES
. MINERAL RESOURCES
. NON-RENEWABLE RESOURCES
. PLANT RESOURCES
. . FOREST RESOURCES
. RENEWABLE RESOURCES
. SOIL RESOURCES
. WATER RESOURCES

NATURAL SCIENCES
. ANATOMY
. . CARDIOVASCULAR SYSTEM

NATURAL SCIENCES<CONT>
. . . HEART
. . DIGESTIVE SYSTEM
. . . LIVER
. . ENDOCRINE SYSTEM
. . HISTOLOGY
. . . CYTOLOGY
. . INTEGUMENTARY SYSTEM
. . . SKIN
. . LYMPHATIC SYSTEM
. . MUSCULOSKELETAL SYSTEM
. . NERVOUS SYSTEM
. . . BRAIN
. . RESPIRATORY SYSTEM
. . UROGENITAL SYSTEM
. ANTHROPOLOGY
. BIOLOGY
. . MICROBIOLOGY
. . . BACTERIOLOGY
. . . VIROLOGY
. BOTANY
. CHEMISTRY
. . BIOCHEMISTRY
. . FOOD CHEMISTRY
. . GEOCHEMISTRY
. . ORGANIC CHEMISTRY
. . PETROCHEMISTRY
. . SOIL CHEMISTRY
. EARTH SCIENCES
. . GEOCHEMISTRY
. . GEOLOGY
. . . HYDROGEOLOGY
. . GEOMORPHOLOGY
. . GEOPHYSICS
. . . CLIMATOLOGY
. . . . BIOCLIMATOLOGY
. . . GEODESY
. . . SEISMOLOGY
. . . SOIL PHYSICS
. . . VULCANOLOGY
. . HYDROLOGY
. . . HYDROGEOLOGY
. . . HYDROGRAPHY
. . METEOROLOGY
. . . CLIMATOLOGY
. . . . BIOCLIMATOLOGY
. . MINERALOGY
. . OCEANOGRAPHY
. . PHYSICAL GEOGRAPHY
. . SOIL SCIENCES
. . . SOIL CHEMISTRY
. . . SOIL PHYSICS
. ECOLOGY
. . ANIMAL ECOLOGY
. . HUMAN ECOLOGY
. . PLANT ECOLOGY
. GENETICS
. PHYSICS
. . ACOUSTICS
. . GEOPHYSICS
. . . CLIMATOLOGY
. . . . BIOCLIMATOLOGY
. . . GEODESY
. . . SEISMOLOGY
. . . SOIL PHYSICS
. . . VULCANOLOGY
. . OPTICS
. PHYSIOLOGY

NATURAL SCIENCES<CONT>
. SPACE SCIENCES
. . ASTRONAUTICS
. . ASTRONOMY
. ZOOLOGY
. . ENTOMOLOGY

NATURE CONSERVATION
. ANIMAL PROTECTION
. . FISHERY CONSERVATION
. . GAME PROTECTION
. ENVIRONMENTAL PROTECTION
. . LANDSCAPE PROTECTION
. . POLLUTION CONTROL
. . . DECONTAMINATION
. . . POLLUTER-PAYS PRINCIPLE
. . . WARNING DEVICES
. PLANT PROTECTION
. . FOREST CONSERVATION

NUTRIENTS
. PROTEINS
. . AMINO ACIDS
. VITAMINS

NUTRITION
. ANIMAL NUTRITION
. HUMAN NUTRITION
. PLANT NUTRITION

OBSERVATION
. REMOTE SENSING

OCEANIA
. AUSTRALIA
. FIJI
. NAURU
. NEW ZEALAND
. PACIFIC ISLANDS AUS
. . PAPUA NEW GUINEA
. PACIFIC ISLANDS FR
. . FRENCH POLYNESIA
. . NEW CALEDONIA
. PACIFIC ISLANDS NZ
. PACIFIC ISLANDS UK
. . NEW HEBRIDES
. PACIFIC ISLANDS USA
. . NEW HEBRIDES
. SAMOA
. TONGA

OILS AND FATS
. ANIMAL OILS
. . FISH OILS
. ESSENTIAL OILS
. FATS
. . ANIMAL FATS
. MARGARINE
. VEGETABLE OILS
. . OLIVE OIL
. . PALM OIL
. . PEANUT OIL

OWNERSHIP
. COLLECTIVE OWNERSHIP
. FOREIGN OWNERSHIP
. . FOREIGN CAPITAL
. LAND OWNERSHIP

OWNERSHIP<CONT>
. PRIVATE OWNERSHIP
. PUBLIC OWNERSHIP

PARAMEDICAL PERSONNEL
. BAREFOOT DOCTORS
. MIDWIVES
. NURSES
. SOCIAL WORKERS

PARENTS
. FATHER
. MOTHER

PENAL SANCTIONS
. CAPITAL PUNISHMENT
. FORCED LABOUR
. PRISONS

PENSION SCHEMES
. OLD AGE BENEFITS

PESTICIDES
. FUNGICIDES
. HERBICIDES
. INSECTICIDES

PHILOSOPHY
. AESTHETICS
. PHILOSOPHY OF EDUCATION

PLANNING
. COMMUNICATION PLANNING
. DEVELOPMENT PLANNING
. ECONOMIC PLANNING
. . AGRICULTURAL PLANNING
. . . FISHERY PLANNING
. . . FORESTRY PLANNING
. . EXPORT PLANNING
. . INDUSTRIAL PLANNING
. . MANPOWER PLANNING
. . MARKET PLANNING
. . PRODUCTION PLANNING
. EDUCATIONAL PLANNING
. FOOD PLANNING
. HEALTH PLANNING
. NATIONAL PLANNING
. PROGRAMME PLANNING
. REGIONAL PLANNING
. RURAL PLANNING
. SOCIAL PLANNING
. TRANSPORT PLANNING
. URBAN PLANNING
. . ZONING

PLANNING SYSTEMS
. DIRECTIVE PLANNING
. SECTORAL PLANNING
. STRATEGIC PLANNING

PLANTS
. AQUATIC PLANTS
. . ALGAE
. FLOWERS
. FUNGI
. GRASSES
. LEGUMINOSAE
. . BEANS

PLANTS<CONT>
. . CHICKPEAS
. . COWPEAS
. . FABA BEANS
. . GROUNDNUTS
. . LENTILS
. . PIGEON PEAS
. . SOYBEANS
. MEDICINAL PLANTS
. SEEDS
. . OILSEEDS
. . . COTTON
. . . FLAX
. . . GROUNDNUTS
. . . RAPE
. . . SOYBEANS
. TREES
. . FOREST TREES
. . FRUIT TREES
. . . BANANA-TREES
. . . COCONUT PALMS
. . . DATE PALMS
. . HEVEAS
. . OIL PALMS
. VEGETABLES
. . ONIONS
. WILD PLANTS

POISONS
. TOXINS

POLITICAL SYSTEMS
. DEMOCRACY
. DICTATORSHIP

POLLUTANTS
. AIR POLLUTANTS
. . AEROSOLS
. . NITROGEN OXIDES
. . SULPHUR DIOXIDE
. HYDROCARBONS
. . BENZENE
. . METHANE
. SOIL POLLUTANTS
. WASTES
. . AGRICULTURAL WASTES
. . DOMESTIC WASTES
. . INDUSTRIAL WASTES
. . . METAL SCRAPS
. . . WOOD WASTES
. . RADIOACTIVE WASTES
. . WASTE WATERS
. WATER POLLUTANTS

POLLUTION
. ACUSTIC POLLUTION
. AIR POLLUTION
. CHEMICAL POLLUTION
. COASTAL POLLUTION
. RADIOACTIVE POLLUTION
. SOIL POLLUTION
. THERMAL POLLUTION
. TRANSFRONTIER POLLUTION
. WATER POLLUTION
. . EUTROPHICATION
. . MARINE POLLUTION
. . RIVER POLLUTION

POLYMERS
. PLASTICS
. . POLYESTER

POPULATION
. ABORIGINAL POPULATION
. . INDIGENOUS POPULATION
. RURAL POPULATION
. . AGRICULTURAL POPULATION
. . . AGRICULTURAL WORKERS
. . . . FARMERS
. . . . . TENANT FARMERS
. . . . FISHERMEN
. . . PEASANTS
. URBAN POPULATION

PRECIPITATIONS
. RAIN
. SNOW

PRECISION INSTRUMENTS
. MEASURING INSTRUMENTS
. . RADAR
. OPTICAL INSTRUMENTS

PRICES
. ADMINISTERED PRICES
. COMMODITY PRICES
. . AGRICULTURAL PRICES
. CONSUMER PRICES
. INDUSTRIAL PRICES
. RETAIL PRICES
. WHOLESALE PRICES

PRIMARY SECTOR
. AGRICULTURAL SECTOR
. MINING
. . COAL MINING
. . DEEP SEA MINING

PROCESSING
. AGRIPRODUCT PROCESSING
. . FOOD PROCESSING
. . . FISHERY PRODUCT PROCESSING
. . . GRAIN PROCESSING
. . . MEAT PROCESSING
. . . MILK PROCESSING
. INFORMATION PROCESSING
. . DATA PROCESSING
. . . DATA ANALYSIS
. . . DATA RETRIEVAL
. . . DATA STORAGE
. . . ELECTRONIC DATA PROCESSING
. REPROCESSING

PRODUCTION
. AGRICULTURAL PRODUCTION
. . ANIMAL PRODUCTION
. . . CATTLE PRODUCTION
. . . FISH PRODUCTION
. . FOREST PRODUCTION
. . . WOOD PRODUCTION
. . PLANT PRODUCTION
. FOOD PRODUCTION
. INDUSTRIAL PRODUCTION
. MASS PRODUCTION
. OVERPRODUCTION
. POWER GENERATION

PRODUCTION CONTROL
. AUTOMATIC CONTROL

PRODUCTION FUNCTIONS
. CAPITAL-LABOUR RATIO
. CAPITAL-OUTPUT RATIO

PRODUCTIVITY
. LABOUR PRODUCTIVITY

PRODUCTS
. BY-PRODUCTS
. COMMODITIES
. . AGRICULTURAL PRODUCTS
. . . ANIMAL PRODUCTS
. . . . ANIMAL FATS
. . . . ANIMAL FIBRES
. . . . . SILK
. . . . . WOOL
. . . ANIMAL OILS
. . . . . FISH OILS
. . . DAIRY PRODUCTS
. . . . BUTTER
. . . . . CHEESE
. . . . . MILK
. . . . . . MILK POWDER
. . . . EGGS
. . . FISHERY PRODUCTS
. . . . FISH MEAL
. . . . . FISH PROTEIN CONCENTRATE
. . . . HIDES AND SKINS
. . . . . FUR
. . . . . LEATHER
. . . . HONEY
. . . . MEAT PRODUCTS
. . . . . MEAT
. . . . . . BEEF
. . . . . . MUTTON
. . . . . . PORK
. . PLANT PRODUCTS
. . . . CEREALS
. . . . . BARLEY
. . . . . MAIZE
. . . . . MILLET
. . . . . RICE
. . . . . RYE
. . . . . SORGHUM
. . . . . TRITICALE
. . . . . WHEAT
. . . FOREST PRODUCTS
. . . . . GUMS
. . . . . . GUM ARABIC
. . . . . RESINS
. . . . . WOOD
. . . . . . CORK
. . . . . . TIMBER
. . . . . WOOD PRODUCTS
. . . . . . CARDBOARD
. . . . . . PAPER
. . . . . . PARTICLE BOARDS
. . . . . . PLYWOOD
. . . . . . PULP
. . . . . . WOOD FIBRES
. . . . FRUITS
. . . . . ALMONDS
. . . . . APPLES
. . . . . BANANAS
. . . . . CASHEW NUTS

PRODUCTS<CONT>
. . . . . CITRUS FRUITS
. . . . . COCONUTS
. . . . . DATES
. . . . . GRAPES
. . . . . GROUNDNUTS
. . . . . OLIVES
. . . . . PEARS
. . . . . PINEAPPLES
. . . . . TOMATOES
. . . . PLANT FIBRES
. . . . . COIR
. . . . . COTTON
. . . . . FLAX
. . . . . HEMP
. . . . . JUTE
. . . . . SISAL
. . . . . WOOD FIBRES
. . . . VEGETABLE OILS
. . . . . OLIVE OIL
. . . . . PALM OIL
. . . . . PEANUT OIL
. . RAW MATERIALS
. COMPETITIVE PRODUCTS
. INDUSTRIAL PRODUCTS
. . MANUFACTURED PRODUCTS
. . . FINISHED PRODUCTS
. . SEMI-MANUFACTURED PRODUCTS
. NATURAL PRODUCTS
. NEW PRODUCTS
. SUBSTITUTE PRODUCTS

PROJECTIONS
. ECONOMIC PROJECTIONS

PROTECTED AREAS
. NATURE RESERVES

PROTECTED RESOURCES
. BOTANICAL GARDENS
. NATIONAL PARKS
. NATURE RESERVES
. ZOOLOGICAL GARDENS

PUBLIC ADMINISTRATION
. ADMINISTRATION OF JUSTICE
. DEVELOPMENT ADMINISTRATION
. ECONOMIC ADMINISTRATION
. . AGRICULTURAL ADMINISTRATION
. . FINANCIAL ADMINISTRATION
. . . FISCAL ADMINISTRATION
. . INDUSTRIAL ADMINISTRATION
. EDUCATIONAL ADMINISTRATION
. HEALTH ADMINISTRATION
. . HEALTH SERVICES
. . . HEALTH CENTRES
. . . HOSPITALS
. . . . MENTAL HOSPITALS
. LABOUR ADMINISTRATION
. SOCIAL ADMINISTRATION
. . SOCIAL SERVICES
. . . CARE OF THE AGED
. . . CHILD CARE
. . . DISABLED CARE
. . . EMERGENCY RELIEF
. . . HEALTH SERVICES
. . . . HEALTH CENTRES
. . . . HOSPITALS

PUBLIC ADMINISTRATION<CONT>
. . . . . MENTAL HOSPITALS
. . . ORPHANAGES

PUBLIC FINANCE
. LOCAL FINANCE
. NATIONAL BUDGET
. . BUDGETARY RESOURCES
. . . TAX REVENUES
. PUBLIC ACCOUNTING
. PUBLIC BORROWING
. PUBLIC DEBT
. PUBLIC EXPENDITURES
. . MILITARY EXPENDITURES
. TAXES
. . CAPITAL TAX
. . CONSUMPTION TAX
. . . IMPORT TAX
. . . VALUE ADDED TAX
. . INCOME TAX
. . . CORPORATION TAX
. . LAND TAX
. . LOCAL TAXES
. . PAYROLL TAX

PUBLIC LAND
. COMMUNAL LAND

PUBLIC SERVICES
. SANITATION SERVICES

PURCHASING
. HIRE PURCHASE

QUALIFICATIONS
. CERTIFICATES
. DIPLOMAS
. OCCUPATIONAL QUALIFICATION
. . JOB REQUIREMENTS
. UNIVERSITY DEGREES

RACIAL SEGREGATION
. APARTHEID

RECRUITMENT
. TEACHER RECRUITMENT

REHABILITATION
. VOCATIONAL REHABILITATION

RELIGIOUS INSTITUTIONS
. RELIGIOUS MISSIONS

RESEARCH
. AGRICULTURAL RESEARCH
. . FISHERY RESEARCH
. . FORESTRY RESEARCH
. APPLIED RESEARCH
. BASIC RESEARCH
. COMMUNICATION RESEARCH
. DEVELOPMENT RESEARCH
. ECOLOGICAL RESEARCH
. ECONOMIC RESEARCH
. EDUCATIONAL RESEARCH
. FIELD RESEARCH
. INDUSTRIAL RESEARCH
. MEDICAL RESEARCH
. NUTRITION RESEARCH

RESEARCH<CONT>
. PEACE RESEARCH
. RESEARCH AND DEVELOPMENT
. SOCIAL RESEARCH

RESEARCH CENTRES
. CAFRAD
. CIMMYT
. ICRISAT
. IDRC
. IRRI
. LABORATORIES
. UNITAR
. UNRISD

RESEARCH METHODS
. COMPARATIVE ANALYSIS
. . COMPARATIVE EDUCATION
. . CROSS CULTURAL ANALYSIS
. DATA COLLECTING
. . CENSUSES
. . . AGRICULTURAL CENSUSES
. . . ECONOMIC CENSUSES
. . . HOUSING CENSUSES
. . . INDUSTRIAL CENSUSES
. . . POPULATION CENSUSES
. . SURVEYS
. . . AERIAL SURVEYS
. . . CADASTRAL SURVEYS
. . . ECONOMIC SURVEYS
. . . GEOLOGICAL SURVEYS
. . . MAIL SURVEYS
. . . SOCIAL SURVEYS
. . . SOIL SURVEYS
. EVALUATION TECHNIQUES
. . TESTS
. EXPERIMENTS
. FORECASTING TECHNIQUES
. INTEGRATED APPROACH
. INTERDISCIPLINARY RESEARCH
. MATHEMATICAL ANALYSIS
. OPERATIONAL RESEARCH
. . SCENARIOS
. SIMULATION
. STATISTICAL ANALYSIS

RESEARCH PROGRAMMES
. RESEARCH PROJECTS

RESOURCES ALLOCATION
. RATIONING

RESOURCES CONSERVATION
. ENERGY CONSERVATION
. SOIL CONSERVATION
. WATER CONSERVATION

RETIREMENT
. EARLY RETIREMENT

ROOT CROPS
. CASSAVA
. POTATOES
. SUGAR BEETS
. SWEET POTATOES

RUBBER
. SYNTHETIC RUBBER

SAFETY
. OCCUPATIONAL SAFETY
. ROAD SAFETY

SAVINGS
. HOARDING

SCIENCES OF EDUCATION
. ECONOMICS OF EDUCATION
. . COST OF EDUCATION
. . . FEES
. . EDUCATIONAL BUDGET
. . EDUCATIONAL FINANCING
. . EDUCATIONAL GRANTS
. . . RESEARCH FELLOWSHIPS
. . . SCHOLARSHIPS
. . . STUDENT LOANS
. . . TRAINING ALLOWANCES
. . FREE EDUCATION
. HISTORY OF EDUCATION
. PHILOSOPHY OF EDUCATION
. PSYCHOLOGY OF EDUCATION
. SOCIOLOGY OF EDUCATION

SCIENTISTS
. AGRONOMISTS
. ANTHROPOLOGISTS
. BIOLOGISTS
. BOTANISTS
. CHEMISTS
. DEMOGRAPHERS
. ECONOMISTS
. GEOGRAPHERS
. GEOLOGISTS
. LINGUISTS
. MATHEMATICIANS
. PHYSICISTS
. POLITICAL SCIENTISTS
. PSYCHOLOGISTS
. SOCIOLOGISTS
. STATISTICIANS

SEASONS
. COLD SEASON
. DRY SEASON
. RAINY SEASON
. WARM SEASON

SECURITIES
. DEBENTURES
. SHARES
. TREASURY BONDS

SERVICE INDUSTRY
. AUTOMOBILE SERVICE
. BANKING SYSTEMS
. HOTEL INDUSTRY
. TOURISM
. TRADE
. . BARTER
. . DOMESTIC TRADE
. . INTERNATIONAL TRADE
. . . EAST-WEST TRADE
. . . FOREIGN TRADE
. . . . EXPORTS
. . . . IMPORTS
. . RETAIL TRADE
. . WHOLESALE TRADE

SERVICE INDUSTRY<CONT>
. TRANSPORT
. . INLAND TRANSPORT
. . INTERNATIONAL TRANSPORT
. . PUBLIC TRANSPORT
. . SCHOOL TRANSPORT
. . URBAN TRANSPORT

SEX
. FEMALES
. MALES

SIZE OF ENTERPRISE
. FARM SIZE

SOCIAL CLASSES
. BOURGEOISIE
. MIDDLE CLASS
. RULING CLASS
. UPPER CLASS
. WORKING CLASS

SOCIAL MOBILITY
. LABOUR MOBILITY
. OCCUPATIONAL MOBILITY

SOCIAL MOVEMENTS
. COOPERATIVE MOVEMENTS
. LABOUR MOVEMENTS
. NATIONAL LIBERATION MOVEMENTS
. PEASANT MOVEMENTS
. STUDENT MOVEMENTS

SOCIAL PARTICIPATION
. STUDENT PARTICIPATION

SOCIAL PROBLEMS
. ACCIDENTS
. . OCCUPATIONAL ACCIDENTS
. ALCOHOLISM
. CORRUPTION
. CRIMES
. . GENOCIDE
. . HOMICIDE
. . WAR CRIMES
. DELINQUENCY
. . JUVENILE DELINQUENCY
. DRUG ADDICTION
. FAMILY DISINTEGRATION
. FAMINE
. MALNUTRITION
. . CALORIE DEFICIENCY
. . PROTEIN DEFICIENCY
. . VITAMIN DEFICIENCY
. POVERTY
. PROSTITUTION
. SOCIAL CONFLICTS
. . LABOUR DISPUTES
. . . LOCKOUTS
. . . STRIKES
. . . . WILDCAT STRIKES
. UNEMPLOYMENT
. . CYCLICAL UNEMPLOYMENT
. . . SEASONAL UNEMPLOYMENT
. . DISGUISED UNEMPLOYMENT
. . STRUCTURAL UNEMPLOYMENT
. . TECHNICAL UNEMPLOYMENT
. . UNDEREMPLOYMENT

SOCIAL PROBLEMS<CONT>
. . YOUTH UNEMPLOYMENT

SOCIAL SCIENCES
. ANTHROPOLOGY
. CRIMINOLOGY
. DEMOGRAPHY
. ECONOMICS
. . AGRICULTURAL ECONOMICS
. . . FISHERY ECONOMICS
. . . FORESTRY ECONOMICS
. . BUSINESS ECONOMICS
. . ECONOMETRICS
. . ECONOMICS OF CULTURE
. . ECONOMICS OF EDUCATION
. . . COST OF EDUCATION
. . . . FEES
. . . EDUCATIONAL BUDGET
. . . EDUCATIONAL FINANCING
. . . EDUCATIONAL GRANTS
. . . . RESEARCH FELLOWSHIPS
. . . . SCHOLARSHIPS
. . . . STUDENT LOANS
. . . . TRAINING ALLOWANCES
. . . FREE EDUCATION
. . ENERGY ECONOMICS
. . ENVIRONMENTAL ECONOMICS
: . FOOD ECONOMICS
. . INDUSTRIAL ECONOMICS
. . LAND ECONOMICS
. . MACROECONOMICS
. . MICROECONOMICS
. . TRANSPORT ECONOMICS
. . WELFARE ECONOMICS
. ETHNOLOGY
. . ETHNOGRAPHY
. . FOLKLORE
. HISTORY
. . ECONOMIC HISTORY
. . HISTORY OF EDUCATION
. . SOCIAL HISTORY
. HUMAN GEOGRAPHY
. . CULTURAL GEOGRAPHY
. . ECONOMIC GEOGRAPHY
. . POLITICAL GEOGRAPHY
. LEGAL SCIENCES
. . JURISPRUDENCE
. . LAW
. . . CIVIL LAW
. . . . FAMILY LAW
. . . COMMERCIAL LAW
. . . COMMON LAW
. . . CRIMINAL LAW
. . . CUSTOMARY LAW
. . . FISCAL LAW
. . . INTERNATIONAL LAW
. . . . LAW OF THE SEA
. . . LABOUR LAW
. . . MARITIME LAW
. . . PATENT LAW
. . . PUBLIC LAW
. . . . ADMINISTRATIVE LAW
. . . . CONSTITUTIONAL LAW
. LINGUISTICS
. POLITICAL GEOGRAPHY
. POLITICAL SCIENCE
. SOCIAL PSYCHOLOGY
. SOCIOLOGY

SOCIAL SCIENCES<CONT>
. . INDUSTRIAL SOCIOLOGY
. . RURAL SOCIOLOGY
. . SOCIOLOGY OF EDUCATION
. . URBAN SOCIOLOGY

SOCIAL SECURITY
. DISABILITY BENEFITS
. EMPLOYMENT INJURIES BENEFITS
. FAMILY ALLOWANCES
. HEALTH INSURANCE
. MATERNITY BENEFITS
. OLD AGE BENEFITS
. SURVIVORS BENEFITS
. UNEMPLOYMENT INSURANCE

SOCIETY
. AFFLUENT SOCIETY

SODA
. CAUSTIC SODA

SPACE
. OUTER SPACE

SPICES
. PEPPER

STABILIZATION
. MARKET STABILIZATION
. PRICE STABILIZATION

STANDARDS
. FOOD STANDARDS
. LABOUR STANDARDS
. PRODUCTION STANDARDS
. QUALITY STANDARDS

STATE AID
. SUBSIDIES
. . EXPORT SUBSIDIES
. TAX EXEMPTION

STATISTICAL DATA
. ECONOMIC STATISTICS
. . AGRICULTURAL STATISTICS
. . . FISHERY STATISTICS
. . . FORESTRY STATISTICS
. . FINANCIAL STATISTICS
. . INDUSTRIAL STATISTICS
. . PRODUCTION STATISTICS
. EDUCATIONAL STATISTICS
. FOOD STATISTICS
. VITAL STATISTICS

STATISTICAL TABLES
. INPUT-OUTPUT TABLES

STOCKS
. BUFFER STOCKS

STORAGE
. FOOD STORAGE
. WATER STORAGE

STUDENTS
. COLLEGE STUDENTS
. . FOREIGN STUDENTS

STUDENTS<CONT>
. . UNDERGRADUATES
. GIFTED STUDENTS
. HANDICAPPED STUDENTS

SUPPLY AND DEMAND
. DEMAND
. . BASIC NEEDS
. . . EDUCATIONAL NEEDS
. . . FOOD REQUIREMENTS
. . . HOUSING NEEDS
. . . INFORMATION NEEDS
. . . WATER REQUIREMENTS
. . CONSUMER DEMAND
. . FINANCIAL NEEDS
. . . INVESTMENT REQUIREMENTS
. . MANPOWER NEEDS
. . POWER DEMAND
. SUPPLY
. . FOOD SUPPLY
. . LABOUR SUPPLY
. . MONEY SUPPLY
. . POWER SUPPLY
. . WATER SUPPLY

SURPLUSES
. AGRICULTURAL SURPLUSES

TEACHING
. DISTANCE STUDY
. . CORRESPONDENCE EDUCATION
. . EDUCATIONAL RADIO
. . EDUCATIONAL TELEVISION
. EXPERIMENTAL TEACHING
. INDIVIDUALIZED TEACHING
. PEER TEACHING
. REMEDIAL TEACHING
. SELF-INSTRUCTION
. TEAM TEACHING

TEACHING METHODS
. PROGRAMMED INSTRUCTION

TEACHING PERSONNEL
. INSTRUCTORS
. TEACHERS

TECHNICAL PERSONNEL
. TECHNICIANS
. . DRAUGHTSMEN

TECHNOLOGY
. ALTERNATIVE TECHNOLOGY
. APPROPRIATE TECHNOLOGY
. INTERMEDIATE TECHNOLOGY
. TRADITIONAL TECHNOLOGY

THEORY
. DEVELOPMENT THEORY
. ECONOMIC THEORY
. EDUCATIONAL THEORY
. INFORMATION THEORY
. POLITICAL THEORY
. POPULATION THEORY
. SOCIAL THEORY

TOILET PREPARATIONS
. COSMETICS

TOILET PREPARATIONS<CONT>
. PERFUMES
. SOAP

TOOLS
. HAND TOOLS
. MACHINE TOOLS

TOWNS
. MIDDLE-SIZED TOWNS
. NEW TOWNS
. SATELLITE TOWNS
. SMALL TOWNS

TRADE BARRIERS
. BOYCOTT
. DUMPING
. EMBARGO
. . ARMS EMBARGO
. RESTRICTIVE BUSINESS PRACTICES
. . CARTELS
. . EXPORT RESTRICTIONS
. . PROTECTIONIST MEASURES
. . . IMPORT RESTRICTIONS
. . . . IMPORT TAX
. . . IMPORT SUBSTITUTION
. . . QUOTA SYSTEM
. TARIFFS
. . PREFERENTIAL TARIFFS
. . . GENERAL SYSTEM OF PREFERENCES

TRADE PROMOTION
. EXPORT PROMOTION
. IMPORT PROMOTION

TRADE VOLUME
. EXPORT VOLUME
. IMPORT VOLUME

TRAFFIC
. AIR TRAFFIC
. RAILWAY TRAFFIC
. ROAD TRAFFIC
. SEA TRAFFIC
. URBAN TRAFFIC

TRAINING
. MANAGEMENT DEVELOPMENT
. TEACHER TRAINING
. TRAINING ABROAD
. VOCATIONAL TRAINING
. . AGRICULTURAL TRAINING
. . APPRENTICESHIP
. . BASIC TRAINING
. . FURTHER TRAINING
. . IN-PLANT TRAINING
. . INDUSTRIAL TRAINING
. . MODULAR TRAINING
. . RETRAINING
. . SANDWICH TRAINING

TRAINING METHODS
. MODULAR TRAINING

TRANSPORT INFRASTRUCTURE
. BRIDGES
. CANALS
. PIPELINES

TRANSPORT INFRASTRUCTURE<CONT>
. PORTS
. . FISHING PORTS
. RAILWAYS
. ROADS
. . MOTORWAYS
. STATIONS
. TUNNELS

TRAVELS
. STUDY TOURS

URBAN CONCENTRATION
. CONURBATION

VETERINARIANS
. ZOOTECHNICIANS

WAGE PAYMENT SYSTEMS
. PAYMENT BY RESULT

WATERWAYS
. INLAND WATERWAYS
. . CANALS
. . LAKES
. . . ARTIFICIAL LAKES
. . RIVERS

WEAPONS
. BACTERIOLOGICAL WEAPONS
. CONVENTIONAL WEAPONS
. NUCLEAR WEAPONS

WOMEN
. FEMALE MANPOWER

WORKERS
. AUXILIARY WORKERS
. CASUAL WORKERS
. DOMESTIC WORKERS
. EMPLOYEES
. . OFFICE WORKERS
. . . ACCOUNTANTS
. . PUBLIC SERVANTS
. . TRANSPORT WORKERS
. . . DOCKERS
. . . PILOTS
. . . SEAFARERS
. . VENDORS
. FEMALE MANPOWER
. FOREIGN WORKERS
. HANDICAPPED WORKERS
. INDUSTRIAL WORKERS
. . CONSTRUCTION WORKERS
. . ELECTRICIANS
. . METALWORKERS
. . MINERS
. . SEMI-SKILLED WORKERS
. . SKILLED WORKERS
. . TEXTILE WORKERS
. . UNSKILLED WORKERS
. MANUAL WORKERS
. MIGRANT WORKERS
. OLDER WORKERS
. RURAL WORKERS
. . AGRICULTURAL WORKERS
. . . FARMERS
. . . . TENANT FARMERS

WORKERS<CONT>
. . . FISHERMEN
. SELF-EMPLOYED
. WAGE EARNERS
. YOUNG WORKERS

WORKSHOPS
. REPAIR SHOPS

YOUTH ORGANIZATIONS
. STUDENT MOVEMENTS

V. KWOC INDEX

ABILITY
    ABILITY GROUPING - 06.04.10

ABORIGINAL
    ABORIGINAL POPULATION - 14.03.01

ABORTION
    ABORTION - 14.05.02
    LEGAL ABORTION - 14.05.02

ABRASIVES
    ABRASIVES - 08.12.08

ABROAD
    TRAINING ABROAD - 06.05.02

ABSENCE
    LEAVE OF ABSENCE - 13.05.00

ABSENTEEISM
    ABSENTEEISM - 13.05.00

ABSORPTIVE
    ABSORPTIVE CAPACITY - 11.02.06

ABSTRACT
    ABSTRACT - 19.02.07

ABUNDANCE
    ABUNDANCE - 03.02.05

ACADEMIC
    ACADEMIC FREEDOM - 04.02.02

ACAST
    ACAST - 01.03.02

ACCELERATED
    ACCELERATED COURSES - 06.05.01

ACCESS
    ACCESS TO CULTURE - 05.02.03
    ACCESS TO EDUCATION - 06.02.02
    ACCESS TO INFORMATION - 19.01.01
    ACCESS TO MARKET - 09.03.01

ACCIDENT
    ACCIDENT INSURANCE - 11.02.03
    ACCIDENT PREVENTION
    - 13.04.00
     USE: OCCUPATIONAL SAFETY

ACCIDENTS
    ACCIDENTS - 02.04.02
    OCCUPATIONAL ACCIDENTS - 13.04.00

ACCLIMATIZATION
    ACCLIMATIZATION - 17.02.01

ACCOUNTANTS
    ACCOUNTANTS - 13.09.09

ACCOUNTING
    ACCOUNTING - 12.09.00
    COST ACCOUNTING - 12.09.00
    NATIONAL ACCOUNTING - 03.02.02
    PUBLIC ACCOUNTING - 11.01.01

ACCOUNTS
    NATIONAL ACCOUNTS - 03.02.02

ACCT
    ACCT - 01.03.03

ACCULTURATION
    ACCULTURATION - 05.02.02

ACCUMULATION
    ACCUMULATION RATE - 03.01.02

ACDA
    ACDA - 01.03.03

ACIDS
    ACIDS - 08.12.04
    AMINO ACIDS - 15.01.03

ACOUSTICS
    ACOUSTICS - 08.14.08

ACQUISITION
    DATA ACQUISITION
    - 18.04.00
     USE: DATA COLLECTING

ACTIVITY
    ACTIVITY ANALYSIS - 12.04.00
    FIELD ACTIVITY - 18.04.00

ACTUARIES
    ACTUARIES - 13.09.09

ACUPUNCTURE
    ACUPUNCTURE - 15.04.04

ACUSTIC
    ACUSTIC POLLUTION - 16.03.04

ADAPTATION
    ADAPTATION - 05.03.03
    ADAPTATION TO CHANGE - 05.03.04
    INDUSTRIAL ADAPTATION - 08.01.02
    SCHOOL ADAPTATION - 06.04.12
    SOCIAL ADAPTATION - 05.03.03
    WORKERS ADAPTATION - 13.02.02

ADC
    ADC - 01.03.03

ADDED
    VALUE ADDED - 12.09.00
    VALUE ADDED TAX - 11.01.02

ADDICTION
    DRUG ADDICTION - 02.04.02

ADDITIVES
    FOOD ADDITIVES - 08.06.02

ADHESIVES
    ADHESIVES - 08.12.08

ADIPA
    ADIPA - 01.03.03

ADJUSTMENT
    ADJUSTMENT
    - 05.03.03
     USE: ADAPTATION

ADMINISTERED
    ADMINISTERED PRICES - 09.02.00

ADMINISTRATION

ADMINISTRATION OF EDUCATION
- 04.03.02
USE: EDUCATIONAL ADMINISTRATION
ADMINISTRATION OF JUSTICE - 04.03.02
AGRICULTURAL ADMINISTRATION - 04.03.02
DEVELOPMENT ADMINISTRATION - 04.03.02
ECONOMIC ADMINISTRATION - 04.03.02
EDUCATIONAL ADMINISTRATION - 04.03.02
FINANCIAL ADMINISTRATION - 04.03.02
FISCAL ADMINISTRATION - 04.03.02
HEALTH ADMINISTRATION - 04.03.02
INDUSTRIAL ADMINISTRATION - 04.03.02
LABOUR ADMINISTRATION - 04.03.02
PERSONNEL ADMINISTRATION
- 13.02.02
USE: PERSONNEL MANAGEMENT
PUBLIC ADMINISTRATION - 04.03.02
SOCIAL ADMINISTRATION - 04.03.02

ADMINISTRATIVE

ADMINISTRATIVE ASPECTS - 04.03.04
ADMINISTRATIVE LAW - 04.01.02
ADMINISTRATIVE REFORMS - 04.03.04

ADMISSION

ADMISSION REQUIREMENTS - 06.04.09

ADOLESCENCE

ADOLESCENCE
- 14.02.02
USE: YOUTH

ADULT

ADULT EDUCATION - 06.03.05

ADULTS

ADULTS - 14.02.02

ADVANCEMENT

ADVANCEMENT
- 13.02.02
USE: PROMOTION
ADVANCEMENT OF EDUCATION
- 06.02.03
USE: EDUCATIONAL DEVELOPMENT

ADVANTAGE

COMPARATIVE ADVANTAGE - 09.05.03

ADVERTISING

ADVERTISING - 09.03.04

AERIAL

AERIAL SURVEYS - 18.04.00

AEROSOLS

AEROSOLS - 16.03.04

AEROSPACE

AEROSPACE INDUSTRY - 08.14.07

AESTHETICS

AESTHETICS - 05.05.02

AFFAIRS

INTERNATIONAL AFFAIRS
- 01.02.01
USE: INTERNATIONAL RELATIONS

AFFILIATION

POLITICAL AFFILIATION - 04.04.02

AFFLUENT

AFFLUENT SOCIETY - 03.02.05

AFFORESTATION

AFFORESTATION - 07.08.03

AFGHAN

AFGHAN - 14.03.02

AFGHANISTAN

AFGHANISTAN - 01.04.06

AFRASEC

AFRASEC - 01.03.03

AFRICA

AFRICA - 01.04.02
AFRICA SOUTH OF SAHARA - 01.04.02
CENTRAL AFRICA - 01.04.02
EAST AFRICA - 01.04.02
ENGLISH SPEAKING AFRICA - 01.04.02
FRENCH SPEAKING AFRICA - 01.04.02
NORTH AFRICA - 01.04.02
SOUTH AFRICA - 01.04.02
SOUTH WEST AFRICA
- 01.04.02
USE: NAMIBIA
SOUTHERN AFRICA - 01.04.02
WEST AFRICA - 01.04.02

AFRICAN

AFRICAN - 14.03.02
AFRICAN DEVELOPMENT BANK - 01.03.03
AFRICAN ORGANIZATIONS - 01.03.03
CENTRAL AFRICAN EMPIRE - 01.04.02
NORTH AFRICAN - 14.03.02
SOUTH AFRICAN - 14.03.02

AGE

AGE - 14.02.02
AGE DISTRIBUTION - 14.02.02
AGE GROUPS - 14.02.02
AGE-SEX DISTRIBUTION - 14.02.01
MINIMUM AGE - 14.02.02
OLD AGE - 14.02.02
OLD AGE BENEFITS - 02.03.02
SCHOOL AGE POPULATION - 14.02.02

AGED

AGED - 14.02.02

AGED<CONT>
    CARE OF THE AGED - 02.05.03

AGEING
    AGEING - 14.02.02

AGENCIES
    FAMILY PLANNING AGENCIES - 14.05.02
    REGIONAL AGENCIES - 01.01.07
    UN AND SPECIALIZED AGENCIES
    - 01.03.02
     USE: UN SYSTEM
    UN SPECIALIZED AGENCIES - 01.03.02

AGENCY
    EUROPEAN SPACE AGENCY - 01.03.03

AGENTS
    CLEANING AGENTS - 08.12.08

AGGLOMERATES
    AGGLOMERATES - 08.10.02

AGGRESSION
    AGGRESSION - 01.02.07

AGRARIAN
    AGRARIAN REFORMS - 07.02.00
    AGRARIAN STRUCTURE - 07.02.00
    AGRARIAN SYSTEMS
    - 07.02.00
     USE: AGRARIAN STRUCTURE

AGREEMENT
    CARTHAGENA AGREEMENT
    - 01.03.03
     USE: ANDEAN GROUP

AGREEMENTS
    CLEARING AGREEMENTS - 11.03.01
    COLLECTIVE AGREEMENTS - 13.06.00
    COMMODITY AGREEMENTS - 09.05.02
    COMPLEMENTARITY AGREEMENTS - 01.02.01
    CULTURAL AGREEMENTS - 05.02.03
    ECONOMIC AGREEMENTS - 09.05.02
    INTERNATIONAL AGREEMENTS - 01.02.04
    MONETARY AGREEMENTS - 11.03.01
    PAYMENT AGREEMENTS - 11.03.02
    TARIFF AGREEMENTS - 09.05.08
    TAX AGREEMENTS - 09.05.09
    TRADE AGREEMENTS - 09.05.02

AGRICULTURAL
    AGRICULTURAL ADMINISTRATION - 04.03.02
    AGRICULTURAL AREAS - 07.05.02
    AGRICULTURAL ASPECTS - 07.01.01
    AGRICULTURAL BANKS - 07.03.03
    AGRICULTURAL CENSUSES - 07.05.01

AGRICULTURAL<CONT>
    AGRICULTURAL COMMODITIES
    - 07.05.05
     USE: AGRICULTURAL PRODUCTS
    AGRICULTURAL COOPERATIVES - 07.03.02
    AGRICULTURAL CREDIT - 07.03.03
    AGRICULTURAL DEVELOPMENT - 07.01.02
    AGRICULTURAL ECONOMICS - 07.01.01
    AGRICULTURAL ECONOMY - 07.01.01
    AGRICULTURAL EDUCATION - 06.03.07
    AGRICULTURAL ENGINEERING - 07.04.00
    AGRICULTURAL ENTERPRISES - 07.03.01
    AGRICULTURAL EQUIPMENT - 07.04.00
    AGRICULTURAL EXTENSION - 07.01.02
    AGRICULTURAL INCOME - 07.03.03
    AGRICULTURAL INDUSTRY
    - 07.01.01
     USE: AGROINDUSTRY
    AGRICULTURAL INSTITUTES - 06.04.06
    AGRICULTURAL INSURANCE - 07.03.03
    AGRICULTURAL INVESTMENTS - 07.03.03
    AGRICULTURAL MACHINERY - 07.04.00
    AGRICULTURAL MANAGEMENT - 07.01.02
    AGRICULTURAL MARKET - 07.01.03
    AGRICULTURAL MECHANIZATION - 07.04.00
    AGRICULTURAL PLANNING - 07.01.02
    AGRICULTURAL POLICY - 07.01.02
    AGRICULTURAL POPULATION - 14.04.02
    AGRICULTURAL POTENTIAL - 07.01.02
    AGRICULTURAL PRICES - 07.01.03
    AGRICULTURAL PRODUCTION - 07.05.01
    AGRICULTURAL PRODUCTS - 07.05.05
    AGRICULTURAL PROJECTS - 07.01.02
    AGRICULTURAL RESEARCH - 07.06.00
    AGRICULTURAL SECTOR - 07.01.01
    AGRICULTURAL STATISTICS - 07.05.01
    AGRICULTURAL SURPLUSES - 07.01.03
    AGRICULTURAL TECHNOLOGY
    - 07.04.00
     USE: AGRICULTURAL ENGINEERING
    AGRICULTURAL TRAINING - 06.03.07
    AGRICULTURAL WASTES - 07.05.05
    AGRICULTURAL WORKERS - 13.09.05

AGRICULTURE
    AGRICULTURE - 07.01.01

AGRIPRODUCT
    AGRIPRODUCT PROCESSING - 08.06.02

AGRIS
    AGRIS - 19.01.02

AGROINDUSTRIAL
    AGROINDUSTRIAL COMPLEX
    - 07.01.01
      USE: AGROINDUSTRY

AGROINDUSTRY
    AGROINDUSTRY - 07.01.01

AGRONOMISTS
    AGRONOMISTS - 13.09.09

AGRONOMY
    AGRONOMY - 07.06.00

AID
    AID BY RELIGIOUS BODIES
    - 01.01.02
      USE: PRIVATE AID
    AID COORDINATION - 01.01.04
    AID EVALUATION - 01.01.04
    AID FINANCING - 01.01.04
    AID IN KIND - 01.01.03
    AID INSTITUTIONS - 01.01.07
    AID PROGRAMMES - 01.01.04
    BILATERAL AID - 01.01.02
    CAPITAL AID
    - 01.01.03
      USE: FINANCIAL AID
    DEVELOPMENT AID - 01.01.01
    ECONOMIC AID - 01.01.03
    FINANCIAL AID - 01.01.03
    FOOD AID - 01.01.03
    FOREIGN AID - 01.01.01
    HEALTH AID - 01.01.03
    LEGAL AID - 04.02.01
    MILITARY AID - 01.02.06
    MULTILATERAL AID - 01.01.02
    PRIVATE AID - 01.01.02
    STATE AID - 11.01.01
    TERMS OF AID - 01.01.04
    TIED AID
    - 01.01.04
      USE: TERMS OF AID

AIDS
    AUDIOVISUAL AIDS - 06.05.03
    INSTRUCTIONAL AIDS
    - 06.05.03
      USE: TEACHING AIDS

AIDS<CONT>
    TEACHING AIDS - 06.05.03

AIMS
    AIMS OF EDUCATION - 06.02.01

AIR
    AIR
    - 17.01.02
      USE: ATMOSPHERE
    AIR PIRACY - 01.02.07
    AIR POLLUTANTS - 16.03.04
    AIR POLLUTION - 16.03.04
    AIR TRAFFIC - 10.08.00
    AIR TRANSPORT - 10.05.00

AIRCRAFT
    AIRCRAFT - 10.04.00
    AIRCRAFT INDUSTRY - 08.14.07

AIRPORTS
    AIRPORTS - 10.03.00

ALBANIA
    ALBANIA - 01.04.05

ALBANIAN
    ALBANIAN - 14.03.02

ALCOHOL
    ALCOHOL - 08.12.04

ALCOHOLIC
    ALCOHOLIC BEVERAGES - 08.06.05
    NON-ALCOHOLIC BEVERAGES - 08.06.05

ALCOHOLISM
    ALCOHOLISM - 02.04.02

ALECSO
    ALECSO - 01.03.03

ALGAE
    ALGAE - 07.10.04

ALGERIA
    ALGERIA - 01.04.02

ALGERIAN
    ALGERIAN - 14.03.02

ALIENATION
    ALIENATION - 05.03.03

ALLERGIES
    ALLERGIES
    - 15.04.02
      USE: IMMUNOLOGIC DISEASES

ALLIANCES
    ALLIANCES - 01.02.01

ALLOCATION
    RESOURCES ALLOCATION - 02.01.02

ALLOWANCES
    FAMILY ALLOWANCES - 02.03.02
    TRAINING ALLOWANCES - 06.04.11

ALLOYS
    ALLOYS - 08.14.02

ALMONDS

    ALMONDS - 07.07.05

ALTERNATIVE

    ALTERNATIVE TECHNOLOGY - 12.06.00

ALTITUDE

    ALTITUDE - 18.06.00

ALUMINIUM

    ALUMINIUM - 08.14.02

    ALUMINIUM INDUSTRY - 08.14.01

    ALUMINIUM ORE
    - 08.13.00
     USE: BAUXITE

AMERICA

    AMERICA - 01.04.03

    CENTRAL AMERICA - 01.04.03

    LATIN AMERICA - 01.04.03

    NORTH AMERICA - 01.04.03

    SOUTH AMERICA - 01.04.03

    UNITED STATES OF AMERICA
    - 01.04.03
     USE: USA

AMERICAN

    AMERICAN - 14.03.02

    AMERICAN ORGANIZATIONS - 01.03.03

    LATIN AMERICAN - 14.03.02

AMERINDIANS

    AMERINDIANS - 14.03.03

AMINO

    AMINO ACIDS - 15.01.03

AMMONIA

    AMMONIA - 08.12.04

AMORTIZATION

    AMORTIZATION - 11.02.05

ANALYSIS

    ACTIVITY ANALYSIS - 12.04.00

    CHEMICAL ANALYSIS - 08.12.02

    COMPARATIVE ANALYSIS - 18.09.00

    CONTENT ANALYSIS - 19.01.02

    COST ANALYSIS - 12.09.00

    COST-BENEFIT ANALYSIS - 12.09.00

    CROSS CULTURAL ANALYSIS - 05.01.02

    DATA ANALYSIS - 19.01.02

    DEMOGRAPHIC ANALYSIS - 14.01.01

    DOCUMENTARY ANALYSIS
    - 19.01.02
     USE: INFORMATION ANALYSIS

    ECONOMIC ANALYSIS - 03.01.02

    FOOD ANALYSIS - 15.03.01

ANALYSIS\<CONT\>

    HISTORICAL ANALYSIS - 05.01.01

    INFORMATION ANALYSIS - 19.01.02

    INPUT-OUTPUT ANALYSIS - 03.02.02

    MATHEMATICAL ANALYSIS - 18.08.00

    NETWORK ANALYSIS - 12.04.00

    REGIONAL ANALYSIS - 17.03.01

    SECTOR ANALYSIS
    - 03.02.02
     USE: INPUT-OUTPUT ANALYSIS

    SOCIOLOGICAL ANALYSIS - 05.01.02

    SOIL ANALYSIS - 17.04.04

    SPATIAL ANALYSIS - 17.03.01

    STATISTICAL ANALYSIS - 18.08.00

    SYSTEMS ANALYSIS - 18.08.00

ANATOMY

    ANATOMY - 15.02.01

ANDEAN

    ANDEAN GROUP - 01.03.03

    ANDEAN INDIANS
    - 14.03.03
     USE: AMERINDIANS

    ANDEAN PACT
    - 01.03.03
     USE: ANDEAN GROUP

    ANDEAN REGION - 01.04.03

ANDORRA

    ANDORRA - 01.04.05

ANGOLA

    ANGOLA - 01.04.02

ANGOLAN

    ANGOLAN - 14.03.02

ANGUILLA

    ST KITTS-NEVIS-ANGUILLA - 01.04.03

ANIMAL

    ANIMAL BREEDING - 07.09.02

    ANIMAL DISEASES - 15.04.01

    ANIMAL ECOLOGY - 16.01.01

    ANIMAL FATS - 08.06.06

    ANIMAL FEEDING - 07.09.03

    ANIMAL FIBRES - 07.09.05

    ANIMAL HUSBANDRY - 07.09.02

    ANIMAL NUTRITION - 07.09.03

    ANIMAL OILS - 08.06.06

    ANIMAL PRODUCTION - 07.09.02

    ANIMAL PRODUCTS - 07.09.05

    ANIMAL PROTECTION - 16.05.01

ANIMAL<CONT>
ANIMAL RESOURCES - 16.02.02

ANIMALS
ANIMALS - 07.09.01
DOMESTIC ANIMALS - 07.09.01
FARM ANIMALS
- 07.09.02
USE: LIVESTOCK
PESTS OF ANIMALS - 16.03.03
WILD ANIMALS - 07.09.01

ANIMATION
CULTURAL ANIMATION - 05.02.03

ANIMISM
ANIMISM - 05.04.03

ANNOTATED
ANNOTATED BIBLIOGRAPHY - 19.02.07

ANNUAL
ANNUAL REPORT - 19.02.08

ANTARCTICA
ANTARCTICA - 01.04.01

ANTHROPOLOGISTS
ANTHROPOLOGISTS - 13.09.09

ANTHROPOLOGY
ANTHROPOLOGY - 05.01.01

ANTIBIOTICS
ANTIBIOTICS - 15.05.00

ANTIGUA
ANTIGUA - 01.04.03

ANTILLES
ANTILLES
- 01.04.03
USE: CARIBBEAN
NETHERLANDS ANTILLES - 01.04.03

ANTITRUST
ANTITRUST LEGISLATION - 12.02.00

APARTHEID
APARTHEID - 04.02.04

APICULTURE
APICULTURE - 07.09.02

APO
APO - 01.03.03

APPELLATION
APPELLATION OF ORIGIN - 12.07.02

APPLES
APPLES - 07.07.05

APPLIANCES
ELECTRIC APPLIANCES - 08.15.02
HOUSEHOLD APPLIANCES - 08.15.02

APPLIED
APPLIED RESEARCH - 18.01.00

APPRAISAL
PROJECT APPRAISAL - 01.01.06

APPRAISAL<CONT>
RESOURCES APPRAISAL
- 16.02.01
USE: RESOURCES INVENTORY

APPRENTICES
APPRENTICES - 13.09.03

APPRENTICESHIP
APPRENTICESHIP - 06.03.07

APPROACH
INTEGRATED APPROACH - 18.03.00

APPROPRIATE
APPROPRIATE TECHNOLOGY - 12.06.00

APTITUDES
APTITUDES - 06.05.04

APU
APU - 01.03.03

AQUACULTURE
AQUACULTURE - 07.10.03

AQUATIC
AQUATIC ENVIRONMENT - 16.01.02
AQUATIC FAUNA - 07.10.04
AQUATIC PLANTS - 07.07.01

AQUEDUCTS
AQUEDUCTS - 17.05.04

ARAB
ARAB COUNTRIES - 01.04.06
ARAB ORGANIZATIONS - 01.03.03
LEAGUE OF ARAB STATES - 01.03.03
LIBYAN ARAB JAMAHIRIYA
- 01.04.02
USE: LIBYA
UNITED ARAB EMIRATES - 01.04.06
YEMEN ARAB REPUBLIC
- 01.04.06
USE: YEMEN

ARABIA
SAUDI ARABIA - 01.04.06

ARABIAN
SAUDI ARABIAN - 14.03.02

ARABIC
ARABIC - 05.06.02
GUM ARABIC - 07.07.08

ARABLE
ARABLE LAND - 07.05.02

ARABS
ARABS - 14.03.02

ARBITRATION
ARBITRATION - 05.03.06

ARCHAEOLOGICAL
ARCHAEOLOGICAL SITES - 05.05.01

ARCHAEOLOGY
ARCHAEOLOGY - 05.05.01

ARCHITECTS
  ARCHITECTS - 13.09.09

ARCHITECTURE
  ARCHITECTURE - 05.05.03

ARCHIVES
  ARCHIVES - 19.01.03

AREA
  AREA STUDY
  - 17.03.01
    USE: REGIONAL ANALYSIS
  FREE TRADE AREA - 09.05.08
  SURVEY AREA - 18.04.00

AREAS
  AGRICULTURAL AREAS - 07.05.02
  COASTAL AREAS
  - 17.03.04
    USE: LITTORAL ZONES
  DEVELOPING AREAS - 03.02.03
  FOREST AREAS - 07.08.03
  INDUSTRIAL AREAS - 08.02.03
  MONETARY AREAS - 11.03.01
  POLLUTED AREAS - 16.03.04
  PROTECTED AREAS - 16.05.01
  RURAL AREAS - 14.04.02
  SUBURBAN AREAS - 14.04.03
  UNDERDEVELOPED AREAS
  - 03.02.03
    USE: DEVELOPING AREAS
  URBAN AREAS - 14.04.03

ARGENTINA
  ARGENTINA - 01.04.03

ARGENTINIAN
  ARGENTINIAN - 14.03.02

ARID
  ARID ZONE - 17.02.03
  SEMI-ARID ZONE - 17.02.03

ARMAMENT
  ARMAMENT - 01.02.06

ARMISTICE
  ARMISTICE - 01.02.07

ARMS
  ARMS EMBARGO - 01.02.06
  ARMS LIMITATION
  - 01.02.06
    USE: DISARMAMENT
  ARMS RACE
  - 01.02.06
    USE: ARMAMENT

ARMY
  ARMY - 01.02.06

ARRANGEMENT
  ARRANGEMENT OF WORKING TIME - 13.03.03

ART
  ART - 05.05.02
  ART EDUCATION - 06.03.07
  DRAMATIC ART - 05.05.03
  FOLK ART - 05.05.02
  WORKS OF ART - 05.05.02

ARTICLE
  ARTICLE - 19.02.06

ARTIFICIAL
  ARTIFICIAL INSEMINATION - 15.02.02
  ARTIFICIAL LAKES - 17.05.04

ARTISTIC
  ARTISTIC CREATION - 05.05.02

ARTISTS
  ARTISTS - 13.09.09

ARTS
  ARTS - 05.05.03
  DECORATIVE ARTS
  - 05.05.03
    USE: FINE ARTS
  FINE ARTS - 05.05.03
  GRAPHIC ARTS - 05.05.03
  PERFORMING ARTS - 05.05.03
  PLASTIC ARTS - 05.05.03
  VISUAL ARTS - 05.05.03

ASBESTOS
  ASBESTOS - 08.10.02

ASEAN
  ASEAN - 01.03.03

ASIA
  ASIA - 01.04.04
  SOUTH ASIA - 01.04.04
  SOUTH EAST ASIA - 01.04.04
  WESTERN ASIA
  - 01.04.06
    USE: MIDDLE EAST

ASIAN
  ASIAN - 14.03.02
  ASIAN DEVELOPMENT BANK - 01.03.03
  ASIAN ORGANIZATIONS - 01.03.03

ASPAC
  ASPAC - 01.03.03

ASPECTS
  ADMINISTRATIVE ASPECTS - 04.03.04
  AGRICULTURAL ASPECTS - 07.01.01
  ECONOMIC ASPECTS - 03.02.01
  EDUCATIONAL ASPECTS - 06.02.01
  FINANCIAL ASPECTS - 11.02.04

ASPECTS<CONT>
- GEOGRAPHICAL ASPECTS - 17.03.02
- INDUSTRIAL ASPECTS - 08.01.01
- JURIDICAL ASPECTS
- - 04.01.01
- *USE:* LEGAL ASPECTS
- LEGAL ASPECTS - 04.01.01
- POLITICAL ASPECTS - 04.04.02
- PSYCHOLOGICAL ASPECTS - 05.03.02
- SOCIAL ASPECTS - 05.03.04
- TECHNICAL ASPECTS - 12.06.00

ASSEMBLY
- ASSEMBLY LINES - 08.14.07
- ASSEMBLY-LINE WORK - 13.03.02
- UN GENERAL ASSEMBLY - 01.03.02

ASSIMILATION
- SOCIAL ASSIMILATION
- - 05.03.03
- *USE:* SOCIAL INTEGRATION

ASSISTANCE
- INTERNATIONAL ASSISTANCE
- - 01.01.01
- *USE:* INTERNATIONAL COOPERATION
- SOCIAL ASSISTANCE
- - 02.05.01
- *USE:* SOCIAL SERVICES
- TECHNICAL ASSISTANCE - 01.01.03
- TRAINING ASSISTANCE - 01.01.03

ASSOCIATED
- WEST INDIES ASSOCIATED STATES - 01.04.03

ASSOCIATION
- FREEDOM OF ASSOCIATION - 04.02.02

ASSOCIATIONS
- ASSOCIATIONS - 05.03.07
- EMPLOYEE ASSOCIATIONS - 13.06.00
- PRODUCERS ASSOCIATIONS - 12.02.00
- PROFESSIONAL ASSOCIATIONS
- - 13.06.00
- *USE:* OCCUPATIONAL ORGANIZATIONS
- TEACHER ASSOCIATIONS - 06.06.02

ASTHMA
- ASTHMA - 15.04.02

ASTRONAUTICS
- ASTRONAUTICS - 17.07.00

ASTRONOMY
- ASTRONOMY - 17.07.00

ATHEISM
- ATHEISM - 05.04.02

ATLANTIC
- ATLANTIC OCEAN - 17.06.00

ATLASES
- ATLASES - 18.07.00

ATMOSPHERE
- ATMOSPHERE - 17.01.02

ATMOSPHERIC
- ATMOSPHERIC POLLUTION
- - 16.03.04
- *USE:* AIR POLLUTION
- ATMOSPHERIC SCIENCES
- - 17.01.01
- *USE:* METEOROLOGY

ATOMIC
- ATOMIC ENERGY
- - 08.11.03
- *USE:* NUCLEAR ENERGY
- ATOMIC WEAPONS
- - 01.02.06
- *USE:* NUCLEAR WEAPONS

ATTENDANCE
- EDUCATIONAL ATTENDANCE - 06.04.12

ATTITUDES
- ATTITUDES - 05.03.02
- EMPLOYEES ATTITUDES - 13.06.00
- EMPLOYERS ATTITUDES
- - 13.06.00
- *USE:* MANAGEMENT ATTITUDES
- MANAGEMENT ATTITUDES - 13.06.00

ATTRACTION
- URBAN ATTRACTION - 14.04.03

AUDIENCE
- AUDIENCE - 05.07.02
- AUDIENCE RATING - 05.07.02

AUDIOVISUAL
- AUDIOVISUAL AIDS - 06.05.03
- AUDIOVISUAL CENTRES - 19.01.03
- AUDIOVISUAL MATERIALS - 19.02.01

AUDITING
- AUDITING - 12.09.00

AUS
- PACIFIC ISLANDS AUS - 01.04.07

AUSTERITY
- AUSTERITY POLICY - 02.01.03

AUSTRALIA
- AUSTRALIA - 01.04.07

AUSTRALIAN
- AUSTRALIAN - 14.03.02

AUSTRIA
- AUSTRIA - 01.04.05

AUSTRIAN
- AUSTRIAN - 14.03.02

AUTHORS
- AUTHORS - 19.02.03

AUTOMATIC
- AUTOMATIC CONTROL - 12.07.02

AUTOMATION
- AUTOMATION - 12.07.02

AUTOMATION<CONT>
    LIBRARY AUTOMATION - 19.01.03

AUTOMOBILE
    AUTOMOBILE INDUSTRY - 08.14.07
    AUTOMOBILE SERVICE - 10.03.00

AUTOMOBILES
    AUTOMOBILES - 10.04.00

AUXILIARY
    AUXILIARY HEALTH WORKERS
    - 13.09.10
      USE: PARAMEDICAL PERSONNEL
    AUXILIARY WORKERS - 13.09.02

AZORES
    AZORES - 01.04.05

BACTERIA
    BACTERIA - 15.01.02

BACTERIOLOGICAL
    BACTERIOLOGICAL WEAPONS - 01.02.06

BACTERIOLOGY
    BACTERIOLOGY - 15.01.01

BAGS
    BAGS - 10.06.00

BAHAMAS
    BAHAMAS - 01.04.03

BAHAMIAN
    BAHAMIAN - 14.03.02

BAHRAIN
    BAHRAIN - 01.04.06

BAKERY
    BAKERY PRODUCTS - 08.06.04

BALANCE
    BALANCE OF PAYMENTS - 11.03.02
    BALANCE OF TRADE - 09.05.03
    ECOLOGICAL BALANCE - 16.01.01

BANANA
    BANANA-TREES - 07.07.05

BANANAS
    BANANAS - 07.07.05

BANGLADESH
    BANGLADESH - 01.04.04

BANK
    AFRICAN DEVELOPMENT BANK - 01.03.03
    ASIAN DEVELOPMENT BANK - 01.03.03
    BANK RATE - 11.02.07
    WORLD BANK
    - 01.03.02
      USE: IBRD

BANKING
    BANKING - 11.02.02
    BANKING SYSTEMS - 11.02.02

BANKRUPTCY
    BANKRUPTCY - 12.09.00

BANKS
    AGRICULTURAL BANKS - 07.03.03
    BANKS - 11.02.02
    CENTRAL BANKS - 11.02.02
    COMMERCIAL BANKS - 09.04.03
    DATA BANKS - 19.01.03
    DEVELOPMENT BANKS - 11.02.02
    INDUSTRIAL BANKS - 08.02.04
    INVESTMENT BANKS - 11.02.06
    SAVINGS BANKS - 11.02.02

BARBADIAN
    BARBADIAN - 14.03.02

BARBADOS
    BARBADOS - 01.04.03

BAREFOOT
    BAREFOOT DOCTORS - 13.09.10

BARGAINING
    COLLECTIVE BARGAINING - 13.06.00

BARLEY
    BARLEY - 07.07.04

BAROMETRIC
    BAROMETRIC PRESSURE - 17.01.02

BARRIER
    LANGUAGE BARRIER - 05.06.01

BARRIERS
    COMMUNICATION BARRIERS - 05.07.01
    TRADE BARRIERS - 09.05.07

BARTER
    BARTER - 09.01.01

BASES
    DATA BASES - 19.01.03
    MILITARY BASES - 01.02.06

BASIC
    BASIC EDUCATION - 06.03.04
    BASIC NEEDS - 02.01.01
    BASIC RESEARCH - 18.01.00
    BASIC TRAINING - 06.03.07

BASINS
    RIVER BASINS - 17.05.02

BAUXITE
    BAUXITE - 08.13.00

BEANS
    BEANS - 07.07.06
    FABA BEANS - 07.07.06

BEEF
    BEEF - 07.09.05

BEER
    BEER - 08.06.05

BEET
    BEET SUGAR - 08.06.04

BEETS
    SUGAR BEETS - 07.07.06

BEHAVIOUR
    BEHAVIOUR - 05.03.02
    CONSUMER BEHAVIOUR - 09.01.03
    ECONOMIC BEHAVIOUR - 03.02.01
    POLITICAL BEHAVIOUR - 04.04.02
    SEXUAL BEHAVIOUR - 14.02.03
    SOCIAL BEHAVIOUR - 05.03.03
    STUDENT BEHAVIOUR - 06.06.01

BEHAVIOURAL
    BEHAVIOURAL SCIENCES - 05.01.01

BELGIAN
    BELGIAN - 14.03.02

BELGIUM
    BELGIUM - 01.04.05

BELIEF
    BELIEF - 05.03.02

BELIZE
    BELIZE - 01.04.03

BENEFIT
    BENEFIT PLANS - 02.03.02
    COST-BENEFIT ANALYSIS - 12.09.00

BENEFITS
    DISABILITY BENEFITS - 02.03.02
    EMPLOYMENT INJURIES BENEFITS - 02.03.02
    FRINGE BENEFITS - 13.07.00
    MATERNITY BENEFITS - 02.03.02
    OLD AGE BENEFITS - 02.03.02
    SENIORITY BENEFITS - 13.07.00
    SURVIVORS BENEFITS - 02.03.02
    UNEMPLOYMENT BENEFITS
    - 02.03.02
      USE: UNEMPLOYMENT INSURANCE

BENELUX
    BENELUX - 01.03.03

BENGALI
    BENGALI - 14.03.02

BENIN
    BENIN - 01.04.02

BENINESE
    BENINESE - 14.03.02

BENZENE
    BENZENE - 08.11.06

BERMUDA
    BERMUDA - 01.04.03

BEVERAGE
    BEVERAGE INDUSTRY - 08.06.05

BEVERAGES
    ALCOHOLIC BEVERAGES - 08.06.05
    BEVERAGES - 08.06.05
    NON-ALCOHOLIC BEVERAGES - 08.06.05

BHUTAN
    BHUTAN - 01.04.04

BHUTANESE
    BHUTANESE - 14.03.02

BIBLIOGRAPHY
    ANNOTATED BIBLIOGRAPHY - 19.02.07
    BIBLIOGRAPHY - 19.02.07

BICYCLES
    BICYCLES - 10.04.00

BIG
    BIG GAME - 07.09.01

BILATERAL
    BILATERAL AID - 01.01.02
    BILATERAL RELATIONS - 01.02.01

BILHARZIASIS
    BILHARZIASIS
    - 15.04.02
      USE: SCHISTOSOMIASIS

BILINGUALISM
    BILINGUALISM - 05.06.01

BIOCHEMISTRY
    BIOCHEMISTRY - 15.01.03

BIOCLIMATOLOGY
    BIOCLIMATOLOGY - 17.01.01

BIODEGRADATION
    BIODEGRADATION - 15.01.03

BIODETERIORATION
    BIODETERIORATION
    - 15.01.03
      USE: BIODEGRADATION

BIOGRAPHIES
    BIOGRAPHIES - 19.02.02

BIOLOGICAL
    BIOLOGICAL EQUILIBRIUM
    - 16.01.01
      USE: ECOLOGICAL BALANCE

BIOLOGISTS
    BIOLOGISTS - 13.09.09

BIOLOGY
    BIOLOGY - 15.01.01
    ENVIRONMENTAL BIOLOGY
    - 16.01.01
      USE: ECOLOGY

BIOMASS
    BIOMASS - 16.01.02

BIOSPHERE
    BIOSPHERE - 16.01.02

BIRDS
    BIRDS - 07.09.01

BIRTH
    BIRTH - 14.05.01
    BIRTH CONTROL - 14.05.02
    BIRTH RATE - 14.05.01
    BIRTH SPACING - 14.05.02

BISSAU
    GUINEA-BISSAU - 01.04.02

BITUMENS
    BITUMENS - 08.10.02

BLACK
    BLACK MARKET - 09.01.02

BLACKS
    BLACKS - 14.03.03

BLINDNESS
    BLINDNESS - 15.04.03
    RIVER BLINDNESS
    - 15.04.02
      USE: ONCHOCERCIASIS

BLOCKADE
    BLOCKADE - 01.02.07

BLOOD
    BLOOD - 15.02.04

BOARDING
    BOARDING SCHOOLS - 06.04.03

BOARDS
    MARKETING BOARDS - 09.03.01
    PARTICLE BOARDS - 08.07.01

BOATS
    BOATS
    - 10.04.00
      USE: SHIPS
    FACTORY BOATS - 07.10.03
    FISHING BOATS
    - 07.10.03
      USE: FISHING VESSELS

BODIES
    AID BY RELIGIOUS BODIES
    - 01.01.02
      USE: PRIVATE AID

BOILERMAKING
    BOILERMAKING - 08.14.01

BOLIVIA
    BOLIVIA - 01.04.03

BOLIVIAN
    BOLIVIAN - 14.03.02

BONDS
    BONDS
    - 11.02.07
      USE: DEBENTURES
    TREASURY BONDS - 11.02.07

BONUSES
    BONUSES
    - 13.07.00
      USE: WAGE INCENTIVES

BOOK
    BOOK INDUSTRY - 08.16.00
    BOOK REVIEW - 19.02.07

BOOKS
    BOOKS - 05.07.03

BOOKSELLING
    BOOKSELLING - 08.16.00

BORDER
    BORDER INTEGRATION - 01.02.01

BORDERS
    BORDERS
    - 01.02.02
      USE: BOUNDARIES

BORROWING
    BORROWING - 11.02.02
    INTERNATIONAL BORROWING - 11.03.01
    PUBLIC BORROWING - 11.01.01

BOTANICAL
    BOTANICAL GARDENS - 16.05.02

BOTANISTS
    BOTANISTS - 13.09.09

BOTANY
    BOTANY - 07.06.00

BOTSWANA
    BOTSWANA - 01.04.02

BOUNDARIES
    BOUNDARIES - 01.02.02

BOURGEOISIE
    BOURGEOISIE - 05.03.05

BOVIDAE
    BOVIDAE - 07.09.01

BOXES
    BOXES - 10.06.00

BOYCOTT
    BOYCOTT - 09.05.07

BRAIN
    BRAIN - 15.02.04
    BRAIN DRAIN - 14.07.00

BRAZIL
    BRAZIL - 01.04.03

BRAZILIAN
    BRAZILIAN - 14.03.02

BREAD
    BREAD - 08.06.04

BREAST
    BREAST FEEDING - 15.03.02

BREEDING
    ANIMAL BREEDING - 07.09.02
    FISH BREEDING - 07.10.04
    PLANT BREEDING - 07.07.01

BREWERY
    BREWERY - 08.06.05

BRICKS
    BRICKS - 08.10.03

BRIDGES
    BRIDGES - 10.03.00

BRITISH
    BRITISH - 14.03.02
    BRITISH HONDURAS
    - 01.04.03
      USE: BELIZE
    BRITISH VIRGIN ISLANDS - 01.04.03

BROADCASTING
    BROADCASTING - 08.16.00

BRUNEI
    BRUNEI - 01.04.04

BUDDHISM
    BUDDHISM - 05.04.03

BUDGET
    BUDGET - 12.09.00
    EDUCATIONAL BUDGET - 06.02.05

BUDGET<CONT>
    FAMILY BUDGET - 03.02.05
    NATIONAL BUDGET - 11.01.01
    TIME BUDGET - 13.03.03

BUDGETARY
    BUDGETARY POLICY - 11.01.01
    BUDGETARY RESOURCES - 11.01.01

BUDGETING
    BUDGETING - 12.09.00
    BUDGETING METHODS - 12.09.00

BUFFALOES
    WATER BUFFALOES - 07.09.01

BUFFER
    BUFFER STOCKS - 09.05.02

BUILDING
    BUILDING INDUSTRY
    - 08.10.01
      USE: CONSTRUCTION INDUSTRY
    BUILDING MACHINERY - 08.14.06
    BUILDING MATERIALS
    - 08.10.02
      USE: CONSTRUCTION MATERIALS

BUILDINGS
    BUILDINGS - 08.10.01
    EDUCATIONAL BUILDINGS - 06.04.07
    FARM BUILDINGS - 07.04.00
    INDUSTRIAL BUILDINGS - 08.03.00
    PREFABRICATED BUILDINGS - 08.10.01
    SCHOOL BUILDINGS - 06.04.07
    UNIVERSITY BUILDINGS - 06.04.07

BULGARIA
    BULGARIA - 01.04.05

BULGARIAN
    BULGARIAN - 14.03.02

BURDEN
    DEBT BURDEN
    - 11.02.02
      USE: INDEBTEDNESS
    DEPENDENCY BURDEN - 14.02.04
    POLLUTANT BURDEN
    - 16.03.04
      USE: POLLUTION LEVEL

BUREAUCRACY
    BUREAUCRACY - 04.03.05

BURMA
    BURMA - 01.04.04

BURMESE
    BURMESE - 14.03.02

BURNS
    BURNS - 15.04.02

BURUNDI
    BURUNDI - 01.04.02

BUSES

BUSES - 10.04.00

BUSINESS

BUSINESS CYCLE - 03.02.04

BUSINESS ECONOMICS - 12.01.00

BUSINESS MANAGEMENT - 12.04.00

BUSINESS ORGANIZATION - 12.04.00

RESTRICTIVE BUSINESS PRACTICES - 09.05.07

BUTTER

BUTTER - 07.09.05

BUYING

BUYING
- 09.03.02
USE: PURCHASING

BY

AID BY RELIGIOUS BODIES
- 01.01.02
USE: PRIVATE AID

BY-PRODUCTS - 12.08.01

MANAGEMENT BY OBJECTIVES - 12.04.00

PAYMENT BY RESULT - 13.07.00

BYELORUSSIAN

BYELORUSSIAN - 14.03.02

BYELORUSSIAN SSR - 01.04.05

CAB

CAB - 01.03.04

CABEI

CABEI - 01.03.03

CABLES

CABLES - 08.14.04

CACEU

CACEU - 01.03.03

CACM

CACM - 01.03.03

CADASTRAL

CADASTRAL SURVEYS - 18.04.00

CADMIUM

CADMIUM - 08.14.02

CAEU

CAEU - 01.03.03

CAFRAD

CAFRAD - 01.03.03

CAICOS

TURKS AND CAICOS ISLANDS - 01.04.03

CALCIUM

CALCIUM - 08.12.04

CALEDONIA

NEW CALEDONIA - 01.04.07

CALORIE

CALORIE DEFICIENCY - 15.03.02

CALORIES

CALORIES - 15.03.02

CALVES

CALVES - 07.09.01

CAMBODIA

CAMBODIA
- 01.04.04
USE: KAMPUCHEA

CAMELS

CAMELS - 07.09.01

CAMEROON

CAMEROON - 01.04.02

CAMEROONIAN

CAMEROONIAN - 14.03.02

CAMPS

CONCENTRATION CAMPS - 02.04.03

CANADA

CANADA - 01.04.03

CANADIAN

CANADIAN - 14.03.02

CANAL

PANAMA CANAL ZONE - 01.04.03

CANALS

CANALS - 10.03.00

CANARY

CANARY ISLANDS - 01.04.05

CANCER

CANCER - 15.04.02

CANE
>CANE SUGAR - 08.06.04
>SUGAR CANE - 07.07.06

CANNED
>CANNED FOOD - 08.06.03

CANNING
>CANNING INDUSTRY - 08.06.01

CAPABILITY
>LAND CAPABILITY - 07.05.02

CAPACITY
>ABSORPTIVE CAPACITY - 11.02.06
>PHYSICAL CAPACITY - 13.02.01
>PRODUCTION CAPACITY - 12.07.01
>STORAGE CAPACITY - 09.03.03

CAPE
>CAPE VERDE - 01.04.02
>CAPE VERDEAN - 14.03.02

CAPITA
>CONSUMPTION PER CAPITA - 09.01.03

CAPITAL
>CAPITAL - 11.02.05
>CAPITAL AID
>- 01.01.03
>*USE:* FINANCIAL AID
>CAPITAL CONCENTRATION - 11.02.05
>CAPITAL COSTS - 12.09.00
>CAPITAL DEPRECIATION - 11.02.05
>CAPITAL EXPENDITURES
>- 12.09.00
>*USE:* CAPITAL COSTS
>CAPITAL FLOWS
>- 11.03.03
>*USE:* CAPITAL MOVEMENTS
>CAPITAL FORMATION - 11.02.05
>CAPITAL GAINS - 12.09.00
>CAPITAL INTENSITY - 12.06.00
>CAPITAL INVESTMENTS
>- 11.02.06
>*USE:* INVESTMENTS
>CAPITAL MARKET
>- 11.02.07
>*USE:* FINANCIAL MARKET
>CAPITAL MOVEMENTS - 11.03.03
>CAPITAL NEEDS
>- 11.02.05
>*USE:* FINANCIAL NEEDS
>CAPITAL PUNISHMENT - 02.04.03
>CAPITAL RESOURCES
>- 11.02.05
>*USE:* FINANCIAL RESOURCES
>CAPITAL TAX - 11.01.02

CAPITAL<CONT>
>CAPITAL TRANSFERS - 11.03.03
>CAPITAL-LABOUR RATIO - 12.07.03
>CAPITAL-OUTPUT RATIO - 12.07.03
>EXPORT OF CAPITAL - 11.03.03
>FOREIGN CAPITAL - 11.03.03
>INDUSTRIAL CAPITAL - 08.02.04
>REPATRIATION OF CAPITAL - 11.03.03
>WORKING CAPITAL - 12.09.00

CAPITALISM
>CAPITALISM - 03.03.01

CAPITALIST
>CAPITALIST - 03.03.01
>CAPITALIST COUNTRIES - 03.03.03
>CAPITALIST ENTERPRISES - 12.01.00

CARBOHYDRATES
>CARBOHYDRATES - 08.06.04

CARD
>CARD FILES - 19.01.04

CARDBOARD
>CARDBOARD - 08.07.02

CARDIOLOGY
>CARDIOLOGY - 15.04.06

CARDIOVASCULAR
>CARDIOVASCULAR SYSTEM - 15.02.04

CARDS
>CARDS - 19.01.04
>PUNCHED CARDS - 19.01.04

CARE
>CARE OF THE AGED - 02.05.03
>CHILD CARE - 02.05.03
>DAY CARE CENTRES - 06.04.02
>DISABLED CARE - 02.05.03
>MEDICAL CARE - 15.04.04
>PRENATAL CARE - 15.04.04

CARGO
>CARGO - 10.06.00
>CARGO SHIPS - 10.04.00

CARIBBEAN
>CARIBBEAN - 01.04.03

CARICOM
>CARICOM - 01.03.03

CARIFTA
>CARIFTA - 01.03.03

CARPETS
>CARPETS - 08.08.01

CARRIERS
>CARRIERS - 10.02.00

CARS
   MOTOR CARS
   - 10.04.00
      USE: AUTOMOBILES

CARTELS
   CARTELS - 12.02.00

CARTHAGENA
   CARTHAGENA AGREEMENT
   - 01.03.03
      USE: ANDEAN GROUP

CARTOGRAPHY
   CARTOGRAPHY
   - 18.07.00
      USE: MAPPING

CASE
   CASE STUDIES - 18.04.00

CASH
   CASH CROPS
   - 07.07.02
      USE: INDUSTRIAL CROPS
   CASH FLOW - 12.09.00
   CASH INCOME
   - 12.09.00
      USE: CASH FLOW

CASHEW
   CASHEW NUTS - 07.07.05

CASSAVA
   CASSAVA - 07.07.06

CASTES
   CASTES - 05.03.05

CASTING
   METAL CASTING - 08.14.03

CASTINGS
   CASTINGS - 08.14.04

CASUAL
   CASUAL WORKERS - 13.09.02

CATALOGUE
   CATALOGUE - 19.02.07

CATALOGUING
   CATALOGUING - 19.01.02

CATERING
   CATERING - 09.03.02

CATTLE
   CATTLE - 07.09.01
   CATTLE PRODUCTION - 07.09.02

CAUSES
   CAUSES OF DEATH - 14.06.00

CAUSTIC
   CAUSTIC SODA - 08.12.04

CAYMAN
   CAYMAN ISLANDS - 01.04.03

CCAQ
   CCAQ - 01.03.02

CDP
   CDP - 01.03.02

CELIBACY
   CELIBACY - 14.02.05

CELLS
   CELLS - 15.02.04

CELLULOSE
   CELLULOSE - 08.07.01

CEMENT
   CEMENT - 08.10.02
   CEMENT INDUSTRY - 08.10.02

CEMLA
   CEMLA - 01.03.04

CENSORSHIP
   CENSORSHIP - 05.07.01

CENSUSES
   AGRICULTURAL CENSUSES - 07.05.01
   CENSUSES - 18.04.00
   ECONOMIC CENSUSES - 03.01.02
   HOUSING CENSUSES - 14.04.01
   INDUSTRIAL CENSUSES - 08.01.01
   POPULATION CENSUSES - 14.01.01

CENTO
   CENTO - 01.03.03

CENTRAL
   CENTRAL AFRICA - 01.04.02
   CENTRAL AFRICAN EMPIRE - 01.04.02
   CENTRAL AMERICA - 01.04.03
   CENTRAL BANKS - 11.02.02
   CENTRAL GOVERNMENT - 04.03.03

CENTRALIZATION
   CENTRALIZATION - 04.03.03

CENTRE
   TOWN CENTRE - 14.04.03

CENTRES
   AUDIOVISUAL CENTRES - 19.01.03
   COMPUTER CENTRES - 18.02.00
   DAY CARE CENTRES - 06.04.02
   DEVELOPMENT CENTRES - 01.01.07
   DOCUMENTATION CENTRES
   - 19.01.03
      USE: INFORMATION SERVICES
   HEALTH CENTRES - 02.05.02
   INFORMATION CENTRES
   - 19.01.03
      USE: INFORMATION SERVICES
   RESEARCH CENTRES - 18.02.00
   RESOURCES CENTRES - 06.05.03
   TRAINING CENTRES - 06.04.06
   YOUTH CENTRES - 05.03.07

CERAMICS
- CERAMICS - 08.10.03
- CERAMICS INDUSTRY - 08.10.03

CEREALS
- CEREALS - 07.07.04

CERN
- CERN - 01.03.03

CERTIFICATE
- SERVICE CERTIFICATE - 13.02.01

CERTIFICATES
- CERTIFICATES - 06.04.13

CEYLON
- CEYLON
- - 01.04.04
  - *USE:* SRI LANKA

CHAD
- CHAD - 01.04.02

CHANGE
- ADAPTATION TO CHANGE - 05.03.04
- CULTURAL CHANGE - 05.02.02
- RESISTANCE TO CHANGE - 05.03.04
- SOCIAL CHANGE - 05.03.04
- TECHNOLOGICAL CHANGE - 12.06.00

CHART
- FLOW CHART - 12.04.00

CHARTING
- CHARTING - 18.07.00

CHARTS
- CHARTS - 18.07.00

CHEESE
- CHEESE - 07.09.05

CHEMICAL
- CHEMICAL ANALYSIS - 08.12.02
- CHEMICAL CONTRACEPTIVES - 14.05.02
- CHEMICAL ENGINEERING - 08.12.02
- CHEMICAL FERTILIZERS - 08.12.05
- CHEMICAL INDUSTRY - 08.12.01
- CHEMICAL POLLUTION - 16.03.04

CHEMICALS
- CHEMICALS - 08.12.04

CHEMISTRY
- CHEMISTRY - 08.12.02
- FOOD CHEMISTRY - 15.03.01
- ORGANIC CHEMISTRY - 08.12.02
- SOIL CHEMISTRY - 17.04.04

CHEMISTS
- CHEMISTS - 13.09.09

CHICKPEAS
- CHICKPEAS - 07.07.06

CHILD
- CHILD CARE - 02.05.03
- CHILD DEVELOPMENT - 06.05.04
- CHILD LABOUR - 13.09.02
- CHILD REARING - 15.03.02
- MATERNAL AND CHILD HEALTH - 15.04.04

CHILDHOOD
- CHILDHOOD - 14.02.02
- EARLY CHILDHOOD - 14.02.02

CHILDREN
- CHILDREN - 14.02.02

CHILE
- CHILE - 01.04.03

CHILEAN
- CHILEAN - 14.03.02

CHINA
- CHINA - 01.04.04

CHINESE
- CHINESE - 14.03.02
- CHINESE LANGUAGE - 05.06.02

CHLORINE
- CHLORINE - 08.12.04

CHOCOLATE
- CHOCOLATE - 08.06.04

CHOICE
- CHOICE OF PRODUCTS - 12.08.02
- CHOICE OF TECHNOLOGY - 12.06.00
- OCCUPATIONAL CHOICE - 13.02.01
- VOCATIONAL CHOICE
- - 13.02.01
  - *USE:* OCCUPATIONAL CHOICE

CHOLERA
- CHOLERA - 15.04.02

CHRISTIANITY
- CHRISTIANITY - 05.04.03

CHROMIUM
- CHROMIUM - 08.14.02

CHROMOSOMES
- CHROMOSOMES - 15.02.03

CHRONIC
- CHRONIC DISEASES - 15.04.02

CHRONOLOGY
- CHRONOLOGY - 18.10.00

CIAT
- CIAT - 01.03.04

CIMMYT
- CIMMYT - 01.03.04

CINEMA
- CINEMA - 05.05.03

CIRCULATION
- MONETARY CIRCULATION - 11.02.01

CITIES
   CITIES
   - 14.04.03
   USE: TOWNS

CITRUS
   CITRUS FRUITS - 07.07.05

CIVIC
   CIVIC EDUCATION - 06.03.04
   CIVIC SERVICE - 04.03.06

CIVIL
   CIVIL ENGINEERING - 12.06.00
   CIVIL LAW - 04.01.02
   CIVIL LIBERTIES - 04.02.02
   CIVIL RIGHTS - 04.02.01
   CIVIL SERVANTS - 13.09.04
   CIVIL SERVICE - 04.03.04
   CIVIL WAR - 01.02.07

CIVILIZATION
   CIVILIZATION - 05.02.01

CLACSO
   CLACSO - 01.03.03

CLADES
   CLADES - 01.03.02

CLAN
   CLAN - 14.02.04

CLASS
   CLASS CONSCIOUSNESS - 05.03.05
   CLASS STRUGGLE - 05.03.06
   LOWER CLASS - 05.03.05
   MIDDLE CLASS - 05.03.05
   RULING CLASS - 05.03.05
   UPPER CLASS - 05.03.05
   WORKING CLASS - 05.03.05

CLASSES
   CLASSES - 06.04.10
   EXPERIMENTAL CLASSES - 06.04.10
   SOCIAL CLASSES - 05.03.05

CLASSIFICATION
   CLASSIFICATION - 19.01.02
   JOB CLASSIFICATION - 13.02.01
   SOIL CLASSIFICATION - 17.04.04

CLAY
   CLAY - 08.10.03

CLEANING
   CLEANING AGENTS - 08.12.08

CLEARING
   CLEARING AGREEMENTS - 11.03.01
   CLEARING SYSTEMS - 11.03.01

CLERGY
   CLERGY - 05.04.04

CLERICAL
   CLERICAL WORKERS
   - 13.09.07
   USE: OFFICE WORKERS

CLIMATE
   CLIMATE - 17.02.01

CLIMATIC
   CLIMATIC INFLUENCE - 17.02.01
   CLIMATIC REGIONS
   - 17.02.03
   USE: CLIMATIC ZONES
   CLIMATIC ZONES - 17.02.03

CLIMATOLOGY
   CLIMATOLOGY - 17.01.01

CLOTHING
   CLOTHING INDUSTRY - 08.08.01

CMEA
   CMEA - 01.03.03

COAL
   COAL - 08.11.05
   COAL GAS - 08.11.05
   COAL MINING - 08.13.00

COAST
   IVORY COAST - 01.04.02

COASTAL
   COASTAL AREAS
   - 17.03.04
   USE: LITTORAL ZONES
   COASTAL FISHING - 07.10.03
   COASTAL POLLUTION - 16.03.04
   COASTAL WATERS - 17.06.00

COASTS
   COASTS - 17.03.04

COATING
   COATING - 08.12.03

COBALT
   COBALT - 08.14.02

COCOA
   COCOA - 07.07.09

COCONUT
   COCONUT PALMS - 07.07.05

COCONUTS
   COCONUTS - 07.07.05

CODE
   LABOUR CODE - 04.01.02

CODES
   CODES - 04.01.01

CODESRIA
   CODESRIA - 01.03.03

COEDUCATIONAL
   COEDUCATIONAL SCHOOLS - 06.04.03

COEXISTENCE
    PEACEFUL COEXISTENCE - 01.02.07

COFFEE
    COFFEE - 07.07.09

COIR
    COIR - 07.07.07

COKE
    COKE - 08.11.05

COLD
    COLD SEASON - 17.02.02
    COLD ZONE - 17.02.03

COLLECTING
    DATA COLLECTING - 18.04.00

COLLECTION
    TAX COLLECTION - 11.01.02

COLLECTIVE
    COLLECTIVE AGREEMENTS - 13.06.00
    COLLECTIVE BARGAINING - 13.06.00
    COLLECTIVE ECONOMY - 03.03.02
    COLLECTIVE FARMING - 07.05.03
    COLLECTIVE HOUSING - 14.04.01
    COLLECTIVE OWNERSHIP - 03.03.05
    COLLECTIVE TRANSPORT
    - 10.01.00
      USE: PUBLIC TRANSPORT

COLLECTIVISM
    COLLECTIVISM - 03.03.01

COLLEGE
    COLLEGE MANAGEMENT - 06.04.08
    COLLEGE STUDENTS - 06.06.01

COLLEGES
    COLLEGES OF EDUCATION - 06.04.05
    TEACHER TRAINING COLLEGES
    - 06.04.05
      USE: COLLEGES OF EDUCATION

COLOMBIA
    COLOMBIA - 01.04.03

COLOMBIAN
    COLOMBIAN - 14.03.02

COLOMBO
    COLOMBO PLAN - 01.03.03

COLONIAL
    COLONIAL COUNTRIES - 01.02.03

COLONIALISM
    COLONIALISM - 03.03.01

COMMENT
    COMMENT - 19.02.07

COMMERCIAL
    COMMERCIAL BANKS - 09.04.03
    COMMERCIAL CREDIT - 09.04.03
    COMMERCIAL EDUCATION - 06.03.07

COMMERCIAL<CONT>
    COMMERCIAL ENTERPRISES - 09.04.03
    COMMERCIAL FARMING - 07.05.03
    COMMERCIAL LAW - 04.01.02
    COMMERCIAL POLICY - 09.04.02
    COMMERCIAL SCHOOLS - 06.04.06

COMMODITIES
    AGRICULTURAL COMMODITIES
    - 07.05.05
      USE: AGRICULTURAL PRODUCTS
    COMMODITIES - 12.08.01

COMMODITY
    COMMODITY AGREEMENTS - 09.05.02
    COMMODITY MARKET - 09.01.02
    COMMODITY PRICES - 09.02.00

COMMON
    COMMON FUND - 09.05.02
    COMMON LAW - 04.01.02
    COMMON MARKET - 01.02.01

COMMONWEALTH
    COMMONWEALTH - 01.03.03

COMMUNAL
    COMMUNAL LAND - 07.02.00

COMMUNICABLE
    COMMUNICABLE DISEASES
    - 15.04.02
      USE: INFECTIOUS DISEASES

COMMUNICATION
    COMMUNICATION - 05.07.01
    COMMUNICATION BARRIERS - 05.07.01
    COMMUNICATION ENGINEERING - 08.16.00
    COMMUNICATION INDUSTRY - 08.16.00
    COMMUNICATION MEDIA
    - 05.07.03
      USE: MEDIA
    COMMUNICATION PLANNING - 05.07.01
    COMMUNICATION POLICY - 05.07.01
    COMMUNICATION RESEARCH - 05.07.01
    COMMUNICATION SATELLITES - 08.16.00
    COMMUNICATION SYSTEMS - 05.07.01
    COMMUNICATION THEORY
    - 18.08.00
      USE: INFORMATION THEORY
    COMMUNICATION USERS
    - 05.07.02
      USE: AUDIENCE
    MASS COMMUNICATION - 05.07.01

COMMUNISM
    COMMUNISM - 03.03.01

COMMUNIST
    COMMUNIST - 03.03.01

COMMUNITIES
    EUROPEAN COMMUNITIES - 01.03.03
    RURAL COMMUNITIES - 14.04.02
    URBAN COMMUNITIES - 14.04.03

COMMUNITY
    COMMUNITY - 14.04.01
    COMMUNITY DEVELOPMENT - 14.04.01
    COMMUNITY RELATIONS - 14.04.01
    SCHOOL-COMMUNITY RELATIONSHIPS - 06.04.12

COMMUTING
    COMMUTING - 14.07.00

COMORIAN
    COMORIAN - 14.03.02

COMOROS
    COMOROS - 01.04.02

COMPARATIVE
    COMPARATIVE ADVANTAGE - 09.05.03
    COMPARATIVE ANALYSIS - 18.09.00
    COMPARATIVE EDUCATION - 06.01.00
    COMPARATIVE STUDY
    - 18.09.00
      USE: COMPARATIVE ANALYSIS

COMPARISON
    COMPARISON - 18.09.00

COMPENSATION
    COMPENSATION
    - 13.07.00
      USE: WAGES
    DAMAGE COMPENSATION - 16.04.01

COMPENSATORY
    COMPENSATORY EDUCATION - 06.03.03
    COMPENSATORY FINANCING - 11.02.04

COMPETITION
    COMPETITION - 09.01.02
    UNFAIR COMPETITION - 09.01.02

COMPETITIVE
    COMPETITIVE PRODUCTS - 12.08.02

COMPILATION
    DATA COMPILATION
    - 18.04.00
      USE: DATA COLLECTING

COMPLEMENTARITY
    COMPLEMENTARITY AGREEMENTS - 01.02.01

COMPLEX
    AGROINDUSTRIAL COMPLEX
    - 07.01.01
      USE: AGROINDUSTRY

COMPOSITION
    FOOD COMPOSITION - 15.03.01
    POPULATION COMPOSITION - 14.02.01

COMPREHENSIVE
    COMPREHENSIVE SCHOOLS - 06.04.03

COMPULSORY
    COMPULSORY EDUCATION - 06.03.03

COMPUTATION
    COMPUTATION - 18.08.00

COMPUTER
    COMPUTER CENTRES - 18.02.00
    COMPUTER PROGRAMMES - 08.15.02
    COMPUTER SCIENCE - 18.08.00

COMPUTERS
    COMPUTERS - 08.15.02
    ELECTRONIC COMPUTERS
    - 08.15.02
      USE: COMPUTERS

CONCENTRATE
    FISH PROTEIN CONCENTRATE - 08.06.04

CONCENTRATION
    CAPITAL CONCENTRATION - 11.02.05
    CONCENTRATION CAMPS - 02.04.03
    CONCENTRATION OF POLLUTANTS
    - 16.03.04
      USE: POLLUTION LEVEL
    ECONOMIC CONCENTRATION - 12.02.00
    INDUSTRIAL CONCENTRATION - 08.02.03
    URBAN CONCENTRATION - 14.04.03

CONCILIATION
    CONCILIATION - 05.03.06

CONCRETE
    CONCRETE - 08.10.02
    CONCRETE CONSTRUCTION - 08.10.01

CONDENSED
    CONDENSED FOOD - 08.06.03

CONDITIONS
    ECONOMIC CONDITIONS - 03.02.01
    LIVING CONDITIONS - 03.02.05
    SOCIAL CONDITIONS - 05.03.04
    WORKING CONDITIONS - 13.03.01

CONDOMS
    CONDOMS - 14.05.02

CONE
    SOUTHERN CONE - 01.04.03

CONF
    CONF - 19.04.00

CONFERENCE
    CONFERENCE - 19.04.00
    CONFERENCE PAPER - 19.02.05
    CONFERENCE REPORT - 19.02.08

CONFLICT
    CONFLICT RESOLUTION
    - 05.03.06
      USE: DISPUTE SETTLEMENT

CONFLICTS
>CONFLICTS - 05.03.06
>RACIAL CONFLICTS - 04.02.04
>SOCIAL CONFLICTS - 05.03.06

CONFUCIANISM
>CONFUCIANISM - 05.04.03

CONGO
>CONGO - 01.04.02

CONGOLESE
>CONGOLESE - 14.03.02

CONSCIOUSNESS
>CLASS CONSCIOUSNESS - 05.03.05

CONSEQUENCES
>ECONOMIC CONSEQUENCES
>- 03.02.01
>>*USE:* ECONOMIC IMPLICATIONS
>SOCIAL CONSEQUENCES
>- 05.03.04
>>*USE:* SOCIAL IMPLICATIONS

CONSERVATION
>CONSERVATION OF CULTURAL HERITAGE - 05.02.02
>ENERGY CONSERVATION - 08.11.01
>FISHERY CONSERVATION - 16.05.01
>FOREST CONSERVATION - 16.05.01
>NATURE CONSERVATION - 16.05.01
>POWER CONSERVATION
>- 08.11.01
>>*USE:* ENERGY CONSERVATION
>RESOURCES CONSERVATION - 16.05.01
>SOIL CONSERVATION - 16.05.01
>WATER CONSERVATION - 16.05.01

CONSERVATISM
>CONSERVATISM - 05.03.02

CONSOLIDATION
>DEBT CONSOLIDATION - 11.02.02

CONSTITUTION
>CONSTITUTION - 04.03.01

CONSTITUTIONAL
>CONSTITUTIONAL COURTS - 04.03.01
>CONSTITUTIONAL LAW - 04.01.02

CONSTRUCTION
>CONCRETE CONSTRUCTION - 08.10.01
>CONSTRUCTION EQUIPMENT
>- 08.14.06
>>*USE:* BUILDING MACHINERY
>CONSTRUCTION INDUSTRY - 08.10.01
>CONSTRUCTION MATERIALS - 08.10.02
>CONSTRUCTION TECHNIQUES - 08.10.01
>CONSTRUCTION WORKERS - 13.09.06
>ROAD CONSTRUCTION - 10.03.00

CONSTRUCTION\<CONT>
>STEEL CONSTRUCTION - 08.10.01
>STONE CONSTRUCTION - 08.10.01
>WOOD CONSTRUCTION - 08.10.01

CONSULTANT
>CONSULTANT REPORT - 19.02.08

CONSULTANTS
>CONSULTANTS - 01.01.07
>MANAGEMENT CONSULTANTS - 12.03.00

CONSUMER
>CONSUMER BEHAVIOUR - 09.01.03
>CONSUMER CREDIT - 11.02.02
>CONSUMER DEMAND - 09.01.03
>CONSUMER EDUCATION - 06.03.04
>CONSUMER EXPENDITURES - 09.01.03
>CONSUMER GOODS - 09.01.03
>CONSUMER PRICES - 09.02.00
>CONSUMER PROTECTION - 09.01.03

CONSUMERS
>CONSUMERS - 09.01.03
>CONSUMERS COOPERATIVES - 09.03.01

CONSUMPTION
>CONSUMPTION - 09.01.03
>CONSUMPTION FUNCTIONS - 09.01.03
>CONSUMPTION PER CAPITA - 09.01.03
>CONSUMPTION TAX - 11.01.02
>DOMESTIC CONSUMPTION - 09.01.03
>ENERGY CONSUMPTION - 08.11.01
>FOOD CONSUMPTION - 15.03.02
>POWER CONSUMPTION
>- 08.11.01
>>*USE:* ENERGY CONSUMPTION
>WATER CONSUMPTION - 17.05.05

CONTAGIOUS
>CONTAGIOUS DISEASES
>- 15.04.02
>>*USE:* INFECTIOUS DISEASES

CONTAINERS
>CONTAINERS - 10.06.00
>TRANSPORT CONTAINERS - 10.06.00

CONTAMINANTS
>CONTAMINANTS
>- 16.03.04
>>*USE:* POLLUTANTS

CONTAMINATION
>FOOD CONTAMINATION - 15.03.01

CONTENT
>CONTENT ANALYSIS - 19.01.02

CONTINENTAL
   CONTINENTAL SHELVES - 17.03.04

CONTINENTS
   CONTINENTS - 17.03.04

CONTINGENCY
   CONTINGENCY FUNDS - 02.03.02

CONTINUING
   CONTINUING EDUCATION
   - 06.03.05
     USE: LIFE-LONG EDUCATION

CONTINUOUS
   CONTINUOUS WORKING DAY - 13.03.03

CONTRACEPTION
   CONTRACEPTION - 14.05.02

CONTRACEPTIVE
   CONTRACEPTIVE METHODS - 14.05.02

CONTRACEPTIVES
   CHEMICAL CONTRACEPTIVES - 14.05.02
   CONTRACEPTIVES - 14.05.02
   ORAL CONTRACEPTIVES - 14.05.02

CONTRACT
   CONTRACT LABOUR - 13.02.01
   LABOUR CONTRACT - 13.02.01

CONTRACTING
   CONTRACTING - 12.07.02

CONTROL
   AUTOMATIC CONTROL - 12.07.02
   BIRTH CONTROL - 14.05.02
   CREDIT CONTROL
   - 11.02.02
     USE: CREDIT POLICY
   DISEASE CONTROL - 15.04.04
   ENVIRONMENTAL CONTROL
   - 19.02.01
     USE: ENVIRONMENTAL MANAGEMENT
   EROSION CONTROL - 16.04.01
   FIRE CONTROL - 16.04.01
   FLOOD CONTROL - 16.04.01
   FOREIGN EXCHANGE CONTROL - 11.03.01
   HEALTH CONTROL - 15.04.04
   INTERNATIONAL CONTROL - 01.02.04
   NOISE CONTROL - 16.04.01
   PEST CONTROL - 16.04.01
   POLLUTION CONTROL - 16.04.01
   PRICE CONTROL - 09.02.00
   PRODUCTION CONTROL - 12.07.02
   QUALITY CONTROL - 12.07.02
   SOCIAL CONTROL - 05.03.04

CONTROL<CONT>
   TRAFFIC CONTROL - 10.08.00
   WEATHER CONTROL - 16.04.01
   WEED CONTROL - 07.05.04

CONURBATION
   CONURBATION - 14.04.03

CONVENIENCE
   FLAGS OF CONVENIENCE - 10.05.00

CONVENTIONAL
   CONVENTIONAL WEAPONS - 01.02.06

CONVENTIONS
   CONVENTIONS - 01.02.04

CONVERTIBILITY
   CONVERTIBILITY - 11.03.01

CONVERTIBLE
   NON-CONVERTIBLE CURRENCIES - 11.03.01

COOKERY
   COOKERY
   - 15.03.01
     USE: FOOD PREPARATION

COOLING
   COOLING - 08.12.03

COOPERATION
   CULTURAL COOPERATION - 05.02.03
   ECONOMIC COOPERATION - 01.02.01
   HORIZONTAL COOPERATION - 01.01.01
   INTERNATIONAL COOPERATION - 01.01.01
   REGIONAL COOPERATION - 01.01.01
   SCIENTIFIC COOPERATION - 18.01.00

COOPERATIVE
   COOPERATIVE FARMING - 07.05.03
   COOPERATIVE MARKETING - 09.03.01
   COOPERATIVE MOVEMENTS - 03.03.04

COOPERATIVES
   AGRICULTURAL COOPERATIVES - 07.03.02
   CONSUMERS COOPERATIVES - 09.03.01
   COOPERATIVES - 03.03.04
   CREDIT COOPERATIVES - 11.02.02
   HOUSING COOPERATIVES - 14.04.01
   MARKETING COOPERATIVES - 09.03.01
   PRODUCTION COOPERATIVES - 12.01.00

COORDINATION
   AID COORDINATION - 01.01.04

COPPER
   COPPER - 08.14.02
   COPPER ORE - 08.13.00

COPYRIGHT
   COPYRIGHT - 19.02.03

CORK
    CORK - 08.07.01

CORPORATION
    CORPORATION TAX - 11.01.02

CORPORATIONS
    TRANSNATIONAL CORPORATIONS
    - 03.03.05
    USE: MULTINATIONAL ENTERPRISES

CORPORATISM
    CORPORATISM - 03.03.01

CORPS
    PEACE CORPS - 01.01.08

CORRECTION
    MONETARY CORRECTION - 11.02.01

CORRECTIONAL
    CORRECTIONAL EDUCATION - 06.03.03
    CORRECTIONAL INSTITUTIONS - 06.04.03

CORRESPONDENCE
    CORRESPONDENCE - 19.02.09
    CORRESPONDENCE EDUCATION - 06.05.03

CORROSION
    CORROSION - 08.12.03

CORRUPTION
    CORRUPTION - 02.04.02

COSMETICS
    COSMETICS - 08.12.08

COST
    COST ACCOUNTING - 12.09.00
    COST ANALYSIS - 12.09.00
    COST OF EDUCATION - 06.02.05
    COST OF LIVING - 03.02.05
    COST-BENEFIT ANALYSIS - 12.09.00

COSTA
    COSTA RICA - 01.04.03
    COSTA RICAN - 14.03.02

COSTS
    CAPITAL COSTS - 12.09.00
    COSTS - 12.09.00
    DISTRIBUTION COSTS - 09.04.01
    EQUIPMENT COSTS - 12.09.00
    LABOUR COSTS - 12.09.00
    OVERHEAD COSTS - 12.09.00
    PRODUCTION COSTS - 12.09.00
    SOCIAL COSTS - 02.02.01

COTTAGE
    COTTAGE INDUSTRY - 08.02.02

COTTON
    COTTON - 07.07.07

COUNCIL
    COUNCIL OF EUROPE - 01.03.03

COUNCIL\<CONT\>
    NORDIC COUNCIL - 01.03.03
    TRUSTEESHIP COUNCIL - 01.03.02
    UN SECURITY COUNCIL - 01.03.02

COUNTERPART
    COUNTERPART - 01.01.05
    COUNTERPART FUNDS - 01.01.05
    COUNTERPART PERSONNEL - 01.01.05

COUNTRIES
    ARAB COUNTRIES - 01.04.06
    CAPITALIST COUNTRIES - 03.03.03
    COLONIAL COUNTRIES - 01.02.03
    DEVELOPED COUNTRIES - 03.02.03
    DEVELOPING COUNTRIES - 03.02.03
    INDUSTRIALIZED COUNTRIES
    - 03.02.03
    USE: DEVELOPED COUNTRIES
    LAND LOCKED COUNTRIES - 17.03.04
    LEAST DEVELOPED COUNTRIES - 03.02.03
    MEDITERRANEAN COUNTRIES - 01.04.05
    OECD COUNTRIES - 01.03.03
    SOCIALIST COUNTRIES - 03.03.03

COURSES
    ACCELERATED COURSES - 06.05.01
    COURSES - 06.05.01
    INTENSIVE COURSES
    - 06.05.01
    USE: ACCELERATED COURSES
    TRAINING COURSES - 06.05.01

COURTS
    CONSTITUTIONAL COURTS - 04.03.01
    LABOUR COURTS - 04.01.02

COWPEAS
    COWPEAS - 07.07.06

COWS
    COWS - 07.09.01

CRAFTSMANSHIP
    CRAFTSMANSHIP - 13.02.01

CRAFTSMEN
    CRAFTSMEN - 13.09.06

CREATION
    ARTISTIC CREATION - 05.05.02
    EMPLOYMENT CREATION - 13.01.03

CREATIVITY
    CREATIVITY - 05.03.02

CREDIT
    AGRICULTURAL CREDIT - 07.03.03
    COMMERCIAL CREDIT - 09.04.03

CREDIT<CONT>

CONSUMER CREDIT - 11.02.02
CREDIT - 11.02.02
CREDIT CONTROL
- 11.02.02
USE: CREDIT POLICY
CREDIT COOPERATIVES - 11.02.02
CREDIT INSURANCE - 11.02.03
CREDIT POLICY - 11.02.02
CREDIT SYSTEMS - 11.02.02
CREDIT UNIONS
- 11.02.02
USE: CREDIT COOPERATIVES
EXPORT CREDIT - 09.05.05
INDUSTRIAL CREDIT - 08.02.04
INSTALMENT CREDIT
- 11.02.02
USE: CONSUMER CREDIT

CRIME

CRIME PREVENTION - 02.04.03

CRIMES

CRIMES - 02.04.02
WAR CRIMES - 01.02.07

CRIMINAL

CRIMINAL LAW - 04.01.02

CRIMINOLOGY

CRIMINOLOGY - 05.01.01

CRISIS

ECONOMIC CRISIS
- 03.02.04
USE: ECONOMIC RECESSION
EDUCATIONAL CRISIS - 06.02.03
ENERGY CRISIS - 08.11.01

CRITICAL

CRITICAL NEEDS
- 05.03.02
USE: BASIC NEEDS
CRITICAL PATH METHOD
- 12.04.00
USE: NETWORK ANALYSIS

CROP

CROP DIVERSIFICATION - 07.05.04
CROP PROSPECTS - 07.05.01
CROP ROTATION - 07.05.04
CROP YIELD - 07.05.01

CROPPING

CROPPING SYSTEMS
- 07.05.04
USE: CULTIVATION SYSTEMS
MULTIPLE CROPPING - 07.05.04

CROPS

CASH CROPS
- 07.07.02
USE: INDUSTRIAL CROPS

CROPS<CONT>

CROPS - 07.05.04
FOOD CROPS - 07.07.02
FORAGE CROPS - 07.07.02
FRUIT CROPS - 07.07.02
INDUSTRIAL CROPS - 07.07.02
LIVESTOCK CROPS
- 07.07.02
USE: FORAGE CROPS
OIL CROPS - 07.07.02
ROOT CROPS - 07.07.02
VEGETABLE CROPS - 07.07.02

CROSS

CROSS CULTURAL ANALYSIS - 05.01.02

CRUSTACEA

CRUSTACEA - 07.10.04

CSTD

CSTD - 01.03.02

CUBA

CUBA - 01.04.03

CUBAN

CUBAN - 14.03.02

CULTIVATED

CULTIVATED LAND - 07.05.02

CULTIVATION

CULTIVATION PRACTICES - 07.05.04
CULTIVATION SYSTEMS - 07.05.04
SHIFTING CULTIVATION - 07.05.04
SOIL CULTIVATION
- 07.05.02
USE: SOIL MANAGEMENT

CULTURAL

CONSERVATION OF CULTURAL HERITAGE - 05.02.02
CROSS CULTURAL ANALYSIS - 05.01.02
CULTURAL AGREEMENTS - 05.02.03
CULTURAL ANIMATION - 05.02.03
CULTURAL CHANGE - 05.02.02
CULTURAL COOPERATION - 05.02.03
CULTURAL DEVELOPMENT - 05.02.03
CULTURAL ENVIRONMENT - 05.02.02
CULTURAL EXPENDITURES - 05.02.03
CULTURAL FACTORS - 05.02.02
CULTURAL GEOGRAPHY - 17.03.01
CULTURAL HERITAGE - 05.02.02
CULTURAL IDENTITY - 05.02.02
CULTURAL INDUSTRY - 05.02.03

CULTURAL\<CONT\>

    CULTURAL INFORMATION - 05.02.03
    CULTURAL INTEGRATION - 05.02.02
    CULTURAL PLURALISM - 05.02.01
    CULTURAL POLICY - 05.02.03
    CULTURAL RELATIONS - 05.02.02
    PARTICIPATION IN CULTURAL LIFE - 05.02.02
    SOCIO-CULTURAL FACILITIES - 05.02.03

CULTURE

    ACCESS TO CULTURE - 05.02.03
    CULTURE - 05.02.01
    DISSEMINATION OF CULTURE - 05.02.03
    ECONOMICS OF CULTURE - 05.02.03
    FISH CULTURE - 07.10.03
    FOLK CULTURE - 05.02.01
    OYSTER CULTURE - 07.10.03
    RIGHT TO CULTURE - 05.02.03
    SCIENTIFIC CULTURE - 05.02.01
    TRADITIONAL CULTURE - 05.02.01

CURRENCIES

    CURRENCIES - 11.02.01
    NON-CONVERTIBLE CURRENCIES - 11.03.01

CURRENCY

    LOCAL CURRENCY - 11.02.01

CURRICULUM

    CURRICULUM - 06.05.01
    CURRICULUM DEVELOPMENT - 06.05.01
    CURRICULUM SUBJECTS - 06.05.01
    CURRICULUM VITAE - 19.02.02
    INTEGRATED CURRICULUM - 06.05.01

CUSTOMARY

    CUSTOMARY LAW - 04.01.02

CUSTOMS

    CUSTOMS - 09.05.08
    CUSTOMS POLICY
    - 09.05.08
    USE: TARIFF POLICY
    CUSTOMS UNION - 09.05.08

CYBERNETICS

    CYBERNETICS - 18.08.00

CYCLE

    BUSINESS CYCLE - 03.02.04

CYCLICAL

    CYCLICAL UNEMPLOYMENT - 13.01.03

CYCLONES

    CYCLONES
    - 17.01.03
    USE: STORMS

CYPRIOT

    CYPRIOT - 14.03.02

CYPRUS

    CYPRUS - 01.04.06

CYTOLOGY

    CYTOLOGY - 15.02.01

CZECHOSLOVAK

    CZECHOSLOVAK - 14.03.02

CZECHOSLOVAKIA

    CZECHOSLOVAKIA - 01.04.05

DAC
>OECD DAC - 01.03.03

DAILY
>DAILY - 19.02.06

DAIRY
>DAIRY INDUSTRY - 08.06.01
>DAIRY PRODUCTS - 07.09.05
>DAIRY PRODUCTS INDUSTRY
>- 08.06.01
>>*USE:* DAIRY INDUSTRY

DAMAGE
>DAMAGE - 16.03.01
>DAMAGE COMPENSATION - 16.04.01

DAMS
>DAMS - 17.05.04

DANCE
>DANCE - 05.05.03

DANGEROUS
>DANGEROUS SUBSTANCES - 16.03.04

DANISH
>DANISH - 14.03.02

DATA
>DATA ACQUISITION
>- 18.04.00
>>*USE:* DATA COLLECTING
>DATA ANALYSIS - 19.01.02
>DATA BANKS - 19.01.03
>DATA BASES - 19.01.03
>DATA COLLECTING - 18.04.00
>DATA COMPILATION
>- 18.04.00
>>*USE:* DATA COLLECTING
>DATA PROCESSING - 19.01.02
>DATA PROTECTION - 19.01.01
>DATA RECORDING - 19.01.02
>DATA RETRIEVAL - 19.01.02
>DATA STORAGE - 19.01.02
>DATA TRANSMISSION - 19.01.02
>ELECTRONIC DATA PROCESSING - 19.01.02
>STATISTICAL DATA - 18.08.00

DATE
>DATE PALMS - 07.07.05

DATES
>DATES - 07.07.05

DAY
>CONTINUOUS WORKING DAY - 13.03.03
>DAY CARE CENTRES - 06.04.02

DC
>OECD DC - 01.03.03

DE
>DE-SCHOOLING - 06.03.02

DEAF
>DEAF-DUMBNESS - 15.04.03

DEAFNESS
>DEAFNESS - 15.04.03

DEALERS
>DEALERS - 13.09.07

DEATH
>CAUSES OF DEATH - 14.06.00
>DEATH - 14.06.00

DEBENTURES
>DEBENTURES - 11.02.07

DEBT
>DEBT - 11.02.02
>DEBT BURDEN
>- 11.02.02
>>*USE:* INDEBTEDNESS
>DEBT CONSOLIDATION - 11.02.02
>DEBT RELIEF - 11.02.02
>DEBT REPAYMENT - 11.02.02
>EXTERNAL DEBT - 11.03.01
>PUBLIC DEBT - 11.01.01

DECADE
>FIRST DEVELOPMENT DECADE - 01.01.01
>SECOND DEVELOPMENT DECADE - 01.01.01

DECENTRALIZATION
>DECENTRALIZATION - 04.03.03

DECISION
>DECISION MAKING - 12.04.00

DECLINE
>FERTILITY DECLINE - 14.05.01
>MORTALITY DECLINE - 14.06.00
>POPULATION DECLINE - 14.01.02

DECOLONIZATION
>DECOLONIZATION - 01.02.03

DECONTAMINATION
>DECONTAMINATION - 16.04.01

DECORATIVE
>DECORATIVE ARTS
>- 05.05.03
>>*USE:* FINE ARTS

DEDUCTION
>TAX DEDUCTION - 11.01.02

DEEP
>DEEP SEA FISHING - 07.10.03
>DEEP SEA MINING - 08.13.00

DEFECTS
>HEREDITARY DEFECTS - 15.02.03

DEFENCE
>DEFENCE - 01.02.06

DEVASTATION

    DEVASTATION - 16.03.01

DEVELOPED

    DEVELOPED COUNTRIES - 03.02.03

    LEAST DEVELOPED COUNTRIES - 03.02.03

DEVELOPING

    DEVELOPING AREAS - 03.02.03

    DEVELOPING COUNTRIES - 03.02.03

DEVELOPMENT

    AFRICAN DEVELOPMENT BANK - 01.03.03

    AGRICULTURAL DEVELOPMENT - 07.01.02

    ASIAN DEVELOPMENT BANK - 01.03.03

    CHILD DEVELOPMENT - 06.05.04

    COMMUNITY DEVELOPMENT - 14.04.01

    CULTURAL DEVELOPMENT - 05.02.03

    CURRICULUM DEVELOPMENT - 06.05.01

    DEVELOPMENT ADMINISTRATION - 04.03.02

    DEVELOPMENT AID - 01.01.01

    DEVELOPMENT BANKS - 11.02.02

    DEVELOPMENT CENTRES - 01.01.07

    DEVELOPMENT PERSONNEL - 01.01.07

    DEVELOPMENT PLANNING - 02.01.02

    DEVELOPMENT PLANS - 02.01.02

    DEVELOPMENT POLICY - 02.01.01

    DEVELOPMENT POTENTIAL - 02.01.01

    DEVELOPMENT PROJECTS - 01.01.06

    DEVELOPMENT RESEARCH - 02.01.01

    DEVELOPMENT STRATEGY - 02.01.01

    DEVELOPMENT STYLES - 02.01.01

    DEVELOPMENT THEORY - 02.01.01

    ECONOMIC AND SOCIAL DEVELOPMENT - 02.01.01

    ECONOMIC DEVELOPMENT - 03.02.03

    EDUCATIONAL DEVELOPMENT - 06.02.03

    FIRST DEVELOPMENT DECADE - 01.01.01

    FISHERY DEVELOPMENT - 07.10.02

    FORESTRY DEVELOPMENT - 07.08.04

    INDUSTRIAL DEVELOPMENT - 08.01.02

    INTEGRATED DEVELOPMENT - 02.01.01

    IRRIGATION DEVELOPMENT - 17.05.03

    MANAGEMENT DEVELOPMENT - 12.04.00

    OBSTACLES TO DEVELOPMENT - 03.02.03

    PERSONALITY DEVELOPMENT - 05.03.01

DEVELOPMENT\<CONT\>

    POLITICAL DEVELOPMENT - 04.04.02

    PRODUCT DEVELOPMENT - 12.08.02

    REGIONAL DEVELOPMENT - 03.02.03

    RESEARCH AND DEVELOPMENT - 18.01.00

    RURAL DEVELOPMENT - 14.04.02

    SECOND DEVELOPMENT DECADE - 01.01.01

    SOCIAL DEVELOPMENT - 05.03.04

    TRADE DEVELOPMENT - 09.05.06

    URBAN DEVELOPMENT - 14.04.03

DEVICES

    INTRAUTERINE DEVICES - 14.05.02

    SAFETY DEVICES - 13.04.00

    WARNING DEVICES - 16.04.01

DEVSIS

    DEVSIS - 19.01.02

DIABETES

    DIABETES - 15.04.02

DIAGNOSIS

    DIAGNOSIS - 15.04.04

DIAGRAMS

    DIAGRAMS - 18.08.00

DIALECTS

    DIALECTS - 05.06.01

DIAMOND

    DIAMOND - 08.13.00

DICTATORSHIP

    DICTATORSHIP - 04.03.01

DICTIONARY

    DICTIONARY - 19.03.00

DIES

    DIES AND JIGS - 08.14.05

DIESEL

    DIESEL ENGINES - 08.14.06

DIET

    DIET - 15.03.02

DIFFUSION

    DIFFUSION OF INNOVATIONS - 12.06.00

DIGESTIVE

    DIGESTIVE SYSTEM - 15.02.04

DIOXIDE

    SULPHUR DIOXIDE - 08.12.04

DIPHTHERIA

    DIPHTHERIA - 15.04.02

DIPLOMACY

    DIPLOMACY - 01.02.05

DIPLOMAS

    DIPLOMAS - 06.04.13

    EQUIVALENCE BETWEEN DIPLOMAS - 06.04.13

DIRECTIVE
DIRECTIVE PLANNING - 02.01.02

DIRECTORY
DIRECTORY - 19.02.07

DISABILITY
DISABILITY - 15.04.03
DISABILITY BENEFITS - 02.03.02

DISABLED
DISABLED CARE - 02.05.03

DISARMAMENT
DISARMAMENT - 01.02.06

DISASTERS
DISASTERS - 16.03.01
MANMADE DISASTERS - 16.03.02
NATURAL DISASTERS - 16.03.02

DISCHARGE
DISCHARGE
- 13.05.00
  USE: DISMISSAL

DISCIPLINE
SCHOOL DISCIPLINE - 06.04.08

DISCOUNT
DISCOUNT - 11.02.07

DISCOVERIES
SCIENTIFIC DISCOVERIES - 12.06.00

DISCRIMINATION
DISCRIMINATION - 04.02.03
ECONOMIC DISCRIMINATION - 02.01.03
RACIAL DISCRIMINATION - 04.02.04

DISCUSSION
GROUP DISCUSSION - 05.03.07

DISEASE
DISEASE CONTROL - 15.04.04
DISEASE TRANSMISSION - 15.04.04
DISEASE VECTORS - 15.04.04

DISEASES
ANIMAL DISEASES - 15.04.01
CHRONIC DISEASES - 15.04.02
COMMUNICABLE DISEASES
- 15.04.02
  USE: INFECTIOUS DISEASES
CONTAGIOUS DISEASES
- 15.04.02
  USE: INFECTIOUS DISEASES
DEFICIENCY DISEASES - 15.04.02
DISEASES - 15.04.01
ENDEMIC DISEASES - 15.04.02
EPIDEMIC DISEASES
- 15.04.02
  USE: INFECTIOUS DISEASES
EYE DISEASES - 15.04.02

DISEASES<CONT>
FUNGUS DISEASES - 15.04.02
IMMUNOLOGIC DISEASES - 15.04.02
INFECTIOUS DISEASES - 15.04.02
INTRACTABLE DISEASES - 15.04.02
MENTAL DISEASES - 15.04.02
MOUTH DISEASES - 15.04.02
OCCUPATIONAL DISEASES - 13.04.00
PARASITIC DISEASES - 15.04.02
PLANT DISEASES - 15.04.01
RICKETTSIAL DISEASES - 15.04.02
STRESS-RELATED DISEASES
- 13.04.00
  USE: OCCUPATIONAL DISEASES
TROPICAL DISEASES - 15.04.02
VENEREAL DISEASES - 15.04.02

DISGUISED
DISGUISED UNEMPLOYMENT - 13.01.03

DISINTEGRATION
FAMILY DISINTEGRATION - 14.02.04

DISLOCATION
JOB DISLOCATION - 13.05.00

DISMISSAL
DISMISSAL - 13.05.00

DISPARITY
ECONOMIC DISPARITY - 03.02.03
REGIONAL DISPARITY - 03.02.03

DISPERSED
DISPERSED HABITAT - 14.04.01

DISPLACEMENT
DISPLACEMENT
- 13.05.00
  USE: LABOUR MOBILITY

DISPOSAL
GARBAGE DISPOSAL
- 16.04.02
  USE: SANITATION SERVICES
SEWAGE DISPOSAL
- 16.04.02
  USE: SANITATION SERVICES
WASTE DISPOSAL - 16.04.02

DISPUTE
DISPUTE SETTLEMENT - 05.03.06

DISPUTES
LABOUR DISPUTES - 13.06.00

DISSEMINATION
DISSEMINATION OF CULTURE - 05.02.03
INFORMATION DISSEMINATION - 19.01.02

DISTANCE
DISTANCE - 18.06.00

350

DISTANCE<CONT>

DISTANCE STUDY - 06.05.03

DISTILLING

DISTILLING - 08.12.03

DISTRIBUTION

AGE DISTRIBUTION - 14.02.02
AGE-SEX DISTRIBUTION - 14.02.01
DISTRIBUTION - 09.04.01
DISTRIBUTION COSTS - 09.04.01
DISTRIBUTION NETWORK - 09.04.01
GEOGRAPHIC DISTRIBUTION - 17.03.02
INCOME DISTRIBUTION - 03.02.05
LAND DISTRIBUTION
- 07.02.00
 USE: LAND TENURE
POPULATION DISTRIBUTION - 14.04.01
POWER DISTRIBUTION - 08.11.01
SEX DISTRIBUTION - 14.02.03
WATER DISTRIBUTION - 17.05.05

DIVERSIFICATION

CROP DIVERSIFICATION - 07.05.04
EXPORT DIVERSIFICATION - 09.05.05
PRODUCTION DIVERSIFICATION - 12.07.01

DIVIDENDS

DIVIDENDS
- 11.02.07
 USE: INVESTMENT RETURNS

DIVISION

DIVISION OF LABOUR - 03.03.01
INTERNATIONAL DIVISION OF LABOUR - 09.05.03

DIVORCE

DIVORCE - 14.02.05

DJIBOUTI

DJIBOUTI - 01.04.02

DOCKERS

DOCKERS - 13.09.08

DOCTORS

BAREFOOT DOCTORS - 13.09.10
MEDICAL DOCTORS
- 13.09.10
 USE: PHYSICIANS

DOCTRINES

ECONOMIC DOCTRINES - 03.03.01
POLITICAL DOCTRINES - 04.04.02

DOCUMENTALISTS

DOCUMENTALISTS - 13.09.09

DOCUMENTARY

DOCUMENTARY ANALYSIS
- 19.01.02
 USE: INFORMATION ANALYSIS

DOCUMENTATION

DOCUMENTATION - 19.01.01
DOCUMENTATION CENTRES
- 19.01.03
 USE: INFORMATION SERVICES

DOCUMENTS

DOCUMENTS - 19.02.01
LIST OF DOCUMENTS - 19.02.05
OFFICIAL DOCUMENTS - 19.02.01
PRIMARY DOCUMENTS - 19.02.01
RESTRICTED DOCUMENTS - 19.02.01
SECONDARY DOCUMENTS - 19.02.01
UNPUBLISHED DOCUMENTS - 19.02.01

DOMESTIC

DOMESTIC ANIMALS - 07.09.01
DOMESTIC CONSUMPTION - 09.01.03
DOMESTIC MARKET - 09.01.02
DOMESTIC TRADE - 09.04.01
DOMESTIC WASTES - 16.03.04
DOMESTIC WORKERS - 13.09.07
GROSS DOMESTIC PRODUCT - 03.02.02

DOMINICA

DOMINICA - 01.04.03

DOMINICAN

DOMINICAN - 14.03.02
DOMINICAN REPUBLIC - 01.04.03

DONKEYS

DONKEYS - 07.09.01

DOUBLE

DOUBLE TAXATION - 09.05.09

DRAIN

BRAIN DRAIN - 14.07.00

DRAINAGE

DRAINAGE - 17.05.03

DRAMATIC

DRAMATIC ART - 05.05.03

DRAUGHTSMEN

DRAUGHTSMEN - 13.09.09

DRAWING

SPECIAL DRAWING RIGHTS - 11.03.01

DREDGING

DREDGING - 17.05.04

DRIED

DRIED FOOD - 08.06.03
DRIED FRUIT - 08.06.04

DRILLING

DRILLING - 17.05.04

DRINKING

DRINKING WATER - 17.05.05

DROPPING

DROPPING OUT - 06.04.12

DROUGHT

DROUGHT - 17.01.03

DRUG

DRUG ADDICTION - 02.04.02

DRUGS

DRUGS - 15.05.00

DRY

DRY SEASON - 17.02.02

DRYING

DRYING - 08.12.03

DUAL

DUAL ECONOMY - 03.03.02

DUAL JOBHOLDING - 13.02.01

DUMBNESS

DEAF-DUMBNESS - 15.04.03

DUMPING

DUMPING - 09.05.07

SEA DUMPING - 16.04.02

DURABLE

DURABLE GOODS - 09.01.03

DURATION

DURATION - 18.10.00

DWELLING

DWELLING
- 14.04.01
USE: HOUSING

DWELLING UNIT
- 14.04.01
USE: HOUSEHOLD

DYNAMICS

GROUP DYNAMICS - 05.03.07

POPULATION DYNAMICS - 14.01.02

EAC

EAC - 01.03.03

EADI

EADI - 01.03.03

EARLY

EARLY CHILDHOOD - 14.02.02

EARLY RETIREMENT - 13.05.00

EARNERS

WAGE EARNERS - 13.07.00

EARNINGS

EXPORT EARNINGS - 09.05.05

EARTH

EARTH SCIENCES - 17.04.01

EARTHMOVING

EARTHMOVING MACHINERY - 08.14.06

EARTHQUAKES

EARTHQUAKES
- 17.04.03
USE: SEISMS

EAST

EAST - 17.03.03

EAST AFRICA - 01.04.02

EAST-WEST TRADE - 09.05.02

FAR EAST - 01.04.04

MIDDLE EAST - 01.04.06

NEAR EAST
- 01.04.06
USE: MIDDLE EAST

SOUTH EAST ASIA - 01.04.04

EASTERN

EASTERN EUROPE - 01.04.05

ECA

ECA - 01.03.02

ECAFE

ECAFE
- 01.03.02
USE: ESCAP

ECE

ECE - 01.03.02

ECLA

ECLA - 01.03.02

ECMT

ECMT - 01.03.03

ECODEVELOPMENT

ECODEVELOPMENT - 16.01.01

ECOLOGICAL

ECOLOGICAL BALANCE - 16.01.01

ECOLOGICAL RESEARCH - 16.01.01

ECOLOGY

ANIMAL ECOLOGY - 16.01.01

ECOLOGY - 16.01.01

HUMAN ECOLOGY - 16.01.01

ECOLOGY<CONT>

    PLANT ECOLOGY - 16.01.01

ECONOMETRIC

    ECONOMETRIC MODELS - 03.01.02

ECONOMETRICS

    ECONOMETRICS - 03.01.02

ECONOMIC

    ECONOMIC ADMINISTRATION - 04.03.02
    ECONOMIC AGREEMENTS - 09.05.02
    ECONOMIC AID - 01.01.03
    ECONOMIC ANALYSIS - 03.01.02
    ECONOMIC AND SOCIAL DEVELOPMENT - 02.01.01
    ECONOMIC ASPECTS - 03.02.01
    ECONOMIC BEHAVIOUR - 03.02.01
    ECONOMIC CENSUSES - 03.01.02
    ECONOMIC CONCENTRATION - 12.02.00
    ECONOMIC CONDITIONS - 03.02.01
    ECONOMIC CONSEQUENCES
    - 03.02.01
     USE: ECONOMIC IMPLICATIONS
    ECONOMIC COOPERATION - 01.02.01
    ECONOMIC CRISIS
    - 03.02.04
     USE: ECONOMIC RECESSION
    ECONOMIC DEPRESSION
    - 03.02.04
     USE: ECONOMIC RECESSION
    ECONOMIC DEVELOPMENT - 03.02.03
    ECONOMIC DISCRIMINATION - 02.01.03
    ECONOMIC DISPARITY - 03.02.03
    ECONOMIC DOCTRINES - 03.03.01
    ECONOMIC EQUILIBRIUM - 03.02.04
    ECONOMIC EVALUATION - 03.01.02
    ECONOMIC FLUCTUATIONS
    - 03.02.04
     USE: BUSINESS CYCLE 006
    ECONOMIC FORECASTS - 03.01.02
    ECONOMIC GEOGRAPHY - 17.03.01
    ECONOMIC GROWTH - 03.02.03
    ECONOMIC HISTORY - 05.01.01
    ECONOMIC IMPLICATIONS - 03.02.01
    ECONOMIC INDICATORS - 03.01.02
    ECONOMIC INFORMATION - 03.01.02
    ECONOMIC INFRASTRUCTURE - 03.02.01
    ECONOMIC INTEGRATION - 01.02.01
    ECONOMIC LEGISLATION - 04.01.02

ECONOMIC<CONT>

    ECONOMIC LOSS - 03.02.04
    ECONOMIC MODELS - 03.01.02
    ECONOMIC PLANNING - 02.01.02
    ECONOMIC POLICY - 02.01.03
    ECONOMIC PROJECTIONS - 03.01.02
    ECONOMIC RECESSION - 03.02.04
    ECONOMIC RECONSTRUCTION - 03.02.03
    ECONOMIC RECOVERY - 03.02.04
    ECONOMIC REFORM - 02.01.03
    ECONOMIC RELATIONS - 01.02.01
    ECONOMIC RESEARCH - 03.01.02
    ECONOMIC RESOURCES - 03.02.01
    ECONOMIC SITUATION
    - 03.02.01
     USE: ECONOMIC CONDITIONS
    ECONOMIC STAGNATION - 03.02.04
    ECONOMIC STATISTICS - 03.01.02
    ECONOMIC STRUCTURE - 03.02.01
    ECONOMIC SURVEYS - 03.01.02
    ECONOMIC SYYYYSTEMS - 03.03.01
    ECONOMIC TAKE OFF - 03.02.03
    ECONOMIC THEORY - 03.01.02
    ECONOMIC THOUGHT - 03.03.01
    NEW INTERNATIONAL ECONOMIC ORDER - 01.02.01

ECONOMICS

    AGRICULTURAL ECONOMICS - 07.01.01
    BUSINESS ECONOMICS - 12.01.00
    ECONOMICS - 03.01.01
    ECONOMICS OF CULTURE - 05.02.03
    ECONOMICS OF EDUCATION - 06.01.00
    EDUCATIONAL ECONOMICS
    - 06.01.00
     USE: ECONOMICS OF EDUCATION
    ENERGY ECONOMICS - 08.11.01
    ENVIRONMENTAL ECONOMICS - 16.04.01
    FISHERY ECONOMICS - 07.10.01
    FOOD ECONOMICS - 15.03.01
    FORESTRY ECONOMICS - 07.08.01
    HOME ECONOMICS - 06.03.04
    INDUSTRIAL ECONOMICS - 08.01.01
    LAND ECONOMICS - 07.02.00
    TRANSPORT ECONOMICS - 10.01.00

ECONOMICS<CONT>
    WELFARE ECONOMICS - 02.02.02

ECONOMISTS
    ECONOMISTS - 13.09.09

ECONOMY
    AGRICULTURAL ECONOMY - 07.01.01
    COLLECTIVE ECONOMY - 03.03.02
    DUAL ECONOMY - 03.03.02
    ECONOMY OF SCALE - 12.09.00
    MARKET ECONOMY - 03.03.01
    MIXED ECONOMY - 03.03.02
    PLANNED ECONOMY - 03.03.02
    POLITICAL ECONOMY
    - 03.01.01
      USE: ECONOMICS
    ZERO GROWTH ECONOMY - 03.02.03

ECOSOC
    ECOSOC - 01.03.02

ECOSYSTEM
    ECOSYSTEM STABILITY
    - 16.01.01
      USE: ECOLOGICAL BALANCE

ECOSYSTEMS
    ECOSYSTEMS - 16.01.02

ECSC
    ECSC - 01.03.03

ECUADOR
    ECUADOR - 01.04.03

ECUADORIAN
    ECUADORIAN - 14.03.02

ECWA
    ECWA - 01.03.02

EDIBLE
    EDIBLE OILS - 08.06.06

EDITORIAL
    EDITORIAL - 19.02.06

EDUCATION
    ACCESS TO EDUCATION - 06.02.02
    ADMINISTRATION OF EDUCATION
    - 04.03.02
      USE: EDUCATIONAL ADMINISTRATION
    ADULT EDUCATION - 06.03.05
    ADVANCEMENT OF EDUCATION
    - 06.02.03
      USE: EDUCATIONAL DEVELOPMENT
    AGRICULTURAL EDUCATION - 06.03.07
    AIMS OF EDUCATION - 06.02.01
    ART EDUCATION - 06.03.07
    BASIC EDUCATION - 06.03.04
    CIVIC EDUCATION - 06.03.04

EDUCATION<CONT>
    COLLEGES OF EDUCATION - 06.04.05
    COMMERCIAL EDUCATION - 06.03.07
    COMPARATIVE EDUCATION - 06.01.00
    COMPENSATORY EDUCATION - 06.03.03
    COMPULSORY EDUCATION - 06.03.03
    CONSUMER EDUCATION - 06.03.04
    CONTINUING EDUCATION
    - 06.03.05
      USE: LIFE-LONG EDUCATION
    CORRECTIONAL EDUCATION - 06.03.03
    CORRESPONDENCE EDUCATION - 06.05.03
    COST OF EDUCATION - 06.02.05
    DEMOCRATIZATION OF EDUCATION - 06.02.02
    ECONOMICS OF EDUCATION - 06.01.00
    EDUCATION - 06.02.01
    EDUCATION OF WOMEN - 06.03.05
    ELEMENTARY EDUCATION
    - 06.03.06
      USE: PRIMARY EDUCATION
    ENVIRONMENTAL EDUCATION - 06.03.04
    FREE EDUCATION - 06.03.03
    GENERAL EDUCATION - 06.03.04
    HEALTH EDUCATION - 06.03.04
    HIGHER EDUCATION - 06.03.06
    HIGHER EDUCATION INSTITUTIONS - 06.04.05
    HISTORY OF EDUCATION - 06.01.00
    LEVELS OF EDUCATION - 06.03.06
    LIFE-LONG EDUCATION - 06.03.05
    MASS EDUCATION - 06.03.04
    MEDICAL EDUCATION - 06.03.07
    NON-FORMAL EDUCATION - 06.03.02
    OUT-OF-SCHOOL EDUCATION - 06.03.02
    PERMANENT EDUCATION
    - 06.03.05
      USE: LIFE-LONG EDUCATION
    PHILOSOPHY OF EDUCATION - 06.01.00
    PHYSICAL EDUCATION - 06.03.04
    PHYSICIAN EDUCATION
    - 06.03.07
      USE: MEDICAL EDUCATION
    PLANNING OF EDUCATION
    - 06.02.04
      USE: EDUCATIONAL PLANNING
    POLITICAL EDUCATION - 06.03.04

EDUCATION<CONT>

POST-SECONDARY EDUCATION - 06.03.06

PRESCHOOL EDUCATION - 06.03.06

PRIMARY EDUCATION - 06.03.06

PRIVATE EDUCATION - 06.03.03

PROFESSIONAL EDUCATION
- 06.03.07
  USE: VOCATIONAL EDUCATION

PSYCHOLOGY OF EDUCATION - 06.01.00

PUBLIC EDUCATION - 06.03.03

QUALITY OF EDUCATION - 06.02.03

RECURRENT EDUCATION - 06.03.05

REFORMS OF EDUCATION
- 06.02.03
  USE: EDUCATIONAL REFORMS

RIGHT TO EDUCATION - 06.02.02

SAFETY EDUCATION - 06.03.04

SCIENCES OF EDUCATION - 06.01.00

SECONDARY EDUCATION - 06.03.06

SEX EDUCATION - 06.03.04

SOCIOLOGY OF EDUCATION - 06.01.00

SPECIAL EDUCATION - 06.03.03

SYSTEMS OF EDUCATION
- 06.03.01
  USE: EDUCATIONAL SYSTEMS

TECHNICAL EDUCATION - 06.03.07

VOCATIONAL EDUCATION - 06.03.07

WORKERS EDUCATION - 06.03.05

EDUCATIONAL

EDUCATIONAL ADMINISTRATION - 04.03.02

EDUCATIONAL ASPECTS - 06.02.01

EDUCATIONAL ATTENDANCE - 06.04.12

EDUCATIONAL BUDGET - 06.02.05

EDUCATIONAL BUILDINGS - 06.04.07

EDUCATIONAL CRISIS - 06.02.03

EDUCATIONAL DEVELOPMENT - 06.02.03

EDUCATIONAL ECONOMICS
- 06.01.00
  USE: ECONOMICS OF EDUCATION

EDUCATIONAL EQUIPMENT - 06.04.07

EDUCATIONAL EXPENDITURES
- 06.02.05
  USE: COST OF EDUCATION

EDUCATIONAL FACILITIES - 06.04.07

EDUCATIONAL FILMS - 06.05.03

EDUCATIONAL FINANCING - 06.02.05

EDUCATIONAL<CONT>

EDUCATIONAL GRANTS - 06.04.11

EDUCATIONAL GUIDANCE - 06.04.09

EDUCATIONAL INNOVATIONS - 06.02.03

EDUCATIONAL INSTITUTIONS - 06.04.01

EDUCATIONAL NEEDS - 06.02.02

EDUCATIONAL OPPORTUNITIES - 06.02.02

EDUCATIONAL OUTPUT - 06.02.05

EDUCATIONAL PLANNING - 06.02.04

EDUCATIONAL POLICY - 06.02.04

EDUCATIONAL PROJECTS - 06.02.03

EDUCATIONAL PSYCHOLOGY
- 06.01.00
  USE: PSYCHOLOGY OF EDUCATION

EDUCATIONAL RADIO - 06.05.03

EDUCATIONAL REFORMS - 06.02.03

EDUCATIONAL RESEARCH - 06.01.00

EDUCATIONAL SCIENCES
- 06.01.00
  USE: SCIENCES OF EDUCATION

EDUCATIONAL SELECTION - 06.04.09

EDUCATIONAL SOCIOLOGY
- 06.01.00
  USE: SOCIOLOGY OF EDUCATION

EDUCATIONAL STATISTICS - 06.01.00

EDUCATIONAL SYSTEMS - 06.03.01

EDUCATIONAL TECHNOLOGY - 06.05.03

EDUCATIONAL TELEVISION - 06.05.03

EDUCATIONAL THEORY - 06.01.00

EEC

EEC - 01.03.03

EFFECTS

ENVIRONMENTAL EFFECTS - 16.03.04

EFFICIENCY

EFFICIENCY - 12.07.03

EFTA

EFTA - 01.03.03

EGGS

EGGS - 07.09.05

EGYPT

EGYPT - 01.04.02

EGYPTIAN

EGYPTIAN - 14.03.02

EIB

EIB - 01.03.03

EL

EL SALVADOR - 01.04.03

ELECTIONS

ELECTIONS - 04.04.02

ELECTORAL

ELECTORAL SYSTEMS - 04.03.01

ELECTRIC

ELECTRIC APPLIANCES - 08.15.02
ELECTRIC LAMPS - 08.15.02
ELECTRIC LIGHTING - 08.15.02
ELECTRIC MOTORS - 08.15.02
ELECTRIC POWER - 08.11.02
ELECTRIC POWER PLANTS - 08.11.02

ELECTRICAL

ELECTRICAL ENGINEERING - 08.11.02
ELECTRICAL EQUIPMENT - 08.15.02
ELECTRICAL INDUSTRY - 08.11.02
ELECTRICAL MACHINERY - 08.15.02
ELECTRICAL MACHINERY INDUSTRY - 08.15.01

ELECTRICIANS

ELECTRICIANS - 13.09.06

ELECTRICITY

ELECTRICITY - 08.11.02

ELECTRIFICATION

ELECTRIFICATION - 08.11.02

ELECTRONIC

ELECTRONIC COMPUTERS
- 08.15.02
  USE: COMPUTERS
ELECTRONIC DATA PROCESSING - 19.01.02
ELECTRONIC ENGINEERING - 08.15.01
ELECTRONIC EQUIPMENT - 08.15.02
ELECTRONIC TUBES - 08.15.02

ELECTRONICS

ELECTRONICS - 08.15.01
ELECTRONICS INDUSTRY - 08.15.01

ELEMENTARY

ELEMENTARY EDUCATION
- 06.03.06
  USE: PRIMARY EDUCATION
ELEMENTARY SCHOOLS
- 06.04.02
  USE: PRIMARY SCHOOLS

ELEPHANTS

ELEPHANTS - 07.09.01

ELITE

ELITE - 05.03.05

EMBARGO

ARMS EMBARGO - 01.02.06
EMBARGO - 09.05.07

EMBRYO

EMBRYO - 15.02.02

EMERGENCY

EMERGENCY RELIEF - 02.05.03

EMIGRANTS

EMIGRANTS - 14.07.00

EMIGRATION

EMIGRATION - 14.07.00

EMIRATES

UNITED ARAB EMIRATES - 01.04.06

EMPIRE

CENTRAL AFRICAN EMPIRE - 01.04.02

EMPLOYED

SELF-EMPLOYED - 13.09.02

EMPLOYEE

EMPLOYEE ASSOCIATIONS - 13.06.00

EMPLOYEES

EMPLOYEES - 13.09.02
EMPLOYEES ATTITUDES - 13.06.00

EMPLOYERS

EMPLOYERS - 12.03.00
EMPLOYERS ATTITUDES
- 13.06.00
  USE: MANAGEMENT ATTITUDES
EMPLOYERS ORGANIZATIONS - 13.06.00

EMPLOYMENT

EMPLOYMENT - 13.01.03
EMPLOYMENT CREATION - 13.01.03
EMPLOYMENT INJURIES BENEFITS - 02.03.02
EMPLOYMENT OPPORTUNITIES - 13.01.02
EMPLOYMENT PLANNING
- 13.01.03
  USE: MANPOWER PLANNING
EMPLOYMENT POLICY - 13.01.03
EMPLOYMENT SECURITY - 13.01.03
EMPLOYMENT SERVICES - 13.02.01
FULL EMPLOYMENT - 13.01.03
PART TIME EMPLOYMENT - 13.01.03
TEMPORARY EMPLOYMENT - 13.01.03
WORLD EMPLOYMENT PROGRAMME - 01.03.02

ENCYCLOPEDIA

ENCYCLOPEDIA - 19.03.00

ENDANGERED

ENDANGERED SPECIES - 16.05.01

ENDEMIC

ENDEMIC DISEASES - 15.04.02

ENDOCRINE

ENDOCRINE SYSTEM - 15.02.04

ENERGY

ATOMIC ENERGY
- 08.11.03
  USE: NUCLEAR ENERGY
ENERGY - 08.11.01
ENERGY CONSERVATION - 08.11.01

ENERGY<CONT>

    ENERGY CONSUMPTION - 08.11.01

    ENERGY CRISIS - 08.11.01

    ENERGY DEMAND
    - 08.11.01
     USE: POWER DEMAND

    ENERGY ECONOMICS - 08.11.01

    ENERGY POLICY - 08.11.01

    ENERGY REQUIREMENTS
    - 08.11.01
     USE: POWER DEMAND

    ENERGY RESOURCES - 16.02.02

    ENERGY SOURCES - 08.11.01

    ENERGY UTILIZATION - 08.11.01

    GEOTHERMAL ENERGY - 08.11.01

    NUCLEAR ENERGY - 08.11.03

    SOLAR ENERGY - 08.11.01

    THERMAL ENERGY - 08.11.01

    TIDAL ENERGY - 08.11.01

    WIND ENERGY - 08.11.01

ENFORCEMENT

    LAW ENFORCEMENT
    - 02.04.03
     USE: PENAL SANCTIONS

ENGINE

    ENGINE FUELS - 08.11.06

ENGINEERING

    AGRICULTURAL ENGINEERING - 07.04.00

    CHEMICAL ENGINEERING - 08.12.02

    CIVIL ENGINEERING - 12.06.00

    COMMUNICATION ENGINEERING - 08.16.00

    ELECTRICAL ENGINEERING - 08.11.02

    ELECTRONIC ENGINEERING - 08.15.01

    ENGINEERING - 12.06.00

    ENGINEERING DESIGN - 12.06.00

    ENVIRONMENTAL ENGINEERING - 16.04.01

    FISHERY ENGINEERING - 07.10.03

    FOOD ENGINEERING
    - 08.06.02
     USE: FOOD TECHNOLOGY

    FOREST ENGINEERING - 07.08.05

    HYDRAULIC ENGINEERING - 17.05.04

    INDUSTRIAL ENGINEERING - 08.03.00

    MINING ENGINEERING - 08.13.00

    NUCLEAR ENGINEERING - 08.11.03

    PETROLEUM ENGINEERING - 08.11.06

ENGINEERS

    ENGINEERS - 13.09.09

ENGINES

    DIESEL ENGINES - 08.14.06

    ENGINES - 08.14.06

    JET ENGINES - 08.14.06

    PETROL ENGINES - 08.14.06

    STEAM ENGINES - 08.14.06

ENGLISH

    ENGLISH LANGUAGE - 05.06.02

    ENGLISH SPEAKING AFRICA - 01.04.02

ENRICHMENT

    FOOD ENRICHMENT - 08.06.02

ENROLMENT

    ENROLMENT - 06.04.09

ENTERPRISE

    SIZE OF ENTERPRISE - 12.02.00

ENTERPRISES

    AGRICULTURAL ENTERPRISES - 07.03.01

    CAPITALIST ENTERPRISES - 12.01.00

    COMMERCIAL ENTERPRISES - 09.04.03

    ENTERPRISES - 12.01.00

    FOREIGN ENTERPRISES - 03.03.05

    INDUSTRIAL ENTERPRISES - 08.02.01

    INTERNATIONAL ENTERPRISES
    - 03.03.05
     USE: MULTINATIONAL ENTERPRISES

    MIXED ENTERPRISES - 03.03.05

    MULTINATIONAL ENTERPRISES - 03.03.05

    NATIONALIZED ENTERPRISES
    - 03.03.05
     USE: PUBLIC ENTERPRISES

    PRIVATE ENTERPRISES - 03.03.05

    PUBLIC ENTERPRISES - 03.03.05

    SMALL ENTERPRISES - 12.01.00

    SOCIALIST ENTERPRISES - 12.01.00

ENTOMOLOGY

    ENTOMOLOGY - 07.06.00

ENTREPRENEURS

    ENTREPRENEURS - 12.03.00

ENVIRONMENT

    AQUATIC ENVIRONMENT - 16.01.02

    CULTURAL ENVIRONMENT - 05.02.02

    ENVIRONMENT - 16.01.02

    FAMILY ENVIRONMENT - 14.02.04

    HUMAN ENVIRONMENT - 16.01.02

    MARINE ENVIRONMENT - 16.01.02

ENVIRONMENT<CONT>

   NATURAL ENVIRONMENT
   - 16.01.02
    USE: PHYSICAL ENVIRONMENT

   PHYSICAL ENVIRONMENT - 16.01.02

   RURAL ENVIRONMENT - 14.04.02

   SCHOOL ENVIRONMENT - 06.04.12

   SOCIAL ENVIRONMENT - 05.03.03

   TERRESTRIAL ENVIRONMENT - 16.01.02

   URBAN ENVIRONMENT - 14.04.03

   WORK ENVIRONMENT - 13.03.01

ENVIRONMENTAL

   ENVIRONMENTAL BIOLOGY
   - 16.01.01
    USE: ECOLOGY

   ENVIRONMENTAL CONTROL
   - 19.02.01
    USE: ENVIRONMENTAL MANAGEMENT

   ENVIRONMENTAL DEGRADATION - 16.03.04

   ENVIRONMENTAL ECONOMICS - 16.04.01

   ENVIRONMENTAL EDUCATION - 06.03.04

   ENVIRONMENTAL EFFECTS - 16.03.04

   ENVIRONMENTAL ENGINEERING - 16.04.01

   ENVIRONMENTAL IMPACT
   - 16.03.04
    USE: ENVIRONMENTAL EFFECTS

   ENVIRONMENTAL MANAGEMENT - 16.04.01

   ENVIRONMENTAL MONITORING
   - 16.04.01
    USE: ENVIRONMENTAL MANAGEMENT

   ENVIRONMENTAL POLICY - 16.04.01

   ENVIRONMENTAL POLLUTION
   - 16.03.04
    USE: POLLUTION

   ENVIRONMENTAL PROTECTION - 16.05.01

   ENVIRONMENTAL QUALITY ENVIRONMENTAL QUALITY
   -
   16.01.02

ENZYMES

   ENZYMES - 15.01.03

EPIDEMIC

   EPIDEMIC DISEASES
   - 15.04.02
    USE: INFECTIOUS DISEASES

EPIDEMICS

   EPIDEMICS - 15.04.04

EPIDEMIOLOGY

   EPIDEMIOLOGY - 15.04.06

EQUAL

   EQUAL OPPORTUNITY - 04.02.03

   EQUAL PAY - 13.07.00

EQUATORIAL

   EQUATORIAL GUINEA - 01.04.02

EQUATORIAL<CONT>

   EQUATORIAL ZONE - 17.02.03

EQUIDAE

   EQUIDAE - 07.09.01

EQUILIBRIUM

   BIOLOGICAL EQUILIBRIUM
   - 16.01.01
    USE: ECOLOGICAL BALANCE

   ECONOMIC EQUILIBRIUM - 03.02.04

   NATURAL EQUILIBRIUM
   - 16.01.01
    USE: ECOLOGICAL BALANCE

EQUIPMENT

   AGRICULTURAL EQUIPMENT - 07.04.00

   CONSTRUCTION EQUIPMENT
   - 08.14.06
    USE: BUILDING MACHINERY

   EDUCATIONAL EQUIPMENT - 06.04.07

   ELECTRICAL EQUIPMENT - 08.15.02

   ELECTRONIC EQUIPMENT - 08.15.02

   EQUIPMENT - 12.05.00

   EQUIPMENT COSTS - 12.09.00

   EQUIPMENT MANAGEMENT - 12.05.00

   FISHING EQUIPMENT - 07.10.03

   FORESTRY EQUIPMENT - 07.08.05

   HYDRAULIC EQUIPMENT - 17.05.04

   INDUSTRIAL EQUIPMENT - 08.03.00

   LABORATORY EQUIPMENT
   - 18.02.00
    USE: RESEARCH EQUIPMENT

   MEDICAL EQUIPMENT
   - 02.05.02
    USE: HEALTH FACILITIES

   OBSOLETE EQUIPMENT - 12.05.00

   PROJECTION EQUIPMENT - 08.15.02

   RESEARCH EQUIPMENT - 18.02.00

   SECOND HAND EQUIPMENT - 12.05.00

   TRANSPORT EQUIPMENT - 10.04.00

EQUIVALENCE

   EQUIVALENCE BETWEEN DIPLOMAS - 06.04.13

ERGONOMICS

   ERGONOMICS - 13.03.01

EROSION

   EROSION - 16.03.02

   EROSION CONTROL - 16.04.01

   SOIL EROSION - 16.03.02

ERUPTIONS

   VOLCANIC ERUPTIONS - 17.04.03

ESCAP

   ESCAP - 01.03.02

ESPIONAGE
    INDUSTRIAL ESPIONAGE - 12.08.02

ESRO
    ESRO
    - 01.03.03
        USE: EUROPEAN SPACE AGENCY

ESSENTIAL
    ESSENTIAL OILS - 08.06.06

ESTIMATING
    ESTIMATING
    - 18.09.00
        USE: EVALUATION

ESTUARIES
    ESTUARIES - 17.03.04

ETHICS
    ETHICS - 05.04.01

ETHIOPIA
    ETHIOPIA - 01.04.02

ETHIOPIAN
    ETHIOPIAN - 14.03.02

ETHNIC
    ETHNIC FACTORS - 14.03.01
    ETHNIC GROUPS - 14.03.01
    ETHNIC MINORITIES - 14.03.01

ETHNICITY
    ETHNICITY - 14.03.01

ETHNOGRAPHY
    ETHNOGRAPHY - 05.01.01

ETHNOLOGY
    ETHNOLOGY - 05.01.01

EURATOM
    EURATOM - 01.03.03

EURODOLLARS
    EURODOLLARS - 11.03.01

EUROPE
    COUNCIL OF EUROPE - 01.03.03
    EASTERN EUROPE - 01.04.05
    EUROPE - 01.04.05
    WESTERN EUROPE - 01.04.05

EUROPEAN
    EUROPEAN - 14.03.02
    EUROPEAN COMMUNITIES - 01.03.03
    EUROPEAN ORGANIZATIONS - 01.03.03
    EUROPEAN PARLIAMENT - 01.03.03
    EUROPEAN SPACE AGENCY - 01.03.03

EUTHANASIA
    EUTHANASIA - 15.04.04

EUTROPHICATION
    EUTROPHICATION - 16.03.04

EVALUATION
    AID EVALUATION - 01.01.04

EVALUATION<CONT>
    ECONOMIC EVALUATION - 03.01.02
    EVALUATION - 18.09.00
    EVALUATION TECHNIQUES - 18.09.00
    JOB EVALUATION - 13.02.01
    PROJECT EVALUATION - 01.01.06
    RESOURCES EVALUATION - 16.02.01

EVAPORATION
    EVAPORATION - 08.12.03

EVASION
    TAX EVASION - 11.01.02

EXAMINATION
    MEDICAL EXAMINATION - 15.04.04

EXAMINATIONS
    EXAMINATIONS - 06.04.13

EXCHANGE
    EXCHANGE RATE - 11.03.01
    FOREIGN EXCHANGE - 11.03.01
    FOREIGN EXCHANGE CONTROL - 11.03.01
    FOREIGN EXCHANGE RESERVE - 11.03.01
    INFORMATION EXCHANGE - 19.01.02
    STOCK EXCHANGE
    - 11.02.07
        USE: FINANCIAL MARKET
    STUDENT EXCHANGE - 06.05.02

EXEMPTION
    TAX EXEMPTION - 11.01.02

EXHIBITIONS
    EXHIBITIONS - 09.03.05

EXODUS
    RURAL EXODUS
    - 14.07.00
        USE: RURAL MIGRATIONS

EXPATRIATE
    EXPATRIATE WORKERS
    - 13.09.02
        USE: FOREIGN WORKERS

EXPENDITURES
    CAPITAL EXPENDITURES
    - 12.09.00
        USE: CAPITAL COSTS
    CONSUMER EXPENDITURES - 09.01.03
    CULTURAL EXPENDITURES - 05.02.03
    EDUCATIONAL EXPENDITURES
    - 06.02.05
        USE: COST OF EDUCATION
    EXPENDITURES - 11.02.05
    MILITARY EXPENDITURES - 01.02.06
    NATIONAL EXPENDITURES - 03.02.02
    PUBLIC EXPENDITURES - 11.01.01

EXPENSES
    MOVING EXPENSES - 13.07.00

EXPERIMENTAL
    EXPERIMENTAL CLASSES - 06.04.10
    EXPERIMENTAL FARMS - 07.03.01
    EXPERIMENTAL SCHOOLS - 06.04.03
    EXPERIMENTAL TEACHING - 06.05.02

EXPERIMENTATION
    EXPERIMENTATION - 18.05.00

EXPERIMENTS
    EXPERIMENTS - 18.05.00

EXPERT
    EXPERT REPORT - 19.02.08

EXPERTS
    EXPERTS - 01.01.07

EXPLOITABILITY
    EXPLOITABILITY - 16.02.01

EXPLOITATION
    RESOURCES EXPLOITATION - 16.02.01

EXPLORATION
    RESOURCES EXPLORATION
    - 16.02.01
     USE: RESOURCES INVENTORY

EXPLOSIONS
    EXPLOSIONS - 16.03.02

EXPLOSIVES
    EXPLOSIVES - 08.12.08

EXPORT
    EXPORT CREDIT - 09.05.05
    EXPORT DIVERSIFICATION - 09.05.05
    EXPORT EARNINGS - 09.05.05
    EXPORT FINANCING - 09.05.05
    EXPORT INSURANCE - 11.02.03
    EXPORT OF CAPITAL - 11.03.03
    EXPORT PLANNING - 09.05.06
    EXPORT PROMOTION - 09.05.06
    EXPORT RESTRICTIONS - 09.05.07
    EXPORT SUBSIDIES - 09.05.05
    EXPORT VALUE - 09.05.05
    EXPORT VOLUME - 09.05.05
    EXPORT-ORIENTED INDUSTRY - 08.01.01

EXPORTS
    EXPORTS - 09.05.05

EXPROPRIATION
    EXPROPRIATION - 03.03.05

EXTENSION
    AGRICULTURAL EXTENSION - 07.01.02
    EXTENSION SERVICES - 19.01.03

EXTENSION<CONT>
    INDUSTRIAL EXTENSION - 08.01.01

EXTENSIVE
    EXTENSIVE FARMING - 07.05.03

EXTERNAL
    EXTERNAL DEBT - 11.03.01

EXTRACTION
    PETROLEUM EXTRACTION - 08.13.00

EYE
    EYE DISEASES - 15.04.02

FABA

FABA BEANS - 07.07.06

FACILITIES

EDUCATIONAL FACILITIES - 06.04.07
HEALTH FACILITIES - 02.05.02
SOCIO-CULTURAL FACILITIES - 05.02.03
SPORTS FACILITIES - 13.08.00

FACTOR

TIME FACTOR - 18.10.00

FACTORIES

FACTORIES
- 08.03.00
  USE: INDUSTRIAL PLANTS

FACTORS

CULTURAL FACTORS - 05.02.02
ETHNIC FACTORS - 14.03.01
LOCATION FACTORS - 02.01.02
PRODUCTION FACTORS - 12.07.01

FACTORY

FACTORY BOATS - 07.10.03
FACTORY LAYOUT - 08.03.00
FACTORY ORGANIZATION - 08.03.00
FACTORY WORKERS
- 13.09.06
  USE: INDUSTRIAL WORKERS

FAIRS

TRADE FAIRS - 09.03.05

FALKLAND

FALKLAND ISLANDS - 01.04.03

FAMILY

FAMILY - 14.02.04
FAMILY ALLOWANCES - 02.03.02
FAMILY BUDGET - 03.02.05
FAMILY DISINTEGRATION - 14.02.04
FAMILY ENVIRONMENT - 14.02.04
FAMILY LAW - 04.01.02
FAMILY PLANNING - 14.05.02
FAMILY PLANNING AGENCIES - 14.05.02
FAMILY PLANNING PROGRAMMES - 14.05.02
FAMILY POLICY - 02.05.03
FAMILY SIZE - 14.02.04

FAMINE

FAMINE - 15.03.02

FAO

FAO - 01.03.02

FAR

FAR EAST - 01.04.04

FARM

FARM ANIMALS
- 07.09.02
  USE: LIVESTOCK

FARM<CONT>

FARM BUILDINGS - 07.04.00
FARM MACHINERY
- 07.04.00
  USE: AGRICULTURAL MACHINERY
FARM MANAGEMENT - 07.03.02
FARM SIZE - 07.03.02

FARMER

FARMER TRAINING
- 06.03.07
  USE: AGRICULTURAL TRAINING

FARMERS

FARMERS - 13.09.05
SHARE FARMERS
- 07.02.00
  USE: TENANT FARMERS
TENANT FARMERS - 07.02.00

FARMING

COLLECTIVE FARMING - 07.05.03
COMMERCIAL FARMING - 07.05.03
COOPERATIVE FARMING - 07.05.03
EXTENSIVE FARMING - 07.05.03
FARMING - 07.05.03
FARMING SYSTEMS - 07.05.03
INTENSIVE FARMING - 07.05.03
MIXED FARMING - 07.05.03
SUBSISTENCE FARMING - 07.05.03

FARMS

EXPERIMENTAL FARMS - 07.03.01
FARMS - 07.03.01
STATE FARMS - 07.03.02

FAROE

FAROE ISLANDS - 01.04.05

FATHER

FATHER - 14.02.04

FATIGUE

FATIGUE - 13.03.04

FATS

ANIMAL FATS - 08.06.06
FATS - 08.06.06
OILS AND FATS - 08.06.06

FAUNA

AQUATIC FAUNA - 07.10.04
FAUNA - 07.09.01

FEASIBILITY

FEASIBILITY STUDIES - 01.01.06

FECUNDITY

FECUNDITY - 15.02.02

FEED

FEED - 07.09.03

FEEDING
>   ANIMAL FEEDING - 07.09.03
>   BREAST FEEDING - 15.03.02
>   FEEDING - 15.03.01

FEES
>   FEES - 06.04.11

FELLOWSHIPS
>   RESEARCH FELLOWSHIPS - 06.04.11

FEMALE
>   FEMALE MANPOWER - 13.09.02

FEMALES
>   FEMALES - 14.02.03

FERMENTATION
>   FERMENTATION - 15.01.03

FERROUS
>   NON-FERROUS METALS - 08.14.02

FERTILITY
>   FERTILITY - 14.05.01
>   FERTILITY DECLINE - 14.05.01
>   SOIL FERTILITY - 07.05.02

FERTILIZATION
>   FERTILIZATION - 15.02.02

FERTILIZER
>   FERTILIZER INDUSTRY - 08.12.05

FERTILIZERS
>   CHEMICAL FERTILIZERS - 08.12.05
>   FERTILIZERS - 08.12.05

FERTILIZING
>   FERTILIZING - 07.05.02

FETISHISM
>   FETISHISM - 05.04.03

FEUDALISM
>   FEUDALISM - 03.03.01

FEVER
>   SCARLET FEVER - 15.04.02
>   YELLOW FEVER - 15.04.02

FIBRES
>   ANIMAL FIBRES - 07.09.05
>   FIBRES - 08.08.01
>   HARD FIBRES - 08.07.01
>   MANMADE FIBRES - 08.08.01
>   NATURAL FIBRES - 08.08.01
>   PLANT FIBRES - 07.07.07
>   SOFT FIBRES - 08.08.01
>   WOOD FIBRES - 08.07.01

FID
>   FID - 01.03.04

FIELD
>   FIELD ACTIVITY - 18.04.00

FIELD<CONT>
>   FIELD RESEARCH - 18.04.00
>   FIELD STUDY
>   - 18.04.00
>   *USE:* FIELD RESEARCH
>   FIELD WORK
>   - 18.04.00
>   *USE:* FIELD ACTIVITY

FIJI
>   FIJI - 01.04.07

FILARIASIS
>   FILARIASIS - 15.04.02

FILES
>   CARD FILES - 19.01.04

FILIPINO
>   FILIPINO - 14.03.02

FILM
>   FILM INDUSTRY - 08.16.00

FILMS
>   EDUCATIONAL FILMS - 06.05.03
>   FILMS - 05.07.03

FINANCE
>   LOCAL FINANCE - 11.01.01
>   PUBLIC FINANCE - 11.01.01

FINANCIAL
>   FINANCIAL ADMINISTRATION - 04.03.02
>   FINANCIAL AID - 01.01.03
>   FINANCIAL ASPECTS - 11.02.04
>   FINANCIAL INSTITUTIONS - 11.02.02
>   FINANCIAL LOSS - 12.09.00
>   FINANCIAL MANAGEMENT - 11.02.04
>   FINANCIAL MARKET - 11.02.07
>   FINANCIAL NEEDS - 11.02.05
>   FINANCIAL POLICY - 11.02.04
>   FINANCIAL RESOURCES - 11.02.05
>   FINANCIAL STATISTICS - 11.02.04
>   FINANCIAL TERMS - 11.02.04

FINANCING
>   AID FINANCING - 01.01.04
>   COMPENSATORY FINANCING - 11.02.04
>   DEFICIT FINANCING - 11.02.05
>   EDUCATIONAL FINANCING - 06.02.05
>   EXPORT FINANCING - 09.05.05
>   FINANCING - 11.02.04
>   FINANCING PROGRAMMES - 11.02.04
>   SELF-FINANCING - 11.02.05

FINE
>   FINE ARTS - 05.05.03

FINISHED

    FINISHED PRODUCTS - 08.04.00

FINLAND

    FINLAND - 01.04.05

FINNISH

    FINNISH - 14.03.02

FIRE

    FIRE CONTROL - 16.04.01

    FIRE INSURANCE - 11.02.03

FIRES

    FIRES - 16.03.02

    FOREST FIRES - 16.03.02

FIRST

    FIRST DEVELOPMENT DECADE - 01.01.01

FISCAL

    FISCAL ADMINISTRATION - 04.03.02

    FISCAL LAW - 04.01.02

    FISCAL POLICY - 11.01.02

FISH

    FISH - 07.10.04

    FISH BREEDING - 07.10.04

    FISH CULTURE - 07.10.03

    FISH MEAL - 08.06.04

    FISH OILS - 08.06.06

    FISH PRESERVATION - 08.06.02

    FISH PRODUCTION - 07.10.04

    FISH PROTEIN CONCENTRATE - 08.06.04

    FISH UTILIZATION - 07.10.04

    FRESHWATER FISH - 07.10.04

    SALT WATER FISH - 07.10.04

FISHERMEN

    FISHERMEN - 13.09.05

FISHERY

    FISHERY - 07.10.01

    FISHERY CONSERVATION - 16.05.01

    FISHERY DEVELOPMENT - 07.10.02

    FISHERY ECONOMICS - 07.10.01

    FISHERY ENGINEERING - 07.10.03

    FISHERY INDUSTRY - 07.10.02

    FISHERY MANAGEMENT - 07.10.02

    FISHERY PLANNING - 07.10.02

    FISHERY POLICY - 07.10.02

    FISHERY PRODUCT PROCESSING - 08.06.02

    FISHERY PRODUCTS - 07.10.04

    FISHERY RESEARCH - 07.10.01

FISHERY<CONT>

    FISHERY RESOURCES - 16.02.02

    FISHERY STATISTICS - 07.10.01

FISHING

    COASTAL FISHING - 07.10.03

    DEEP SEA FISHING - 07.10.03

    FISHING - 07.10.03

    FISHING BOATS
    - 07.10.03
     USE: FISHING VESSELS

    FISHING EQUIPMENT - 07.10.03

    FISHING FLEET
    - 07.10.03
     USE: FISHING VESSELS

    FISHING GEAR
    - 07.10.03
     USE: FISHING EQUIPMENT

    FISHING GROUNDS - 07.10.03

    FISHING PORTS - 07.10.03

    FISHING RIGHTS - 07.10.02

    FISHING VESSELS - 07.10.03

    INLAND FISHING - 07.10.03

    MARINE FISHING - 07.10.03

FLAGS

    FLAGS OF CONVENIENCE - 10.05.00

FLAX

    FLAX - 07.07.07

FLEET

    FISHING FLEET
    - 07.10.03
     USE: FISHING VESSELS

    MERCHANT FLEET
    - 10.05.00
     USE: MERCHANT MARINE

FLEXIBLE

    FLEXIBLE HOURS OF WORK - 13.03.03

FLOOD

    FLOOD CONTROL - 16.04.01

FLOODS

    FLOODS - 16.03.02

FLORA

    FLORA - 07.07.01

FLOUR

    FLOUR - 08.06.04

FLOW

    CASH FLOW - 12.09.00

    FLOW CHART - 12.04.00

FLOWERS

    FLOWERS - 07.07.01

FLOWS

    CAPITAL FLOWS
    - 11.03.03
     USE: CAPITAL MOVEMENTS

FLUCTUATIONS

    ECONOMIC FLUCTUATIONS
    - 03.02.04
    USE: BUSINESS CYCLE
    SEASONAL FLUCTUATIONS - 03.02.04

FLUORINE

    FLUORINE - 08.12.04

FODDER

    FODDER - 07.09.03

FOETUS

    FOETUS - 15.02.02

FOLK

    FOLK ART - 05.05.02
    FOLK CULTURE - 05.02.01

FOLKLORE

    FOLKLORE - 05.01.01

FOOD

    CANNED FOOD - 08.06.03
    CONDENSED FOOD - 08.06.03
    DEHYDRATED FOOD - 08.06.03
    DRIED FOOD - 08.06.03
    FOOD - 15.03.01
    FOOD ADDITIVES - 08.06.02
    FOOD AID - 01.01.03
    FOOD ANALYSIS - 15.03.01
    FOOD CHEMISTRY - 15.03.01
    FOOD COMPOSITION - 15.03.01
    FOOD CONSUMPTION - 15.03.02
    FOOD CONTAMINATION - 15.03.01
    FOOD CROPS - 07.07.02
    FOOD ECONOMICS - 15.03.01
    FOOD ENGINEERING
    - 08.06.02
    USE: FOOD TECHNOLOGY
    FOOD ENRICHMENT - 08.06.02
    FOOD HYGIENE - 15.03.02
    FOOD INDUSTRY - 08.06.01
    FOOD INSPECTION - 15.03.01
    FOOD IRRADIATION - 08.06.02
    FOOD PLANNING - 15.03.01
    FOOD POLICY - 15.03.01
    FOOD PREPARATION - 15.03.01
    FOOD PRESERVATION - 08.06.02
    FOOD PROCESSING - 08.06.02
    FOOD PRODUCTION - 08.06.01

FOOD\<CONT\>

    FOOD PRODUCTS
    - 15.03.01
    USE: FOOD
    FOOD REQUIREMENTS - 15.03.02
    FOOD RESERVES - 15.03.01
    FOOD SCIENCE - 08.06.02
    FOOD SHORTAGE - 15.03.01
    FOOD SPOILAGE - 15.03.01
    FOOD STANDARDS - 15.03.02
    FOOD STATISTICS - 15.03.02
    FOOD STERILIZATION - 08.06.02
    FOOD STORAGE - 08.06.02
    FOOD SUPPLY - 15.03.01
    FOOD TECHNOLOGY - 08.06.02
    FROZEN FOOD - 08.06.03
    IRRADIATED FOOD - 08.06.03
    PERISHABLE FOOD - 15.03.01
    PROTEIN RICH FOOD - 15.03.01
    WORLD FOOD PROGRAMME - 01.03.02

FOOTWEAR

    FOOTWEAR
    - 08.08.02
    USE: SHOE INDUSTRY

FORAGE

    FORAGE CROPS - 07.07.02

FORCE

    LABOUR FORCE
    - 13.01.02
    USE: MANPOWER

FORCED

    FORCED LABOUR - 02.04.03

FORECASTING

    FORECASTING TECHNIQUES - 18.10.00
    TECHNOLOGICAL FORECASTING - 12.06.00

FORECASTS

    ECONOMIC FORECASTS - 03.01.02
    FORECASTS - 18.10.00
    WEATHER FORECASTS - 17.01.01

FOREIGN

    FOREIGN AID - 01.01.01
    FOREIGN CAPITAL - 11.03.03
    FOREIGN ENTERPRISES - 03.03.05
    FOREIGN EXCHANGE - 11.03.01
    FOREIGN EXCHANGE CONTROL - 11.03.01
    FOREIGN EXCHANGE RESERVE - 11.03.01
    FOREIGN INTERVENTION - 01.02.05

FOREIGN<CONT>
FOREIGN INVESTMENTS - 11.03.03
FOREIGN OWNERSHIP - 03.03.05
FOREIGN POLICY - 01.02.05
FOREIGN RELATIONS - 01.02.01
FOREIGN SERVICE - 01.02.05
FOREIGN STUDENTS - 06.06.01
FOREIGN TRADE - 09.05.01
FOREIGN WORKERS - 13.09.02

FOREIGNERS
FOREIGNERS - 14.07.00

FOREMEN
FOREMEN
- 13.09.03
USE: SUPERVISORS

FOREST
FOREST AREAS - 07.08.03
FOREST CONSERVATION - 16.05.01
FOREST ENGINEERING - 07.08.05
FOREST FIRES - 16.03.02
FOREST MANAGEMENT - 07.08.04
FOREST NURSERIES - 07.08.03
FOREST POLICY - 07.08.04
FOREST PRODUCTION - 07.08.06
FOREST PRODUCTS - 07.08.06
FOREST RESOURCES - 16.02.02
FOREST TREES - 07.08.06
FOREST UTILIZATION - 07.08.03

FORESTRY
FORESTRY - 07.08.01
FORESTRY DEVELOPMENT - 07.08.04
FORESTRY ECONOMICS - 07.08.01
FORESTRY EQUIPMENT - 07.08.05
FORESTRY INDUSTRY - 07.08.01
FORESTRY PLANNING - 07.08.04
FORESTRY RESEARCH - 07.08.02
FORESTRY STATISTICS - 07.08.02

FORESTS
FORESTS - 07.08.01
MANMADE FORESTS - 07.08.03

FORGING
FORGING - 08.14.03

FORMAL
NON-FORMAL EDUCATION - 06.03.02

FORMATION
CAPITAL FORMATION - 11.02.05

FORWARDING
FREIGHT FORWARDING - 10.06.00

FOSSIL
FOSSIL FUELS - 08.11.01

FRAMEWORK
INSTITUTIONAL FRAMEWORK - 04.03.01

FRANCE
FRANCE - 01.04.05

FREE
FREE EDUCATION - 06.03.03
FREE PORTS - 09.05.08
FREE TRADE AREA - 09.05.08

FREEDOM
ACADEMIC FREEDOM - 04.02.02
FREEDOM - 04.02.02
FREEDOM OF ASSOCIATION - 04.02.02
FREEDOM OF INFORMATION - 04.02.02
FREEDOM OF OPINION - 04.02.02
FREEDOM OF SPEECH - 04.02.02
RELIGIOUS FREEDOM - 04.02.02

FREEZING
FREEZING - 08.12.03

FREIGHT
FREIGHT - 10.09.00
FREIGHT FORWARDING - 10.06.00
FREIGHT MARKET - 10.09.00

FRENCH
FRENCH - 14.03.02
FRENCH GUIANA - 01.04.03
FRENCH LANGUAGE - 05.06.02
FRENCH POLYNESIA - 01.04.07
FRENCH SPEAKING AFRICA - 01.04.02

FRESHWATER
FRESHWATER - 17.05.05
FRESHWATER FISH - 07.10.04

FRIGID
FRIGID ZONE - 17.02.03

FRINGE
FRINGE BENEFITS - 13.07.00

FRONTIER
FRONTIER MIGRATIONS - 14.07.00

FRONTIERS
FRONTIERS
- 01.02.02
USE: BOUNDARIES

FROZEN
FROZEN FOOD - 08.06.03

FRUIT
DRIED FRUIT - 08.06.04

FRUIT<CONT>
    FRUIT CROPS - 07.07.02
    FRUIT JUICES - 08.06.05
    FRUIT TREES - 07.07.05

FRUITS
    CITRUS FRUITS - 07.07.05
    FRUITS - 07.07.05

FUEL
    NUCLEAR FUEL - 08.11.03

FUELS
    ENGINE FUELS - 08.11.06
    FOSSIL FUELS - 08.11.01
    FUELS - 08.11.01

FULL
    FULL EMPLOYMENT - 13.01.03
    FULL TIME - 13.03.03

FUNCTIONAL
    FUNCTIONAL LITERACY - 06.03.04

FUNCTIONS
    CONSUMPTION FUNCTIONS - 09.01.03
    PRODUCTION FUNCTIONS - 12.07.01

FUND
    COMMON FUND - 09.05.02

FUNDS
    CONTINGENCY FUNDS - 02.03.02
    COUNTERPART FUNDS - 01.01.05
    PENSION FUNDS - 11.02.02

FUNGI
    FUNGI - 07.07.01

FUNGICIDES
    FUNGICIDES - 08.12.05

FUNGUS
    FUNGUS DISEASES - 15.04.02

FUR
    FUR - 08.08.02
    FUR INDUSTRY - 08.08.02

FURNITURE
    FURNITURE - 08.07.03
    FURNITURE INDUSTRY - 08.07.03

FURTHER
    FURTHER TRAINING - 06.03.07

FUTURE
    FUTURE - 18.10.00

GABON
    GABON - 01.04.02

GABONESE
    GABONESE - 14.03.02

GAINS
    CAPITAL GAINS - 12.09.00

GAMBIA
    GAMBIA - 01.04.02

GAMBIAN
    GAMBIAN - 14.03.02

GAME
    BIG GAME - 07.09.01
    GAME PROTECTION - 16.05.01
    SMALL GAME - 07.09.01

GARBAGE
    GARBAGE DISPOSAL
    - 16.04.02
    USE: SANITATION SERVICES

GARDENING
    GARDENING - 07.07.02

GARDENS
    BOTANICAL GARDENS - 16.05.02
    ZOOLOGICAL GARDENS - 16.05.02

GAS
    COAL GAS - 08.11.05
    NATURAL GAS - 08.11.06

GASOLINE
    GASOLINE
    - 08.11.06
    USE: PETROL

GATT
    GATT - 01.03.02

GEAR
    FISHING GEAR
    - 07.10.03
    USE: FISHING EQUIPMENT

GENEALOGY
    GENEALOGY - 14.02.04

GENERAL
    GENERAL EDUCATION - 06.03.04
    GENERAL SYSTEM OF PREFERENCES - 09.05.08
    UN GENERAL ASSEMBLY - 01.03.02

GENERATION
    POWER GENERATION - 08.11.01

GENERATIONS
    GENERATIONS - 14.02.02

GENES
    GENES - 15.02.03

GENETIC
    GENETIC IMPROVEMENT - 15.02.03

GENETICS
    GENETICS - 15.02.01

GENOCIDE
    GENOCIDE - 14.03.01

GEOCHEMISTRY
  GEOCHEMISTRY - 17.04.01

GEODESY
  GEODESY - 17.04.01

GEOGRAPHERS
  GEOGRAPHERS - 13.09.09

GEOGRAPHIC
  GEOGRAPHIC DISTRIBUTION - 17.03.02

GEOGRAPHICAL
  GEOGRAPHICAL ASPECTS - 17.03.02

GEOGRAPHY
  CULTURAL GEOGRAPHY - 17.03.01
  ECONOMIC GEOGRAPHY - 17.03.01
  GEOGRAPHY - 17.03.01
  HUMAN GEOGRAPHY - 17.03.01
  PHYSICAL GEOGRAPHY - 17.03.01
  POLITICAL GEOGRAPHY - 17.03.01

GEOLOGICAL
  GEOLOGICAL MAPS - 18.07.00
  GEOLOGICAL SURVEYS - 17.04.04

GEOLOGISTS
  GEOLOGISTS - 13.09.09

GEOLOGY
  GEOLOGY - 17.04.01

GEOMORPHOLOGY
  GEOMORPHOLOGY - 17.04.01

GEOPHYSICS
  GEOPHYSICS - 17.04.01

GEOTHERMAL
  GEOTHERMAL ENERGY - 08.11.01

GERMAN
  GERMAN - 14.03.02
  GERMAN DR - 01.04.05

GERMANY
  GERMANY - 01.04.05
  GERMANY FR - 01.04.05

GHANA
  GHANA - 01.04.02

GHANAIAN
  GHANAIAN - 14.03.02

GIBRALTAR
  GIBRALTAR - 01.04.05

GIFTED
  GIFTED STUDENTS - 06.06.01

GLACIERS
  GLACIERS - 17.05.02

GLASS
  GLASS - 08.10.04
  GLASS INDUSTRY - 08.10.04

GLOSSARY
  GLOSSARY - 19.03.00

GOATS
  GOATS - 07.09.01

GOLD
  GOLD - 08.14.02
  GOLD STANDARD - 11.03.01

GOODS
  CONSUMER GOODS - 09.01.03
  DURABLE GOODS - 09.01.03
  GOODS - 10.02.00
  HOUSEHOLD GOODS
  - 08.15.02
    USE: HOUSEHOLD APPLIANCES
  LEATHER GOODS - 08.08.02
  PRODUCTION GOODS - 11.02.05

GOVERNMENT
  CENTRAL GOVERNMENT - 04.03.03
  GOVERNMENT - 04.03.02
  GOVERNMENT POLICY - 04.03.02
  LOCAL GOVERNMENT - 04.03.03
  REGIONAL GOVERNMENT - 04.03.03

GOVERNMENTAL
  NON-GOVERNMENTAL ORGANIZATIONS - 01.03.01

GRADUATES
  GRADUATES - 06.06.01

GRAIN
  GRAIN PROCESSING - 08.06.02

GRAINS
  GRAINS
  - 07.07.04
    USE: CEREALS

GRANTS
  EDUCATIONAL GRANTS - 06.04.11
  GRANTS - 01.01.04
  GRANTS IN KIND
  - 01.01.03
    USE: AID IN KIND

GRAPES
  GRAPES - 07.07.05

GRAPHIC
  GRAPHIC ARTS - 05.05.03

GRAPHS
  GRAPHS - 18.08.00

GRASSES
  GRASSES - 07.09.03

GRASSLAND
  GRASSLAND - 07.07.02

GRAZING
  GRAZING - 07.07.02

GREECE
  GREECE - 01.04.05

GREEK
  GREEK - 14.03.02

GREEN
GREEN REVOLUTION - 07.01.02

GREENHOUSES
GREENHOUSES - 07.04.00

GREENLAND
GREENLAND - 01.04.05

GRENADA
GRENADA - 01.04.03

GROSS
GROSS DOMESTIC PRODUCT - 03.02.02
GROSS NATIONAL PRODUCT - 03.02.02

GROUNDNUTS
GROUNDNUTS - 07.07.05

GROUNDS
FISHING GROUNDS - 07.10.03

GROUNDWATER
GROUNDWATER - 17.05.05

GROUP
ANDEAN GROUP - 01.03.03
GROUP DISCUSSION - 05.03.07
GROUP DYNAMICS - 05.03.07
GROUP WORK - 13.03.02

GROUPING
ABILITY GROUPING - 06.04.10

GROUPS
AGE GROUPS - 14.02.02
ETHNIC GROUPS - 14.03.01
GROUPS - 05.03.07
INTEREST GROUPS - 04.04.02
MINORITY GROUPS - 05.03.07
PRESSURE GROUPS
- 04.04.02
   USE: INTEREST GROUPS
RELIGIOUS GROUPS - 05.04.02

GROWTH
ECONOMIC GROWTH - 03.02.03
GROWTH MODELS - 03.01.02
GROWTH POLES - 02.01.02
GROWTH POLICY - 02.01.03
GROWTH RATE - 03.01.02
INDUSTRIAL GROWTH
- 08.01.02
   USE: INDUSTRIAL DEVELOPMENT
ZERO GROWTH ECONOMY - 03.02.03

GUADELOUPE
GUADELOUPE - 01.04.03

GUARANTEED
GUARANTEED WAGE
- 13.07.00
   USE: MINIMUM WAGE

GUARANTEES
INVESTMENT GUARANTEES - 11.02.06

GUATEMALA
GUATEMALA - 01.04.03

GUATEMALAN
GUATEMALAN - 14.03.02

GUERRILLA
GUERRILLA - 01.02.07

GUIANA
FRENCH GUIANA - 01.04.03

GUIDANCE
EDUCATIONAL GUIDANCE - 06.04.09
VOCATIONAL GUIDANCE - 06.03.07

GUINEA
EQUATORIAL GUINEA - 01.04.02
GUINEA - 01.04.02
GUINEA-BISSAU - 01.04.02
PAPUA NEW GUINEA - 01.04.07

GUINEAN
GUINEAN - 14.03.02

GULF
PERSIAN GULF STATES - 01.04.06

GULFS
GULFS - 17.03.04

GUM
GUM ARABIC - 07.07.08

GUMS
GUMS - 07.07.08

GUYANA
GUYANA - 01.04.03

GUYANESE
GUYANESE - 14.03.02

GYNAECOLOGY
GYNAECOLOGY - 15.04.06

HABITAT
  DISPERSED HABITAT - 14.04.01
  HABITAT - 14.04.01

HAITI
  HAITI - 01.04.03

HAITIAN
  HAITIAN - 14.03.02

HAND
  HAND TOOLS - 08.14.05
  SECOND HAND EQUIPMENT - 12.05.00

HANDBOOK
  HANDBOOK
  - 19.02.09
  USE: MANUAL

HANDICAPPED
  HANDICAPPED - 15.04.05
  HANDICAPPED STUDENTS - 06.06.01
  HANDICAPPED WORKERS - 13.09.02
  MENTALLY HANDICAPPED - 15.04.05
  PHYSICALLY HANDICAPPED - 15.04.05

HANDICRAFT
  HANDICRAFT - 08.02.02
  HANDICRAFT PROMOTION - 08.01.02

HANDLING
  HANDLING - 10.06.00
  MATERIALS HANDLING
  - 10.06.00
  USE: HANDLING

HARBOURS
  HARBOURS
  - 10.03.00
  USE: PORTS

HARD
  HARD FIBRES - 08.07.01

HARDWARE
  HARDWARE
  - 08.15.02
  USE: ELECTRONIC EQUIPMENT

HARMFUL
  HARMFUL SUBSTANCES
  - 16.03.04
  USE: DANGEROUS SUBSTANCES

HARVESTING
  HARVESTING - 07.05.04

HAVENS
  TAX HAVENS - 11.01.02

HAWAII
  HAWAII - 01.04.07

HEALTH
  AUXILIARY HEALTH WORKERS
  - 13.09.10
  USE: PARAMEDICAL PERSONNEL
  HEALTH - 15.04.01
  HEALTH ADMINISTRATION - 04.03.02

HEALTH<CONT>
  HEALTH AID - 01.01.03
  HEALTH CENTRES - 02.05.02
  HEALTH CONTROL - 15.04.04
  HEALTH EDUCATION - 06.03.04
  HEALTH FACILITIES - 02.05.02
  HEALTH INDICATORS - 02.05.02
  HEALTH INSURANCE - 02.03.02
  HEALTH PLANNING - 02.05.02
  HEALTH POLICY - 02.05.02
  HEALTH SERVICES - 02.05.02
  MATERNAL AND CHILD HEALTH - 15.04.04
  MENTAL HEALTH - 15.04.01
  PUBLIC HEALTH - 15.04.01

HEART
  HEART - 15.02.04

HEATING
  HEATING - 08.12.03

HEAVY
  HEAVY INDUSTRY - 08.01.01

HEBRIDES
  NEW HEBRIDES - 01.04.07

HELENA
  ST HELENA - 01.04.02

HELICOPTERS
  HELICOPTERS - 10.04.00

HELP
  SELF-HELP - 14.04.01

HEMISPHERE
  NORTHERN HEMISPHERE - 01.04.01
  SOUTHERN HEMISPHERE - 01.04.01

HEMP
  HEMP - 07.07.07

HERBICIDES
  HERBICIDES - 08.12.05

HEREDITARY
  HEREDITARY DEFECTS - 15.02.03

HEREDITY
  HEREDITY - 15.02.03

HERITAGE
  CONSERVATION OF CULTURAL HERITAGE - 05.02.02
  CULTURAL HERITAGE - 05.02.02

HEVEAS
  HEVEAS - 07.07.08

HIDES
  HIDES AND SKINS - 08.08.02

HIGHER
  HIGHER EDUCATION - 06.03.06

HIGHER<CONT>
HIGHER EDUCATION INSTITUTIONS - 06.04.05

HILLS
HILLS - 17.03.04

HINDUISM
HINDUISM - 05.04.03

HIRE
HIRE PURCHASE - 09.03.02

HISTOLOGY
HISTOLOGY - 15.02.01

HISTORICAL
HISTORICAL ANALYSIS - 05.01.01

HISTORY
ECONOMIC HISTORY - 05.01.01
HISTORY - 05.01.01
HISTORY OF EDUCATION - 06.01.00
SOCIAL HISTORY - 05.01.01

HOARDING
HOARDING - 11.02.05

HOLDERS
SCHOLARSHIP HOLDERS - 06.06.01

HOLIDAYS
HOLIDAYS - 13.08.00
SCHOOL HOLIDAYS - 06.04.12

HOLY
HOLY SEE
- 01.04.05
USE: VATICAN

HOME
HOME ECONOMICS - 06.03.04
HOME TRADE
- 09.04.01
USE: DOMESTIC TRADE
WORK AT HOME - 13.03.02

HOMICIDE
HOMICIDE - 02.04.02

HONDURAN
HONDURAN - 14.03.02

HONDURAS
BRITISH HONDURAS
- 01.04.03
USE: BELIZE
HONDURAS - 01.04.03

HONEY
HONEY - 07.09.05

HONG
HONG KONG - 01.04.04

HORIZONTAL
HORIZONTAL COOPERATION - 01.01.01
HORIZONTAL INTEGRATION - 12.02.00

HORMONES
HORMONES - 15.02.04

HORSES
HORSES - 07.09.01

HORTICULTURE
HORTICULTURE - 07.07.02

HOSPITALIZATION
HOSPITALIZATION - 15.04.04

HOSPITALS
HOSPITALS - 02.05.02
MENTAL HOSPITALS - 02.05.02

HOSTAGES
HOSTAGES - 01.02.07

HOTEL
HOTEL INDUSTRY - 09.04.05

HOURS
FLEXIBLE HOURS OF WORK - 13.03.03
HOURS OF WORK - 13.03.03

HOUSEHOLD
HOUSEHOLD - 14.04.01
HOUSEHOLD APPLIANCES - 08.15.02
HOUSEHOLD GOODS
- 08.15.02
USE: HOUSEHOLD APPLIANCES

HOUSING
COLLECTIVE HOUSING - 14.04.01
HOUSING - 14.04.01
HOUSING CENSUSES - 14.04.01
HOUSING COOPERATIVES - 14.04.01
HOUSING NEEDS - 14.04.01
HOUSING POLICY - 14.04.01

HOW
KNOW HOW - 12.06.00

HUMAN
HUMAN ECOLOGY - 16.01.01
HUMAN ENVIRONMENT - 16.01.02
HUMAN GEOGRAPHY - 17.03.01
HUMAN NUTRITION - 15.03.02
HUMAN RELATIONS - 05.03.01
HUMAN RESOURCES - 13.01.02
HUMAN RIGHTS - 04.02.01
HUMAN SETTLEMENTS - 14.04.01

HUMANIZATION
HUMANIZATION OF WORK - 13.03.01

HUMID
HUMID ZONE - 17.02.03

HUMIDITY
HUMIDITY - 17.01.03

HUNGARIAN
HUNGARIAN - 14.03.02

HUNGARY
　　HUNGARY - 01.04.05

HUNTING
　　HUNTING - 07.09.04

HUSBAND
　　HUSBAND - 14.02.05

HUSBANDRY
　　ANIMAL HUSBANDRY - 07.09.02

HYBRIDIZATION
　　HYBRIDIZATION - 15.02.03

HYDRAULIC
　　HYDRAULIC ENGINEERING - 17.05.04
　　HYDRAULIC EQUIPMENT - 17.05.04

HYDROCARBONS
　　HYDROCARBONS - 08.11.06

HYDROELECTRIC
　　HYDROELECTRIC POWER - 08.11.02
　　HYDROELECTRIC POWER PLANTS - 08.11.02

HYDROGEN
　　HYDROGEN - 08.12.04

HYDROGEOLOGY
　　HYDROGEOLOGY - 17.05.01

HYDROGRAPHY
　　HYDROGRAPHY - 17.05.01

HYDROLOGICAL
　　HYDROLOGICAL NETWORK - 17.05.02

HYDROLOGY
　　HYDROLOGY - 17.05.01

HYGIENE
　　FOOD HYGIENE - 15.03.02
　　HYGIENE - 15.04.04
　　OCCUPATIONAL HYGIENE - 13.04.00

IAEA
　　IAEA - 01.03.02

IBE
　　IBE - 01.03.02

IBRD
　　IBRD - 01.03.02

ICAO
　　ICAO - 01.03.02

ICE
　　ICE - 17.05.05

ICELAND
　　ICELAND - 01.04.05

ICELANDIC
　　ICELANDIC - 14.03.02

ICEM
　　ICEM - 01.03.03

ICFTU
　　ICFTU - 01.03.04

ICJ
　　ICJ - 01.03.02

ICRISAT
　　ICRISAT - 01.03.04

ICSSD
　　ICSSD - 01.03.04

ICSU
　　ICSU - 01.03.04

ICVA
　　ICVA - 01.03.04

IDA
　　IDA - 01.03.02

IDB
　　IDB - 01.03.03

IDCAS
　　IDCAS - 01.03.03

IDENTITY
　　CULTURAL IDENTITY - 05.02.02

IDEOLOGIES
　　IDEOLOGIES - 05.03.02
　　POLITICAL IDEOLOGIES - 04.04.02

IDRC
　　IDRC - 01.03.04

IEA
　　IEA - 01.03.04
　　OECD IEA - 01.03.03

IFAP
　　IFAP - 01.03.04

IFC
　　IFC - 01.03.02

IFHP
　　IFHP - 01.03.04

IFIP
　　IFIP - 01.03.04

IFLA
    IFLA - 01.03.04

IIEP
    IIEP - 01.03.02

ILLITERACY
    ILLITERACY - 06.02.02

ILLITERATES
    ILLITERATES - 06.06.01

ILLUSTRATIONS
    ILLUSTRATIONS - 19.02.04

ILO
    ILO - 01.03.02

ILPES
    ILPES - 01.03.03

IMCO
    IMCO - 01.03.02

IMF
    IMF - 01.03.02

IMMIGRANTS
    IMMIGRANTS - 14.07.00

IMMIGRATION
    IMMIGRATION - 14.07.00

IMMUNIZATION
    IMMUNIZATION - 15.04.04

IMMUNOLOGIC
    IMMUNOLOGIC DISEASES - 15.04.02

IMMUNOLOGY
    IMMUNOLOGY - 15.04.04

IMPACT
    ENVIRONMENTAL IMPACT
    - 16.03.04
      USE: ENVIRONMENTAL EFFECTS

IMPERIALISM
    IMPERIALISM - 01.02.01

IMPLEMENTATION
    PLAN IMPLEMENTATION - 02.01.02
    PROJECT IMPLEMENTATION - 01.01.06

IMPLICATIONS
    ECONOMIC IMPLICATIONS - 03.02.01
    SOCIAL IMPLICATIONS - 05.03.04

IMPORT
    IMPORT PROMOTION - 09.05.06
    IMPORT RESTRICTIONS - 09.05.07
    IMPORT SUBSTITUTION - 09.05.04
    IMPORT TAX - 11.01.02
    IMPORT VOLUME - 09.05.04

IMPORTS
    IMPORTS - 09.05.04

IMPOVERISHMENT
    IMPOVERISHMENT - 03.02.05

IMPROVEMENT
    GENETIC IMPROVEMENT - 15.02.03

IMPROVEMENT<CONT>
    SOIL IMPROVEMENT - 07.05.02

IN
    AID IN KIND - 01.01.03
    GRANTS IN KIND
    - 01.01.03
      USE: AID IN KIND
    IN-PLANT TRAINING - 06.03.07
    PARTICIPATION IN CULTURAL LIFE - 05.02.02

INBREEDING
    INBREEDING - 15.02.03

INCENTIVES
    TAX INCENTIVES - 11.01.02
    WAGE INCENTIVES - 13.07.00

INCOME
    AGRICULTURAL INCOME - 07.03.03
    CASH INCOME
    - 12.09.00
      USE: CASH FLOW
    INCOME - 03.02.05
    INCOME DISTRIBUTION - 03.02.05
    INCOME REDISTRIBUTION - 03.02.05
    INCOME TAX - 11.01.02
    LOW INCOME - 03.02.05
    NATIONAL INCOME - 03.02.02

INCOMES
    INCOMES POLICY - 02.01.03

INCREASE
    POPULATION INCREASE - 14.01.02
    PRODUCTION INCREASE - 12.07.01

INDEBTEDNESS
    INDEBTEDNESS - 11.02.02

INDEPENDENCE
    INDEPENDENCE - 01.02.03

INDEPENDENT
    INDEPENDENT WORKERS
    - 13.09.02
      USE: SELF-EMPLOYED

INDEX
    INDEX - 19.02.07
    INDEX NUMBERS - 18.08.00
    POLLUTION INDEX - 16.04.01
    PRICE INDEX - 09.02.00

INDEXATION
    INDEXATION - 03.02.05

INDEXING
    INDEXING - 19.01.02
    SUBJECT INDEXING
    - 19.01.02
      USE: INDEXING

INDIA

INDIA - 01.04.04

INDIAN

INDIAN - 14.03.02
INDIAN OCEAN - 17.06.00
WEST INDIAN - 14.03.02

INDIANS

ANDEAN INDIANS
- 14.03.03
USE: AMERINDIANS

INDICATORS

ECONOMIC INDICATORS - 03.01.02
HEALTH INDICATORS - 02.05.02
SOCIAL INDICATORS - 05.01.02

INDIES

WEST INDIES
- 01.04.03
USE: CARIBBEAN
WEST INDIES ASSOCIATED STATES - 01.04.03

INDIGENOUS

INDIGENOUS POPULATION - 14.03.01

INDIVIDUALIZED

INDIVIDUALIZED TEACHING - 06.05.02

INDIVIDUALS

INDIVIDUALS - 05.03.01

INDOCHINA

INDOCHINA - 01.04.04

INDONESIA

INDONESIA - 01.04.04

INDONESIAN

INDONESIAN - 14.03.02

INDUCED

INDUCED MUTATIONS - 15.02.03

INDUSTRIAL

INDUSTRIAL ADAPTATION - 08.01.02
INDUSTRIAL ADMINISTRATION - 04.03.02
INDUSTRIAL AREAS - 08.02.03
INDUSTRIAL ASPECTS - 08.01.01
INDUSTRIAL BANKS - 08.02.04
INDUSTRIAL BUILDINGS - 08.03.00
INDUSTRIAL CAPITAL - 08.02.04
INDUSTRIAL CENSUSES - 08.01.01
INDUSTRIAL CONCENTRATION - 08.02.03
INDUSTRIAL CREDIT - 08.02.04
INDUSTRIAL CROPS - 07.07.02
INDUSTRIAL DESIGN - 08.03.00
INDUSTRIAL DEVELOPMENT - 08.01.02
INDUSTRIAL ECONOMICS - 08.01.01

INDUSTRIAL<CONT>

INDUSTRIAL ENGINEERING - 08.03.00
INDUSTRIAL ENTERPRISES - 08.02.01
INDUSTRIAL EQUIPMENT - 08.03.00
INDUSTRIAL ESPIONAGE - 12.08.02
INDUSTRIAL EXTENSION - 08.01.01
INDUSTRIAL GROWTH
- 08.01.02
USE: INDUSTRIAL DEVELOPMENT
INDUSTRIAL INFORMATION - 08.01.01
INDUSTRIAL INTEGRATION - 01.02.01
INDUSTRIAL INVESTMENTS - 08.02.04
INDUSTRIAL LOCATION
- 08.02.03
USE: LOCATION OF INDUSTRY
INDUSTRIAL MANAGEMENT - 08.02.04
INDUSTRIAL PLANNING - 08.01.02
INDUSTRIAL PLANTS - 08.03.00
INDUSTRIAL POLICY - 08.01.02
INDUSTRIAL POTENTIAL - 08.01.02
INDUSTRIAL PRICES - 08.02.04
INDUSTRIAL PROCESSES - 08.03.00
INDUSTRIAL PRODUCTION - 08.04.00
INDUSTRIAL PRODUCTS - 08.04.00
INDUSTRIAL PROFILES - 08.03.00
INDUSTRIAL PROJECTS - 08.01.02
INDUSTRIAL PROMOTION - 08.01.02
INDUSTRIAL PROPERTY - 08.05.00
INDUSTRIAL PSYCHOLOGY - 13.03.01
INDUSTRIAL RELATIONS
- 13.06.00
USE: LABOUR RELATIONS
INDUSTRIAL RESEARCH - 08.05.00
INDUSTRIAL SECTOR - 08.01.01
INDUSTRIAL SOCIOLOGY - 13.03.01
INDUSTRIAL STATISTICS - 08.01.01
INDUSTRIAL STRUCTURE - 08.01.02
INDUSTRIAL TRAINING - 06.03.07
INDUSTRIAL WASTES - 08.04.00
INDUSTRIAL WORKERS - 13.09.06

INDUSTRIALIZATION

INDUSTRIALIZATION - 08.01.02
INDUSTRIALIZATION POLICY - 08.01.02

INDUSTRIALIZED

INDUSTRIALIZED COUNTRIES
- 03.02.03
USE: DEVELOPED COUNTRIES

INDUSTRIES

    MANUFACTURING INDUSTRIES
    - 08.01.01
     USE: INDUSTRY

INDUSTRY

    AEROSPACE INDUSTRY - 08.14.07
    AGRICULTURAL INDUSTRY
    - 07.01.01
     USE: AGROINDUSTRY
    AIRCRAFT INDUSTRY - 08.14.07
    ALUMINIUM INDUSTRY - 08.14.01
    AUTOMOBILE INDUSTRY - 08.14.07
    BEVERAGE INDUSTRY - 08.06.05
    BOOK INDUSTRY - 08.16.00
    BUILDING INDUSTRY
    - 08.10.01
     USE: CONSTRUCTION INDUSTRY
    CANNING INDUSTRY - 08.06.01
    CEMENT INDUSTRY - 08.10.02
    CERAMICS INDUSTRY - 08.10.03
    CHEMICAL INDUSTRY - 08.12.01
    CLOTHING INDUSTRY - 08.08.01
    COMMUNICATION INDUSTRY - 08.16.00
    CONSTRUCTION INDUSTRY - 08.10.01
    COTTAGE INDUSTRY - 08.02.02
    CULTURAL INDUSTRY - 05.02.03
    DAIRY INDUSTRY - 08.06.01
    DAIRY PRODUCTS INDUSTRY
    - 08.06.01
     USE: DAIRY INDUSTRY
    ELECTRICAL INDUSTRY - 08.11.02
    ELECTRICAL MACHINERY INDUSTRY - 08.15.01
    ELECTRONICS INDUSTRY - 08.15.01
    EXPORT-ORIENTED INDUSTRY - 08.01.01
    FERTILIZER INDUSTRY - 08.12.05
    FILM INDUSTRY - 08.16.00
    FISHERY INDUSTRY - 07.10.02
    FOOD INDUSTRY - 08.06.01
    FORESTRY INDUSTRY - 07.08.01
    FUR INDUSTRY - 08.08.02
    FURNITURE INDUSTRY - 08.07.03
    GLASS INDUSTRY - 08.10.04
    HEAVY INDUSTRY - 08.01.01
    HOTEL INDUSTRY - 09.04.05
    INDUSTRY - 08.01.01

INDUSTRY<CONT>

    INSTRUMENTATION INDUSTRY - 08.14.08
    IRON AND STEEL INDUSTRY - 08.14.01
    LEATHER INDUSTRY - 08.08.02
    LIGHT INDUSTRY - 08.01.01
    LOCATION OF INDUSTRY - 08.02.03
    MACHINE TOOL INDUSTRY - 08.14.05
    MACHINERY INDUSTRY - 08.14.06
    MEAT INDUSTRY - 08.06.01
    MEDIUM-SCALE INDUSTRY - 08.02.02
    METALWORKING INDUSTRY - 08.14.01
    MILLING INDUSTRY - 08.06.01
    MOTOR VEHICLE INDUSTRY - 08.14.07
    NATIONALIZED INDUSTRY - 08.02.01
    OPTICAL INDUSTRY - 08.14.08
    PETROCHEMICAL INDUSTRY - 08.12.01
    PETROLEUM INDUSTRY - 08.11.06
    PHARMACEUTICAL INDUSTRY - 08.12.06
    PLASTICS INDUSTRY - 08.12.07
    POWER INDUSTRY - 08.11.01
    PRINTING INDUSTRY - 08.16.00
    PULP AND PAPER INDUSTRY - 08.07.02
    RECORD INDUSTRY - 08.16.00
    ROPE INDUSTRY - 08.08.01
    RUBBER INDUSTRY - 08.09.00
    RURAL INDUSTRY - 08.02.02
    SERVICE INDUSTRY - 09.01.01
    SHOE INDUSTRY - 08.08.02`
    SMALL-SCALE INDUSTRY - 08.02.02
    STEEL INDUSTRY
    - 08.14.01
     USE: IRON AND STEEL INDUSTRY
    SUGAR INDUSTRY - 08.06.01
    TANNING INDUSTRY - 08.08.02
    TELECOMMUNICATION INDUSTRY - 08.16.00
    TEXTILE INDUSTRY - 08.08.01
    TOBACCO INDUSTRY - 08.06.01
    WATCHMAKING INDUSTRY - 08.14.08
    WOODWORKING INDUSTRY - 08.07.01

INEQUALITY

    SOCIAL INEQUALITY - 05.03.05

INFANT

    INFANT MORTALITY - 14.06.00

INFANTS

INFANTS - 14.02.02

INFECTIOUS

INFECTIOUS DISEASES - 15.04.02

INFLATION

INFLATION - 11.02.01

INFLUENCE

CLIMATIC INFLUENCE - 17.02.01

SOCIAL INFLUENCE - 05.03.03

INFORMAL

INFORMAL SECTOR - 08.02.02

INFORMATICS

INFORMATICS
- 18.08.00
USE: COMPUTER SCIENCE

INFORMATION

ACCESS TO INFORMATION - 19.01.01

CULTURAL INFORMATION - 05.02.03

ECONOMIC INFORMATION - 03.01.02

FREEDOM OF INFORMATION - 04.02.02

INDUSTRIAL INFORMATION - 08.01.01

INFORMATION - 19.01.01

INFORMATION ANALYSIS - 19.01.02

INFORMATION CENTRES
- 19.01.03
USE: INFORMATION SERVICES

INFORMATION DISSEMINATION - 19.01.02

INFORMATION EXCHANGE - 19.01.02

INFORMATION NEEDS - 19.01.01

INFORMATION NETWORK - 19.01.01

INFORMATION POLICY - 19.01.01

INFORMATION PROCESSING - 19.01.02

INFORMATION RECORDING - 19.01.02

INFORMATION SCIENCES - 19.01.01

INFORMATION SERVICES - 19.01.03

INFORMATION SOURCES - 19.01.01

INFORMATION SYSTEMS - 19.01.02

INFORMATION THEORY - 18.08.00

INFORMATION USERS - 19.01.01

MANAGEMENT INFORMATION SYSTEM - 12.04.00

SCIENTIFIC INFORMATION - 19.01.01

SOCIAL INFORMATION - 05.01.02

TECHNICAL INFORMATION - 19.01.01

TECHNOLOGICAL INFORMATION
- 19.01.01
USE: TECHNICAL INFORMATION

INFRASTRUCTURE

ECONOMIC INFRASTRUCTURE - 03.02.01

TRANSPORT INFRASTRUCTURE - 10.03.00

INIS

INIS - 19.01.02

INJURIES

EMPLOYMENT INJURIES BENEFITS - 02.03.02

WOUNDS AND INJURIES - 15.04.02

INLAND

INLAND FISHING - 07.10.03

INLAND NAVIGATION
- 10.05.00
USE: INLAND WATER TRANSPORT

INLAND TRADE
- 09.04.01
USE: DOMESTIC TRADE

INLAND TRANSPORT - 10.07.00

INLAND WATER TRANSPORT - 10.05.00

INLAND WATERWAYS - 10.03.00

INNOVATIONS

DIFFUSION OF INNOVATIONS - 12.06.00

EDUCATIONAL INNOVATIONS - 06.02.03

INNOVATIONS - 12.06.00

INPUT

INPUT-OUTPUT - 03.02.02

INPUT-OUTPUT ANALYSIS - 03.02.02

INPUT-OUTPUT TABLES - 03.02.02

INSECT

INSECT PESTS - 16.03.03

INSECTICIDES

INSECTICIDES - 08.12.05

INSECTS

INSECTS - 16.03.03

INSEMINATION

ARTIFICIAL INSEMINATION - 15.02.02

INSPECTION

FOOD INSPECTION - 15.03.01

LABOUR INSPECTION - 13.02.02

INSTALLATIONS

NUCLEAR INSTALLATIONS - 08.11.03

INSTALMENT

INSTALMENT CREDIT
- 11.02.02
USE: CONSUMER CREDIT

INSTITUTES

AGRICULTURAL INSTITUTES - 06.04.06

RESEARCH INSTITUTES
- 18.02.00
USE: RESEARCH CENTRES

TECHNOLOGICAL INSTITUTES - 06.04.06

INSTITUTIONAL

INSTITUTIONAL FRAMEWORK - 04.03.01

INSTITUTIONS
AID INSTITUTIONS - 01.01.07
CORRECTIONAL INSTITUTIONS - 06.04.03
EDUCATIONAL INSTITUTIONS - 06.04.01
FINANCIAL INSTITUTIONS - 11.02.02
HIGHER EDUCATION INSTITUTIONS - 06.04.05
RELIGIOUS INSTITUTIONS - 05.04.04
WELFARE INSTITUTIONS
- 02.05.01
USE: SOCIAL SERVICES

INSTRUCTION
INSTRUCTION
- 06.05.02
USE: TEACHING
PROGRAMMED INSTRUCTION - 06.05.03
SELF-INSTRUCTION - 06.05.02

INSTRUCTIONAL
INSTRUCTIONAL AIDS
- 06.05.03
USE: TEACHING AIDS
INSTRUCTIONAL MEDIA
- 06.05.03
USE: TEACHING AIDS
INSTRUCTIONAL PROGRAMMES
- 06.05.01
USE: TEACHING PROGRAMMES
INSTRUCTIONAL RADIO
- 06.05.03
USE: EDUCATIONAL RADIO
INSTRUCTIONAL STAFF
- 06.06.02
USE: TEACHING PERSONNEL

INSTRUCTORS
INSTRUCTORS - 13.09.09

INSTRUMENTATION
INSTRUMENTATION INDUSTRY - 08.14.08

INSTRUMENTS
MEASURING INSTRUMENTS - 08.14.08
MUSICAL INSTRUMENTS - 05.05.03
OPTICAL INSTRUMENTS - 08.14.08
PRECISION INSTRUMENTS - 08.14.08

INSURANCE
ACCIDENT INSURANCE - 11.02.03
AGRICULTURAL INSURANCE - 07.03.03
CREDIT INSURANCE - 11.02.03
EXPORT INSURANCE - 11.02.03
FIRE INSURANCE - 11.02.03
HEALTH INSURANCE - 02.03.02
INSURANCE - 11.02.03
INVESTMENT INSURANCE
- 11.02.06
USE: INVESTMENT GUARANTEES

INSURANCE<CONT>
LIFE INSURANCE - 11.02.03
SICKNESS INSURANCE
- 02.03.02
USE: HEALTH INSURANCE
SOCIAL INSURANCE
- 02.03.01
USE: SOCIAL SECURITY
UNEMPLOYMENT INSURANCE - 02.03.02

INTECOL
INTECOL - 01.03.04

INTEGRATED
INTEGRATED APPROACH - 18.03.00
INTEGRATED CURRICULUM - 06.05.01
INTEGRATED DEVELOPMENT - 02.01.01

INTEGRATION
BORDER INTEGRATION - 01.02.01
CULTURAL INTEGRATION - 05.02.02
ECONOMIC INTEGRATION - 01.02.01
HORIZONTAL INTEGRATION - 12.02.00
INDUSTRIAL INTEGRATION - 01.02.01
POLITICAL INTEGRATION - 04.04.02
REGIONAL INTEGRATION - 01.02.01
SOCIAL INTEGRATION - 05.03.03
VERTICAL INTEGRATION - 12.02.00

INTEGUMENTARY
INTEGUMENTARY SYSTEM - 15.02.04

INTELLECTUAL
INTELLECTUAL PROPERTY - 19.02.03

INTELLECTUALS
INTELLECTUALS - 05.03.05

INTELLIGENCE
INTELLIGENCE QUOTIENT - 06.05.04

INTENSITY
CAPITAL INTENSITY - 12.06.00
LABOUR INTENSITY - 12.06.00

INTENSIVE
INTENSIVE COURSES
- 06.05.01
USE: ACCELERATED COURSES
INTENSIVE FARMING - 07.05.03

INTERCROPPING
INTERCROPPING - 07.05.04

INTERCULTURAL
INTERCULTURAL RESEARCH
- 05.01.02
USE: CROSS CULTURAL ANALYSIS

INTERDISCIPLINARY
INTERDISCIPLINARY RESEARCH - 18.03.00

INTEREST
INTEREST - 11.02.07

INTEREST<CONT>
    INTEREST GROUPS - 04.04.02
    INTEREST RATE - 11.02.07

INTERETHNIC
    INTERETHNIC RELATIONS - 14.03.01

INTERGOVERNMENTAL
    INTERGOVERNMENTAL ORGANIZATIONS - 01.03.01

INTERGROUP
    INTERGROUP RELATIONS - 05.03.06

INTERMEDIATE
    INTERMEDIATE TECHNOLOGY - 12.06.00

INTERNAL
    INTERNAL MIGRATIONS - 14.07.00

INTERNATIONAL
    INTERNATIONAL AFFAIRS
    - 01.02.01
     USE: INTERNATIONAL RELATIONS
    INTERNATIONAL AGREEMENTS - 01.02.04
    INTERNATIONAL ASSISTANCE
    - 01.01.01
     USE: INTERNATIONAL COOPERATION
    INTERNATIONAL BORROWING - 11.03.01
    INTERNATIONAL CONTROL - 01.02.04
    INTERNATIONAL COOPERATION - 01.01.01
    INTERNATIONAL DIVISION OF LABOUR - 09.05.03
    INTERNATIONAL ENTERPRISES
    - 03.03.05
     USE: MULTINATIONAL ENTERPRISES
    INTERNATIONAL INVESTMENTS - 11.03.03
    INTERNATIONAL LAW - 01.02.04
    INTERNATIONAL LIQUIDITY - 11.03.01
    INTERNATIONAL MARKET - 09.05.03
    INTERNATIONAL MIGRATIONS - 14.07.00
    INTERNATIONAL MONETARY REFORM - 11.03.01
    INTERNATIONAL MONETARY SYSTEM - 11.03.01
    INTERNATIONAL NEGOTIATION - 01.02.04
    INTERNATIONAL ORGANIZATIONS - 01.03.01
    INTERNATIONAL PAYMENTS - 11.03.02
    INTERNATIONAL POLITICS - 01.02.01
    INTERNATIONAL RELATIONS - 01.02.01
    INTERNATIONAL SCHOOLS - 06.04.04
    INTERNATIONAL TRADE - 09.05.01
    INTERNATIONAL TRANSPORT - 10.07.00
    INTERNATIONAL WATERWAYS - 17.05.02
    NEW INTERNATIONAL ECONOMIC ORDER - 01.02.01

INTERNATIONALISM
    PROLETARIAN INTERNATIONALISM - 01.02.01

INTERVENTION
    FOREIGN INTERVENTION - 01.02.05
    STATE INTERVENTION - 04.03.01

INTERVIEWS
    INTERVIEWS - 18.04.00

INTRACTABLE
    INTRACTABLE DISEASES - 15.04.02

INTRAUTERINE
    INTRAUTERINE DEVICES - 14.05.02
    INTRAUTERINE MORTALITY - 14.06.00

INVENTIONS
    INVENTIONS - 12.06.00

INVENTORIES
    INVENTORIES - 09.03.03

INVENTORS
    INVENTORS - 12.06.00

INVENTORY
    RESOURCES INVENTORY - 16.02.01

INVESTMENT
    INVESTMENT BANKS - 11.02.06
    INVESTMENT GUARANTEES - 11.02.06
    INVESTMENT INSURANCE
    - 11.02.06
     USE: INVESTMENT GUARANTEES
    INVESTMENT POLICY - 11.02.06
    INVESTMENT PROMOTION - 11.02.06
    INVESTMENT REQUIREMENTS - 11.02.06
    INVESTMENT RETURNS - 11.02.07
    RATE OF INVESTMENT - 11.02.06

INVESTMENTS
    AGRICULTURAL INVESTMENTS - 07.03.03
    CAPITAL INVESTMENTS
    - 11.02.06
     USE: INVESTMENTS
    FOREIGN INVESTMENTS - 11.03.03
    INDUSTRIAL INVESTMENTS - 08.02.04
    INTERNATIONAL INVESTMENTS - 11.03.03
    INVESTMENTS - 11.02.06
    PRIVATE INVESTMENTS - 11.02.06
    PUBLIC INVESTMENTS - 11.02.06

INVISIBLE
    INVISIBLE TRANSACTIONS - 11.03.03

IONISING
    IONISING RADIATION - 08.11.04

IPPF
    IPPF - 01.03.04

IPSA
    IPSA - 01.03.04

IRAN
    IRAN - 01.04.06

IRANIAN
    IRANIAN - 14.03.02

IRAQ
    IRAQ - 01.04.06

IRAQI
    IRAQI - 14.03.02

IRELAND
    IRELAND - 01.04.05

IRISH
    IRISH - 14.03.02

IRON
    IRON - 08.14.02
    IRON AND STEEL INDUSTRY - 08.14.01
    IRON ORE - 08.13.00

IRRADIATED
    IRRADIATED FOOD - 08.06.03

IRRADIATION
    FOOD IRRADIATION - 08.06.02
    IRRADIATION - 08.12.03

IRRI
    IRRI - 01.03.04

IRRIGATED
    IRRIGATED LAND - 07.05.02

IRRIGATION
    IRRIGATION - 17.05.03
    IRRIGATION DEVELOPMENT - 17.05.03
    IRRIGATION SYSTEMS - 17.05.03

ISA
    ISA - 01.03.04

ISIS
    ISIS - 19.01.02

ISLAM
    ISLAM - 05.04.03

ISLAND
    REUNION ISLAND - 01.04.02

ISLANDS
    BRITISH VIRGIN ISLANDS - 01.04.03
    CANARY ISLANDS - 01.04.05
    CAYMAN ISLANDS - 01.04.03
    FALKLAND ISLANDS - 01.04.03
    FAROE ISLANDS - 01.04.05
    ISLANDS - 17.03.04
    PACIFIC ISLANDS
    - 01.04.07
     USE: OCEANIA
    PACIFIC ISLANDS AUS - 01.04.07
    PACIFIC ISLANDS FR - 01.04.07
    PACIFIC ISLANDS NZ - 01.04.07
    PACIFIC ISLANDS UK - 01.04.07

ISLANDS<CONT>
    PACIFIC ISLANDS USA - 01.04.07
    TURKS AND CAICCCCOS ISLANDS - 01.04.03
    UNITED STATES VIRGIN ISLANDS - 01.04.03

ISO
    ISO - 01.03.04

ISOLATIONISM
    ISOLATIONISM - 01.02.01

ISOTOPES
    ISOTOPES - 08.11.04

ISRAEL
    ISRAEL - 01.04444.06

ISRAELI
    ISRAELI -   14.03.02

ISSA
    ISSA - 01.03.04

ISSC
    ISSC - 01.03.04

ITALIAN
    ITALIAN - 14.03.02

ITALY
    ITALY - 01.04.05

ITC
    ITC - 01.03.02

ITEM
    NEWS ITEM - 19.02.06

ITU
    ITU - 01.03.02

IUAES
    IUAES - 01.03.04

IUSSP
    IUSSP - 01.03.04

IVORY
    IVORY COAST - 01.04.02

JAMAHIRIYA

LIBYAN ARAB JAMAHIRIYA
- 01.04.02
USE: LIBYA

JAMAICA

JAMAICA - 01.04.03

JAMAICAN

JAMAICAN - 14.03.02

JAPAN

JAPAN - 01.04.04

JAPANESE

JAPANESE - 14.03.02

JET

JET ENGINES - 08.14.06

JIGS

DIES AND JIGS - 08.14.05

JOB

JOB CLASSIFICATION - 13.02.01
JOB DESCRIPTION - 13.02.01
JOB DISLOCATION - 13.05.00
JOB EVALUATION - 13.02.01
JOB REQUIREMENTS - 13.02.01
JOB ROTATION
- 13.05.00
USE: REASSIGNMENT
JOB SATISFACTION - 13.03.04
JOB SEARCHING - 13.02.01
JOB SEEKERS - 13.02.01
ON-THE-JOB TRAINING
- 06.03.07
USE: IN-PLANT TRAINING

JOBHOLDING

DUAL JOBHOLDING - 13.02.01

JOINT

JOINT MANAGEMENT
- 13.06.00
USE: WORKERS PARTICIPATION
JOINT PROJECTS - 01.01.06
JOINT VENTURES - 03.03.05

JORDAN

JORDAN - 01.04.06

JORDANIAN

JORDANIAN - 14.03.02

JOURNAL

JOURNAL
- 19.02.06
USE: PERIODICALS

JOURNALISTS

JOURNALISTS - 13.09.09

JUDAISM

JUDAISM - 05.04.03

JUDGES

JUDGES - 13.09.09

JUICES

FRUIT JUICES - 08.06.05

JURIDICAL

JURIDICAL ASPECTS
- 04.01.01
USE: LEGAL ASPECTS

JURISPRUDENCE

JURISPRUDENCE - 04.01.01

JUSTICE

ADMINISTRATION OF JUSTICE - 04.03.02
SOCIAL JUSTICE - 02.02.01

JUTE

JUTE - 07.07.07

JUVENILE

JUVENILE DELINQUENCY - 02.04.02

KAMPUCHEA
>KAMPUCHEA - 01.04.04

KEEPING
>PEACE KEEPING - 01.02.07

KENYA
>KENYA - 01.04.02

KENYAN
>KENYAN - 14.03.02

KIND
>AID IN KIND - 01.01.03
>GRANTS IN KIND
>- 01.01.03
>*USE:* AID IN KIND

KINGDOM
>UNITED KINGDOM - 01.04.05

KINSHIP
>KINSHIP - 14.02.04

KITTS
>ST KITTS-NEVIS-ANGUILLA - 01.04.03

KNOW
>KNOW HOW - 12.06.00

KONG
>HONG KONG - 01.04.04

KOREA
>KOREA - 01.04.04
>KOREA DPR - 01.04.04
>KOREA NORTH
>- 01.04.04
>*USE:* KOREA DPR
>KOREA R - 01.04.04
>KOREA SOUTH
>- 01.04.04
>*USE:* KOREA R

KOREAN
>KOREAN - 14.03.02

KUWAIT
>KUWAIT - 01.04.06

KUWAITI
>KUWAITI - 14.03.02

LABELLING
>LABELLING - 10.06.00

LABORATORIES
>LABORATORIES - 18.02.00
>LANGUAGE LABORATORIES - 06.04.07

LABORATORY
>LABORATORY EQUIPMENT
>- 18.02.00
>*USE:* RESEARCH EQUIPMENT

LABOUR
>CAPITAL-LABOUR RATIO - 12.07.03
>CHILD LABOUR - 13.09.02
>CONTRACT LABOUR - 13.02.01
>DIVISION OF LABOUR - 03.03.01
>FORCED LABOUR - 02.04.03
>INTERNATIONAL DIVISION OF LABOUR - 09.05.03
>LABOUR - 13.01.01
>LABOUR ADMINISTRATION - 04.03.02
>LABOUR CODE - 04.01.02
>LABOUR CONTRACT - 13.02.01
>LABOUR COSTS - 12.09.00
>LABOUR COURTS - 04.01.02
>LABOUR DISPUTES - 13.06.00
>LABOUR FORCE
>- 13.01.02
>*USE:* MANPOWER
>LABOUR INSPECTION - 13.02.02
>LABOUR INTENSITY - 12.06.00
>LABOUR LAW - 04.01.02
>LABOUR LEGISLATION - 04.01.02
>LABOUR MARKET - 13.01.02
>LABOUR MIGRATIONS - 14.07.00
>LABOUR MOBILITY - 13.05.00
>LABOUR MOVEMENTS - 13.06.00
>LABOUR POLICY - 13.01.01
>LABOUR PRODUCTIVITY - 13.02.02
>LABOUR REDUNDANCY - 13.05.00
>LABOUR RELATIONS - 13.06.00
>LABOUR REQUIREMENTS
>- 13.01.02
>*USE:* MANPOWER NEEDS
>LABOUR SHORTAGE - 13.01.02
>LABOUR STANDARDS - 13.03.01
>LABOUR SUPPLY - 13.01.02
>LABOUR UNIONS
>- 13.06.00
>*USE:* TRADE UNIONS

LABOUR<CONT>

    LABOUR-MANAGEMENT RELATIONS
    - 13.06.00
     USE: LABOUR RELATIONS

LAFTA

    LAFTA - 01.03.03

LAKES

    ARTIFICIAL LAKES - 17.05.04
    LAKES - 17.05.02

LAMPS

    ELECTRIC LAMPS - 08.15.02

LAND

    ARABLE LAND - 07.05.02
    COMMUNAL LAND - 07.02.00
    CULTIVATED LAND - 07.05.02
    DEFORESTED LAND - 07.08.03
    IRRIGATED LAND - 07.05.02
    LAND CAPABILITY - 07.05.02
    LAND DISTRIBUTION
    - 07.02.00
     USE: LAND TENURE
    LAND ECONOMICS - 07.02.00
    LAND LOCKED COUNTRIES - 17.03.04
    LAND OWNERSHIP - 07.02.00
    LAND RECLAMATION - 07.05.02
    LAND REFORMS - 07.02.00
    LAND RENT - 07.03.03
    LAND SETTLEMENT - 14.04.02
    LAND SPECULATION - 07.02.00
    LAND TAX - 11.01.02
    LAND TENURE - 07.02.00
    LAND USE - 07.05.02
    LAND UTILIZATION
    - 07.05.02
     USE: LAND USE
    PUBLIC LAND - 07.02.00

LANDOWNERS

    LANDOWNERS - 07.02.00

LANDSCAPE

    LANDSCAPE PROTECTION - 16.05.01

LANGUAGE

    CHINESE LANGUAGE - 05.06.02
    ENGLISH LANGUAGE - 05.06.02
    FRENCH LANGUAGE - 05.06.02
    LANGUAGE BARRIER - 05.06.01
    LANGUAGE LABORATORIES - 06.04.07
    LANGUAGE MINORITIES - 05.06.01

LANGUAGE<CONT>

    LANGUAGE TEACHING - 06.03.07
    RUSSIAN LANGUAGE - 05.06.02
    SPANISH LANGUAGE - 05.06.02

LANGUAGES

    LANGUAGES - 05.06.01
    OFFICIAL LANGUAGES - 05.06.01
    VERNACULAR LANGUAGES - 05.06.01

LANKA

    SRI LANKA - 01.04.04

LANKAN

    SRI LANKAN - 14.03.02

LAO

    LAO - 14.03.02
    LAO PDR - 01.04.04

LATEX

    LATEX - 07.07.08

LATIN

    LATIN AMERICA - 01.04.03
    LATIN AMERICAN - 14.03.02

LAW

    ADMINISTRATIVE LAW - 04.01.02
    CIVIL LAW - 04.01.02
    COMMERCIAL LAW - 04.01.02
    COMMON LAW - 04.01.02
    CONSTITUTIONAL LAW - 04.01.02
    CRIMINAL LAW - 04.01.02
    CUSTOMARY LAW - 04.01.02
    FAMILY LAW - 04.01.02
    FISCAL LAW - 04.01.02
    INTERNATIONAL LAW - 01.02.04
    LABOUR LAW - 04.01.02
    LAW - 04.01.01
    LAW ENFORCEMENT
    - 02.04.03
     USE: PENAL SANCTIONS
    LAW OF THE SEA - 01.02.04
    MARITIME LAW - 04.01.02
    PATENT LAW - 04.01.02
    PUBLIC LAW - 04.01.02

LAWYERS

    LAWYERS - 13.09.09

LAYOFF

    LAYOFF - 13.05.00

LAYOUT

    FACTORY LAYOUT - 08.03.00

LEAD
    LEAD - 08.14.02

LEADERSHIP
    LEADERSHIP - 05.03.05
    POLITICAL LEADERSHIP - 04.04.02

LEAGUE
    LEAGUE OF ARAB STATES - 01.03.03

LEARNING
    LEARNING - 06.05.04
    PROGRAMMED LEARNING
    - 06.05.03
    USE: PROGRAMMED INSTRUCTION

LEAST
    LEAST DEVELOPED COUNTRIES - 03.02.03

LEATHER
    LEATHER - 08.08.02
    LEATHER GOODS - 08.08.02
    LEATHER INDUSTRY - 08.08.02

LEAVE
    LEAVE OF ABSENCE - 13.05.00
    MATERNITY LEAVE - 13.05.00

LEAVERS
    SCHOOL LEAVERS - 06.06.01

LEAVING
    LEAVING SCHOOL - 06.04.12

LEBANESE
    LEBANESE - 14.03.02

LEBANON
    LEBANON - 01.04.06

LEGAL
    LEGAL ABORTION - 14.05.02
    LEGAL AID - 04.02.01
    LEGAL ASPECTS - 04.01.01
    LEGAL PROTECTION - 04.01.01
    LEGAL SCIENCES - 04.01.01
    LEGAL STATUS - 04.02.01

LEGISLATION
    ANTITRUST LEGISLATION - 12.02.00
    ECONOMIC LEGISLATION - 04.01.02
    LABOUR LEGISLATION - 04.01.02
    LEGISLATION - 04.01.01
    SOCIAL LEGISLATION - 02.02.01

LEGUMINOSAE
    LEGUMINOSAE - 07.07.06

LEISURE
    LEISURE - 13.08.00

LENTILS
    LENTILS - 07.07.06

LEONE
    SIERRA LEONE - 01.04.02

LEONEAN
    SIERRA LEONEAN - 14.03.02

LEPROSY
    LEPROSY - 15.04.02

LESOTHO
    LESOTHO - 01.04.02

LEVEL
    LOCAL LEVEL - 04.03.03
    NATIONAL LEVEL - 04.03.03
    POLLUTION LEVEL - 16.03.04

LEVELS
    LEVELS OF EDUCATION - 06.03.06

LIABILITY
    LIABILITY - 04.02.03

LIBERALISM
    LIBERALISM - 03.03.01

LIBERALIZATION
    TRADE LIBERALIZATION - 09.05.07

LIBERATION
    LIBERATION - 04.02.02
    NATIONAL LIBERATION MOVEMENTS - 04.04.02

LIBERIA
    LIBERIA - 01.04.02

LIBERIAN
    LIBERIAN - 14.03.02

LIBERTIES
    CIVIL LIBERTIES - 04.02.02

LIBRARIANS
    LIBRARIANS - 13.09.09

LIBRARIES
    LIBRARIES - 19.01.03

LIBRARY
    LIBRARY AUTOMATION - 19.01.03
    LIBRARY SCIENCE - 19.01.01

LIBYA
    LIBYA - 01.04.02

LIBYAN
    LIBYAN - 14.03.02
    LIBYAN ARAB JAMAHIRIYA
    - 01.04.02
    USE: LIBYA

LICENSING
    LICENSING - 08.05.00

LIECHTENSTEIN
    LIECHTENSTEIN - 01.04.05

LIFE
    LIFE - 15.02.02
    LIFE INSURANCE - 11.02.03
    LIFE STYLES - 05.03.01
    LIFE TABLES - 14.06.00
    LIFE-LONG EDUCATION - 06.03.05

LIFE<CONT>
    PARTICIPATION IN CULTURAL LIFE   - 05.02.02
    QUALITY OF LIFE - 05.03.01
    WORKING LIFE - 13.03.03

LIGHT
    LIGHT INDUSTRY - 08.01.01

LIGHTING
    ELECTRIC LIGHTING - 08.15.02

LIME
    LIME - 08.10.02

LIMITATION
    ARMS LIMITATION
    - 01.02.06
     USE: DISARMAMENT

LINE
    ASSEMBLY-LINE WORK - 13.03.02

LINEAR
    LINEAR PROGRAMMING - 12.04.00

LINES
    ASSEMBLY LINES - 08.14.07

LINGUISTICS
    LINGUISTICS - 05.06.01

LINGUISTS
    LINGUISTS - 13.09.09

LIQUIDITY
    INTERNATIONAL LIQUIDITY - 11.03.01
    LIQUIDITY - 11.02.01

LIST
    LIST OF DOCUMENTS - 19.02.05
    LIST OF PARTICIPANTS - 19.02.05
    PRICE LIST - 09.02.00

LITERACY
    FUNCTIONAL LITERACY - 06.03.04
    LITERACY - 06.03.04

LITERATURE
    LITERATURE - 05.05.03
    LITERATURE SURVEY - 19.02.07

LITTORAL
    LITTORAL ZONES - 17.03.04

LIVER
    LIVER - 15.02.04

LIVESTOCK
    LIVESTOCK - 07.09.02
    LIVESTOCK CROPS
    - 07.07.02
     USE: FORAGE CROPS

LIVING
    COST OF LIVING - 03.02.05
    LIVING CONDITIONS - 03.02.05
    STANDARD OF LIVING - 03.02.05

LOADING
    LOADING - 10.06.00

LOANS
    LOANS - 11.02.02
    STUDENT LOANS - 06.04.11

LOCAL
    LOCAL CURRENCY - 11.02.01
    LOCAL FINANCE - 11.01.01
    LOCAL GOVERNMENT - 04.03.03
    LOCAL LEVEL - 04.03.03
    LOCAL TAXES - 11.01.02

LOCATION
    INDUSTRIAL LOCATION
    - 08.02.03
     USE: LOCATION OF INDUSTRY
    LOCATION FACTORS - 02.01.02
    LOCATION OF INDUSTRY - 08.02.03

LOCKED
    LAND LOCKED COUNTRIES - 17.03.04

LOCKOUTS
    LOCKOUTS - 13.06.00

LOCOMOTIVES
    LOCOMOTIVES - 10.04.00

LOCUSTS
    LOCUSTS - 16.03.03

LOGGING
    LOGGING - 07.08.03

LOGIC
    LOGIC - 18.08.00

LONG
    LIFE-LONG EDUCATION - 06.03.05
    LONG TERM - 18.10.00

LOSS
    ECONOMIC LOSS - 03.02.04
    FINANCIAL LOSS - 12.09.00

LOW
    LOW INCOME - 03.02.05

LOWER
    LOWER CLASS - 05.03.05

LUBRICANTS
    LUBRICANTS - 08.11.06

LUCIA
    ST LUCIA - 01.04.03

LUXEMBOURG
    LUXEMBOURG - 01.04.05

LYMPHATIC
    LYMPHATIC SYSTEM - 15.02.04

MACAO
MACAO - 01.04.04

MACHINE
MACHINE TOOL INDUSTRY - 08.14.05
MACHINE TOOLS - 08.14.05

MACHINERY
AGRICULTURAL MACHINERY - 07.04.00
BUILDING MACHINERY - 08.14.06
EARTHMOVING MACHINERY - 08.14.06
ELECTRICAL MACHINERY - 08.15.02
ELECTRICAL MACHINERY INDUSTRY - 08.15.01
FARM MACHINERY
- 07.04.00
  USE: AGRICULTURAL MACHINERY
MACHINERY - 08.14.06
MACHINERY INDUSTRY - 08.14.06

MACHINES
OFFICE MACHINES - 08.14.06

MACHINING
MACHINING - 08.14.03

MACROECONOMICS
MACROECONOMICS - 03.01.01

MADAGASCAR
MADAGASCAR - 01.04.02

MADEIRA
MADEIRA - 01.04.05

MAGAZINE
MAGAZINE
- 19.02.06
  USE: PERIODICALS

MAGIC
MAGIC - 05.04.02

MAGNESIUM
MAGNESIUM - 08.12.04

MAIL
MAIL SURVEYS - 18.04.00

MAINTENANCE
MAINTENANCE AND REPAIR - 12.05.00

MAIZE
MAIZE - 07.07.04

MAKING
DECISION MAKING - 12.04.00
POLICY MAKING - 04.03.02

MALADJUSTMENT
MALADJUSTMENT - 05.03.03

MALAGASY
MALAGASY - 14.03.02

MALARIA
MALARIA - 15.04.02

MALAWI
MALAWI - 01.04.02

MALAWIAN
MALAWIAN - 14.03.02

MALAYSIA
MALAYSIA - 01.04.04

MALAYSIAN
MALAYSIAN - 14.03.02

MALDIVES
MALDIVES - 01.04.04

MALDIVIAN
MALDIVIAN - 14.03.02

MALES
MALES - 14.02.03

MALI
MALI - 01.04.02

MALIAN
MALIAN - 14.03.02

MALNUTRITION
MALNUTRITION - 15.03.02

MALTA
MALTA - 01.04.05

MALTESE
MALTESE - 14.03.02

MANAGEMENT
AGRICULTURAL MANAGEMENT - 07.01.02
BUSINESS MANAGEMENT - 12.04.00
COLLEGE MANAGEMENT - 06.04.08
ENVIRONMENTAL MANAGEMENT - 16.04.01
EQUIPMENT MANAGEMENT - 12.05.00
FARM MANAGEMENT - 07.03.02
FINANCIAL MANAGEMENT - 11.02.04
FISHERY MANAGEMENT - 07.10.02
FOREST MANAGEMENT - 07.08.04
INDUSTRIAL MANAGEMENT - 08.02.04
JOINT MANAGEMENT
- 13.06.00
  USE: WORKERS PARTICIPATION
LABOUR-MANAGEMENT RELATIONS
- 13.06.00
  USE: LABOUR RELATIONS
MANAGEMENT - 12.04.00
MANAGEMENT ATTITUDES - 13.06.00
MANAGEMENT BY OBJECTIVES - 12.04.00
MANAGEMENT CONSULTANTS - 12.03.00
MANAGEMENT DEVELOPMENT - 12.04.00
MANAGEMENT INFORMATION SYSTEM - 12.04.00
MANAGEMENT TECHNIQUES - 12.04.00
MIDDLE MANAGEMENT - 12.03.00
PERSONNEL MANAGEMENT - 13.02.02

MANAGEMENT<CONT>
    PROJECT MANAGEMENT - 01.01.06
    RESOURCES MANAGEMENT - 16.02.01
    SCHOOL MANAGEMENT - 06.04.08
    SCIENTIFIC MANAGEMENT - 12.04.00
    SELF-MANAGEMENT - 12.04.00
    SOIL MANAGEMENT - 07.05.02
    TOP MANAGEMENT - 12.03.00
    WASTE MANAGEMENT - 16.04.02
    WATER MANAGEMENT - 17.05.05
    WORKERS SELF-MANAGEMENT - 13.06.00

MANAGERS
    MANAGERS - 12.03.00

MANGANESE
    MANGANESE - 08.14.02

MANMADE
    MANMADE DISASTERS - 16.03.02
    MANMADE FIBRES - 08.08.01
    MANMADE FORESTS - 07.08.03

MANPOWER
    FEMALE MANPOWER - 13.09.02
    MANPOWER - 13.01.02
    MANPOWER NEEDS - 13.01.02
    MANPOWER PLANNING - 13.01.03
    MANPOWER POLICY
    - 13.01.03
     USE: EMPLOYMENT POLICY
    MANPOWER SERVICES
    - 13.022.0
     USE: EMPLOYMENT SERVICES

MANUAL
    MANUAL - 19.02.09
    MANUAL WORKERS - 13.09.02

MANUFACTURED
    MANUFACTURED PRODUCTS - 08.04.00
    SEMI-MANUFACTURED PRODUCTS - 08.04.00

MANUFACTURING
    MANUFACTURING - 08.01.01
    MANUFACTURING INDUSTRIES
    - 08.01.01
     USE: INDUSTRY

MAPPING
    MAPPING - 18.07.00

MAPS
    GEOLOGICAL MAPS - 18.07.00
    MAPS - 18.07.00
    SOIL MAPS - 18.07.00

MARGARINE
    MARGARINE - 08.06.06

MARGINALISM
    MARGINALISM - 03.03.01

MARGINALITY
    MARGINALITY - 05.03.03

MARINE
    MARINE ENVIRONMENT - 16.01.02
    MARINE FISHING - 07.10.03
    MARINE POLLUTION - 16.03.04
    MARINE RESOURCES - 16.02.02
    MERCHANT MARINE - 10.05.00

MARINO
    SAN MARINO - 01.04.05

MARITAL
    MARITAL STATTTTUS - 14.02.05

MARITIME
    MARITIME LAW - 04.01.02
    MARITIME QUESTIONS - 10.05.00
    MARITIME TRANSPORT
    - 10.05.00
     USE: SEA TRANSPORT

MARKET
    ACCESS TO MARKET - 09.03.01
    AGRICULTURAL MARKET - 07.01.03
    BLACK MARKET - 09.01.02
    CAPITAL MARKET
    - 11.02.07
     USE: FINANCIAL MARKET
    COMMODITY MARKET - 09.01.02
    COMMON MARKET - 01.02.01
    DOMESTIC MARKET - 09.01.02
    FINANCIAL MARKET - 11.02.07
    FREIGHT MARKET - 10.09.00
    INTERNATIONAL MARKET - 09.05.03
    LABOUR MARKET - 13.01.02
    MARKET - 09.01.02
    MARKET ECONOMY - 03.03.01
    MARKET PLANNING - 09.01.02
    MARKET STABILIZATION - 09.01.02
    MARKET STUDIES - 09.03.01
    MONEY MARKET - 11.02.07

MARKETING
    COOPERATIVE MARKETING - 09.03.01
    MARKETING - 09.03.01
    MARKETING BOARDS - 09.03.01
    MARKETING COOPERATIVES - 09.03.01
    RETAIL MARKETING - 09.03.01

MARKETING<CONT>
WHOLESALE MARKETING - 09.03.01

MARKS
TRADE MARKS - 09.03.04

MARRIAGE
MARRIAGE - 14.02.05

MARRIED
MARRIED PERSONS - 14.02.05

MARTINIQUE
MARTINIQUE - 01.04.03

MARXISM
MARXISM - 03.03.01

MASS
MASS COMMUNICATION - 05.07.01
MASS EDUCATION - 06.03.04
MASS MEDIA - 05.07.03
MASS PRODUCTION - 12.07.01

MASTERCRAFTSMEN
MASTERCRAFTSMEN - 13.09.03

MATERIALS
AUDIOVISUAL MATERIALS - 19.02.01
BUILDING MATERIALS
- 08.10.02
 USE: CONSTRUCTION MATERIALS
CONSTRUCTION MATERIALS - 08.10.02
MATERIALS HANDLING
- 10.06.00
 USE: HANDLING
RADIOACTIVE MATERIALS - 08.11.04
RAW MATERIALS - 12.08.01
REFERENCE MATERIALS - 19.02.07$_5$
REFRACTORY MATERIALS - 08.10.03
TEACHIING MTERIALS
- 06.05.03
 USE: TEACHING AIDS

MATERNAL
MATERNAL AND CHILD HEALTH - 15.04.04

MATERNITY
MATERNITY BENEFITS - 02.03.02
MATERNITY LEAVE - 13.05.00

MATHEMATICAL
MATHEMATICAL ANALYSIS - 18.08.00
MATHEMATICAL MODELS - 18.08.00

MATHEMATICIANS
MATHEMATICIANS - 13.09.09

MATHEMATICS
MATHEMATICS - 18.08.00

MAURITANIA
MAURITANIA - 01.04.02

MAURITANIAN
MAURITANIAN - 14.03.02

MAURITIAN
MAURITIAN - 14.03.02

MAURITIUS
MAURITIUS - 01.04.02

MEAL
FISH MEAL - 08.06.04
MEAL PREPARATION
- 15.03.01
 USE: FOOD PREPARATION

MEANS
MEANS OF PRODUCTION - 12.07.01
MEANS OF TRANSPORT - 10.04.00

MEASLES
MEASLES - 15.04.02

MEASUREMENT
MEASUREMENT - 18.06.00
MEASUREMENT SYSTEMS - 18.06.00

MEASURES
PROTECTIONIST MEASURES - 09.05.07

MEASURING
MEASURING
- 18.06.00
 USE: MEASUREMENT
MEASURING INSTRUMENTS - 08.14.08

MEAT
MEAT - 07.09.05
MEAT INDUSTRY - 08.06.01
MEAT PROCESSING - 08.06.02
MEAT PRODUCTS - 07.09.05

MECHANIZATION
AGRICULTURAL MECHANIZATION - 07.04.00
MECHANIZATION - 12.05.00

MEDIA
COMMUNICATION MEDIA
- 05.07.03
 USE: MEDIA
INSTRUCTIONAL MEDIA
- 06.05.03
 USE: TEACHING AIDS
MASS MEDIA - 05.07.03
MEDIA - 05.07.03

MEDICAL
MEDICAL CARE - 15.04.04
MEDICAL DOCTORS
- 13.09.10
 USE: PHYSICIANS
MEDICAL EDUCATION - 06.03.07
MEDICAL EQUIPMENT
- 02.05.02
 USE: HEALTH FACILITIES
MEDICAL EXAMINATION - 15.04.04
MEDICAL PERSONNEL - 13.09.10

MEDICAL<CONT>
    MEDICAL RESEARCH - 15.04.06
    MEDICAL SCIENCES - 15.04.06
    MEDICAL TREATMENT
    - 15.04.04
     USE: MEDICAL CARE

MEDICINAL
    MEDICINAL PLANTS - 15.05.00

MEDICINE
    MEDICINE - 15.04.06
    OCCUPATIONAL MEDICINE - 13.04.00
    PREVENTIVE MEDICINE - 15.04.04
    TRADITIONAL MEDICINE - 15.04.06
    VETERINARY   MEDICINE - 15.04.06

MEDITERRANEAN
    MEDITERRANEAN - 17.06.00
    MEDITERRANEAN COUNTRIES - 01.04.05

MEDIUM
    MEDIUM TERM - 18.10.00
    MEDIUM-SCALE INDUSTRY - 08.02.02

MEETING
    MEETING PAPER
    - 19.02.05
     USE: CONFERENCE PAPER
    MEETING REPORT
    - 19.02.08
     USE: CONFERENCE REPORT

MELANESIA
    MELANESIA
    - 01.04.07
     USE: OCEANIA

MEMBER
    MEMBER STATES - 01.03.01

MEMORANDUM
    MEMORANDUM - 19.02.05

MEN
    MEN - 14.02.03

MENINGITIS
    MENINGITIS - 15.04.02

MENTAL
    MENTAL DISEASES - 15.04.02
    MENTAL HEALTH - 15.04.01
    MENTAL HOSPITALS - 02.05.02
    MENTAL RETARDATION - 06.05.04
    MENTAL STRESS - 13.03.04

MENTALLY
    MENTALLY HANDICAPPED - 15.04.05

MERCHANT
    MERCHANT FLEET
    - 10.05.00
     USE: MERCHANT MARINE
    MERCHANT MARINE - 10.05.00

MERCURY
    MERCURY - 08.14.02

MERGERS
    MERGERS - 12.02.00

MESTIZOS
    MESTIZOS - 14.03.03

METABOLISM
    METABOLISM - 15.02.04

METAL
    METAL CASTING - 08.14.03
    METAL PRODUCTS - 08.14.01
    METAL SCRAPS - 08.14.04
    METAL SHEETS - 08.14.04
    SHEET-METAL WORKING - 08.14.01

METALLURGY
    METALLURGY - 08.14.03

METALS
    METALS - 08.14.02
    NON-FERROUS METALS - 08.14.02
    PRECIOUS METALS - 08.14.02
    TOXIC METALS - 15.05.00

METALWORKERS
    METALWORKERS - 13.09.06

METALWORKING
    METALWORKING INDUSTRY - 08.14.01

METEOROLOGY
    METEOROLOGY - 17.01.01
    METEOROLOGY SERVICES - 17.01.01

METHANE
    METHANE - 08.11.06

METHOD
    CRITICAL PATH METHOD
    - 12.04.00
     USE: NETWORK ANALYSIS

METHODOLOGY
    METHODOLOGY - 18.03.00

METHODS
    BUDGETING METHODS - 12.09.00
    CONTRACEPTIVE METHODS - 14.05.02
    PLANNING METHODS - 02.01.02
    RESEARCH METHODS - 18.03.00
    TEACHING METHODS - 06.05.02
    TRAINING METHODS - 06.05.02

METRIC
    METRIC SYSTEM - 18.06.00

METROLOGY
    METROLOGY - 18.06.00

MEXICAN
    MEXICAN - 14.03.02

MEXICO
MEXICO - 01.04.03

MICROBES
MICROBES - 15.01.02

MICROBIOLOGY
MICROBIOLOGY - 15.01.01

MICROECONOMICS
MICROECONOMICS - 03.01.01

MICROFICHES
MICROFICHES - 19.01.04

MICROFILMS
MICROFILMS - 19.01.04

MICRONESIA
MICRONESIA
- 01.04.07
USE: OCEANIA

MICROORGANISMS
MICROORGANISMS - 15.01.02

MIDDLE
MIDDLE CLASS - 05.03.05
MIDDLE EAST - 01.04.06
MIDDLE MANAGEMENT - 12.03.00
MIDDLE-SIZED TOWNS - 14.04.03

MIDWIVES
MIDWIVES - 13.09.10

MIGRANT
MIGRANT WORKERS - 13.09.02

MIGRANTS
MIGRANTS - 14.07.00

MIGRATION
MIGRATION POLICY - 14.07.00

MIGRATIONS
FRONTIER MIGRATIONS - 14.07.00
INTERNAL MIGRATIONS - 14.07.00
INTERNATIONAL MIGRATIONS - 14.07.00
LABOUR MIGRATIONS - 14.07.00
MIGRATIONS - 14.07.00
RETURN MIGRATIONS - 14.07.00
RURAL MIGRATIONS - 14.07.00
SEASONAL MIGRATIONS - 14.07.00

MILITARY
MILITARY - 01.02.06
MILITARY AID - 01.02.06
MILITARY BASES - 01.02.06
MILITARY EXPENDITURES - 01.02.06
MILITARY SERVICE - 01.02.06

MILK
MILK - 07.09.05
MILK POWDER - 07.09.05

MILK<CONT>
MILK PROCESSING - 08.06.02
MILK PRODUCTS
- 07.09.05
USE: DAIRY PRODUCTS

MILLET
MILLET - 07.07.04

MILLING
MILLING INDUSTRY - 08.06.01

MINERAL
MINERAL OILS - 08.11.06
MINERAL RESOURCES - 16.02.02
MINERAL WATERS - 08.06.05

MINERALOGY
MINERALOGY - 17.04.01

MINERALS
MINERALS - 08.13.00

MINERS
MINERS - 13.09.06

MINES
MINES - 08.13.00

MINIMUM
MINIMUM AGE - 14.02.02
MINIMUM WAGE - 13.07.00

MINING
COAL MINING - 08.13.00
DEEP SEA MINING - 08.13.00
MINING - 08.13.00
MINING ENGINEERING - 08.13.00

MINORITIES
ETHNIC MINORITIES - 14.03.01
LANGUAGE MINORITIES - 05.06.01
RELIGIOUS MINORITIES - 05.04.02

MINORITY
MINORITY GROUPS - 05.03.07

MIQUELON
ST PIERRE AND MIQUELON - 01.04.03

MISSION
MISSION REPORT - 19.02.08

MISSIONS
RELIGIOUS MISSIONS - 05.04.04
TRADE MISSIONS - 09.05.06

MIXED
MIXED ECONOMY - 03.03.02
MIXED ENTERPRISES - 03.03.05
MIXED FARMING - 07.05.03

MOBILE
MOBILE SCHOOLS - 06.04.03

MOBILITY
LABOUR MOBILITY - 13.05.00

MOBILITY<CONT>
    OCCUPATIONAL MOBILITY - 13.02.01
    SOCIAL MOBILITY - 05.03.05

MODELS
    ECONOMETRIC MODELS - 03.01.02
    ECONOMIC MODELS - 03.01.02
    GROWTH MODELS - 03.01.02
    MATHEMATICAL MODELS - 18.08.00
    MODELS - 18.08.00

MODERNIZATION
    MODERNIZATION - 05.03.04

MODES
    MODES OF PRODUCTION - 12.07.01
    MODES OF TRANSPORTATION - 10.05.00

MODULAR
    MODULAR TRAINING - 06.05.02

MOISTURE
    MOISTURE
    - 17.01.03
     USE: HUMIDITY

MOLASSES
    MOLASSES - 08.06.04

MOLLUSCS
    MOLLUSCS - 07.10.04

MONACO
    MONACO - 01.04.05

MONEGASQUE
    MONEGASQUE - 14.03.02

MONETARY
    INTERNATIONAL MONETARY REFORM - 11.03.01
    INTERNATIONAL MONETARY SYSTEM - 11.03.01
    MONETARY AGREEMENTS - 11.03.01
    MONETARY AREAS - 11.03.01
    MONETARY CIRCULATION - 11.02.01
    MONETARY CORRECTION - 11.02.01
    MONETARY POLICY - 11.02.01
    MONETARY RELATIONS - 11.03.01
    MONETARY SYSTEMS - 11.02.01
    MONETARY TRANSFERS - 11.03.01
    MONETARY UNIONS
    - 11.03.01
     USE: MONETARY AREAS

MONEY
    MONEY
    - 11.02.01
     USE: CURRENCIES
    MONEY MARKET - 11.02.07
    MONEY SUPPLY - 11.02.01

MONGOLIA
    MONGOLIA PR - 01.04.04

MONGOLIAN
    MONGOLIAN - 14.03.02

MONITORING
    ENVIRONMENTAL MONITORING
    - 16.04.01
     USE: ENVIRONMENTAL MANAGEMENT

MONOGRAPH
    MONOGRAPH - 19.02.09

MONOPOLIES
    MONOPOLIES - 12.02.00

MONSOON
    MONSOON
    - 17.02.02
     USE: RAINY SEASON

MONTHLY
    MONTHLY - 19.02.06

MONTSERRAT
    MONTSERRAT - 01.04.03

MORBIDITY
    MORBIDITY - 15..04.1

MOROCCAN
    MOROCCAN - 14.03.02

MOROCCO
    MOROCCO - 01.04.02

MORTALITY
    INFANT MORTALITY - 14.06.00
    INTRAUTERINE MORTALITY - 14.06.00
    MORTALITY - 14.06.00
    MORTALITY DECLINE - 14.06.00
    OCCUPATIONAL MORTALITY - 14.06.00

MORTGAGES
    MORTGAGESS - 11.02.02

MOTHER
    MOTHER - 14.02.04

MOTIVATIONS
    MOTIVATIONS - 05.03.02

MOTOR
    MOTOR CARS
    - 10.04.00
     USE: AUTOMOBILES
    MOTOR VEHICLE INDUSTRY - 08.14.07
    MOTOR VEHICLES - 10.04.00

MOTORCYCLES
    MOTORCYCLES - 10.04.00

MOTORIZED
    NON-MOTORIZED TRANSPORT - 10.04.00

MOTORS
    ELECTRIC MOTORS - 08.15.02
    MOTORS
    - 08.14.06
     USE: ENGINES

MOTORWAYS
    MOTORWAYS - 10.03.00

MOUNTAINS
    MOUNTAINS - 17.03.04

MOUTH
    MOUTH DISEASES - 15.04.02

MOVEMENTS
    CAPITAL MOVEMENTS - 11.03.03
    COOPERATIVE MOVEMENTS - 03.03.04
    LABOUR MOVEMENTS - 13.06.00
    NATIONAL LIBERATION MOVEMENTS - 04.04.02
    PEASANT MOVEMENTS - 05.03.07
    SOCIAL MOVEMENTS - 05.03.07
    STUDENT MOVEMENTS - 06.06.01

MOVING
    MOVING EXPENSES - 13.07.00

MOZAMBICAN
    MOZAMBICAN - 14.03.02

MOZAMBIQUE
    MOZAMBIQUE - 01.04.02

MPCC
    MPCC - 01.03.03

MULTILATERAL
    MULTILATERAL AID - 01.01.02
    MULTILATERAL RELATIONS - 01.02.01

MULTILINGUALISM
    MULTILINGUALISM - 05.06.01

MULTIMODAL
    MULTIMODAL TRANSPORT - 10.05.00

MULTINATIONAL
    MULTINATIONAL ENTERPRISES - 03.03.05

MULTIPLE
    MULTIPLE CROPPING - 07.05.04

MULTIPURPOSE
    MULTIPURPOSE PROJECTS - 01.01.06

MUSCULOSKELETAL
    MUSCULOSKELETAL SYSTEM - 15.02.04

MUSEUMS
    MUSEUMS - 05.05.01

MUSIC
    MUSIC - 05.05.03

MUSICAL
    MUSICAL INSTRUMENTS - 05.05.03

MUTATIONS
    INDUCED MUTATIONS - 15.02.03
    MUTATIONS - 15.02.03

MUTTON
    MUTTON - 07.09.05

MYTHOLOGY
    MYTHOLOGY - 05.04.02

NAMIBIA
    NAMIBIA - 01.04.02

NAMIBIAN
    NAMIBIAN - 14.03.02

NARCOTICS
    NARCOTICS - 15.05.00

NATION
    NATION - 04.03.01

NATIONAL
    GROSS NATIONAL PRODUCT - 03.02.02
    NATIONAL ACCOUNTING - 03.02.02
    NATIONAL ACCOUNTS - 03.02.02
    NATIONAL BUDGET - 11.01.01
    NATIONAL EXPENDITURES - 03.02.02
    NATIONAL INCOME - 03.02.02
    NATIONAL LEVEL - 04.03.03
    NATIONAL LIBERATION MOVEMENTS - 04.04.02
    NATIONAL PARKS - 16.05.02
    NATIONAL PLANNING - 02.01.02
    NATIONAL PLANS - 02.01.02
    NATIONAL POLICY - 04.03.03

NATIONALISM
    NATIONALISM - 03.03.01

NATIONALIST
    NATIONALIST - 03.03.01

NATIONALIZATION
    NATIONALIZATION - 03.03.05

NATIONALIZED
    NATIONALIZED ENTERPRISES
    - 03.03.05
     USE: PUBLIC ENTERPRISES
    NATIONALIZED INDUSTRY - 08.02.01

NATIVE
    NATIVE RESERVATION - 14.03.01

NATIVES
    NATIVES
    - 14.03.01
     USE: INDIGENOUS POPULATION

NATO
    NATO - 01.03.03

NATURAL
    NATURAL DISASTERS - 16.03.02
    NATURAL ENVIRONMENT
    - 16.01.02
     USE: PHYSICAL ENVIRONMENT
    NATURAL EQUILIBRIUM
    - 16.01.01
     USE: ECOLOGICAL BALANCE
    NATURAL FIBRES - 08.08.01
    NATURAL GAS - 08.11.06

NATURAL<CONT>
NATURAL PRODUCTS - 12.08.01
NATURAL RESOURCES - 16.02.02
NATURAL SCIENCES - 17.04.01

NATURE
NATURE CONSERVATION - 16.05.01
NATURE PROTECTION
- 16.05.01
USE: NATURE CONSERVATION
NATURE RESERVES - 16.05.02

NAURU
NAURU - 01.04.07

NAURUAN
NAURUAN - 14.03.02

NAVIGATION
INLAND NAVIGATION
- 10.05.00
USE: INLAND WATER TRANSPORT

NEA
OECD NEA - 01.03.03

NEAR
NEAR EAST
- 01.04.06
USE: MIDDLE EAST

NEEDS
BASIC NEEDS - 02.01.01
CAPITAL NEEDS
- 11.02.05
USE: FINANCIAL NEEDS
CRITICAL NEEDS
- 05.03.02
USE: BASIC NEEDS
EDUCATIONAL NEEDS - 06.02.02
FINANCIAL NEEDS - 11.02.05
HOUSING NEEDS - 14.04.01
INFORMATION NEEDS - 19.01.01
MANPOWER NEEDS - 13.01.02

NEGOTIATION
INTERNATIONAL NEGOTIATION - 01.02.04

NEGOTIATIONS
TARIFF NEGOTIATIONS - 09.05.08
TRADE NEGOTIATIONS - 09.05.02

NEIGHBOURHOOD
NEIGHBOURHOOD - 14.04.03

NEOCOLONIALISM
NEOCOLONIALISM - 03.03.01

NEPAL
NEPAL - 01.04.04

NEPALESE
NEPALESE - 14.03.02

NERVOUS
NERVOUS SYSTEM - 15.02.04

NETHERLANDER
NETHERLANDER - 14.03.02

NETHERLANDS
NETHERLANDS - 01.04.05
NETHERLANDS ANTILLES - 01.04.03

NETWORK
DISTRIBUTION NETWORK - 09.04.01
HYDROLOGICAL NETWORK - 17.05.02
INFORMATION NETWORK - 19.01.01
NETWORK ANALYSIS - 12.04.00
RAILWAY NETWORK - 10.03.00
ROAD NETWORK - 10.03.00

NEUTRALISM
NEUTRALISM - 01.02.01

NEUTRALITY
NEUTRALITY - 01.02.01

NEVIS
ST KITTS-NEVIS-ANGUILLA - 01.04.03

NEW
NEW CALEDONIA - 01.04.07
NEW HEBRIDES - 01.04.07
NEW INTERNATIONAL ECONOMIC ORDER - 01.02.01
NEW PRODUCTS - 12.08.01
NEW TOWNS - 14.04.03
NEW ZEALAND - 01.04.07
NEW ZELANDER - 14.03.02
PAPUA NEW GUINEA - 01.04.07

NEWS
NEWS - 19.01.01
NEWS ITEM - 19.02.06

NEWSLETTER
NEWSLETTER - 19.02.06

NICARAGUA
NICARAGUA - 01.04.03

NICARAGUAN
NICARAGUAN - 14.03.02

NICKEL
NICKEL - 08.14.02

NIGER
NIGER - 01.04.02

NIGERIA
NIGERIA - 01.04.02

NIGERIAN
NIGERIAN - 14.03.02

NIGHT
NIGHT SCHOOLS - 06.04.03
NIGHT WORK - 13.03.03

NITRATES
NITRATES - 08.12.04

NITROGEN
  NITROGEN - 08.12.04
  NITROGEN OXIDES - 08.12.04

NOISE
  NOISE - 16.03.04
  NOISE CONTROL - 16.04.01

NOMADISM
  NOMADISM - 14.07.00

NOMADS
  NOMADS - 14.07.00

NORDIC
  NORDIC COUNCIL - 01.03.03

NORMATIVE
  NORMATIVE PLANNING
  - 02.01.02
    USE: DIRECTIVE PLANNING

NORMS
  SOCIAL NORMS - 05.04.01

NORTH
  KOREA NORTH
  - 01.04.04
    USE: KOREA DPR
  NORTH - 17 03.03
  NORTH AFRICA - 01.04.02
  NORTH AFRICAN - 14.03.02
  NORTH AMERICA - 01.04.03

NORTHERN
  NORTHERN HEMISPHERE - 01.04.01

NORWAY
  NORWA - 01.04.05

NORWEGIAN
  NORWEGIAN - 14.03.02

NUCLEAR
  NUCLEAR ENERGY - 08.11.03
  NUCLEAR ENGINEERING - 08.11.03
  NUCLEAR FUEL - 08.11.03
  NUCLEAR INSTALLATIONS - 08.11.03
  NUCLEAR POWER
  - 08.11.03
    USE: NUCLEAR ENERGY
  NUCLEAR POWER PLANTS - 08.11.03
  NUCLEAR REACTORS - 08.11.03
  NUCLEAR WAR - 01.02.07
  NUCLEAR WEAPONS - 01.02.06

NUMBERS
  INDEX NUMBERS - 18.08.00

NUPTIALITY
  NUPTIALITY - 14.02.05

NURSERIES
  FOREST NURSERIES - 07.08.03

NURSERY
  NURSERY SCHOOLS - 06.04.02

NURSES
  NURSES - 13.09.10

NUTRIENTS
  NUTRIENTS - 15.03.02

NUTRITION
  ANIMAL NUTRITION - 07.09.03
  HUMAN NUTRITION - 15.03.02
  NUTRITION - 15.03.02
  NUTRITION POLICY - 15.03.02
  NUTRITION RESEARCH - 15.03.02
  PLANT NUTRITION - 07.07.01

NUTRITIVE
  NUTRITIVE VALUE - 15.03.02

NUTS
  CASHEW NUTS - 07.07.05

NZ
  PACIFIC ISLANDS NZ - 01.04.07

OAPEC
    OAPEC - 01.03.03

OAS
    OAS - 01.03.03

OASES
    OASES - 17.03.04

OAT
    OAT - 07.07.04

OAU
    OAU - 01.03.03

OBJECTIVES
    MANAGEMENT BY OBJECTIVES - 12.04.00

OBSERVATION
    OBSERVATION - 18.04.00

OBSOLESCENCE
    TECHNOLOGICAL OBSOLESCENCE - 12.06.00

OBSOLETE
    OBSOLETE EQUIPMENT - 12.05.00

OBSTACLES
    OBSTACLES TO DEVELOPMENT - 03.02.03

OCAM
    OCAM - 01.03.03

OCAS
    OCAS - 01.03.03

OCCUPATIONAL
    OCCUPATIONAL ACCIDENTS - 13.04.00
    OCCUPATIONAL CHOICE - 13.02.01
    OCCUPATIONAL DISEASES - 13.04.00
    OCCUPATIONAL HYGIENE - 13.04.00
    OCCUPATIONAL MEDICINE - 13.04.00
    OCCUPATIONAL MOBILITY - 13.02.01
    OCCUPATIONAL MORTALITY - 14.06.00
    OCCUPATIONAL ORGANIZATIONS - 13.06.00
    OCCUPATIONAL QUALIFICATION - 13.02.01
    OCCUPATIONAL SAFETY - 13.04.00
    OCCUPATIONAL SATISFACTION
    - 13.03.04
      USE: JOB SATISFACTION
    OCCUPATIONAL STRUCTURE - 13.01.03
    OCCUPATIONAL TRAINING
    - 06.03.07
      USE: VOCATIONAL TRAINING

OCCUPATIONS
    OCCUPATIONS - 13.09.01

OCEAN
    ATLANTIC OCEAN - 17.06.00
    INDIAN OCEAN - 17.06.00
    PACIFIC OCEAN - 17.06.00

OCEANIA
    OCEANIA - 01.04.07

OCEANOGRAPHY
    OCEANOGRAPHY - 17.06.00

OECD
    OECD - 01.03.03
    OECD COUNTRIES - 01.03.03
    OECD DAC - 01.03.03
    OECD DC - 01.03.03
    OECD IEA - 01.03.03
    OECD NEA - 01.03.03

OFFENDERS
    OFFENDERS - 02.04.02

OFFICE
    OFFICE MACHINES - 08.14.06
    OFFICE WORKERS - 13.09.07

OFFICIAL
    OFFICIAL DOCUMENTS - 19.02.01
    OFFICIAL LANGUAGES - 05.06.01

OFFPRINTS
    OFFPRINTS - 19.02.04

OIL
    OIL CROPS - 07.07.02
    OIL PALMS - 07.07.05
    OLIVE OIL - 08.06.06
    PALM OIL - 08.06.06
    PEANUT OIL - 08.06.06
    SHALE OIL - 08.11.06

OILS
    ANIMAL OILS - 08.06.06
    EDIBLE OILS - 08.06.06
    ESSENTIAL OILS - 08.06.06
    FISH OILS - 08.06.06
    MINERAL OILS - 08.11.06
    OILS AND FATS - 08.06.06
    VEGETABLE OILS - 08.06.06

OILSEEDS
    OILSEEDS - 07.07.05

OLD
    OLD AGE - 14.02.02
    OLD AGE BENEFITS - 02.03.02

OLDER
    OLDER PEOPLE
    - 14.02.02
      USE: AGED
    OLDER WORKERS - 13.09.02

OLIVE
    OLIVE OIL - 08.06.06

OLIVES
    OLIVES - 07.07.05

OMAN
OMAN - 01.04.06

OMANI
OMANI - 14.03.02

OMBUDSMAN
OMBUDSMAN - 04.03.02

ON
ON-THE-JOB TRAINING
- 06.03.07
USE: IN-PLANT TRAINING

ONCHOCERCIASIS
ONCHOCERCIASIS - 15.04.02

ONIONS
ONIONS - 07.07.06

OPEC
OPEC - 01.03.03

OPERATION
PLANS OF OPERATION - 01.01.06

OPERATIONAL
OPERATIONAL RESEARCH - 12.04.00

OPINION
FREEDOM OF OPINION - 04.02.02
OPINION - 05.03.02
PUBLIC OPINION - 04.04.02

OPIUM
OPIUM - 07.07.09

OPPORTUNITIES
EDUCATIONAL OPPORTUNITIES - 06.02.02
EMPLOYMENT OPPORTUNITIES - 13.01.02

OPPORTUNITY
EQUAL OPPORTUNITY - 04.02.03

OPPOSITION
POLITICAL OPPOSITION - 04.04.02

OPTICAL
OPTICAL INDUSTRY - 08.14.08
OPTICAL INSTRUMENTS - 08.14.08

OPTICS
OPTICS - 08.14.08

OPTIMUM
POPULATION OPTIMUM - 14.01.02

ORAL
ORAL CONTRACEPTIVES - 14.05.02

ORDER
NEW INTERNATIONAL ECONOMIC ORDER - 01.02.01

ORE
ALUMINIUM ORE
- 08.13.00
USE: BAUXITE
COPPER ORE - 08.13.00
IRON ORE - 08.13.00

ORES
ORES
- 08.13.00
USE: MINERALS

ORGANIC
ORGANIC CHEMISTRY - 08.12.02

ORGANIZATION
BUSINESS ORGANIZATION - 12.04.00
FACTORY ORGANIZATION - 08.03.00
ORGANIZATION OF RESEARCH - 18.02.00
WORK ORGANIZATION - 13.03.01

ORGANIZATIONS
AFRICAN ORGANIZATIONS - 01.03.03
AMERICAN ORGANIZATIONS - 01.03.03
ARAB ORGANIZATIONS - 01.03.03
ASIAN ORGANIZATIONS - 01.03.03
EMPLOYERS ORGANIZATIONS - 13.06.00
EUROPEAN ORGANIZATIONS - 01.03.03
INTERGOVERNMENTAL ORGANIZATIONS - 01.03.01
INTERNATIONAL ORGANIZATIONS - 01.03.01
NON-GOVERNMENTAL ORGANIZATIONS - 01.03.01
NON-PROFIT ORGANIZATIONS - 05.03.07
OCCUPATIONAL ORGANIZATIONS - 13.06.00
REGIONAL ORGANIZATIONS - 01.03.01
VOLUNTARY ORGANIZATIONS - 05.03.07
WOMEN'S ORGANIZATIONS - 05.03.07
YOUTH ORGANIZATIONS - 05.03.07

ORIENTED
EXPORT-ORIENTED INDUSTRY - 08.01.01

ORIGIN
APPELLATION OF ORIGIN - 12.07.02

ORPHANAGES
ORPHANAGES - 02.05.03

OUT
DROPPING OUT - 06.04.12
OUT-OF-SCHOOL EDUCATION - 06.03.02

OUTER
OUTER SPACE - 17.07.00

OUTPUT
CAPITAL-OUTPUT RATIO - 12.07.03
EDUCATIONAL OUTPUT - 06.02.05
INPUT-OUTPUT - 03.02.02
INPUT-OUTPUT ANALYSIS - 03.02.02
INPUT-OUTPUT TABLES - 03.02.02

OVEREMPLOYMENT
OVEREMPLOYMENT
- 13.01.02
USE: LABOUR SHORTAGE

OVEREXPLOITATION
OVEREXPLOITATION - 16.02.01

394

OVERHEAD
>OVERHEAD COSTS - 12.09.00

OVERPOPULATION
>OVERPOPULATION - 14.01.02

OVERPRODUCTION
>OVERPRODUCTION - 12.07.01

OVERSEAS
>OVERSEAS TERRITORIES - 01.02.03

OVERTIME
>OVERTIME - 13.03.03

OVIDAE
>OVIDAE - 07.09.01

OWNERSHIP
>COLLECTIVE OWNERSHIP - 03.03.05
>FOREIGN OWNERSHIP - 03.03.05
>LAND OWNERSHIP - 07.02.00
>OWNERSHIP - 03.03.05
>PRIVATE OWNERSHIP - 03.03.05
>PUBLIC OWNERSHIP - 03.03.05
>WORKERS STOCK OWNERSHIP - 13.07.00

OXIDES
>NITROGEN OXIDES - 08.12.04

OXYGEN
>OXYGEN - 08.12.04

OYSTER
>OYSTER CULTURE - 07.10.03

OZONE
>OZONE - 08.12.04

PACIFIC
>PACIFIC ISLANDS
>- 01.04.07
>USE: OCEANIA
>PACIFIC ISLANDS AUS - 01.04.07
>PACIFIC ISLANDS FR - 01.04.07
>PACIFIC ISLANDS NZ - 01.04.07
>PACIFIC ISLANDS UK - 01.04.07
>PACIFIC ISLANDS USA - 01.04.07
>PACIFIC OCEAN - 17.06.00
>PACIFIC REGION - 01.04.07

PACKAGING
>PACKAGING - 10.06.00

PACT
>ANDEAN PACT
>- 01.03.03
>USE: ANDEAN GROUP

PAHO
>PAHO - 01.03.03

PAINTS
>PAINTS AND VARNISHES - 08.12.08

PAKISTAN
>PAKISTAN - 01.04.04

PAKISTANI
>PAKISTANI - 14.03.02

PALM
>PALM OIL - 08.06.06

PALMS
>COCONUT PALMS - 07.07.05
>DATE PALMS - 07.07.05
>OIL PALMS - 07.07.05

PAMPA
>PAMPA - 17.03.04

PANAMA
>PANAMA - 01.04.03
>PANAMA CANAL ZONE - 01.04.03

PANAMANIAN
>PANAMANIAN - 14.03.02

PAPER
>CONFERENCE PAPER - 19.02.05
>MEETING PAPER
>- 19.02.05
>USE: CONFERENCE PAPER
>PAPER - 08.07.02
>PULP AND PAPER INDUSTRY - 08.07.02

PAPUA
>PAPUA NEW GUINEA - 01.04.07

PARAGUAY
>PARAGUAY - 01.04.03

PARAGUAYAN
>PARAGUAYAN - 14.03.02

PARAMEDICAL
    PARAMEDICAL PERSONNEL - 13.09.10

PARASITES
    PARASITES - 15.01.02

PARASITIC
    PARASITIC DISEASES - 15.04.02

PARASITOLOGY
    PARASITOLOGY - 15.01.01

PARENTS
    PARENTS - 14.02.04

PARKS
    NATIONAL PARKS - 16.05.02

PARLIAMENT
    EUROPEAN PARLIAMENT - 01.03.03
    PARLIAMENT - 04.03.01

PARLIAMENTARY
    PARLIAMENTARY PROCEDURE - 04.03.01

PART
    PART TIME - 13.03.03
    PART TIME EMPLOYMENT - 13.01.03

PARTICIPANTS
    LIST OF PARTICIPANTS - 19.02.05

PARTICIPATION
    PARTICIPATION IN CULTURAL LIFE - 05.02.02
    POLITICAL PARTICIPATION - 04.04.02
    SOCIAL PARTICIPATION - 05.03.03
    STATE PARTICIPATION - 11.01.01
    STUDENT PARTICIPATION - 06.06.01
    WORKERS PARTICIPATION - 13.06.00

PARTICLE
    PARTICLE BOARDS - 08.07.01

PARTIES
    POLITICAL PARTIES - 04.04.02

PARTS
    SPARE PARTS - 12.05.00

PASSENGER
    PASSENGER RATE - 10.09.00

PASSENGERS
    PASSENGERS - 10.02.00

PASTEURIZATION
    PASTEURIZATION - 08.06.02

PATENT
    PATENT LAW - 04.01.02

PATENTS
    PATENTS - 08.05.00

PATH
    CRITICAL PATH METHOD
    - 12.04.00
      USE: NETWORK ANALYSIS

PATHOLOGY
    PATHOLOGY
    - 15.04.01
      USE: DISEASES

PATHOLOGY\<CONT>
    PLANT PATHOLOGY - 07.07.01

PATIENTS
    PATIENTS - 15.04.05

PATTERN
    SETTLEMENT PATTERN
    - 14.04.01
      USE: HABITAT

PAY
    EQUAL PAY - 13.07.00
    SEVERANCE PAY - 13.07.00

PAYMENT
    PAYMENT AGREEMENTS - 11.03.02
    PAYMENT BY RESULT - 13.07.00
    PAYMENT SYSTEMS - 11.03.02
    WAGE PAYMENT SYSTEMS - 13.07.00

PAYMENTS
    BALANCE OF PAYMENTS - 11.03.02
    INTERNATIONAL PAYMENTS - 11.03.02

PAYROLL
    PAYROLL TAX - 11.01.02

PAYS
    POLLUTER-PAYS PRINCIPLE - 16.04.01

PEACE
    PEACE - 01.02.07
    PEACE CORPS - 01.01.08
    PEACE KEEPING - 01.02.07
    PEACE RESEARCH - 01.02.07

PEACEFUL
    PEACEFUL COEXISTENCE - 01.02.07

PEANUT
    PEANUT OIL - 08.06.06

PEARS
    PEARS - 07.07.05

PEAS
    PIGEON PEAS - 07.07.06

PEASANT
    PEASANT MOVEMENTS - 05.03.07

PEASANTS
    PEASANTS - 05.03.05

PEDAGOGY
    PEDAGOGY
    - 06.01.00
      USE: SCIENCES OF EDUCATION

PEDESTRIANS
    PEDESTRIANS - 10.02.00

PEDIATRICIANS
    PEDIATRICIANS - 13.09.10

PEDIATRICS
    PEDIATRICS - 15.04.06

PEDOLOGY
    PEDOLOGY
    - 17.04.04
      USE: SOIL SCIENCES

PEER

PEER TEACHING - 06.05.02

PENAL

PENAL SANCTIONS - 02.04.03

PENSION

PENSION FUNDS - 11.02.02
PENSION SCHEMES - 02.03.02

PENSIONS

RETIREMENT PENSIONS - 02.03.02

PEOPLE

OLDER PEOPLE
- 14.02.02
USE: AGED

PEPPER

PEPPER - 07.07.09

PERFORMANCE

STANDARD PERFORMANCE - 13.02.02

PERFORMERS

PERFORMERS - 13.09.09

PERFORMING

PERFORMING ARTS - 05.05.03

PERFUMES

PERFUMES - 08.12.08

PERIOD

PROBATION PERIOD - 13.02.01
REST PERIOD - 13.03.03

PERIODICALS

PERIODICALS - 19.02.06

PERISHABLE

PERISHABLE FOOD - 15.03.01

PERMANENT

PERMANENT EDUCATION
- 06.03.05
USE: LIFE-LONG EDUCATION

PERMIT

WORK PERMIT - 13.02.01

PERSIAN

PERSIAN GULF STATES - 01.04.06

PERSONALITY

PERSONALITY - 05.03.01
PERSONALITY DEVELOPMENT - 05.03.01

PERSONNEL

COUNTERPART PERSONNEL - 01.01.05
DEVELOPMENT PERSONNEL - 01.01.07
MEDICAL PERSONNEL - 13.09.10
PARAMEDICAL PERSONNEL - 13.09.10
PERSONNEL ADMINISTRATION
- 13.02.02
USE: PERSONNEL MANAGEMENT
PERSONNEL MANAGEMENT - 13.02.02
SCIENTIFIC PERSONNEL - 13.09.03
TEACHING PERSONNEL - 06.06.02

PERSONNEL<CONT>

TECHNICAL PERSONNEL - 13.09.03

PERSONS

MARRIED PERSONS - 14.02.05

PERT

PERT
- 12.04.00
USE: NETWORK ANALYSIS

PERU

PERU - 01.04.03

PERUVIAN

PERUVIAN - 14.03.02

PEST

PEST CONTROL - 16.04.01

PESTICIDE

PESTICIDE RESIDUES - 08.12.05

PESTICIDES

PESTICIDES - 08.12.05

PESTS

INSECT PESTS - 16.03.03
PESTS OF ANIMALS - 16.03.03
PESTS OF PLANTS - 16.03.03

PETROCHEMICAL

PETROCHEMICAL INDUSTRY - 08.12.01

PETROCHEMICALS

PETROCHEMICALS - 08.12.04

PETROCHEMISTRY

PETROCHEMISTRY - 08.12.02

PETRODOLLARS

PETRODOLLARS - 11.03.01

PETROL

PETROL - 08.11.06
PETROL ENGINES - 08.14.06

PETROLEUM

PETROLEUM - 08.11.06
PETROLEUM ENGINEERING - 08.11.06
PETROLEUM EXTRACTION - 08.13.00
PETROLEUM INDUSTRY - 08.11.06
PETROLEUM PRODUCTS - 08.11.06
PETROLEUM REFINERIES - 08.11.06
PETROLEUM RESOURCES - 16.02.02

PHARMACEUTICAL

PHARMACEUTICAL INDUSTRY - 08.12.06

PHARMACEUTICALS

PHARMACEUTICALS - 08.12.06

PHARMACISTS

PHARMACISTS - 13.09.10

PHARMACOLOGY

PHARMACOLOGY - 15.05.00

PHILIPPINES

PHILIPPINES - 01.04.04

PHILOSOPHY

    PHILOSOPHY - 05.01.01

    PHILOSOPHY OF EDUCATION - 06.01.00

PHOSPHATES

    PHOSPHATES - 08.12.04

PHOSPHORUS

    PHOSPHORUS - 08.12.04

PHOTOGRAMMETRY

    PHOTOGRAMMETRY - 18.07.00

PHOTOGRAPHS

    PHOTOGRAPHS - 19.02.04

PHYSICAL

    PHYSICAL CAPACITY - 13.02.01

    PHYSICAL EDUCATION - 06.03.04

    PHYSICAL ENVIRONMENT - 16.01.02

    PHYSICAL GEOGRAPHY - 17.03.01

    PHYSICAL PROPERTIES - 18.06.00

    PHYSICAL WORK - 13.03.02

PHYSICALLY

    PHYSICALLY HANDICAPPED - 15.04.05

PHYSICIAN

    PHYSICIAN EDUCATION
    - 06.03.07
     USE: MEDICAL EDUCATION

PHYSICIANS

    PHYSICIANS - 13.09.10

PHYSICISTS

    PHYSICISTS - 13.09.09

PHYSICS

    PHYSICS - 17.04.01

    SOIL PHYSICS - 17.04.04

PHYSIOLOGY

    PHYSIOLOGY - 15.02.01

PHYTOPATHOLOGY

    PHYTOPATHOLOGY
    - 15.04.01
     USE: PLANT DISEASES

PIECE

    PIECE WORK
    - 13.07.00
     USE: PAYMENT BY RESULT

PIERRE

    ST PIERRE AND MIQUELON - 01.04.03

PIGEON

    PIGEON PEAS - 07.07.06

PIGS

    PIGS
    - 07.09.01
     USE: SWINE

PILOT

    PILOT PROJECTS - 01.01.06

PILOTS

    PILOTS - 13.09.08

PINEAPPLES

    PINEAPPLES - 07.07.05

PIPELINE

    PIPELINE TRANSPORT - 10.05.00

PIPELINES

    PIPELINES - 10.03.00

PIPES

    PIPES - 08.14.04

PIRACY

    AIR PIRACY - 01.02.07

PLACEMENT

    PLACEMENT SERVICES
    - 13.02.01
     USE: EMPLOYMENT SERVICES

PLAGUE

    PLAGUE - 15.04.02

PLAINS

    PLAINS - 17.03.04

PLAN

    COLOMBO PLAN - 01.03.03

    PLAN IMPLEMENTATION - 02.01.02

PLANNED

    PLANNED ECONOMY - 03.03.02

PLANNERS

    PLANNERS - 02.01.02

PLANNING

    AGRICULTURAL PLANNING - 07.01.02

    COMMUNICATION PLANNING - 05.07.01

    DEVELOPMENT PLANNING - 02.01.02

    DIRECTIVE PLANNING - 02.01.02

    ECONOMIC PLANNING - 02.01.02

    EDUCATIONAL PLANNING - 06.02.04

    EMPLOYMENT PLANNING
    - 13.01.03
     USE: MANPOWER PLANNING

    EXPORT PLANNING - 09.05.06

    FAMILY PLANNING - 14.05.02

    FAMILY PLANNING AGENCIES - 14.05.02

    FAMILY PLANNING PROGRAMMES - 14.05.02

    FISHERY PLANNING - 07.10.02

    FOOD PLANNING - 15.03.01

    FORESTRY PLANNING - 07.08.04

    HEALTH PLANNING - 02.05.02

    INDUSTRIAL PLANNING - 08.01.02

    MANPOWER PLANNING - 13.01.03

    MARKET PLANNING - 09.01.02

    NATIONAL PLANNING - 02.01.02

    NORMATIVE PLANNING
    - 02.01.02
     USE: DIRECTIVE PLANNING

PLANNING<CONT>

PLANNING - 02.01.02

PLANNING METHODS - 02.01.02

PLANNING OF EDUCATION
- 06.02.04
  USE: EDUCATIONAL PLANNING

PLANNING SYSTEMS - 02.01.02

PRODUCTION PLANNING - 12.07.01

PROGRAMME PLANNING - 12.04.00

PROJECT PLANNING
- 01.01.06
  USE: PROJECT DESIGN

REGIONAL PLANNING - 02.01.02

RURAL PLANNING - 14.04.02

SECTORAL PLANNING - 02.01.02

SOCIAL PLANNING - 02.02.01

STRATEGIC PLANNING - 02.01.02

TOWN PLANNING
- 14.04.03
  USE: URBAN PLANNING

TRANSPORT PLANNING - 10.01.00

URBAN PLANNING - 14.04.03

PLANS

BENEFIT PLANS - 02.03.02

DEVELOPMENT PLANS - 02.01.02

NATIONAL PLANS - 02.01.02

PLANS OF OPERATION - 01.01.06

REGIONAL PLANS - 02.01.02

PLANT

IN-PLANT TRAINING - 06.03.07

PLANT BREEDING - 07.07.01

PLANT DISEASES - 15.04.01

PLANT ECOLOGY - 16.01.01

PLANT FIBRES - 07.07.07

PLANT NUTRITION - 07.07.01

PLANT PATHOLOGY - 07.07.01

PLANT PRODUCTION - 07.07.03

PLANT PRODUCTS - 07.07.03

PLANT PROTECTION - 16.05.01

PLANT RESOURCES - 16.02.02

PLANT SHUTDOWN - 13.05.00

PLANTATIONS

PLANTATIONS - 07.03.01

PLANTING

PLANTING - 07.05.04

PLANTS

AQUATIC PLANTS - 07.07.01

ELECTRIC POWER PLANTS - 08.11.02

HYDROELECTRIC POWER PLANTS - 08.11.02

INDUSTRIAL PLANTS - 08.03.00

MEDICINAL PLANTS - 15.05.00

NUCLEAR POWER PLANTS - 08.11.03

PESTS OF PLANTS - 16.03.03

PLANTS - 07.07.01

POWER PLANTS - 08.11.01

PUMPING PLANTS - 17.05.04

THERMAL POWER PLANTS - 08.11.02

WILD PLANTS - 07.07.01

PLASTIC

PLASTIC ARTS - 05.05.03

PLASTICS

PLASTICS - 08.12.07

PLASTICS INDUSTRY - 08.12.07

PLATE

TIN PLATE - 08.14.04

PLATEAUS

PLATEAUS - 17.03.04

PLATING

PLATING - 08.12.03

PLATINUM

PLATINUM - 08.14.02

PLURALISM

CULTURAL PLURALISM - 05.02.01

PLUTONIUM

PLUTONIUM - 08.14.02

PLYWOOD

PLYWOOD - 08.07.01

PNEUMOCONIOSIS

PNEUMOCONIOSIS - 15.04.02

PNEUMONIA

PNEUMONIA - 15.04.02

POISONING

POISONING - 15.04.02

POISONS

POISONS - 15.05.00

POLAND

POLAND - 01.04.05

POLES

GROWTH POLES - 02.01.02

POLICE

POLICE - 04.03.02

POLICY

AGRICULTURAL POLICY - 07.01.02

AUSTERITY POLICY - 02.01.03

POLICY<CONT>

BUDGETARY POLICY - 11.01.01
COMMERCIAL POLICY - 09.04.02
COMMUNICATION POLICY - 05.07.01
CREDIT POLICY - 11.02.02
CULTURAL POLICY - 05.02.03
CUSTOMS POLICY
- 09.05.08
 USE: TARIFF POLICY
DEFENCE POLICY - 01.02.06
DEVELOPMENT POLICY - 02.01.01
ECONOMIC POLICY - 02.01.03
EDUCATIONAL POLICY - 06.02.04
EMPLOYMENT POLICY - 13.01.03
ENERGY POLICY - 08.11.01
ENVIRONMENTAL POLICY - 16.04.01
FAMILY POLICY - 02.05.03
FINANCIAL POLICY - 11.02.04
FISCAL POLICY - 11.01.02
FISHERY POLICY - 07.10.02
FOOD POLICY - 15.03.01
FOREIGN POLICY - 01.02.05
FOREST POLICY - 07.08.04
GOVERNMENT POLICY - 04.03.02
GROWTH POLICY - 02.01.03
HEALTH POLICY - 02.05.02
HOUSING POLICY - 14.04.01
INCOMES POLICY - 02.01.03
INDUSTRIAL POLICY - 08.01.02
INDUSTRIALIZATION POLICY - 08.01.02
INFORMATION POLICY - 19.01.01
INVESTMENT POLICY - 11.02.06
LABOUR POLICY - 13.01.01
MANPOWER POLICY
- 13.01.03
 USE: EMPLOYMENT POLICY
MIGRATION POLICY - 14.07.00
MONETARY POLICY - 11.02.01
NATIONAL POLICY - 04.03.03
NUTRITION POLICY - 15.03.02
POLICY MAKING - 04.03.02
POPULATION POLICY - 14.01.02

POLICY<CONT>

PRICE POLICY - 09.02.00
PRODUCTIVITY POLICY - 12.07.03
RACIAL POLICY - 04.02.04
REGIONAL POLICY - 02.01.02
RESEARCH POLICY - 18.01.00
SCIENCE AND TECHNOLOGY POLICY
- 18.01.00
 USE: SCIENCE POLICY
SCIENCE POLICY - 18.01.00
SOCIAL POLICY - 02.02.01
TARIFF POLICY - 09.05.08
TRADE POLICY - 09.05.06
TRANSPORT POLICY - 10.01.00
WAGE POLICY - 13.07.00

POLIOMYELITIS

POLIOMYELITIS - 15.04.02

POLISH

POLISH - 14.03.02

POLITICAL

POLITICAL AFFILIATION - 04.04.02
POLITICAL ASPECTS - 04.04.02
POLITICAL BEHAVIOUR - 04.04.02
POLITICAL DEVELOPMENT - 04.04.02
POLITICAL DOCTRINES - 04.04.02
POLITICAL ECONOMY
- 03.01.01
 USE: ECONOMICS
POLITICAL EDUCATION - 06.03.04
POLITICAL GEOGRAPHY - 17.03.01
POLITICAL IDEOLOGIES - 04.04.02
POLITICAL INTEGRATION - 04.04.02
POLITICAL LEADERSHIP - 04.04.02
POLITICAL OPPOSITION - 04.04.02
POLITICAL PARTICIPATION - 04.04.02
POLITICAL PARTIES - 04.04.02
POLITICAL POWER - 04.03.01
POLITICAL PROBLEMS - 04.04.02
POLITICAL SCIENCE - 04.04.01
POLITICAL SCIENTISTS - 13.09.09
POLITICAL STABILITY - 04.04.02
POLITICAL SYSTEMS - 04.03.01
POLITICAL THEORY - 04.04.01

POLITICS

INTERNATIONAL POLITICS - 01.02.01

POLITICS<CONT>
POLITICS - 04.04.02

POLLUTANT
POLLUTANT BURDEN
- 16.03.04
USE: POLLUTION LEVEL

POLLUTANTS
AIR POLLUTANTS - 16.03.04
CONCENTRATION OF POLLUTANTS
- 16.03.04
USE: POLLUTION LEVEL
POLLUTANTS - 16.03.04
SOIL POLLUTANTS - 16.03.04
WATER POLLUTANTS - 16.03.04

POLLUTED
POLLUTED AREAS - 16.03.04

POLLUTER
POLLUTER-PAYS PRINCIPLE - 16.04.01

POLLUTION
ACUSTIC POLLUTION - 16.03.04
AIR POLLUTION - 16.03.04
ATMOSPHERIC POLLUTION
- 16.03.04
USE: AIR POLLUTION
CHEMICAL POLLUTION - 16.03.04
COASTAL POLLUTION - 16.03.04
ENVIRONMENTAL POLLUTION
- 16.03.04
USE: POLLUTION
MARINE POLLUTION - 16.03.04
POLLUTION - 16.03.04
POLLUTION CONTROL - 16.04.01
POLLUTION INDEX - 16.04.01
POLLUTION LEVEL - 16.03.04
POLLUTION SOURCES - 16.03.04
RADIOACTIVE POLLUTION - 16.03.04
RIVER POLLUTION - 16.03.04
SOIL POLLUTION - 16.03.04
THERMAL POLLUTION - 16.03.04
TRANSFRONTIER POLLUTION - 16.03.04
WATER POLLUTION - 16.03.04

POLYANDRY
POLYANDRY - 14.02.05

POLYESTER
POLYESTER - 08.12.07

POLYGAMY
POLYGAMY - 14.02.05

POLYMERS
POLYMERS - 08.12.04

POLYNESIA
FRENCH POLYNESIA - 01.04.07
POLYNESIA
- 01.04.07
USE: OCEANIA

POPULATION
ABORIGINAL POPULATION - 14.03.01
AGRICULTURAL POPULATION - 14.04.02
INDIGENOUS POPULATION - 14.03.01
POPULATION - 14.01.02
POPULATION CENSUSES - 14.01.01
POPULATION COMPOSITION - 14.02.01
POPULATION DECLINE - 14.01.02
POPULATION DENSITY - 14.01.02
POPULATION DISTRIBUTION - 14.04.01
POPULATION DYNAMICS - 14.01.02
POPULATION INCREASE - 14.01.02
POPULATION OPTIMUM - 14.01.02
POPULATION POLICY - 14.01.02
POPULATION SIZE - 14.01.02
POPULATION THEORY - 14.01.02
POPULATION TRANSFERS - 14.07.00
RURAL POPULATION - 14.04.02
SCHOOL AGE POPULATION - 14.02.02
STATIONARY POPULATION - 14.01.02
URBAN POPULATION - 14.04.03

PORK
PORK - 07.09.05

PORTS
FISHING PORTS - 07.10.03
FREE PORTS - 09.05.08
PORTS - 10.03.00

PORTUGAL
PORTUGAL - 01.04.05

PORTUGUESE
PORTUGUESE - 14.03.02
PORTUGUESE TIMOR - 01.04.04

POST
POST-SECONDARY EDUCATION - 06.03.06
POST-SECONDARY SCHOOLS
- 06.04.05
USE: HIGHER EDUCATION INSTITUTIONS

POSTAL
POSTAL SERVICES - 08.16.00

POTASH
POTASH - 08.12.04

POTASSIUM
POTASSIUM - 08.12.04

POTATOES
POTATOES - 07.07.06
SWEET POTATOES - 07.07.06

POTENTIAL
AGRICULTURAL POTENTIAL - 07.01.02
DEVELOPMENT POTENTIAL - 02.01.01
INDUSTRIAL POTENTIAL - 08.01.02

POTTERY
POTTERY - 08.10.03

POULTRY
POULTRY - 07.09.01

POVERTY
POVERTY - 03.02.05

POWDER
MILK POWDER - 07.09.05

POWER
ELECTRIC POWER - 08.11.02
ELECTRIC POWER PLANTS - 08.11.02
HYDROELECTRIC POWER - 08.11.02
HYDROELECTRIC POWER PLANTS - 08.11.02
NUCLEAR POWER
- 08.11.03
 USE: NUCLEAR ENERGY
NUCLEAR POWER PLANTS - 08.11.03
POLITICAL POWER - 04.03.01
POWER CONSERVATION
- 08.11.01
 USE: ENERGY CONSERVATION
POWER CONSUMPTION
- 08.11.01
 USE: ENERGY CONSUMPTION
POWER DEMAND - 08.11.01
POWER DISTRIBUTION - 08.11.01
POWER GENERATION - 08.11.01
POWER INDUSTRY - 08.11.01
POWER PLANTS - 08.11.01
POWER PRODUCTION
- 08.11.01
 USE: POWER GENERATION
POWER RESOURCES
- 16.02.02
 USE: ENERGY RESOURCES
POWER SUPPLY - 08.11.01
POWER UTILIZATION
- 08.11.01
PURCHASING POWER - 03.02.05
THERMAL POWER PLANTS - 08.11.02

PRACTICE
RELIGIOUS PRACTICE - 05.04.02
TEACHING PRACTICE - 06.05.02

PRACTICES
CULTIVATION PRACTICES - 07.05.04
RESTRICTIVE BUSINESS PRACTICES - 09.05.07

PRAIRIE
PRAIRIE - 17.03.04

PRECIOUS
PRECIOUS METALS - 08.14.02
PRECIOUS STONES - 08.13.00

PRECIPITATIONS
PRECIPITATIONS - 17.01.03

PRECISION
PRECISION INSTRUMENTS - 08.14.08

PREFABRICATED
PREFABRICATED BUILDINGS - 08.10.01

PREFERENCES
GENERAL SYSTEM OF PREFERENCES - 09.05.08

PREFERENTIAL
PREFERENTIAL TARIFFS - 09.05.08

PREGNANCY
PREGNANCY - 14.05.01

PREINVESTMENT
PREINVESTMENT SURVEYS - 11.02.06

PRENATAL
PRENATAL CARE - 15.04.04

PREPARATION
FOOD PREPARATION - 15.03.01
MEAL PREPARATION
- 15.03.01
 USE: FOOD PREPARATION

PREPARATIONS
TOILET PREPARATIONS - 08.12.08

PRESCHOOL
PRESCHOOL EDUCATION - 06.03.06

PRESERVATION
FISH PRESERVATION - 08.06.02
FOOD PRESERVATION - 08.06.02

PRESIDENCY
PRESIDENCY - 04.03.01

PRESS
PRESS - 05.07.03
PRESS RELEASE - 19.02.06

PRESSURE
BAROMETRIC PRESSURE - 17.01.02
PRESSURE GROUPS
- 04.04.02
 USE: INTEREST GROUPS

PREVENTION
ACCIDENT PREVENTION
- 13.04.00
 USE: OCCUPATIONAL SAFETY

PREVENTION<CONT>
    CRIME PREVENTION - 02.04.03

PREVENTIVE
    PREVENTIVE MEDICINE - 15.04.04

PRICE
    PRICE CONTROL - 09.02.00
    PRICE INDEX - 09.02.00
    PRICE LIST - 09.02.00
    PRICE POLICY - 09.02.00
    PRICE STABILIZATION - 09.02.00
    PRICE SUPPORT - 09.02.00
    TRANSPORT PRICE
    - 10.09.00
     USE: FREIGHT

PRICES
    ADMINISTERED PRICES - 09.02.00
    AGRICULTURAL PRICES - 07.01.03
    COMMODITY PRICES - 09.02.00
    CONSUMER PRICES - 09.02.00
    INDUSTRIAL PRICES - 08.02.04
    PRICES - 09.02.00
    RETAIL PRICES - 09.02.00
    WHOLESALE PRICES - 09.02.00

PRICING
    PRICING - 12.09.00

PRIMARY
    PRIMARY DOCUMENTS - 19.02.01
    PRIMARY EDUCATION - 06.03.06
    PRIMARY PRODUCTS
    - 12.08.01
     USE: COMMODITIES
    PRIMARY SCHOOLS - 06.04.02
    PRIMARY SECTOR - 07.01.01

PRINCIPE
    SAO TOME AND PRINCIPE - 01.04.02

PRINCIPLE
    POLLUTER-PAYS PRINCIPLE - 16.04.01

PRINTING
    PRINTING INDUSTRY - 08.16.00

PRISONERS
    PRISONERS - 02.04.03

PRISONS
    PRISONS - 02.04.03

PRIVACY
    PRIVACY PROTECTION - 05.03.01

PRIVATE
    PRIVATE AID - 01.01.02
    PRIVATE EDUCATION - 06.03.03

PRIVATE<CONT>
    PRIVATE ENTERPRISES - 03.03.05
    PRIVATE INVESTMENTS - 11.02.06
    PRIVATE OWNERSHIP - 03.03.05
    PRIVATE SCHOOLS - 06.04.04
    PRIVATE SECTOR - 03.03.05

PROBABILITY
    PROBABILITY - 18.08.00

PROBATION
    PROBATION PERIOD - 13.02.01

PROBLEMS
    POLITICAL PROBLEMS - 04.04.02
    SOCIAL PROBLEMS - 02.04.01

PROCEDURE
    PARLIAMENTARY PROCEDURE - 04.03.01

PROCESSES
    INDUSTRIAL PROCESSES - 08.03.00

PROCESSING
    AGRIPRODUCT PROCESSING - 08.06.02
    DATA PROCESSING - 19.01.02
    ELECTRONIC DATA PROCESSING - 19.01.02
    FISHERY PRODUCT PROCESSING - 08.06.02
    FOOD PROCESSING - 08.06.02
    GRAIN PROCESSING - 08.06.02
    INFORMATION PROCESSING - 19.01.02
    MEAT PROCESSING - 08.06.02
    MILK PROCESSING - 08.06.02
    PROCESSING - 12.07.02
    WOOD PROCESSING - 08.07.01

PROCUREMENT
    WEAPON PROCUREMENT - 01.02.06

PRODUCERS
    PRODUCERS - 12.03.00
    PRODUCERS ASSOCIATIONS - 12.02.00

PRODUCT
    FISHERY PRODUCT PROCESSING - 08.06.02
    GROSS DOMESTIC PRODUCT - 03.02.02
    GROSS NATIONAL PRODUCT - 03.02.02
    PRODUCT DESIGN - 12.08.02
    PRODUCT DEVELOPMENT - 12.08.02

PRODUCTION
    AGRICULTURAL PRODUCTION - 07.05.01
    ANIMAL PRODUCTION - 07.09.02
    CATTLE PRODUCTION - 07.09.02
    FISH PRODUCTION - 07.10.04

PRODUCTION<CONT>

    FOOD PRODUCTION - 08.06.01

    FOREST PRODUCTION - 07.08.06

    INDUSTRIAL PRODUCTION - 08.04.00

    MASS PRODUCTION - 12.07.01

    MEANS OF PRODUCTION - 12.07.01

    MODES OF PRODUCTION - 12.07.01

    PLANT PRODUCTION - 07.07.03

    POWER PRODUCTION
    - 08.11.01
     USE: POWER GENERATION

    PRODUCTION - 12.07.01

    PRODUCTION CAPACITY - 12.07.01

    PRODUCTION CONTROL - 12.07.02

    PRODUCTION COOPERATIVES - 12.01.00

    PRODUCTION COSTS - 12.09.00

    PRODUCTION DIVERSIFICATION - 12.07.01

    PRODUCTION FACTORS - 12.07.01

    PRODUCTION FUNCTIONS - 12.07.01

    PRODUCTION GOODS - 11.02.05

    PRODUCTION INCREASE - 12.07.01

    PRODUCTION PLANNING - 12.07.01

    PRODUCTION SPECIALIZATION - 12.07.01

    PRODUCTION STANDARDS - 12.07.02

    PRODUCTION STATISTICS - 12.07.01

    PRODUCTION TARGETS - 12.07.02

    WOOD PRODUCTION - 07.08.06

PRODUCTIVITY

    LABOUR PRODUCTIVITY - 13.02.02

    PRODUCTIVITY - 12.07.03

    PRODUCTIVITY POLICY - 12.07.03

PRODUCTS

    AGRICULTURAL PRODUCTS - 07.05.05

    ANIMAL PRODUCTS - 07.09.05

    BAKERY PRODUCTS - 08.06.04

    BY-PRODUCTS - 12.08.01

    CHOICE OF PRODUCTS - 12.08.02

    COMPETITIVE PRODUCTS - 12.08.02

    DAIRY PRODUCTS - 07.09.05

    DAIRY PRODUCTS INDUSTRY
    - 08.06.01
     USE: DAIRY INDUSTRY

    FINISHED PRODUCTS - 08.04.00

PRODUCTS<CONT>

    FISHERY PRODUCTS - 07.10.04

    FOOD PRODUCTS
    - 15.03.01
     USE: FOOD

    FOREST PRODUCTS - 07.08.06

    INDUSTRIAL PRODUCTS - 08.04.00

    MANUFACTURED PRODUCTS - 08.04.00

    MEAT PRODUCTS - 07.09.05

    METAL PRODUCTS - 08.14.01

    MILK PRODUCTS
    - 07.09.05
     USE: DAIRY PRODUCTS

    NATURAL PRODUCTS - 12.08.01

    NEW PRODUCTS - 12.08.01

    PETROLEUM PRODUCTS - 08.11.06

    PLANT PRODUCTS - 07.07.03

    PRIMARY PRODUCTS
    - 12.08.01
     USE: COMMODITIES

    PRODUCTS - 12.08.01

    SEMI-MANUFACTURED PRODUCTS - 08.04.00

    SUBSTITUTE PRODUCTS - 12.08.01

    WOOD PRODUCTS - 08.07.01

PROFESSIONAL

    PROFESSIONAL ASSOCIATIONS
    - 13.06.00
     USE: OCCUPATIONAL ORGANIZATIONS

    PROFESSIONAL EDUCATION
    - 06.03.07
     USE: VOCATIONAL EDUCATION

PROFESSIONALS

    PROFESSIONALS - 13.09.03

PROFESSORS

    PROFESSORS
    - 13.09.09
     USE: TEACHERS

PROFILES

    INDUSTRIAL PROFILES - 08.03.00

PROFIT

    NON-PROFIT ORGANIZATIONS - 05.03.07

    PROFIT SHARING - 13.07.00

PROFITABILITY

    PROFITABILITY - 12.09.00

PROFITS

    PROFITS - 12.09.00

PROGRAMME

    PROGRAMME PLANNING - 12.04.00

    WORK PROGRAMME - 19.02.05

    WORLD EMPLOYMENT PROGRAMME - 01.03.02

PROGRAMME<CONT>
WORLD FOOD PROGRAMME - 01.03.02

PROGRAMMED
PROGRAMMED INSTRUCTION - 06.05.03
PROGRAMMED LEARNING
- 06.05.03
USE: PROGRAMMED INSTRUCTION

PROGRAMMES
AID PROGRAMMES - 01.01.04
COMPUTER PROGRAMMES - 08.15.02
FAMILY PLANNING PROGRAMMES - 14.05.02
FINANCING PROGRAMMES - 11.02.04
INSTRUCTIONAL PROGRAMMES
- 06.05.01
USE: TEACHING PROGRAMMES
RESEARCH PROGRAMMES - 18.01.00
TEACHING PROGRAMMES - 06.05.01
TRAINING PROGRAMMES - 06.05.01

PROGRAMMING
LINEAR PROGRAMMING - 12.04.00

PROGRESS
PROGRESS REPORT - 19.02.08
SCIENTIFIC PROGRESS - 18.01.00
SOCIAL PROGRESS
- 05.03.04
USE: SOCIAL DEVELOPMENT
TECHNICAL PROGRESS
- 12.06.00
USE: TECHNOLOGICAL CHANGE

PROJECT
PROJECT APPRAISAL - 01.01.06
PROJECT DESIGN - 01.01.06
PROJECT EVALUATION - 01.01.06
PROJECT IMPLEMENTATION - 01.01.06
PROJECT MANAGEMENT - 01.01.06
PROJECT PLANNING
- 01.01.06
USE: PROJECT DESIGN
PROJECT REPORT - 19.02.08
PROJECT REQUEST - 01.01.06
PROJECT SELECTION - 01.01.06

PROJECTION
PROJECTION EQUIPMENT - 08.15.02

PROJECTIONS
ECONOMIC PROJECTIONS - 03.01.02
PROJECTIONS - 18.10.00

PROJECTS
AGRICULTURAL PROJECTS - 07.01.02
DEVELOPMENT PROJECTS - 01.01.06

PROJECTS<CONT>
EDUCATIONAL PROJECTS - 06.02.03
INDUSTRIAL PROJECTS - 08.01.02
JOINT PROJECTS - 01.01.06
MULTIPURPOSE PROJECTS - 01.01.06
PILOT PROJECTS - 01.01.06
RESEARCH PROJECTS - 18.01.00

PROLETARIAN
PROLETARIAN INTERNATIONALISM - 01.02.01

PROLETARIAT
PROLETARIAT - 05.03.05

PROMOTION
EXPORT PROMOTION - 09.05.06
HANDICRAFT PROMOTION - 08.01.02
IMPORT PROMOTION - 09.05.06
INDUSTRIAL PROMOTION - 08.01.02
INVESTMENT PROMOTION - 11.02.06
PROMOTION - 13.02.02
SALES PROMOTION
- 09.03.01
USE: MARKETING
TRADE PROMOTION - 09.05.06

PROPAGANDA
PROPAGANDA - 04.04.02

PROPERTIES
PHYSICAL PROPERTIES - 18.06.00

PROPERTY
INDUSTRIAL PROPERTY - 08.05.00
INTELLECTUAL PROPERTY - 19.02.03

PROPHYLAXIS
PROPHYLAXIS - 15.04.04

PROSPECTS
CROP PROSPECTS - 07.05.01

PROSTITUTION
PROSTITUTION - 02.04.02

PROTECTED
PROTECTED AREAS - 16.05.01
PROTECTED RESOURCES - 16.05.01
PROTECTED SPECIES - 16.05.01

PROTECTION
ANIMAL PROTECTION - 16.05.01
CONSUMER PROTECTION - 09.01.03
DATA PROTECTION - 19.01.01
ENVIRONMENTAL PROTECTION - 16.05.01
GAME PROTECTION - 16.05.01
LANDSCAPE PROTECTION - 16.05.01
LEGAL PROTECTION - 04.01.01

PROTECTION<CONT>

NATURE PROTECTION
- 16.05.01
 USE: NATURE CONSERVATION
PLANT PROTECTION - 16.05.01
PRIVACY PROTECTION - 05.03.01
RADIATION PROTECTION - 16.04.01
SOCIAL PROTECTION
- 02.03.01
 USE: SOCIAL SECURITY
WILDLIFE PROTECTION
- 16.05.01
 USE: NATURE CONSERVATION

PROTECTIONISM

PROTECTIONISM - 09.05.07

PROTECTIONIST

PROTECTIONIST MEASURES - 09.05.07

PROTEIN

FISH PROTEIN CONCENTRATE - 08.06.04
PROTEIN DEFICIENCY - 15.03.02
PROTEIN RICH FOOD - 15.03.01

PROTEINS

PROTEINS - 15.01.03

PROTOTYPES

PROTOTYPES - 12.08.02

PSYCHIATRY

PSYCHIATRY - 15.04.06

PSYCHOLOGICAL

PSYCHOLOGICAL ASPECTS - 05.03.02

PSYCHOLOGISTS

PSYCHOLOGISTS - 13.09.09

PSYCHOLOGY

EDUCATIONAL PSYCHOLOGY
- 06.01.00
 USE: PSYCHOLOGY OF EDUCATION
INDUSTRIAL PSYCHOLOGY - 13.03.01
PSYCHOLOGY - 05.01.01
PSYCHOLOGY OF EDUCATION - 06.01.00
SOCIAL PSYCHOLOGY - 05.01.01

PUBERTY

PUBERTY - 15.02.02

PUBLIC

PUBLIC ACCOUNTING - 11.01.01
PUBLIC ADMINISTRATION - 04.03.02
PUBLIC BORROWING - 11.01.01
PUBLIC DEBT - 11.01.01
PUBLIC EDUCATION - 06.03.03
PUBLIC ENTERPRISES - 03.03.05
PUBLIC EXPENDITURES - 11.01.01
PUBLIC FINANCE - 11.01.01

PUBLIC<CONT>

PUBLIC HEALTH - 15.04.01
PUBLIC INVESTMENTS - 11.02.06
PUBLIC LAND - 07.02.00
PUBLIC LAW - 04.01.02
PUBLIC OPINION - 04.04.02
PUBLIC OWNERSHIP - 03.03.05
PUBLIC RELATIONS - 09.03.04
PUBLIC SECTOR - 03.03.05
PUBLIC SERVANTS - 13.09.04
PUBLIC SERVICES - 04.03.06
PUBLIC TRANSPORT - 10.01.00
PUBLIC UTILITIES
- 04.03.06
 USE: PUBLIC SERVICES
PUBLIC WORKS - 04.03.06

PUBLISHING

PUBLISHING - 08.16.00

PUERTO

PUERTO RICAN - 14.03.02
PUERTO RICO - 01.04.03

PULP

PULP - 08.07.02
PULP AND PAPER INDUSTRY - 08.07.02

PUMPING

PUMPING PLANTS - 17.05.04

PUMPS

PUMPS - 17.05.04

PUNCHED

PUNCHED CARDS - 19.01.04

PUNISHMENT

CAPITAL PUNISHMENT - 02.04.03

PUPILS

PUPILS
- 06.06.01
 USE: STUDENTS

PURCHASE

HIRE PURCHASE - 09.03.02

PURCHASING

PURCHASING - 09.03.02
PURCHASING POWER - 03.02.05

QATAR

QATAR - 01.04.06

QUALIFICATION

OCCUPATIONAL QUALIFICATION - 13.02.01

QUALIFICATIONS

QUALIFICATIONS - 06.04.13

QUALITY

ENVIRONMENTAL QUALITY ENVIRONMENTAL QUALITY
-
16.01.02
QUALITY CONTROL - 12.07.02
QUALITY OF EDUCATION - 06.02.03
QUALITY OF LIFE - 05.03.01
QUALITY STANDARDS - 12.07.02
WATER QUALITY - 17.05.05

QUARANTINE

QUARANTINE - 15.04.04

QUARRYING

QUARRYING - 08.10.01

QUARTERLY

QUARTERLY - 19.02.06

QUATERNARY

QUATERNARY - 17.04.02

QUESTIONNAIRES

QUESTIONNAIRES - 18.04.00

QUESTIONS

MARITIME QUESTIONS - 10.05.00

QUOTA

QUOTA SYSTEM - 09.05.07

QUOTIENT

INTELLIGENCE QUOTIENT - 06.05.04

RACE

ARMS RACE
- 01.02.06
USE: ARMAMENT
RACE RELATIONS - 04.02.04

RACIAL

RACIAL CONFLICTS - 04.02.04
RACIAL DISCRIMINATION - 04.02.04
RACIAL POLICY - 04.02.04
RACIAL SEGREGATION - 04.02.04

RACISM

RACISM - 04.02.04

RADAR

RADAR - 08.15.02

RADIATION

IONISING RADIATION - 08.11.04
RADIATION PROTECTION - 16.04.01
SOLAR RADIATION - 17.01.03

RADICALISM

RADICALISM - 04.04.02

RADDDDIO

EDUCATIONAL RADIO - 06.05.03
INSTRUCTIONAL RADIO
- 06.05.03
USE: EDUCATIONAL RADIO
RADIO - 05.07.03
RADIO RECEIVERS - 08.16.00

RADIOACTIVE

RADIOACTIVE MATERIALS - 08.11.04
RADIOACTIVE POLLUTION - 16.03.04
RADIOACTIVE WASTES - 08.11.04

RADIOACTIVITY

RADIOACTIVITY - 08.11.04

RADIOISOTOPES

RADIOISOTOPES - 08.11.04

RADIOLOGY

RADIOLOGY - 15.04.06

RAILWAY

RAILWAY NETWORK - 10.03.00
RAILWAY TRAFFIC - 10.08.00
RAILWAY TRANSPORT - 10.05.00

RAILWAYS

RAILWAYS - 10.03.00

RAIN

RAIN - 17.01.03

RAINY

RAINY SEASON - 17.02.02

RAPE

RAPE - 07.07.06

RATE

ACCUMULATION RATE - 03.01.02

RATE<CONT>
    BANK RATE - 11.02.07
    BIRTH RATE - 14.05.01
    EXCHANGE RATE - 11.03.01
    GROWTH RATE - 03.01.02
    INTEREST RATE - 11.02.07
    PASSENGER RATE - 10.09.00
    RATE OF INVESTMENT - 11.02.06
    WAGE RATE - 13.07.00

RATING
    AUDIENCE RATING - 05.07.02

RATIO
    CAPITAL-LABOUR RATIO - 12.07.03
    CAPITAL-OUTPUT RATIO - 12.07.03

RATIONALIZATION
    RATIONALIZATION - 12.04.00

RATIONING
    RATIONING - 03.02.05

RAW
    RAW MATERIALS - 12.08.01

REACTORS
    NUCLEAR REACTORS - 08.11.03

READING
    READING - 06.03.04

REARING
    CHILD REARING - 15.03.02

REASSIGNMENT
    REASSIGNMENT - 13.05.00

RECEIVERS
    RADIO RECEIVERS - 08.16.00
    TELEVISION RECEIVERS - 08.16.00

RECESSION
    ECONOMIC RECESSION - 03.02.04

RECLAMATION
    LAND RECLAMATION - 07.05.02

RECOMMENDATION
    RECOMMENDATION - 19.02.05

RECONSTRUCTION
    ECONOMIC RECONSTRUCTION - 03.02.03

RECORD
    RECORD INDUSTRY - 08.16.00

RECORDING
    DATA RECORDING - 19.01.02
    INFORMATION RECORDING - 19.01.02

RECOVERY
    ECONOMIC RECOVERY - 03.02.04
    RECOVERY - 12.07.02

RECRUITMENT
    RECRUITMENT - 13.02.01

RECRUITMENT<CONT>
    TEACHER RECRUITMENT - 06.06.02

RECURRENT
    RECURRENT EDUCATION - 06.03.05

RECYCLING
    WASTE RECYCLING - 16.04.02

REDISTRIBUTION
    INCOME REDISTRIBUTION - 03.02.05

REDUCTIONS
    TARIFF REDUCTIONS - 09.05.08

REDUNDANCY
    LABOUR REDUNDANCY - 13.05.00

REEXPORT
    REEXPORT - 09.05.05

REFERENCE
    REFERENCE MATERIALS - 19.02.07

REFINERIES
    PETROLEUM REFINERIES - 08.11.06

REFINING
    REFINING - 08.12.03

REFORESTATION
    REFORESTATION - 07.08.03

REFORM
    ECONOMIC REFORM - 02.01.03
    INTERNATIONAL MONETARY REFORM - 11.03.01
    SOCIAL REFORM - 02.02.01

REFORMS
    ADMINISTRATIVE REFORMS - 04.03.04
    AGRARIAN REFORMS - 07.02.00
    EDUCATIONAL REFORMS - 06.02.03
    LAND REFORMS - 07.02.00
    REFORMS OF EDUCATION
    - 06.02.03
      USE: EDUCATIONAL REFORMS
    TARIFF REFORMS - 09.05.08
    TAX REFORMS - 11.01.02

REFRACTORY
    REFRACTORY MATERIALS - 08.10.03

REFRIGERATION
    REFRIGERATION - 08.12.03

REFUGEES
    REFUGEES - 14.07.00

REGION
    ANDEAN REGION - 01.04.03
    PACIFIC REGION - 01.04.07

REGIONAL
    REGIONAL AGENCIES - 01.01.07
    REGIONAL ANALYSIS - 17.03.01
    REGIONAL COOPERATION - 01.01.01
    REGIONAL DEVELOPMENT - 03.02.03

REGIONAL<CONT>

    REGIONAL DISPARITY - 03.02.03

    REGIONAL GOVERNMENT - 04.03.03

    REGIONAL INTEGRATION - 01.02.01

    REGIONAL ORGANIZATIONS - 01.03.01

    REGIONAL PLANNING - 02.01.02

    REGIONAL PLANS - 02.01.02

    REGIONAL POLICY - 02.01.02

    REGIONAL SCIENCE
    - 17.03.01
     USE: REGIONAL ANALYSIS

REGIONALIZATION

    REGIONALIZATION - 02.01.02

REGIONS

    CLIMATIC REGIONS
    - 17.02.03
     USE: CLIMATIC ZONES

REGULATION

    STAFF REGULATION - 13.02.02

REGULATIONS

    REGULATIONS - 04.01.01

REHABILITATION

    REHABILITATION - 15.04.04

    VOCATIONAL REHABILITATION - 13.05.00

REINSURANCE

    REINSURANCE - 11.02.03

REINVESTMENTS

    REINVESTMENTS - 11.02.06

RELATED

    STRESS-RELATED DISEASES
    - 13.04.00
     USE: OCCUPATIONAL DISEASES

RELATIONS

    BILATERAL RELATIONS - 01.02.01

    COMMUNITY RELATIONS - 14.04.01

    CULTURAL RELATIONS - 05.02.02

    ECONOMIC RELATIONS - 01.02.01

    FOREIGN RELATIONS - 01.02.01

    HUMAN RELATIONS - 05.03.01

    INDUSTRIAL RELATIONS
    - 13.06.00
     USE: LABOUR RELATIONS

    INTERETHNIC RELATIONS - 14.03.01

    INTERGROUP RELATIONS - 05.03.06

    INTERNATIONAL RELATIONS - 01.02.01

    LABOUR RELATIONS - 13.06.00

    LABOUR-MANAGEMENT RELATIONS
    - 13.06.00
     USE: LABOUR RELATIONS

    MONETARY RELATIONS - 11.03.01

RELATIONS<CONT>

    MULTILATERAL RELATIONS - 01.02.01

    PUBLIC RELATIONS - 09.03.04

    RACE RELATIONS - 04.02.04

    TRADE RELATIONS - 09.05.02

RELATIONSHIPS

    SCHOOL-COMMUNITY RELATIONSHIPS - 06.04.12

    TEACHER-STUDENT RELATIONSHIPS - 06.06.02

RELEASE

    PRESS RELEASE - 19.02.06

RELIANCE

    SELF-RELIANCE - 02.01.01

RELIEF

    DEBT RELIEF - 11.02.02

    EMERGENCY RELIEF - 02.05.03

RELIGION

    RELIGION - 05.04.02

RELIGIOUS

    AID BY RELIGIOUS BODIES
    - 01.01.02
     USE: PRIVATE AID

    RELIGIOUS FREEDOM - 04.02.02

    RELIGIOUS GROUPS - 05.04.02

    RELIGIOUS INSTITUTIONS - 05.04.04

    RELIGIOUS MINORITIES - 05.04.02

    RELIGIOUS MISSIONS - 05.04.04

    RELIGIOUS PRACTICE - 05.04.02

REMEDIAL

    REMEDIAL TEACHING - 06.05.02

REMOTE

    REMOTE SENSING - 18.04.00

RENEWABLE

    NON-RENEWABLE RESOURCES - 16.02.02

    RENEWABLE RESOURCES - 16.02.02

RENEWAL

    URBAN RENEWAL - 14.04.03

RENT

    LAND RENT - 07.03.03

    RENT
    - 11.02.07
     USE: INVESTMENT RETURNS

REPAIR

    MAINTENANCE AND REPAIR - 12.05.00

    REPAIR SHOPS - 08.03.00

REPATRIATION

    REPATRIATION OF CAPITAL - 11.03.03

REPAYMENT

    DEBT REPAYMENT - 11.02.02

REPORT

    ANNUAL REPORT - 19.02.08

REPORT<CONT>

CONFERENCE REPORT - 19.02.08
CONSULTANT REPORT - 19.02.08
EXPERT REPORT - 19.02.08
MEETING REPORT
- 19.02.08
  USE: CONFERENCE REPORT
MISSION REPORT - 19.02.08
PROGRESS REPORT - 19.02.08
PROJECT REPORT - 19.02.08
RESEARCH REPORT - 19.02.08
TECHNICAL REPORT - 19.02.08

REPORTING

REPORTING SYSTEMS - 19.01.02

REPRESENTATION

WORKERS REPRESENTATION - 13.06.00

REPROCESSING

REPROCESSING - 12.07.02

REPRODUCTION

REPRODUCTION - 15.02.02

REPTILES

REPTILES - 07.09.01

REPUBLIC

DOMINICAN REPUBLIC - 01.04.03
YEMEN ARAB REPUBLIC
- 01.04.06
  USE: YEMEN

REPUBLICS

UNION OF SOVIET SOCIALIST REPUBLICS
- 01.04.05
  USE: USSR

REQUEST

PROJECT REQUEST - 01.01.06

REQUIREMENTS

ADMISSION REQUIREMENTS - 06.04.09
ENERGY REQUIREMENTS
- 08.11.01
  USE: POWER DEMAND
FOOD REQUIREMENTS - 15.03.02
INVESTMENT REQUIREMENTS - 11.02.06
JOB REQUIREMENTS - 13.02.01
LABOUR REQUIREMENTS
- 13.01.02
  USE: MANPOWER NEEDS
WATER REQUIREMENTS - 17.05.05

RESEARCH

AGRICULTURAL RESEARCH - 07.06.00
APPLIED RESEARCH - 18.01.00
BASIC RESEARCH - 18.01.00
COMMUNICATION RESEARCH - 05.07.01

RESEARCH<CONT>

DEVELOPMENT RESEARCH - 02.01.01
ECOLOGICAL RESEARCH - 16.01.01
ECONOMIC RESEARCH - 03.01.02
EDUCATIONAL RESEARCH - 06.01.00
FIELD RESEARCH - 18.04.00
FISHERY RESEARCH - 07.10.01
FORESTRY RESEARCH - 07.08.02
INDUSTRIAL RESEARCH - 08.05.00
INTERCULTURAL RESEARCH
- 05.01.02
  USE: CROSS CULTURAL ANALYSIS
INTERDISCIPLINARY RESEARCH - 18.03.00
MEDICAL RESEARCH - 15.04.06
NUTRITION RESEARCH - 15.03.02
OPERATIONAL RESEARCH - 12.04.00
ORGANIZATION OF RESEARCH - 18.02.00
PEACE RESEARCH - 01.02.07
RESEARCH - 18.01.00
RESEARCH AND DEVELOPMENT - 18.01.00
RESEARCH CENTRES - 18.02.00
RESEARCH EQUIPMENT - 18.02.00
RESEARCH FELLOWSHIPS - 06.04.11
RESEARCH INSTITUTES
- 18.02.00
  USE: RESEARCH CENTRES
RESEARCH METHODS - 18.03.00
RESEARCH POLICY - 18.01.00
RESEARCH PROGRAMMES - 18.01.00
RESEARCH PROJECTS - 18.01.00
RESEARCH REPORT - 19.02.08
RESEARCH RESULTS - 18.03.00
RESEARCH WORKERS - 13.09.09
SCIENTIFIC RESEARCH
- 18.01.00
  USE: RESEARCH
SOCIAL RESEARCH - 05.01.02

RESEARCHERS

SCIENTIFIC RESEARCHERS
- 13.09.09
  USE: RESEARCH WORKERS

RESERVATION

NATIVE RESERVATION - 14.03.01

RESERVE

FOREIGN EXCHANGE RESERVE - 11.03.01

RESERVES

FOOD RESERVES - 15.03.01

REVIEW
    BOOK REVIEW - 19.02.07

REVOLUTION
    GREEN REVOLUTION - 07.01.02
    REVOLUTION - 05.03.04

RHODESIA
    RHODESIA - 01.04.02

RICA
    COSTA RICA - 01.04.03

RICAN
    COSTA RICAN - 14.03.02
    PUERTO RICAN - 14.03.02

RICE
    RICE - 07.07.04

RICH
    PROTEIN RICH FOOD - 15.03.01

RICKETTSIAL
    RICKETTSIAL DISEASES - 15.04.02

RICO
    PUERTO RICO - 01.04.03

RIGHT
    RIGHT TO CULTURE - 05.02.03
    RIGHT TO EDUCATION - 06.02.02
    RIGHT TO STRIKE - 13.06.00
    RIGHT TO WORK - 13.02.01

RIGHTS
    CIVIL RIGHTS - 04.02.01
    FISHING RIGHTS - 07.10.02
    HUMAN RIGHTS - 04.02.01
    SPECIAL DRAWING RIGHTS - 11.03.01
    WOMEN'S RIGHTS - 04.02.01

RIVER
    RIVER BASINS - 17.05.02
    RIVER BLINDNESS
    - 15.04.02
      USE: ONCHOCERCIASIS
    RIVER POLLUTION - 16.03.04

RIVERS
    RIVERS - 17.05.02

ROAD
    ROAD CONSTRUCTION - 10.03.00
    ROAD NETWORK - 10.03.00
    ROAD SAFETY - 10.08.00
    ROAD TRAFFIC - 10.08.00
    ROAD TRANSPORT - 10.05.00

ROADS
    ROADS - 10.03.00

RODENTS
    RODENTS - 16.03.03

ROLE
    SOCIAL ROLE - 05.03.03

ROLLING
    ROLLING - 08.14.03
    ROLLING STOCK - 10.04.00

ROMANIA
    ROMANIA - 01.04.05

ROMANIAN
    ROMANIAN - 14.03.02

ROOT
    ROOT CROPS - 07.07.02

ROPE
    ROPE INDUSTRY - 08.08.01

ROTATION
    CROP ROTATION - 07.05.04
    JOB ROTATION
    - 13.05.00
      USE: REASSIGNMENT

ROYALTIES
    ROYALTIES - 11.02.07

RUBBER
    RUBBER - 08.09.00
    RUBBER INDUSTRY - 08.09.00
    SYNTHETIC RUBBER - 08.09.00

RUBELLA
    RUBELLA - 15.04.02

RULES
    WORK RULES - 13.03.01

RULING
    RULING CLASS - 05.03.05

RUMINANTS
    RUMINANTS - 07.09.01

RURAL
    RURAL - 14.04.02
    RURAL AREAS - 14.04.02
    RURAL COMMUNITIES - 14.04.02
    RURAL DEVELOPMENT - 14.04.02
    RURAL ENVIRONMENT - 14.04.02
    RURAL EXODUS
    - 14.07.00
      USE: RURAL MIGRATIONS
    RURAL INDUSTRY - 08.02.02
    RURAL MIGRATIONS - 14.07.00
    RURAL PLANNING - 14.04.02
    RURAL POPULATION - 14.04.02
    RURAL SCHOOLS - 06.04.04
    RURAL SOCIOLOGY - 14.04.02
    RURAL WORKERS - 13.09.05
    RURAL YOUTH - 14.04.02

RUSSIAN

    RUSSIAN - 14.03.02

    RUSSIAN LANGUAGE - 05.06.02

RWANDA

    RWANDA - 01.04.02

RWANDESE

    RWANDESE - 14.03.02

RYE

    RYE - 07.07.04

SAFETY

    OCCUPATIONAL SAFETY - 13.04.00

    ROAD SAFETY - 10.08.00

    SAFETY - 16.04.01

    SAFETY DEVICES - 13.04.00

    SAFETY EDUCATION - 06.03.04

SAHARA

    AFRICA SOUTH OF SAHARA - 01.04.02

    SAHARA - 01.04.02

SAHEL

    SAHEL - 01.04.02

SALARY

    SALARY
    - 13.07.00
     USE: WAGES

SALES

    SALES - 09.03.02

    SALES PROMOTION
    - 09.03.01
     USE: MARKETING

    SALES TAX
    - 11.01.02
     USE: CONSUMPTION TAX

SALESMEN

    SALESMEN
    - 13.09.07
     USE: VENDORS

SALT

    SALT - 08.12.04

    SALT WATER - 17.05.05

    SALT WATER FISH - 07.10.04

SALVADOR

    EL SALVADOR - 01.04.03

SALVADORIAN

    SALVADORIAN - 14.03.02

SAMOA

    SAMOA - 01.04.07

SAMOAN

    SAMOAN - 14.03.02

SAMPLE

    SAMPLE - 18.04.00

SAN

    SAN MARINO - 01.04.05

SANCTIONS

    PENAL SANCTIONS - 02.04.03

SAND

    SAND - 08.10.02

SANDWICH

    SANDWICH TRAINING - 06.03.07

SANITATION

    SANITATION - 16.04.02

    SANITATION SERVICES - 16.04.02

SAO
    SAO TOME AND PRINCIPE - 01.04.02

SATELLITE
    SATELLITE TOWNS - 14.04.03

SATELLITES
    COMMUNICATION SATELLITES - 08.16.00

SATISFACTION
    JOB SATISFACTION - 13.03.04
    OCCUPATIONAL SATISFACTION
    - 13.03.04
      USE: JOB SATISFACTION

SAUDI
    SAUDI ARABIA - 01.04.06
    SAUDI ARABIAN - 14.03.02

SAVANNA
    SAVANNA - 17.03.04

SAVINGS
    SAVINGS - 11.02.05
    SAVINGS BANKS - 11.02.02

SCALE
    ECONOMY OF SCALE - 12.09.00
    MEDIUM-SCALE INDUSTRY - 08.02.02
    SMALL-SCALE INDUSTRY - 08.02.02
    WAGE SCALE - 13.07.00

SCANDINAVIA
    SCANDINAVIA - 01.04.05

SCANDINAVIAN
    SCANDINAVIAN - 14.03.02

SCARLET
    SCARLET FEVER - 15.04.02

SCENARIOS
    SCENARIOS - 02.01.01

SCHEMES
    PENSION SCHEMES - 02.03.02

SCHISTOSOMIASIS
    SCHISTOSOMIASIS - 15.04.02

SCHOLARSHIP
    SCHOLARSHIP HOLDERS - 06.06.01

SCHOLARSHIPS
    SCHOLARSHIPS - 06.04.11

SCHOOL
    LEAVING SCHOOL - 06.04.12
    OUT-OF-SCHOOL EDUCATION - 06.03.02
    SCHOOL ADAPTATION - 06.04.12
    SCHOOL AGE POPULATION - 14.02.02
    SCHOOL BUILDINGS - 06.04.07
    SCHOOL DISCIPLINE - 06.04.08
    SCHOOL ENVIRONMENT - 06.04.12
    SCHOOL HOLIDAYS - 06.04.12

SCHOOL<CONT>
    SCHOOL LEAVERS - 06.06.01
    SCHOOL MANAGEMENT - 06.04.08
    SCHOOL SEGREGATION - 06.04.12
    SCHOOL SYSTEMS
    - 06.03.01
      USE: EDUCATIONAL SYSTEMS
    SCHOOL TRANSPORT - 06.04.07
    SCHOOL-COMMUNITY RELATIONSHIPS - 06.04.12
    TRANSITION FROM SCHOOL TO WORK - 06.03.07

SCHOOLING
    DE-SCHOOLING - 06.03.02
    SCHOOLING - 06.03.02

SCHOOLS
    BOARDING SCHOOLS - 06.04.03
    COEDUCATIONAL SCHOOLS - 06.04.03
    COMMERCIAL SCHOOLS - 06.04.06
    COMPREHENSIVE SCHOOLS - 06.04.03
    ELEMENTARY SCHOOLS
    - 06.04.02
      USE: PRIMARY SCHOOLS
    EXPERIMENTAL SCHOOLS - 06.04.03
    INTERNATIONAL SCHOOLS - 06.04.04
    MOBILE SCHOOLS - 06.04.03
    NIGHT SCHOOLS - 06.04.03
    NURSERY SCHOOLS - 06.04.02
    POST-SECONDARY SCHOOLS
    - 06.04.05
      USE: HIGHER EDUCATION INSTITUTIONS
    PRIMARY SCHOOLS - 06.04.02
    PRIVATE SCHOOLS - 06.04.04
    RURAL SCHOOLS - 06.04.04
    SCHOOLS - 06.04.02
    SECONDARY SCHOOLS - 06.04.02
    SPECIAL SCHOOLS - 06.04.03
    SUMMER SCHOOLS - 06.04.03
    TECHNICAL SCHOOLS - 06.04.06
    VOCATIONAL SCHOOLS - 06.04.06

SCIENCE
    COMPUTER SCIENCE - 18.08.00
    FOOD SCIENCE - 08.06.02
    LIBRARY SCIENCE - 19.01.01
    POLITICAL SCIENCE - 04.04.01
    REGIONAL SCIENCE
    • 17.03.01
      USE: REGIONAL ANALYSIS

SCIENCE<CONT>

SCIENCE - 18.01.00

SCIENCE AND TECHNOLOGY POLICY
- 18.01.00
USE: SCIENCE POLICY

SCIENCE POLICY - 18.01.00

SCIENCES

ATMOSPHERIC SCIENCES
- 17.01.01
USE: METEOROLOGY

BEHAVIOURAL SCIENCES - 05.01.01

EARTH SCIENCES - 17.04.01

EDUCATIONAL SCIENCES
- 06.01.00
USE: SCIENCES OF EDUCATION

INFORMATION SCIENCES - 19.01.01

LEGAL SCIENCES - 04.01.01

MEDICAL SCIENCES - 15.04.06

NATURAL SCIENCES - 17.04.01

SCIENCES OF EDUCATION - 06.01.00

SOCIAL SCIENCES - 05.01.01

SOIL SCIENCES - 17.04.04

SPACE SCIENCES - 17.07.00

SCIENTIFIC

SCIENTIFIC COOPERATION - 18.01.00

SCIENTIFIC CULTURE - 05.02.01

SCIENTIFIC DISCOVERIES - 12.06.00

SCIENTIFIC INFORMATION - 19.01.01

SCIENTIFIC MANAGEMENT - 12.04.00

SCIENTIFIC PERSONNEL - 13.09.03

SCIENTIFIC PROGRESS - 18.01.00

SCIENTIFIC RESEARCH
- 18.01.00
USE: RESEARCH

SCIENTIFIC RESEARCHERS
- 13.09.09
USE: RESEARCH WORKERS

SCIENTISTS

POLITICAL SCIENTISTS - 13.09.09

SCIENTISTS - 13.09.09

SCRAPS

METAL SCRAPS - 08.14.04

SDI

SDI - 19.01.02

SEA

DEEP SEA FISHING - 07.10.03

DEEP SEA MINING - 08.13.00

LAW OF THE SEA - 01.02.04

SEA<CONT>

SEA - 17.06.00

SEA DUMPING - 16.04.02

SEA TRAFFIC - 10.08.00

SEA TRANSPORT - 10.05.00

SEABED

SEABED - 17.06.00

SEAFARERS

SEAFARERS - 13.09.08

SEARCHING

JOB SEARCHING - 13.02.01

SEASON

COLD SEASON - 17.02.02

DRY SEASON - 17.02.02

RAINY SEASON - 17.02.02

WARM SEASON - 17.02.02

SEASONAL

SEASONAL FLUCTUATIONS - 03.02.04

SEASONAL MIGRATIONS - 14.07.00

SEASONAL UNEMPLOYMENT - 13.01.03

SEASONAL WORKERS - 13.09.02

SEASONS

SEASONS - 17.02.02

SEATO

SEATO - 01.03.03

SEAWEEDS

SEAWEEDS
- 07.10.04
USE: ALGAE

SECOND

SECOND DEVELOPMENT DECADE - 01.01.01

SECOND HAND EQUIPMENT - 12.05.00

SECONDARY

POST-SECONDARY EDUCATION - 06.03.06

POST-SECONDARY SCHOOLS
- 06.04.05
USE: HIGHER EDUCATION INSTITUTIONS

SECONDARY DOCUMENTS - 19.02.01

SECONDARY EDUCATION - 06.03.06

SECONDARY SCHOOLS - 06.04.02

SECONDARY SECTOR
- 08.01.01
USE: INDUSTRIAL SECTOR

SECRETARIAT

UN SECRETARIAT - 01.03.02

SECTOR

AGRICULTURAL SECTOR - 07.01.01

INDUSTRIAL SECTOR - 08.01.01

INFORMAL SECTOR - 08.02.02

SECTOR<CONT>
>   PRIMARY SECTOR - 07.01.01
>   PRIVATE SECTOR - 03.03.05
>   PUBLIC SECTOR - 03.03.05
>   SECONDARY SECTOR
>   - 08.01.01
>   *USE:* INDUSTRIAL SECTOR
>   SECTOR ANALYSIS
>   - 03.02.02
>   *USE:* INPUT-OUTPUT ANALYSIS
>   TERTIARY SECTOR
>   - 09.01.01
>   *USE:* SERVICE INDUSTRY

SECTORAL
>   SECTORAL PLANNING - 02.01.02

SECULARIZATION
>   SECULARIZATION - 05.04.04

SECURITIES
>   SECURITIES - 11.02.07

SECURITY
>   EMPLOYMENT SECURITY - 13.01.03
>   SOCIAL SECURITY - 02.03.01
>   UN SECURITY COUNCIL - 01.03.02

SEE
>   HOLY SEE
>   - 01.04.05
>   *USE:* VATICAN

SEEDS
>   SEEDS - 07.07.01

SEEKERS
>   JOB SEEKERS - 13.02.01

SEGREGATION
>   RACIAL SEGREGATION - 04.02.04
>   SCHOOL SEGREGATION - 06.04.12

SEISMOLOGY
>   SEISMOLOGY - 17.04.03

SEISMS
>   SEISMS - 17.04.03

SELECTION
>   EDUCATIONAL SELECTION - 06.04.09
>   PROJECT SELECTION - 01.01.06

SELF
>   SELF-DETERMINATION - 01.02.03
>   SELF-EMPLOYED - 13.09.02
>   SELF-FINANCING - 11.02.05
>   SELF-HELP - 14.04.01
>   SELF-INSTRUCTION - 06.05.02
>   SELF-MANAGEMENT - 12.04.00
>   SELF-RELIANCE - 02.01.01
>   WORKERS SELF-MANAGEMENT - 13.06.00

SELLING
>   SELLING
>   - 09.03.01
>   *USE:* MARKETING

SEMEN
>   SEMEN - 15.02.02

SEMI
>   SEMI-ARID ZONE - 17.02.03
>   SEMI-MANUFACTURED PRODUCTS - 08.04.00
>   SEMI-SKILLED WORKERS - 13.09.03

SEMINAR
>   SEMINAR - 19.04.00

SENEGAL
>   SENEGAL - 01.04.02

SENEGALESE
>   SENEGALESE - 14.03.02

SENIORITY
>   SENIORITY BENEFITS - 13.07.00

SENSING
>   REMOTE SENSING - 18.04.00

SEPTICEMIA
>   SEPTICEMIA - 15.04.02

SERIALS
>   SERIALS - 19.02.06

SERUMS
>   SERUMS - 15.05.00

SERVANTS
>   CIVIL SERVANTS - 13.09.04
>   PUBLIC SERVANTS - 13.09.04

SERVICE
>   AUTOMOBILE SERVICE - 10.03.00
>   CIVIC SERVICE - 04.03.06
>   CIVIL SERVICE - 04.03.04
>   FOREIGN SERVICE - 01.02.05
>   MILITARY SERVICE - 01.02.06
>   SERVICE CERTIFICATE - 13.02.01
>   SERVICE INDUSTRY - 09.01.01

SERVICES
>   EMPLOYMENT SERVICES - 13.02.01
>   EXTENSION SERVICES - 19.01.03
>   HEALTH SERVICES - 02.05.02
>   INFORMATION SERVICES - 19.01.03
>   MANPOWER SERVICES
>   - 13.02.01
>   *USE:* EMPLOYMENT SERVICES
>   METEOROLOGY SERVICES - 17.01.01
>   PLACEMENT SERVICES
>   - 13.02.01
>   *USE:* EMPLOYMENT SERVICES
>   POSTAL SERVICES - 08.16.00

SERVICES<CONT>
    PUBLIC SERVICES - 04.03.06
    SANITATION SERVICES - 16.04.02
    SOCIAL SERVICES - 02.05.01
    STATISTICAL SERVICES - 18.02.00
    TRANSLATION SERVICES - 19.01.03
    VOLUNTARY SERVICES - 01.01.08

SETTLEMENT
    DISPUTE SETTLEMENT - 05.03.06
    LAND SETTLEMENT - 14.04.02
    SETTLEMENT PATTERN
    - 14.04.01
     USE: HABITAT

SETTLEMENTS
    HUMAN SETTLEMENTS - 14.04.01

SEVERANCE
    SEVERANCE PAY - 13.07.00

SEWAGE
    SEWAGE
    - 16.03.04
     USE: WASTE WATERS
    SEWAGE DISPOSAL
    - 16.04.02
     USE: SANITATION SERVICES

SEX
    AGE-SEX DISTRIBUTION - 14.02.01
    SEX - 14.02.03
    SEX DISTRIBUTION - 14.02.03
    SEX EDUCATION - 06.03.04

SEXUAL
    SEXUAL BEHAVIOUR - 14.02.03

SEXUALITY
    SEXUALITY - 14.02.03

SEYCHELLES
    SEYCHELLES - 01.04.02

SHALE
    SHALE OIL - 08.11.06

SHARE
    SHARE FARMERS
    - 07.02.00
     USE: TENANT FARMERS

SHAREHOLDERS
    SHAREHOLDERS - 11.02.07

SHARES
    SHARES - 11.02.07

SHARING
    PROFIT SHARING - 13.07.00

SHEEP
    SHEEP - 07.09.01

SHEEPMEAT
    SHEEPMEAT
    - 07.09.05
     USE: MUTTON

SHEET
    SHEET-METAL WORKING - 08.14.01

SHEETS
    METAL SHEETS - 08.14.04

SHELVES
    CONTINENTAL SHELVES - 17.03.04

SHIFT
    SHIFT WORK - 13.03.03

SHIFTING
    SHIFTING CULTIVATION - 07.05.04

SHINTOISM
    SHINTOISM - 05.04.03

SHIPBUILDING
    SHIPBUILDING - 08.14.07

SHIPOWNERS
    SHIPOWNERS - 10.05.00

SHIPPING
    SHIPPING
    - 10.05.00
     USE: SEA TRANSPORT

SHIPS
    CARGO SHIPS - 10.04.00
    SHIPS - 10.04.00

SHOE
    SHOE INDUSTRY - 08.08.02

SHOP
    SHOP STEWARDS - 13.06.00

SHOPS
    REPAIR SHOPS - 08.03.00
    SHOPS - 09.04.04

SHORT
    SHORT TERM - 18.10.00

SHORTAGE
    FOOD SHORTAGE - 15.03.01
    LABOUR SHORTAGE - 13.01.02
    TEACHER SHORTAGE - 06.06.02

SHRIMPS
    SHRIMPS - 07.10.04

SHUTDOWN
    PLANT SHUTDOWN - 13.05.00

SICKNESS
    SICKNESS INSURANCE
    - 02.03.02
     USE: HEALTH INSURANCE
    SLEEPING SICKNESS
    - 15.04.02
     USE: TRYPANOSOMIASIS

SID
    SID - 01.03.04

SIECA
    SIECA - 01.03.03

SIERRA
    SIERRA LEONE - 01.04.02

SIERRA<CONT>
    SIERRA LEONEAN - 14.03.02

SIKKIM
    SIKKIM - 01.04.04

SILICON
    SILICON - 08.12.04

SILK
    SILK - 07.09.05

SILKWORMS
    SILKWORMS - 07.09.01

SILOS
    SILOS - 07.04.00

SILVER
    SILVER - 08.14.02

SILVICULTURE
    SILVICULTURE - 07.08.01

SIMULATION
    SIMULATION - 18.08.00

SINGAPORE
    SINGAPORE - 01.04.04

SINGAPOREAN
    SINGAPOREAN - 14.03.02

SISAL
    SISAL - 07.07.07

SITES
    ARCHAEOLOGICAL SITES - 05.05.01

SITUATION
    ECONOMIC SITUATION
    - 03.02.01
      USE: ECONOMIC CONDITIONS

SIZE
    FAMILY SIZE - 14.02.04
    FARM SIZE - 07.03.02
    POPULATION SIZE - 14.01.02
    SIZE OF ENTERPRISE - 12.02.00

SIZED
    MIDDLE-SIZED TOWNS - 14.04.03

SKILLED
    SEMI-SKILLED WORKERS - 13.09.03
    SKILLED WORKERS - 13.09.03

SKIN
    SKIN - 15.02.04

SKINS
    HIDES AND SKINS - 08.08.02

SLAUGHTERHOUSES
    SLAUGHTERHOUSES - 07.09.04

SLAUGHTERING
    SLAUGHTERING - 07.09.04

SLAVERY
    SLAVERY - 05.03.05

SLEEPING
    SLEEPING SICKNESS
    - 15.04.02
      USE: TRYPANOSOMIASIS

SLIDES
    SLIDES - 19.02.04

SLUMS
    SLUMS - 14.04.03

SMALL
    SMALL ENTERPRISES - 12.01.00
    SMALL GAME - 07.09.01
    SMALL TOWNS - 14.04.03
    SMALL-SCALE INDUSTRY - 08.02.02

SMALLPOX
    SMALLPOX - 15.04.02

SNOW
    SNOW - 17.01.03

SOAP
    SOAP - 08.12.08

SOCIAL
    ECONOMIC AND SOCIAL DEVELOPMENT - 02.01.01
    SOCIAL ADAPTATION - 05.03.03
    SOCIAL ADMINISTRATION - 04.03.02
    SOCIAL ASPECTS - 05.03.04
    SOCIAL ASSIMILATION
    - 05.03.03
      USE: SOCIAL INTEGRATION
    SOCIAL ASSISTANCE
    - 02.05.01
      USE: SOCIAL SERVICES
    SOCIAL BEHAVIOUR - 05.03.03
    SOCIAL CHANGE - 05.03.04
    SOCIAL CLASSES - 05.03.05
    SOCIAL CONDITIONS - 05.03.04
    SOCIAL CONFLICTS - 05.03.06
    SOCIAL CONSEQUENCES
    - 05.03.04
      USE: SOCIAL IMPLICATIONS
    SOCIAL CONTROL - 05.03.04
    SOCIAL COSTS - 02.02.01
    SOCIAL DEVELOPMENT - 05.03.04
    SOCIAL ENVIRONMENT - 05.03.03
    SOCIAL HISTORY - 05.01.01
    SOCIAL IMPLICATIONS - 05.03.04
    SOCIAL INDICATORS - 05.01.02
    SOCIAL INEQUALITY - 05.03.05
    SOCIAL INFLUENCE - 05.03.03
    SOCIAL INFORMATION - 05.01.02
    SOCIAL INSURANCE
    - 02.03.01
      USE: SOCIAL SECURITY

SOCIAL<CONT>

SOCIAL INTEGRATION - 05.03.03
SOCIAL JUSTICE - 02.02.01
SOCIAL LEGISLATION - 02.02.01
SOCIAL MOBILITY - 05.03.05
SOCIAL MOVEMENTS - 05.03.07
SOCIAL NORMS - 05.04.01
SOCIAL PARTICIPATION - 05.03.03
SOCIAL PLANNING - 02.02.01
SOCIAL POLICY - 02.02.01
SOCIAL PROBLEMS - 02.04.01
SOCIAL PROGRESS
- 05.03.04
  USE: SOCIAL DEVELOPMENT
SOCIAL PROTECTION
- 02.03.01
  USE: SOCIAL SECURITY
SOCIAL PSYCHOLOGY - 05.01.01
SOCIAL REFORM - 02.02.01
SOCIAL RESEARCH - 05.01.02
SOCIAL ROLE - 05.03.03
SOCIAL SCIENCES - 05.01.01
SOCIAL SECURITY - 02.03.01
SOCIAL SERVICES - 02.05.01
SOCIAL STATUS - 05.03.05
SOCIAL STRATIFICATION - 05.03.05
SOCIAL STRUCTURE - 05.03.04
SOCIAL SURVEYS - 05.01.02
SOCIAL SYSTEM - 05.03.01
SOCIAL THEORY - 02.02.02
SOCIAL WORK - 02.05.01
SOCIAL WORKERS - 13.09.10

SOCIALISM

SOCIALISM - 03.03.01

SOCIALIST

SOCIALIST - 03.03.01
SOCIALIST COUNTRIES - 03.03.03
SOCIALIST ENTERPRISES - 12.01.00
UNION OF SOVIET SOCIALIST REPUBLICS
- 01.04.05
  USE: USSR

SOCIALIZATION

SOCIALIZATION - 05.03.03

SOCIETY

AFFLUENT SOCIETY - 03.02.05

SOCIETY<CONT>

SOCIETY - 05.03.01

SOCIO

SOCIO-CULTURAL FACILITIES - 05.02.03

SOCIOLOGICAL

SOCIOLOGICAL ANALYSIS - 05.01.02

SOCIOLOGISTS

SOCIOLOGISTS - 13.09.09

SOCIOLOGY

EDUCATIONAL SOCIOLOGY
- 06.01.00
  USE: SOCIOLOGY OF EDUCATION
INDUSTRIAL SOCIOLOGY - 13.03.01
RURAL SOCIOLOGY - 14.04.02
SOCIOLOGY - 05.01.01
SOCIOLOGY OF EDUCATION - 06.01.00
URBAN SOCIOLOGY - 14.04.03

SODA

CAUSTIC SODA - 08.12.04
SODA - 08.12.04

SODIUM

SODIUM - 08.12.04

SOFT

SOFT FIBRES - 08.08.01

SOFTWARE

SOFTWARE
- 08.15.02
  USE: COMPUTER PROGRAMMES

SOIL

SOIL ANALYSIS - 17.04.04
SOIL CHEMISTRY - 17.04.04
SOIL CLASSIFICATION - 17.04.04
SOIL CONSERVATION - 16.05.01
SOIL CULTIVATION
- 07.05.02
  USE: SOIL MANAGEMENT
SOIL EROSION - 16.03.02
SOIL FERTILITY - 07.05.02
SOIL IMPROVEMENT - 07.05.02
SOIL MANAGEMENT - 07.05.02
SOIL MAPS - 18.07.00
SOIL PHYSICS - 17.04.04
SOIL POLLUTANTS - 16.03.04
SOIL POLLUTION - 16.03.04
SOIL RESOURCES - 16.02.02
SOIL SCIENCES - 17.04.04
SOIL SURVEYS - 17.04.04
SOIL TYPES - 17.04.04

SOILS
> SOILS - 17.04.04

SOLAR
> SOLAR ENERGY - 08.11.01
> SOLAR RADIATION - 17.01.03

SOLVENTS
> SOLVENTS - 08.12.08

SOMALI
> SOMALI - 14.03.02

SOMALIA
> SOMALIA - 01.04.02

SORGHUM
> SORGHUM - 07.07.04

SOURCES
> ENERGY SOURCES - 08.11.01
> INFORMATION SOURCES - 19.01.01
> POLLUTION SOURCES - 16.03.04

SOUTH
> AFRICA SOUTH OF SAHARA - 01.04.02
> KOREA SOUTH
> - 01.04.04
> > *USE:* KOREA R
> SOUTH - 17.03.03
> SOUTH AFRICA - 01.04.02
> SOUTH AFRICAN - 14.03.02
> SOUTH AMERICA - 01.04.03
> SOUTH ASIA - 01.04.04
> SOUTH EAST ASIA - 01.04.04
> SOUTH WEST AFRICA
> - 01.04.02
> > *USE:* NAMIBIA
> SOUTH YEMEN
> - 01.04.06
> > *USE:* YEMEN PDR

SOUTHERN
> SOUTHERN AFRICA - 01.04.02
> SOUTHERN CONE - 01.04.03
> SOUTHERN HEMISPHERE - 01.04.01

SOVIET
> SOVIET - 14.03.02
> UNION OF SOVIET SOCIALIST REPUBLICS
> - 01.04.05
> > *USE:* USSR

SOWING
> SOWING - 07.05.04

SOYBEANS
> SOYBEANS - 07.07.06

SPACE
> EUROPEAN SPACE AGENCY - 01.03.03
> OUTER SPACE - 17.07.00

SPACE<CONT>
> SPACE - 17.07.00
> SPACE SCIENCES - 17.07.00

SPACING
> BIRTH SPACING - 14.05.02

SPAIN
> SPAIN - 01.04.05

SPANISH
> SPANISH - 14.03.02
> SPANISH LANGUAGE - 05.06.02

SPARE
> SPARE PARTS - 12.05.00

SPATIAL
> SPATIAL ANALYSIS - 17.03.01

SPC
> SPC - 01.03.03

SPEAKING
> ENGLISH SPEAKING AFRICA - 01.04.02
> FRENCH SPEAKING AFRICA - 01.04.02

SPECIAL
> SPECIAL DRAWING RIGHTS - 11.03.01
> SPECIAL EDUCATION - 06.03.03
> SPECIAL SCHOOLS - 06.04.03

SPECIALIZATION
> PRODUCTION SPECIALIZATION - 12.07.01

SPECIALIZED
> UN AND SPECIALIZED AGENCIES
> - 01.03.02
> > *USE:* UN SYSTEM
> UN SPECIALIZED AGENCIES - 01.03.02

SPECIES
> ENDANGERED SPECIES - 16.05.01
> PROTECTED SPECIES - 16.05.01

SPECIFICATIONS
> SPECIFICATIONS - 12.07.02

SPECULATION
> LAND SPECULATION - 07.02.00

SPEECH
> FREEDOM OF SPEECH - 04.02.02

SPICES
> SPICES - 07.07.09

SPINNING
> SPINNING - 08.08.01

SPOILAGE
> FOOD SPOILAGE - 15.03.01

SPORT
> SPORT - 13.08.00

SPORTS
> SPORTS FACILITIES - 13.08.00

SQUATTERS
> SQUATTERS - 14.04.01

SRI

  SRI LANKA - 01.04.04
  SRI LANKAN - 14.03.02

SSR

  BYELORUSSIAN SSR - 01.04.05
  UKRAINIAN SSR - 01.04.05

ST

  ST HELENA - 01.04.02
  ST KITTS-NEVIS-ANGUILLA - 01.04.03
  ST LUCIA - 01.04.03
  ST PIERRE AND MIQUELON - 01.04.03
  ST VINCENT - 01.04.03

STABILITY

  ECOSYSTEM STABILITY
  - 16.01.01
    USE: ECOLOGICAL BALANCE
  POLITICAL STABILITY - 04.04.02

STABILIZATION

  MARKET STABILIZATION - 09.01.02
  PRICE STABILIZATION - 09.02.00
  STABILIZATION - 03.02.04

STAFF

  INSTRUCTIONAL STAFF
  - 06.06.02
    USE: TEACHING PERSONNEL
  STAFF - 13.02.02
  STAFF REGULATION - 13.02.02

STAGNATION

  ECONOMIC STAGNATION - 03.02.04

STANDARD

  GOLD STANDARD - 11.03.01
  STANDARD OF LIVING - 03.02.05
  STANDARD PERFORMANCE - 13.02.02

STANDARDIZATION

  STANDARDIZATION - 12.07.02

STANDARDS

  FOOD STANDARDS - 15.03.02
  LABOUR STANDARDS - 13.03.01
  PRODUCTION STANDARDS - 12.07.02
  QUALITY STANDARDS - 12.07.02
  STANDARDS - 12.07.02

STARCH

  STARCH - 08.06.04

STARVATION

  STARVATION
  - 15.03.02
    USE: FAMINE

STATE

  STATE - 04.03.01

STATE\<CONT\>

  STATE AID - 11.01.01
  STATE FARMS - 07.03.02
  STATE INTERVENTION - 04.03.01
  STATE PARTICIPATION - 11.01.01

STATEMENT

  STATEMENT - 19.02.05

STATES

  LEAGUE OF ARAB STATES - 01.03.03
  MEMBER STATES - 01.03.01
  PERSIAN GULF STATES - 01.04.06
  TRUCIAL STATES
  - 01.04.06
    USE: UNITED ARAB EMIRATES
  UNITED STATES OF AMERICA
  - 01.04.03
    USE: USA
  UNITED STATES VIRGIN ISLANDS - 01.04.03
  WEST INDIES ASSOCIATED STATES - 01.04.03

STATIONARY

  STATIONARY POPULATION - 14.01.02

STATIONS

  STATIONS - 10.03.00

STATISTICAL

  STATISTICAL ANALYSIS - 18.08.00
  STATISTICAL DATA - 18.08.00
  STATISTICAL SERVICES - 18.02.00
  STATISTICAL TABLES - 18.08.00

STATISTICIANS

  STATISTICIANS - 13.09.09

STATISTICS

  AGRICULTURAL STATISTICS - 07.05.01
  ECONOMIC STATISTICS - 03.01.02
  EDUCATIONAL STATISTICS - 06.01.00
  FINANCIAL STATISTICS - 11.02.04
  FISHERY STATISTICS - 07.10.01
  FOOD STATISTICS - 15.03.02
  FORESTRY STATISTICS - 07.08.02
  INDUSTRIAL STATISTICS - 08.01.01
  PRODUCTION STATISTICS - 12.07.01
  STATISTICS - 18.08.00
  VITAL STATISTICS - 14.01.01

STATUS

  LEGAL STATUS - 04.02.01
  MARITAL STATUS - 14.02.05
  SOCIAL STATUS - 05.03.05

STATUS<CONT>
    TEACHER STATUS - 06.06.02

STEAM
    STEAM ENGINES - 08.14.06

STEEL
    IRON AND STEEL INDUSTRY - 08.14.01
    STEEL - 08.14.02
    STEEL CONSTRUCTION - 08.10.01
    STEEL INDUSTRY
    - 08.14.01
      USE: IRON AND STEEL INDUSTRY

STEPPES
    STEPPES - 17.03.04

STERILITY
    STERILITY - 15.02.02

STERILIZATION
    FOOD STERILIZATION - 08.06.02

STEWARDS
    SHOP STEWARDS - 13.06.00

STOCK
    ROLLING STOCK - 10.04.00
    STOCK EXCHANGE
    - 11.02.07
      USE: FINANCIAL MARKET
    WORKERS STOCK OWNERSHIP - 13.07.00

STOCKS
    BUFFER STOCKS - 09.05.02
    STOCKS - 09.03.03

STONE
    STONE - 08.10.02
    STONE CONSTRUCTION - 08.10.01

STONES
    PRECIOUS STONES - 08.13.00

STORAGE
    DATA STORAGE - 19.01.02
    FOOD STORAGE - 08.06.02
    STORAGE - 09.03.03
    STORAGE CAPACITY - 09.03.03
    WATER STORAGE - 17.05.05

STORMS
    STORMS - 17.01.03

STRAITS
    STRAITS - 17.03.04

STRATEGIC
    STRATEGIC PLANNING - 02.01.02

STRATEGY
    DEVELOPMENT STRATEGY - 02.01.01

STRATIFICATION
    SOCIAL STRATIFICATION - 05.03.05

STREAMING
    STREAMING
    - 06.04.10
      USE: ABILITY GROUPING

STRESS
    MENTAL STRESS - 13.03.04
    STRESS-RELATED DISEASES
    - 13.04.00
      USE: OCCUPATIONAL DISEASES

STRIKE
    RIGHT TO STRIKE - 13.06.00

STRIKERS
    STRIKERS - 13.06.00

STRIKES
    STRIKES - 13.06.00
    WILDCAT STRIKES - 13.06.00

STRUCTURAL
    STRUCTURAL UNEMPLOYMENT - 13.01.03

STRUCTURE
    AGRARIAN STRUCTURE - 07.02.00
    ECONOMIC STRUCTURE - 03.02.01
    INDUSTRIAL STRUCTURE - 08.01.02
    OCCUPATIONAL STRUCTURE - 13.01.03
    SOCIAL STRUCTURE - 05.03.04

STRUGGLE
    CLASS STRUGGLE - 05.03.06

STUDENT
    STUDENT BEHAVIOUR - 06.06.01
    STUDENT EXCHANGE - 06.05.02
    STUDENT LOANS - 06.04.11
    STUDENT MOVEMENTS - 06.06.01
    STUDENT PARTICIPATION - 06.06.01
    TEACHER-STUDENT RELATIONSHIPS - 06.06.02

STUDENTS
    COLLEGE STUDENTS - 06.06.01
    FOREIGN STUDENTS - 06.06.01
    GIFTED STUDENTS - 06.06.01
    HANDICAPPED STUDENTS - 06.06.01
    STUDENTS - 06.06.01

STUDIES
    CASE STUDIES - 18.04.00
    FEASIBILITY STUDIES - 01.01.06
    MARKET STUDIES - 09.03.01

STUDY
    AREA STUDY
    - 17.03.01
      USE: REGIONAL ANALYSIS
    COMPARATIVE STUDY
    - 18.09.00
      USE: COMPARATIVE ANALYSIS
    DISTANCE STUDY - 06.05.03
    FIELD STUDY
    - 18.04.00
      USE: FIELD RESEARCH

422

STUDY<CONT>
  STUDY TOURS - 06.05.02
  TIME STUDY
  - 13.03.01
    USE: WORK STUDY
  WORK STUDY - 13.03.01

STYLES
  DEVELOPMENT STYLES - 02.01.01
  LIFE STYLES - 05.03.01

SUBCONTRACTING
  SUBCONTRACTING - 12.07.02

SUBCULTURE
  SUBCULTURE - 05.02.01

SUBJECT
  SUBJECT INDEXING
  - 19.01.02
    USE: INDEXING

SUBJECTS
  CURRICULUM SUBJECTS - 06.05.01

SUBSIDIES
  EXPORT SUBSIDIES - 09.05.05
  SUBSIDIES - 11.02.02

SUBSISTENCE
  SUBSISTENCE FARMING - 07.05.03

SUBSTANCES
  DANGEROUS SUBSTANCES - 16.03.04
  HARMFUL SUBSTANCES
  - 16.03.04
    USE: DANGEROUS SUBSTANCES
  TOXIC SUBSTANCES - 15.05.00

SUBSTITUTE
  SUBSTITUTE PRODUCTS - 12.08.01

SUBSTITUTION
  IMPORT SUBSTITUTION - 09.05.04

SUBTROPICAL
  SUBTROPICAL ZONE - 17.02.03

SUBURBAN
  SUBURBAN AREAS - 14.04.03

SUBURBS
  SUBURBS
  - 14.04.03
    USE: SUBURBAN AREAS

SUDAN
  SUDAN - 01.04.02

SUDANESE
  SUDANESE - 14.03.02

SUGAR
  BEET SUGAR - 08.06.04
  CANE SUGAR - 08.06.04
  SUGAR - 08.06.04
  SUGAR BEETS - 07.07.06
  SUGAR CANE - 07.07.06

SUGAR<CONT>
  SUGAR INDUSTRY - 08.06.01

SULPHATES
  SULPHATES - 08.12.04

SULPHUR
  SULPHUR - 08.12.04
  SULPHUR DIOXIDE - 08.12.04

SUMMER
  SUMMER SCHOOLS - 06.04.03

SUPERMARKETS
  SUPERMARKETS - 09.04.04

SUPERSTITION
  SUPERSTITION - 05.04.02

SUPERVISORS
  SUPERVISORS - 13.09.03

SUPPLIERS
  SUPPLIERS - 09.03.02

SUPPLY
  FOOD SUPPLY - 15.03.01
  LABOUR SUPPLY - 13.01.02
  MONEY SUPPLY - 11.02.01
  POWER SUPPLY - 08.11.01
  SUPPLY - 09.01.01
  SUPPLY AND DEMAND - 09.01.01
  WATER SUPPLY - 17.05.05

SUPPORT
  PRICE SUPPORT - 09.02.00

SURGERY
  SURGERY - 15.04.06

SURINAM
  SURINAM - 01.04.03

SURINAMESE
  SURINAMESE - 14.03.02

SURPLUSES
  AGRICULTURAL SURPLUSES - 07.01.03
  SURPLUSES - 12.08.01

SURVEY
  LITERATURE SURVEY - 19.02.07
  SURVEY AREA - 18.04.00

SURVEYORS
  SURVEYORS - 13.09.09

SURVEYS
  AERIAL SURVEYS - 18.04.00
  CADASTRAL SURVEYS - 18.04.00
  ECONOMIC SURVEYS - 03.01.02
  GEOLOGICAL SURVEYS - 17.04.04
  MAIL SURVEYS - 18.04.00
  PREINVESTMENT SURVEYS - 11.02.06

SURVEYS<CONT>
SOCIAL SURVEYS - 05.01.02
SOIL SURVEYS - 17.04.04
SURVEYS - 18.04.00

SURVIVORS
SURVIVORS BENEFITS - 02.03.02

SWAMPS
SWAMPS - 17.05.02

SWAZI
SWAZI - 14.03.02

SWAZILAND
SWAZILAND - 01.04.02

SWEDEN
SWEDEN - 01.04.05

SWEDISH
SWEDISH - 14.03.02

SWEET
SWEET POTATOES - 07.07.06

SWINE
SWINE - 07.09.01

SWISS
SWISS - 14.03.02

SWITZERLAND
SWITZERLAND - 01.04.05

SYNTHETIC
SYNTHETIC RUBBER - 08.09.00

SYRIA
SYRIA - 01.04.06

SYRIAN
SYRIAN - 14.03.02

SYSTEM
CARDIOVASCULAR SYSTEM - 15.02.04
DIGESTIVE SYSTEM - 15.02.04
ENDOCRINE SYSTEM - 15.02.04
GENERAL SYSTEM OF PREFERENCES - 09.05.08
INTEGUMENTARY SYSTEM - 15.02.04
INTERNATIONAL MONETARY SYSTEM - 11.03.01
LYMPHATIC SYSTEM - 15.02.04
MANAGEMENT INFORMATION SYSTEM - 12.04.00
METRIC SYSTEM - 18.06.00
MUSCULOSKELETAL SYSTEM - 15.02.04
NERVOUS SYSTEM - 15.02.04
QUOTA SYSTEM - 09.05.07
RESPIRATORY SYSTEM - 15.02.04
SOCIAL SYSTEM - 05.03.01
UN SYSTEM - 01.03.02
UROGENITAL SYSTEM - 15.02.04

SYSTEMS
AGRARIAN SYSTEMS
- 07.02.00
USE: AGRARIAN STRUCTURE
BANKING SYSTEMS - 11.02.02
CLEARING SYSTEMS - 11.03.01
COMMUNICATION SYSTEMS - 05.07.01
CREDIT SYSTEMS - 11.02.02
CROPPING SYSTEMS
- 07.05.04
USE: CULTIVATION SYSTEMS
CULTIVATION SYSTEMS - 07.05.04
ECONOMIC SYSTEMS - 03.03.01
EDUCATIONAL SYSTEMS - 06.03.01
ELECTORAL SYSTEMS - 04.03.01
FARMING SYSTEMS - 07.05.03
INFORMATION SYSTEMS - 19.01.02
IRRIGATION SYSTEMS - 17.05.03
MEASUREMENT SYSTEMS - 18.06.00
MONETARY SYSTEMS - 11.02.01
PAYMENT SYSTEMS - 11.03.02
PLANNING SYSTEMS - 02.01.02
POLITICAL SYSTEMS - 04.03.01
REPORTING SYSTEMS - 19.01.02
SCHOOL SYSTEMS
- 06.03.01
USE: EDUCATIONAL SYSTEMS
SYSTEMS ANALYSIS - 18.08.00
SYSTEMS DESIGN - 12.04.00
SYSTEMS OF EDUCATION
- 06.03.01
USE: EDUCATIONAL SYSTEMS
SYSTEMS THEORY
- 18.08.00
USE: CYBERNETICS
TAX SYSTEMS - 11.01.02
TEACHING SYSTEMS
- 06.03.01
USE: EDUCATIONAL SYSTEMS
VALUE SYSTEMS - 05.04.01
WAGE PAYMENT SYSTEMS - 13.07.00

TABLES
    INPUT-OUTPUT TABLES - 03.02.02
    LIFE TABLES - 14.06.00
    STATISTICAL TABLES - 18.08.00

TAIWAN
    TAIWAN - 01.04.04

TAKE
    ECONOMIC TAKE OFF - 03.02.03

TANKERS
    TANKERS - 10.04.00

TANNING
    TANNING INDUSTRY - 08.08.02

TANZANIA
    TANZANIA - 01.04.02

TANZANIAN
    TANZANIAN - 14.03.02

TAOISM
    TAOISM - 05.04.03

TARGETS
    PRODUCTION TARGETS - 12.07.02

TARIFF
    TARIFF AGREEMENTS - 09.05.08
    TARIFF NEGOTIATIONS - 09.05.08
    TARIFF POLICY - 09.05.08
    TARIFF REDUCTIONS - 09.05.08
    TARIFF REFORMS - 09.05.08

TARIFFS
    PREFERENTIAL TARIFFS - 09.05.08
    TARIFFS - 09.05.08

TAX
    CAPITAL TAX - 11.01.02
    CONSUMPTION TAX - 11.01.02
    CORPORATION TAX - 11.01.02
    IMPORT TAX - 11.01.02
    INCOME TAX - 11.01.02
    LAND TAX - 11.01.02
    PAYROLL TAX - 11.01.02
    SALES TAX
    - 11.01.02
    USE: CONSUMPTION TAX
    TAX AGREEMENTS - 09.05.09
    TAX COLLECTION - 11.01.02
    TAX DEDUCTION - 11.01.02
    TAX EVASION - 11.01.02
    TAX EXEMPTION - 11.01.02
    TAX HAVENS - 11.01.02
    TAX INCENTIVES - 11.01.02

TAX<CONT>
    TAX REFORMS - 11.01.02
    TAX REVENUES - 11.01.02
    TAX SYSTEMS - 11.01.02
    VALUE ADDED TAX - 11.01.02

TAXATION
    DOUBLE TAXATION - 09.05.09
    TAXATION - 11.01.02

TAXES
    LOCAL TAXES - 11.01.02
    TAXES - 11.01.02

TAXPAYERS
    TAXPAYERS - 11.01.02

TEA
    TEA - 07.07.09

TEACHER
    TEACHER ASSOCIATIONS - 06.06.02
    TEACHER RECRUITMENT - 06.06.02
    TEACHER SHORTAGE - 06.06.02
    TEACHER STATUS - 06.06.02
    TEACHER TRAINING - 06.06.02
    TEACHER TRAINING COLLEGES
    - 06.04.05
    USE: COLLEGES OF EDUCATION
    TEACHER-STUDENT RELATIONSHIPS - 06.06.02

TEACHERS
    TEACHERS - 13.09.09

TEACHING
    EXPERIMENTAL TEACHING - 06.05.02
    INDIVIDUALIZED TEACHING - 06.05.02
    LANGUAGE TEACHING - 06.03.07
    PEER TEACHING - 06.05.02
    REMEDIAL TEACHING - 06.05.02
    TEACHING - 06.05.02
    TEACHING AIDS - 06.05.03
    TEACHING MATERIALS
    - 06.05.03
    USE: TEACHING AIDS
    TEACHING METHODS - 06.05.02
    TEACHING PERSONNEL - 06.06.02
    TEACHING PRACTICE - 06.05.02
    TEACHING PROGRAMMES - 06.05.01
    TEACHING SYSTEMS
    - 06.03.01
    USE: EDUCATIONAL SYSTEMS
    TEAM TEACHING - 06.05.02

TEAM
    TEAM TEACHING - 06.05.02

TEAM<CONT>
TEAM WORK - 13.03.02

TECHNICAL
TECHNICAL ASPECTS - 12.06.00
TECHNICAL ASSISTANCE - 01.01.03
TECHNICAL EDUCATION - 06.03.07
TECHNICAL INFORMATION - 19.01.01
TECHNICAL PERSONNEL - 13.09.03
TECHNICAL PROGRESS
- 12.06.00
 USE: TECHNOLOGICAL CHANGE
TECHNICAL REPORT - 19.02.08
TECHNICAL SCHOOLS - 06.04.06
TECHNICAL UNEMPLOYMENT - 13.01.03

TECHNICIANS
TECHNICIANS - 13.09.03

TECHNIQUE
TECHNIQUE
- 12.06.00
 USE: TECHNOLOGY

TECHNIQUES
CONSTRUCTION TECHNIQUES - 08.10.01
EVALUATION TECHNIQUES - 18.09.00
FORECASTING TECHNIQUES - 18.10.00
MANAGEMENT TECHNIQUES - 12.04.00

TECHNOCRACY
TECHNOCRACY - 04.03.05

TECHNOLOGICAL
TECHNOLOGICAL CHANGE - 12.06.00
TECHNOLOGICAL FORECASTING - 12.06.00
TECHNOLOGICAL INFORMATION
- 19.01.01
 USE: TECHNICAL INFORMATION
TECHNOLOGICAL INSTITUTES - 06.04.06
TECHNOLOGICAL OBSOLESCENCE - 12.06.00

TECHNOLOGY
AGRICULTURAL TECHNOLOGY
- 07.04.00
 USE: AGRICULTURAL ENGINEERING
ALTERNATIVE TECHNOLOGY - 12.06.00
APPROPRIATE TECHNOLOGY - 12.06.00
CHOICE OF TECHNOLOGY - 12.06.00
EDUCATIONAL TECHNOLOGY - 06.05.03
FOOD TECHNOLOGY - 08.06.02
INTERMEDIATE TECHNOLOGY - 12.06.00
SCIENCE AND TECHNOLOGY POLICY
- 18.01.00
 USE: SCIENCE POLICY
TECHNOLOGY - 12.06.00

TECHNOLOGY<CONT>
TECHNOLOGY TRANSFER - 12.06.00
TRADITIONAL TECHNOLOGY - 12.06.00
WOOD TECHNOLOGY - 08.07.01

TELECOMMUNICATION
TELECOMMUNICATION INDUSTRY - 08.16.00

TELECOMMUNICATIONS
TELECOMMUNICATIONS - 05.07.03

TELEGRAPH
TELEGRAPH - 08.16.00

TELEPHONE
TELEPHONE - 08.16.00

TELEVISION
EDUCATIONAL TELEVISION - 06.05.03
TELEVISION - 05.07.03
TELEVISION RECEIVERS - 08.16.00

TELEX
TELEX - 08.16.00

TEMPERATE
TEMPERATE ZONE - 17.02.03

TEMPERATURE
TEMPERATURE - 18.06.00

TEMPORARY
TEMPORARY EMPLOYMENT - 13.01.03

TENANT
TENANT FARMERS - 07.02.00

TENURE
LAND TENURE - 07.02.00

TERM
LONG TERM - 18.10.00
MEDIUM TERM - 18.10.00
SHORT TERM - 18.10.00

TERMINOLOGY
TERMINOLOGY - 19.03.00

TERMS
FINANCIAL TERMS - 11.02.04
TERMS OF AID - 01.01.04
TERMS OF TRADE - 09.05.03

TERRESTRIAL
TERRESTRIAL ENVIRONMENT - 16.01.02

TERRITORIAL
TERRITORIAL WATERS - 17.06.00

TERRITORIES
OVERSEAS TERRITORIES - 01.02.03
TRUST TERRITORIES - 01.02.03

TERRORISM
TERRORISM - 01.02.07

TERTIARY
TERTIARY - 17.04.02
TERTIARY SECTOR
- 09.01.01
 USE: SERVICE INDUSTRY

TESTING
> TESTING - 18.09.00

TESTS
> TESTS - 18.09.00

TEXTBOOK
> TEXTBOOK - 19.02.09

TEXTILE
> TEXTILE INDUSTRY - 08.08.01
> TEXTILE WORKERS - 13.09.06

TEXTILES
> TEXTILES - 08.08.01

THAI
> THAI - 14.03.02

THAILAND
> THAILAND - 01.04.04

THEATRE
> THEATRE - 05.05.03

THEORY
> COMMUNICATION THEORY
> - 18.08.00
>   *USE:* INFORMATION THEORY
> DEVELOPMENT THEORY - 02.01.01
> ECONOMIC THEORY - 03.01.02
> EDUCATIONAL THEORY - 06.01.00
> INFORMATION THEORY - 18.08.00
> POLITICAL THEORY - 04.04.01
> POPULATION THEORY - 14.01.02
> SOCIAL THEORY - 02.02.02
> SYSTEMS THEORY
> - 18.08.00
>   *USE:* CYBERNETICS
> THEORY - 18.03.00

THERMAL
> THERMAL ENERGY - 08.11.01
> THERMAL POLLUTION - 16.03.04
> THERMAL POWER PLANTS - 08.11.02

THESAURUS
> THESAURUS - 19.03.00

THESIS
> THESIS - 19.02.09

THOUGHT
> ECONOMIC THOUGHT - 03.03.01

TIDAL
> TIDAL ENERGY - 08.11.01
> TIDAL WAVES - 17.04.03

TIDES
> TIDES - 17.06.00

TIED
> TIED AID
> - 01.01.04
>   *USE:* TERMS OF AID

TIMBER
> TIMBER - 08.07.01

TIME
> ARRANGEMENT OF WORKING TIME - 13.03.03
> FULL TIME - 13.03.03
> PART TIME - 13.03.03
> PART TIME EMPLOYMENT - 13.01.03
> TIME BUDGET - 13.03.03
> TIME FACTOR - 18.10.00
> TIME STUDY
> - 13.03.01
>   *USE:* WORK STUDY

TIMOR
> PORTUGUESE TIMOR - 01.04.04

TIN
> TIN - 08.14.02
> TIN PLATE - 08.14.04

TITANIUM
> TITANIUM - 08.14.02

TOBACCO
> TOBACCO - 07.07.09
> TOBACCO INDUSTRY - 08.06.01

TOBAGO
> TRINIDAD AND TOBAGO - 01.04.03

TOGO
> TOGO - 01.04.02

TOGOLESE
> TOGOLESE - 14.03.02

TOILET
> TOILET PREPARATIONS - 08.12.08

TOMATOES
> TOMATOES - 07.07.05

TOME
> SAO TOME AND PRINCIPE - 01.04.02

TONGA
> TONGA - 01.04.07

TONGAN
> TONGAN - 14.03.02

TONNAGE
> TONNAGE - 10.06.00

TOOL
> MACHINE TOOL INDUSTRY - 08.14.05

TOOLS
> HAND TOOLS - 08.14.05
> MACHINE TOOLS - 08.14.05
> TOOLS - 08.14.05

TOP
> TOP MANAGEMENT - 12.03.00

TOPOGRAPHY
> TOPOGRAPHY - 18.07.00

TORTURE

    TORTURE - 02.04.03

TOURISM

    TOURISM - 09.04.05

TOURS

    STUDY TOURS - 06.05.02

TOWN

    TOWN CENTRE - 14.04.03
    TOWN PLANNING
    - 14.04.03
     USE: URBAN PLANNING

TOWNS

    MIDDLE-SIZED TOWNS - 14.04.03
    NEW TOWNS - 14.04.03
    SATELLITE TOWNS - 14.04.03
    SMALL TOWNS - 14.04.03
    TOWNS - 14.04.03

TOXIC

    TOXIC METALS - 15.05.00
    TOXIC SUBSTANCES - 15.05.00

TOXICITY

    TOXICITY - 15.05.00

TOXINS

    TOXINS - 15.03.02

TOYS

    TOYS - 08.07.03

TRACTORS

    TRACTORS - 07.04.00

TRADE

    BALANCE OF TRADE - 09.05.03
    DOMESTIC TRADE - 09.04.01
    EAST-WEST TRADE - 09.05.02
    FOREIGN TRADE - 09.05.01
    FREE TRADE AREA - 09.05.08
    HOME TRADE
    - 09.04.01
     USE: DOMESTIC TRADE
    INLAND TRADE
    - 09.04.01
     USE: DOMESTIC TRADE
    INTERNATIONAL TRADE - 09.05.01
    RETAIL TRADE - 09.04.04
    TERMS OF TRADE - 09.05.03
    TRADE - 09.01.01
    TRADE AGREEMENTS - 09.05.02
    TRADE BARRIERS - 09.05.07
    TRADE DEVELOPMENT - 09.05.06
    TRADE FAIRS - 09.03.05

TRADE<CONT>

    TRADE LIBERALIZATION - 09.05.07
    TRADE MARKS - 09.03.04
    TRADE MISSIONS - 09.05.06
    TRADE NEGOTIATIONS - 09.05.02
    TRADE POLICY - 09.05.06
    TRADE PROMOTION - 09.05.06
    TRADE RELATIONS - 09.05.02
    TRADE UNIONISM - 13.06.00
    TRADE UNIONS - 13.06.00
    TRADE VOLUME - 09.05.03
    WHOLESALE TRADE - 09.04.04
    WORLD TRADE
    - 09.05.01
     USE: INTERNATIONAL TRADE

TRADERS

    TRADERS
    - 13.09.07
     USE: DEALERS

TRADITION

    TRADITION - 05.02.01

TRADITIONAL

    TRADITIONAL CULTURE - 05.02.01
    TRADITIONAL MEDICINE - 15.04.06
    TRADITIONAL TECHNOLOGY - 12.06.00

TRAFFIC

    AIR TRAFFIC - 10.08.00
    RAILWAY TRAFFIC - 10.08.00
    ROAD TRAFFIC - 10.08.00
    SEA TRAFFIC - 10.08.00
    TRAFFIC - 10.08.00
    TRAFFIC CONTROL - 10.08.00
    URBAN TRAFFIC - 10.08.00

TRAINEES

    TRAINEES - 06.06.01

TRAINING

    AGRICULTURAL TRAINING - 06.03.07
    BASIC TRAINING - 06.03.07
    FARMER TRAINING
    - 06.03.07
     USE: AGRICULTURAL TRAINING
    FURTHER TRAINING - 06.03.07
    IN-PLANT TRAINING - 06.03.07
    INDUSTRIAL TRAINING - 06.03.07
    MODULAR TRAINING - 06.05.02
    OCCUPATIONAL TRAINING
    - 06.03.07
     USE: VOCATIONAL TRAINING

TRAINING<CONT>

ON-THE-JOB TRAINING
- 06.03.07
USE: IN-PLANT TRAINING
SANDWICH TRAINING - 06.03.07
TEACHER TRAINING - 06.06.02
TEACHER TRAINING COLLEGES
- 06.04.05
USE: COLLEGES OF EDUCATION
TRAINING - 06.02.01
TRAINING ABROAD - 06.05.02
TRAINING ALLOWANCES - 06.04.11
TRAINING ASSISTANCE - 01.01.03
TRAINING CENTRES - 06.04.06
TRAINING COURSES - 06.05.01
TRAINING METHODS - 06.05.02
TRAINING PROGRAMMES - 06.05.01
TRAINING WORKSHOPS
- 06.04.06
USE: TRAINING CENTRES
VOCATIONAL TRAINING - 06.03.07

TRAINS

TRAINS - 10.04.00

TRANSACTIONS

INVISIBLE TRANSACTIONS - 11.03.03

TRANSFER

TECHNOLOGY TRANSFER - 12.06.00

TRANSFERS

CAPITAL TRANSFERS - 11.03.03
MONETARY TRANSFERS - 11.03.01
POPULATION TRANSFERS - 14.07.00

TRANSFRONTIER

TRANSFRONTIER POLLUTION - 16.03.04

TRANSISTORS

TRANSISTORS - 08.15.02

TRANSIT

TRANSIT - 10.07.00

TRANSITION

TRANSITION FROM SCHOOL TO WORK - 06.03.07

TRANSLATION

TRANSLATION - 05.06.01
TRANSLATION SERVICES - 19.01.03

TRANSLATORS

TRANSLATORS - 13.09.09

TRANSMISSION

DATA TRANSMISSION - 19.01.02
DISEASE TRANSMISSION - 15.04.04

TRANSNATIONAL

TRANSNATIONAL CORPORATIONS
- 03.03.05
USE: MULTINATIONAL ENTERPRISES

TRANSPORT

AIR TRANSPORT - 10.05.00
COLLECTIVE TRANSPORT
- 10.01.00
USE: PUBLIC TRANSPORT
INLAND TRANSPORT - 10.07.00
INLAND WATER TRANSPORT - 10.05.00
INTERNATIONAL TRANSPORT - 10.07.00
MARITIME TRANSPORT
- 10.05.00
USE: SEA TRANSPORT
MEANS OF TRANSPORT - 10.04.00
MULTIMODAL TRANSPORT - 10.05.00
NON-MOTORIZED TRANSPORT - 10.04.00
PIPELINE TRANSPORT - 10.05.00
PUBLIC TRANSPORT - 10.01.00
RAILWAY TRANSPORT - 10.05.00
ROAD TRANSPORT - 10.05.00
SCHOOL TRANSPORT - 06.04.07
SEA TRANSPORT - 10.05.00
TRANSPORT - 10.01.00
TRANSPORT CONTAINERS - 10.06.00
TRANSPORT ECONOMICS - 10.01.00
TRANSPORT EQUIPMENT - 10.04.00
TRANSPORT INFRASTRUCTURE - 10.03.00
TRANSPORT PLANNING - 10.01.00
TRANSPORT POLICY - 10.01.00
TRANSPORT PRICE
- 10.09.00
USE: FREIGHT
TRANSPORT WORKERS - 13.09.08
URBAN TRANSPORT - 10.07.00

TRANSPORTATION

MODES OF TRANSPORTATION - 10.05.00
TRANSPORTATION
- 10.01.00
USE: TRANSPORT

TRAVELS

TRAVELS - 09.04.05

TRAWLERS

TRAWLERS - 07.10.03

TREASURY

TREASURY BONDS - 11.02.07

TREATIES

TREATIES
- 01.02.04
USE: INTERNATIONAL AGREEMENTS

TREATMENT

MEDICAL TREATMENT
- 15.04.04
USE: MEDICAL CARE

TREATMENT<CONT>
>WASTE TREATMENT - 16.04.02
>WATER TREATMENT - 17.05.05

TREES
>BANANA-TREES - 07.07.05
>FOREST TREES - 07.08.06
>FRUIT TREES - 07.07.05
>TREES - 07.07.01

TRENDS
>TRENDS - 18.10.00

TRIBE
>TRIBE - 14.03.01

TRINIDAD
>TRINIDAD AND TOBAGO - 01.04.03

TRITICALE
>TRITICALE - 07.07.04

TROPICAL
>TROPICAL DISEASES - 15.04.02
>TROPICAL ZONE - 17.02.03

TRUCIAL
>TRUCIAL STATES
>- 01.04.06
> USE: UNITED ARAB EMIRATES

TRUCKS
>TRUCKS - 10.04.00

TRUST
>TRUST TERRITORIES - 01.02.03

TRUSTEESHIP
>TRUSTEESHIP COUNCIL - 01.03.02

TRUSTS
>TRUSTS - 12.02.00

TRYPANOSOMIASIS
>TRYPANOSOMIASIS - 15.04.02

TUBERCULOSIS
>TUBERCULOSIS - 15.04.02

TUBES
>ELECTRONIC TUBES - 08.15.02

TUNDRA
>TUNDRA - 17.03.04

TUNGSTEN
>TUNGSTEN - 08.14.02

TUNISIA
>TUNISIA - 01.04.02

TUNISIAN
>TUNISIAN - 14.03.02

TUNNELS
>TUNNELS - 10.03.00

TURBINES
>TURBINES - 08.14.06

TURKEY
>TURKEY - 01.04.06

TURKISH
>TURKISH - 14.03.02

TURKS
>TURKS AND CAICOS ISLANDS - 01.04.03

TURNOVER
>TURNOVER - 09.03.02

TYPES
>SOIL TYPES - 17.04.04

TYPHOID
>TYPHOID - 15.04.02

TYPHOONS
>TYPHOONS
>- 17.01.03
> USE: STORMS

TYPHUS
>TYPHUS - 15.04.02

TYRES
>TYRES - 08.09.00